TORN MUSIC

TORN MUSIC

REJECTED FILM SCORES

a Selected History

BY GERGELY HUBAI

SILMAN-JAMES PRESS LOS ANGELES

This book's author and editors have extended their best efforts to ensure that the material contained herein is factual. They have relied on information culled from professional sources (such as the IMDb), books and articles by scholars and authorities on the subject of film music, and the sometimes conflicting memories of those who witnessed and/or participated in the creation of the films discussed here. With a project of this scope, however, involving a living and evolving collaborative art—one that has often been underappreciated and underdocumented—the inclusion of a few errors is probably inevitable despite our best intentions. The author and publisher welcome documented notice of any errors that readers may find herein and will endeavor to remedy these in future editions of the book.

First Edition

10 9 8 7 6 5 4 3 2 1

Library of Congress Cataloging-in-Publication Data

Hubai, Gergely, 1984-
Torn music : rejected film scores, a select history / by Gergely Hubai. -- 1st ed.
p. cm.
Includes bibliographical references and index.
ISBN 978-1-935247-05-0 (alk. paper)
1. Motion picture music--History and criticism. I. Title.
ML2075.H82 2012
781.5'4209--dc23
2011052526

Cover design by Wade Lageose
Layout and typesetting by William Morosi

Printed and bound in the United States of America

Silman-James Press
1181 Angelo Drive
Beverly Hills, CA 90210

To Anna, my family and everybody who put
up with the life of a researcher

Contents

Foreword by Christopher Young

Though I am so honored that Gergely asked me to write the Foreword for this incredible and unique book, I can't help but wonder, based on the subject matter, whether it will be replaced by another composer's intro. If that happens, well, *c'est la vie*, for this book is about every film composer's most dreaded nightmare: the rejected score.

There's a saying in Hollywood that you're not a real film composer until you've had at least one entire score thrown out. This is most certainly true. But, having said that, to the best of my knowledge John Williams has never suffered that fate (though I bet you he's had at least a few cues canned)—and he is one hell of a real film composer.

There's also a saying that there are five categories of score that a composer will probably never forget: They include the first score (the firstborn!), the personal favorites, the most awarded ones (how can you argue with an Oscar?), and the ones that bring back great memories of a positive experience with everybody involved. But the fifth category—rejected scores—leaves the longest and strongest impressions.

As you will learn while reading this book, my history with rejected scores started with Tobe Hooper's remake of *Invaders from Mars* (1986). At the time, I was obsessed with an urge to incorporate my love for musique concrète into a score, and I mistakenly thought that this score might be my first opportunity to go all out and deliver something very strange. I've often humorously said that the reason my score was ultimately rejected was that they were looking for music *about* Mars, and not *from* Mars. After its rejection, I felt that I had given birth to an idiot bastard son that needed to be locked in the basement and forever forgotten. Needless to say, I was very depressed and assumed my career was over. Like many of my beloved peers, however, I emerged from the experience to discover that in fact it is not the end of the world.

There are numerous reasons why scores get thrown out. Usually it happens because music is the last thing that can be altered in a troubled movie to make it appear better. But while a score may be able to dress up a corpse, it can never revive it. It is good to know, however, that music has a tremendous impact on the perception of the movie, so it makes sense that scores frequently get the ax. I hear that it is happening more now than ever, but I remember a point when the replacing of scores was so frequent that, in the case of one major film company, I would regularly ask the music department head, not who they had hired to score the movie, but who they were hiring to *replace* the score.

There are some other highlights in my own personal affair with rejected scores. When I was a student at UCLA, for example, my trial by fire with New World Pictures was rescoring the film *Highpoint* (1982), which was the first film I worked on that had major actors in it. I was asked to replace a fantastic score by the Academy Award–winning composer John Addison, because the intent of the movie had been completely rethought. Don't think I wasn't scared shitless. Ten years later, a similar situation came up when I was asked to replace Maurice Jarre's score for *Jennifer 8*. This was my first real studio movie—and I was scared shitless again.

I may be the only composer in film music's short history who was fired, replaced, and then rehired again to replace his own replaced score. I'm also probably the only composer who's had a score replaced by his own ex-student. Believe it or not, in that case I was excited for the replacement composer—after all, the decision to replace my score was final, it had to be replaced anyway, so why not by my ex-student?

My composer friends unanimously agree that Gergely has come up with a great idea for a book, even though he does collect, like the *National Enquirer* (albeit in a very scholarly way), the bad moments in many film composers' creative lives. *Torn Music* is thoroughly researched and extremely well written. The great news is that it also helps all of us film composers who've had a score rejected realize that we are not alone.

Your friend,
Christopher Young

Acknowledgments

Researching this book was difficult. Since it covers scores from Golden Age classics to modern pictures, from megabuck "events" to low-budget features to television series, I had to contact many people in order to find the answers I needed. I most heartily thank the following composers, filmmakers, record producers, musicians, estates, and fellow researchers (all listed alphabetically), who kindly gave of their time and knowledge to help me finish this book.

Mark Adler, David Amram, John Badham, Marco Beltrami, David Bergeaud, Charles Bernstein, Peter Bernstein, Stephen Bishop, Larry Blank, Chris Boardman, Justin Boggan, Whitney Branan, Glenn Branca, Joep de Bruijn, Geoffrey Burgon, Carter Burwell, Tristram Cary, Brooke Casey, Andrea Chin, Eric Colvin, Charles Cunningham, Mason Daring, Carl Davis, Chris Dedrick, Colette Delerue, Tom DeMary, John R. Docherty, George Dreyfus, Megan Durden, Kathy Durning, Franck Ernould, Robin Esterhammer, Guy Farley, Robert Folk, Nicholas S. Folsom, Clément Fontaine, Kathe Garbrick, Ron Geesin, Richard Gibbs, Paul Gilreath, Paul Glass, Adam Glasser, Frank Harris, Tony Hinnigan, Stephen Hopkins, Michael Hoppé, Kenneth V. Jones, Andrew Kemp, Lukas Kendall, Dimitri Kennaway, Christopher Klatman, Guenther Koegebehn, Phillip Lambro, Joseph LoDuca, Paul MacLean, Harry Manfredini, David Mansfield, Raz Mesinai, Patrick Moraz, Alan More, Angela Morley, Michael Perilstein, James Phillips, Paul Phillips, Stu Phillips, Dave Platt, Allison Ravenscroft, Doug Raynes, Nick Redman, Robert Rich, William Richert, Kendall Roclord, Kecia Rodi, Bruce Rowland, Donald Rubinstein, Craig Safan, David Schecter, Lalo Schifrin, Gerard Schurmann, John Scott, Peter Sculthorpe, Walter E. Sear, Jonathan Sheffer, Graham Sheriff, Warren Sherk, Ron Shillingford, Neil R. Sinyard, Graeme Skinner, Lynn Small, Scott Stambler, Charles Strouse, Elizabeth Swados, Isabel Syed, Ernest Thompson, Ken Thorne, Didier Thunus, Robert Townson, Richie Unterberger, Otto Vavrin II, Chris Villars, David and Sue Whitaker, David C. Williams, Dan Wool, Andreas Wostrack, Michael Wurtz, Stefano Zanni.

Introduction

A book could be written about all the insane things that go on in terms of score politics, but it would have to be written by someone who doesn't need the work anymore.

—John Ottman

Film scoring has been an often overlooked aspect of the moviemaking process for decades. However, thanks to the efforts of such record labels as Varèse Sarabande, Film Score Monthly, Intrada, and many other companies, there have never been so many film music recordings available as nowadays. Every month, more and more classic and recent scores are released, no doubt draining their collectors' wallets. These releases have also had a positive effect on film music literature: Today, more books on the subject are in print than ever before.

But one important topic that these books have yet to cover in detail is rejected scores (a popular subject for rumor and gossip among film music enthusiasts). The time has come for a comprehensive volume of score-replacement stories. Because tales of rejected scores can often be both muddy and complicated, past discussions of them have often been riddled with misinformation, inaccuracies, and simple lies. *Torn Music* aims to accurately reveal the circumstances surrounding 300 of these ill-fated scores. Not that there have been no more rejected scores than that—there are probably well more than twice that number.

The movies and television shows discussed herein range from classic films and highly rated TV shows to little-seen independent productions and cult pictures. They are presented chronologically, from 1932 through the present. Every film genre is represented, and the list of composers whose tossed-aside works are discussed includes the greatest names in the business, as well as composers you've probably never heard of before. In writing this book, I've tried to collect the most interesting cases I've encountered, many of which involve famous movies and well-known composers. I hope my selection is eclectic enough to appeal to all its readers.

Before going any further, I should address a couple of possible misconceptions about rejected scores. First, these works are not necessarily bad or even inappropriate for their respective movies. In fact, you might find many of them to be better than the scores that replaced them. All that's usually required for a score's demise is one person—a powerful decision-maker attached to a project—who thinks otherwise.

On the other side of the coin, replacement scores aren't inherently inferior, either. While some film music journalists seem to enjoy pointing out how a rejected work was much better than its replacement (thus often taking a shot at the Hollywood system), it's worth noting that quite a lot of rejected scores were truly inappropriate for the movies they were written for. When possible and where applicable, *Torn Music* tries to provide comparisons between used and unused scores, describing how each composer's work added to or detracted from a given picture.

A third common misconception is that having a score replaced is a shameful experience, or even a career killer, and therefore shouldn't be discussed. In my talks with composers, I've found that very, very few of them believe this. In fact, a popular film music insider's adage says that you're nobody until you've had a score rejected. Scores by Bernard Herrmann, Jerry Goldsmith, John Barry, and Elmer Bernstein have been replaced in a number of films, yet these composers' talents would never be questioned based on those rejections. Bottom line: It can—and usually does—happen to everyone in the business.

This Introduction's epigraph, from film composer, editor, and director John Ottman, may go a long way toward explaining why there haven't been any previous books devoted to the subject of rejected film scores. It's a tricky topic to discuss, and often it's hard to find all the information necessary to understand the political and/or aesthetic issues involved in a score replacement. I would like to think that the very fact that studios, production companies, and distributors have spent so many, many thousands of dollars replacing scores is actually a backhanded compliment to and statement about the importance of film music. I hope that *Torn Music* will be useful and educational—and fun—for all, including casual movie fans, diehard soundtrack enthusiasts, researchers, and industry professionals as well.

Gergely Hubai

The Most Dangerous Game (1932)

Original composer: **W. Franke Harling**
Replacement composer: **Max Steiner**

As surprising as it may sound, the history of replaced movie scores begins before the appearance of recorded sound. Even during the age of silent movies, filmmakers and studios often commissioned alternate soundtracks for their pictures, and music replacement was practiced on the local level as well. Theater owners frequently made changes to the music assigned to silent films, so the same picture was rarely shown the same way in two different towns, or even in two different showings in the same town.

The appearance of recorded sound, a gradual process that culminated in the success of *The Jazz Singer* (1927), changed the way pictures were assembled and soon forced the studios to provide recorded scores for their movies. The short time period between *The Jazz Singer* and *King Kong* (1933) saw much research into how this new element—the score—could be utilized in the "talkies."

Thus, the art of film scoring quickly developed from scratch, and by 1932 there was enough music consciousness in the business to bring about the first important score replacement in Hollywood since the appearance of the sound film.

Producer Merian C. Cooper took charge at RKO Pictures during the Great Depression, a period that happened to coincide with the most important developments in sound film. Among Cooper's earliest projects during these bleak times were two extravagant jungle adventures: *The Most Dangerous Game* and *King Kong*. While these were very risky ventures in an age of financial insecurity, studio executives trusted Cooper because he had a reputation for delivering quality products while shaving budgets. One of his great ideas was to tackle two simultaneous jungle movies by shooting day and night on the same sets: Daytime was devoted to the giant ape Kong, while the night was reserved for *The Most Dangerous Game*, which concerns a most unusual hunt in which human beings are the prey.

Composer Max Steiner, the head of RKO's music department, wanted to write new scores for both these seminal movies. RKO's chiefs, however, thought that the usual "library music" (recorded music that the studio had previously used with other films) would suit both projects well enough. In the end, Steiner, willing to work at a decreased fee, insisted on writing an original score for *King Kong*. *The Most Dangerous Game* was then assigned to W. Franke Harling, who wrote a score—of sorts.

Harling was a minor celebrity in Hollywood for having composed *A Light from St. Agnes*, a popular "jazz" opera that had been performed throughout the United States and in Paris. In the world of film music, he was best known for scoring *Rango* (1931), a nature drama starring orangutans that interact with humans. The movie relied heavily on music in telling its story, so Harling seemed a good fit for the jungle-themed *The Most Dangerous Game* as well. Unfortunately, his approach didn't suit Cooper, who thought the score was too Broadway-influenced and did not match the picture's tone. The composer's light operatic music may have worked well for a group of humanized orangutans, but it wasn't dramatic enough for a more serious adventure.

Despite financial constraints, Cooper persuaded Steiner to write the score for *The Most Dangerous Game* based on his excellent work for King Vidor's *Bird of Paradise.* Steiner had an extremely strict deadline on this new commission; he started writing *King Kong* in the summer, and the new score had to be finished by early autumn. Because of *The Most Dangerous Game*'s earlier premiere, Steiner's work on it actually predates his groundbreaking achievements on *King Kong.*

The music for Kong's adventures is often said to mark the birth of the original film score, so it's ironic that the first important film music replacement occurred almost simultaneously.

In contrast with Harling's light approach, Steiner's music for *The Most Dangerous Game* downplays the romance in the picture, in favor of creating an atmosphere of overwhelming danger through the use of eerie textures and a menacing ten-note melody that functions throughout the score as a leitmotif for the deranged hunter, Count Zaroff. This main melody is also cleverly incorporated into the film's piece of "source music" (music emanating from an onscreen source, aka diegetic music) titled "Russian Waltz." This technique would come to be used in countless movies as a clever way to intertwine source music and underscore material. While the music for *The Most Dangerous Game* is definitely a lesser work than that of *King Kong,* possibly because a lack of time didn't allow for the best development of the material, film history's premier replacement score is still worthy of a listen.

■ **Don Quixote** (1933)

Original composer: **Maurice Ravel**
Replacement composer: **Jacques Ibert**

In 1946, producer David O. Selznick had the brilliant idea of holding auditions for the scoring of his next prestigious production, *Duel in the Sun.* His concept was simple: Ask Hollywood's greatest composers to score a scene from the Western in under two weeks, and the winner would go on to score the entire movie.

The contest didn't go down too well with the resident maestros, however. Miklós Rózsa, for instance, thought the idea was both outrageous and insulting, especially since Selznick already knew his work through Alfred Hitchcock's *Spellbound.* Erich Wolfgang Korngold also declined the offer, fearing he might actually win the contest and be stuck with a movie he had no interest in. The picture eventually received an underscore from Dimitri Tiomkin, who got the job without taking part in the humiliating competition.

Little did these Hollywood composers know that, about a decade before Selznick proposed his contest, a similar event had been organized in Europe, with scandalous consequences.

In 1933, director G. W. Pabst decided to make the first screen adaptation of Miguel de Cervantes' classic novel, *Don Quixote,* with none other than the legendary bass Feodor Chaliapin in the title role. Chaliapin had already played this character in Jules Massenet's opera version of the tale in 1910, but Pabst didn't want to make an adaptation of the opera itself. Instead, he wanted an original score and a couple of songs written for the picture.

Five composers were contacted. The hopeful contenders included Darius Milhaud, Marcel Delannoy, Maurice Ravel, Jacques Ibert, and Manuel de Falla (who had already written a short puppet-opera titled *El Retablo de Maese Pedro* based on chapter 26 from the novel's second part). The composers were asked to submit their concepts for the music without being informed of the contest; each believed that his music would actually be used in the picture.

The secret competition's winner was Maurice Ravel, who immediately began work on the songs that would eventually become the three-part song cycle *Don Quichotte à Dulcinée.* Unfortunately, the composer's health was in decline, made even worse by a minor accident in which he had injured his head. Ravel started to complain about various symptoms that left him unable to work. He had difficulty focusing on the musical ideas he heard in his head, he said, and became almost incapable of putting anything down on paper.

Pabst feared that Ravel wasn't giving his full attention to the project, especially after the composer interrupted the work to supervise the European tour of his Piano Concerto in G. Unsatisfied with his choice's pace, the director eventually awarded a new commission to French composer Jacques Ibert, who happened to be a friend of Ravel's. Once revealed, the circumstances of the competition outraged both Ibert and Ravel, who even threatened to file a lawsuit against the production but later gave up on this idea.

Pabst went on to direct three versions of *Don Quixote* at the same time—one in English, one in French, and one in German. All three variations starred Chaliapin, although many of the other cast members were changed. All three utilized the same sets, translations of the same screenplay, and Ibert's same music.

Ibert conducted the recording used in the picture. The four songs ("Chanson du depart," "Chanson à Dulcinée," "Chanson du Duc," and "Chanson de la mort"), based on texts by Pierre de Ronsard and Alexandre Arnaux, relied on guitars and metric asymmetry for their distinctly Spanish flavor. They became immensely popular after the premiere and received multiple recordings under the title *Chansons de Don Quichotte, for Voice and Piano.* (A fifth song, "Chanson de Sancho," was only discovered and recorded for the first time in 1990 by Swiss conductor Adriano for a compilation CD focusing on Ibert's film music.)

As for Ravel's unused music, the composer continued to work on the songs long after Pabst replaced him. His "Chanson romanesque," "Chanson épique," and "Chanson à boire" are settings of poems by Paul Morand and cover different aspects of the story than Ibert's work. Ravel completed their orchestration in 1934, grouping them as a song cycle under the title *Don Quichotte à Dulcinée,* which premiered on 1 December 1934, in Paris, conducted by Paul Paray and performed by Martial Singher. By this time Ravel was seriously ill, but he could at least enjoy the success of the songs for which Pabst had refused to wait. Like Ibert's songs, *Don Quichotte à Dulcinée* has enjoyed many performances and been recorded several times. The cycle's stature in Ravel's output is elevated by the fact that it turned out to be his last finished composition.

■ The Good Earth (1937)

Original composer: **Arnold Schoenberg**
Replacement composer: **Herbert Stothart**

World War II made a serious impact on the history of American film scoring by forcing some of Europe's most talented musicians to flee to the New World. There, Hollywood would "discover" two groups of composers. The first included the likes of Bronislau Kaper and Miklós Rózsa, immigrants who managed to get the gist of the system and become established, in-demand composers.

The second group included great artists such as Arnold Schoenberg and Igor Stravinsky, who, despite being established concert composers before escaping to Los Angeles, never "clicked" with the Hollywood studio system. The result was some unused sketches for various film projects, not to mention numerous interesting and amusing anecdotes.

Schoenberg's is a particularly interesting case. He was widely known as the inventor of the twelve-tone technique, a revolutionary and extremely influential twentieth-century compositional process. But although he was intrigued by the notion of writing film music, his concept of what a movie should be didn't always match Hollywood's. Furthermore, his high opinion of his own talents made him often difficult to deal with and unresponsive to criticism.

The musical misunderstandings surrounding *The Good Earth* (based on Pearl S. Buck's best-selling novel) started as soon as producer Irving J. Thalberg decided he would hire the legendary Schoenberg to score it, instead of one of the readily available staff composers. Given the prestige of the source novel, Thalberg hoped that a prestigious composer like Schoenberg would be interested in the commission. Contact with the Austrian composer was easy, since he was living in California at the time, teaching courses at both USC and UCLA.

While Schoenberg was quite interested in writing music for film, learning exactly what his role was supposed to be eventually left him bitterly disappointed. Anecdotes from the period describe Schoenberg as so oblivious to Hollywood film-scoring practices that he felt he should be working together with the actors, and that Thalberg should shoot the movie to his music without changing a note. While he never recorded anything for *The Good Earth* with an orchestra, he spent a good deal of time researching and writing many sketches in two small notebooks (Sk833-858 and Sk859-865 in the Schoenberg collection).

The following communiqué was sent to Thalberg after he left the composer hanging for a month about *The Good Earth* (original spelling retained):

> When I left you, about three weeks ago, you told me you would answer in a few days. Having got no answer untill today, I can not believ, this is your intention: to give me no answer at all. Maybe you are disappointed about the price I asked. But you will agree, it is not my fault, you did not ask me before and only so late, that I had already spent so much time, coming twice to you, reading the book, trying out how I could compose it and making sketches. I should be very, very sorry if I had to realize, that you do not only not pay attention to the respectfull way in which I am accostumed do be treated as a person of international reputation, but even not for the time I have spent on this occasion. And I would be very sorry if you should write me, it were only a mistake of an officer, that I got not an answer in time, because I came personally to you and have the right to expect, that you personally examine whether I have been answered so as it is fitting to my rank. As beforesaid, I cannot believe it is your intention not to give me an answer at all. But even in case you are still considering to make me a proposition, I wanted to ask you to give me your decision or at least to write me a letter.

Schoenberg never got a satisfactory explanation of why he hadn't been contacted again regarding *The Good Earth*, but educated guesses can be made. From what we can gather from surviving records, it seems that Schoenberg became too involved in the picture after a merely informal inquiry from Thalberg. He didn't even have a written contract.

The two key issues that often proved to be the source of Hollywood's problem with concert composers were money and time. Schoenberg and many of his colleagues usually overpriced themselves, not recognizing that Hollywood already had its share of capable composers who wrote scores for a fraction of those fees. Concert composers were also used to laboring and deliberating over a forty-five- to sixty-minute orchestra score for a fairly long time. But even when a producer was willing to shell out the large fee, he could not afford to wait as long—often as much as a year—as a composer of Stravinsky's or Schoenberg's stature often demanded, especially when his own music department could turn out something usable in a week (quality notwithstanding).

■ Union Pacific (1939)

Original composer: **George Antheil**
Replacement composers: **Sigmund Krumgold, John Leipold**

George Antheil, self-described as the "bad boy of music," was one of the most notorious composers in the history of American music. A man of many talents, he also was a world-touring concert pianist (often performing his own technically demanding piano works); the author of a crime novel, a book on forensic endocrinology, and a best-selling autobiography; an advice-to-the-lovelorn columnist; and even the designer (in collaboration with actress Hedy Lamarr) of a patented torpedo guidance system.

As a concert composer, Antheil was best known for his *Ballet mécanique*, a piece that was originally conceived in 1924 to accompany an abstract film of the same title by noted artist Fernand Léger and producer/director Dudley Murphy. For numerous reasons Antheil's score did not find its way into the film at the time (the two were finally paired decades later), so the composer turned this wild, colorful, rhythmically driven, Futurist-influenced music into a concert work that he would reorchestrate a number of times throughout his life. His original orchestration included sixteen player pianos, a battery of percussion instruments, a siren, and three (high-, medium-, and low-pitched) airplane propellers. A more modest orchestration, replacing most of the player pianos with human pianists, was premiered in Paris in 1926. It was subsequently performed at New York City's Carnegie Hall in 1927, where it caused a scandal and was a critical disaster.

Soon after the Carnegie Hall debacle, Antheil changed his music's style. Gone were its avant-garde leanings, replaced by a less scandal-prone neoclassical approach. In 1936 he moved to Hollywood, where he became involved in traditional Hollywood film scoring.

Antheil's earliest Hollywood score was written for Ben Hecht and Charles MacArthur's *The Scoundrel* (1935). While the picture is listed in Antheil's filmography, the finished print carried a credit to "musical director" Frank Tours, who had selected a number of classical pieces to be included in the picture's score. Primary among these was Rachmaninoff's Second Piano Concerto, substituting for what may have been an overly modern score from the "bad boy."

That qualified success notwithstanding, Antheil soon found himself in the deep end of the business through his association with Boris Morros, the head of Paramount's music department, who introduced him to epic-specialist director Cecil B. DeMille. Antheil and the director successfully collaborated on the Western hodgepodge *The Plainsman* (1936) and the spectacular retelling of the Battle of New Orleans *The Buccaneer* (1938).

In 1939, Antheil eagerly took on the job of scoring DeMille's next picture, *Union Pacific*. Till then he had had minimal interference from Paramount's music department, meaning DeMille and Morros usually accepted all the music he wrote. With *Union Pacific*, things were about to change.

> Up until now, let me emphasize that I had had no trouble with the Paramount music department. But, too, up until now, Boris Morros had been in charge. Now he left Paramount in order to become a producer at another studio, and I was suddenly to learn how difficult it is to make a few extra dollars via movie scoring. When I brought my first sketches for *Union Pacific* to Projection Room Number One of Paramount Studios, I noticed something very strange. Previously I could have played any amount of sketches for DeMille without ever encountering a single other movie composer in that projection room; now, however, every movie composer or arranger working at Paramount at that time was mysteriously present! Now C. B. DeMille is a man, if he will forgive my saying so, who likes to keep in touch with the public's pulse; to cut to the chase, he likes to make his pictures by public vote. He is much influenced by everything everybody tells him—especially en masse.

Paramount was always ready to use its staff composers to fix whatever musical problems came up in their distributed titles. For instance, the original music for Alexander Korda's 1931 picture *Service for Ladies* by British composer Percival Mackey was replaced by the stock cues of Karl Hajos, Rudolph Kopp, and John Leipold in the American version. One of the more famous titles tinkered with by the Paramount staff composers is Fritz Lang's criminal romance *You and Me*, which originally had a score by Kurt Weill. Of this, only three songs were retained—the rest was replaced by the music of W. Franke Harling, John Leipold, and an uncredited Leo Shuken.

When Boris Morros was named head of Paramount's music department, he tore down this carefully layered system by firing half the staff composers while he kept on inviting "outsiders" like Antheil. When Morros was later removed from his position, the whole musical department was ready to avenge their treatment by taking care of the last remaining renegade. In his autobiography, Antheil claims that DeMille was initially quite enthusiastic after he presented his *Union Pacific* themes. But then...

> He looked around to see how the rest of the music department liked it. Their faces were a study. I looked at DeMille. I could see him thinking. "Good God, if even his own music department doesn't like it..." "What do you think of it?" he asked them, point-blank. The jury hemmed and hawed. You could see they really didn't like to say, really... DeMille turned around to me and said, not unkindly, "Well, George, perhaps you weren't feeling too well last night. Go home and try again." I was still ace-high with him. The next day I found the projection room filled again. The same jury. They didn't like my sketches again, not really... "They're not bad, you know, but really, Mr. DeMille..." So I went home that night and rewrote everything again. I worked myself silly. Ditto the next night, and the next. Inside of one week I was ready to say "uncle."

The final score for *Union Pacific* was provided by Paramount staffers Sigmund Krumgold and John Leipold, with uncredited input by Gerard Carbonara, Leo Shuken, and Victor Young.

It is interesting to note that Boris Morros actually lost his job because of a similar controversy surrounding the classic 1939 version of *Stagecoach*. Here the original music was written by composer Louis Gruenberg and two other unnamed composers, but producer Walter Wanger didn't like the results, so he commissioned a new score from reliable staff composers. The replacement score, credited to five composers (John Leipold, Leo Shuken, Richard Hageman, Gerard Carbonara, and W. Franke Harling), went on to receive an Academy Award, providing a dramatic end to Morros's attempts at modernizing his studio's film music department.

Paramount continued to use staff composers to alter other composers' film scores even after World War II, when the studio had half of William Alwyn's music for the 1948 British drama *So Evil My Love* rewritten by Victor Young. This practice gradually died out with the fading of the studio system, severely impairing the possibility of quick fixes for individual projects.

■ **The Westerner** (1940)

Original composer: **Dimitri Tiomkin**
Additional composer: **Alfred Newman**

When a film's main titles credit two composers, chances are they either collaborated on the project or helped one another meet a strict deadline. The 20th Century Fox epic *The Egyptian* (1954), for which Alfred Newman and Bernard Herrmann receive joint scoring credit, is a good example of this practice. Sometimes, however, a dual scoring credit is a memento of a partial rescoring.

In 1939, director William Wyler finished shooting *The Westerner*, an unusual Western with a strangely likeable villain in the form of the obsessed Judge Roy Bean, whose only wish in life is to see stage star Lillie Langtry. Producer Samuel Goldwyn, however, held up the picture's release for two reasons. First, he was engaged in arguments with his theatrical distributor, United Artists (which he left in 1941 for RKO), and *The Westerner* was caught up in this turmoil. The second problem concerned the music, as Goldwyn had very conservative musical tastes that were hard to satisfy.

During the extended post-production of *The Westerner*, Goldwyn reconsidered the original score written by Dimitri Tiomkin and deemed most of it too modern. So he called in his favorite composer—Alfred Newman—to make adjustments.

Tiomkin's music for *The Westerner* was largely based on American folk songs. "Buffalo Skinners," "Sweet Betsy from Pike," "Git Along Little Dogie," and "Arkansas Traveler," were all incorporated into his original material. While the adaptations worked well in the traditional framework of Golden Age Westerns, it was Tiomkin's original material that was the source of Goldwyn's dissatisfaction. The producer was unable to express his objections in musical terminology, but he had a problem with Tiomkin's (unusual for Hollywood) chords, which contained what he felt were disturbing added tones that were largely absent from the vernacular of that period's film music.

Alfred Newman's job on *The Westerner* was to bring a more conventional "Western" sound to the picture. As the busy head of 20th Century Fox's music department, he only took the commission as a friendly gesture toward Goldwyn, who was his foremost advocate.

The original Tiomkin sketches are included in USC's Tiomkin collection (no commercially available recording of the score exists at the moment). Based on this collection's cue sheets, Newman took arranger credit for almost half of the composer's work but in fact extensively rewrote those portions. While some of Newman's material also utilizes classic folk tunes, his rearrangements were written in a more conservative fashion and usually didn't reference any of Tiomkin's work. Judging from the cue sheets, Newman primarily reworked the underscore after the first act, including making new arrangements of Stephen Foster's song "Nell and I."

Ironically, the Russian-born and -trained Tiomkin would soon became a real innovator of music for Hollywood Westerns, and to this day other film composers quote from his classic genre pieces. He worked on some of the greatest Westerns ever made; his scores for *Red River (1948)*, *Duel in the Sun (1947)*, and *High Noon (1952)* contain some of the best-known melodies of the genre.

Later in his career, Tiomkin had to bow out of two potential blockbusters. In 1962 he had to turn down John Ford's *How the West Was Won* due to eye surgery, so the score was written by Alfred Newman. Then, in 1964, he was poised to define the sound of the television Western as well by providing the theme song to *The Wild Wild West*, for which he was also to score the pilot episode.

As he was known to do, Tiomkin toyed with the press by announcing that he was going to use ten zithers in the pilot score, claiming that Hollywood had mistreated the instrument up to that point. Ultimately, however, nothing came of the idea, as Tiomkin failed to deliver a theme song that satisfied the show's creators. Producer Michael Garrison hated his "The Ballad of Jim West" and the alternate tune "Wild West," both of which he considered too old-fashioned. The pilot and the main title were eventually completed by Richard Markowitz, although Tiomkin was paid $7,500 for his troubles and was permitted to keep his compositions.

Orchestrator Patrick Russ reconstructed both failed songs for a recording of Tiomkin's film music in 2004, and a suite from *The Westerner* is still in the works.

■ The Thief of Bagdad (1940)

Original composer: **Oscar Straus**
Replacement composer: **Miklós Rózsa**

The subtitle of *The Thief of Bagdad* promised "An Arabian Fantasy in Technicolor," and it was definitely an adventure everybody remembered. Utilizing a series of special effects that are still quite effective, the movie featured djinns, wizards, flying horses, and a story so magical that it remained a popular title decades after its premiere.

The Thief of Bagdad was produced by the pioneering London Films, which presented groundbreaking movies in England. The most surprising thing about the firm was that almost its entire production team consisted of Hungarian immigrants, led by the three Korda brothers: Alexander (producer), Zoltán (director), and Vincent (art director). London Films hired many talented Hungarians, including screenwriter Lajos Bíró and young composer Miklós Rózsa, who had scored *Knight Without Armour* (1937) and *The Four Feathers* (1939) for the company.

Alexander wanted to hire Rózsa for their latest extravagant venture as well, but director Ludwig Berger insisted on using Austrian composer Oscar Straus, with whom he had previously worked on *Ein Waltztraum* (1925) and *Les Trois valses* (1938). It was decided that Straus would provide all the music, including the songs to be performed in the picture, but it would be up to Rózsa to adapt this material to fit the screen. This was an important condition because Straus wasn't available on-site: He sent all his material from the French town of Vichy, where he was taking a cure. A composer of operettas and an array of films with "waltz" in their titles, Straus proved an unlucky choice, as his music leaned toward what Rózsa described as "turn-of-the-century Viennese candy-floss."

Shortly after Straus's sketches arrived in London, the production was brought to a halt by Muir Mathieson's open criticism of the music, which he found incompetent. Rózsa was advised by Korda not to say anything, and after a stormy meeting in the producer's office, a conspiracy was put in motion to change Berger's mind about the music.

> He [Korda] said, "Go home now and re-write everything Straus has done. When you're ready, call me." Which I did, and he then told me, "We will install a piano in the office next to Dr. Berger's. Go there and play your songs whenever he is in there until he comes in to find out what you're doing. Meanwhile not a word to anyone about this, not even to Muir Mathieson." So, at 9 a.m. the next morning I did as instructed, settled myself in the little office and thumped at the piano with all my might. This went on for the whole day, and the next—I played and worked, played and worked, always fortissimo. The secretaries all started complaining that they couldn't type or make phone calls, but I simply referred them to Mr. Korda. Anyway, on the third day the door opened and in came Dr. Berger. He asked me what I was playing and I told him: "Oh, just a few ideas of mine for the picture." "Well, play them to me!" So I played him Sabu's song, the love-theme, The Silvermaid's Dance—everything that I had done so far. I could sense immediately there had been a breakthrough of some kind, and when I had finished I noticed beads of perspiration on his forehead. He said, "How am I going to tell Straus?" Then and there he went to Korda, who told him that if he wanted me, he could have me.

After Berger's change of heart, Straus was sent a telegram dismissing him from the production. The composer was furious and threatened to sue Korda, subsequently dropping this idea after he was paid his full fee. Rózsa's songs and score went on to become classics. Dozens of compositions were written during the production and then abandoned after scene changes. Today, these pieces survive in manuscript form only.

Despite the resolution of the musical situation, *The Thief of Bagdad* had more than its share of problems throughout its creation. British newspapers poked fun at the fact that one of the country's chief diplomatic advisers, Alexander Korda's friend Sir Robert Vansittart, spent the early years of World War II writing song lyrics for it. Also, the bombing of London caused the whole production to be transferred from Britain to Hollywood. Nonetheless, Rózsa's score managed to become an instant classic, and the movie's trip across the Atlantic began his prolific Hollywood career.

■ **Commandos Strike at Dawn** (1942)

Original composer: **Igor Stravinsky**
Replacement composer: **Louis Gruenberg**

In the early 1940s, composer Igor Stravinsky was recovering from a series of personal tragedies and sought refuge from the war in America. Although he made a few acquaintances at MGM during his 1935 visit, he obtained no film work until 1942, when he received a serious commission from Columbia to score a war picture titled *Commandos Strike at Dawn,* about the Norwegian resistance during World War II.

While war movies as a genre had a very specific sound, usually utilizing heroic marches for the Allies and easily identifiable descending motives for the Nazis, Stravinsky approached the project from a completely different perspective, focusing on the conflict's victims rather than its heroes. Being a refugee from the war himself, he felt sympathy for the survivors of war and gave the score an almost bucolic feeling at some points, depicting the idyllic life of the Norwegians that had ended with the Nazi invasion.

Stravinsky bought a book of Norwegian song adaptations that contained ten pieces, three of which were adapted by Edvard Grieg. He chose these songs as his starting point, but since he was not well versed in the medium of film scoring, he engaged the help of more experienced film composers. Miklós Rózsa remembers his discussions with Stravinsky:

> One night, [Alexandre] Tansman and Stravinsky told me that they had been offered a film; since Stravinsky had never written a film score Tansman had been engaged as his assistant and adviser. It was a war picture called *The Commandos Strike at Dawn,* set in Norway. They asked my advice on all sorts of technical matters, while I was more interested in establishing whether or not they had received contracts. No, they said, but their agent said it was all settled. A month later I met them again. There was still no contract, but they showed me the Prelude Stravinsky had written based on Norwegian folk songs. It was in full score, in his immaculate hand, on paper where, as always, he had drawn his own staves with a little gadget of his own design. I read it through— it was a lovely

> little piece—and asked again about the contract. Nothing. At last it became apparent that the producer had cold feet. His alleged reason for not engaging the man he called "the great Maestro" was that he knew that the Maestro would need a huge orchestra to do justice to his magnificent music (in fact, after *The Rite of Spring,* Stravinsky's orchestra tended to be smaller than average, rather than larger) and the budget could only run to a small one.

His ideas of shifting the score's focus from the attackers to the victims apart, Stravinsky's working methods were also strange by Hollywood standards. He started writing without a contract and before seeing a frame of the movie, yet finished the last cleanups long after he was fired from the picture. He had, it turned out, other plans for the music: The score for *Commandos Strike at Dawn* was recycled into *Four Norwegian Moods,* which premiered on 13 January 1944 in Boston, conducted by Stravinsky himself. The four movements are titled "Intrada," "Song," "Wedding Dance," and "Cortége."

The replacement composer for the project was Louis Gruenberg. Gruenberg was also of Russian descent, but he had different roots from Stravinsky's, coming to the United States at the age of two and having little direct connection with the war that currently raged around the globe. His quickly delivered score was not only to Columbia's taste, but also that of the Motion Picture Academy, which nominated it for an Oscar in 1944.

After the failed experiment with *Commandos Strike at Dawn,* Stravinsky had no film work to keep him in Hollywood until a particular neighbor got him a more substantial commission.

Stravinsky lived next door to author Franz Werfel, whose latest novel, *The Song of Bernadette,* had been quickly optioned by 20th Century Fox for a feature adaptation. The studio spent $2 million on the picture, a small fraction of which went toward commissioning music from Stravinsky. As with *Commandos Strike at Dawn,* though, nothing came through. The composer was attracted to the project, but he backed out because of clashes with Darryl F. Zanuck. The music he composed for the "Apparition of the Virgin" scene would later form the middle section of his *Symphony in Three Movements,* while the first and third movements were based on music written for MGM war shorts about Japan's scorched-earth tactics in China and Allied victories.

Stravinsky had one more shot at Hollywood, but the music he wrote for Orson Welles's *Jane Eyre* never made it into the picture (it later became part of the composer's *Gloria*). Despite not finding the right niche with the studios, Stravinsky remained in Los Angeles until 1969.

■ **Hitler's Madman** (1943)

Original composer: **Karl Hajos**
Replacement composers: **Nathaniel Shilkret, Mario Castelnuovo-Tedesco, Eric Zeisl, Arthur Morton**

While Warner Bros., Paramount, and MGM were busy rescoring their films to improve their quality, Hollywood's smaller and more obscure studios of the era had their own problems. These "poverty row" studios operated with minuscule budgets and produced B-movies as quickly as they could, in order to satisfy the need for new features every week. Their movies starred reliable character actors with long-term contracts, in cheap productions of almost every genre from Western to jungle adventure to horror, or whatever the public was most keen on at the moment.

In this fiscally tight situation, the companies hired temporarily available composers or utilized library cues to score their movies. These and other cost-cutting measures reflected negatively on the little studios, but occasionally one of their projects would rise above its humble origins and begin a new life under the distribution of a bigger studio, with a bigger budget.

One such title was the 1943 production *Hitler's Hangman*, by Producers Releasing Corporation. PRC was a big fish in a small pond, as they managed not only to produce their own movies but to distribute them as well. *Hitler's Hangman* was their greatest hit. Directed by Douglas Sirk shortly after he and his wife escaped from Nazi Germany, the movie told the story of Colonel Reinhardt Heydrich, Hitler's appointed "Protector" to Prague and the Czech territories, whose tyranny was avenged by the resistance. *Hitler's Hangman* was a powerful production, particularly due to Sirk's excellent handling, far above the level of the average poverty row picture.

Word soon got out that PRC might have done something special this time, and MGM informed the company that it would be interested in picking up the movie as its own release. Since PRC didn't have the necessary resources to exploit the picture to its fullest, the company agreed to the deal and handed over *Hitler's Hangman* to MGM. The new owners first renamed it *Hitler's Madman*, and then, hoping to make it sound more like a genuine studio feature, they replaced most of the music.

The original score was provided by Austrian-born Karl Hajos, who worked as a staff composer for Paramount and often engaged in freelance writing for the various poverty row productions. The new main titles were done by a young Arthur Morton, who later became one of Jerry Goldsmith's regular orchestrators. Others whose music was featured in this musical mixture included MGM staff composers Nathaniel Shilkret, Mario Castelnuovo-Tedesco, and Eric Zeisl, with bits and pieces of Hajos' score left in where it was suitable.

To our ears the change of score makes little sense, given that the musical approaches differ very little. However, this was a question of prestige for MGM, and the work of its staff composers forms a musical continuity between the "outsider"

Hitler's Madman and the studio's other features. For that reason alone, the change of composers is understandable, although it doesn't make the differences any more noticeable to the contemporary ear.

■ Since You Went Away (1944)

Original composer: **Alexandre Tansman**
Replacement composer: **Max Steiner**

Since You Went Away was David O. Selznick's Oscar bait for the 1944 season. It told the story of a loyal wife left at home while her husband fought for his country. As was typical with his productions, Selznick personally took charge of all its aspects, from scripting to overseeing the music. But it seems he was out of his depth in finding the perfect composer for this assignment.

As late as early 1943, Selznick showed interest in employing MGM's in-house composer Herbert Stothart, as well as the up-and-coming Bernard Herrmann, based on the latter composer's work on *Citizen Kane* and *The Devil and Daniel Webster*. After receiving a telegram from Herrmann stating that he thought he'd be unsuitable for the job, Selznick ordered a list of all the available Hollywood composers and a short resumé for each of them. From this list, he chose Polish composer Alexandre Tansman, whose single credit was Universal's *Flesh and Fantasy*.

Selznick eventually selected two additional people from the list: He hired Charles Previn to be the conductor, and musical director Louis Forbes to oversee the production's source music. Forbes played a key part as Selznick and his musical advisors selected a couple of popular tunes for the picture. These had to be recorded in advance of shooting, so the first work for Tansman and Previn was to record a couple of versions of "Together," a 1928 song by Buddy G. DeSylva, Lew Brown, and Ray Henderson. The song was to be a cornerstone of the movie's music: It would be used in the big dance sequence, played by a music box, and whistled by Joseph Cotten.

Initially enthusiastic over Tansman's score, Selznick then seems to have had second thoughts. He sent the following memo to production manager Richard Johnston on 13 March 1944:

> Would you please get together with Hal Kern immediately and discuss with him my desire that the Tansman score of SYWA should not be done continuously but that the first sessions should be limited to whatever is the minimum required from a cost standpoint. Also it should, of course, be handled diplomatically and be kept between ourselves so as not to frighten or discourage Tansman. My purpose is to hear a couple reels of his music before he proceeds with the whole picture, so that if I am going to get any shocks or disappointments it will be limited to these few reels and I will know with the least possible delay whether or not I have to make a switch. I have the highest possible hopes for Tansman's work but I don't know enough about it not to want to be absolutely sure that I am right about him before the whole picture is scored.

Obeying the producer's wishes, Tansman produced a temporary recording for the movie's first couple of reels. This early predecessor of today's mockup practice was unique in that Tansman had to reorchestrate his score for the reduced forces of a chamber ensemble. Naturally, a handful of players cannot project the force of a full orchestra, and the thinness of the sound, when it was presented to Selznick, sealed Tansman's fate.

Although every memo the producer wrote on the subject claimed that he liked the tunes, the orchestration of the temporary track left him unmoved. He appreciated Tansman's talent, but believed the Polish composer simply didn't have the background in Hollywood to realize the full scope of an important project like *Since You Went Away*.

Abe Meyer of MCA Artists tried to champion Tansman's score. In a letter dated 14 April 1944, he listed a couple of reasons why Selznick should have given Tansman a second chance:

> Mr. Tansman's actual work on this consisted of only five or six minutes of music, principally arrangements of the song, "Together." This music was not timed to fit the actual scenes in the picture, but the work was done in accordance with the instructions received from your editing department. Tansman was simply requested to make several arrangements of "Together," given the approximate length of the whole scene and the general mood of the scene. Neither Tansman nor Charlie Previn were consulted for the application of these recordings to the scenes, and they had no idea as to how they were used. I would also like to mention that the recording of the temporary track was made with a small orchestra at Mr. Selznick's explicit request and, naturally, these tracks could not sound as full as the other tracks which were made with music larger orchestras. It might be this comparison which caused Mr. Selznick's disappointment.

Two weeks later, Selznick's mind was made up. He rang up his composer friend Max Steiner and asked him to come in and do the score. Abe Meyer, who had delivered all the Tansman music, recommended Victor Young as a replacement, but Selznick didn't want any more musical exploration and even rejected the prospect of Bernard Herrmann doing the score. He wanted Steiner to come in and save the day.

Steiner was going through hard times with his wife, Louise Klos (the two divorced the next year), and Selznick was very appreciative of Steiner's undertaking the work under such circumstances, not to mention the severe time constraints and the additional baggage of Tansman's score, from which a recording of "Together" was retained.

One hopes that the Academy Award Steiner received for the music, which happened to be the only one awarded to *Since You Went Away*, made him forget his troubles for a while. Unfortunately, this is one of the many Steiner scores lacking a legitimate CD release.

■ **Caesar and Cleopatra** (1945)

Original composer: **Arthur Bliss**
Replacement composer: **Georges Auric**

Based on the play by George Bernard Shaw, *Caesar and Cleopatra* was the most expensive British film produced up to that point. (One of the stories about its excessive budget claims that the crew brought sand from Egypt in order to have truly authentic sets!)

While the movie was well received for its visual extravagance, contemporary reviewers took issue with its many flaws, all of which were attributable to the man in charge, producer/director Gabriel Pascal. Pascal had previously produced two other G. B. Shaw adaptations, *Pygmalion* and *Major Barbara*. A legendary craftsman, he was tough and uncompromising in all departments of production, especially in music.

Many, however, felt that Pascal's concepts were often unclear, and that he devoted too much energy to pointless changes. In 1940, for instance, he spent a large amount of money getting portions of William Walton's *Major Barbara* score rewritten by fellow Hungarian Miklós Rózsa. Among Rózsa's challenges were rearranging the main theme, "Onward, Christian Soldiers," to sound more comical. He achieved this by adding a pizzicato string counterpoint to Walton's arrangement.

Rózsa writes of his work with Pascal:

> I had to redo another scene, where Walton had underlined every funny remark with a "wah-wah" on the trumpet. He wasn't to blame—it was the style of the time, and I had done exactly the same in *The Divorce of Lady X* on the advice of Muir Mathieson, who told me that we had to learn from Hollywood. Pascal wanted me to produce a different sort of "wah-wah," and I spent half an hour with the trumpeter trying every possible sort of "kva-kva" (as Pascal called it). Nothing satisfied him. We tried every sort of mute, every conceivable way of playing, but nothing was any good. At last, Pascal shouted, "It's hopeless! The man has no sense of humour!" When we saw the finished edit, the "kva-kva" we had finally chosen (after endless wasting of time and Korda's money) was inaudible under the dialogue.

This little anecdote gives a good example of the sorts of things that both composers for *Caesar and Cleopatra* had to put up with.

Unverified rumors at the time named the acclaimed William Walton, Benjamin Britten, and Sergei Prokofiev as composers whom Shaw had approached to do the score. But on 6 June 1944, composer Arthur Bliss finally signed a contract to do it, making his deal with the author rather than the director. Bliss was a well-established composer of classical concert music with only a few movies to his name. His filmography, however, contained the most expensive film of its time, H. G. Wells's *Things to Come*, whose score would have been a milestone in British film scoring had it not been ruined by the constant re-editing of the picture and the poor quality of contemporary dubbing technology.

All the communication regarding the music for *Caesar and Cleopatra* was conducted by Shaw, whose background as a music critic led to some helpful suggestions. In two letters to Bliss, he advised the composer to write his own music in his own style and not produce a clichéd imitation of Egyptian music. Shaw went on to offer Bliss additional advice:

> Be careful not to let yourself be placed in the position of an employee of Pascal or of the film company, as anything you compose for them in that capacity will belong to them and not to you. If I were a composer writing for a film I should make a skeleton piano score of an orchestral suite consisting of overture, nocturne, barcarole, intermezzo, and finale. I should copyright this in my own name in England and America. Then, being in an impregnable position as sole owner of the music, I should license the film people to use the material as an accompaniment to their film for a stated period on stated terms, giving them no rights whatever.... Remember that an orchestral suite by you will long survive Pascal's film and become a standard concert piece quite independently of my play, like Grieg's *Peer Gynt*. Let no parasite fasten on it.

Bliss wrote 100 pages of music and, following Shaw's advice, didn't bother much with the conventional film music styles of the era. He made use of a lot of diegetic music, with tracks such as "Ftatateeta," "Soldiers' Chorus," and "Barcarolle," some of which included the only exotic instrument the score called for, an ancient Roman wind instrument called the *buccina*.

Of this work, only a seventeen-minute suite in eight movements was ever recorded. It contains both orchestral underscore and source music in the following sections: a grand ceremonial "Overture," two moody tracks ("The Sea" and "Memphis at Night"), three dance interludes of varying intensity written for the banquet, and, finally "Supply Sequence," which was later reused in a short film produced by the Ministry of Information titled *Présence au combat* (aka *La France combattante*).

None of this music, however, was used in *Caesar and Cleopatra*; Bliss bowed out of the project once he got to know Gabriel Pascal. His replacement, noted French concert composer and film composer Georges Auric, found it harder to capture the exoticism of Egypt without using traditional Egyptian instruments. His strategy was to employ an interesting orchestra lineup that included piano, celesta, xylophone, bells, harp, and even a saxophone, and his music proved to be one of the highlights of an otherwise flawed production.

Like Bliss's work, selections of Auric's music for this film have been rerecorded and issued on a compilation.

■ **The Naked City** (1948)

Original composer: **George Bassman**
Replacement composers: **Miklós Rózsa, Frank Skinner**

The Naked City is one of the classic film noirs of the 1940s, a brutally honest look at the criminal underbelly of New York City. The two driving forces behind this groundbreaking movie were producer Mark Hellinger and director Jules Dassin.

Hellinger had been a New York newspaper columnist before building a career in Hollywood, first producing for Warner Bros. and then for Universal. He became famous for such hard-hitting film noirs as director Richard Siodmak's *The Killers* (1946) and Dassin's *Brute Force* (1947).

After hiring Dassin to direct *The Naked City*, Hellinger, accustomed to giving his directors a lot of artistic freedom, laid down only one important condition for the director, that he use Miklós Rózsa as the film's composer. Rózsa had previously scored both *The Killers* and *Brute Force*. But before there could be a third Hellinger-Rózsa collaboration, Dassin decided against it.

Rózsa wrote about this change of plans:

> One day, though, he [Hellinger] called me in and explained frankly that he was in a quandary: Dassin wanted him to use instead a composer friend who had also lost his job at MGM, though for a different reason. I remembered Berger, Straus, and *The Thief of Bagdad*, so I told him that, if that was what Dassin wanted, it was all right with me; there would be other opportunities for us to work together in the future, and I would have no hard feelings. Hellinger was such a sweet man; he embraced me (it was early in the morning and he had a few brandies already) and said, "You're really not mad at me?" "How could I be," I replied, "when I love you?" So that was that, or so I thought.

The tumult of the production of *The Naked City*, famous for its uncompromising use of actual locations (a practice that was very unusual at the time), proved too much for Hellinger: He suffered a heart attack while working in New York. Despite his doctors' advice to rest for six weeks, he continued with the production and eventually attended the recording sessions of the musical score, conducted by the composer chosen by Dassin, George Bassman. Bassman was a famed MGM arranger and composer who had scored three earlier Dassin films: *Young Ideas* (1943), *A Letter for Evie* (1946), and *Two Smart People* (1946).

During the recording sessions, Hellinger began to believe that the score sounded similar to a certain Aaron Copland composition. (Bassman had studied with Copland.) Knowing Bassman's background as an arranger, he was afraid the composer might simply have reworked already-existing music, a situation that could have legal consequences. Bassman stated, however, that his music was completely original; further, he accused Hellinger of knowing nothing about music. This infuriated the producer, who immediately called Rózsa and asked him to replace Bassman as quickly as he could. Rózsa wrote of this dust-up:

> Dassin's friend (whom I didn't know personally) was really an arranger, and when Hellinger heard this man's score at the recording session he almost had another heart attack. He ranted and raved and swore that, come what may, that music would never go into his picture. The next day I received a call with the familiar voice at the other end. He began by asking if I had finished the picture I was working on [*Desert Fury*] and whether I had heard about what had happened the previous day. I said I had, and there was a long dramatic pause during which he searched for the right words. In the end he just said, "Would you...?" and my heart overflowed. "You know I would, Mark," I replied. "Bless you," he said. That was our last conversation together: next morning I heard on the radio that he had died during the night of another heart attack.

The producer's death (at age 44) didn't stop the system for a moment—Rózsa watched and spotted *The Naked City* in the studio just one hour after Hellinger's funeral service. The head of Universal's music department, Milton Schwarzwald, consulted with Rózsa on the score and gave him a strict deadline that left him only two weeks to complete the entire job on his own. Rózsa initially refused the idea of employing an additional composer but later accepted Schwarzwald's offer to bring in Universal staff composer Frank Skinner.

Skinner received screen credit in the movie, scoring the less music-dependent dialogue scenes, while Rózsa worked on the more musically important sequences. Thus, Hellinger's last wish of having a Rózsa score for *The Naked City* was fulfilled. Shortly after completion of the picture, Rózsa created a testament to his friend in the form of a symphonic poem he called *Mark Hellinger Suite*, which contained two cues each from the scores of *The Killers*, *Brute Force*, and *The Naked City*. Today this piece is known as *Background to Violence*, a title assigned to it when it was recorded by Decca Records (USA).

Interestingly, both Dassin and his first-choice composer, Bassman, would soon be blacklisted for their political beliefs and activities. Dassin directed only two more films—the dark classics *Thieves Highway* (1949) and *Night and the City* (1950)—before his 1950 blacklisting, after which he moved to Europe and didn't direct again for five years. (In 1952, he refused to testify before the House Un-American Activities Committee.) After his *Naked City* spat with Hellinger, Bassman felt unwelcome in Hollywood, so he moved to New York City, where he worked on major Broadway productions. (In 1952, he too was called before the House Un-American Activities Committee, where he testified to his—as well as his mother's and ex-wife's—earlier involvement with the Communist Party.)

■ **Michurin** (1948)

Original composer: **Gavril Popov**
Replacement composer: **Dmitri Shostakovich**

Ivan Vladimirovich Michurin, an agricultural innovator who introduced more than 300 new types of fruits to the working class, was a hero of Soviet science who, like all deserving Soviet heroes, was awarded his own biographical picture. What makes this film remarkable is that its music became the focal point of a political discussion. In order to understand why, we need a bit of historical background.

The original composer selected for the Michurin story was Gavril Nikolayevich Popov, who was born in 1904 and studied in the Leningrad Conservatory during the early Soviet years, from 1922 to 1930. From the start of his career, and especially after the premiere of his *Septet/Chamber Symphony*, he was regarded as the likely successor to Dmitri Shostakovich. Yet after the premiere of his Symphony No. 1 (op. 7), Popov was accused of "formalism," a mortal sin in the eyes of the Soviet authorities. As a result, he—like many twentieth-century Soviet composers—imposed boundaries on his own creativity. In Popov's case, this self-censorship led to alcoholism.

Accusations of "formalism" (more a political charge than an artistic one) affected many artists whose work was deemed too highbrow and artsy to appeal to the masses. In 1946, when Central Committee secretary Andrei Zhdanov was given control of his country's cultural policies and took the government's campaign against formalism to greater lengths, Soviet composers found themselves in an even more difficult situation. Zhdanov, whose motto was, "The only possible conflict in Soviet culture is the conflict between good and best," introduced a doctrine that bears his name. "Zhdanovism" required that artists working in all fields adhere to the government's choice of proper style, usually meaning some form of Socialist Realism.

In 1948, Zhdanov extended the reach of his doctrine from primarily literary works to music with the Central Committee's censorship of Vano Muradeli's opera *The Great Friendship*. The upshot of this change was that forward-thinking Soviet composers no longer had a platform for their works. Dmitri Shostakovich, Sergei Prokofiev, Aram Khachaturian, and many others who didn't adhere tightly enough to the party's dictates were directed toward writing film music. Zhdanov felt that doing film music brought composers into the service of a higher cause, teaching them to produce something useful instead of what he considered pointless, self-serving symphonies and chamber works. The low number of available movie assignments, however, forced the composers to compete for jobs.

Michurin (written and directed by Aleksandr Dovzhenko) represented Popov's first opportunity to work under the Zhdanovistic regime, so he had little idea how far he could go with his musical score.

The key musical figure at the time was Tikhon Nikolayevich Khrennikov, leader of the Union of Soviet Composers. It was his job to supervise the musical aspects of his country's prestige pictures. Khrennikov had serious reservations about Popov, and when he heard Popov's finished score, he tarred it with the formalism brush, claiming that well-known traditional tunes were barely recognizable because of Popov's modifications, making the score unworthy of inclusion.

Since *Michurin*'s production was overseen by Stalin himself (though he didn't get executive producer credit), Khrennikov quickly handed the movie to Shostakovich. The new composer was better versed in what was expected of him, allowing him to duly fulfill the wishes of Khrennikov, who was extremely pleased with the new score. While not a particular fan of the film's director, Shostakovich enjoyed the actual shooting of the film, and later used it as an inspiration for *The Song of the Forests*. The composing process itself proved more difficult, though, as the composer suffered frequent headaches and found little creative challenge in the movie.

Michurin is often labeled as Shostakovich's worst film score. That may reflect the severe limitations under which he worked. With Popov's ill-fated earlier score as a guide to the allowable boundaries, he simplified everything he could and resorted to writing filler material between folk songs, which he didn't dare modify. As a final neat touch, he inserted his earlier composition "Song of the Counterplan" into the score, as it was favored by the authorities. In the movie, the song is performed by a group of peasants who are led by the agronomist into a better future.

Soviet composers' own better future finally arrived on May 28, 1958, when those who had been persecuted under the Zhdanov doctrine were formally declared rehabilitated.

Shostakovich's score was later organized into a suite by his student Lev Atovmian and recorded on a compilation focusing on lesser film works.

■ Night and the City (1950)

Composer for British version: **Benjamin Frankel**
Composer for American version: **Franz Waxman**

While the American film industry was running at full power during World War II, the British film industry was less active. Following the war, coproductions involving studios in both countries grew in frequency, as did clashes between American and British film production methods, especially with regard to scoring. These clashes resulted in a couple of score replacements almost every year, starting with *Night and the City*, a picture that would become a classic of the film noir genre.

Night and the City was done as an Anglo-American joint venture because producer Darryl F. Zanuck wanted to help blacklisted director Jules Dassin. To secure him some work outside Hollywood, he gave him this film, which was to be shot largely in London. But Zanuck's English partners asked for some favors in return. Because it was a coproduction, 20th Century Fox was contractually obliged to employ a given percentage of British crew. One of those "quota crewmembers" was Benjamin Frankel, the composer who would later write the first serial film score for Hammer's *The Curse of the Werewolf* (1961).

With his roots in jazz, Frankel's produced a forty-five-minute score for *Night and the City* that combined jazz-influenced orchestral music and stylistically fitting source music. Its highlights are the pulsating "Main Title," the more romantic "Mary's Apartment," and the climactic "Harry Escapes from Figler."

Fox, however, was averse to using Frankel's music for business reasons that had nothing to do with the music's quality. The film was, therefore, rescored for its American release, and only the version screened in British territories retained Frankel's music.

British and American film composers of that era were compensated for their work in different ways. American composers generally received more money for their scores, but their music became the property of the studios. British composers, on the other hand, were paid less but retained their music's copyright, allowing them to, for example, arrange a film score into a suite and perform it in concert or for recordings without studio interference.

When American companies started to coproduce more films with Great Britain and employ more British composers as part of their quota deals, music ownership became a sensitive issue. To illustrate this situation, the surviving records show that Frankel received £750 for writing the music for *Night and the City* (to which he retained the copyright), while his eventual American counterpart, Franz Waxman, was paid $12,500 for both his composing efforts and his rights.

Jules Dassin returned to America during *Night and the City*'s postproduction and worked only with Waxman, the American studio's pick. Waxman began writing his music four weeks after the British composer had completed his score, and in fact, Dassin didn't even learn about Frankel's score until decades later.

Waxman worked under most unusual circumstances, consulting with Dassin on the telephone without actually meeting the blacklisted director. The American score has perhaps more of a Hollywood style to it and is about sixty minutes long, almost a quarter of an hour longer than Frankel's. Waxman's work also includes both source music and underscore, but with a more dominant orchestral presence, especially from the strings, which provide a dark melancholy that envelops the picture.

Night and the City was soon followed by rescored pictures of all kinds. The Bette Davis mystery story *Another Man's Poison* (1951) originally had a score by John Greenwood, but by the time it reached America it had music by Paul Sawtell. The British version of the Warner Bros. picture *His Majesty O'Keefe* (1954) had a score by Robert Farnon, but the composer for the American release was Dimitri Tiomkin, who also penned the movie's song "Emerald Island." The period saw many examples of Anglo-American joint productions with scores that differed in different releasing territories.

The music for *Night and the City* has been much discussed by film music fans because both its British and American scores have been released on a double CD, allowing easy comparison. (Unfortunately, Criterion's DVD release of *Night and the City* could only include a couple of bonus scenes with Frankel's score, as the British print was withdrawn in 1962 and only recovered in 2002–03.)

■ A Place in the Sun (1951)

Original composer: **Franz Waxman**
Additional composers: **Daniele Amfitheatrof, Victor Young**

George Stevens's *A Place in the Sun* was based on Theodore Dreiser's *An American Tragedy*. Since this 1949 production was considered an Oscar contender, Paramount reportedly held up its release so it wouldn't have to compete with *Sunset Blvd.*, another surefire hit released in 1950. Both movies were scored by Franz Waxman, who became the first composer to win two successive Academy Awards for them.

But what's rarely mentioned about *A Place in the Sun* is that it was the first prestige picture to pose major postproduction problems for the music department. Previous problem titles had either been of lesser importance, or (as in the case of *Since You Went Away*) had faced their biggest musical difficulties before the recording of their original scores were undertaken.

A Place in the Sun saw almost a third of its music replaced, becoming one of the first publicized examples of a score being tampered with by a higher power—in this case, director George Stevens. Considering how much controversy it generated within the business at the time, it's surprising that concerns about the film's music are all but forgotten today, thanks to the ingeniousness of Waxman's music and the fact that the replaced bits are barely noticeable.

In Hollywood's Golden Age, just who wrote what part of a movie's music was not as sensitive an issue as it is today. There are numerous examples of ghost-writing, music directors credited and awarded on projects they didn't contribute to, and so on. In fact, a good deal of film music literature prides itself on uncovering the horrific truth about legendary films.

But such practices were commonplace in yesterday's Hollywood. They are only shocking when considered within the context of present-day thinking about the composer as a freelance artist with a commitment to individualism. That outlook only emerged with the passing of the old studio system.

Franz Waxman wrote and recorded a complete score for *A Place in the Sun*. George Stevens, however, had a hard time with the music in one of the scenes. He felt that a particular cue was too subtle and wanted something more dramatic.

The first rewrite composer to be hired was Daniele Amfitheatrof, who produced new music for the scene. But soon more of Waxman's music was discarded, and by the end of the editing process, almost a third of his score had been replaced by Amfitheatrof and Victor Young, head of the Paramount music department. Some anecdotes claim Young refused to betray another composer, but the cue sheets reveal that both he and Amfitheatrof wrote around a dozen cues for the project. Apart from their work, stock music by Frank Skinner and Miklós Rózsa also appeared in the mix, not to mention the many stock cues that were utilized as source music.

While this may not look like a lot of music tampering, especially when compared with most other titles in this book, it created enough controversy at the time to make it historically important. The situation was made all the more problematic by Waxman, who was so committed to his artistic integrity that he didn't even want to rewrite a single cue.

A Place in the Sun's delayed premiere (mentioned above) allowed for a lot of tinkering by Stevens, who was responsible for the final musical mixture. While Waxman's most memorable theme ("Vickers' Theme") was retained almost intact, the Oscar the composer received was scant compensation for the atrocities committed on the rest of the score.

In 1965, George Stevens once again created a film music controversy when he made similar changes in Alfred Newman's score for *The Greatest Story Ever Told*. In this case, several sections of the original score were replaced with reprises of Handel's "Hallelujah" and excerpts from Verdi's *Requiem*. This was the first partial score replacement to merit its own book, *Hollywood Holyland: The Filming and Scoring of the Greatest Story Ever Told*, penned by Newman associate and choral supervisor Ken Darby. The book goes into great detail about how Stevens butchered music that Darby felt was more appropriate for the picture than any of the replacement cues.

The scandal was all the more noticeable because replacing prolific composers' scores was still largely unheard of. Even though *Torn Curtain* and *2001: A Space Odyssey* were just around the corner, the fact that the legendary head of the 20th Century Fox music department would have to endure even a partial replacement of his music was unbelievable to contemporary reviewers. Both Waxman and Newman were committed to artistic integrity, but in the following years that would prove to be an exceptionally hard commitment to maintain in Hollywood.

■ **Distant Drums** (1951)

Original composer: **Alex North**
Replacement composer: **Max Steiner**

Produced by Milton Sperling's United States Film Productions, *Distant Drums* is a Western that takes place in Florida during the Second Seminole War. A largely forgotten picture today, its most interesting aspect is its muddled musical history, which began with an ill-advised marketing concept that took the title *Distant Drums* very much to heart.

The Warner Bros. publicity department made big news of the upcoming score, going so far as to claim that the film would have "the first all-percussion symphony as the background score," in which music director Ray Heindorf would "employ drums from all the world." It is not known whether Heindorf actually wrote anything like that for the picture; even if he did, no such material survived. It's very likely that the "symphony" made up of "exotic percussion" and "jungle noises" was only imagined by an eager publicist.

Up-and-coming composer Alex North was contracted to do the picture on 9 July 1951, fresh from his success with *A Streetcar Named Desire* (1951), one of the first jazz scores written for a movie. Looking forward to scoring both *Viva Zapata!* and *Death of a Salesman*, North had to first finish *Distant Drums* (an assignment he had accepted mainly because it didn't require a lot of music) by 5 August. The picture was spotted sparsely, which was very unusual for a Western. The composer wrote only eleven cues, not scoring a single second of the first or last two reels. The entire score would have been twenty-five minutes long, but only seven cues, fifteen minutes of music, were recorded.

North avoided using a string section, guitars, Indian drums, or harmonicas, going instead with woodwinds and brass in their lower registers, timpani, and xylophones performing dissonant harmonies in odd meters—that is, basically what one might expect from him. However, someone at United States Film obviously didn't know the composer's stylistic predilections, because North was fired after just one day of recording, without finishing the score.

According to a widely circulated anecdote, Milton Sperling, the person behind the rejection, considered the music too modern, saying it sounded like "Barstock" (meaning Hungarian composer Béla Bartók).

North's contract was terminated. Of his $8,000 fee, he received only $5,000 because he hadn't finished the recording. The original contract specified that he was to be paid even if the producer decided not to use his score, and that copyright in every composition not used in the finished film would revert back to North. The rejection changed everything, so the composer opted for a swift solution. Paying back the $5,000, he retained full copyright in all his music. Thanks to some friendly encouragement from Elia Kazan, who suggested that the people dismissing his music should "swim in their own shit and choke to death in it," he survived the episode relatively unscathed.

Just one week after North's recording day, Sperling hired composer Max Steiner, who was not only a Warner Bros. veteran but had also worked on four earlier United States Pictures titles. Steiner's more traditional score for *Distant Drums* has been released along with his other USP works, but North's music has not been released commercially, even though it survives in multiple copies. The Alex North Collection at the Margaret Herrick Library holds not only the original scores and sketches but also acetate discs and an open-reel tape, which together contain various takes of all seven recorded cues. A tape can also be found in the Ray Heindorf Collection of the Film Music Society. These cues all survived from the 14 August recording session, which Heindorf conducted.

Actually, fans of Alex North already have heard parts of *Distant Drums*. Having retained all the copyrights, the composer mined the music for some of his best-known scores. Portions of the unused *Distant Drums* score appeared in *Viva Zapata!* (1952), *Pony Soldier* (1952), and *South Seas Adventure* (1958). We can only hope that one day this score, by itself, will be released for an interesting look at some of Alex North's earlier work.

■ **Crest of the Wave/Seagulls over Sorrento** (1954)

Original composer: **Hans May**
Composer for American version: **Miklós Rózsa**

Crest of the Wave, which was released as *Seagulls over Sorrento* in the United States, starred Gene Kelly in a story about the tensions that flare between American and British sailors working together on an experimental torpedo. The drama, directed by Roy and John Boulting, was an Anglo-American coproduction. To score it, the Boultings chose a composer they had worked with in the past, Austrian-born Hans May, who had fled to England when the Nazis took over his home country. Among his previous credits were Roy Boulting's *Thunder Rock* (1942) and John Boulting's *Brighton Rock* (1947). His score leaned heavily on the popular Italian song "Torna a Surriento," which is performed on screen and also provided an important recurring motif in his underscore. (This song, written by Ernesto and Giambattista De Curtis in 1905, has had a long life, providing a popular vehicle for a variety of performers, from Elvis Presley, Dean Martin, and Meatloaf to Mario Lanza, Placido Domingo, and Luciano Pavarotti.)

For the picture's American release, MGM asked Miklós Rózsa to provide new music, which he did. His score, which lasts only about fifteen minutes, also used "Torna a Surriento" as its basis, blending the song with a couple of patriotic-sounding themes. Film Score Monthly released this music on the fifteen-CD set titled *Miklós Rózsa Treasury (1949–1968)*. This compilation also includes a five-minute suite from Hans May's score.

Interestingly, when Rózsa signed his contract with MGM in 1948, he was very specific about the conditions of his employment. Among these conditions was that he would not rewrite the work of other composers and that other composers would not rewrite his. However, his contractual defense of his artistic integrity did not completely insulate him from the occasional rescoring. (In the case of *Crest of the Wave,* it's highly likely that he didn't know about May's work.)

Rózsa provided MGM with partial rescores for a few English-American coproductions. In 1948, he provided four new cues to John Wooldridge's music for *Edward, My Son*. In 1954, producer Sam Zimbalist, who also produced the Rózsa-scored films *Quo Vadis?* (1951) and *Ben-Hur* (1959), had Rózsa assist with the music for the *Beau Brummell,* which had been scored by Richard Addinsell. Rózsa rewrote the film's main title and entire finale, but insisted on receiving no credit for this work.

Summer with Monika/Sommaren med Monika (1955)

Original composer (1953): **Erik Nordgren**
Composer for the American version (1955): **Les Baxter**

Monika and Harry are a young couple who escape the city and the adult world for one summer, spending the season around Stockholm's islands. Unfortunately, not only does the summer end, but the couple are awakened from their lives of sweet carelessness by Monika's pregnancy. Directed by Swedish legend Ingmar Bergman, this small movie, which he wrote as a vehicle for actress Harriet Andersson, is perhaps, with the possible exception of *The Seventh Seal*, the work of his that most influenced popular culture.

Sommaren med Monika was picked up for American distribution in 1955 by the notorious Kroger Babb, who focused on only one thing, its groundbreaking nudity. Forget its moving story and heartbreaking depiction of characters coming of age; Harriet Andersson bared a lot more than any American actress previously had, and to exploit this, Babb implemented a major overhaul for the movie.

First, he cut out all of its character-building scenes, reducing the ninety-six-minute feature to a mere sixty-two minutes. (The shortened length allowed this import to be paired up with Babb's new sensation, *Mixed-Up Women*, a retitling of the 1950 picture *One Too Many*.) Then, with his advertising, he tried to turn Harriet Andersson into a pinup, retitling the film *Monika, the Story of a Bad Girl* and retaining the "k" in her name for a touch of Nordic exoticism. The advertisements proclaimed that she is "naughty and nineteen" and that "The Devil controls her by radar!" Her age was also upped—in the movie she was only 17, but it would not do for the object of desire to be underage.

Finally, Babb made one last touch-up, the music. The composer for the original Swedish version was Ingmar Bergman's regular collaborator Erik Nordgren, who had scored most of the director's movies. His subtle music for this film, referencing the story's emotional aspects, was out of place for Babb's erotic adventure. Besides, many scenes had already been cut out and English dialogue was soon to be dubbed in. So the entire soundtrack was scrapped, in favor of an erotically charged jazz score composed by none other than exotica legend Les Baxter!

Since his first score for the sailboat travelogue *Tanga Tika* (1953), Baxter had been getting a number of similarly themed assignments, but *Summer with Monika* was his first rescoring of a foreign movie. A couple of years later this would become Baxter's specialty, as he rescored dozens of films for American International Pictures.

After its 1955 debut, *Monika, the Story of a Bad Girl* became a huge hit and opened a mini-wave of U.S. distribution for other Swedish pictures. Movies such as Arne Ragneborn's *Farlig frihet* (*The Vicious Breed*), which also featured a Les Baxter replacement score for its U.S. release, were often rescored by U.S. distributors, chipping away the dramatic edges from the stories to highlight the more superficial and titillating aspects.

In time, rescoring seemed less and less necessary, since the Swedish imports often ceased to have any purpose apart from exploiting bare flesh. With the arrival of another "sinful" picture titled *Hon dansade en sommar* (*One Summer of Happiness*), Sweden became, for the American audience, a sexually liberated country where everybody was ready to shed their clothes at any time for a swim.

It's sad to note that Babb's massacred version of *Sommaren med Monika* remains Ingmar Bergman's most widely seen movie in America. But as they say, sex sells.

■ **Storm Over the Nile** (1955)

Original composer: **Buxton Orr (adapting Miklós Rózsa)**
Replacement composer: **Benjamin Frankel**

The Four Feathers (1939) was one of the most important pictures for the Korda brothers' London Films because, in a way, all of their exotic adventures, such as *The Thief of Bagdad* (1940) and *The Jungle Book* (1942), were dependent on it. When director Zoltán Korda shot *The Four Feathers* in Egypt and Sudan, he shot a huge amount of footage, and much of it was later incorporated into other London Films productions that happened to have exotic settings. This kind of cost cutting was very popular in those days, and Zoltán was complimented by his brothers on the way he took advantage of *The Four Feathers*' once-in-a-lifetime filming opportunity.

A. E. W. Mason's novel *The Four Feathers* had been filmed a number of times (1915, 1921, 1929, 1939), often remade as a direct response to the arrival of new technologies, such as synchronized sound and color film. In the 1950s, pictures like *The Robe* or *How to Marry a Millionaire* rocked the box office on both sides of the Atlantic with their spectacular widescreen presentations. The technical innovation seemed custom-made for epic period films. Its success persuaded Zoltán Korda to give up his planned screen adaptation of *The King's General* in favor of a widescreen version of the ever-popular *The Four Feathers*.

Renaming his remake *Storm Over the Nile*, Korda devised an ingenious but strange method of cutting costs. By blowing up and stretching his 1939 Sudan footage, he managed to concoct a widescreen version of his exotic material, with codirector Terence Young reshooting the rest of movie with a brand-new cast. Clever editing was applied in an effort to hide the incorporation of so much earlier material, but the technological limitations of the day resulted in several poorly stretched and almost unrecognizably expanded images being included in the final print.

Korda's first idea about the music was to simply rework and reuse Miklós Rózsa's score for *The Four Feathers*. This had been a frequent movie business practice when remaking classic pictures in color or widescreen. For instance, when the Selznick International Pictures 1937 version of *The Prisoner of Zenda* was remade shot-by-shot by MGM in 1952, using the same script with a different cast and new color photography techniques, MGM also wanted to use Alfred Newman's score from the original. But they couldn't, because its recording was timed to the original film and didn't work well with the new footage. In order to make the old score fit the new picture, arranger Conrad Salinger and conductor Johnny Green recorded a new version that used the original themes and re-created the cues with only marginal changes. (Sadly, Newman's original 1937 recording for this film is missing, so only the 1952 MGM recording can be released on CD.)

In the case of *Storm Over the Nile*, use of the Rózsa's score from *The Four Feathers* seemed an even easier undertaking, since a lot of the older film's footage had been reused. For scenes such as the complete and unchanged take of the battle, it seemed natural to utilize the original score as recorded. For the newly shot scenes, British composer Buxton Orr was hired.

Born in Glasgow, Orr had trained to be a doctor before giving up that profession and learning composition from Benjamin Frankel. *Storm Over the Nile* would have been his first score, and all he had to do was rework and rerecord Rózsa's music to fit the new scenes. There were a few problems, however. Because the new footage had different timings and sometimes even different shots, Orr struggled with creating an adaptation of the original score. Although the movie changed very little, there were just enough new cuts and shots to make the young composer's job nearly impossible.

Eventually the whole idea of adapting Rózsa's music throughout the film was dropped, because of Orr's inability to make it fit the picture. Korda then turned to a more seasoned composer to provide a new original score for the new scenes—Orr's former teacher Benjamin Frankel.

Frankel didn't deviate much from Rózsa's sound, his job being to provide original music that matched the reused cues. And his connecting material successfully substituted for the Hungarian composer's original music.

Despite its use of new CinemaScope footage, the technically updated *Storm Over the Nile* never matched the quality of its predecessor: *The Four Feathers* remains the most recommended version of A. E. W. Mason's tale.

■ **Forbidden Planet** (1956)

Original composer: **David Rose**
Replacement composers: **Louis and Bebe Barron**

Forbidden Planet is one of those rare examples of a science-fiction movie daring to test the limits of its genre. Two good reasons for the movie's success were its Academy Award–winning special effects (including Robby the Robot, the most expensive prop of its time) and the picture's unique score/sound design, created by Louis and Bebe Barron.

The Barrons were a New York–based couple who had been experimenting with electronic music since 1948, when they received their first tape recorder as a wedding gift. They are often credited with committing the first purely electronically generated music to tape.

Their electronic music, which grew out of musique concrète techniques, was the result of Louis's prowess as an experimenter with and designer/builder of electronic circuits (oscillators, filters, ring modulators), combined with Bebe's talent at utilizing, as a composer, the sounds that Louis's circuits produced. Theirs was a process of trial and error, capturing on tape the usually unpredictable sounds—both the wonderful and the humdrum—that their circuits produced, and then laboriously sorting through them and editing them into compelling streams of music. The unusual electronic soundscapes the couple created made them notable figures in Greenwich Village's avant-garde scene in the 1950s.

In December 1955, one of Louis and Bebe's performances was witnessed by Dore Schary, an executive producer of the upcoming sci-fi film *Forbidden Planet.* The producer offered them a contract on the spot, even though the Barrons couldn't travel to Los Angeles for recording.

Between January and March of 1956, they worked on the movie's score in their New York City home, using an unfinished workprint and collaborating via telephone with editor Ferris Webster and sound effects editor Franklin Milton. The soundtrack they created delighted Schary, who loved all the strange sounds they came up with, from the wailing of the Id Monster to the planet's ambient sonic atmosphere.

Unfortunately, before the Barrons had been hired to do *Forbidden Planet*'s score, Hollywood composer Dave Rose, head of MGM Records and perhaps best-known for penning the popular tune "The Stripper," had been assigned the project. Acting on the belief that *Forbidden Planet* was his movie, Rose had already begun sketching its main title and score. Schary had to break the news about the Barrons' music to Rose.

The rejection came as a real blow, and Rose (rumor has it) spent that evening playing piano, drinking champagne, and burning all his score sketches for the movie, with the exception of the main title theme.

But as head of MGM Records, he decided to make some money from his affiliation with the picture. He recorded his title theme with his own musicians and released it as a record. In order to milk the film's release publicity, Rose subtitled the record "Inspired by the MGM CinemaScope film." To further emphasize the association with *Forbidden Planet,* he asked the MGM sound-effects people to re-create the robot sounds from the Barrons' score and mix them into his theme music. Interestingly, Rose's rerecorded main theme can be synchronized with the movie credits, and even the electronic beeps end up in the right places as each credit appears onscreen.

Rose's music was also heard in the movie's theatrical trailer, which was compiled around March 1956, when the studio required additional music to sell their coming attraction. (Rose's *Forbidden Planet* track was originally released with Bronislau

Kaper's *The Swan* on the flipside. It can also be found on the compilation *The Very Best of David Rose.*)

The Barrons had an unfortunately limited career in the world of film music in Hollywood, where they were treated with animosity: Not being accepted into the Musicians Union, they weren't eligible for an Academy Award nomination, and they didn't even get a real composer credit for *Forbidden Planet*—their credit reads "Electronic Tonalities" instead of "Music" or "Musical Score."

Despite these setbacks, they did create more interesting electronic scores. One of their best was written for Shirley Clarke's experimental movie *Bridges-Go-Round,* a four-minute montage of images of New York City's bridges. For this short film, Clarke commissioned two scores: an electronic one by the Barrons and a jazz-tinged one by famed composer/arranger/saxophonist and Columbia Records producer Teo Macero. The film is meant to be played twice, once with each score. It thus provides a marvelous illustration of how music influences the way we perceive and react to a film. Macero's score makes New York City feel like a bustling, swinging urban center, while the Barrons' tends to abstract the bridges into isolated, alien life forms. *Bridges-Go-Round* is one of the few movies in which double scores represented an artistic concept, not a panicked decision by a studio executive.

■ **The Barretts of Wimpole Street** (1957)

Composer for British version: **Malcolm Arnold**
Composer for American version: **Bronislau Kaper**

The Barretts of Wimpole Street was the farewell effort of director Sidney Franklin, who decided to end his career with a color remake of his best picture, which had been released in 1934.

Like many British-American coproductions of the era, this MGM title became the focal point of an argument about the differing salary and copyright demands of American and British composers. Several failed attempts were made to normalize these issues in the mid-'50s, but no resolution was ever reached. As a result, British scores were commonly replaced with American ones.

The 1957 version of *The Barretts of Wimpole Street* was first scored by the popular British composer of concert and film music Malcolm Arnold, who wrote his Academy Award–winning score for *The Bridge on the River Kwai* in the same year. Sadly, there's insufficient documentation to establish exactly why Arnold's *Wimpole* score was rejected. One can conjecture, however, that there's a very good chance it fell prey to the ongoing salary and copyright issues mentioned above.

To replace Arnold's score, MGM hired its staff composer Bronislau Kaper, who could always be counted on to provide a new score for a troubled production. In 1954, for instance, Kaper had rescored the British-American coproduction *Betrayed,* a World War II Dutch resistance melodrama that was Clark Gable's final turn with

Lana Turner. Here the composer replaced Walter Goehr's original work, although the United Kingdom prints still featured Goehr's music.

Even MGM's highest-paid composer, Miklós Rózsa, was sometimes asked to rewrite British composers' music, such as the finale of Richard Addinsell's *Beau Brummel* (1954). Rózsa claimed he did that particular job only as a friendly favor to producer Sam Zimbalist, and that, out of a commitment to artistic integrity, he never again rewrote anyone else's music. Given this, it's likely he wasn't aware that there had been an original score to the British war movie *Seagulls over Sorrento* (1954), for which the movie's twin-brother directors, John and Roy Boulting, had hired composer Hans May (with whom they had worked on more than one occasion). But May's music was replaced, as was the movie's title: It was distributed in the States as *Crest of the Wave*.

While films like *Night and the City* (1950), *Betrayed*, and *Another Man's Poison* (1951) retained both British and American scores, depending on which side of the Atlantic they were screened, this was usually not true for the MGM film library. True to form, *The Barretts of Wimpole Street* and its MGM counterparts were shown with their American scores only, while the British scores went missing in action.

■ **Saddle the Wind** (1958)

Original composer: **Jeff Alexander**
Replacement composer: **Elmer Bernstein**

Saddle the Wind is a powerful tale set during the waning days of the Wild West. Written by Rod Serling, it's the story of a retired gunfighter (Robert Taylor) who must confront a wild younger brother (John Cassavetes) who has an itchy trigger finger.

Soon after MGM commenced the film's production in June of 1957, the studio began to have doubts about the picture's quality. A planned Christmas release date was canceled, and MGM requested script changes from Serling. But his revisions were not accepted, and other writers (Karl Tunberg and editor Margaret Booth) eventually were brought onto the project. The rewritten movie's additions included new relationship dynamics between the brothers and a new ending in which the younger brother shoots himself to protect his sibling.

Five months after the completion of *Saddle the Wind*'s original principal photography, MGM reshot many of its scenes. These reshoots, which were quickly done on the studio's soundstage rather than returning to locations, were poorly made, with the cast often shot in front of obvious back projections.,The picture was ultimately cut down to eighty-four minutes, which required many changes of various kinds throughout the film, including in its music.

The musical focus at this point was the title song, "Saddle the Wind," performed by co-star Julie London. A separate entity in itself, it received no input from the composers who would work on the picture's score. Written by Jay Livingston and Ray Evans, the song made such an impact on the producers that the movie's original title, *Three Guns,* was changed to match it.

The original version of the song, as written for the picture, was orchestrated by Alexander Courage and recorded by André Previn on 13 June 1957. Another version was then recorded by Johnny Mann for Julie London's label, Liberty Records. For obvious marketing reasons, this latter version found its way into the movie as well, in a separate vocal track that London recorded on 19 July. The singer also performed a third version of the song, which appears in the movie when she uses it in an attempt to calm down Tony, the wild brother.

The picture's original extended cut had been scored by composer Jeff Alexander. Alexander had already had some bad experiences on an MGM Western, working in 1953 on *Escape from Fort Bravo,* a Civil War story about escaped Confederate soldiers. One of Alexander's earliest credited scores, *Fort Bravo* gave him special problems. He recorded his initial score in the summer of 1953, but was then required to rewrite almost every cue in September, after the movie's first test screenings. Whereas his original music had underscored both the beauty of the Arizona landscape and the threat of the Mescaleros with exotic percussion, the second one focused more on the soldiers and their upbeat song "Yellow Stripes," omitting most of first's menacing material. Luckily, the movie wasn't changed significantly, so Alexander could rewrite the score quickly.

For *Saddle the Wind,* he wasn't so lucky, and his music for it would go unheard until Film Score Monthly released it alongside the music by Elmer Bernstein that was eventually used instead.

Jeff Alexander recorded his *Saddle the Wind* score on 3 and 8 October 1957, employing frequent Goldsmith collaborator Arthur Morton (who at that time was moonlighting at MGM) as an orchestrator. This original cut of the film included several shots that were later eliminated, including a breathtaking closing shot that ended with an image of barbed wire, officially shutting down the Old West for good. With the picture's many subsequent changes, the original music lost its relevance and would have required a thorough butchering to make it fit.

The recut version was scored by Elmer Bernstein, who recorded his music in two segments: the first half on 23 December 1957, the second on 28 January of the next year. During his work on *Saddle the Wind,* Bernstein never met any of the filmmakers—his only "boss" was MGM's head of the music department, Johnny Green. Needless to say, the primary reason for the composer change was the recuts—the two scores were spotted almost the same way, and both composers approached the picture similarly.

The movie's only surviving piece of Alexander's music is a whistling source cue. All the rest was changed.

MGM was lucky in commissioning this picture's new score when it did, since an unforeseeable event would force the studio to do something unprecedented in the spring of 1958 with one of its other Western titles. That year saw a musicians strike that posed some unusual challenges to Hollywood. Even though the studios could have original scores written for their pictures, nobody was there to record them. MGM's latest Western, *The Law and Jake Wade* (which also happened to star Robert Taylor), was facing such a problem but solved it in its own way. Composer Bronislau Kaper had started working on the picture, but in the end he never finished it: The studio decided not to have original music and bought a selection of cues from Capitol Records with which they could "score" the whole movie. *The Law and Jake Wade* was marketed as the first major studio feature to use a "canned" soundtrack, and in doing so it delivered a message to striking musicians. The protest ended soon, though not necessarily because of *The Law and Jake Wade.*

Similar strikes would continue to shake up Hollywood's music departments from time to time. MGM provided an unsavory example of how to overcome such obstacles, and an original score became the victim.

■ **Saboteur** (German Version) (1958)

Original composer (1942): **Frank Skinner**
Composer for German version (1958): **Kurt Heuser**

Changing movie scores in foreign markets such as Germany's is a rather common phenomenon that hasn't been written about much. This controversial process has affected countless American movies; even classics like *Casablanca* have not been spared strange, seemingly pointless, rescorings for European cinema presentation and home video release. *Saboteur*'s treatment in Germany, however, was an unusual case. Far more thought was put into its rescoring than most rescored titles, which were usually butchered beyond recognition.

Saboteur was Alfred Hitchcock's first film for Universal Pictures in America, and it essentially served as the blueprint for his superior *North by Northwest.* In *Saboteur,* a factory worker (Robert Cummings) is wrongfully accused of arson and, to clear his name, is forced to race across the United States in pursuit of the real saboteur. He ends up in a nearly literal cliffhanger, atop the Statue of Liberty. A memorable, menacing score was provided by Universal staff composer Frank Skinner, but in some countries where the movie was shown, his music was never heard.

After World War II, as Germany was recovering from the scars of war, watching foreign movies wasn't a prominent feature of German cultural life. But in the 1950s, more and more American movies (both new and classic) arrived at the local *Kinos.* To draw an appreciable audience, the pictures usually had to be dubbed into German. But German distributors often didn't have access to the original music and sound effects "stems"—isolated audio tracks (i.e., not mixed with each other or with the dialogue). The lack of these essential elements meant that dubbed foreign releases had to re-create entire soundtracks from scratch. While the dialogue was newly recorded by local actors, the original sound effects were edited out from a composite soundtrack and/or replaced with stock library effects.

The music, however, was more problematic. In the case of David Raksin's score for *Laura* (1944), for example (the first monothematic film score), the music plays an important role. Yet in the film's German-dubbed version, the original music was retained only in the dialogue-free sequences. Whenever music played against dialogue, the original music could not be used, and library music was dropped in to replace it.

Compared with such a hodgepodge, *Saboteur* was lucky. For the German version, Frank Skinner's entire score was tossed out, with the exception of the movie's final half-minute. It was replaced with a score by Kurt Heuser, a screenwriter and regular contributor to Nordwestdeutscher Rundfunk (NWDR) who had a couple of scores to his name. Although Heuser's work had its own themes, he developed his motifs much like Skinner did and utilized similar orchestration. Also, both versions of the picture are spotted in almost the same way. The most noticeable difference between Skinner's and Heuser's scores is tone: Heuser's music is less powerful and more melancholic, less striking. The difference is quite noticeable when Skinner's music returns for the finale, where it now seems jarringly out of place.

Another small problem with the picture's new music was that it disregarded most of the subtle musical hints that Hitchcock planted in the narrative. For example, in the scene when the protagonist meets a blind pianist, the pianist plays *Summer Night on the River* by Frederick Delius, a British composer who was himself visually impaired. The onscreen pianist even acknowledges Delius's blindness while complimenting the composer. In the German print, however, the spoken reference to Delius is retained but his music is not. A completely different piece, not by Delius, is heard in its place. Another scene where the German version of *Saboteur* horribly mismatches music and onscreen activities is found during a party sequence. In this case, the original score's wild swing music, which incorporated Skinner's main melody, is replaced with a slow waltz, showing no regard for the onscreen revelers uptempo dancing.

The German version of *Saboteur* with Heuser's music is still the one available on German home video releases, including the most recent DVD editions. While several classics, such as *Casablanca, Laura,* and *Notorious,* now have their classic American soundtracks restored to their new German dubs, Hitchcock's *Saboteur* still shows in Germany with Heuser's score.

It's important to note that the foreign-market rescoring phenomenon has affected several countries, so buyers of foreign DVDs should be prepared for a few nasty surprises. A recent Spanish DVD release of *The Song of Bernadette,* for instance, had Alfred Newman's Oscar-winning score replaced with uncredited stock music, so the Spanish-speaking population that saw only this version missed out on quite a bit of the movie's impact. When buying a DVD with foreign language options, it is interesting to skip around among the channels and hear the often-different musical scores. Though not always as drastic as the aforementioned cases, foreign-market rescoring happens to more movies than you'd think.

■ **The Horse's Mouth** (1958)

Original composer: **Tristram Cary**
Replacement composer: **Kenneth V. Jones (adapting Sergei Prokofiev)**

The Horse's Mouth is the third book of Joyce Cary's "First Trilogy." It focuses on the exploits of painter Gulley Jimson, who somehow can never make ends meet. The novel was picked up for a movie adaptation by director Ronald Neame. Actor Alec Guinness wrote its screenplay, which closely followed the original storyline but shifted its focus from the social context (an important element in the novel) to Jimson. The screenplay's Jimson was mostly Guinness's creation and had little in common with Cary's character.

While the movie was somewhat successful and nominated for an Academy Award, the change in its story's perspective troubled the first composer brought onto the project, the novelist's son, Tristram Cary, a young, rising composer fresh off the success of *The Ladykillers* (which also happened to feature Guinness leading its cast). Tristram Cary wrote:

> Ronald Neame commissioned a score from me, but when I saw the rough cut of the film, I realized that the film company's interpretation of Gulley Jimson completely misunderstood the way my father had drawn his character. I should have refused the commission then and there, but rather foolishly went on it (as usual, I needed the money!). I wrote what I still consider was a very good score, but I think I was representing my father's Gulley rather than Alec Guinness's. We had one day's recording (which I still have in my archive), but it was clear that the music was fine for me but not at all fine for them. Most of my music was never recorded. I don't even have the scores; they would have been chucked in the bin.

With the rejection of Cary's score, the whole idea of an original score was scrapped as well. Neame loved and wanted to use the famous concert composer Sergei Prokofiev's music from *Lieutenant Kijé* (1934), a forgotten Soviet picture whose only claim to fame is the popular orchestral suite that the composer assembled from his score. Neame asked Cary to adapt this suite into cues that he could use for the picture. When Cary refused, the director turned to composer Kenneth V. Jones.

The resulting score is serviceable, but it's easy to see how music written for a Soviet comedy has very little to do with Gulley Jimson. Jones wrote some original music for the picture as well, which is nicely mixed in with the Prokofiev. Hidden in the movie is a single remaining Cary cue, which plays when Jimson has a bad hangover.

His bad experience with *The Horse's Mouth*, which came close on the heels of his father's death in 1957, left a mark on Tristram Cary: He didn't get a major film assignment for two years after this rejection. But in time he successfully reestablished himself, going on to write numerous film and television scores, as well as concert pieces, and becoming one of Britain's leading experts in the field of electronic music (an interest he developed while working as a radar engineer during WWII).

Kenneth V. Jones went on to become a much sought-after composer for score replacement and rewrite jobs. The best title from his "secret filmography" must be Jack Clayton's *The Innocents* (1961), a stylish horror film adapted from Henry James's *The Turn of the Screw*. Jones wrote about half of the underscore after the director felt that Georges Auric's original work wasn't scary enough at some points. The rescoring occurred in secret—even the original composer wasn't told it was going to happen. After his 1962 appointment as director of the Opéra National de Paris, Auric paid less attention to film scoring, making *The Innocents* one of his last dozen works in the field and establishing Jones as one of the unsung "musical doctors" of British cinema.

■ **Green Mansions** (1959)

Original composer: **Heitor Villa-Lobos**
Replacement composer: **Bronislau Kaper**

While many of Europe's great concert composers sought refuge in America during World War II, several of them had bad experiences when attempting to work in Hollywood. Arnold Schoenberg with *The Good Earth* and Igor Stravinsky with *Commandos Strike at Dawn* are good examples of how noted concert composers often couldn't get used to the rules of film scoring and sometimes couldn't finish even a single project.

Before coming to Hollywood, the highly regarded Brazilian composer Heitor Villa-Lobos was no stranger to film scoring, as he had in his youth played cello in a band accompanying silent films and later had written music for the Brazilian propaganda/historical movie *Descombrimento do Brasil* (1937). His composing method, however, was completely different from the traditional American film scoring process. The difference would cause some controversy once he signed on to write music for the 1959 MGM production *Green Mansions*, a drama set in the Amazon jungle.

By the time he arrived in America to see the picture, Villa-Lobos had already written what he considered to be its score. Composer colleague Miklós Rózsa remembers his meeting with the Brazilian maestro:

> I met him when he arrived in Hollywood, asked him whether he had yet seen the film, and how much time they were allowing him to write the music. He was going to see the picture tomorrow, he said, and the music was already completed. They had sent him a script, he told me, translated into Portuguese, and he had followed that, just as if he had been writing a ballet or opera. I was dumbfounded; apparently nobody had bothered to explain the basic techniques to him. "But Maestro," I said, "what will happen if your music doesn't match the picture exactly?" Villa-Lobos was obviously talking to a complete idiot. "In that case, of course, they will adjust the picture," he replied. Well, they didn't. They paid him his fee and sent him back to Brazil. Bronislau Kaper, an experienced MGM staff composer, fitted his music to the picture as best he could.

MGM initially sought out Villa-Lobos because they knew of his background in writing what some called "jungle music" (exotically colored, rhythmically complex and driving music). But the composer only scored a handful of his *Green Mansions* cues to the movie's actual timing. This meant that, while some of his cues could be used almost without change, a great deal of the material would have to be adapted and refitted by Kaper, who also added a plethora of his own new material. The finished movie's underscore mixed together the work of both Villa-Lobos and Kaper, resulting in a strange hybrid that was a lot more traditional-sounding than the Brazilian's initial music.

Despite not being used in the movie the way he intended it, Villa-Lobos's music became a legendary score. (In an interview, Jerry Goldsmith later remembered discovering so much Villa-Lobos music written for the movie based on the script alone that he and André Previn had wanted to raid the unused material.) While Kaper was credited with the score, Villa-Lobos gained a confusing credit for providing "special music" for the picture.

The Brazilian composer didn't let his unused material go to waste, however, capitalizing on it by turning it into a concert piece, the orchestral suite *Forest of the Amazons*—a moniker that deliberately bore no connection to the picture's title, for legal reasons. The first recording of this suite, which has gone on to be recorded several more times, was one of the first releases of United Artists Records. It featured Brazilian soprano Bidu Sayão, a male choir, and the popular Symphony of the Air, who performed the piece at the Manhattan Towers Hotel in New York.

Villa-Lobos also extracted four songs from his *Green Mansions* score. These have appeared frequently on various Brazilian compilation albums. Unfortunately for the composer, he never got to enjoy the popularity of these pieces, as UA's *Forest of the Amazons* turned out to be one of his last recordings before his death in late 1959. The score itself, as used in the picture, was released decades later by Film Score Monthly.

■ **Jack the Ripper** (1959)

Composer for British version: **Stanley Black**
Composers for American version: **Jimmy McHugh and Pete Rugolo**

This British production of Jack the Ripper's story, directed by Robert Baker, adopted the popular theory of placing a vengeful doctor in the role of the legendary serial killer. It was brought to the American market by producing genius Joseph E. Levine, who had devised a novel way to make money out of foreign releases: He picked up their U.S. distribution rights dirt cheap, then spent enormous sums on marketing those movies to American audiences. The previous year, he had picked up the Italian movie *Le Fatiche di Ercole*, which he retitled *Hercules* and provided with "saturation booking"—opening it in 600 theaters across America. Levine made his money back from this marketing gamble within a few days of the film's premiere. He then went on to make a fortune on all its subsequent runs and reruns.

In 1959, Levine set his sights on *Jack the Ripper,* which had done good business in Britain and, he felt, with a little tinkering, could do well in the United States too. He initiated a number of changes to the picture, including providing a gimmicky ending for the black-and-white movie by inserting shots recolored with unrealistically red blood in the last reel (even at the cost of disrupting the movie's continuity). Some of the sex and violence were also cut for the more conservative American market; shots of exposed breasts had to be removed completely, for example. A final important change was the removal of the original musical score by the well-regarded Stanley Black, a popular band and orchestra leader and prolific film composer.

The British score had emphasized the film's Gothic nature by stressing a tragic and urgent-sounding main theme, which was later transformed into quieter melodies. While the opening with powerful brass and pounding kettledrums is noteworthy, the remainder of the score—a combination of tense and romantic music—is quite typical of the era. (A three-movement suite from it was released in 2005 on the Chandos compilation *The Film Music of Stanley Black.*)

For the picture's new music, Levine hired film-scoring newcomer Pete Rugolo, best known as an arranger for Stan Kenton's band, and veteran songwriter Jimmy McHugh, who had written songs that appeared in hundreds of films and composed Universal's musical logo in 1935. They followed Levine's request for a more noticeable score, one that was loud and emphasized the action. The resulting music is bombastic, exciting, and colorful, if not too coherent. The score features haunting carnival music as background for everyday London, a lot of eerie Theremin for the mysterious murderer, and many other oddities. Among the strangest aspects are the brassy themes—sounding like a big band starting to improvise—that underscore many of Jack's killings. Rugolo and McHugh also provided a selection of crowd-pleasing numbers, including a sappy love theme and a fun can-can.

The soundtrack album put out by RCA Victor was also a masterful promotional tool. Featuring Joseph E. Levine's name in a rather prominent place, it advertised the record as having a "miracle surface" that should only be played on RCA's very own Victrola phonograph. As an added bonus, the liner notes gave advice on how to listen to the record under ideally creepy circumstances.

Preparing for *Jack the Ripper*'s blockbuster American premiere, Levine set his marketing machine into full swing. He organized a luncheon for his distributors, where he pulled the publicity stunt of bringing a million dollars in cash into the room. Standing next to the money, he explained that he would spend this sum on marketing the movie—an unheard-of amount at that time, when most movies were *made* for less than a million. In reality, Levine had only borrowed the money to show it off, hoping the publicity stunt would help him re-create his success with *Hercules.*

It didn't. "We dropped dead in every [theater]!" Levine would lament. "You'd think somewhere, a small town maybe, someplace, it would have done business. But no. That's a record they'll never come close to."

After this failure, Levine essentially stopped importing foreign movies and went on to produce his own pictures instead. His prestigious filmography contains such titles as *Zulu, The Graduate, The Lion in Winter,* and *A Bridge Too Far.*

■ Goliath and the Barbarians/Il Terrore dei barbari (1959)

Composer for Italian version: **Carlo Innocenzi**
Composer for American version: **Les Baxter**

After Joseph E. Levine made himself a rich man by starting the fad of marketing small-budget Italian epics such as *Le Fatiche di Ercole* (aka *Hercules,* 1958) in the United States, others quickly learned his tricks. Soon James H. Nicholson and Samuel Z. Arkoff of American International Pictures (AIP) became the leading importers/ marketers of these so-called "sword and sandal" or "peplum" (from the Greek word for "tunic") movies.

AIP started its importing spree with *Il Terrore dei barbari,* a peplum starring Steve Reeves that got into financial trouble during production. After a private screening of its finished portions, Nicholson and Arkoff immediately bought American distribution rights to it, handing enough funds to its producers to complete it. Luckily for AIP, Levine's promotional campaign for *Hercules* had elevated Reeves' status at the box office, so AIP simply rode Levine's wave of phenomenal marketing, and *Il Terrore dei barbari* became one of the distributor's most successful imports upon its release.

Before arriving in America, however, this Italian picture had to undergo several crucial changes. First, the title was changed to *Goliath and the Barbarians,* in hopes that American audiences would be more interested in a Biblical giant than in some fellow named Emiliano (as the character was called in the Italian version). The ploy worked, and although the movie didn't have anything to do the Biblical Goliath, it was still a success. Nicholson and Arkoff also changed the musical score. The Italian version's muscular music was written by the prolific film music composer Carlo Innocenzi, who was nearing the end of his almost three-decade career, and conducted by Franco Ferrara. Together, Innocenzi and Ferrara created the template for how these movies would be scored in Italy.

Italian film scores, however, had a horrible reputation in many parts of the world. Bronislau Kaper, who rescored Angelo Francesco Lavagnino's *The Angel Wore Red* for producer Sol Siegel, said that Italian music was "stupid, arrogant, monotonous, tasteless." The producers at AIP apparently shared his opinion, and their decision to rescore *Il Terrore dei barbari* led to dozens of collaborations between AIP and their favorite composer, musical exotica legend Les Baxter.

During his long career, Baxter wrote new music for dozens of AIP-imported Italian movies, starting with the most ambitious, *Goliath and the Barbarians*:

> I was sent to London to do *Goliath and the Barbarians*, and there was a union problem. Things that were done in London had to be conducted by an English conductor. It was very difficult in some of the foreign countries, Italy as well, to bring in a composer from the States to conduct his own work, owing to union restrictions. I was delighted to have Muir [Mathieson] do it—he conducted the music beautifully and I enjoyed working with him. He was a very strong-willed person and even changed the tempo of certain things in Goliath, which was startling because I wrote the music to fit the picture. But we had many wonderful conversations together as he was Scottish and I am Scottish.

For AIP, there were many more sword-and-sandal epics to come: *La Vendetta di Ercole* (Italian score by Alessandro Derewitsky) was renamed *Goliath and the Dragon* (1960) because Levine still retained the "Hercules" name for himself. Then AIP bought such pictures as *Maciste alla corte del Gran Khan* (Italian score by Carlo Innocenzi), aka *Samson and the Seven Miracles of the World* (1961); *Gli Invasori* (original music by Roberto Nicolosi), aka *Erik the Conqueror* (1961); and three pictures scored in Italy by Angelo Francesco Lavagnino (*Marco Polo*, 1961; *Maciste contro il Vampiro*, aka *Goliath and the Vampires*, 1961; and *Zorro contro Maciste*, aka *Samson and the Slave Queen*, 1963). Baxter rescored all of these, as well as such pictures as the Japanese animated feature *Alakazam the Great* (1960) and Denmark's first creature feature, *Reptilicus* (1961).

It's important to note that not all of Baxter's rescorings led to totally new original scores. His most popular work, *Goliath and the Barbarians*, was recycled into a couple of other peplum pictures. Its music became an in-house favorite temporary score at AIP, and portions of it were used in almost all of the peplums that went through Nicholson and Arkoff's hands. Baxter remembers this chaotic period at AIP, and its policy of reusing music and retitling pictures:

> Things were done at great speed there, and the fact is I never even met Ronald Stein! I was there 15 years, so was he, and I spoke to him perhaps once on the telephone. Offhand I don't recall working on *Warriors Five* or *Premature Burial*, although the studio sometimes used my left-over cues or took my cues illicitly from other pictures. I don't think I worked on *Samson and the Slave Queen*, but if you watch the film you can hear practically half the music from *Goliath and the Barbarians*. Actually, some of the titles in my filmography are things I could never dream of scoring... *Dagmar's Hot Pants, Inc.* [1971]... what on earth's that? Presumably they used my cues from another film and played them in the picture. And maybe another reason I don't recognize some of my film titles is they get re-titled. I did *Tambourine* for Nicholas Ray, but some genius decided to call it *Hot Blood* [1956], which sounds more like a vampire picture.

To this day, most of Les Baxter's film music remains unreleased. *Goliath and the Barbarians*, a rare exception, was released on LP, and later on CD, by Intrada. Since most of the original musical tapes are missing or have deteriorated, there are precious few samples available of this busy composer's work. Unfortunately, the same is true for the AIP output of fellow composer Ronald Stein, who worked on such pictures as the Italian schlock costume movies *Il Terrore dei Mari* (*Guns of the Black Witch*, 1961) and *La Guerra continua* (*Warriors Five*, 1962), and the Danish sci-fi *Journey to the Seventh Planet* (1962).

■ Black Sunday/La Maschera del Demonio (1960)

Composer for Italian version: **Roberto Nicolosi**
Composer for American version: **Les Baxter**

Apart from rescoring Italian peplums for American release, another of Les Baxter's many areas of expertise was the writing of new music for the American versions of films by cult Italian director Mario Bava. Like most Bava features, *Black Sunday*—titled in Italy *La Maschera del Demonio*—was picked up for distribution by American International Pictures.

After a screening in Rome, AIP producers James H. Nicholson and Samuel Z. Arkoff acquired the film's foreign distribution rights for $100,000, considerably more than the film's actual budget. They then quickly went to work on it, preparing it for an American audience. Even in its original submission of the film to the Motion Picture Association of America (MPAA), AIP presented a changed version retitled *Black Sunday* with some objectionable content, such as the incestuous overtones of the Asa/Javuto relationship, already eliminated. Apart from objections to a few graphic shots involving mangled faces, the movie got off easy. (Thanks to censorship boards around the world, there are now about half a dozen versions of this film in circulation with different edits, different dubs, and, naturally, different scores.)

The picture's original composer was Roberto Nicolosi, but AIP insisted on having their version rescored by Baxter, whose "new" music didn't turn out all that different. The differences between the two scores are not particularly noticeable in the themes, but they come to prominence in the way the composers created contrasting atmospheres while using similar sound palettes. Nicolosi's score, which is much more subdued than Baxter's, allows Bava's visuals to breathe and provides suspense only when needed. The Italian composer scored only about a quarter of the movie, generally using short cues that follow the action and provide most of the "boo" moments. Recurring events (such as the resurrections) are accompanied by similar music, emphasizing ties between the past and the present.

In contrast, Baxter's music steps into the spotlight, sometimes overpowering the director's images. Baxter's mixture of tragic brass and anxious strings provides the movie with a disturbing atmosphere that goes against the original intentions of both Bava and Nicolosi.

In the next decade, Baxter worked on several Bava movies, replacing their original scores according to the wishes of American International Pictures. In the cases of *I*

Tre volti della Paura (aka *Black Sabbath*, 1963) and *La Ragazza che sapeva troppo* (aka *The Evil Eye*, 1963), Baxter basically re-created the mood of Roberto Nicolosi scores by adapting whatever was acceptable from the original work and then providing original music as needed.

The American and Italian versions of *Black Sabbath*, a trilogy of terror tales, are quite different: AIP not only switched the order in which the three vignettes are presented, it also added a newly shot comic ending that lends an additional campy layer to the whole work. Nicolosi's music, which matched each story's individual style, was replaced with a more uniform and homogenous horror-movie sound that, nonetheless, still borrowed from the original Italian score.

In 2005, Digitmovies issued Nicolosi's score, along with his music for *La Ragazza che sapeva troppo* (1963). A suite from Baxter's score, paired with a suite from his *Baron Blood* (1972) score, was released by Bay Cities in 1992 and reissued by Citadel Records in 1997. Baxter's complete *Black Sunday* score is available from Kritzerland.

AIP continued its practice of rescoring horror movies until 1977's *Tentacles*, when Stelvio Cipriani's music was replaced with a score by Elliot Kaplan, who took the job despite the fact that new contractual agreements kept him from both getting credit and collecting royalties for his work.

■ **Surprise Package** (1960)

Original composer: **Benjamin Frankel**
Replacement composer: **Kenneth V. Jones**

As American and British coproductions became more and more frequent by the early 1960s, the rights issues of British composers continued to pose special problems for producers. While American composers always gave up the rights of their scores and recordings to the studios, British ones were accustomed to retaining their copyright in return for smaller composing fees than their American colleagues received. This difference in practices had been the source of myriad legal battles, and when things turned ugly, the studios mostly backed out.

In a famous rights dispute, Gail Kubik, a successful composer of both concert and film music, requested all rights to his score to MGM's *I Thank a Fool* (1962). MGM refused his request, deciding to have the movie rescored by Ron Goodwin instead. In a similar earlier dispute, the studio retained Benjamin Frankel's score for *Night and the City* (1950) only in British territories and commissioned new Franz Waxman music for the United States, purely to have a score to which they owned the rights.

On 9 January 1960, the Composers' Guild of Great Britain passed a unanimous regulation declaring that their members would never sign any contract that would infringe their copyrights. Some British composers, therefore, couldn't accept the best coproductions they were offered.

Cracks soon began to appear in the system. That year, MGM's *The Day They Robbed the Bank of England* encountered a scoring problem when conductor/musical director Muir Mathieson contracted a composer who didn't work out for the film's producers. The studio needed a quick replacement, but because of the aforementioned Guild agreement, they couldn't find any big-name British composers (including Frankel) who were willing to sign on. MGM did find a young composer named Ted Astley (Edwin Astley, later composer of *The Saint* television series), who was willing to write the music and sign the studio's contract. Astley's name soon became feared in the world of British composer representatives, who couldn't provide their clients the best projects because another "Ted Astley" might snap up the job—not owing to his professionalism so much as his willingness to compromise his copyright ownership.

Benjamin Frankel found himself in a troubling situation with his score for Columbia's *Surprise Package*, a Stanley Donen comedy about an exiled ruler who is all too happy to sell his prized possessions for a little cash. The composer completed his score, including a number of rewritten cues requested by the director, by January 1960. Despite Frankel's work being finished and the agreed-upon payment of £1,500 received, the music was not passed on, since Columbia was interested in the score only if it could own all the rights, not just the rights to its inclusion in *Surprise Package*.

This rights problem only became apparent in February, at which time Frankel's solicitor, Eric Goodhead, got into a heated argument with Donen's solicitor over what to do with the music. While he was defensive of his client during his discussions with Stanley Donen Ltd., Goodhead secretly asked Frankel if he'd be the "guinea pig" in a rights negotiation if the Composers' Guild agreed to join the battle.

As luck would have it, the composer's and his solicitor's attention was soon diverted by another issue: Frankel's music was slowly disappearing from the movie. It's not known how aware Donen was of the conflicting rights interests and studio politics, but he soon started to replace most of Frankel's cues with uncredited contributions by Kenneth V. Jones, a composer/conductor who was available on short notice. Even though legal complications might have eventually lead the studio to replace Frankel's score, Donen was replacing it for aesthetic reasons—he wanted a darker sound with more underlying menace and a dash of humor.

By the time the political game with the studio was finished, Frankel had only nine minutes of his music in the picture, while twenty-three minutes were composed by others. The cuts to his score included the main titles and the end credits. Changes were also made to the song "Surprise Package," penned by famous songwriters Sammy Cahn and Jimmy Van Heusen and performed by Noel Coward in the role of the exiled monarch.

The songwriters' credits were secure, but it was up to Frankel to decide whether he wanted to retain his score credit, since most of the movie's music was by Jones.

In May, Frankel decided to remove his name from the credits. (Incidentally, not even Stanley Donen Ltd. could keep track of the musical changes, so in the summer they contacted Frankel to inquire whether the jazzy arrangement of the theme tune that appears as a source piece in the motel room was by him or someone else.)

After all this business had been taken care of, a final big surprise came when the main titles (designed by Maurice Binder of James Bond movies fame) rolled for the first time. Instead of Frankel or Jones, the only person to receive credit for the musical score was Muir Mathieson, whose contribution was credited as "music under the direction of," or, to be more precise, the person who sorted out the musical mess of *Surprise Package*.

■ **Something Wild** (1961)

Original composer: **Morton Feldman**
Replacement composer: **Aaron Copland**

When it was released in 1961, Jack Garfein's *Something Wild* received a mixed critical reception, and even the critics who liked it admitted that the movie would most likely be seen by only a handful of people. This moving tale of the depressed Mary Ann Robinson was one of the early movies shot almost exclusively on the streets and in the actual buildings of New York City, not on a studio lot masquerading as the Big Apple.

Seeking special music for his special film, Garfein initially commissioned a score from the iconoclastic modernist composer Morton Feldman. Feldman's idiosyncratic music was characterized by slow tempos and quiet dynamics, the combination of which resulted in intimate pieces that were often likened to notes painted across a canvas of time. Feldman's previous film music credit was Hans Namuth's short documentary on abstract expressionist Jackson Pollock (*Jackson Pollock*, 1951), in which he replaced a recording of gamelan music that hadn't resonated with the painter. The films Feldman wrote for, and that best suited his sound, were short documentaries or somewhat experimental works (*The Sin of Jesus*, 1961; *Willem de Kooning*, 1963; *Time of the Locust*, 1966). *Something Wild* was an unusual project for him to take on.

The only music ever released from Feldman's score is a single three-minute cue called "Mary Ann's Theme," for celesta, horn, and string quartet. This rather traditional-sounding piece in slow waltz time is a heartbreaking statement of pain and isolation, written to underscore the tragic results of the heroine's rape. The cue opens and closes with a repetitive celesta solo. Between the celesta statements, simple melodic material is alternately presented by violin and horn accompanied by a repetitive, unassuming, harmonically static string-trio figure.

Garfein wasn't so keen on the theme, and he had a problem with one instrument in particular: "My wife is being raped and you write celesta music?!" (Mary Ann was played by Carroll Baker, Garfein's real-life wife.) A short argument quickly ended the collaboration, but the director didn't give up on noted concert music composers. He eventually hired the legendary Aaron Copland, much of whose music, rich with vernacular-sounding themes, had come to define the sound of overtly populist American music.

Although he had successfully scored some highly regarded (now classic) movies (including *Of Mice and Men*, 1939; *Our Town*, 1940; and *The Red Pony*, 1949), at this point in his career, the composer had soured on Hollywood and had practically retired from writing for films. The reason was that important parts of his music for William Wyler's *The Heiress* had ended up on the cutting room floor, replaced by other music. Extremely upset by the director's meddling with his score, Copland demanded that his name be removed from *The Heiress*, but the studio would not agree to that. Adding irony to insult, the score went on to win the 1950 Academy Award, which he never picked up.

For *The Heiress*, Copland devised a very precise score with strictly used leitmotifs, the only time he had ever done this in his film-scoring career. He also produced, working with in-house arranger Nathan Van Cleave, diegetic music for the nineteenth-century story. Copland and Wyler seemed to get along well during their collaboration, with the exception of one thing: Wyler insisted that his picture include the popular French song "Plaisir d'amour." (Written by Jean-Paul-Gilles Martini, 1741–1816, this song's melody would later become the basis of Elvis Presley's hit "Can't Help Falling in Love with You.") Once the music recording was done and Copland left the project, Wyler had his way with the score, cutting out Copland's music from the main titles and inserting the French theme, as arranged by Van Cleave.

Wyler also replaced another of Copland's cues with "Plaisir d'Amour." This incident, a scandal in the music community, was one reason why the composer turned his back on Hollywood and left film scoring behind. Considering this, it was surprising that, even twelve years later, Copland agreed to score another film. He gave the following reasons:

> It's an excellent film for music. It's wide open for music, which of course is a great advantage for the composer, because normally you have to hold your music down, because of the amount of dialogue, the amount of rain or the amount of traffic noise or the crickets at night. There's always something to compete with, it's seldom quiet enough in a film so that you can listen in an undisturbed fashion to the music. In *Something Wild*, they have a very basic kind of story that's quite understandable without the use of much dialogue and that means there's plenty of opportunity for the music to show, to count in the dramatic effect of the whole.

Copland's music to *Something Wild* is one of the great forgotten scores. It is full of his trademark Americana feeling, but modernized a bit by the introduction of jazzy elements and a rawness that matched Garfein's groundbreaking film, which unfortunately failed to find an audience when it was released in the 1960s.

The composer later extracted a suite titled *Music for a Great City* from this score. It was released on the Columbia LP *Copland Conducts Copland.* In 2003, the original score was finally released, taken from the private session recordings preserved by Jack Garfein. This release is a testament to Copland's place in American film music. Since the movie hasn't been released on VHS or DVD even to this day, Copland's score is the best way to feel the spirit of this forgotten production.

■ **El Cid** (1961)

Original composer: **Mario Nascimbene**
Replacement composer: **Miklós Rózsa**

Starring Charlton Heston in the title role and the gorgeous Sophia Loren as his wife, this 1961 production, directed by Anthony Mann, was a successful continuation of MGM's favorite genre, the large-scale historical epic. *El Cid* was produced by Samuel Bronston, who had previously produced the Jesus epic *King of Kings* (1961), a movie partially financed by MGM, which took over its distribution in order to postpone its premiere to avoid direct competition with the studio's *Ben-Hur* (1959).

Bronston's new epic, however, was produced by his own company, Samuel Bronston Productions, in association with The Rank Organization (UK) and the Italian company Dear Film Produzione. In order to get it made without MGM's assistance, the producer struck a distribution deal with Allied Artists Pictures Corporation. The lack of MGM's control gave Bronston more creative freedom, but the deal he made with his Italian coproducers required that he compromise in certain areas. Composer Miklós Rózsa remembers:

> The film was an Italian coproduction, which meant that in return for the subsidy from the Italian government, a certain number of Italian artists and technicians had to be employed. Originally an Italian composer had been engaged, but Bronston intensely disliked his music and had rejected him in favor of me. Now the Italians were insisting that an Italian composer's name [Carlo Savina] be on the credits. Bronston couldn't afford to lose all the Italian money, so he asked that on the Italian prints an Italian composer's name should appear together with mine.

Selected to be the "phantom composer" was Carlo Savina, an Italian composer who had recorded the LP version of the *Ben-Hur* soundtrack with the Symphony Orchestra of Rome. Savina never actually worked on *El Cid.* However, another Italian composer, Mario Nascimbene, was brought to work on it. Nascimbene was well versed in the genre, having scored a number of popular sword-and-sandal pictures, from *The Vikings* (1958) to *Solomon and Sheba* (1959) and *Carthage in Flames* (1960). When pushed by the Italian government and the picture's Italian coproducers, Bronston gave Nascimbene some work, just to keep him busy while the producer figured out how to get music from Rózsa, his first and only composer choice.

As an MGM contract composer, Rózsa was supposed to start working soon on the score for the studio's Marlon Brando vehicle *Mutiny on the Bounty* (1962), for which he already had recorded a couple of source cues. While Bronston attended to getting his chosen composer out of his *Bounty* obligations, Nascimbene was given the task of writing temporary music for *El Cid*. He wrote:

> Bronston called me and asked me to score *El Cid*, which was being shot by Anthony Mann. I read the screenplay first, and they told me to write some dance music themes only. The music had to accompany a kind of fighting dance for scenes taking place on the beach, so I wrote some cues for tympani, with rather brutal, violent rhythm, without any real melody. Director Mann liked what I had written and shot his scenes, using [my] cues as background. [...] When shooting *El Cid* was about halfway, I was asked to come to Malaga to discuss the score itself. Samuel Bronston met me there when I arrived, showed me a pile of records of Massenet's *El Cid* and told me: "This is the music for the film." Apparently I had to sort of "adapt" Massenet's music for the film. Samuel Bronston behaved in an offensive way, and I told him that I am used to discussing the score with a director, and with him only. So I returned to Rome, where I tore up the contract already made.

Nascimbene received cool, almost cruel, treatment from the producer, whose request that the composer adapt Massenet's music was apparently insincere. Bronston never asked Rózsa to even listen to the opera as a reference, so the producer's passion for Massenet was most likely a ruse meant to squeeze the Italian composer into a situation that would force him to resign.

In time to score *El Cid*, Bronston cleared Rózsa of his obligation to MGM's *Bounty*. (*Mutiny on the Bounty* was eventually scored by Bronislau Kaper, MGM's second-in-command composer, who had helped out Rózsa when Rózsa left *The Swan* to work on *Lust for Life*, a movie that interested him much more.) Rózsa would prove lucky to have left the sinking *Bounty* when he did: The picture turned out to be an excruciating experience for Kaper, who worked on it for more than a year, continuously rewriting portions of the score.

It's very rare that a producer goes to such lengths to get his composer of choice. But Bronston and Rózsa had developed a very good relationship when collaborating on *King of Kings*, which they both felt to be an exceptional film with an exceptional score. Rózsa was given uniquely first-class treatment on *El Cid*, being flown to Málaga to take in the Spanish atmosphere and research medieval music.

What started out as another great collaboration with Bronston, however, was jeopardized by the director, Mann, and his sound editor, who not only buried some of Rózsa's best battle cues under layers of sound effects but also left out a number of worthy cues (many of which went unheard until Tadlow Records produced a new recording of the score in 2008). Due to this heavy editing of his music, Rózsa canceled his publicity tour to promote *El Cid*, claiming he couldn't "talk about something that was not in the film anymore." It would be the last of Rózsa's epic scores.

Nascimbene's curious legacy, however, doesn't end with not scoring *El Cid*. Throughout the years, he was rumored to work on a number of pictures he actually had nothing to do with. One was *Jason and the Argonauts* (1963), for which Columbia's early publicity material listed Nascimbene as the composer. Although he was never involved in the project, rumors circulated that he had had a full *Jason* score rejected. A more outrageous claim concerned the Italian version of Stanley Kubrick's *Spartacus* (1960), which an Italian film directory claimed was scored by Nascimbene, and then went so far as to analyze the score! This, of course, is also not true—the basis of this publication's claim was Kirk Douglas's offer to Nascimbene to score the picture based on their great work together on *The Vikings*. The composer, still working on King Vidor's *Solomon and Sheba*, declined the *Spartacus* offer, but the story nonetheless was picked up and published in several reference books. Considering that Italian and American versions of the same movies have frequently had different scores, perhaps it's not surprising that this particular myth lived on for so long.

■ Hatari! (1962)

Original composer: **Hoagy Carmichael**
Replacement composer: **Henry Mancini**

In the 1950s and 1960s, a gradual and somewhat radical revolution in film music brought previously unheard sounds to movie theaters. The dominance of orchestral, leitmotif-driven scores was over, and a new audience was ready to accept both jazz and slightly experimental music in film soundtracks.

During postproduction of his lavish hunting story *Hatari!*, director Howard Hawks was eager to use his usual composer, Dimitri Tiomkin, who had scored almost all of his movies since 1948's *Red River*. According to an anecdote from a Hawks biography, the director wanted an unusual musical score for *Hatari!*, so he asked his composer to completely leave out the string and woodwind sections, replacing them with native African instruments. When Tiomkin, one of Hollywood's more conservative composers, realized that Hawks wasn't joking, the two of them parted company.

The director then decided to hire a composer who had never scored a film before and, thus, was not tied by the conventions that made Tiomkin think largely in terms of big, bombastic orchestral forces. He chose popular songwriter Hoagy Carmichael (whose songs have been heard in more than 150 films). It was in Hawks's *To Have and Have Not* (1944) that Carmichael had made his big-time acting debut, performing his own music as the pianist/bandleader character named Cricket.

Carmichael was honored to have Hawks give him the chance to score a feature film. He put together his score—lots of colorful, exotic tunes to match the strange world of African hunters and the wildlife they pursue—in his Sunset Boulevard apartment. When he presented his material to Hawks, the director seemed happy at first. But then Hawks began coming up with his own musical ideas. He proposed modifying

Carmichael's music to fit the individual scenes, and bringing in a second composer with more scoring experience to work with the famed songwriter. Carmichael's son remembered an incident in which Hawks brought in his own lyrics, which for a Hoagy Carmichael composition were childish and pointless. It has been suggested that this may have been one of the reasons Carmichael quit the film.

His replacement was Henry Mancini, who had fond recollections of the project:

> Shortly after I started into the score, Howard called and told me he had a lot of musical instruments he had brought back from Africa. He asked if I wanted to take a look at them. Of course I did! I went over to see him. He dragged out a big box and opened it, an absolute treasure chest of authentic African musical instruments, including the thumb piano, shell gourds, and giant pea pods. [...] I was entranced and immediately decided to use them in the score. Howard also had some tapes of chants of the Masai, and so, with those instruments and tapes from which to adapt authentic material, I was in pretty good shape to score the animal scenes, of which there were many. [...] Howard shot a lot of material without knowing exactly where or even if he was going to use it. And he shot one such scene with Elsa Martinelli, a sort of cameo or vignette.

This particular scene featured three baby elephants taking a walk with their human companions and having some fun in the mud as they did so. Hawks was proud of the scene, but he couldn't find a good place for it in the movie. He contemplated removing it unless Mancini could come up with some worthwhile musical moment that would salvage it. The result was the colorful track titled "Baby Elephant Walk," a piece said to be influenced by the popular boogie-woogie song "Down the Road a Piece." The track became one of the film's best-remembered musical moments and one of Mancini's most popular compositions.

It is interesting to note that on the soundtrack recording, "Baby Elephant Walk" is followed by a song called "Just for Tonight," which was Hoagy Carmichael's reworking of "A Perfect Paris Night." This song was the only element retained from the original composer's work, and, unfortunately, some editions of the soundtrack fail to even mention Carmichael in connection with it. The rest of his music can be found in the Hoagy Carmichael Collection at Indiana University.

■ The Day of the Triffids (1962)

Original composer: **Ron Goodwin**
Additional composer: **Johnny Douglas**

Based on John Wyndham's famous science-fiction novel of the same name, *The Day of the Triffids* is about a mysterious alien plant species that tries to take over Earth once a meteor shower has rendered most of humanity blind. The picture, a coproduction of Allied Artists (USA) and the Rank Organization (UK), was a so-called quota film, an Eady Plan production, which meant that in order for it to obtain certain British government financial benefits, a sizable percentage of its cast and crew had to be British. Because of this, the picture's credits are not altogether accurate: The names of some members of the crew had to disappear from the opening titles. Among these were American producer Bernard Glasser, whose name was replaced by that of British producer George Pitcher, whose exact involvement in the film is unknown. Because of his blacklisted status, American screenwriter Bernard Gordon also went uncredited. Hungarian-born veteran filmmaker Steve Sekely directed the film, and the score was provided by British composer Ron Goodwin.

Goodwin was hired to do *Triffids* because he had scored John Wyndham's previous book-to-screen, *Village of the Damned* (1960), a box-office success. (Following *Triffids*, he would go on to score *Children of the Damned*, *Village*'s 1964 sequel.)

When *Triffids* was first screened for its distributors, they complained that some shots of the Triffids (ambulatory monster plants bent on ruling our planet) were unconvincing. Executive producer Philip Yordan, also a screenwriter (and sometimes a front for blacklisted writers), worked with American editor Lester A. Sansom to prune the film of its less successful scenes and shots. By the time they finished their trimming, more than 20 minutes had been cut, leaving the picture only 57 minutes long, too short for theatrical presentation.

To remedy this, Yordan, a gifted "idea man," came up with an ingenious new subplot to interweave with the original story. It was the tale of a couple, both scientists, who are stranded in an isolated lighthouse, where they are attacked by Triffids. Gordon wrote and produced these new scenes; noted cinematographer and director Freddie Francis directed them. Under editor Sansom's guidance, the new material was intercut with the old, resulting in a 96-minute movie that included 70 minutes of the original picture and 26 minutes of new material.

By this point, composer Goodwin was busy on another project. Interestingly, his absence for this revised version of *Triffids* was highlighted by writer Gordon, who named his newly created lighthouse hero Tom Goodwin, after the composer who, as fate would have it, wouldn't score the lighthouse scenes.

Although some of Goodwin's music was replaced in the reconstituted picture, due to continuity changes and the addition of new story material most of it remains in the film. Only about five minutes was removed (e.g., the music that accompanies the appearance of a Triffid in the hospital and that accompanies the fog sequence). Johnny Douglas, a composer/arranger/conductor perhaps best known for his work in the easy-listening genre, was hired to score the remaining scenes. These included the electric fence sequence, romantic scenes in the lighthouse, and the scenes of London in chaos. Originally, Douglas was brought on to supply music for the new lighthouse scenes only, but the picture had been changed so much since Goodwin's original scoring that Douglas needed to produce additional music for early scenes as well.

Both Goodwin's and Douglas's music is often energetic. Except for the scenes with Betina, the blind girl—which were scored by Goodwin—the romantic music (such as during the "rest" scene at the lighthouse) all belongs to Douglas, who also scored the last thirty minutes of the film, including the Triffids' exodus and the ending at the church.

Of note is how close Douglas's music often came to matching Goodwin's sound. This, in part, was Douglas's mandate, and only on close examination can one tell the two composers' work apart on this film. By economics or by choice, *The Day of the Triffids* is one of the few movies in which two composers' scores coexist so comfortably. And, just as the two interweaving stories (the original plot and the lighthouse tale) lend the picture greater breadth, each composer's music enhances the work of the other.

The main titles tried to resolve the two-composer issue by crediting Goodwin with "music composed and conducted by" and Douglas with "additional music composed and directed by." In the final accounting, the second composer supplied more music than originally planned, and his contribution proved longer than what was left of Goodwin's score. A look at the final cue sheets shows Douglas with three more minutes of music than Goodwin; if we disregard the source music, the original composer's surviving work amounts to about fifteen minutes of underscore.

Douglass *Triffids* work was so successful that he was invited to score producer Yordan's next sci-fi yarn, *Crack in the World* (1965), which also reunited him with Triffids filmmakers Glasser and Sansom.

(In 2006, a rerecording of Goodwin's *Triffids* score was released on CD by Monstrous Movie Music. Unfortunately, Douglas's score will never receive the same treatment, because the composer discarded most of his film scores, with the exception of some love themes he deemed reusable. With this act, a part of British film scoring history disappeared as well.)

■ **I Thank a Fool** (1962)

Original composer: **Gail Kubik**
Replacement composer: **Ron Goodwin**

Gail Kubik was an influential American composer and a Pulitzer Prize winner, yet recordings of his film music and concert music are largely unavailable today.

One of Kubik's favorite film directors was William Wyler, with whom he worked on two Air Force documentaries—*The Memphis Belle* (1944) and *Thunderbolt* (1947)—before collaborating with him on a feature film, Paramount's *The Desperate Hours* (1955), starring Humphrey Bogart in one of his last screen performances.

During its recording, some studio executives found Kubik's wild and percussive music too modern. His composer friend Miklós Rózsa told him, "If you get away with this, you will be the greatest man in Hollywood." Paramount's head of production, Don Hartman, told him his score would probably be thrown out after the first screening. And Hartman was pretty nearly right: Although Kubik retained his screen credit, most of the picture was ultimately scored with original music by Daniele Amfitheatrof and stock cues by Victor Young, Joseph J. Lilley, and Paul Weston.

In 1957, Paramount generously handed back to Kubik the rights to his *Desperate Hours* music, as well as publishing and promoting the suite he created with it, *Scenario for Orchestra*. Nevertheless, Kubik left Hollywood for good that year, relocating to New York City, where he scored two episodes of the CBS Television documentary series *The Twentieth Century*, "Hiroshima" (1958) and "The Silent Sentinel" (1959).

Kubik always believed that film music and concert music were cut from the same cloth, so he never sacrificed his personal voice when working in either medium. In fact, he often reworked his film music into concert pieces. Even his Pulitzer Prize–winning *Symphony Concertante* was derived from his score to the 1949 movie *C-Man*. This would cause him problems when trying to work within the Hollywood system, because the studios wanted to keep at least half of a film score's publishing rights. The best that most Hollywood composers could get away with was arranging a suite of score excerpts to be performed on the concert stage.

Kubik, by contrast, always tried to hang on to all the rights to his film music, and he was unusually successful at it, gaining full ownership of all his scores, including the Oscar-winning popular animated adventure *Gerald McBoing-Boing* (1951) and his mostly discarded score for *The Desperate Hours*.

In 1961, Kubik moved to Paris, where he was contacted by writer-turned-producer Anatole de Grunwald, who was working for MGM London at that time. The producer asked Kubik to write music for his new film, *I Thank a Fool*, a thriller about a doctor, played by Susan Hayworth, who is convicted of euthanasia. Although still smarting from his Hollywood experiences, the composer decided to give the American-financed British movie a shot.

The contract he signed to compose this film's score contained a number of unusual provisions, starting with his commission price of $12,500. The lengthy legal document also required MGM to bear all his traveling and housing costs in Paris and London during the composing and recording process, and even cover his wife's travel expenses to attend the film's premiere. It also specified that the composer's credit, "MUSIC COMPOSED AND CONDUCTED BY GAIL KUBIK," must appear on the screen in print the same size as that of director Robert Stevens's name. Perhaps the oddest aspect of this contract was that MGM left the issue of the ownership of the music's rights unresolved. (It would remain unresolved until the score was completed.)

Kubik worked on the score in the comfort of his Paris home. As the time neared when he would have to travel to London to record it, there was still material to write, so he contacted his friend Gerard Schurmann to orchestrate the score as well as compose some of its minor cues. With Schurmann's help, Kubik's romantic score was ready on time to be recorded by the London Philharmonic Orchestra.

Kubik believed that, with the movie's premiere date already set, he could negotiate the retention of rights in his score. But when MGM finally got around to tackling the rights issue, it took into consideration his large commission fee and kid-gloves treatment and said no to his request for complete ownership. The studio demanded that he either sacrifice part of his salary or give up his ownership demands, neither of which he was willing to do. Encouraged by its achievements in sorting out music ownership dilemmas with British composers in previous years, MGM decided not to make an exception for Kubik and dropped his music from the film. Ron Goodwin was hired to quickly replace it. This expensive venture finished Kubik's film career for good, and it even cost the head of MGM's British studios his job.

After his Pyrrhic victory, Kubik adapted his *I Thank a Fool* score into the concert piece *Scenes for Orchestra* in 1962.

■ **Dr. No** (1962)

Original composer with multiple scores: **Monty Norman**
Arranger of "James Bond Theme": **John Barry**

When the first James Bond movie, *Dr. No*, came out, 007 didn't have a musical tradition—no blueprint for its composer to follow, no "James Bond Theme."

The composer given the job of creating Bond's musical identity was the successful theater composer and lyricist Monty Norman, the Tony Award–winning (1961) coauthor of the English book and lyrics for *Irma la Douce*, whose one previous film-scoring credit was the Hammer Film production *The Two Faces of Dr. Jekyll* (1960). Norman was also the composer of the short-lived West End musical *Belle or The Ballad of Dr. Crippen* (1961), a show that counted among its chief financial backers Albert R. "Cubby" Broccoli, a film producer who had just partnered with fellow producer Harry Saltzman to create EON Productions, a company that chose the film version of Ian Fleming's novel *Dr. No* as its first project. (EON and the Broccoli family would go on to produce almost all the Bond movies.)

Because he admired *Belle*, Broccoli hired Norman to write *Dr. No*'s music. In keeping with the story's setting, the composer traveled with the production crew to Jamaica to mine the island's musical heritage. He took a song-centered approach to the score, basing it upon a few Caribbean-influenced songs, particularly his jolly "Kingston Calypso" (based on the "Three Blind Mice" nursery song), the party track "Jump Up," and the addictive love song "Underneath the Mango Tree." Somewhat as if it were a musical, Norman's score was essentially constructed from the recordings of these tunes that he made in Jamaica, along with their instrumental versions and a couple of unrelated mood pieces.

Editor Peter Hunt remembers the orchestra sessions in London, during which it became apparent that Norman's music wasn't working well with the picture:

> We go through all the musical requirements with Monty Norman, we give him all the timings and cues and so on, and we think we can manage about two sessions with an orchestra to record it in—we're quite short of money by this point, remember—a morning and afternoon and maybe we could manage an extra hour or so if absolutely necessary, just to finish everything off. So we start the first session and the music comes up—there's just myself, a couple of assistants, and the mixer there—well, it just doesn't

> seem to fit the picture somehow. Anyway, Terence [Young, the director] arrives a bit late and says, "How's it going, boys?" "Well," I say, "I think we better have a little talk, I really don't think it's working." Monty had used the Jamaican sound, and it was very good in its own right but just not quite appropriate for the film as we saw it.

Among the score's problems was the lack of a distinctive theme for the hero. To remedy this, Norman revamped the theme from the Indian-influenced, sitar-driven song "Good Sign, Bad Sign," which he had written for the unproduced musical *A House for Mr. Biswas* (based on V. S. Naipaul's acclaimed novel). After some minor modifications, the song's eight-note motif (dum de-de-dum-dum, dum dum dum) became the basis of the series-defining "James Bond Theme." This 007 music was then incorporated into a new orchestral underscore written to replace some of the Caribbean material. The new portions were orchestrated by Norman's associate Burt Rhodes and conducted by Eric Rogers. Some of the cues drew upon the Caribbean material (such as orchestral treatments of the song "The Island Speaks"), but most of the orchestral underscore sounds like 1950s library music. Its hints at the "James Bond Theme" are subtle, usually small brass bursts of the main riff utilized when danger is imminent.

The version of the "James Bond Theme" that was finally used in the film, however, was arranged and orchestrated by John Barry, whose previous single film credit was the youth-counterculture flick *Beat Girl*, starring Gillian Hills. Barry was recommended to the production by Noel Rogers, head of United Artists Music, the publishing arm of UA Records. Peter Hunt remembers Barry's involvement:

> Monty Norman had done a "James Bond Theme" of sorts, but John didn't like it very much, and I said, "Well, it's not a bad tune really," and we had a long discussion about it—you must remember we had a lot of long discussions about everything because John was still very new to the game. Anyway, he finally said, "Well, I'll use it, but I'd like it to be something else with a new arrangement, a guitar, different accompaniments, and so forth." So I said fine, let's go ahead, because we didn't have much time by now. We set up another session and completely re-did the score and it worked like a dream. From then on, we've been great friends, and he's gone on to do marvelous things and we always enjoyed working together.

Barry's arrangement (track 1 on the official soundtrack album) inventively used and expanded on Norman's original tune, and became one of the world's most recognizable movie themes. It has been used on countless occasions to invoke Bond's presence. EON Productions used this 1962 version of the theme to patch musical holes in their subsequent Bond movies up until 1969, and featured it in their trailers until 1989.

Barry added the underlying four-note vamp that runs in the background, the snarling guitar orchestration of the theme (played by Vic Flick), the glorious brass stabs in the middle part of the arrangement, the similarly joyous bridge, and the coda, which perfectly ends this great track. The newly arranged theme was so popular with the filmmakers that much of the Jamaican-flavored music was replaced with edited takes of this single theme: It can be heard when 007 introduces himself in the casino, when he arrives at the airport, at the beginning of the car chase, and several other places. While Barry went on to compose the scores for eleven more Bond pictures, as well as many, many other films, Norman's film-composing career ended during the scoring of the 1963 movie *Call Me Bwana*:

> My next film with Saltzman/Broccoli was not a Bond film, it was a Bob Hope film called *Call Me Bwana*. They asked me to do that while I was still doing *Dr. No*. We completed the score and recorded it all. Then I went to Harry, who seemed to have been avoiding me, and said, "I've done all the work, Harry," which he praised, "so isn't it time we talked money?" And he replied with a wonderful Sam Goldwynesque line: "Monty, If you want to talk money, we can't do business." Follow that. For some reason, he took offence. I didn't do any more Bonds. A stupid situation really. Of course, we should have worked out a deal before we started, but as I knew them so well, I didn't expect problems. Cubby had very little to do with *Call Me Bwana*. Harry was the main producer.

The question of authorship of the "James Bond Theme" made its way into court more than once. Most famously, in 2001, Monty Norman filed a lawsuit against the *Sunday Times*, which had claimed that John Barry was the sole composer of the memorable theme and that Norman had very little to do with it. The case brought together all the story's living participants, including Norman and Barry. At the end of this widely reported case, Norman prevailed and was awarded his costs plus £30,000 in damages.

(The fact that *Dr. No*'s official soundtrack only contains music from the Caribbean recordings with irrelevant song titles confuses buyers, who believe they are getting the music as it was heard in the movie. In fact, the film's actual orchestral underscore hasn't been released to this day, with the exception of a rerecorded suite produced by Silva Screen. The multiple scores for *Dr. No* add up to a puzzle that even Bond would be hard-pressed to solve.)

■ **Lawrence of Arabia** (1962)

Composer: **Maurice Jarre**
Orchestrator/arranger: **Gerard Schurmann**
Alternate composer of unused material: **Richard Rodgers**

For producer Sam Spiegel, director David Lean's *Lawrence of Arabia* wasn't just a movie, it was a special event, a chance to gather a full creative team of famous individuals. Spiegel's primary goal in the area of music was to secure a big-name composer, and he traveled half the globe in a quest to interest composers in the project. One of his early choices was Bernard Herrmann, but Herrmann's demand for a $50,000 salary eliminated him from consideration. Years later, Herrmann would make several negative comments about the film, claiming it presented a "complete distortion" of the real events of T. E. Lawrence's life. He also disliked Maurice Jarre's score, which he, never one to mince words, deemed "cheap." He went so far in his criticism as to suggest that it might have been partially ghostwritten. (Jarre felt that Herrmann's comments were directed at him because of his work with Hitchcock on the 1969 film *Topaz,* after the director had ended his long collaboration with Herrmann.)

While Spiegel had his own hiring agenda, David Lean hoped to reunite with highly respected concert and film composer Malcolm Arnold, who had written the music for his *The Bridge on the River Kwai* (1957), a film that won Academy Awards for both the director and the composer. However, Spiegel insisted on what he felt was a bigger name, so a compromise was proposed: The producer would hire Sir William Walton (well known for his concert music, particularly Symphony No. 1 and *Façade*) as the primary composer for the movie, and Malcolm Arnold would write additional cues based on Walton's themes. It's not known whether Spiegel knew that the two composers were great friends, but in the end it would not matter, because the deal never came about. Walton and Arnold looked at roughly edited portions of *Lawrence of Arabia* and weren't impressed; both declined to take part in the project. (In 1969, Walton and Arnold would collaborate on *Battle of Britain,* which would prove to be the finale to both of their film music careers.)

Once he couldn't get Walton, Spiegel decided to hire three composers whose combined name value he felt would equal Walton's. His idea was to have each of the three write different parts of the score, and combine them into a musical tour de force. Malcolm Arnold proposed Russian composer (and expert in Arabic music) Aram Khachaturian, known for his very popular *Sabre Dance,* to write the Arabic-influenced music. Highly regarded concert composer Benjamin Britten (renowned for such works as *The Young Person's Guide to the Orchestra,* the opera *Peter Grimes,* and *War Requiem*) was contacted for patriotic British music. The third composer was the relative newcomer Maurice Jarre, nominated on the basis of his work on the film *Sundays and Cybele* (1962).

Both Khachaturian and Britten were unavailable. But by the time this was determined, barely six weeks remained for Jarre to complete all the music. With the two big names out of the running, Gerard Schurmann was hired to work with Jarre on the score, while Spiegel continued to troll for a well-known composer who might lend his name to the project.

Of the long list of composers contacted about the job, the only one who ended up writing music for the film was the legendary Richard Rodgers, composer of such classic Broadway musicals as *Oklahoma!, South Pacific,* and *The Sound of Music.* Asked to try his hand at *Lawrence of Arabia*'s Eastern-sounding music, Rodgers began his work almost simultaneously with Jarre. But David Lean eventually made the call to leave Rodgers' music out.

(Rodgers' unused sketches for the movie are housed in the Richard Rodgers Collection at the Library of Congress. They present a challenge to researchers, because the *Lawrence of Arabia* material is bundled with two other projects, and the staff must rely on educated guesses as to which sketches belongs to which project. Currently, about ten Rodgers compositions are in the *Lawrence of Arabia* file. These include Arabic-sounding pieces, British marches, and some cues that were definitely not written for this film. In fact, the library's notes about the other cues do not connect them with Lean's picture, speculating instead that they were written for some sort of documentary.)

Originally, both Jarre and Schurmann were to cowrite the film's music, but a fast-approaching deadline changed the plan: Now Jarre would write it in sketch form and Schurmann would extract a score and orchestrate it. Initially intended to receive a co-composer credit, Schurmann finally had to settle for an orchestration credit. The workload was immense, and the orchestrator later complained that he had had to work from very loose sketches in which only the percussion parts were rendered in detail (a trademark of Jarre, who was originally a percussionist). The collaboration later generated a lot of debate as to the extent of Schurmann's involvement, a subject on which Jarre remained ever defensive.

The London Philharmonic Orchestra was hired to record the score, and in order to receive a subsidy from the British government, Spiegel had to hire a British conductor. He chose the legendary Sir Adrian Boult, who ended up conducting only the Overture. Jarre conducted the rest, with Schurmann filling in on some cues, even though the movie's credits would list Boult as the conductor. (On the initial soundtrack recording, Jarre receives conductor credit.)

Numerous subsequent releases and re-recordings of *Lawrence of Arabia*'s soundtrack have demonstrated that this Academy Award–winning music's troubled path to completion did little to affect its popularity.

■ Contempt/Le Mépris/Il Disprezzo (1963)

Composer for international version: **Georges Delerue**
Composer for Italian version: **Piero Piccioni**

Jean-Luc Godard's *Contempt* (French title: *Le Mépris*), based on Alberto Moravia's novel *Il Disprezzo*, is a film about the making of a film. While its backdrop is a fictional international production of a movie based on Homer's *The Odyssey*, its primary focus is on the relationships among its characters (the movie's cast and crew).

Interestingly, the challenge of dealing with artistic compromise in the film industry, as depicted in the fictional film-within-the-film, found a counterpart in *Contempt*'s actual production. Producer Carlo Ponti and director Godard disagreed about commercialism and artistry in much the same way as the film's fictional producer (played by Jack Palance) and its director, Fritz Lang (played by Lang himself).

Godard originally wanted American stars Kim Novak and Frank Sinatra to play the leads. Ponti, however, wanted Sophia Loren and Marcello Mastroianni. A casting compromise gave the leads to Brigitte Bardot, one of the most famous international stars at that time, and Michel Piccoli.

Other production and postproduction departments, including music, had to settle for compromises as well, since Godard and Ponti (and uncredited coproducer Joseph E. Levine, who demanded the inclusion of a nude scene for Bardot) apparently had quite different concepts of the picture. *Contempt*'s international version has a vastly different musical underscore from the one distributed in Italy under the title *Il Disprezzo.*

The composer for the international version was Georges Delerue, who wrote a romantic score that highlighted the character Camille (Bardot), a woman who is stuck in an increasingly demanding relationship with her husband, the fictional film's screenwriter (Piccoli), and has a fling with its powerful producer (Palance). Delerue's haunting music perfectly captures Camille's disintegrating relationship and the beauty of her character. His score made the movie feel like a French picture, which was one of the reasons that Carlo Ponti commissioned an alternate score for use only in the Italian market.

The Italian version was scored by Italian composer Piero Piccioni, based on Ponti's instructions. As opposed to Delerue's romantic approach, Piccioni's work is rooted in an Italian psychedelia, with a heavy reliance on the Hammond organ (which soon becomes an intrusive entity in the movie and makes the soundtrack a challenging listen). While Delerue's relatively sparse score focuses on the romance and tragedy of the film's characters, Piccioni's work is detached, lending the picture a distinctly Italian, distinctly dreamlike quality. (When Piccioni's score was released by specialist label Digitmovies as their second CD and their first individual movie soundtrack, it sold out rather quickly, making it a hard-to-find album—not bad for a score that made its only appearance in Italy.)

Rescoring a movie for the Italian market was an everyday occurrence for international productions in the 1960s. Spanish composer Manuel Parada, for instance, wrote music for a dozen Spanish-Italian coproductions, knowing that his scores would be heard only in Spain, while Italian scores (often by Francesco De Masi) would be used in the Italian and international prints. With Italian-German coproductions, the Germans frequently commissioned new scores, many composed by Heinz Gietz (e.g., *Man Called Gringo* and *Alla conquista dell' Arkansas*). Similarly, dozens of Italian-French productions from the 1950s and '60s were rescored when prints were prepared for release in one territory or another. And in the late 1950s, Giovanni Fusco made a small career out of rescoring English movies for the American market.

Apart from a comparison of *Contempt*'s two scores, perhaps nothing speaks so vividly to the differences in musical tastes around the world than Nico Fidenco's strangely upbeat theme song for *Hud* (1963), which replaced Elmer Bernstein's somber guitar music in Italian prints of director Martin Ritt's classic modern-day Western drama starring Paul Newman and Patricia Neal.

■ **Seven Days in May** (1964)

Original composer: **David Amram**
Replacement composer: **Jerry Goldsmith**

Seven Days in May, directed by John Frankenheimer, painted a frightening picture of a military coup attempting to overthrow an unpopular U.S. President. For this picture, the director chose to revive his partnership with noted concert and jazz composer David Amram, who had penned the influential, heavily jazz-tinged score for his earlier political thriller *The Manchurian Candidate* (1962), a film about the assassination of a U.S. Presidential candidate. (Always his own man, when he was besieged by movie offers after the success of *The Manchurian Candidate*, the composer chose to focus on his concert work and take only selected projects that particularly interested him.)

The two men had a history beyond that single film: In 1959, Amram had provided the music for Frankenheimer's TV adaptation of Henry James's *The Turn of the Screw*, and in 1961 he wrote the music for Frankenheimer's *The Young Savages* (1961).

For *Seven Days in May*, Amram delivered music that was markedly different from that of *The Manchurian Candidate*. Although it still had its jazzy moments, it was predominantly an orchestral score. Unfortunately, it didn't work out, as Amram relates:

> John Frankenheimer at that point was in such a big rush that he had to run off [to Paris] before I recorded the score.... When he wasn't there, the producer [Edward Lewis] didn't like my music. I don't think he liked me either, because he didn't feel I was a Hollywood-type person. I never wanted to become a Hollywood hack, with ghost-writers and orchestrators doing my work. I did it all myself. The producer decided that since I wouldn't have someone else come in and use a bunch of old Hollywood schlock music cues droning in the background, he would just have no music at all, so what he did was he got Jerry Goldsmith, who was a terrific composer, to come in and just have snare drum beats playing. Almost the entire score is nothing but snare drums. In a sense, the producer almost tried to write the score himself. There's one part in the film where there's a jukebox playing a jazz piece I wrote, and you can hear that for two and a half minutes. I called John while he was in Paris, but he said "There's nothing I could do." He said, "I'm under the gun now, I have all these deadlines to keep." I was stuck.

It was evidently the producer's call. Frankenheimer was taken by Amram's music, even if he makes only passing mention of it in his audio commentary accompanying the film's DVD release, while praising Goldsmith's score as "minimal, but effective" and commenting on its use of snare drums and its sparseness. (While one of Amram's source cues was retained in *Seven Days in May*, he did not receive an onscreen credit for it.)

Seven Days in May established a relationship between Frankenheimer and the new composer that would extend to two subsequent pictures, *Seconds* (1966) and *The Challenge* (1982). Later, Goldsmith would be tapped for Frankenheimer's last two theatrical features, *Ronin* (1998) and *Reindeer Games* (2000), but he wouldn't complete either one. With *Ronin* he ran into scheduling conflicts and had to bow out at the last minute before writing anything, leaving composer Elia Cmiral only a couple of weeks to deliver almost seventy-five minutes of music. As for *Reindeer Games*, Goldsmith wrote and recorded a demo, but when Michael Crichton called him for help on his troubled *The 13th Warrior* (1999), the composer chose that picture over *Reindeer Games*, which was eventually scored by Alan Silvestri.

■ The Man Who Laughs/L'Uomo che ride (1966)

Original composer: **Piero Piccioni**
Replacement composer: **Carlo Savina**

L'Uomo che ride was Italy's film version of the classic Victor Hugo novel *The Man Who Laughs*. Directed by Sergio Corbucci, the production featured breathtaking color photography, but it horribly bastardized the tale it was based on. The time frame was reset from 17th-century England to Renaissance Italy, historical characters were changed, the main character's name was changed, and the novel's tragic ending was dropped.

Meant to be a crowd pleaser, the film failed miserably, particularly when compared with the 1928 silent version (starring Conrad Veidt), which remains the best of the story's four movie adaptations. *L'Uomo che ride* demonstrates that despite forty years of advances in film technology, nothing can substitute for good cinematic storytelling. With nearly a half-dozen writers tinkering with its script, the film ended up a complete mess, made even worse by budget restrictions and production changes.

Piero Piccioni, whose biggest hit at that time was the Italian score for *Il Disprezzo* (1963), was hired to provide the music for *L'Uomo che ride*. (He would become one of the great names of Italian film music, providing interesting, Italy-only alternate scores for several films that were coproduced with other nations. See my discussion of the 1966 film *After the Fox* later in this book for a noteworthy example.) Best known for his pop-oriented scores, Piccioni enjoyed penning the music for *L'Uomo che ride* because it offered him a chance to write a rich orchestral underscore. Nonetheless, his music, like so many aspects of this movie, proved ill-fated. The producer, Joseph Fryd, deemed it inappropriate for the picture, and Piccioni would recall the unfortunate and upsetting experience decades after the picture itself had fallen into obscurity:

> Corbucci actually told me that he liked the work that I had done for the movie, but the producer, whose name I forget and is no longer important, decided to have another composer write the score. I was rather young and inexperienced at the time, so I did not challenge his decision. Needless to say, I went on to score many more movies, and he went on to do other work, which was more fitting to his aptitude and position—cleaning toilets, I think.

Prolific film composer Carlo Savina, who had worked with Corbucci and "forgot-his-name" producer Fryd on their previous picture, *Johnny Oro* (1966), was quickly brought in to write a replacement score that very few people would hear, for a movie very few people would see. Savina's music, a bit more lighthearted than Piccioni's, was perhaps a better match for the watered-down and refitted Hugo story, which now featured a happy ending!

In a curious twist of fate, a track from Piccioni's rejected score was issued before Savina's music was made available. The rare compilation album *Splendido Il Piccioni 3* featured the old-fashioned love theme Piccioni penned for the film. In 2011, however, GDM/Legend released both composers' scores on a single CD.

■ **Torn Curtain** (1966)

Original composer: **Bernard Herrmann**
Replacement composer: **John Addison**

Torn Curtain boasts one of the most famous rejected scores of all time. Its director, Alfred Hitchcock, had grown increasingly aloof with age, and seemed to harbor doubts about this new picture following the poor audience reaction to his previous film, the "erotic thriller" *Marnie* (1964). Taking advantage of these doubts, Universal, and in particular producer Lew Wasserman, began to make its presence felt during postproduction. The studio and Hitchcock held differing views on the film's tone and concept, and in the course of their battles, the director began listening more attentively to the studio's opinions. He gave in to them on a number of significant points, and one victim of these compromises would be renowned composer Bernard Herrmann, with whom Hitchcock had worked on eight movies in the previous eleven years (including *The Trouble with Harry*, *The Wrong Man*, *The Man Who Knew Too Much*, *Vertigo*, *North by Northwest*, and *Psycho*).

Despite their celebrated productive relationship, the duo had begun to argue about music long before *Torn Curtain*'s production began: They had disagreed on the music for *Psycho* (1960), for which the director wanted a jazzy score, and Hitchcock mostly blamed Herrmann's music for *Marnie*'s poor box-office showing, claiming that its old-fashioned style ruined his cutting-edge "sex mystery."

In a 4 November 1965 telegram to Herrmann (who at that time was living in England), Hitchcock first addressed what he thought the music for *Torn Curtain* should sound like. "Dear Benny," he wrote,

> To follow up Peggy [Robertson]'s conversation with you, let me say at first I am very anxious for you to do the music on *Torn Curtain*. However, I am particularly concerned with the need to break away from the old-fashioned cued-in type music that we have been using for so long. I was extremely disappointed when I heard the score of *Joy in the Morning*, not only did I find it conforming to the old pattern, but extremely reminiscent of the *Marnie* music. Unfortunately for we artists, we do not have the freedom that we would like to have, because we are catering to an audience and that is why you get your money and I get mine. This audience is very different from the one to which we used

> to cater; it is young, vigorous and demanding. It is this fact that has been recognized by almost all of the European film makers where they have sought to introduce a beat and a rhythm that is more in tune with the requirements of the aforesaid audience. This is why I am asking you to approach this problem with a receptive and if possible enthusiastic mind. If you cannot do this then I am the loser. I have made up my mind that this approach to the music is extremely essential, I also have very definite ideas as to where music should go in the picture and there is not too much. So often have I been asked, for example by Tiomkin, to come and listen to a score and when I express my disapproval, his hands were thrown up and with the cry of "But you can't do anything now, it has all been orchestrated." It is this kind of frustration that I am rather tired of. By that I mean getting music scored on a take it or leave it basis. Another problem: This music has got to be sketched in, in advance, because we have an urgent problem of meeting a tax date. We will not finish shooting until the middle of January at the earliest and Technicolor requires the completed picture by February first.

Citing the failed 1965 romance *Joy in the Morning* (one of the worst films Herrmann ever worked on) and the failed *Marnie* (a score Hitchcock disliked) to indicate what Hitchcock didn't want in his new movie, this communiqué's primary point seems to be, "Introduce a beat and a rhythm that is more in tune with the requirements of the aforesaid audience." This is certainly a reference to the popular soundtracks of the day—like the ones accompanying the James Bond and Beatles movies—music with a jazz- or rock-influenced beat that spoke directly to a young mid-'60s audience. LPs of such scores not only sold well but often were strong marketing tools to lure young viewers into theaters. Such additional help for *Torn Curtain* was of growing interest to Hitchcock, who now, under the influence of Universal, began to view his old musical collaborator as a potential threat to his picture's success.

After receiving this cable, Herrmann tried to remain upbeat and, accepting a $17,500 fee, promised to write a "vigorous beat" score. In his note to Hitchcock's assistant Peggy Robertson, dated November 18, 1965, Herrmann updated her on his current situation and requested crucial material for his work:

> As of today I have not received the script and am anxious to have it as it will allow me to get down to work on it. I would also like to have Hitch indicate where he wishes music and also his ideas about the kind of music for each cue. If he could describe these in the same manner as he does when he gives the sound dept. his notes on sound. However, if he is too busy to do this now—could you at least send me the script as soon as possible. Also, bear in mind that I can quickly compose the score so as not to be too far behind Hitchcock's shooting. When would he like me to return to begin on the film? I could start on December 27 (Monday) and be ready to record on 19th of January—which gives us the week of January 24th for dubbing and therefore making the Technicolor date of February 1st. This plan allows me 3 weeks for composing, 2 or 3 days for the orchestra scoring—and a full week for dubbing—or if needed one could start dubbing on Friday, January 21. Please let me know how the above plans meet with Hitch's plans and approval...

In this letter, the normally outspoken Herrmann seems shy and accommodating.

After finally receiving the script in late November, the composer wrote a few sketches and, on 27 December, flew to Los Angeles, where he sat down with the director for a short and not-too-positive meeting. Herrmann's sketches were deemed too "heavy" by Hitchcock, who also made a series of other demands: Write no music for the murder scene, add a melodic love theme, and avoid Richard Straussisms.

Hitchcock's formal music notes, which the composer received in mid-February 1966, were brief and nearly generic. For example, he wrote that the main theme should be "an exciting, arresting, and rhythmic piece of music ... to rivet the audience's attention." Herrmann, sequestered at the Sportsmen's Lodge (a San Fernando Valley hotel with a long history as a celebrity hangout), finished the score in March.

While the music didn't have the pop flavor requested in the director's 4 November telegram, it definitely had a unique sound, due principally to Herrmann's extremely unorthodox orchestration: twelve "terrifying" flutes, sixteen French horns, nine trombones, two tubas, two sets of timpani, eight cellos, eight basses, and a small contingent of violins and violas. Its darkly powerful, rhythmically driven main theme becomes synonymous with the film's oppressive East German authorities. The whole score has an interesting and unusual darkness about it. Even the romantic cues ("Sarah," "Dawn," and "The Hill"), scored for strings and flutes, are fairly dark and gloomy and not overly melodic. Yet by contrast they seem gentle, since they're not weighed down by the powerful brass. The nostalgically romantic "Valse Lente," source music to accompany Michael and Sarah's discussion in a Copenhagen restaurant, sounds a bit like a weak sister of "Memory Waltz" from the composer's score for *The Snows of Kilimanjaro* (1952). The music Herrmann wrote for the murder scene, built on the interval of the minor third, is both brash and unnerving.

On March 24, the first of two days scheduled for recording his score at Goldwyn Studios, Herrmann conducted the recording of "Prelude," "The Killing," and about a half-dozen other cues. The music and its unusual orchestration delighted the studio musicians, who, after recording the main title track, gave the composer a standing ovation. Their enthusiasm, however, was not contagious. The outlandish sound and nature of the score had "disaster" written all over it. After Hitchcock heard a playback of "Prelude," he complained that it was exactly what he hadn't wanted. He was also upset to learn that Herrmann had scored the murder scene, which he had specifically requested be left without music.

Hitchcock left the Goldwyn Studios and drove to Universal, where he announced to the producers that he had been wrong about hiring Herrmann in the first place, and he canceled the next day's recording sessions. (It's said that, to show his contriteness to the studio, he even offered to cover Herrmann's fee out of his own pocket.)

Later that same day, Hitchcock, still quite angry, phoned the composer to carp about his score's lack of a pop tune. Herrmann would later say that he replied, "Hitch,...you don't make pop pictures.... I don't write pop music."

After the conversation, Herrmann met with his friend Norman Lloyd, executive producer of *Alfred Hitchcock Presents*, who later recalled their meeting:

> So we met at a little hamburger joint on Ventura Boulevard. And to sit at a deserted hamburger joint on Ventura Boulevard at 2:30 in the afternoon, on a sunny California day, was like being relegated to a corner in Dante's hell. Benny arrived and told me what had happened—and that day I saw him as an almost totally destroyed human being. To Benny, his relationship with Hitchcock and his history with Welles were the two greatest things in his life. He considered himself a very good friend of Hitchcock's, and he felt it was over. So we debated the issue—was there anything could be done? Could we enlist the music department at Universal? Then we realized they were the ones who had set up the whole situation, so there was no hope there. And there was no way that Hitch was going to listen to another note of the score. So one just held Benny's hand; the situation was one of total destruction.

Until his death, Herrmann claimed he just wanted the best for the movie, in order to make the characters seem real, not like "ludicrous TV characters." But Hitchcock wasn't receptive.

After all was said and done, Herrmann was off the picture, and a new composer was needed as soon as possible. Right away, possible replacement composers were knocking on the director's door. Dimitri Tiomkin quickly stepped up to offer his services, but Hitchcock declined, despite the fact that they had already worked on four movies, including the classics *Shadow of a Doubt* (1943), *Strangers on a Train* (1951), and *Dial M for Murder* (1954).

On March 29, Hitchcock received a filmography from British composer John Addison, a list of roughly forty titles, including the recent *The Amorous Adventures of Moll Flanders* (1965) and *Tom Jones* (1963), for which Addison had won an Academy Award.

Addison was hired for a fee of $12,500 and flown to Los Angeles to start work immediately. Stanley Wilson, Musical Director at Universal, briefed him on the situation. and to speed up the process, orchestrator Edward B. Powell was brought in to help. Hitchcock prepared new musical notes for Addison, and the two communicated via telephone. Addison recalls:

> I like to play the stuff over on the piano to the director, and I didn't want to make any exception with Hitch, but he was going to London to do the promotion of the film as he always does. When I mentioned this problem to him, his reaction was immediate. "Right, we will have the telephone company make a setup at the studios here at Universal and you can bring in a pianist and play the stuff to me as you wish to do, I will listen to it in my hotel in London and make my comments." And that's what we did. Now I really don't know what Hitchcock got out of this, but it made me feel better. Most of the time he would just say, "Right." but occasionally he would make a comment and I would then consider it and act as I thought. We recorded at the old Goldwyn sound stage and he attended all of the recordings. I found him excellent to work with; he treated me with great respect and politeness. But that is not to say he wouldn't have fired me if he hadn't liked what I was doing.

Addison delivered a more traditional, less gloomy score than his predecessor. It opens with an energetic, rhythmically driven main title theme (not radically unlike the approach Herrmann took with his "Prelude") in 3/4 time. Its love theme, which appears in all kinds of incarnations, is nicely introduced during a bedroom scene but becomes overused during Sarah's shopping spree. Also overused is the dramatic fanfare accompanying every appearance of the Greek letter π, which is associated with an espionage organization. Furthermore, Addison, like Herrmann, felt that Gromek's murder needed underscoring, despite Hitchcock's desire not to have any music there. (Addison's cue "The Murder of Gromek" went unused in the movie but can be heard on the official soundtrack recording.) Ultimately, the film's most memorable musical moment wasn't contributed by Addison. It was the climactic ballet performance set to Tchaikovsky's tone poem *Francesca da Rimini*, recorded by conductor Stanley Wilson.

As for the pop song that Lew Wasserman and Universal craved, it simply didn't work out. The horribly dated "Love Theme from *Torn Curtain* (Green Years)," penned by the songwriting duo of Jay Livingston and Ray Evans (three-time Academy Award winners who were famous for such songs as "Mona Lisa" and "Que Sera, Sera," the latter song making an important appearance in Hitchcock's 1956 version of *The Man Who Knew Too Much*), was not used in the movie. And it didn't make the pop charts either. Anything but hip and contemporary, it was, in the era of the Beatles, an awkward reminder of the music that a youthful audience's parents might have danced to.

Though *Torn Curtain* became Hitchcock's second-most-successful movie (after *Psycho*) at the box office, it was an artistic failure. In the years since its release, the movie (like many of Hitchcock's lesser pictures) has been reevaluated and has grown in critical stature, but for hard-core fans, particularly film score fans, the most interesting aspect is the "what if" of Bernard Herrmann's music. The two rerecordings of his rejected score (covering most of the material he wrote) have probably sold many more copies than the picture's actual Addison soundtrack.

In 1977, Elmer Bernstein released a recording of his reconstruction of Herrmann's score as an LP in his *Elmer Bernstein Film Music Collection* series. This rerecording, however, wasn't complete—a good number of cues, including most of the romantic material written for the movie's Berlin scenes, were not included, and many other cues were combined into suites. In 1998, Joel McNeely recorded a new version of *Torn Curtain* with the National Philharmonic Orchestra for the Varése Sarabande label. This recording included all the original cues, with the exception of two small pieces with running lengths of less than half a minute each, and featured the most important previously unreleased material, the Berlin cues ("The Blurring," "Hotel Berlin," "Sarah Alone," and "Dawn"). In the absence of Herrmann's original recordings, the reconstructions were based on the material available in UCLA's film score collection.

Herrmann's *Torn Curtain* has also lived on through reworkings of its materials into other scores. The composer himself reused the opening bars of his cue "The Killing" in the "The Turning Point" cue from his score for *Battle of Neretva* (1969). Elmer Bernstein made use of a few of the cues in Martin Scorsese's remake of *Cape*

Fear (1991), though the bulk of the film's music consisted of his reorchestration of Herrmann's score to the original 1962 version of *Cape Fear*. Bernstein's *Cape Fear* cue "The Fight" was essentially a combination of Herrmann's *Torn Curtain* cues "The Fall," "The Killing," and "The Corridor." Herrmann's *Torn Curtain* would also have an impact on the next generation of composers: It served as inspiration for Christopher Young's score for *Torment* (1986).

Universal's DVD release of *Torn Curtain* dedicates a large portion of its documentary to the unused Herrmann music, even showing some scenes to which that score has been restored, finally reuniting the original music and images.

■ **One of Our Spies Is Missing** (1966)

Original composers: **Gerald Fried and Robert Drasnin (stock music)**
Replacement composer: **Gerald Fried**

During the spy-movie mania of the 1960s, while the Cold War between the United States and the U.S.S.R. continued to simmer, movie studios capitalized on it in the craziest ways, and the television networks soon followed suit. Therefore, it wasn't surprising when MGM decided to produce a feature-length motion picture version of its most popular television program, NBC's *The Man from U.N.C.L.E.* (a series that aired from mid-1964 through early 1968). The movie *To Trap a Spy* (1964) was the first attempt to turn this series' episodes into a theatrically released film. It added footage to the two-part, sixty-seven-minute pilot episode "The Vulcan Affair" and turned it into a ninety-two-minute feature, which was premiered in foreign markets, where it did phenomenal business given its minuscule budget. In the following years, seven more of the series' two-part episodes also became movies. But due to competition from a proliferation of actual spy pictures and an increasingly negative audience reaction to recutting television shows into movies, most such "features" showed only in overseas markets.

These bottom-rung movies were essentially television programs beefed up with a bit of added sex and violence. Depending on the movie, the music from the original episodes was altered or replaced or kept in tact to varying degrees. *To Trap a Spy*, for instance, barely changed Jerry Goldsmith's score for the original episode. *The Spy with My Face* (1965) featured additional scoring by the episode's original composer, Morton Stevens. *One Spy Too Many* (1966), like its TV version, "Alexander the Greater Affair," featured music by Gerald Fried that underwent only minor changes in its journey to the big screen. This was also true for *The Spy in the Green Hat* (1966), built from "The Concrete Overcoat Affair" episode, which was scored by Nelson Riddle. *The Helicopter Spies* (1968) and *How to Steal the World* (1968) retained their episodes' original Richard Shores music, with the addition of a couple of bits of preexisting music from other sources to fill in the blank spots.

MGM reconsidered its musical approach with the fourth and sixth of its *U.N.C.L.E.* movies. The series' "The Bridge of Lions Affair" episode, which became the film *One of Our Spies Is Missing* (1966), had not had original music written for it; instead, it was scored entirely with preexisting cues culled from other second-season *U.N.C.L.E.* episodes, composed by Gerald Fried and Robert Drasnin. For the movie, however, it was decided that a completely new score that better fit the picture was needed. That job was handled by Fried, whose new score, written for fifteen musicians, had a lighter, jazzier feel than the more dramatic television episode's music. This was in line with the series' increasingly lighthearted tone and helped the picture a great deal.

The Karate Killers (1967) movie, built from the TV episode "The Five Daughters Affair," had a similar problem: The original had been largely scored with cues from previous seasons' episodes composed by Fried, Riddle, and Drasnin. As with *One of Our Spies Is Missing*, two-thirds of *The Karate Killers* was given a new score by Gerald Fried, and the remaining third of the score utilized the old TV cues. (The additional music from these eight pictures is available on the compilation *The Spy with My Face: The Man from U.N.C.L.E. Movies*.)

■ **Chappaqua** (1966)

Original composer: **Ornette Coleman**
Replacement composer: **Ravi Shankar**

"Chappaqua" is an Algonquian Indian word meaning "the rustling land" or "the land where nothing is heard except the rustling of the wind in the leaves." It is also the name of a quiet hamlet in Westchester County, New York. For the film *Chappaqua*'s main character, Russell Harwick (played by writer/director/actor Conrad Rooks), this peaceful hamlet represents the innocence of his early life in suburbia, before he descended into the crazed world of drug addiction. The film's story is autobiographical, tracing Rooks's journey through addiction and rehab in a series of over-the-top, psychedelic, image-driven scenes/hallucinations that jump back and forth between black-and-white and color, as filmed by famed photographer Robert Frank.

Rooks, born into a wealthy family (his father was CEO of Avon Corporation), managed to assemble some fantastic talents for his little picture, resulting in appearances by beatnik hero writers William S. Burroughs, Allen Ginsberg, and Peter Orlovsky; 1960s counterculture guru Swami Satchidananda; celebrated French stage and screen star Jean-Louis Barrault; the notorious rock band the Fugs; composer Moondog; and world-famous innovative musicians Ornette Coleman and Ravi Shankar. While most of these celebrities provided only cameo appearances, both Coleman and Shankar also wrote music for the picture. In the end, though, only one of their scores was used.

Rooks originally hired Coleman to provide music for *Chappaqua* utilizing Coleman's trio—the alto saxophonist accompanied by drummer Charles Moffett and bassist

David Izenson. But the movie seemed to need more than just the trio, so Coleman called in tenor saxophonist Pharoah Sanders and, working with a limited music budget, an eleven-piece chamber orchestra to record his energetic, harmonically dense score. Coleman's music was arranged for this three-day session by Joseph Tekula.

Coleman solved the challenges of combining his trio with an orchestra without sacrificing his own sound by allowing the trio to float rather freely over and through the larger ensemble's intermittent verticalities and quiet murmurings/rustlings. It was exciting and, for its time, innovative music, but it didn't make it to the finished picture. Although Rooks liked Coleman's score, finding it very beautiful, he felt that it just didn't work with his movie. So he quickly hired another music legend, Ravi Shankar, to compose a new score.

At this point in time, the music of composer and sitar virtuoso Shankar, the most visible exponent of Indian classical music in the West, was just starting to have an impact on the Western popular music world. He soon would be a fixture at rock music festivals, popularizing his instrument in the process (the sitar would find its way into hit songs by the Beatles, the Rolling Stones, and others).

The replacement music, performed by Shankar, who was accompanied by master tabla players Alla Rakha and Keshau Sathe and assisted by composer Philip Glass (in Glass's first foray into film music), consisted of fairly traditional Indian material, less dramatic and emotionally charged than Coleman's score. By its very nature, its meditative flavor, it was less likely to be at odds with or dramatically "color" onscreen activities. Furthermore, thanks to the sitar's newfound association with psychedelia in Western pop music, its use in *Chappaqua*, accompanying wild scenes depicting drug "tripping," made it a perfect cultural match for its time.

For the film, Shankar's music was written and performed as "wild" tracks, meaning it was not synched to what transpired onscreen. This allowed the director simply to cut in the music wherever he felt it worked best with the picture.

Glass's work with Shankar on this project would have far-reaching ramifications for his own music. It provided him with firsthand, in-depth knowledge of Indian music and its additive processes, knowledge that would have a great impact on the development of his music from that point on.

Incidentally, Ravi Shankar's music for Rooks's film is still unavailable on CD, although it was issued by Columbia Records on vinyl in 1966. Ornette Coleman's music for this film, presented on record as *Chappaqua Suite*, a work in four movements, has been a collector's item in jazz circles since its first vinyl release in 1965 by Columbia Records and on through its later reissues on CD. *Chappaqua Suite* is rather unusual in that it has stood the test of time much better than the movie it was written for.

■ After the Fox/Caccia alla volpe (1966)

Composer for Italian version: **Piero Piccioni**
Composer for American version: **Burt Bacharach**

Famed playwright Neil Simon had been writing for television since the late 1940s, but *After the Fox* was his first screenplay (although hit Broadway shows of his such as *Barefoot in the Park* and *The Odd Couple* would later be turned into movies). Originally intended as a spoof of art-house cinema, the script evolved into a comic crime caper that generously poked fun at film directors (particularly Italian ones) and actors as well as starstruck audiences. Three years earlier, Jean-Luc Godard's *Contempt* had portrayed the making of a movie within a movie, and *After the Fox*, filled with inside jokes and cameo appearances by noted film personages, could be seen as a wildly comic counterpart to that film. Simon originally envisioned an Italian actor in the part of protagonist Aldo Vanucci, a crafty criminal who undertakes an elaborate fake film production as a cover-up for a gold heist, but then an enthusiastic Peter Sellers came along. Sellers loved the script and helped to get the movie made. He also was responsible for getting renowned neorealist director Vittorio De Sica to sign on to direct it.

Soon, Simon's role in the project was overtaken by the star and the director. De Sica had his own agenda: He saw the movie as a parable about money's corrupting influence on the purity of art, and he populated the production with his regular collaborators, including screenwriter Cesare Zavattini, brought on to help emphasize the director's viewpoint in the script. But collaboration proved difficult, as neither Simon nor Zavattini spoke each other's language. Editor Adriana Novelli didn't speak English either, and Simon came to believe that some of his best jokes ended up badly timed in the edit because she didn't get the punch lines. (The film eventually would be re-edited by Russell Lloyd.)

The music for *After the Fox* is now remembered for one feature: Burt Bacharach's title tune, with lyrics by Hal David. Performed by the Hollies and Peter Sellers, the silly though effective "After the Fox" is a sort of call-and-response between the band and the actor. Sadly, the rest of Bacharach's music was not as inspired as his title song, whose theme floats through his underscore. To highlight the picture's Italian setting, he leaned heavily on ethnic musical clichés delivered with a lighthearted feel. All things considered, this score is miles behind Bacharach's best comedy score, the memorable music for *Casino Royale*, the 1967 spy-movie spoof with an all-star cast also featuring Peter Sellers.

The music for the film's Italian version was provided by composer Piero Piccioni, who had previously scored De Sica's *Il Boom* (1963) and would later work on the director's *Le Streghe* (1967) and *Le Coppie* (1970). While Piccioni could claim numerous successes in his career, his score for *After the Fox* (which still exists in the Italian print) is both forgettable and forgotten. It traffics in the same Italian clichés as Bacharach's score, but with less emphasis on jazz and exotic percussion elements. Both scores try to provide comic music for the suspense sequences, and both succeed on the same minimal level. The only substantial difference is that Piccioni's lacks the strong title tune of Bacharach's. The song Piccioni wrote for the picture, "Guarda un po' chi c'è," is a dime-a-dozen tune. Similar songs appeared in the comedies of Ennio Morricone and Bruno Nicolai, often sung in a high-pitched female voice.

Although Piccioni's changes in the score are not at all radical, the fact that a separate Italian score exists makes for an interesting tidbit of film-scoring trivia. Incidentally, the Italian version's credits still list only Bacharach as the composer.

"Guarda un po' chi c'è" and "Il Bikini," an Oriental-tinged spy spoof cue that incorporates the vamp from the "James Bond Theme," are the only commercially released cues from Piccioni's score. They appear on the compilation *Splendido il Piccioni 3*.

■ The Bible: In the Beginning (1966)

Original composers: **Ennio Morricone, Goffredo Petrassi**
Replacement composer: **Toshirô Mayuzumi**

The Bible: In the Beginning was Italian producer Dino De Laurentiis's extravagant, three-hour-long movie based on the first twenty-two chapters of the Book of Genesis. Written by celebrated playwright Christopher Fry and directed by John Huston (whose previous credits included such classics as *The Maltese Falcon*, *The Treasure of the Sierra Madre*, *Key Largo*, and *The Misfits*), this fractured, episodic production's tone swings wildly from an effects-laden depiction of the creation of the earth to an exploitative Adam and Eve segment to a lighthearted telling of the Noah's Ark tale. De Laurentiis amassed a sizable budget for this production, enabling him to secure a top-drawer cast (including Richard Harris, George C. Scott, Ava Gardner, and Peter O'Toole) and crew for what would turn out to be an often laughable feature. His composer of choice was Ennio Morricone.

Morricone and the producer had a good working relationship, despite the fact that at the beginning of the composer's career, De Laurentiis had rejected his score for *Le Pillole di Ercole* (1962). Although it's not likely that Morricone ever regretted the absence of this lame romantic comedy from his 400-plus-title filmography, he did provide a few details about it that may be of interest to young composers whose first works are similarly rejected:

> Salce [the film's director] knew me because I made the arrangements for a broadcast directed by Luciano Salce and Ettore Scola, *Le canzoni di tutti*, so he called me [for music] for two plays and then for a movie, *Le Pillole d'Ercole*. I wrote the score and we recorded in Salsomaggiore, after which the producer, Dino De Laurentiis, didn't want me because he didn't know me. "Who's that Morricone guy?" And the music was done by Lavagnino [Armando Trovaioli], then in fashion. *Il federale* [1961] was the following movie from Salce: the producers Broggi and Libassi didn't have any difficulty in accepting me.

The Bible was supposed to be the fourth collaboration between Morricone and De Laurentiis, but after the composer started working on it, an irresolvable legal problem arose: Morricone had an exclusive contract with RCA Records to release his music, but the film production had a contract with 20th Century Fox to release the soundtrack. By the time it became clear that Morricone's music couldn't be used, the composer had already recorded a few tracks ("La Creazione," "Deliquio," "La Voce," and "Torre di Babele," conducted by Franco Ferrara), whose ownership he retained after he was taken off the film.

Some have conjectured that these tracks were lost forever, but that's not true; the recordings were later used by Morricone in other projects. Even before *The Bible* was released, Morricone had already used "La Creazione" in the 1965 Western *Il Ritorno di Ringo*, in which the cue was titled "L'Incontro con la figlia" ("The Meeting with the Daughter"). In 1967, Morricone used some of his *Bible* cues, with slight alterations, in Silvano Agosti's picture *Il Giardino delle delizie*. "Deliquio" and "La Voce" remained relatively unchanged, while "La Creazione" was given a new vocal overlay by Edda Dell'Orso. The cue "Torre di Babele" was first released on LP as part of the 1970 noncommercial album *Ennio Morricone*. It would enter the composer's filmography nearly two decades after its recording, when Morricone would reuse both it and "La Creazione" in the television miniseries *The Secret of the Sahara* (1987), titling these haunting choral works "The Golden Door" and "The Mountain," respectively.

Once it was determined that Morricone's score for *The Bible* couldn't be used, the producers contacted two other composers—Toshirô Mayuzumi and Goffredo Petrassi—with the intention of splitting the scoring of the film between them. Mayuzumi, one of Japan's foremost 20th-century composers, employed a highly eclectic style in both his concert works and film scores. Early in his career, he had been deeply interested in Western avant-garde techniques, and he was one of the first Japanese composers to create *musique concrète* and electronic works. Later in life, he embraced a pan-Asian style that combined elements of traditional Japanese music with Western avant-garde and experimental music. At the time he was hired for *The Bible*, his most famous pieces were probably *Nirvana Symphony* and his electronic work commissioned for the 1964 Tokyo Olympics, *Olympic Campanology*, but he had also written nearly eighty film scores, mostly for Japanese productions.

Petrassi was an extremely well-known composer of neoclassical concert works. He was also a respected conductor and teacher (Ennio Morricone was one of his students). At the time he was hired for *The Bible*, he had written only four film scores, but his Italian nationality and home-turf fame were pluses from the perspective of the coproduction deals supporting the picture.

Petrassi recorded his half of the film's music first. But it wasn't well received by the people in charge, so the whole picture was given to Mayuzumi. Mayuzumi's score (nominated for an Academy Award and a Golden Globe) was a strange brew of traditional epic film music and contemporary techniques and sounds. His majestic main theme reoccurs throughout the film to connect the twenty-two chapters, but the individual episodes have underscores that vary greatly from chapter to chapter, ranging from the experimentalism of the creation scenes to the touching romanticism of the Abraham sequence. The destruction of Sodom allows for some great orchestral mayhem, and the vividly colorful music for Noah's Ark even contains moments of comedic mickey-mousing. Mayuzumi's score, which remains one of his best-known film efforts, is a slightly disjointed work in support of a movie suffering from the same problem but on a much, much greater scale.

Fulfilling the contract that had required Morricone's dismissal, Mayuzumi's music was released by 20th Century Fox's record label.

■ **Bonnie and Clyde** (1967)

Original composer: **George Bassman**
Replacement composer: **Charles Strouse**

Bonnie and Clyde, the romanticized story of a notorious Depression Era bank-robbing duo, was produced by Warren Beatty and directed by Arthur Penn, and starred Beatty and Faye Dunaway. It was an extremely influential film, particularly in its tone and editing style, which were partially influenced by the French New Wave movement (interestingly, the film was offered to French directors Truffaut and Godard before Penn), and its balletic depiction of violence. Controversial at the time of its release for its depiction of sex and violence, it was nonetheless nominated for eight Academy Awards.

Veteran Hollywood and Broadway composer George Bassman was hired to write *Bonnie and Clyde*'s score. The title of Charles Goldman's exhaustive article about Bassman, "Rhapsody in Black," aptly describes the composer's career, one characterized by both incredible highs and abysmal lows.

After his formal music studies (including composition lessons with David Diamond, Aaron Copland, and Nadia Boulanger), Bassman began writing and arranging for big bands. He worked with Fletcher Henderson's band and cowrote the Tommy Dorsey Orchestra's hit "I'm Getting Sentimental over You." In the 1930s he moved to Hollywood, where he began working in various capacities—conducting, orchestrating, arranging, composing—for myriad productions at RKO and then MGM (he was the latter's music director for twelve years, starting in 1937). He penned music for a few Marx Brothers films, including *A Day at the Races* (1937), and orchestrated a number of popular musicals that featured Judy Garland, including *Babes in Arms* (1938), *The Wizard of Oz* (1939), and *For Me and My Gal* (1942). For *The Wizard of Oz*, he also wrote the underscore music for the cyclone, the poppy field, and the Emerald City. Among his other notable achievements, Bassman scored the noir classic *The Postman Always Rings Twice* (1946).

While scoring *The Naked City* (1948), a movie noted for its gritty New York City location shots, Bassman ran afoul of producer Mark Hellinger, who accused him of plagiarism. The two had huge fights over the music, and some in Hollywood said that these fights helped bring on Hellinger's second—this time fatal—heart attack. Bassman's score for *The Naked City* was replaced by Miklós Rózsa and Frank Skinner.

Convinced that Hellinger's death had rendered him persona non grata in Hollywood, Bassman moved to New York, where he busied himself with arranging and writing for Broadway, including orchestrating the original production of the hit musical *Guys and Dolls* (which premiered in New York in 1950). Hollywood's doors closed to him decisively, however, after he was called before the House Un-American Activities Committee in January 1952, where he admitted that he had been a member of the Communist Party (as had his mother). As of that point, no Hollywood studio producer could hire him.

While continuing his Broadway work, Bassman conducted and wrote music for a few New York–based television shows, including the monthly drama-anthology series *Producer's Showcase* (1956–57). He also found a little bit of work with independent filmmakers based in New York: He wrote additional music for the Oscar-winning *Marty* (1955), penned by legendary screenwriter Paddy Chayefsky, and provided the full score for another Chayevsky-scripted film (and another portrayal of grim loneliness), *Middle of the Night* (1959).

In the early 1960s, Bassman weathered a stormy relationship with Hollywood director Sam Peckinpah to score the highly regarded Western *Ride the High Country* (1962). And he continued to score a few television shows. Among them was "Survival" (1963), the only episode of the WWII series *Combat* that was not composed by Leonard Rosenman. Bassman was hired by the episode's director, Robert Altman, to provide out-of-the-ordinary music for its controversially grim and hallucinatory story. (Reportedly because of this show, Altman was fired from the series.)

But score rejections would soon dog Bassman again. In 1965 he was hired by producer Stephen Alexander to score Sydney Pollack's directorial debut, *The Slender Thread*, the tense story of a novice volunteer at a suicide help-line. However, before Bassman completed this score, Pollack changed his mind about the music, rejecting the composer's work, choosing instead to score the entire movie with improvised trumpet. By the time this experiment proved a failure, the use of Bassman's music was no longer an option, and Quincy Jones was hired to provide a jazz-flavored score.

But the next year, Hollywood gave Bassman another shot: He was hired to score *Bonnie and Clyde*. Unfortunately, the opportunity would prove illusory. Starting in the mid-1960s, a new Hollywood came into being with the advent of an influential group of independent filmmakers, who often maintained an unusual relationship with film music. This can be seen in such pictures as William Friedkin's *The French Connection*, in which Don Ellis's music is scattered liberally throughout the picture, but rarely in the spots where the composer intended it.

Arthur Penn had a similar approach in mind for *Bonnie and Clyde*. But Bassman wouldn't go along with this sort of treatment of his music, so he was replaced by successful Broadway musicals composer Charles Strouse (winner of three Tony Awards, for *Bye, Bye Birdie*; *Applause*; and *Annie*). Strouse wrote a highly effective, although quite short, score. With the exception of a dreamlike sequence, most of *Bonnie and Clyde*'s score consists of bluegrass music, notably Earl Scruggs's 1949 "Foggy Mountain Breakdown" (performed by the duo Flatt and Scruggs), playing under Bonnie and Clyde's escape sequences, while the most important scenes—including the famous final shootout—are left unaccompanied. (Soon, fast-picking bluegrass would become synonymous with rural chase scenes in innumerable Hollywood productions, and its use quickly became a cliché.)

His experiences with *The Slender Thread* and *Bonnie and Clyde* ultimately proved fatal for George Bassman's career, leaving him unable to work in either the old or the new Hollywood.

■ A Time for Killing (1967)

Original composer: **Van Alexander**
Replacement composer: **Mundell Lowe**

One of Our Spies Is Missing (1966) and the rest of the *U.N.C.L.E.* movies showed that by the mid-1960s, some television shows had production values that (debatably) made them fit for the big screen. On the opposite side of the coin, this same period saw the production of many movies intended for theatrical release that simply didn't make the grade. Such doomed efforts often skipped theatrical release altogether, appearing on television without much delay.

A Time for Killing is an unremarkable Western starring Glenn Ford and Inger Stevens that is remembered primarily for being Harrison Ford's first credited screen appearance. Its original composer, Van Alexander, regularly worked for Columbia Pictures and had composed scores for a number of B movies (including William Castle's cheesy terror escapade *Strait-Jacket*, starring Joan Crawford) and quite a few television series (including *The Donna Reed Show*, *Bewitched*, and *I Dream of Jeannie*). *A Time for Killing* was meant to be his big break, but that was not to be. Alexander's own tale of woe illustrates the problems he faced:

> They had changed directors in the middle of it, as well as writers. The picture was really in trouble. Following those four or five independent projects for Columbia, they said, "Why don't we give Van a chance? Maybe he can save the picture." They gave me a very good price and I had plenty of time to do it. I was given an office at the studio. I did the score in about six or seven weeks. I had a big orchestra, and they were all there at the scoring session (Mike Frankovich and the head of the music department, Joni Taps). They raved about the music and said, "My God. You've saved the picture!" I was on cloud nine. So now they had what they called a "preview" of the picture. This is where they show it to the public and try to get some feedback. With my wife and two daughters, we all went to a theater out here in the San Fernando Valley for the showing. Well, it was a disaster. People were laughing in the serious parts and were hissing the villain. I wanted to crawl under the table. I thought that I had written a pretty good score, and everyone at the scoring stage had approved. And now the Columbia brass sees the result in the

> theater! Two days later, Mike Frankovich calls and tells me that he doesn't think that the music is right for the picture! I asked him if they wanted to change anything and he said, "No, I think that we're going to throw it all out and rescore it with ten guitars and make it a real Western." So they hired Mundell Lowe, who is a great guitar player. He brought in ten guitars, but that didn't help the picture either. It never played in a theater, but was on television about three weeks later. That made me feel a little better, but I felt as if I'd never do another picture!

Alexander's assessment wasn't far from the truth—this would be the last score he wrote for a theatrical release.

Replacement composer Mundell Lowe was a well-known jazz guitarist and composer who, before moving to Los Angeles, had played with many jazz giants, including Charlie Parker, Sonny Rollins, and Sarah Vaughn. In LA he wrote music for many television shows. His score for *A Time for Killing* was simple and guitar-based. (*Note*: A song that Alexander wrote for the film, "A Long Ride Home," sung by Eddy Arnold, remained in the film.)

A Time for Killing wasn't the only theatrical Western to be turned into a television movie and get a new score in the process. For example, in 1968, television director Jud Taylor shot a unique film called *Fade-In* on the set of the Paramount Pictures Western *Blue* (1968). The picture was about an on-set love story taking place during *Blue's* shooting and featured several cast members (including Ricardo Montalban, Sally Kirkland, and Terence Stamp) playing themselves. *Blue*'s composer, Manos Hatzidakis, provided the music, mining *Blue*'s score for music for the secondary feature.

But Paramount took *Fade-In* away from director Taylor and edited the hell out of it. (After the director objected to this re-edit and requested that his name be removed from the final picture, *Fade-In* became one of the first movies to bear the fictional director name "Alan Smithee," an insider's signal that the director disowns the picture.) Among the many things Paramount changed was Hatzidakis's music, replacing it with the work of staff composers and orchestrators Jack Hayes, Ken Lauber, and Leo Shuken. In the end, *Fade-In* the experimental "movie-about-a-movie" became *Fade-In* the television Movie-of-the-Week.

■ **Bora Bora** (1968)

Composer for Italian version: **Piero Piccioni**
Composer for American version: **Les Baxter**

In 1966, American International Pictures (AIP), famous for producing and distributing B movies and repackaged foreign pictures (including Toho Studios' Godzilla pictures) for American audiences, acquired the rights to the Japanese spy movie *International Secret Police: Key of Keys* (1965) for a mere $66,000. It was just one of the company's many cheap foreign acquisitions, but this particular picture turned out to be incomprehensible to the American audience. So comedy writer Woody Allen was hired to re-edit it, combining it with footage from another Japanese film, *International Secret Police: A Barrel of Gunpowder*, and write and record new, comical dialogue for it. The result was *What's Up, Tiger Lily?*, a very broad comedy that leans heavily on puns and sight gags. The original film's score, by Sadao Bekku, hadn't been targeted for replacement, but in an attempt to make the movie longer, AIP added (against Allen's wishes) footage of the popular band the Lovin' Spoonful. The band's songs eventually were used as the movie's soundtrack, which became quite popular and had an effect on some of the studio's later features. While peplum and horror movie rescoring seemingly reflected AIP's dislike of foreign scores, the success of the *Tiger Lily* experiment suggested the studio should try producing best-selling soundtracks for its comedies regardless of whether the films were good or not.

Following the success of *What's Up, Tiger Lily?*, AIP's in-house composer Les Baxter began to be assigned to rescore foreign comedies. One of Baxter's early comedy assignments was the Italian production *Dr. Goldfoot and the Girl Bombs* (1966), a strange spinoff of a successful American teen comedy directed by Norman Taurog (best known for directing the early-sixties Elvis vehicles *G.I. Blues* and *Blue Hawaii*), *Dr. Goldfoot and the Bikini Machine* (1965). Both *Goldfoot* movies starred Vincent Price as the devilish doctor, but the less successful Italian-made sequel (directed by celebrated horror-movie maker Mario Bava) seems to have been primarily designed as a vehicle for Italian comedians Franco Franchi and Ciccio Ingrassia. Since Les Baxter had written the music for the first *Goldfoot* film, he was the natural choice to replace the movie's original score by Coriolano Gori as AIP prepared a version of the picture for American audiences. To create the new score, Baxter recycled bits from his *Dr. Goldfoot and the Bikini Machine* music and added some new material.

A slew of similar movies would keep Baxter busy for years to come, with the rarely seen *Bora Bora* a standout among them. *Bora Bora* is a gem for eager collectors of 1960s scores, since two albums are available of music written for the same movie. These are not really soundtracks, but more like "exotica" records whose musical content happened to appear in an Italian film that almost nobody saw. ("Exotica" was a musical genre that Les Baxter pioneered and popularized in the 1950s, particularly via his 1951 album *Ritual of the Savage*. It combined lush, easy-listening orchestral music with a touch of jazz and a heavy dose of multilayered ethnic percussion playing a Western composer's imagined version of Afro-Cuban and Pacific Island rhythms. As long as tiki bars were popular, kitschy exotica music had a home.)

The movie *Bora Bora* is long gone, and with no video releases to date, its two scores—the original Italian one by Piero Piccioni and its American replacement by Baxter—are all that are available to us. Piccioni's score is quite psychedelic, utilizing his favored Hammond organ, though it now takes a backseat to "tribal" percussion and funky instrumental tunes. The film's breathtaking shots of the island's natural beauty are accented by faint female vocals, a sound frequently employed by Italian composers. The score evokes the island's atmosphere, and while it contains its fair share of traditional elements, it is not overpowered by them. (The recording of

Piccioni's music received deluxe treatment in Japan, making it one of the composer's most sought-after releases.)

When AIP picked up *Bora Bora* in 1970, they dubbed it into English and shortened it by seven minutes. The job of creating new music was handed over to their usual musical repairman, Les Baxter, who produced a score consisting chiefly of a series of mood pieces with, surprisingly, fewer "tribal" instruments than Piccioni had employed.

Both composers' soundtracks are recommended for fans of tropical/exotica music. (The original LP of Baxter's score did a respectable business at the time of its release because the composer was fairly well known outside the film music community, but no CD of it has ever been issued.)

■ 2001: A Space Odyssey (1968)

Original composers: **Frank Cordell, Alex North**
Replacement music: **Classical compositions by various composers**

While developing and writing the script for his unique science fiction film *2001: A Space Odyssey* with author and futurist Arthur C. Clarke, the innovative director and avid record collector Stanley Kubrick (acclaimed for such earlier films as *Paths of Glory*, *Lolita*, and *Dr. Strangelove*) busied himself with finding the right music for the picture. His passion for classical music led him to believe that he didn't need an original score—he could simply make use of the great wealth of music that already existed.

He bought and listened to all kinds of classical records, looking for music that might convey the concepts underpinning his movie. One of his favorite pieces was German composer Carl Orff's popular cantata *Carmina Burana*, which frequently played on the phonograph while he and Clarke worked on their script. The dramatic feel of the piece whetted Kubrick's interest in Orff, and, while still in the preproduction stage he approached the composer about writing the film's score. Orff declined, claiming that his age (71) prevented him from taking on such a big task. Dutch composer Dick Raaymakers claims he too was asked to work on the picture, but declined due to other commitments.

Another theme in Kubrick's search was music directly associated with German philosopher Friedrich Nietzsche, an influence on the director and his movie. He became interested in Gustav Mahler's Third Symphony, not only because he felt its sound would be right for his film, but also because the work's fourth movement is a setting of Nietzsche's "Midnight Song," a poem from his influential novel *Also sprach Zarathustra*. Kubrick asked British composer Frank Cordell (best known for his work on the 1966 movie *Khartoum*) to adapt the Third Symphony for his film. Cordell spent a year analyzing, editing, and even recording parts of the symphony, Mahler's longest work, but his adaptation was not used. (After being dropped from the film, Cordell hoped to release what he had adapted and recorded, but the project did not come to fruition before his death in 1980. His estate is still trying to get these recordings issued.)

With the Third Symphony discarded, Kubrick constructed an elaborate temporary score out of various classical pieces. Among them were contemporary Hungarian composer György Ligeti's dense, simmering, wordless choral pieces Requiem for Soprano, Mezzo Soprano, Two Mixed Choirs and Orchestra; *Lux Aeterna*; and *Atmosphères*. These proved very effective in enhancing the mysteriousness of the film's monolith. Other pieces in the temp score included Johann Strauss's popular *The Blue Danube* waltz and Aram Khachaturian's *Gayane* ballet, which accompanied the endless voyaging through space. The key composition, however, was Richard Strauss's famous tone poem *Also sprach Zarathustra*, which was of course inspired by Nietzsche. Its dramatic opening would become the movie's signature music, used not only in the main title sequence but in the memorable scene in which ape man Moon-Watcher takes over leadership of mankind with the bones of a deceased animal.

Still, despite Kubrick's careful selection of existing pieces, MGM's brass decided that a movie of great stature needed an original score by a big-name composer. Alex North, with whom the director had worked on *Spartacus* (1960), was selected. The composer remembers:

> I was living in the Chelsea Hotel in New York (where Arthur Clarke was living) and got a phone call from Kubrick from London asking my availability to come over and do a score for *2001*. He told me that I was the film composer he most respected, and he looked forward to working together. I was ecstatic at the idea of working with Kubrick again (*Spartacus* was an extremely exciting experience for me), as I regard Kubrick as the most gifted of the younger-generation directors, and that goes for the older as well. And to do a film score where there were about twenty-five minutes of dialogue and no sound effects! What a dreamy assignment, after *Who's Afraid of Virginia Woolf?*, loaded with dialogue.
>
> I flew over to London for two days in early December to discuss music with Kubrick. He was direct and honest with me concerning his desire to retain some of the "temporary" music tracks which he had been using for the past years. I realized that he liked these tracks, but I couldn't accept the idea of composing part of the score interpolated with other composers. I felt I could compose music that had the ingredients and essence of what Kubrick wanted and give it a consistency and homogeneity and contemporary feel. In any case, I returned to London December 24th [1967] to start work for recording on January 1, after having seen and discussed the first hour of film for scoring. Kubrick arranged a magnificent apartment for me on the Chelsea Embankment, and furnished me with all the things to make me happy: record player, tape machine, good records, etc. I worked day and night to meet the first recording date, but with the stress and strain, I came down with muscle spasms and back trouble. I had to go to the recording in an ambulance, and the man who helped me with the orchestration, Henry Brant, conducted while I was in the control room. Kubrick was present, in and out; he was pressured for time as well. He made very good suggestions, musically. I had written two sequences for the opening, and he was definitely favorable to one, which was

> my favorite as well. So I assumed all was going well, what with his participation and interest in the recording. But somehow I had the hunch that whatever I wrote to supplant *Zarathustra* would not satisfy Kubrick, even though I used the same structure but brought it up to date in idiom and dramatic punch. Also, how could I compete with Mendelssohn's "Scherzo" from *Midsummer Night's Dream*? Well, I thought I did pretty damned well in that respect.
>
> In any case, after having composed and recorded over forty minutes of music in those two weeks, I waited around for the opportunity to look at the balance of the film, spot the music, etc. During that period I was rewriting some of the stuff that I was not completely satisfied with, and Kubrick even suggested over the phone certain changes that I could make in the subsequent recording. After eleven tense days of waiting to see more film in order to record in early February, I received word from Kubrick that no more score was necessary, that he was going to use breathing effects for the remainder of the film. It was all very strange, and I thought perhaps I would still be called upon to compose more music; I even suggested to Kubrick that I could do whatever necessary back in LA at the MGM studios. Nothing happened. I went to a screening in New York, and there were most of the "temporary" tracks.

In Alex North's original score, the only place a temp selection really bleeds through is in his cue "Bones," obviously based on *Also sprach Zarathustra*. The piece was recorded for the ape's bone-crushing scene, since the movie didn't have main titles at that point. Four other scenes that North scored ("The Foraging," "The Bluff," "Night Terrors," and "Eat Meat and Kill") would be left without music in the film's final cut. For one of these, the composer developed two variations: "The Foraging" had a more powerful alternate version called "Dawn of Man," but both the composer and the director preferred the subtler one. The second half of North's score contained the provocative space ballet "Space Station Docking," written for a scene that was originally temped with the scherzo from Mendelssohn's *A Midsummer Night's Dream* and later replaced by *The Blue Danube*, and three more cues: the gentle "Space Talk," "Trip to the Moon" (which would be replaced by the Strauss waltz), and "Moon Rocket Bus," which featured soprano Mary Thomas, a cue Kubrick apparently disliked. On the director's insistence, North was not asked to write anything beyond the film's seventh reel (about halfway through the film) as Kubrick already had decided that nothing from the composer's original music would be used. Kubrick remembered:

> When I had completed the editing of *2001: A Space Odyssey*, I had laid in temporary music tracks for almost all of the music which was eventually used in the film. Then, in the normal way, I engaged the services of a distinguished film composer to write the score. Although he and I went over the picture very carefully, and he listened to these temporary tracks (Strauss, Ligeti, Khachaturian) and agreed that they worked fine and would serve as a guide to the musical objectives of each sequence, he, nevertheless, wrote and recorded a score which could not have been more alien to the music we had listened to, and much more serious than that, a score which, in my opinion, was completely inadequate for the film. With the premiere looming up, I had no time left even to think about another score being written, and had I not been able to use the music

> I had already selected for the temporary tracks I don't know what I would have done. The composer's agent phoned Robert O'Brien, the then-head of MGM, to warn him that if I didn't use his client's score the film would not make its premiere date. But in that instance, as in all others, O'Brien trusted my judgment. He is a wonderful man, and one of the very few film bosses able to inspire genuine loyalty and affection from his filmmakers.

After the rejection of his score, North was devastated, calling it the most humiliating experience of his life. He later found ways to make use of elements of his great *2001* score, most notably "Bones," in other pieces. North's later film scores influenced by his *2001* material include the religious epic *Shoes of the Fisherman* (1968), the macabre comedy *Shanks* (1974), and the fantasy adventure *Dragonslayer* (1981). North had planned to build his *2001* material into his Third Symphony, to be dedicated to the Apollo 13 astronauts, but that work was never finished.

North's full *2001* score was resurrected in 1993 when record producer and film score specialist Robert Townson put together a new recording of it conducted by Jerry Goldsmith. (By this point, the original recordings, engineered by Ken Cameron at his Anvil Studios in Denham, were said to have been destroyed. According to recording engineer Eric Tomlinson, the 35mm magnetic film masters were erased before Anvil closed its gates.) When the rerecording hit record store shelves, it triggered a debate about whether North's score would have added to or detracted from the picture's massive impact.

When the Stanley Kubrick collection was released on DVD by Warner Bros., the company planned to issue a CD compilation under the title *Music from the Films of Stanley Kubrick*. The project never materialized, but the idea of the compilation prompted film score producer Nick Redman to reinvestigate the case of North's original *2001* recordings. He found that the composer had retained a set of mono tapes of the score, which he had donated to the Academy of Motion Picture Arts and Sciences' Margaret Herrick Library. In 2003, North's widow gave permission for the tapes to be released. Redman tried to get the music included as a bonus on the movie's 2006 DVD reissue, but Warner Bros. wasn't interested in licensing a score that didn't belong to them. A CD of the original recordings was eventually released by Intrada in 2007.

More than forty years after the film's creation, film score buffs are divided into two camps: Those who prefer North's score to Kubrick's classical music compilation usually claim that the director treated the composer unfairly and that North's music would have greatly improved the picture. Those on the other side insist that *2001* didn't need a narrative score to help it along, and that the audience's preconceived notions about the well-known classical pieces often aided Kubrick's cause rather than hindering it. It's important to note, however, that the idea of having an original score had been forced on the director in the first place.

■ **The Lost Continent** (1968)

Original composer: **Benjamin Frankel**
Replacement composer: **Gerard Schurmann**

The Lost Continent was the most ambitious film to come out of Hammer Film Productions. Accordingly, it looks nothing like what we have come to expect from the leading British horror-movie studio. Based on Dennis Wheatley's novel *Uncharted Seas*, the film tells the story of a ship that gets lost and sails into uncharted seas, where its crew faces man-eating plants, sea monsters, mutated conquistadors, and all manner of other marvelously absurd impediments.

Directed and cowritten by Michael Carreras (son of studio founder James Carreras), *The Lost Continent* is one of the oddest titles in Hammer's catalogue, for more than one reason. Its original score was composed by Benjamin Frankel, who had previously worked on such Hammer titles as *The Curse of the Werewolf* (1961), for which he provided Britain's first commercial film score to employ serial techniques, *I Only Arsked* (1958), and *The Old Dark House* (1963). This time, however, Frankel's work was overseen by Hammer music director Philip Martell, who disagreed with most of the composer's choices. Because Frankel was a successful concert composer, with numerous symphonies, concertos, and string quartets to his credit, Martell was convinced that he didn't know how to write "proper film music." After Frankel presented his score, Martell visited him at his home to instruct him on how to do the job properly. The lecture quickly turned into an argument, Martell was shown the door, and Frankel never worked for Hammer again.

A replacement score for *The Lost Continent* was provided by Gerard Schurmann, who had worked on Hammer's *The Camp on Blood Island* (1958). In fact, director Carreras had offered Schurmann the movie first, but he wasn't available. Once Frankel was out of the picture, the director still wanted Schurmann badly enough to wait six months until he was free again. Schurmann was known for vibrant, harsh, evocative horror scores that had a way of making low-budget productions seem bigger and better than they actually were. In this case, however, his score was ruined by a bad final sound mix, an event that would cause Schurmann to leave the field of film scoring for a couple of decades:

> With the use of a very much larger orchestra, our carefully laid musical schemes and preparations were in the end totally undone by the most ruinous final dub it has ever been my misfortune to encounter. The man in charge was, I believe, the supervising editor, who had impressed me before I ever started to write the music by his rudely arrogant and patronizing manner. So utterly appalled was I by this gentleman's demeanor that I refused to go to any of the dubbing sessions. I now admit that had I been there I might perhaps have been able to prevent some of the very worst from happening, but it just seemed to me to be a lost cause at the time.

Though Philip Martell's uncompromising attitude had been behind the score replacement on *The Lost Continent*, he was in fact a capable and talented musical director, as he demonstrated three years later, on the film *Dr. Jekyll & Sister Hyde* (1971). Producer Albert Fennell had originally wanted Laurie Johnson to score the movie, but ended up instead with veteran Hammer composer Harry Robinson. The producer asked Robinson for a ninety-minute score, essentially "wall-to-wall" music, from which he intended to toss out unneeded and unwanted cues later. But the composer insisted on the tried-and-true method—spotting the picture and writing the exact amount of needed music—and after he delivered all of the picture's source music, he and Fennell clashed. Robinson left the project in anger, and Martell quickly hired as his replacement David Whitaker, who came up with a fitting underscore. Considering Hammer's many titles, it's surprising how few scores the studio replaced. They probably had Philip Martell to thank for that.

■ Land of the Giants: "The Crash" (1968)

Original composer: **Alexander Courage**
Replacement composer: **John Williams**

Producer Irwin Allen had numerous popular television fantasy series under his belt, including *The Time Tunnel* (1966–67), *Voyage to the Bottom of the Sea* (1964–68), and *Lost in Space* (1965–68). With each show he pushed the television production envelope a little further, producing fantastic stories with exceptional effects—and on a strict budget. On the heels of these successful programs, in 1968 he created, produced, and launched a new show, *Land of the Giants*. This sci-fi series, set in the year 1983, followed the adventures of a group of travelers who mysteriously ended up on a planet of seventy-foot-tall humanoid giants and had to cope with their new Lilliputian status. The show utilized state-of-the-art cinematography (nominated for an Emmy) and featured a wide variety of stunning gigantic props. It also happened to undergo multiple score rejections, as Allen flip-flopped over where to go with the show's music.

The first composer hired was Alexander Courage, whose main gig was scoring *Star Trek* and who had worked on selected episodes of Irwin's programs. In the last days of 1967, Courage recorded a main theme and score for the pilot episode of *Land of the Giants*, "The Crash." In this opening story, the spaceship *Spindrift* gets lost in an ethereal haze and is forced to land in a strange dystopia populated by giants. Allen was not satisfied with the main theme and commissioned a rewrite by Joseph Mullendore, who had previously contributed a handful of scores to other Irwin shows. But Mullendore's offering, recorded in January, also was rejected (and unfortunately has disappeared).

After a hiatus, the show's whole musical concept was rethought, resulting in the scrapping of Courage's entire score. Next, Allen turned to his frequent musical collaborator Johnny Williams, regular composer for *The Time Tunnel* and *Lost in Space*.

Williams wrote and recorded a first-episode score and a main theme. The latter became the show's signature fanfare through its first season.

Williams's score brought relatively fresh musical ideas to television science fiction scores and proved popular with Allen. Compared with Courage's unused work, it simply sounds fresher. Portions of the rejected work recycle television clichés, such as typical "mine disaster" music for *Spindrift*'s panic and Carl Stalling–like "sneaking" music that accentuates a character's every step. By comparison, Williams's score strayed from the run-of-the-mill television sound, and while it can't be called cinematic, it wasn't slavishly reliant on the era's standard TV-music ideas.

After *Land of the Giants*' first season, Allen asked Williams to write a new theme to accompany the redesigned titles, which featured scenes from previous episodes. Not long after this, "Johnny" Williams would become John Williams, and his collaborations with Allen would lead to more rewarding film assignments.

(The GNP Crescendo label has released both scores for the first episode of *Land of the Giants* on a single CD.)

■ **Barbarella** (1968)

Original composer: **Michel Magne**
Replacement composer: **Charles Fox**

Based on a popular French comic-book character, *Barbarella* was produced by Dino De Laurentiis and directed by Roger Vadim (a French filmmaker perhaps best remembered for launching the career of his first wife, Brigitte Bardot, in his 1956 film *And God Created Woman*). This comically psychedelic sci-fi tale of the fortieth century, with its abundance of sex and drugs—definitely a product of the 1960s!—starred Jane Fonda, Vadim's third wife.

French composer Michel Magne (an Academy Award nominee for his music for *Gigot*) had worked with Vadim on three previous films and was hired to score *Barbarella*. Vadim encouraged Magne to be as experimental as he could and come up with something new for the genre. His score centered on a baroque-style fugue that morphed from a traditional classical performance into an easy-listening, lounge-music version. Light bossa nova–rhythm pieces are also scattered throughout his soundtrack. Magne's "Barbarella's Song" is a light pop effort that asks in its lyrics if she is "merely a girl" or "from another world."

Aided by assistants Jean-Claude Petit and Jean-Claude Vannier, Magne wrote and recorded his score, and then presented it to the producers at Paramount, the movie's American distributor and actual financiers. But the music wasn't well received at Paramount. While Vadim had encouraged Magne to try new things, the studio/distributor preferred a different, more comedic approach. Film and television composer/songwriter Charles Fox, known for the sunny pop sound of his songs, was hired to create a lightly psychedelic score based on four bouncy songs that he cowrote with

Bob Crewe (a songwriter responsible for four of the Four Seasons' number-one hits). The rest of Fox's score was more or less upbeat, pop-ish lounge music, some of it treated with futuristic and adventurous electronics.

The film's inventive main credits—under which Barbarella undresses in zero gravity—do not make any mention of the musical contributors. Magne, however, is erroneously listed by several sources as the uncredited conductor of Fox's score. This is the result of confusing press releases that removed Magne's composer credit but inadvertently left his conductor credit. This incorrect information appears on even the latest CD reissues of Fox's *Barbarella* score.

The recordings of both scores share a troubled release history. It took quite some time for Magne's widow to get her late husband's unused music released in proper fashion. While a teaser track appeared on the 1998 retrospective *Michel Magne: 25 ans de musique de film* compilation, the full score was only issued in 2007 on the selection *Bandes originales des films de Roger Vadim*, which collected music from four films, including *Don Juan ou Si Don Juan était une femme*, a movie Magne scored for Vadim five years after being dropped from *Barbarella*.

After its initial success on a Dynovoice LP, a recording on which tracks bleed into each other, providing a forty-minute pseudo-psychedelic trip (courtesy of the Bob Crewe Generation Orchestra), Fox's score was reissued on CD in 2002 by Harkit Records. But despite the inclusion of several bonus tracks, the CD's serious sound problems and unusual cuts kept it from becoming a hot item. A 2004 CD reissue corrected some of these problems, but the bad press surrounding the previous CD hurt the label's reputation in soundtrack circles.

Sinful Davey (1969)

Original composer: **John Barry**
Replacement composer: **Ken Thorne**

Between the release of Tony Richardson's Academy Award–winning *Tom Jones* (1963) and Stanley Kubrick's masterful *Barry Lyndon* (1975), the British film industry maintained a steady output of stories about lovable rogues who wander the countryside stealing money and/or hearts, always ending their wayward journeys with a moral lesson. However, few of these pictures were actually good, and *Sinful Davey*, a tale of an early-18th-century Scottish highwayman, directed by the great John Huston, is one example of a decently made movie that lacks that extra something—in the acting? the screenplay? the music?—needed for success. (This despite its inspired tagline: "The Seven Deadly Sins have never been so lively! Grave-robbing, Maid-snatching, Jail-breaking, Jewel-thieving, Smuggling, Piracy, and Wife-stealing. Leave it to Davey to invent No. 8!")

The first composer on the picture was John Barry, at that time still best known to the general audience for his James Bond scores, and the hit songs associated with them. That track record, combined with his two Academy Award–winning scores—*Born Free* (1966) and *The Lion in Winter* (1968)—and the Academy Award–winning title song from the former movie, made the producers of *Sinful Davey* think they had a surefire winner on board.

The producers had a lighthearted score in mind, possibly even with a hit theme song, however, Barry's take on the project proved substantially different. He composed a fairly dark score based mostly on the historical music of the era—think *Barry Lyndon* with less reliance on classical music and more varied themes. This just didn't click with the MGM executives, who discarded his work, leaving director Huston to look for new, lighter music for his picture. He hired composer Ken Thorne (known at the time for his music for director Richard Lester's *Help!*, *How I Won the War*, and *A Funny Thing Happened on the Way to the Forum*). Thorne remembers:

> John Barry's score was considered too dark for John Huston's liking, and he approached me to initially write a "test" piece of the Market Scene. I did this and, having recorded it, we sat in "the booth" waiting for John Huston to arrive! I was very nervous! Suddenly he appeared, dressed entirely in green! Without a word he sat down and we ran the section for him. There was complete silence at the end for what seemed to me to be a long time, and then he stood up and said, "Perfect!!" So I then completed the rest of the score in the following weeks. But I still feel that my lighthearted approach didn't really add anything to the movie! It just wasn't another *Tom Jones*.

The most lasting element of Thorne's contribution is the pop ballad "Sinful Davey," cowritten with lyricist Don Black (known at the time for his lyrics for the title songs from *Born Free* and *Thunderball*). The song, a strange testament to the virtues of the titular outlaw, was performed by the popular Israeli chanteuse Esther Ofarim. Targeted at the pop charts, it was perhaps what the MGM executives had in mind when they first hired Barry, hoping he might pen another "Goldfinger" or "Born Free." But *Sinful Davey* the movie never did big business, and "Sinful Davey" the song wasn't particularly successful either: It appeared as an obscure single that became a collectible for fans of Esther Ofarim. As for John Barry's original score, unfortunately the recording was destroyed in a flood at the CTS Studios storage facility, so a future release is unlikely.

■ **Age of Consent** (1969)

Original composer: **Peter Sculthorpe**
Replacement composer: **Stanley Myers**

Age of Consent was based on the semiautobiographical novel of the same name by Australian artist Norman Lindsay. Shot in Australia, the movie was coproduced by two Englishmen: its star, James Mason, and its director, the legendary Michael Powell (creator of such masterpieces as *Black Narcissus*, *The Red Shoes*, and *Peeping Tom*). Columbia Pictures signed on as the international distributor. Powell, keen on utilizing Australian talent on the picture, hired composer Peter Sculthorpe, one of Australia's leading concert composers.

Sculthorpe was at first reluctant to participate, because he was busy with his ballet *Sun Music*. Still, he ended up actively involved in *Age of Consent* fairly early on, even visiting the set during filming on the Great Barrier Reef in April 1968 (which he recalled as the most pleasant aspect of the entire process). He didn't formally sign onto the production until the following month, and not before determining that the movie needed only a half-hour of music, allowing him to spend time on his concert compositions. His fee for the score was $1,500, but he expected to make a lot more from royalties, not to mention the free publicity it offered him.

Sculthorpe wrote the picture's music in June and July, with recording commencing in the latter month. His score drew on some of his previous works, including his 1963 chamber ensemble piece *Small Town*. The gallery sequence from early in the picture makes use of Sculthorpe's more avant-garde String Quartet No. 7, which was written while the composer was a Harkness Fellow composer-in-residence at Yale in 1966. The music heard during the young actress Helen Mirren's nude swim is based on his 1968 Balinese gamelan–influenced *Tabuh-tabuhan*. Other cues were also influenced by gamelan music, in accordance with the composer's strong interest in the music of Australia's neighboring Asian cultures. (Further influences on Sculthorpe's music, over his career, have been Aboriginal music and culture, as well as Australia's geography.)

In return for his efforts, the film's distributor turned its back on Sculthorpe's score, and in the international release his music was replaced. The reasons for this may be complex, but the official version is that Columbia Pictures' London management found the score poorly recorded and the tape faulty. The studio cabled Sculthorpe in September 1968 to request that a new recording be delivered in time for the American premiere in May 1969, but the composer was away in Japan. (He later recalled that, even had he been home, he would not have been inclined to work further on the score.) The film was rescored by British composer Stanley Myers, who completely discarded Sculthorpe's approach and wrote a more subdued, slightly romantic underscore. The replacement angered director Powell, who went so far as to refer to Myers as a "Hollywood hack" in the notes that accompanied the film's VHS release, produced by Trevor Williams.

Sculthorpe comments on the incident and its aftermath:

> When a new score for *Age of Consent* was written by Stanley Myers, I had no reason to believe that my music was rejected because it wasn't commercial enough. It should also be said that I wasn't overly disappointed because at that time I was rather disappointed with the film. I've always been fond of the score that I wrote. When I had a letter from Michael Powell's widow, Thelma Schoonmaker, telling me of plans to restore the music to the film, I was truly elated. By coincidence, a print of the original, with my music, was located at the National Film and Sound Archive of Australia. I then saw the film again and I must confess that I found it to be full of charm and a sensitive treatment of a somewhat risqué subject.

In 2005, a restored *Age of Consent* was reunited with Sculthorpe's score and premiered at the Sydney Film Festival. This new/old cut not only reinstated Sculthorpe's music but also put back previously cut nude footage of Helen Mirren, as well as the opening bedroom scenes, which had been edited from international prints by British film censors. For years, the only available print of the picture on VHS had been the Columbia edit with Myers' score, so the restored rerelease was quite a revelation. *Age of Consent* had now completed its global trek, having gone halfway around the world only to be mutilated, but now returning to Australia in the form the director envisioned, almost forty years later. Thanks to Martin Scorsese's Film Foundation, the restored movie, supervised by Powell's widow, the award-winning editor Schoonmaker, has recently been released in its original format, with Sculthorpe's music.

■ The Appointment (1969)

Original composer: **Michel Legrand**
Replacement composers: **John Barry and Don Walker**
Composer for U.S. television airing (1972): **Stu Phillips**

The Appointment is a psychological drama about a lawyer whose suspicions about his wife lead to disaster. Its director, Sidney Lumet (whose credits prior to this film included the critically acclaimed *12 Angry Men, The Pawnbroker,* and *Fail-Safe*), claims it wasn't one of his favorite movies; in fact, he has said that he signed on primarily so he could experiment with color photography and spend some pleasant months in Rome.

The production was supervised by producer Martin Poll, who personally selected its first composer, Michel Legrand, with whom he had worked on the picture *Love Is a Ball* (1963). Legrand wasn't only an inspired choice but a convenient one as well for Poll. Because the producer had another production, *The Lion in Winter* (1969), shooting at the same time in France, he could easily check up on the composer once in a while. Legrand wrote almost an hour of score based around a single motif that was meant to represent the protagonist's obsession. All his cues are derived from various permutations of this theme. Legrand recorded the rather simple score with the Paris Opera Orchestra and Chorus, experimenting during the recording, sometimes taping the same cues with different orchestrations.

When played with the picture, however, the music proved to be an audience-preview disaster. Legrand remembers this incident:

> I worked closely with Lumet. I wrote a score I really liked, and [he liked it too]. They preview the film, and it gets a negative response from the audience. They call for a production meeting and someone then suggests it must be because the music is sad. This is precisely a deeply sad story! So they decided to change the music, but the film wasn't more successful. It's easy to fall on the composer, for he's the last one on the line. They think then that if the movie doesn't work, it's his fault. They know nothing about it!

> Directors, producers, you know, they figure they're all a bit [like] actors, writers, technicians—but they're not musicians! They don't have a clue about what the music does.

The producer quickly sought out the composer who was working on his parallel French production, John Barry, to rescore *The Appointment*. Even though Barry was still busy with the medieval-period picture and was preparing for the upcoming Bond movie *On Her Majesty's Secret Service* (1969), he agreed to write a theme for *The Appointment*, which would later be arranged by Don Walker (who'd receive an "additional music" credit on the picture). The score marked one of the rare instances in which Barry didn't orchestrate and conduct his own work; Don Walker and Harry Rabowitz took care of those duties.

This hasty replacement score was, like its predecessor, chiefly monothematic. The new theme, however, was warmer and provided more emotional backing for the story's destructive romance. Now everyone was satisfied with the score, and the picture was nominated for a Palme d'Or at Cannes.

The recording of the new score had pushed back the film's delivery date, which in turn cost Lumet his right to the movie's final cut as stipulated in his contract. *The Appointment* was taken over by veteran editor Margaret Booth (at one time the MGM editor-in-chief, she is reported to have been the first "cutter" to be called an "editor"), who took great liberties with it. The picture had a very limited U.S. theatrical release, after which MGM decided to do a television version, recutting it and adding Italian scenery shots from unrelated films.

When all was said and done, a dramatic, tormented tale had been turned into a happy love story. This meant it required new music as well, resulting in the unusual creation of a score for a television version of a movie that was different from that of its cinema counterpart. Composer Stu Phillips was called in by Bob Justman, president of MGM's Television Division. Phillips worked directly with Margaret Booth, but he was initially confused by instructions to make the score more contemporary. To make matters more confusing, when he screened the movie with Barry's score, he found that it still fit the story:

> At the conclusion of the screening, I turned to Margaret and asked, "What is it you want me to do that John Barry didn't do?" They explained that the studio wanted a score to be more contemporary and hipper. Since it was '69, we're talking flower power and flower children. They said that the version of the film that Michel Legrand had scored ran too long. They edited it shorter and hired John Barry because they thought he could bring a contemporary sound to the music, as he did with the Bond pictures. But obviously John looked at the picture the same way Michel did and said, "Hey, this is an opera"—which it basically is, and without any problem you could write a bunch of arias and make it into an opera.

Phillips took advantage of his background as a pop music producer to record two songs with lyrics by Bob Stone, "Solo é triste" and "The Beauty of Beginning." These became themes for the film's obsessed lawyer and the romance, respectively. The new score, still romantic, boasted a more optimistic sound that suited the modified tone of the new edit. And yet it would go largely unheard: The TV version of the movie debuted on CBS in 1972 and was rerun a few times, but it has since disappeared. All available copies of *The Appointment* contain Barry's music. Surprisingly, after all its problems, *The Appointment* became a minor hit in Europe, allowing it to earn back its budget.

(Selections from all three scores were released on a CD by Film Score Monthly.)

■ **Battle of Neretva/Bitka na Neretvi** (1969)

Composer for Yugoslavian version: **Vladimir Kraus-Rajteric**
Composer for American version: **Bernard Herrmann**

There's a saying about too many cooks, and director Veljko Bulajic's *Battle of Neretva* illustrates it perfectly. A big-budget, multinationally financed epic about a World War II battle that pitted Yugoslav partisans against a large Axis force, the film was a collaboration by parties from around the world, all of them interested in modifying it to fit their own tastes and nationalities.

The original Yugoslavian cut of the picture ran 175 minutes, but its European and overseas production/distribution companies thought that was too long: No matter how popular the war movie genre was at the time, a three-hour account of an obscure (for non-Yugoslavs), albeit glorious, battle would simply be too much for the average audience. In Germany, Columbia Film-Verleih cut the film down to 142 minutes. The Italian version by the International Film Company ran 134 minutes, and the Commonwealth version (the best English-language release, on VHS), was 127. The most drastic edits, though, were made in the American print, distributed by American International Pictures: It lasted a mere 102 minutes!

The film's original score, by Yugoslav composer Vladimir Kraus-Rajteric, was largely serviceable, but its understated nature was at odds with Hollywood's epic war-movie scoring traditions. Its two main components were a selection of marches and some Slavic ethnic singing, neither of which particularly excited international distributors. Another problem with Kraus-Rajteric's score was its brevity—it ran for only minutes at a time, leaving important, vast sections of the original three-hour epic (including major battle sequences) in musical silence.

To elevate the movie's profile (it already had a big-name international cast that included Orson Welles and Yul Brynner), American producers Henry T. Weinstein and Steve Previn came up with the idea of hiring one of the greatest living film composers, Bernard Herrmann, to rescore it. The composer, who was in London at the time, initially thought little of the picture, comparing it to a "great big roast beef" from which every collaborating nation "cuts off the piece they like...one bit's well done, another bit's overdone...and everybody's happy." But after the producers agreed to pay him a larger-than-normal fee and to give him the opportunity to vacation with his wife in Yugoslavia, Herrmann accepted the job.

The strong, furious "Prelude" turned out to be one of the best pieces Herrmann wrote during his self-imposed London exile, and the London Philharmonic provided a forceful performance. The love theme, "From Italy," grew out of the composer's *Clarinet Quintet—Souvenirs de Voyage*, written two years before. The obligatory marches include "Chetnik's March" and "Partisan's March," both of which nicely expand on ideas from the "Prelude." But the most interesting cue is "The Turning Point." This track reprises material from Herrmann's *Torn Curtain* score, particularly the cue titled "The Killing."

Battle of Neretva was nominated for a Best Foreign Language Film Oscar. While the longer Yugoslavian version of the movie has a better narrative than the heavily truncated American cut, it is sadly underserved by Kraus-Rajteric's short score. For film music fans, the American version with Herrmann's superior music provides the most memorable experience. Aficionados of Herrmann's score can find the original recording on the Southern Cross label, or get an excellent 2010 re-recording of it (along with a suite from his score for *The Naked and the Dead*) performed by the Moscow Symphony Orchestra on the Tribute Film Classics label.

■ **Battle of Britain** (1969)

Original composer: **William Walton**
Replacement composer: **Ron Goodwin**

When he was asked to score director Guy Hamilton's star-studded World War II film, *Battle of Britain*, about the Royal Air Force's struggle against the Luftwaffe for air supremacy over London, legendary British concert composer Sir William Walton was already familiar with the medium. He had scored a handful of propaganda shorts as well as *The First of the Few* (1942), a drama about the development of the RAF's Spitfire fighter plane. But in the time since his work on Laurence Olivier's Shakespeare adaptations—*Henry V* (1944), *Hamlet* (1948), and *Richard III* (1955)—Walton had steered clear of film scoring and focused on concert music. His one-act comic opera *The Bear* had been a great success at the 1967 Aldenburgh Festival, and he had been receiving important commissions from such orchestras as the New York Philharmonic and the San Francisco Symphony.

Thus it took some persuasion to get Walton back into the film scoring business, but he had good friends who helped sway him: Laurence Olivier was the lead in *Battle of Britain*, and on the musical side, he was offered assistance from his longtime friend Malcolm Arnold (perhaps best known in the film world for his popular 1957 score for *The Bridge on the River Kwai*), who would not only orchestrate and conduct Walton's film score but write additional material as well.

Walton composed a complex and compelling score in his post-Romantic style, providing a welcome musical departure for a genre dominated by preexisting marches and stylistically unvarying underscores. All of the cues flowed perfectly from one to the next, forming something of a tone poem that was not overly circumscribed by the film's visuals. (Much of Malcolm Arnold's duties involved fitting his friend's ideas to the movie itself.) The highlight is undeniably Walton's noble "Battle of Britain March," which resembles such previous marches by the composer as "Orb and Sceptre" (a march written for the coronation of Queen Elizabeth II) and *Granada Prelude*.

Director Hamilton firmly supported Walton's approach and appreciated that the composer came up with imaginative set pieces. But the studio, United Artists (UA), had other ideas. According to its official word on the subject, the score was simply too sparse, not even long enough to make up a proper LP. With this rationale provided to the newspapers, the studio hoped to avoid bruising Walton's ego when a replacement score was ordered.

One month before the film's scheduled premiere, the studio commissioned a new score from Ron Goodwin, composer of such World War II film scores as *Where Eagles Dare* (1968) and *Operation Crossbow* (1965). Goodwin took the commission only after doubling his usual fee and securing an agreement that none of Walton's score would be used in the finished picture.

Goodwin's "patented" rousing style is highlighted in his 6/8-time "Luftwaffe March." This particular piece became so popular later on that it was retitled "Ace High March," so it could appear in British brass band programs without a war-related title. It is nicely paralleled by Goodwin's "Battle of Britain March," which evokes urgency and action, in contrast with Walton's more noble and somber work of the same name. The key to Goodwin's score is his various arrangements and reorchestrations of these two marches. For example, variations of the "Luftwaffe March" are heard in the tracks "Work and Play" and "Threat." His "Battle of Britain March" would become a staple of military bands across the country, and was even used as a bumper for commentator G. Gordon Liddy's syndicated radio program. Goodwin explains some of the score's influences:

> When I first went to see Ben Fisz, the producer, he said he wanted a clearly identifiable German theme, as there had been some confusion as to which planes you were watching in the air battles. I found a lot of German military music to help get a fairly authentic feel. I didn't have a lot of time to do that, of course.

News of the music replacement quickly spread among the production's crew. Everyone seemed to know about it except the original composer, who by this time had moved back to his Italian home in Ischia. In fact, he only learned of it when a journalist rang him up to ask about it! Back in England, Laurence Olivier stood up for Walton's music, threatening to remove his credit from the picture if Walton's score wasn't acknowledged by the inclusion of at least one of its cues. UA gave in to Olivier, and Walton's cue "Battle in the Air" appeared in the movie during a battle sequence.

When Goodwin learned this at the film's press premiere, he wanted to bail out of the entire project, even offering to repay his fee and withdraw his score. But legal threats from the studio caused him to reconsider his position.

To help mend fences with Walton, UA offered him the option of putting together a suite of his *Battle of Britain* music. But he declined, and tried to put this humiliating experience behind him. His friend Malcolm Arnold was so troubled by the experience that he practically turned his back on film scoring, taking very few assignments from that point on. As for Goodwin, he became the scapegoat in the controversy, and many contemporary reviews slammed his score purely because it had replaced Walton's music. Goodwin reflected on his score's reception:

> I think with the benefits of hindsight, if anyone ever asked me to rewrite the score, I would say no, because whatever you do there are bound to be odious comparisons. I must say I get a bit fed up when critics, etc., go around saying, "Poor old William Walton being replaced by this unknown composer." I mean, what about poor old Ron Goodwin? The basic fact is that he wrote something that for whatever reason was considered to be unsatisfactory. That is why they got another composer in, and it happened to be me.

In 1969, Goodwin's soundtrack was released on LP. But if the brevity of Walton's score had been a problem, then Goodwin's score must have been a disappointment as well. The LP contained just over thirty-five minutes of music, five of which were taken up by Walton's sole retained cue, "Battle in the Air." In other words, at least on record, there was no great difference between the two score's running lengths.

Walton's "Battle in the Air" became a popular piece on its own, and the rest of his score had an interesting afterlife: The manuscript was rescued from the scrap heap through the personal intervention of Prime Minister Edward Heath and released to Oxford University Press. Bernard Herrmann, an admirer of the music, planned to record it as a suite in 1975, but his untimely death that same year aborted the project. In 1985, composer and record producer Colin Matthews put together a suite from the manuscript and, together with conductor Carl Davis, recorded it for the album *Walton: Film Music*, marking the first time Walton's score was made available in any format.

In 2004, MGM reissued some of its classic war movies on DVD to commemorate the fiftieth anniversary of D-Day. Among them was *Battle of Britain*, which offered an unusual extra: In addition to viewing the film with Goodwin's score, one could view an alternative version with Walton's. The production of this special bonus, for which thanks are due to editor Timothy Gee (first assistant editor on the original production) and recording engineer Eric Tomlinson (music recordist on the original production), took a couple of years to accomplish. Gee's expertise came in particularly handy: He knew exactly where each piece of the unused score was supposed to appear. The combined efforts of these two men has allowed us the rare opportunity to see and hear two competing scores in action.

■ The Red Tent/Krasnaya palatka/La Tenda rossa (1969)

Composer for Russian version: **Aleksandr Zatsepin**
Composer for international version: **Ennio Morricone**

The late 1960s and early '70s saw a rise in the number of coproductions between Eastern and Western countries. One of the most ambitious of these was *The Red Tent*, a Soviet-Italian collaboration directed by Soviet filmmaker Mikhail Kalatozov. *The Red Tent* presents a fictionalized version of the 1928 tragedy of the airship *Italia*, which, under the command of its designer, Umberto Nobile, crashed while attempting to reach the North Pole, killing several of its crew. The explorer Roald Amundsen—the first man to reach the South Pole—led one of the many rescue teams that set out to find the downed airship's survivors, but ironically, the Amundsen group disappeared during the operation. In Kalatozov's highly unusual dramatization, the surviving Nobile (played by Peter Finch) is confronted by his past through the intervention of ghosts (Amundsen's ghost is played by Sean Connery), who try to determine whether Nobile should be held responsible for those who lost their lives due to the *Italia*'s crash and the subsequent rescue missions.

Produced mostly in the Soviet Union (under the supervision of the KGB), the Soviet version differed from the Italian version in both editing and music. It had a running time of more than two and one-half hours, of which its producers seemed reluctant to cut a single second. The Italians, on the other hand, not only trimmed the movie to a more reasonable length (which allowed more showings per day), but they also took issue with the music, even though Russian composer Aleksandr Zatsepin's work evoked both Russian and Italian film scoring traditions. Side by side with unmistakably Eastern-sounding melodies, he produced such cues as "Deer Run," which sounded like a track from a contemporary Italian film, right down to the campy vocals.

Zatsepin's score was quite melodic, but it had to go for two reasons. The first was the heavy editing of the Italian version. The second was the fact that Italian coproduction company Vides Cinematografica could get Ennio Morricone to score their picture, lending name value to the project. The internationally released version of the movie (which was picked up by Paramount for the U.S. market) is two hours long and cuts out a lot of the Russian material.

While the Italian score features some traditional Morricone love themes and a main theme that reuses the ending of the cue "1+1+1=4" from his *Menage all'italiana* (1965) score, the big surprise is "Altri, dopo di noi." This twenty-two-minute suite, which channels Arctic isolation with cold precision, features some of the composer's strangest, most atonal work and makes use of chimes, wind effects, and radarlike pings. As a recording, the score was released both on its own and combined with Zatsepin's, but the two-score CD edits down the Italian composer's long suite (which is a shame).

The Red Tent is not the only instance in which Morricone was recruited for a rescoring, and his efforts were usually successful. In 1972, Euro International Film and Dunov Film coproduced a film version of Mikhail Bulgakov's novel *The Master and Margherita* (*Il Maestro e Margherita*), starring Ugo Tognazzi. The original score, provided by Yugoslav composer Ljiljana Popovic, leaned heavily on some disturbing a cappella material, heard here and there throughout the movie. When Morricone rescored the film for wider release, he provided a lyrical monothematic score with an addictive romantic theme. He reused this great theme in 1995, as "Sicilia" in the television series *Il Barone*. While the original version of *Il Maestro e Margherita* with Popovic's music is still shown occasionally on television, the version that has Morricone's score is the better-known one.

The final rescoring gig for Morricone came in 1975, when he wrote music for *Spazio: 1999*, a feature created from re-edited episodes of Gerry Anderson's sci-fi television series *Space: 1999*, a British-Italian collaboration. The series' Italian coproducers decided to reuse the episodes "Breakaway," "Ring around the Moon," and "Another Time, Another Place" to create their a movie for theatrical release. For this feature, TV series composer Barry Gray's music was replaced with Morricone's, which was a combination of original material and library tracks. He also provided a theme song, "Un treno in più," which was performed by Italian pop singer Patty Pravo. Morricone would later reuse this song in a disco arrangement for the 1978 film *Cosi come sei*, and as "Le train" in the 1979 French miniseries *Orient-Express*.

(*Note:* The film *Spazio: 1999* is much harder to find than its source material, the individual episodes of *Space: 1999*, which feature Barry Gray's music.)

■ **The Reivers** (1969)

Original composer: **Lalo Schifrin**
Replacement composer: **John Williams**

The Reivers, a skillfully directed film adaptation of William Faulkner's Pulitzer Prize–winning 1962 novel of the same name, is a picaresque coming-of-age fable that stars Steve McQueen, who reportedly was allowed a great deal of input during the film's postproduction, greatly influencing how it was finally shaped and scored.

Director Mark Rydell hired Lalo Schifrin for the music. Schifrin had provided the director's previous picture (his directorial debut), the risqué *The Fox*, with a lovely, intimate score that was nominated for an Academy Award.

While *The Reivers* was being edited, the filmmakers assembled a temp track with a rich Americana sound that ranged from lush orchestra music to raunchy jazzy numbers. But Schifrin never got to hear this temporary music before writing his score (which he recorded with a small chamber ensemble that included several traditional American instruments), and, alas, his music didn't work for the filmmakers. They had grown fond of their expansive temp tracks. His intimate music struck them as weak in comparison; it seemed to lack the sweep that a "Steve McQueen movie" needed, particularly one over which the star had so much say. So a new composer was hired.

That composer was John Williams. Williams was primarily known at that time for scoring comedies, but he had also written the music for Universal's Western *The Rare Breed* (1966). For him, *The Reivers* was an avenue to a more mature sound, and a welcome break from a string of comedies. He wrote a score that was lush, nostalgic, and generally upbeat, often referencing folk idioms and instruments (e.g., harmonica and banjo), and even quoting Stephen Foster's "Camptown Races" during the picture's finale. It was a masterful demonstration of what he could bring to the right project, and it garnered Williams his first Academy Award nomination for an original score, as well as opportunities for further work with Rydell: *The Cowboys* (1972), *Cinderella Liberty* (1973), and *The River* (1984).

Going back to *The Reivers*, it should be noted that Schifrin's score wasn't the film's only music to fall by the wayside. After leaving the Byrds in 1966, singer-songwriter Gene Clark (cowriter of "Eight Miles High" and other Byrds hits) joined banjo player Doug Dillard in a new country-rock band called Dillard & Clark. As revealed in Clark's autobiography, the new group needed publicity, and since Clark was a friend of Steve McQueen's, the actor helped the band get a gig recording a song for *The Reivers*—"The World Is Wide Open," penned by hit-makers Alan and Marilyn Bergman. But while the style of the song meshed with the sound of Schifrin's original score, it didn't work in the context of Williams's broader, lusher music, and Dillard & Clark were dismissed from the project.

■ The Molly Maguires (1970)

Original composer: **Charles Strouse**
Replacement composer: **Henry Mancini**

Martin Ritt's movie *The Molly Maguires* tells the story of an Irish-born Pinkerton agent infiltrating the Molly Maguires, a secret society of Irish immigrant miners in 19th-century Pennsylvania, who (precursors to union organizers) struggled violently against atrocious working conditions and low pay imposed by exploitative mine owners. (Ritt had by this point in his career directed such powerful features as *Paris Blues*, *The Spy Who Came in from the Cold*, and *Hombre*.) This well-made, well-financed drama, written by Walter Benjamin and starring Sean Connery and Richard Harris, would have great appeal for two established songsmiths hoping for a chance to show off their dramatic underscoring skills.

Tony Award–winning Broadway composer Charles Strouse had made his movie scoring debut in 1967 with his bluegrass-inspired music for *Bonnie and Clyde*. He appeared poised for a successful career in film scoring, but *The Molly Maguires*, it turned out, would not offer that opportunity. He was fired from the film because, ironically, he hadn't played to his forte—songwriting. His fairly authentic-sounding

Irish score was dramatic enough to please the director, but he was dismissed because he hadn't delivered a song. Strouse remembers:

> I thought the score was really good, but I was fired for the only time in my life by Bob Evans, who was the head of Paramount [the film's producing studio]. The reason, among numerous other things, was that I was instructed by Martin Ritt to write a very sad score that was about the ugliness of the revolution. I thought I did that and I liked the score very much. When Bob Evans saw the first screening, he just came out of *Love Story*, which had a love ballad in it. Then he said, "Where is the big love song?" I turned to Martin Ritt and I said, "You never told me to write anything like that!" This was probably my fault—I should have thought beyond him and written something like that, but I was under Martin's direction, and he never said anything about a big sweeping ballad. So Bob fired me.

According to Ritt's biography, the director was so chagrined by the firing that he sent an apology letter to the reportedly outraged mother of the "neglected composer." Still, the music had to go. After leaving Paramount, Strouse didn't even bother to pick up his score's tapes or sheet music—a move he would come to regret, since the music was unique in his career.

The composer hired to replace Strouse was also well known for his songwriting talents: Henry Mancini, among whose earlier scores were such now-classic titles as *Touch of Evil* (1958), *Days of Wine and Roses* (1962), *Charade* (1963), and *Wait until Dark* (1967). If there was one Hollywood composer who could deliver a heartbreaking love theme, it was Mancini. But while procuring a popular song for the picture was the studio's reason for hiring him, the composer himself accepted the job for the chance to show off his skills at dramatic orchestral underscoring.

Nonetheless, fans of Mancini's song-based scores will not be disappointed by *The Molly Maguires*. It has a lovely central theme, played on the pennywhistle with harp accompaniment, which was inspired by traditional Irish music. The action cues that accompany the strike scenes also carry a strong Irish flavor: Instead of heavy brass and drum hits, these powerful themes are mostly carried by strings, an orchestration choice that allowed the fusion of Americana and Irish sounds, representing the lead character's suspension between the two cultures. Finally, the score contains a heavy dose of native-style instrumentals—such tracks as "Fiddle and Fife" and "Pennywhistle Jig"—which usually appear as source cues. The LP of the score (and its later CD reissue) stands as a forgotten Mancini masterpiece that merits the attention of his fans.

■ **Cry of the Banshee** (1970)

Composer for British version: **Wilfred Josephs**
Composer for American version: **Les Baxter**

By 1970, domestic productions by American International Pictures had started to become routine affairs because they always utilized the same people. But AIP's London office worked quite differently. Run by Louis M. "Deke" Heyward, the English branch soon surpassed the American headquarters in producing successful movies. This was due to a more experimental approach.

In the case of *Cry of the Banshee*, starring Vincent Price, Heyward and director Gordon Hessler had two novel ideas: The first was to hire Monty Python's Terry Gilliam to produce animated opening titles for the picture. The British comedy troupe was enjoying its first success on television, and Heyward felt that Gilliam's animation would be fresh and crowd-pleasing. The second novel idea was to procure a score from Wilfred Josephs, an extremely prolific concert and film composer (twelve symphonies, twenty-two concertos, operas, ballets, chamber music, and many film and television scores) who had worked as a dentist before devoting himself full-time to music.

The score Josephs created for *Cry of the Banshee*, including its source cues, was very nicely rooted in an Elizabethan period sound, yet it also firmly connected with the picture's horror elements. And Gilliam provided the expected innovative titles. But once the film crossed the Atlantic and landed at AIP's home office, Heyward's and Hessler's imaginative work was undone: The titles gave way to winged creatures and name cards, and Josephs' score was replaced with music by none other than Les Baxter.

Gordon Hessler never learned what really happened to bring about the change of scores, though he had his hunches:

> I suspect that Les Baxter was a great friend of somebody high up at AIP and was doing scores for them at the time. Perhaps he or someone else saw it and criticized the music, so they were advised to change it. Wilfred Josephs is perhaps not the greatest composer in the world, but he certainly did a good job. The music is very important to these movies, and to take it off after spending so much money was a huge decision by somebody. But to have Les Baxter do a kind of period picture where you have minuet dancing and that sort of thing, it's ludicrous. You really have to have somebody who has an idea of that time period.

While the people at AIP were always very critical of the movies delivered to them and had rescored them on countless occasions, they had no option with *Cry of the Banshee*: In addition to removing Gilliam's main titles, they had cruelly recut the whole picture, speeding up the narrative, repositioning some sequences (including the coven massacre), and removing most of the British version's generous supply of gratuitously bared breasts. With all these edits made, Josephs' score had to go, and Les Baxter was the studio's obvious choice to replace him.

But Baxter's new score doesn't disappoint, and the composer considered *Banshee* among his best film music efforts. (It's no surprise that this is one of his few scores available on CD.) It largely makes use of strings evocatively performed in both traditional and modernist ways, producing sounds that range from plucking to tormented shrieks. A tambourine is put to good use in the movie's opening, adding period color to the grim story before we're treated to some of Baxter's most unorthodox writing, particularly when it represents the banshee and the eerie dark woods.

Despite the quality of Baxter's work, the latest DVD release of *Cry of the Banshee* drops his music and retains Josephs', much to the delight of cinema purists. Sadly, the latter composer remains underrepresented in the soundtrack recording market: The only film music of his ever released on CD is an unused title theme and one cue from Patrick McGoohan's *The Prisoner* television series.

■ **Le Cercle rouge** (1970)

Original composer: **Michel Legrand**
Replacement composer: **Éric Demarsan**

French director Jean-Pierre Melville had been planning his caper movie *Le Cercle rouge* for decades, but repeatedly postponed its production because similar movies kept showing up in cinemas. Eventually, long after John Huston's *The Asphalt Jungle* (1950) and Jules Dassin's *Rififi* (1955) had left the theaters, Melville was ready to shoot his own stylish film noir jewel-heist picture, featuring an all-star cast that included Alain Delon and Yves Montand. To score the complex action of his lengthy movie's multiple plotlines and double-crosses, the director hired composer Michel Legrand.

Legrand already ranked as one of the leading French film composers, and his celebrated scores previous to 1970 included *The Umbrellas of Cherbourg* (1964) and *The Thomas Crown Affair* (1968). Although he had had numerous bad experiences with American and British productions (e.g., *The Man Who Loved Cat Dancing, Robin and Marian,* and *The Hunter*), he felt safe at home among his many French filmmaker friends. That is, until he went to work on *Le Cercle rouge*. Composer Éric Demarsan takes up the story:

> They [Legrand and Melville] didn't get along at all. So Melville called me. You know, he was a really odd man. He said, "Come to the studio on such and such a day. Be discreet"—I used to wear flashy ruffled shirts—"wear a little gray suit." He didn't want the news of his dispute with Legrand to spread.... He gave me lots of tips—and I needed them because I had very little time. For nights on end, he made me watch reels from [1959's] *Odds Against Tomorrow*, a noir movie with Harry Belafonte, in his studio. He was hypnotized by the way it used music. He told me he wanted a similar ambience. In that case, it meant taking a format like that of the Modern Jazz Quartet and putting some strings and brass around it.

Demarsan had previously worked with Melville on *L'Armée des ombres* (1969), a film about the French Resistance during World War II, so communication between the two was good. Although Melville couldn't describe what he wanted in the score in musical terms, he requested that the music reflect the notion "trapped by fate." He cited John Lewis's score for Robert Wise's film *Odds Against Tomorrow* as an example of what he meant.

As opposed to the swinging soundtracks that were in fashion for the caper pictures of the day, Demarsan's score is loaded with tension and claustrophobia. The composer also wrote a selection of lighter pieces to ease the tension, but it is his complex textures that make *Le Cercle rouge* one of the quintessential crime-movie jazz scores. Additions to the jazz quartet are minimal—a small string and brass section, and a harmonica to provide local color to the French setting.

A cue from Legrand's unused score for *Le Cercle rouge*, "Chassés-croisés," was released on the compilation *Le Cinéma de Michel Legrand*, but it varies little stylistically from the Demarsan music.

Despite his work's failure to find its way into Melville's movie, Legrand was in fact one of the leading "music doctors" of French cinema, called on to rescore numerous features whose composers and directors had reached an impasse. The best-known of these jobs was the irresistible score he wrote for Robert Mulligan's *Summer of '42* (1971). (Unfortunately, the composer and nature of the original score have never been revealed.) In the same year, Legrand wrote replacement music for director Philippe de Broca's *La Poudre d'escampette*. De Broca had originally hired seventy-five-year-old French pianist and composer Jean Wiener (composer of more than 100 film scores and, in his younger days, a friend of Erik Satie, Darius Milhaud, and other influential French concert composers), but the composer arrived at the scoring session completely unprepared. Instead, Wiener started improvising to the picture and was fired on the spot. Luckily, the movie didn't need much music, and Legrand quickly penned a melancholic theme for its unusual love triangle.

■ **Love Story** (1970)

Original composer: **Jimmy Webb**
Replacement composer: **Francis Lai**

In the late 1960s, Hollywood showed great enthusiasm for hiring popular singer/songwriters to score movies, hoping to increase soundtrack sales at the same time. One such artist to embark on a career in film scoring at that time was Jimmy Webb. By 1969, his long list of light-pop hits included "By the Time I Get to Phoenix," "Up, Up and Away," and "MacArthur Park."

Webb's first actual film-scoring assignment was *Love Story*, which proved problematic for him. Directed by Arthur Hill and starring Ali MacGraw and Ryan O"Neal, the picture was a sentimental tragedy based on Erich Segal's best-selling novel of the same name. Webb was expected to concentrate his efforts on writing a hit song, But, like many a pop musician taking on a scoring project, he instead took a fairly experimental approach. One of the few ideas of his to survive the project would be the strange car-horn organ, which was central to his score. In the liner notes of the box set of recordings *The Moon's a Harsh Mistress: Jimmy Webb in the Seventies*, musician Fred Tackett remembers the unique solution:

> We did a beautiful soundtrack for *Love Story*. Jimmy came up with an astonishing thing for one scene. We went out and recorded all these automobile horns, then put them

> through a VSO (variable speed oscillator) and tuned each to a different pitch. We had 16 tracks of car horns, which Jimmy played like an organ, making chords by moving the faders up and down. In the scene where Ali MacGraw has just learned she's dying, she comes out of the doctor's office into the street, when these haunting minor chords that Jimmy played on this car horn organ begin to well up out of the natural traffic noise. That gave me chills. Unfortunately, they weren't interested in innovative score music. They wanted a nice little pop song to push.

As far as the people in charge were concerned, Webb's score was a failure. Although he was reportedly given another chance to write something different, the producers finally hired Francis Lai, composer of many French film scores, who went on to provide *Love Story* with a chart-topping pop score that collected a Golden Globe, a Grammy, and an Academy Award.

Lai's music, particularly the hit song derived from *Love Story*'s main theme, "Where Do I Begin" (lyrics by Carl Sigman), was so influential that suddenly every producer in Hollywood wanted a similar song for his or her film. The effects were felt directly on other films, such as *The Molly Maguires* (1970), which lost its first score when Paramount production head Robert Evans saw *Love Story* and decided he wanted just such a hit tune for his picture as well, no matter how inappropriate it might be.

As close as he got with his opportunity to score *Love Story*, Jimmy Webb never broke into the film scoring scene with any major success; he can claim only a dozen film and television scoring credits. Incidentally, the car-horn organ can be heard in the instrumental lead-in to Webb's composition "Songseller (Music from an Unmade Movie, Pt. 1)" on his album *Words & Music*.

■ The Go-Between (1970)

Original composer: **Richard Rodney Bennett**
Replacement composer: **Michel Legrand**

The Go-Between (screenplay by Harold Pinter) is based on a popular novel by L. P. Hartley. It tells the story of 13-year-old Leo's summer holiday in 1900, spent at the home of a rich, upper-class boarding school classmate. While there, Leo befriends his classmate's older sister, who enlists him to pass secret messages between her and her lover—a rough tenant farmer whom, thanks to her acquiescence to the British class system, she will never be permitted to marry. As Leo comes to understand the situation and his role in it, he grows disillusioned about love and fidelity.

Director Joseph Losey was an American expatriate whose blacklisting had forced him to relocate to England to work. To score *The Go-Between*, he hired composer Richard Rodney Bennett, with whom he'd worked on a few pictures, including *Blind Date* (1959), *Secret Ceremony* (1968), and *Figures in a Landscape* (1970). To convey his vision of the mood of Hartley's novel, Losey sought a nostalgic look for the film, shooting some of the most beautiful scenery in rural Britain. He felt that the book's sociological subtext, about the rotten core of the class system and how it victimizes young Leo, who is initially unaware of his role as a pawn, could somehow be signaled by the music, but Losey wasn't able to communicate his specific musical intentions to Bennett. At the time, the director was interested in avant-garde jazz, and he even invited one of its famous practitioners, trumpeter Don Cherry, to the set to help with musical ideas.

Bennett, who knew the dark novel well and was puzzled by Losey's desire to pair some form of contemporary jazz with his beautiful, bucolic film, remembers:

> I have always felt that *The Go-Between* was a very frightening novel and wasn't at all what you saw on the screen. That is to say that there were very dark undercurrents to that beautiful landscape. Joe had for some reason got involved with avant-garde jazz and told me that he wanted an avant-garde jazz score to that film! I simply couldn't believe my ears! He said he didn't exactly want jazz—he wanted something very primitive, and I simply couldn't understand him, so I came up with a score which I thought was right which was very, very dark and offbeat; it was, in fact, a serial piece for chamber ensemble, and it wasn't what they wanted. They wanted a hit tune, so Michel Legrand did it. I don't know if they got their hit tune, but they certainly got something quite different from what I had written.

Although Losey wanted to give Bennett a chance to rewrite his score, the composer had to leave England to fulfill a teaching engagement at Baltimore's Peabody Institute. So the director hired composer Michel Legrand, who had worked with him on the erotically charged *Eva* (1962), a film that also depicted a twisted love relationship.

Today, *The Go-Between* is as famous for its score as for anything else. Legrand's music, which relies heavily on piano and strings, is built on an unusual but fetching theme of alternating perfect fifths and minor sixths (and their inversions), which recurs in variation throughout the score. This simple but compelling theme became a minor hit and was subsequently released on LP as a suite of variations. While it rates as some of Legrand's most memorable work, not everyone was a fan of it—in a 2002 article, Richard Rodney Bennett accused Legrand's score of being "terribly wrong" for the film.

As an interesting postscript to the story, Losey invited Bennett to work on *A Doll's House* (1973), starring Jane Fonda, an adaptation of Henrik Ibsen's popular play. After viewing the picture, Bennett said that he believed it didn't need any music at all: "You must not put music in this picture. There is nothing music can do, and even for the money I won't do a picture where I don't think music is necessary or possible." With Bennett unwilling, the director once again called on Legrand for a score. But time proved Bennett right: Apart from musically framing it, Legrand's score adds nothing to the picture. (*Note:* 1973 saw the release of another film adaptation of the same Ibsen play, starring Claire Bloom and featuring a lush score by John Barry.)

■ A New Leaf (1971)

Original composer: **Johnny Mandel**
Replacement music: **Preexisting music by Neal Hefti**

Before discussing *A New Leaf,* some background information is required. In 1965, Paramount Pictures produced the bizarre little comedy *Oh Dad, Poor Dad, Mama's Hung You in the Closet and I'm Feeling So Sad* (1967), based on Arthur Kopit's popular play of the same name. The story is about an eccentric woman who travels to Jamaica with her husband and their grown-up son. But there's a hitch: Her husband is dead, and she has had him stuffed and totes him around like baggage.

Paramount found the movie a bit too odd and shelved it for two years. At that time it carried a score by George Duning, composer of such classics as *From Here to Eternity* (1953), *Picnic* (1955), and *3:10 to Yuma* (1957). He and *Oh Dad, Poor Dad* director Richard Quine had also worked together on nine feature films, including *Bell, Book and Candle* (1958) and *The World of Suzie Wong* (1960).

During the film's two-year hiatus, *Oh Dad, Poor Dad* went through numerous changes, including the addition of a narration voiced by Jonathan Winters and the commissioning of a new, jollier score. The new music was penned by Neal Hefti, source of such lovable tunes as the "Batman Theme" from the Adam West television series (which aired from 1966 through 1968) and the music to *The Odd Couple* movie (1968) and TV series (1970 through 1975). Director Quine and Hefti had previously worked together on *Sex and the Single Girl* (1964) and *How to Murder Your Wife* (1965). Hefti's music for *Oh Dad, Poor Dad* mixed Caribbean musical elements with popular rock 'n' roll tunes of the era and included a campy theme song.

Four years after the eventual release of *Oh Dad, Poor Dad,* Paramount Pictures found itself having problems with *A New Leaf,* the directorial debut of Elaine May (who had been half of the extremely popular comedy duo Nichols and May from the mid-1950s through 1961). Her quirky comedy film starred Walter Matthau as a New York playboy who has to find a means of supporting his expensive lifestyle once his inheritance is depleted. His solution is to marry a rich girl and murder her. For all the charm of the debuting director's movie, it also had two major problems. First, it went well over its budget. Second, after forty days of additional shooting and ten months of postproduction, it was three hours long! The studio wasn't happy, and Paramount production head Robert Evans had the picture recut, eliminating a major subplot.

The new, trim running time of 108 minutes meant a number of changes would be needed on the musical front as well. The original score for *A New Leaf* had been written by Johnny Mandel, at the time best known for his music for Robert Altman's *M*A*S*H* (1970). Both Mandel's score and the theme song, "Suicide Is Painless" (lyrics by Mike Altman), became immensely popular, and the theme reappeared in the *M*A*S*H* TV series (1972–83). Previously, the composer had written a gorgeous score for *The Sandpiper* (1965), and Mandel was also well known for numerous popular, now-classic songs, including "The Shadow of Your Smile" (lyrics by Paul Francis Webster) and "Emily" (lyrics by Johnny Mercer).

Just before taking the *A New Leaf* job, Mandel wrote music for the Warren Beatty/Elizabeth Taylor gambling drama *The Only Game in Town* (1970), but it went unused. Taylor had demanded that the production be moved to Paris, so she could be near her husband, Richard Burton, who was shooting a picture there. Relocating from Las Vegas caused the production budget to soar; it also led to French composer Maurice Jarre's being brought in, and he wrote a melancholic jazz score to replace Mandel's.

Paramount's cut of *A New Leaf* was fitted with many new musical cues pulled from another Paramount score, namely, that of Neal Hefti's *Oh Dad, Poor Dad*. But some of Mandel's cues remained in May's drastically altered comedy, with the result that the composer didn't view his score as "rejected," referring to it as a "decapitated" work instead. Hefti claimed that his music had been used only to patch up a number of blank spots, and that that was done without his direct involvement. The most noticeable example of the patchwork effect is the use of the cue "Old Dad Calypso" for the go-kart trip after the wedding, but a lack of scoring in several other spots becomes quite distracting as well. No composer's name appears in the movie's credits, and in fact, owing to the work's savage editing, Elaine May wanted her name removed from the credits too!

Hefti's music from *Oh Dad, Poor Dad* also made its way into other productions, including Neil Simon's *Last of the Red Hot Lovers* (1973) and the television series *The Odd Couple*.

■ **See No Evil** (1971)

Original composer: **André Previn**
Replacement composer: **David Whitaker**
Replacement of replacement composer: **Elmer Bernstein**

See No Evil, also known as *Blind Terror*, is a largely forgotten chiller starring Mia Farrow as a young blind girl staying with her aunt and uncle in their English country mansion. While she is away from their home for an evening, her aunt and uncle are brutally murdered, and when she returns, the killer is still there. This very tense film from Columbia Pictures (UK and USA) was directed by Richard Fleischer, who had also directed such edge-of-your-seat movies as *The Boston Strangler* (1968) and *Narrow Margin* (1952).

See No Evil was scored by Farrow's then-husband, composer-conductor-pianist André Previn. At the time, Previn could already claim four Oscars and five Grammys; he was also the conductor of the London Symphony Orchestra. His music for the film, recorded by the LSO, did indeed project "blind terror" by combining *Psycho*-like strings with electronic overlays. A synthesizer helped convey both the horror of the lonely girl and the sinisterness of her silent stalker.

Columbia didn't like Previn's score, though associate producer Basil Appleby told him the studio gave no specific reasons. (In retrospect, the composer guessed they had wanted something more melodic, with a catchy tune.) Columbia asked Previn to take a second look at the picture and consider rescoring it, but LSO commitments put him in Moscow when the rewrites were to take place. (British TV viewers would get a chance to hear an extract from Previn's original score when he conducted the LSO, with Howard Blake on Moog synthesizer, during an episode of the BBC's 1976–1984 television series *André Previn's Music Night.*)

Columbia Pictures UK then hired British composer-arranger-conductor David Whitaker to write a new score. Known for his work with many pop performers, including Johnny Hallyday and the Rolling Stones, the composer had also worked in the horror/thriller genre before, most notably providing the music for Gordon Hessler's *Scream and Scream Again* (1970). His *See No Evil* score made use of a large orchestra augmented with such "exotic" instruments as the Hungarian cimbalom (basically a large, classy hammered dulcimer), Jew's harp, harmonica, and tuned cowbells. The story's idyllic rural setting was acknowledged through his melodic style and solo piano writing. This lovely music was then transformed, with the help of the nonorchestral instruments, into an increasingly bizarre soundscape in conjunction with each of the killer's actions.

Both Columbia UK and director Fleischer were enthusiastic about the music, but back in America, Columbia was not satisfied. As in Previn's case, no reasons for the rejection were revealed, but a likely guess is that the problem lay in the key U.S. decision-makers' desire for control over the composing and recording (both of which were done in Britain).

Elmer Bernstein was hired to write and record a third score in Los Angeles, closer to the Columbia brass. The music he provided was the exact opposite of Previn's subtle score and shared only marginal similarities with Whitaker's unused work. The Bernstein score basically juggled two styles of music: a crime-jazz sound like that found in his score for *McQ* (1974) to accompany the violence, and romantic orchestral material to underscore the film's pristine country setting. The clash of the two styles apparently symbolizes conflict within the killer, whose violent actions are usually traced by dramatic, jazz-influenced music, as in such scenes as the opening murder shown on television, which gives him the idea to kill, and his attack on the blind girl on horseback.

Oddly, for all the trouble over its scoring, *See No Evil* ended up as a motion picture whose effectiveness depends on the use of chilling silence. The scenes that work best are those accompanied solely by simple, natural sounds, such as footsteps, running water, a ticking clock, chirping birds, etc. Looking back, the considerable energy devoted to scoring it seems like rather silly and wasteful exercises.

■ Tang shan da xiong/The Big Boss (1971)

Original composer: **Wang Fu-ling**
Replacement composer for British version: **Peter Thomas**
Replacement composer for Japanese version: **Joseph Koo**

In 1970, two executives of the Hong Kong–based Shaw Brothers studio formed the production-distribution company Golden Harvest, in an attempt to provide more artistic freedom to directors and actors who didn't want to sign the more exploitative deals offered by Shaw. Over the next decade Golden Harvest would surpass its competition, landing its first big punch in 1971 with *The Big Boss*, martial arts master Bruce Lee's first major motion picture. (In the late 1960s, Lee had worked as a character actor in American television, perhaps most notably in the role of Kato on *The Green Hornet* TV series. Before signing with the new Golden Harvest company, he turned down a contract offer from Shaw Brothers.) The movie made the martial artist an overnight sensation, and his subsequent films helped the studio rise to prominence, even though Lee himself was to die only two years later. The actor's enigmatic death as well as the incredible number of extant alternate cuts of *The Big Boss* (none of them complete) help lend a mythical aura to the production.

While several Hong Kong martial arts movies have featured alternate scores for versions edited for screening in different countries, *The Big Boss* stands out because it featured original music by several composers written especially for the picture. This contrasts with the standard practice, which was simply to recycle back-catalog tracks.

The original composer, assigned to the so-called Mandarin cut was Wang Fu-ling, a veteran Shaw Brothers composer who provided his typical, relatively derivative martial-arts score. While Wang is the only composer credited on the film, the similarities between some of his cues and composer Chen Yung-yu's score for *The Duel* (1971) lead some experts to believe that Chen provided uncredited additional music for *The Big Boss*. Strangely, throughout its numerous re-edits and alternate versions, Wang remained the only credited composer on the film, regardless of whether his music was utilized or not.

The original Wang score popped up in a number of places, even in Europe: The movie's first English dub made use of it, as did the French theatrical trailer. However, the voiceover work for first English dub was deemed too much like the notoriously hilarious voiceovers of many other Hong Kong imports, so a second dub with higher production values was commissioned.

For this second dub, German film composer Peter Thomas wrote new music that fused a 1960s spy-jazz sound with traditional Asian instrumentals, creating a soundscape that reflected the setting while retaining a musical language familiar to Western ears. Thomas's music was meant to upgrade the production values (similar to how the redubbing was supposed to work), and it became a widely used alternate score—although all the composer credit still went to Wang Fu-ling!

Released in 2005 on iTunes, the Thomas score was an important bit of film music that failed to receive a CD release (as a consequence, it largely went unnoticed among collectors). While this online release featured close to forty-five minutes of music, a couple of the film's cues were released only on compilations—the song "Moontown" was on the album *Orion 2000* and a rerelease of Thomas's *Raumpatrouille,* while "Communication in Hyperspace" and "EKG" are on the composer's album *Warp Back to Earth.*

The so-called Cantonese edit of *The Big Boss,* done in 1983, features an even stranger musical mixture. Half of the music is Thomas's, while the other half was written by Joseph Koo, another veteran Golden Harvest composer who reportedly composed his score for a 1974 Japanese version of the film. Typical of Hong Kong martial arts pictures, the Cantonese edit also uses unlicensed, preexisting music. For example, this version of *The Big Boss* contains music from Pink Floyd ("Time," "Obscured by Clouds," and "The Grand Vizier's Garden Party (Entertainment)") and King Crimson ("Larks' Tongues in Aspic, Part Two"). When Koo's music was issued, these unlicensed pieces were not included. Wang Fu-ling's original score, meanwhile, hasn't been released to this day.

■ Brother Sun, Sister Moon/Fratello Sole, Sorella Luna (1972)

Composer for Italian version: **Riz Ortolani**
Composers for British version: **Donovan, and Ken Thorne**

By 1971, director Franco Zeffirelli was well known for his Academy Award–nominated version of *Romeo and Juliet* (1968) and *The Taming of the Shrew* (1967), the latter starring Elizabeth Taylor and Richard Burton. His *Brother Sun, Sister Moon* was not just a religious costume drama about Saint Francis of Assisi, it also was a sociopolitical statement very much tied to its day. Francis, just returned from a war—like Vietnam veterans in 1971—finds peace with God in a form of Christianity stripped of pomposity. Zeffirelli's underlying concept, drawing parallels between Francis's time and the present, as well as between St. Francis's life of poverty and innocence and the hippie movement of the late 1960s and early 1970s, was difficult to communicate, and he hoped to enlist the aid of the film's music.

To this end, Zeffirelli went as far as trying to cast famous musical performers for his picture. In his autobiography, he wrote that he considered the Beatles for the main roles, though scheduling conflicts ultimately prevented this. Another performer rumored for the lead role was Brazilian singer-songwriter Caetano Veloso, famous as a champion of the *Tropicalismo* movement in music, who similarly couldn't sacrifice his recording career for a movie appearance. With the casting of singers proving difficult, Zeffirelli gave the lead to screen novice Graham Faulkner. For the music, he hired Italian composer Riz Ortolani.

Ortolani's traditional score has a religious flavor, with beautiful melodies highlighting Francis's humanity. Its main theme is often played by woodwinds against a lush string background. There are a couple of simple songs that match the sensibilities of the era, performed by Claudio Baglioni, and also a beautiful choral piece performed by the Coro dei Cantori delle Basiliche di Roma, "Francesco Goes Alone Round the World."

However, Ortolani's score made it only into the Italian prints, where its use was secured thanks to a coproduction deal that required the composer's music be used in at least the Italian version of the movie. Otherwise, the picture was completely recut before it arrived in theaters. It ended up fourteen minutes longer, with many scene sequences changed, and the dialogue often changed too.

For this new cut, both director and production company agreed to try something different with the music. For the British market, a song-score (a very unusual idea for a religious epic) was commissioned from popular Scottish singer-songwriter Donovan (known for such psychedelic-folk hits as "Mellow Yellow," "Hurdy Gurdy Man," "Season of the Witch," "Sunshine Superman," and "There Is a Mountain") and composer Ken Thorne, whose credits at the time included *Help!* (1965), *How I Won the War* (1967), and *The Magic Christian* (1969). The cowriting concept was simple: have Donovan write songs that tied into Zeffirelli's message, feature them prominently in the film, and have Thorne adapt the material into an orchestral underscore. Nine songs were written for the picture, headlined by the titular "Brother Sun, Sister Moon." Thorne's strong film-scoring talents came in handy as he reworked the songs around dialogue-heavy scenes. The composer remembers signing onto the film:

> I got involved through my agent, Vic Lewis, who called and asked if I was interested in writing the score. It seemed, from what he said, that there had been, for reasons unknown, difficulty with the musical approach. He told me that Ortolani had been the first composer to be hired by Franco Zeffirelli and there had also been an English composer engaged for a while, so I was the third choice!! I remember being in an elevator with another fellow on our way to meet with Franco. He asked who I was and I told him that I was the third composer for *Brother Sun, Sister Moon*. He then told me that he was the twenty-fourth scriptwriter to be hired for the project!

Interestingly, Donovan never released an album of his original recordings for the picture. Despite how popular the score was, and how well suited to the movie, no recording of the original soundtrack ever materialized. The title theme earned Donovan generous royalties, however, when Sister Janet Mead (the period's second "singing nun," the first being Sister Luc-Gabrielle, known for her hit "Dominique" under the name "Soeur Sourire") covered the song on the B-side of her U.S. hit single "The Lord's Prayer," which sold millions of copies in 1974.

In 2004, Donovan released newly recorded versions of his *Brother Sun, Sister Moon* songs. Unable to obtain the rights to release the original recordings, he tried to satisfy public demand by issuing a cover album of his own songs. While the tunes and lyrics are the same, this album is more intimate—just Donovan's guitar and voice—than the film score.

Frenzy (1972)

Original composer: **Henry Mancini**
Replacement composer: **Ron Goodwin**

After the failures of his espionage movies *Torn Curtain* (1966) and *Topaz* (1969), Alfred Hitchcock returned to England to shoot his next picture, *Frenzy*, based on Arthur La Berne's novel about a serial killer roaming London, *Goodbye Piccadilly, Farewell Leicester Square.*

For this picture, Hitchcock made what some might consider a surprising choice for composer: Henry Mancini. While Mancini is still best known for writing the infectiously upbeat "The Pink Panther Theme," his music had a darker side as well. That aspect of his work is in evidence in his score for *Wait Until Dark* (1967), in which he used out-of-tune pianos to portray terror, as well as his scores for *Touch of Evil* (1958), *Days of Wine and Roses* (1962), and *Charade* (1963).

After signing on for a fee of $25,000, Mancini traveled to England to discuss the music's style with Hitchcock. But the director proved more concerned with the placement of the music than what it should sound like.

Four days were scheduled at CTS Bayswater Studios to record Mancini's score, but only two days of sessions were completed. The director attended these sessions but remained disconcertingly silent, although he reportedly nodded after each cue was recorded. Hitchcock later decided that the score was too "macabre" and eventually came to the conclusion that the placement of the music was wrong as well.

An apocryphal anecdote relates that once Hitchcock heard Mancini's Gothic score, he told him, "If I had wanted Bernard Herrmann, I would have hired him!"(Herrmann himself was said to be a disseminator of this story.) True or not, the story helps illustrate Hitchcock's difficulty in articulating what he wanted musically. The director let Mancini go and hired Ron Goodwin, a respected composer of film scores of every genre.

The new composer had pleasant recollections of meeting Hitchcock:

> Well, first of all I was asked to go to Pinewood Studios to meet him, and I was bit nervous about meeting him. But he was very relaxed, very humorous, and told me some funny stories; he was very, very friendly and made me feel welcome and relaxed. But he was very, very meticulous about what kind of music he wanted. I mean, I left to rewind the film and his secretary transcribed all the notes of our conversation [...] He went back to Hollywood before we recorded the music, having said that he would like the first-stage recording sent by courier to him so that he could run it with the picture and see how it went. To my great surprise, it was quite late in the evening of the first recording, and my first ring was a call from him from Hollywood just to say that he'd run the first reel and he was very pleased with it, so I thought that was very kind and a nice thing to do. I don't think many directors would be able to do that.

Key to respotting the film before Goodwin began work was Hitchcock's decision to leave most of the intense, gruesome, and memorable scenes without music. These included one disturbingly silent rape sequence, and numerous offscreen murders that serve to contrast the killer's atrocities with everyday life in London. In one hilariously macabre moment—again mostly without underscore—the serial killer desperately tries to recover some incriminating evidence from a truck hauling sacks of potatoes.

Goodwin, supplied with extensive notes from the director, even discussed the picture with Mancini. He came to the conclusion that the Mancini-Hitchcock problem had been one of "a breakdown in communication."

Despite his score's replacement, Mancini retained fond memories of Hitchcock:

> If I were doing the score again, I really don't know what I would do differently. It turned out that Hitchcock wanted a lighter score, which also confused me, because he and I discussed the musical requirements beforehand, and seemed to be in agreement. He afterwards hired Ron Goodwin, who is a friend of mine and with whom I later discussed the situation. Ron read me a detailed analysis of what Hitchcock had in mind after he decided he wanted another score. It was interesting, because I wish I had been given something like that to go by. It might have been a different story. [...] Apart from the film, I found Mr. Hitchcock to be a gracious and generous man. During lunch one day, we got into a discussion about a mutual interest we had, wine. The next day, a case of Château Haut-Brion—magnums—was delivered to me. Come to think of it, I guess the whole adventure was not a total loss after all. I still think what I did on *Frenzy* was good—a score completely without themes, because it seemed to me the film didn't require any.

To appreciate the differences in Mancini's and Goodwin's approaches, one only needs to look at the film's opening, a breathtaking aerial shot of London that takes viewers down the Thames and between the Tower Bridge's towers as it descends. Mancini's main theme (which can be heard as a rerecording on *Mancini in Surround*) is a dark, ominous piece with Gothic textures and heavy organ use, seeming to depict modern-day London as a dark city of the Middle Ages. By contrast, Goodwin's "London Theme" is an optimistic piece that celebrates the greatness of the city; it would make any tourist bureau proud. Hitchcock said that it should be "grandiose in style, symbolizing the entry through the gates into London." In accordance with this, the opening shot depicts the capital as a beautiful city, an impression aided by Sir George's celebratory speech, which the audience drops in on once the aerial camera lands.

But this glorious feeling is quickly confounded when a naked female body is spotted floating in the Thames with a necktie around her neck. We're now in a sinister London where a new Jack the Ripper is plying his trade.

■ **Sounder** (1972)

Original composer: **Alex North**
Replacement composer: **Taj Mahal**

Sounder, directed by Martin Ritt, is a heartfelt film adaptation of William H. Armstrong's Newbery Award–winning young-adult novel of the same name. It's a young African-American boy's coming-of-age story set in Depression Era Louisiana. The son of a poor sharecropper, the boy undertakes journeys of discovery in search of his dog, Sounder, and his father, who has been sentenced to a work gang for committing a petty crime. Along the way, he learns the values of education and perseverance. The movie was nominated for four Academy Awards.

This wasn't the first time Martin Ritt had visited the American South in his movies. His usual musical accompanist for these trips was the influential and highly original film composer Alex North. The director and the composer had previously worked on two movies inspired by the writings of renowned Southern novelist William Faulkner: *The Long, Hot Summer* (1958) and *The Sound and the Fury* (1959). Both pictures made great use of North's knowledge of jazz and his understanding of effective spotting. (Their third feature together, 1964's *The Outrage,* took advantage of another of North's specialties, Mexican-influenced music.)

Although North's score was undoubtedly appropriate for *Sounder*'s Southern setting, the filmmakers decided not to use a through-composed score after all, opting instead for an intimate, song-based rural blues score by the popular blues artist Taj Mahal (born Henry Saint Clair Fredericks), who also played the character Ike in the movie.

Sounder was Taj Mahal's first venture into film music. His score is a collection of sometimes tender and sometimes lively blues tunes featuring banjo, guitar, harmonica, and vocals skillfully performed by the composer. This period-style music feels like a natural part of the film's rural landscape and adds a sense of authenticity to the production. Taj Mahal's *Sounder* music was released on LP by Columbia Records, and his "Sounder Medley" appeared on compilations.

Incidentally, *Sounder* wasn't the last time a score by Alex North would be rejected. In 1980 the composer scored the family Western *Cattle Annie and Little Britches,* directed by Lamont Johnson, with whom he had worked previously on the comedy flop *Somebody Killed Her Husband* (1978). But *Cattle Annie* was a troubled production, and North's score didn't survive. New music was eventually provided by Sahn Berti and Tom Slocum—a pair whose only notable credit is this picture.

■ Columbo: "The Greenhouse Jungle" (1972)

Original composer: **Paul Glass**
Replacement composer: **Oliver Nelson**

While the film world is replete with rejected scores, the phenomenon makes only occasional appearances in the small-screen world. Tight, strict television network deadlines and unchangeable airtimes simply don't allow for major musical overhauls. Even when a television composer fails to deliver music on time, the networks can rely on vast libraries of old cues to fill in any empty spaces.

However, pilot episodes and season starters enjoy the luxury of more available time for postproduction changes, and though the rescoring of such episodes is very rare, it does happen. Examples include Alexander Courage's music for the pilot of *Land of the Giants* (a sci-fi series that aired from 1968 to 1970) and Jerry Fielding's music for the season opener of *McMillan & Wife* (a lighthearted crime drama that aired from 1971 to 1977).

In a handful of interesting instances, scorers were changed because the original music was too far "outside the box." Generally speaking, television scoring allows for creativity only as long as a composer stays within the guidelines of what middle-Americans expect to hear coming from their TV sets. The most important rule in this regard is that any distinctly unpleasant or outrageously weird music that might drive a viewer to change channels must be excluded.

An illustration of this problem is Paul Glass's score to the second episode of the second season of the series *Columbo* (a quirky detective show that ran from 1971 to 1990), "The Greenhouse Jungle," which featured Ray Milland as an eccentric orchid specialist who kills his nephew. Milland's odd character inspired Glass to try something unusual—introduce a rarely heard instrument. Glass explains:

> The episode was about this guy who collected flowers. He seemed to be such a difficult person that I thought it would be a good idea to write a kind of concerto for heckelphone, named so because it was produced by the Czechoslovakian Heckel factory. This very strange-sounding low oboe was possibly the reason the producers didn't like the music. I found out about the replacement whilst I was doing another film called *Sandcastles*. I was recording that at 20th Century Fox when they rang me and said the music was not acceptable. Since I was doing the other music, I really didn't worry about it all that much.

Glass's score was deemed unsuitable by the studio's executives because it butted heads with the conventions of television music's instrumentation. The episode's replacement score was provided by prolific television composer and former jazz performer-composer-arranger Oliver Nelson, in what would be his only contribution to the *Columbo* series.

In a similar vein, author-composer Elizabeth Swados's score for the television biopic *Gauguin the Savage* (1980) was thrown out after the network decided it sounded too much like Stravinsky—an intended insult that Swados, a composer of dance, theater, television, and film music, took as a compliment. The show eventually received a conventional television underscore penned by prolific small-screen composer Gerald Fried.

■ The Getaway (1972)

Original composer: **Jerry Fielding**
Replacement composer: **Quincy Jones**

The fruitful partnership of director Sam Peckinpah and composer Jerry Fielding was underappreciated until recently. Their collaborations started in 1966 with the one-hour television movie *Noon Wine* (presented on the show *ABC Stage 67*). They subsequently worked together on five movies, two of which—*The Wild Bunch* (1969) and *Straw Dogs* (1971)—earned Oscar nominations for the composer.

In 1972, while making the picture *Junior Bonner*, Peckinpah and Fielding crossed paths with the third main character of our score-replacement tale, actor Steve McQueen.

McQueen was one of America's hottest actors in the late sixties and early seventies. In 1968 he played a character who was the epitome of coolness in the hit film *Bullitt*, and that same year he starred in yet another hit, *The Thomas Crown Affair*.

A few years later, taking stock of his back-to-back mega-hit movies from 1968, McQueen couldn't help but note how much less successful his subsequent projects had by comparison. Even the critically acclaimed *Junior Bonner* didn't do well at the box office. So he set out not only to star in his next movie, *The Getaway*, but also to supervise all areas of its production, including the music. His incredible star status at that time allowed him to wield such unusually strong decision-making power.

The Getaway, based on Jim Thompson's novel of the same name, adapted for the screen by Walter Hill and directed by Sam Peckinpah, is a tale of double crosses on top of double crosses. (McQueen vetoed Thompson's own film adaptation because he felt it was too dark.)

Hired to score *The Getaway*, Jerry Fielding worked with his friend Peckinpah on determining the music's role and, most importantly, where it should appear. The composer saw the picture as melancholic and thought that its music shouldn't be overwhelming—on the contrary, it should be kept to a minimum. The turbulent romance between husband and wife Doc (McQueen) and Carol (Ali McGraw) McCoy, a modern-day (circa 1970s) Bonnie and Clyde, became his score's focal point, and since the romance was unusual, so was his quasi-love theme. In the story, Doc and Carol haven't seen each other during the four years Doc has been in prison, and their separation has alienated them from one another. So Fielding wrote an intentionally awkward theme for the couple. It is heard near the beginning of the movie, just before they make love for the first time in years. The theme's payoff is the cue "Texas Trash Heap," which is heard after the couple survives numerous double crossings and shootouts, during their attempt to escape the clutches of a horde of thugs and live happily (and richly) ever after.

The rest of the score is fairly typical of Fielding and provides a tense underpinning for the film's suspenseful moments. Much as in *Straw Dogs*, he maintains a sense of suspense through such lengthy cues as "Bag Theft" and "The Bank Robbery" though the use of martial drumming and tense string textures. (Incidentally, "The Bank Robbery" is the only one of Fielding's cues found married to the film in its original dub. This cue, on a single reel of the film, is in the Jerry Fielding collection of Brigham Young University. The print shows how Peckinpah and Fielding envisioned the music. Surprisingly, an already sparse underscore was cut even leaner in this dub—a minute of the full robbery cue was left out. The music plays incredibly well with the scene: The martial motifs lend an air of professionalism to the bank robbery, and the music underscores each minor onscreen incident.)

Fielding's score was recorded in October and November of 1972, conducted by the composer. (The orchestrators on this complex project were Greig McRitchie and Lennie Niehaus.) The film's associate producer Gordon Dawson praised the music, saying, "It was like a man in a green suit walking in a forest."

Posters with Fielding's name on them were printed, and the movie's prescreenings received favorable reviews. But Steve McQueen had problems with Fielding's score. The actor apparently believed that his cool movie deserved a hipper soundtrack, one that was more commercial. He asked his friend Quincy Jones to provide replacement music as quickly as possible. Jones was good at replacing film scores on short notice, as he had done on *The New Centurions* (1972) and *A Dandy in Aspic* (1968), and although he had decided to take on fewer such assignments, he couldn't decline the request of an old friend.

There was no time to respot the film for Jones, so he worked from the same spotting as Fielding had. However, as a result of changes in the cues' starting and ending points during the dub, Jones's jazzy score, which featured harmonica virtuoso Toots Thielemans, ended up even shorter than Fielding's. Jones's music presented a more lighthearted view of the film, and moved away from the calculated tension-building so prevalent in Fielding's score. (Jones's score recording is unreleased to this day, with the exception of a single issued by A&M Records.)

The rejection of his score for *The Getaway* took a toll on Fielding, who vowed never to replace a composer friend on another project, because he now knew how it felt to be on the short end of the stick. As a testament to his high regard for Fielding's score, Peckinpah took out a full-page ad in the November 17, 1972, issue of *Daily Variety* in which he praised his friend's rejected music:

> I know you will be pleased that the second preview of *Getaway* was as great as the first. In fact, it was even more enthusiastically received. Which is surprising since it was attended mostly by industry people. I want to thank you for the beautiful job you did with the music. I have heard many marvelous comments, particularly on the second showing. Possibly because no one there had impaired hearing and we had no problem with malfunctioning equipment. Once again, congratulations. I am looking forward to the next one.

Peckinpah's experience on *The Getaway* wasn't much better than Fielding's. The famously cantankerous director's desire to get a percentage of the movie's profits led to a bitter argument that tainted his relationship with McQueen. After the humiliating experiences they shared on *The Getaway*, Peckinpah and Fielding worked together on two more films: the ultrastrange *Bring Me the Head of Alfredo Garcia* (1974) and *The Killer Elite* (1975).

While *The Killer Elite* is usually listed as their last joint venture, the pair collaborated on some music demos for Peckinpah's 1978 picture *Convoy*, for which the composer wrote and recorded a couple of tunes. However, Fielding was never hired to score the movie; instead, the job went to Chip Davis (cofounder of Mannheim Steamroller), who cowrote the hit tune "Convoy," on which the movie was based, with Bill Fries (aka C. W. McCall) in 1974.

While it took more than thirty years for Fielding's *The Getaway* soundtrack to be released, now it is not only available on CD, but it's also one of the few rejected scores that, thanks to a recent Blu-ray release, can be viewed together with the picture and such other pertinent extras as Nick Redman's documentary *Main Title 1M1: Jerry Fielding, Sam Peckinpah and The Getaway* .

■ **The Neptune Factor** (1973)

Original composer: **William McCauley**
Replacement composer: **Lalo Schifrin**

Riding the popularity wave of producer-writer-director Irwin Allen's *The Poseidon Adventure* (1972), Canada's *The Neptune Factor* lived up to the cheesy disaster genre's expectations in almost every department. Directed by Daniel Petrie, it tells the tale of marine biologists trapped under the sea by an earthquake and the mission undertaken to rescue them. Selected to write its music was Canadian composer-conductor William McCauley. McCauley enjoyed a long and fruitful career in his homeland, scoring 125 pictures and even commercials. He was known to deliver good music for a budget price, thus allowing *The Neptune Factor* to hire better (and more expensive) actors—including *The Poseidon Adventure*'s Ernest Borgnine and star of *Voyage to the Bottom of the Sea* (1961 film version) Walter Pidgeon—and create tolerable special effects (which still looked like bathroom toys).

To cover the entire job (including copyists, an orchestra, and recording), McCauley was given $25,000. For this amount he wrote, orchestrated, conducted, and recorded (at Toronto's now-defunct Manta Sound studio) his entire score in less than a month, with the exception of two short cues composed by his son, Matthew. The music is thematically rich and quite atypical of disaster scores, a field dominated by John Williams (who scored *The Poseidon Adventure, Earthquake,* and *The Towering Inferno*). Like Williams, McCauley composed a lush main theme to capture the beauty of the story's setting before havoc breaks loose. Onscreen, the underwater world is presented as a magnificent place to carry out research, and McCauley's romantic score perfectly captures this. Forget the monster fishes and the impending danger, this score is a hymn to the sea. It may not be groundbreaking, but it's music that should be heard.

Unfortunately, when 20th Century Fox picked up the picture for distribution, they packaged it as a double-feature with *Battle for the Planet of the Apes* (1973) and ordered a new score that would better match the genre's conventions. Discarding most of McCauley's work, producer Sandy Howard commissioned a new score from Lalo Schifrin, who approached the picture as he would any other disaster movie—his music reflecting the danger, excitement, and camp values (especially during the action sequences) expected from such films. A couple of McCauley cues—mostly scene-painting tracks with pleasing melodies—were kept in the picture, and for these the Canadian composer received due credit. For the rest of the movie, Schifrin provided tense but predictable music written under a tight deadline. His main theme is a set of fanfares sounding like the poor nephew of Richard Strauss's *Also sprach Zarathustra*. In the end, this score doesn't rank as one of the composer's greatest achievements. And the mix buries most of Schifrin's music under heavy sound effects, especially during the underwater scenes.

In 2007, the original music for *The Neptune Factor* was finally brought to light on a DVD produced by Nick Redman and released by 20th Century Fox. This disc features William McCauley's complete score as an isolated stereo track and Schifrin's music married to the film's sound effects as an isolated mono track (tracks for the music alone were lost by the studio). Because McCauley's name recognition is too low to warrant a CD release, presenting his *Neptune Factor* score as an isolated track on this DVD was a special treat for score collectors.

■ The Man Who Loved Cat Dancing (1973)

Original composer: **Michel Legrand**
Replacement composer: **John Williams**

The strange Western *The Man Who Loved Cat Dancing* had a troubled production: Among other problems, the coproducers sued each other, the star was seriously injured while filming a fight scene, and a crew member died under mysterious circumstances. Based on Marilyn Durham's best-selling novel of the same title, the beautifully photographed movie featured an all-star cast headed up by Burt Reynolds (fresh off his success in *Deliverance*) and Sarah Miles. It told the story of a train robber and killer (Reynolds) who is haunted by his past. He's on a journey to reclaim the children from his marriage to his now-dead Native American wife, Cat Dancing. Along the way, accompanied by a band of desperate criminals, he kidnaps a woman (Miles) who is fleeing from her husband and from the bounty hunter her husband has hired to find her.

French composer Michel Legrand was taken on to provide the music. It was his first Western score, and he wrote it in Paris, traveling to Hollywood only for the recording sessions. His music mixed a medium-size orchestra—augmented by a variety of out-of-the-ordinary instruments including cimbalom, ocarina, recorder, sarod, and electric guitar—with Native American–style chant that he performed himself. Through his music, which lacked the traditional Western genre feel, the composer hoped to evoke a sense of Native American spirituality, signifying the dead wife, Cat Dancing. Legrand remembers how his approach confused the filmmakers:

> About *Dancing*, when they pitched the film to me, I had an idea that I thought was absolutely great. I submitted it to the director and he was enthusiastic. I start with some Indian chant, and progressively it merges into symphonic music, first with a handful of

players, then twenty, forty, and seventy by the end. But when they heard it, those stupid producers said, "What's this, we don't get it." I finish recording, then they discard the score and ask John Williams to replace me. Poor John, I think he had something like eight days to come up with something. [It was] not one of his greatest works.

Director Richard C. Sarafian auditioned a few composers, including Miklós Rózsa, while seeking Legrand's replacement. John Williams was ultimately selected, under the condition that he would write all the music (about forty minutes' worth) in less than a week. Williams was no stranger to the Western genre: Before *Cat Dancing* he had scored *The Cowboys* (1972), *The Rare Breed* (1966), and episodes of such television shows as *Wagon Train* and *Tales of Wells Fargo*. Despite *Cat Dancing*'s insane deadline, the composer managed to pen a tuneful score featuring distinct melodies for its two main characters and their romance. Written for a medium-size orchestra (forty-two players at its peak), the music mixed standard suspense scoring with the use of such traditional Americana instruments as harmonica, guitar, and banjo.

The score's love theme was later developed into the song "Dream Away," with lyrics by Paul Williams, who later released it on his album *Here Comes Inspiration*, conducted by John Williams himself! This was the only piece of music available from the movie until 2002, when Film Score Monthly released a CD containing Williams's original score, including unused pieces and alternate takes, together with Legrand's.

Legrand's music on this recording stands in distinct contrast to the suspense cues that characterize much of Williams's work. Unfortunately, Legrand's entire score was never recorded, but what exists of it (twenty-plus minutes) was organized for the CD into a main theme and two suites. Presenting two composers' work side by side, this release is recommended to film music fans who wish to compare a rejected score with its replacement. Sadly, the cue titles for Legrand's music didn't survive, so only the cue numbers offer hints as to which piece goes where in the picture.

Legrand discussed the release:

> One day the FSM staff calls me to ask if they could put my music on the same album with John's. I told them I agree. That it would be fun. Later, I happen to put that CD on. Listening to John's score, which I had never heard before, nothing in my humble opinion really interesting. Then I write to John, who's a very good friend, and I tell him, "John, now that this CD is out, your career's over, for when they start noticing my score's much better than yours, they'll hire you no more!" He got a good laugh out of it.

■ **Hex** (1973)

Original composer: **Patrick Williams**
Replacement composer: **Charles Bernstein**

Hex, an arty biker/horror/Western film with early-1970s psychedelic overtones, features performances by Keith Carradine, Gary Busey, and Scott Glenn. It's the strange tale of six World War I veterans traveling through Nebraska on motorcycles.

They soon run afoul of the townspeople of Bingo and flee to the safe haven of a farm run by two sisters of Native American heritage. Hopped up on locally grown locoweed, one of the men rapes one of the women, and her sister responds by putting an Indian shaman's hex on the whole biker bunch. One by one, they meet their fates in bizarre ways, such as being clawed to death by an owl. (Critics have suggested that the filmmakers themselves must have been sampling the local weed when they made this flick.)

Written and directed by newcomer Leo Garen, and his only major movie credit, *Hex* was produced by Max L. Raab, a clothier (once dubbed by *The New York Times* "Dean of the Prep Look") turned filmmaker (executive producer of 1971's *A Clockwork Orange* and *Walkabout*) for 20th Century Fox. Since the film was made for Fox, the rookie director received musical guidance from Lionel Newman, the head of its music department (previously headed by his brother Alfred).

Newman often aided filmmakers by selecting composers for them. For *Hex* he suggested Patrick Williams, a talented composer who had mostly done television work. Williams had scored Abraham Polonsky's unusual Western *Tell Them Willie Boy Is Here* (1969), which featured Robert Redford hunting down the titular Paiute Indian. But his traditional Western genre music was not what the filmmakers had in mind, and it was replaced with a more introspective score by Dave Grusin, who scrambled to invent some Native American–like music without having sufficient time to explore the subject. Grusin's score focused more on the Native American protagonist than did Williams's.

Something similar happened in the case of *Hex*. Director Garen was unsatisfied with Williams's score, preferring music that was not so traditional, not so genre-bound. At this point, Charles Bernstein's involvement with *Hex* began:

> I think that Pat Williams was a choice largely supported by Lionel Newman and the studio, but the director wanted to do something more adventurous and unconventional with the music. I was suggested, so I came in and supplied a less conventional score using odd percussion, women's voices, harmonica, as well as regular instruments recorded over at Fox. Pat's score was more conventional in the orchestral sense; it played more of the elements of the old West in a traditional manner than it did the sort of oddball, anachronistic time-travel factor where you had elements from the 1960s mixed with the 1800s.

Both *Hex* and *Tell Them Willie Boy Is Here* are interesting examples of safe, traditional scores being replaced by edgier, less genre-specific scores more in tune with their directors' overall cinematic visions. Grusin's ersatz ethnic music for *Tell Them Willie Boy Is Here* and Bernstein's crazy *Hex* music demonstrate alternative ways to score pictures that are a bit off the beaten path. It's just an unlucky coincidence for Patrick Williams that both of these movies' first scores were by him. (Neither replacement score has been released on a recording, so the only chance to hear them is at the rare showing of these features.)

■ Hell Up in Harlem (1973)

Original composers: **James Brown and Fred Wesley**
Replacement composer: **Edwin Starr**

Despite his tremendous achievements in the world of popular music, James Brown's efforts at film scoring didn't meet with unqualified success. Whereas Isaac Hayes and Curtis Mayfield helped define the blaxploitation genre (Hayes with his *Shaft* score in 1971, whose title song received an Oscar, and Mayfield with *Super Fly* in 1972), the Godfather of Soul's foray into the business didn't go so smoothly.

Brown's first scoring assignment was *Black Caesar*, a loose remake of the classic 1931 film *Little Caesar*. Written, directed, and produced by Larry Cohen and starring Fred Williamson, *Black Caesar* is the story of Tommy Gibbs (Williamson), who violently works his way from shoeshine boy to kingpin of Harlem's crime world. A survivor and ghetto cult hero, he directs much of his wrath at the racist society he was born into. But power corrupts, and Gibbs eventually brings about his own downfall.

Cohen and his music coordinator, songwriter–music producer Barry De Vorzon, went straight to the top when they wanted a funky score for their film, hiring James Brown. The problem was, Brown wrote only about thirty percent of the film's required music (extracted from his sketches and arranged by Fred Wesley, Brown's longtime trombonist and musical director, and cowriter of the hit "Hot Pants"). For the rest of the score, Brown planned to reuse some of his earlier recordings, such as "Try Me" and "I Lost Someone." This approach would have been fraught with creative and legal problems, so Wesley, without consulting Brown, wrote all the remaining music needed to fulfill the contract.

Unaware that his old songs had not been used after all, Brown got a shock when he attended the movie's premiere. He threatened to fire Wesley on the spot, but compliments he received on the music changed his mind, and Brown ended up congratulating his team on the great work they had done.

The film was a huge success and naturally paved the way for a sequel, *Revenge*, the further adventures of Tommy Gibbs. In the follow-up, Tommy, aided by his estranged father, Papa Gibbs, establishes a new crime empire in New York. When a traitor in his gang drives a wedge between father and son, Tommy moves to California, leaving Papa as the boss. But then Papa is murdered, and Tommy returns to New York driven by a rage for vengeance.

When it came time to hire a composer for his hastily produced sequel, Larry Cohen once again turned to James Brown and his team. Since Fred Williamson was busy making other movies and Cohen himself was already working on *It's Alive* (1974), much of *Revenge* had to be shot on weekends, utilizing a stand-in for the star whenever other commitments made him unavailable. In the meantime, Brown started work on the movie's theme song, "Revenge," which he eventually retitled "The Payback." Once again the score was a team effort by Brown, Wesley, and company. Fred Wesley recalls delivering the tape to Larry Cohen:

> I went straight to Larry's office in order to complete my business right away, then have a little time to spend with my family before heading back to the East Coast. I didn't anticipate any problems. Larry put the tape on and heard what was now titled "The Payback." He played about half of it, then skipped to the next track, played a little of that, then stopped listening altogether. He looked me straight in the face and said, "This isn't funky enough, Fred." I retorted, "Isn't funky enough? I don't know what kind of Hollywood game you're beginning to play, but I do know that this is extremely funky music." He began to try to explain something to me when I stopped him and asked to use the telephone. I figured that if he were going to play games I had better get the best game-player I knew of to be on my team. I dialed the phone. "Hello, Mr. Brown? This is Fred. Larry says that the music isn't funky enough."

The phone conversation resulted in Brown's withdrawal from the project. The music he wrote and recorded for *Revenge*—soon to be retitled *Hell Up in Harlem*—was turned into the double album *The Payback*, which reached 34th position on Billboard's pop album charts. Its title song became an R&B chart topper.

The song "The Payback" was to have a long life of its own. It would be sampled by several bands, including En Vogue, which used its "beats" in two songs, "Hold On" and "My Lovin' (You're Never Gonna Get It)." And in 1980, Brown himself reworked it as "Rapp Payback (Where Iz Moses)."

Few contemporary reviews mentioned *The Payback*'s origin as film music, so many speculated that Brown's hospitalization and the tragic death of his oldest son were its primary inspirations. But despite being rarely considered as a movie soundtrack, it is in fact the greatest blaxploitation score that never made it to the screen.

Hell Up in Harlem was eventually scored by singer-songwriter Edwin Starr (perhaps best known for his 1969 anti–Vietnam War song "War," which hit the number one slot on the pop charts). Starr's glossily produced score is funky and puts his high-pitched, growling voice to good use. Its title theme "Ain't It Hell Up in Harlem," works well to bring the audience into the movie's world. Still, the music barely registered on the pop charts.

■ **The Seven-Ups** (1973)

Original composer: **Johnny Mandel**
Replacement composer: **Don Ellis**

The Seven-Ups, produced and directed by Philip D'Antoni, was a quasi-sequel to director William Friedkin's *The French Connection* starring Roy Scheider (named Buddy, as he is in *The French Connection*) as the leader of an elite undercover New York City police squad known for its unorthodox methods. The movie follows the squad—known as the Seven-Ups, because the criminals it nabbed were up for seven or more years in prison—on an investigation that becomes entangled in a series of kidnappings of mobsters for ransom, and results in the death of one of the squad members.

First-time director D'Antoni had previously produced, back to back, two popular and now classic crime films, *Bullitt* (1968) and *The French Connection* (1971). Like both of those movies, *The Seven-Ups* features a wild, edge-of-your-seat car chase, which begins in Manhattan and finishes out in the countryside. As in the other films, *The Seven-Ups'* chase sequence was designed by stuntman Bill Hickman. Returning from *The French Connection* as well were Academy Award–winning editor Jerry Greenberg and, eventually, composer Don Ellis.

Legendary popular jazz trumpeter-composer Don Ellis has relatively few film scores to his name. His only soundtracks released on CD are *The French Connection* and its 1975 sequel *French Connection II* (directed by John Frankenheimer and produced by Robert L. Rosen—and a decidedly lesser picture than the original). Although Ellis's work on *The French Connection* was stunning, it was an unfortunate introduction to mainstream scoring for him, because the director's cinematic vision simply didn't allow for musical accompaniment to any of the film's big scenes. Friedkin cut up Ellis's thirty-seven-minute score and used only half of it, with little regard for its thematic integrity. Only when the original soundtrack of *The French Connection* was released would fans get the chance to assess the composer's original intentions.

The music functioned for the director as a collection of effective musical moods that he could draw upon to underscore a given onscreen event. Such musical cut-and-paste, essentially creating a score in the editing room, became somewhat popular in the 1970s, when many directors (especially Friedkin in *The Exorcist*) denied the need for scene-specific underscores and instead utilized whatever music and sound design seemed to best communicate a scene's underlying emotions, often without specifically hitting its dramatic turns.

Regardless of such editing-room butchery, *The French Connection* was widely praised for its music, an unusual, edgy blend that seamlessly united elements of contemporary jazz with avant-garde concert music to effectively underscore the movie's grittiness.

In 1972, Ellis worked on another gritty police drama, this time set in Los Angeles, *The New Centurions*. But his score didn't make it to the final print, eventually being replaced by music by Quincy Jones.

Despite his early film scoring setbacks, Ellis was willing to step up again and score *The Seven-Ups* in a style similar to *The French Connection*, where the music's experimental nature heighten's the edginess of the film's story and sometimes brutal images. Learning from his experience with Friedkin, he wrote a fairly short score for *The Seven-Ups*, and since *The French Connection* music had been so heavily cut and moved about, he chose to make the new score less dependent on the film's specific visuals. (Even so, his cues for this movie were matched more or less to the scenes the way Ellis had intended them.) The most telling cues are the somewhat experimental-sounding "Car Wash," "Main Title," and "Coffin," the last a demanding cue featuring the string section. Just as in *The French Connection*, the film's largest action scene—the car chase—is left without music.

Curiously, given Ellis's successful past with the filmmakers, he had not been their first choice for composer. Johnny Mandel had been taken on before him, and he produced a safe, traditional underscore that employed a heroic theme throughout the picture. Not only was his musical vocabulary more traditional than Ellis's, but so was his overall approach, namely, in that the cues were highly specific to the screen action. It's worth pointing out that the two scores also differ with regard to their spotting: Mandel's score is slightly shorter than Ellis's, because he left four scenes unaccompanied (including the two car chases). Ellis, in turn, skipped two scenes for which Mandel had written slightly inappropriate and superfluous cues.

Both composers' scores were released on the same CD (from Intrada), allowing film music fans to make their own comparisons.

■ The Exorcist (1973)

Original composer: **Lalo Schifrin**
Replacement composer: **Jack Nitzsche (plus existing works by many composers, including Mike Oldfield, Anton Webern, George Crumb, Krzysztof Penderecki, Hans Werner Henze, and David Borden)**

One of the all-time most popular and most profitable horror movies, *The Exorcist* was nominated for ten Academy Awards, winning two (for its sound and its screenplay). Based on the best-selling novel by William Peter Blatty, who also wrote the screenplay, this record-breaking picture about a demonically possessed little girl struck a nerve with moviegoers around the world, leading to two (inferior) sequels and a prequel that exists in two versions.

Director William Friedkin's musical saga with this picture actually began with another horror movie, Brian De Palma's *Sisters* (1973). That film's Bernard Herrmann score heralded the composer's big return to American screens after his break with Alfred Hitchcock over his rejected score for *Torn Curtain* (1966). Herrmann's music for *Sisters*, which made extensive use of a shrieking, spine-chilling choir, helped smooth out that movie's rough edges, and one of the many who took notice of this exceptionally thrilling score was William Friedkin, who wanted Herrmann for *The Exorcist*. Friedkin met with the composer, and the meeting went well. Relates Friedkin:

> [Herrmann] flew in from England; I showed him the rough cut and he loved the picture, and he wanted to do it, except he said he would not work in California. He didn't like California's musicians. He didn't want to work in Hollywood. He had been through all that and to hell with it. He had to record it in London and he had to get St. Giles Church, which has the greatest sound in there. I thought that was a marvelous idea if I

> had six months to finish the movie and let him just mail me the score. But I was making changes in the picture throughout and I wanted to dub the picture [in New York] because I love the facilities here.... I couldn't be in London and here, so I had to not use Bernard Herrmann. I didn't know who the hell to use then.

The reason the collaboration fell through will never be absolutely clear, and many apocryphal stories purport to apply to the situation. According to Christopher Palmer, writing on the composer's behalf when he was ill, Herrmann wanted to record in St. Giles because of its wonderful acoustics and because of its organ, which he hoped to use in his score; the problem was not displeasure with Los Angeles musicians. Palmer also wrote that Herrmann "hated the film and never really wanted to do it." According to director Larry Cohen (who immediately hired Herrmann to score his 1974 low-budget horror flick, *It's Alive*), Friedkin told the composer that he wanted a score that was better than the one Herrmann had written for *Citizen Kane*. To which the composer replied, "Well, why didn't you make a better picture than *Citizen Kane*?" and walked out. Given Herrmann's reputation for testiness and Friedkin's rather substantial ego, this movie could have been an interesting partnership.

After his first choice didn't work out, Friedkin decided to hire Lalo Schifrin, an Argentinian-born composer with a strong jazz background (he wrote, arranged, and played piano for Dizzy Gillespie in the late fifties and early sixties) who was best known at that time for his *Mission: Impossible* TV series theme, as well as scores for such popular films as *Cool Hand Luke* (1967), *Bullitt* (1968), and a half-dozen Clint Eastwood films, including *Dirty Harry* (1971) and *Magnum Force* (1973). Friedkin hoped to bring out the composer's experimentalist side, as heard in his score for George Lucas's *THX-1138*.

Schifrin attended a spotting session for the movie. But, expecting to have an intimate talk with the director about the musical approach needed, the composer found himself in the distracting presence of the dozen or so people Friedkin had brought along, who chatted and walked in and out of the screening room while the movie was playing. Following that jarring presentation, composer and director sat down to exchange ideas about how the score should work. Friedkin, for starters, envisioned "music that would operate in textures" and wanted to leave the movie's big scenes unscored, an idea that would grow into a major point of contention between him and Schifrin.

As he worked on the score, Schifrin would play through its cues on the piano for Friedkin. But the director was never completely sure of their applicability to the picture as he envisioned it. The first of Schifrin's music to be recorded was a six-minute piece for the trailer. Unfortunately, this first trailer's combination of terrifying images and intense music was deemed too disturbing and never made it into theaters.

Schifrin then prepared a number of cues (some for scenes that would eventually be left unscored). He wrote music for the opening in Iraq and Regan's hypnosis, as well as cues relating to the character of Father Karras. His most devilish idea was to have

Karras's dream sequence scored with a whispered Latin text to be played backward. At times he put in horror tags for "boo" moments; at others he provided pulsating suspense music.

A recording of what is now known as *Suite from the Unused Score to "The Exorcist"*—intense, dissonant music scored for string orchestra, five percussionists, keyboards, harp, and voices, which the composer considered "one of the best [scores] I've ever done"—was presented to Friedkin. Favoring textures and timbres over themes, the dramatic score leaned heavily on high, keening clusters, scurrying *divisi* passages, glissandi, and such out-of-the-ordinary techniques as *col legno battuto* bowing. The story of its reception by the director is convoluted, with each participant offering a different recollection of events. Following is how a few members of the production remember the situation.

Lalo Schifrin:

> So, [after viewing the trailer] the Warner Bros. executives told Friedkin to tell me that I must write a less dramatic and softer score. I could easily have done what they wanted perfectly well because it was way too simple in relation to what I'd previously written, but Friedkin didn't tell me what they said. Finally, I wrote the music for the film in the same vein as the trailer. In fact, when I wrote the trailer I was in the studio with Friedkin and he congratulated me for it. So, I thought I was in the right direction...but the truth was very different.

Mixer Robert "Buzz" Knudson:

> We were just starting work doing some predubbing on the picture, and Billy got a phone call from Lalo. He [Friedkin] said, "Come on, Buzz, we're going to go over and listen to the main title, they've just finished doing it." So we went over to hear what was going on. And over on the scoring stage there was, I believe, a ninety-piece orchestra. So Billy said, "OK, Lalo, let's hear it." Anyhow, Lalo was sitting there and they played this score, which was a beautiful score, but a big, full score that would have dominated the movie. When it was over, there was a kind of silence. And Billy got out of his chair and said, "Well, Lalo, it's never going to be in my movie." And that was it.

Editor Bud Smith:

> [Friedkin said,]"Sounds like f****** Mexican marimba music. I hate f****** Mexican music." And he threw it all out. Six weeks later on a dubbing stage at Todd-AO, he needed a piece of music. He said, "I remember something that Lalo did that maybe we can use here." The techie put the reel on, Friedkin listened to it, and hated it so much he went back in the machine room, grabbed the reel, ran out the front door, and threw it as far as he could into the parking lot across the street, saying, "That's where that f****** marimba music belongs."

After firing Schifrin, the director complained that his score had been "big, loud, scary, wall-to-wall, accent, accent." What he wanted, Friedkin said, was music that was "subtle and small. Not to scare audiences." He stated that "The music should be like a cold hand on the back of your neck, a chill presence that would never assert itself." At one point he even considered having no score for his picture at all, just demonic sound effects from sound consultant Ken Nordine. Nordine, a voiceover artist, was known at that time for recordings of his surreal stories with jazz accompaniment by members of Chico Hamilton's group, e.g., the album *Word Jazz*. For *The Exorcist,* he both provided some special sound effects and acted as star Linda Blair's vocal coach.

But the director eventually realized he needed some sort of music. After rejecting Schifrin's work, Friedkin called on Jack Nitzsche to write some short atonal pieces. Nitzsche was a legendary composer-arranger-conductor-producer who had worked with some of pop music's biggest names, including Phil Spector, the Beach Boys, the Rolling Stones, Neil Young, and many others. However, he provided only the opening cue, "Iraq" (which blended his own music with material by Krzysztof Penderecki), and a few short cues that utilized rubbed crystal wineglasses, producing a sound like that of the glass harmonica; these are heard, for example, during Father Merrin's arrival at the house. Nitzsche booked ten sessions with the London Symphony Orchestra but failed to deliver any more music due to a hand injury.

Another composer to become involved in this long musical saga was David Borden, a composer with strong minimalist and experimental leanings, perhaps best known as the founder of the early synthesizer ensemble Mother Mallard's Portable Masterpiece Co. Borden produced two pieces that would make their way into the picture, "Study No. 1" and "Study No. 2." Friedkin eventually went with what he called a "music score by Tower Records." Using head editor Jordan Leondopoulos's temp tracks (which featured some avant-garde and experimental-sounding compositions) as a guide, a highly unusual score for the picture was cobbled together from many existing recordings, à la the music for Stanley Kubrick's *2001: A Space Odyssey*. This would become one of the greatest anthology scores in film music history—though film music fans still debate its effectiveness in comparison with what we know of Schifrin's unused work.

Friedkin's musical vision for *The Exorcist* became a sampling of preexisting recordings of unusual music from contemporary and modern composers. Probably the best known of these recordings is Mike Oldfield's 1973 progressive-rock classic *Tubular Bells*. The other works come from some of the biggest names in twentieth-century concert music: Anton Webern (Five Pieces for Orchestra), Hans Werner Henze (Fantasia for Strings), George Crumb (*Black Angels*), and Krzysztof Penderecki (*Polymorphia*, String Quartet No 1, Cello Concerto, *The Devils of Loudun*, and *Kanon for Orchestra and Tape*).

The movie's original soundtrack LP became a best seller in no small part due to the inclusion of *Tubular Bells*, and yet the twenty-fifth anniversary release of the CD omitted the Oldfield material. For the first time, however, it contained whatever survived of Lalo Schifrin's music.

■ **Chinatown** (1974)

Original composer: **Phillip Lambro**
Replacement composer: **Jerry Goldsmith**

Chinatown, an intensely engaging and complex homage to the film noir genre, is a crime-filled story about how power and greed intersected with the challenge of bringing water to a rapidly expanding Los Angeles in the 1930s. It was written by Robert Towne, who would receive an Oscar for his work; produced by legendary former Paramount Pictures production head Robert Evans; and directed by Roman Polanski, in his first film made in America since the infamous 1969 murder of his wife, Sharon Tate. Polanski's previous credits included such critically acclaimed films as *Knife in the Water* (1962), *Repulsion* (1965), *Cul-de-Sac* (1966), and *Rosemary's Baby* (1968). *Chinatown* starred Jack Nicholson, Faye Dunaway, and John Huston and would be nominated for eleven Academy Awards.

For previous scores, Polanski had often turned to composer Krzysztof Komeda, but Komeda had died in a car accident in 1969. Musically rudderless, the director turned to Phillip Lambro for *Chinatown*. Lambro and Polanski had first met on the set of *Rosemary's Baby*, when actor-director John Cassavetes was considering hiring the composer to score his movie *Faces* (1968).

The twenty-plus minutes of jazz-based music Lambro came up with for *Chinatown* featured a main title theme played on saxophone and an infectious love theme for the relationship between Jake Gittes (Nicholson) and Evelyn Mulwray (Dunaway). The final reel's music, which the both the director and the composer were excited about, introduced some Chinese percussion instruments, musically anchoring the story's conclusion in Los Angeles's Chinatown.

Everyone seemed happy with the music. In fact, the composer wrote in his autobiography, *Close Encounters of the Worst Kind*, that Evans awarded him a $1,000 bonus for a job well done. But at that point Polanski reportedly invited one of his friends—the legendary Polish-born composer Bronislau Kaper, famous for scoring such classic movies as *Gaslight*, *Green Dolphin Street*, *The Red Badge of Courage*, the 1962 version of *Mutiny on the Bounty*, and *Lord Jim*—to take a sneak peak at the picture and offer his feedback.

Although enthusiastic about the movie, Kaper intensely disliked the score, especially the final reel. Surprisingly, given the reported bonus, Robert Evans joined him in his criticisms, saying he didn't understand how Polanski could have allowed his "rinky dink friend" to score the picture in the first place. Evans decided on the spot to have the movie rescored. (It may be worth noting that screenwriter Joe Eszterhas once wrote of Evans, "All lies ever told anywhere about Robert Evans are true.") Only two weeks remained till the picture's premiere, and the director initially objected, but he didn't have the final word.

Composer Jerry Goldsmith was invited to Evans's house to discuss writing a replacement score before Polanski left for Italy to direct a production of Alban Berg's opera *Lulu*. Previously, Goldsmith had scored such critical and box-office hits as *Seven Days in May* (1964), *The Sand Pebbles* (1966), *Planet of the Apes* (1968), *Tora! Tora! Tora!* (1970), and *Papillon* (1973). The film was spotted for Goldsmith in much the same way it had been for Lambro, and its sound was determined early on. Goldsmith remembers:

> In *Chinatown*, Bob Evans had fallen in love with "I Can't Get Started" by Bunny Berigan, and he thought the whole picture and the music should really have that flavor. Well, now that's tangible, we can pinpoint it. I explained, "I don't feel that that would be right for the film because the picture is the 1930s all over again, I grew up in Los Angeles, and that's amazingly enough the way it looked. I can remember this whole ambience as a kid. It's too much of a reemphasis of the thirties with that kind of music. Let me go into another direction." He understood and said, "You're right!" So here was one means of communication because we had the plans already set up.

For the underscore, written in just ten days, Goldsmith assembled an unusual ensemble: four harps, four pianos, strings, percussion, and solo trumpet. The latter instrument was played by Uan Rasey, whose sensitive performances would give the movie its heart and soul. Although rather short—clocking under thirty minutes for a two-hour movie—*Chinatown* remains one of the all-time most effective scores, an achievement that is all the more remarkable in view of the incredible time constraints faced by its composer. Polanski was pleased with Goldsmith's beautiful, laid-back, sun-bleached music, which combined sultry neo-noir jazz with evocative orchestral textures, and Evans went so far as to say the music saved the picture. The score earned Goldsmith his seventh Academy Award nomination (but he lost out to Nino Rota and Carmine Coppola, who took home the Oscar for their music for *The Godfather: Part II*).

In an odd turn of events, Paramount Pictures' promotions office decided it wanted to use parts of Lambro's score in its *Chinatown* television and radio ads and theatrical trailer. The composer seized on this opportunity to fetch back the rights to his work from the studio. In an unusual deal, he obtained total ownership of his score in return for allowing the studio to use it promotionally. The agreement contained an interesting additional condition: Should the score ever be released as a recording, that release could not contain any references to *Chinatown*.

Having previously issued the composer's *Crypt of the Living Dead* (1973) and *Murph the Surf* (1975), Robin Esterhammer and Perseverance Records hoped to issue Lambro's *Chinatown* score, with the idea of rerecording it in Prague on a $19,000 budget. To measure interest in the project as well as gather the needed capital, Perseverance announced a plan to reserve copies for anyone who invested ten dollars in the project. Only about a dozen people were willing to make that investment, so the planned release was canceled.

■ **Moses the Lawgiver** (1974)

Original composer: **Anthony Burgess**
Replacement composer: **Ennio Morricone**

Celebrated British author-critic-composer-translator Anthony Burgess first got involved with adapting Bible stories for television when he moved to Italy in 1970 and met producer Vincenzo Labella. (Burgess is famous for his many novels, among the best-known of which are his four Enderby books and *A Clockwork Orange*. Britain's *The Times* placed him on its list of "50 Greatest British Writers Since 1945.") With the help of British producer Sir Lew Grade and his Incorporated Television Co., and Radiotelevisione Italiana, Labella made a six-part television miniseries based on the book of Exodus, *Moses the Lawgiver,* starring Burt Lancaster. Between 1972 and 1974, Burgess wrote the series' six scripts. (A few years later he would publish an epic poem based on these screenplays, *Moses: A Narrative.*) While the production was under way in exotic locations, Burgess also worked on a musical score.

Despite his claim that he wrote an extensive amount of music for the series, Burgess's notebook shows that, out of a number of little pieces, only one was expanded beyond a piano sketch. In the end, his music for the production was never recorded or heard; instead, the series was eventually scored by the legendary Italian composer Ennio Morricone.

In his book *This Man and Music*, Burgess referred to "Music for television series *Moses* (unacceptable to Sir Lew Grade)." The author expanded upon that statement in *You've Had Your Time*, his second volume of autobiography:

> Having long had an ambition to write film-music, I inserted one or two little songs into the script. These, surprisingly, turned up in the workshop projection. One of them should not have turned up. I wrote it as a discardable obscene joke, but there it was, a marching song for the infanticidal Egyptian troops, trilled loudly in a variety of Palestinian accents.... I had a bigger and not at all coarse musical intention for *Moses*, and that was an entire orchestral score. I wrote a good deal of it, but the closed shop went into operation. Ennio Morricone composed the music, and Lew Grade tried to soothe me by commissioning words for the main theme, these to be sung by Barbra Streisand. It was decided finally that she had better not sing them.

Burgess's *Moses* music is discussed in detail by Paul Phillips in his book *A Clockwork Counterpoint: The Music and Literature of Anthony Burgess*. Phillips, who describes the types of music Burgess wrote for the series, reports that the writer-composer penned eighteen pieces totaling twenty-six pages in length. The only one expanded beyond its piano sketch was "Title Music," which, stylistically, builds on the Golden Age traditions of *Ben-Hur* (1959) and various other swashbuckling movies. Burgess also wrote two pieces that he later incorporated into his Third Symphony's first movement: His cheerful "Moses' Song" was written for the last episode of the show (and its words reprinted in *Moses: A Narrative*); "The Egyptian March" (reprinted in Phillips's book) seems to be another exercise in Golden Age–style composing, though its full impact is impossible to grasp from the sketch. The rest of the simple one-page sketches were mostly medieval-sounding chants and ancient-sounding dances.

A decade later, Burgess wrote several pieces of music for another Biblical television series produced by his friend Labella, *A.D.* (1985). Based on Burgess's historical novel *The Kingdom of the Wicked* and the screenplay he adapted from it, this British-Italian miniseries tells the stories of Saints Peter and Paul after the death of Jesus. Burgess's piece "Prelude" makes heavy use of the notes A and D, as in the title (and the Gregorian calendar). His other compositions for the picture include a solo organ piece for the amphitheater, two songs ("Roman Lullaby" and "Nero's Song"), "Roman March," and several cues for a full orchestra.

Producer Labella was keen to use whatever music Burgess had written, but both director Stuart Cooper and music producer Gilbert Marouani opposed the idea, hiring famous film composer Lalo Schifrin to provide the score. Since Marouani had previously said he was satisfied with Burgess's forty minutes' worth of music, Labella was in a difficult position. The series' credits list both Schifrin and Burgess as composers—Burgess receiving an "additional music" credit. However, the commercially available nine-hour version of the series doesn't contain any of his music. It's possible that the twelve-hour version has some of it, but it's also likely Labella wanted to be kind to his friend by at least giving him credit for the music he worked on, even if it didn't find its way into the picture. This and several other bad experience left Burgess frustrated and disillusioned with the film business for a good while.

An interesting final note: *Moses the Lawgiver* and *A.D.* form the first and last parts of a trilogy of Bible-based miniseries with screenplays by Burgess. The middle one is director Franco Zeffirelli's two-part *Jesus of Nazareth* (1977), produced by Lew Grade. Burgess's historical novel *Man of Nazareth* is based on his screenplay for this production.

■ **S*P*Y*S** (1974)

Composer for British version: **John Scott**
Composer for American version: **Jerry Goldsmith**

After their great success in Robert Altman's film *M*A*S*H* (1970), actors Donald Sutherland and Elliot Gould were paired once again for another comedy, *S*P*Y*S*. Unfortunately S*P*Y*S fell far short of *M*A*S*H* on every conceivable level; other than the aforementioned actors, the only things the two pictures had in common were their asterisks.

A critical disaster and box-office bomb, *S*P*Y*S* was produced by Irwin Winkler, Robert Chartoff, and Joseph Edwards and directed by Irvin Kirshner, whose notable previous credits included *Hoodlum Priest* (1961), *A Fine Madness* (1966), and *Up the Sandbox* (1972). At its heart, this transatlantic coproduction was nothing more than a series of loosely assembled, sadly unfunny scenes in which Sutherland and Gould, playing CIA agents, exchanged insults while entangled in an inexplicable international conspiracy. The picture also featured the 1960s iconic French model-turned-singer-turned-actress Zouzou, as a sexy anarchist.

Veteran British film composer John Scott was hired to pen the score. His music generally had a bit of a James Bond feel—the obligatory spy sound of its day—and his carousel-like main theme provided a comic nod toward Anton Karas's famous score for *The Third Man* (1949). Scott's score was quite an integral part of the movie, as the characters even sing his main theme as the end credits start rolling. This would seem to make its replacement a bit difficult.

Scott briefly discusses his work on *S*P*Y*S*:

> Director Irvin Kirshner briefed me on this film. He was very exact in communicating what he wanted the music to do. However, he was getting mixed messages from his producers. The film was fun. I thought there were hilarious moments. However, the outcome was that the Americans wanted one film and the Europeans wanted another. I have never heard Jerry Goldsmith's score, but he, without doubt, was my hero. Of course I was devastated when I heard that my score had been replaced for the U.S. version.

The people at 20th Century Fox didn't think Scott's score was overtly funny enough. With the action itself not being especially funny, Fox hoped the situation could be improved with the help of a new musical score, one that leaped out at the audience and tickled the funny bone in an obvious way. So the company quickly commissioned Jerry Goldsmith to come up with a replacement score for the American print.

And what a score Goldsmith delivered: campy musical silliness that is simply addictive, hilarious 1970s kitsch, and electronics that sound like baby premonitions of *Gremlins* (1984) and *Link* (1986). Among its best moments are the whispering ensemble cue ("spyhyhys") and the Oriental-sounding adaptation of Beethoven's Fifth Symphony ("Who's Paying"). Throughout, Goldsmith's musical puns respond to visual cues, desperately trying to make us chuckle. (When this short score appeared on the six-disc celebratory compilation *Jerry Goldsmith at 20th Century Fox*, the composer had only one thing to say: "Wow. You also found *S*P*Y*S*.")

Two decades later, composer John Scott would find himself in another intercontinental film-music dispute, this time regarding the picture *North Star* (1996). For this bleak adventure set during the Alaskan gold rush, Scott composed muscular orchestral music in the vein of old Western scores. But American production company Regency Enterprises failed to appreciate it, and commissioned Australian composer Bruce Rowland to write a new score solely for the American market (the film's European prints retained Scott's music). Rowland recorded his music, an orchestral-style synth-score, in his home studio. His synthesized music was meant to emphasize the picture's cold setting and offer audiences a slightly more modern sound. *North Star* is regularly shown with both scores, but Scott's music is better known because he released it on his own JOS Records label. Unfortunately his *S*P*Y*S* music remains unreleased (as does Rowland's *North Star* score).

■ Profondo Rosso/Deep Red (1975)

Original composer: **Giorgio Gaslini**
Replacement composer: **Goblin**

Music has always been important to acclaimed Italian horror movie director Dario Argento, and by 1975 (still very early in his career), he had worked with a couple of very good composers, including Ennio Morricone, who scored his *Bird with the Crystal Plumage* (1970) and *Cat o' Nine Tails* (1971). By 1971, however, the director's tastes were turning away from the conventional film music sound, and for his film *Four Flies on Grey Velvet* (1971) he wanted to hire the British rock band Deep Purple (who agreed to the commission). But it turned out that Argento was contractually obligated to use an Italian composer, and he again went with Morricone, who delivered a score that was quite different from his usual fare, one that clearly demonstrated Argento's interest in moving beyond traditional orchestral film music.

For the 1975 *Profondo Rosso*, the director sought the services of Italian composer Giorgio Gaslini, a well-known pianist-composer and pioneering figure in Italian jazz and avant-garde improvised music, with whom Argento had worked on his 1973 black comedy *La Cinque giornate* and two episodes of the 1973 Italian television show *Door into Darkness* ("Il Tram" and "Testimone oculare").

But the Argento-Gaslini collaboration didn't go smoothly this time. Music has a pivotal role in *Profondo Rosso*—a melody played on the piano becomes a key to finding a killer—and Argento had very specific ideas about it. Gaslini's source cues worked out just fine, with the composer himself appearing in the movie to play them. He also provided the memorable leitmotif for the killer. But the rest of Gaslini's music did not jibe with the director's vision for this movie; Argento liked it but envisioned his film with a more pop and rock sound. To achieve this, he turned to the group Goblin, which had enjoyed some success in the world of alternative rock but had little experience in film scoring.

Goblin—known as Cherry Five before working on *Profondo Rosso*—was a progressive rock group inspired by such bands as Yes, King Crimson, and Emerson, Lake & Palmer. At the time of this, their first film score, their personnel was Claudio Simonetti (keyboards), Massimo Morante (guitars), Fabio Pignatelli (bass guitar), and Walter Martino (drums). The band recalls taking on this type of work for the first time:

> All began from some arguments between Dario Argento (who wanted a more modern sound) and Gaslini, who didn't feel able to satisfy him. So they called us.... [W]e spent three days composing the music of the film in Claudio's house. So "Profondo rosso," "Death Dies," and "Mad Puppet" are all by us. "Wild Session" and "Deep Shadows" are our performances of Gaslini's songs, while "School at Night" and "Gianna" have been left in their original composition and execution.... Suddenly Argento asked us to compose some real rock songs, which had to be different from the usual "hard" arrangement of a ready-made melody. That very night, while playing in Claudio's house, we wrote the song which sold more than one million copies!

In the final film, about half of the music is—in one form or another—Gaslini's. Some cues from his original orchestral score were retained, as was some source music (including the jazz ensemble music heard at the opening). But a good deal of his material was rescored by Goblin, who performed it on electric guitars and synthesizers, stylistically reinterpreting it in their own unique fashion. Other cues are original songs by Goblin, and the inclusion of these not only opened a new chapter in Italian film scoring, but it proved influential on a broader scale: One can hear a definite Goblin influence on John Carpenter's genre-defining music for his early horror movies.

The resulting *Profondo Rosso* soundtrack sold more than a million copies and lasted fifty-two weeks on the Italian music charts, proving the commercial viability of Argento's ideas about nontraditional horror movie scoring. The director himself came under the spell of Goblin and employed the group on many of his future projects.

■ Robin and Marian (1976)

Original composer: **Michel Legrand**
Replacement composer: **John Barry**

Robin and Marian is an unusual cinematic telling of the Robin Hood legend, showing its lead characters in the autumn years of their lives, though still involved with such old familiar folk as the Sheriff of Nottingham, Richard the Lionheart, and Little John. And at the end of this version of the tale, both Robin and Marian, played by Sean Connery and Audrey Hepburn, perish tragically. Directed by Richard Lester (known in the 1960s for his Beatles movies, *A Hard Day's Night* and *Help!*, and such comedies as *A Funny Thing Happened on the Way to the Forum* and *How I Won the War*), *Robin and Marian* enjoyed mixed reviews and mediocre box-office returns.

Director Lester's initial choice for composer was Michel Legrand, with whom he had worked on *The Three Musketeers* (1973). Legrand reportedly based his *Robin and Marian* score on highly regarded British concert composer Sir Michael Tippett's early string works (probably his popular Concerto for Double String Orchestra, *Little Music for Strings*, and perhaps *Fantasia Concertante on a Theme of Corelli*, all of which feature intricate counterpoint). But on presenting his finished work to the director, he received mixed messages. Lester generally liked the score, but felt that some of its complicated cues were too busy. A second session was held to rerecord the problem cues, which the composer had now simplified—but even that music was deemed inappropriate for the film. Legrand remembers being disheartened and perplexed by the director's reactions:

> Lester's a weird fellow; I didn't get along with him. He chickens out, he worries all the time. I wrote for Robin a concerto grosso for solo violin, solo cello, and double string orchestra, and he told me my music was so good that, if he uses it, it'll distract from the film. I told him he was wrong, that it'd be the opposite, that it would add something more.

Executive producer Ray Stark (producer of such films as *Night of the Iguana*, *Funny Girl*, and *The Way We Were*) found Legrand's contribution to be underwhelming (although he stated this with harsher words). With only two weeks to spare before the movie's release, Stark approached Maurice Jarre to write a new score, but the French composer was intimidated by the prospect of replacing Legrand's score, not to mention having only fourteen days in which to do it. Stark then turned to John Barry, an institution in British film scoring, with whom Lester had already worked on such pictures as *The Knack...and How to Get It* (1965) and *Petulia* (1968). (Incidentally, Lester had reservations about hiring Barry, despite the fact that the composer had written some of his most innovative works for his pictures.)

There was little communication between the composer and the filmmakers, who relied on their knowledge of Barry's previous work as an indication of what he would do on *Robin and Marian*: In short, they expected a memorable love theme and some action music. Barry remembers writing the score:

> Richard could not stay in Los Angeles, he had another movie [*The Ritz*] he had started in London, and so it was telephone conversations. It was one of those rush jobs: I had literally [no time] from seeing the movie to recording it, because they had a release date.... I wrote it in the Beverly Hills Hotel, Bungalow 15, and I think Richard was happy with some of it and unhappy with other parts. It's very difficult when you're doing a movie and the director sits 6,000 miles away. Columbia were delighted with the score I did, a romantic adventure score.

While Barry's score does have a memorable if relatively subdued love theme, its main characteristic is not the lush string themes the composer is known for. In *Robin and Marian* the woodwinds take center stage, nicely fitting the romance of the gracefully aging couple. There is, of course, action music as well, with thumping tympani and rousing brass for the battles and riding sequences. Barry's original bare-bones approach to the action writing was pumped up by American television composer Richard Shores, who was called in by Columbia Pictures to do some last-minute revisions so the music would fit Ray Stark's expectations. What Shores did was basically reorchestrate some of Barry's cues, often adding more percussion. He also composed one original track—which sounds out of place in the picture—providing a final twist in the long and varied musical saga of *Robin and Marian*. Looking back, Barry would be all but dismissive about his score, because of the way it had been twisted and recast by Stark and Shores.

For soundtrack-collector completists, Legrand's rejected score was released by Universal France, along with his music for the 1973 version of *The Three Musketeers*. A short suite of Legrand's unused music, titled "Sean and Audrey," is also available on the compilation CD *Le Cinéma de Michel Legrand*.

■ **Todo modo** (1976)

Original composer: **Charles Mingus**
Replacement composer: **Ennio Morricone**

Bassist-composer-bandleader Charles Mingus is one of the most important figures in jazz history, yet his film music output is rarely discussed, even though he worked on several interesting projects. For instance, he was the first composer on John Cassavetes' 1959 story of interracial romance, *Shadows*, which was eventually scored with improvised saxophone solos by Shafi Hadi, who performed and recorded frequently with Mingus. (Mingus has an "additional music" credit on *Shadows*.)

His frustrating experience on *Shadows* kept Mingus away from further film scoring until he met Italian producer Daniel Senatore and his filmmaking partner, director Elio Petri. Together, the two had helmed the Oscar-winning crime story *Investigation of a Citizen Above Suspicion* (1970), which dealt with police corruption and cover-ups. This producer-director duo was about to tap into an even more controversial topic with their adaptation of Leonardo Sciascia's novel *Todo modo* (whose title comes from St. Ignatius of Loyola's statement "All means are good to find the divine will"). The surreal picture was a powerful indictment of Italy's anticommunist, Roman Catholic–allied Christian Democratic Party and its leader at the time, Prime Minister Aldo Moro. It satirized Italy's power elite and the unholy union of church and state through the story of a retreat run by a world-weary priest (played by Marcello Mastroianni), to which Italy's power moguls come for enlightenment but instead are murdered.

While director Petri wasn't particularly involved with the film's music, Senatore, who hired Mingus, was quite passionate about it, and felt that the jazz legend's involvement would bring added publicity, because the often outspoken composer was considered to be something of a social activist. Senatore asked Mingus to write a jazz score that blended Italian musical elements with his own distinct voice. And that's just what the composer did—without seeing a single frame of the movie.

The Third Stream–ish score utilized a *Godfather*-like theme to establish the film's Italian setting and provide links between musical Mingusisms. Mingus also incorporated an upbeat, bluesy version of his "Peggy's Blue Skylight," which acted as interesting counterpoint to some of the screen's macabre moments.

Mingus traveled to Italy to record his music on March 29 and 30 at Umiliani Studios and then on March 31 and April 1 at the Dirmaphon Studio, where the film could be projected and he would finally get the chance to see how his music worked with the picture. His ensemble consisted of regular Mingus collaborators George Adams (tenor sax, flute), Jack Walrath (trumpet), Danny Mixon (piano, organ), and Dannie Richmond (drums), along with local musicians hired to play oboe, bass clarinet, bassoon, alto sax, and trombone; Mingus took care of the bass part himself. After recording his score, the composer flew back to America.

And then his score was dropped from the picture. The often-repeated rumor about why it was cut claims that director Petri, who wasn't wild about the idea of a jazz score to begin with, jettisoned Mingus's music when popular entertainer and musician Renzo Arbore claimed that it used some of his old music. Although Arbore later denied this statement, Petri quickly commissioned a new score from Ennio Morricone, who had provided the music for Petri's *Investigation of a Citizen Above Suspicion*. Morricone wrote a new score in a matter of days.

Two years after *Todo modo*'s premiere, Aldo Moro was kidnapped and murdered by the Red Brigades. Because the character who represented Moro in *Todo modo* was killed at the end of the picture as well, the movie was banned from Italian television, and no home video was released. Consequently, it is almost impossible to see, and its music is one of the few Morricone scores not released on disc. However, twenty-two minutes of Charles Mingus's score lived on (on a CD titled *Cumbia & Jazz Fusion*) and eventually became one of the composer's own favorites.

(*Note*: Despite Mingus's frustrated film-scoring efforts, recordings of him performing his own compositions are heard in a number of feature films, including *One True Thing*, *Jerry Maguire*, and *The Notorious Bettie Page*.)

■ The Last Hard Men (1976)

Original composer: **Leonard Rosenman**
Replacement music: **Excerpts from Jerry Goldsmith Western scores**

The Last Hard Men, a Western starring Charlton Heston and James Coburn, is the violent tale of an escaped convict who wreaks vicious and protracted revenge on the retired lawman who arrested him and killed his wife. It was directed by Andrew V. McLaglen, who had a long history of directing both film and television Westerns, particularly John Wayne movies, including *McLintock!* (1963), *Cahill U.S. Marshall* (1965), and *Chisum* (1970), as well as such Jimmy Stewart Westerns as *Shenandoah* (1965) and *The Rare Breed* (1966).

The picture was scored by Leonard Rosenman, whose previous film credits included *East of Eden* (1955), *The Cobweb* (1955, considered the first major Hollywood film score to use twelve-tone techniques extensively), *Fantastic Voyage* (1966), *A Man Called Horse* (1970), and 151 episodes of the television series *Combat*. Although he could write lush, traditional fare, his influential modernist scores that employed an elegant style of atonality were greatly responsible for revitalizing and updating the Hollywood music scene. (Interesting note: When he was a young New York concert composer, Rosenman was drawn into film music by his friend and piano student actor James Dean, who introduced him to Elia Kazan, who hired him to score *East of Eden*. Throughout his life, Rosenman kept one foot in the concert music world, and he succinctly delineated that music's difference from film music: "In the concert field, everything is related to form. In the film field, the form is that of the film.")

The Last Hard Men was not destined to be one of the composer's successes. The composer himself felt the picture was "dreadful," but he was intrigued by director McLaglen's proposal to score it with modernist music. The version first shown to Rosenman had even been temped with a crazy-quilt of avant-garde music. The director's aesthetic reasoning was that, since the story takes place in the early twentieth century, when atonal music was a novel and exciting device, the film's music should break away from the Hollywood Western's usual Americana-type underscoring and saloon music and instead reflect that era's musical innovations.

Rosenman responded with a score that contained, in his words, "the wildest way-out music," and 20th Century Fox responded by throwing it out and replacing it with music from the studio's vault. The replacement score, credited to Jerry Goldsmith, utilized material from his scores for *100 Rifles* (1969) and *Stagecoach* (1966, a remake of the 1939 classic). His credit on the film is simply "music," as opposed to the common "original music." (Incidentally, at the same time that his old scores were finding a new home in *The Last Hard Men*, Goldsmith was working on what would be his Academy Award–winning music for *The Omen*.) *The Last Hard Men*'s use of preexisting music obviously wasn't publicized when the picture was released, and it was up to serious Goldsmith fans to piece together the music's true sources. In the end, amid the movie's mostly negative reviews, its score would be one of the few elements to meet with a positive reaction.

Today, almost every film of any importance has an original score written specifically for it. The primary exceptions are films furnished with what could be called anthology scores, compiled from great and/or popular and/or unique music found on preexisting recordings. Among the most notable cases of this approach are *2001: A Space Odyssey* (1968), *The Exorcist* (1973), and *Goodfellas* (1990).

■ Fun with Dick and Jane (1977)

Original composer: **Billy Goldenberg**
Replacement composer: **Ernest Gold**

Composer-conductor-arranger-pianist-songwriter Billy Goldenberg arrived in Hollywood in the 1960s and soon became one of its most reliable television composers. He scored an endless number of series, pilots, main themes, and other projects, including episodes of *Columbo* and *Kojak*, and received twenty-two Emmy nominations for his work. One of Goldenberg's most famous scores was written for director Steven Spielberg's strange television movie *Duel* (1971), for which the composer provided strikingly eerie music. (Earlier, he had worked with the director on a couple of episodes of the television series *Night Gallery* and *The Name of the Game*.)

Goldenberg became known as a musical doctor who could save problematic projects. One of these was the Barbra Streisand movie *Up the Sandbox* (1972). Goldenberg had worked as an arranger on Streisand's 1965 hit television special *My Name is Barbra*, and when she proved dissatisfied with *Sandbox*'s two previous scores (by famed jazz and television composer-arrangers Neal Hefti and Nelson Riddle), she brought him in to write a third.

In Goldenberg's next encounter with a replacement score, the score being replaced would be his own. After a disastrous test screening of *Peeper* (1975), director Peter Hyams' failed spoof of 1940s detective movies, producer Irwin Winkler asked the composer to rewrite his music to make it more overtly comedic. Goldenberg refused, and his material was replaced with a score by television composer Richard Clements.

Not long afterward came director Ted Kotcheff's *Fun with Dick and Jane*, which starred George Segal and Jane Fonda as Dick and Jane Harper, a down-on-their-luck rich couple who turn to a life of crime to reclaim their social status. Goldenberg took the assignment during a period when he was coping with an especially heavy workload, and *Fun with Dick and Jane* turned out to be one of the worst scores of his career. Even the composer himself called it terrible. He was eventually fired from the project, to be replaced by the Oscar-winning composer for such classics as *On the Beach* (1959) and *Exodus* (1960), Ernest Gold. Gold penned an amusing score that included the title credits song "Ahead of the Game."

Even though Goldenberg saw his *Fun with Dick and Jane* score rejection coming and even seemed to agreed with it, the firing took a toll on him, triggering a creative dry spell that would last for almost a year. Once recovered from his disappointment, he would work steadily as a Hollywood composer for two more decades. But his disillusionment with the business and the changes in the way television scores were produced eventually led this remarkable composer to retire from this sort of composing, with unfortunately few CD releases of his scores.

■ The White Buffalo (1977)

Original composer: **David Shire**
Replacement composer: **John Barry**

In the wake of Steven Spielberg's mega-successful *Jaws* (1975), Dino De Laurentiis produced a trio of movies about huge, rampaging beasts—*King Kong* (1976), *The White Buffalo* (1977), *and Orca* (1977). His reimagining of the classic 1933 *King Kong* conquered theater box offices faster than its eponymous ape climbed the World Trade Center.

The White Buffalo, starring action hero Charles Bronson, was directed by J. Lee Thompson, whose previous credits included three now-classic Gregory Peck films: *The Guns of Navarone* (1961), *Cape Fear* (1962), and *Mackenna's Gold* (1969). Misjudging the film, De Laurentiis marketed it as yet another rampaging beast flick, just like his *King Kong*. But instead of a havoc-wreaking buffalo, audiences were treated to an artsy philosophical and symbolic tale not unlike *Moby Dick* set on the American plains, about Wild Bill Hickok (and his fear of impending death), the declining West, and sacred Native American culture. This inappropriate marketing caused *The White Buffalo* to meet an untimely box-office death. (In a further misguided bit of marketing, the movie would be retitled *Hunt to Kill* for its network television premiere—perpetrating an even sillier deception on unsuspecting viewers.)

To score the movie, De Laurentiis turned to David Shire, a busy composer noted for his unique, beautiful, and hypnotic solo piano score for Francis Ford Coppola's *The Conversation* (1974); his funky *The Taking of Pelham One Two Three* (1974) score, which employed serial techniques; his sultry music for *Farewell, My Lovely* (1975); and his minimal score for *All the President's Men* (1976). In contrast with his unusual and innovative music for those films, however, and perhaps guided by De Laurentiis's concept of the picture, Shire saw *The White Buffalo* as an opportunity to try his hand at the more conventional Western genre.

But, the film's screenwriter, Richard Sale, who had adapted his own novel for the film, didn't view the picture as a Western per se. He apparently lobbied De Laurentiis for a new score, one less beholden to the Western's traditions. In fact, Sale specifically requested British composer John Barry. Barry's sole previous Western score—for *Monte Walsh* (1970)—employed an emotional voice that differed from the typical Americana sound. Barry remembers hearing from De Laurentiis and Sale:

> *White Buffalo* was finished just before Christmas, and somebody had done a score prior to that, but it wasn't working out. Dino was frantic. He called me and said, "John, this score is not working. You have to do *The White Buffalo* for me!" He also said that the guy who kept asking for me was the writer. Dino said: "I want to call the writer up on Christmas Day and say, 'Your Christmas present is John Barry, the composer, all right already?!'" I said, "Sure." Dino gave the happy writer my phone number, and we talked a long time on Christmas Day.

Barry (who had, incidentally, previously scored De Laurentiis's *King Kong*) provided one of his most unusual scores for *The White Buffalo*. It had an atonal main theme and many exciting percussion-heavy cues (not all of which would make it onto the soundtrack's official CD). There also is, of course, the obligatory love theme.

Sadly, most of John Barry's score cannot be enjoyed to its fullest as a soundtrack recording. Lacking master tapes, Chris Neel and Prometheus Records had to resurrect the music from monaural mix-downs and a dubbing tape, with the unwelcome result that a few tracks have faint dialogue in the background. As for Shire's score, it was never released, apart from two chunks of source music that he arranged and conducted and that were retained in the picture. These are "Camptown Medley #1" and "Camptown Medley #2," which appear on the Prometheus CD.

■ Shoot the Sun Down (1978)

Original composer: **Bruce Langhorne**
Replacement composers: **Ed Bogas and Judy Munsen**

The little-known film *Shoot the Sun Down* was first-time writer/director David Leeds's take on the spaghetti Western genre, and his only feature film. An independent picture shot on a minimal budget, it is the tale of a motley assortment of characters who search for, find, and try to get away with a cache of Aztec gold. It is notable for an early Christopher Walken performance, just before he made it big with his Oscar-winning role in *The Deer Hunter* (1978). It also featured Margot Kidder just before her big break in *Superman* (1978).

Nearly all of *Shoot the Sun Down*'s score was provided by legendary folk-rock session guitarist/multi-instrumentalist Bruce Langhorne. In the 1960s, Langhorne was heard on recordings by Bob Dylan, Richie Havens, Joan Baez, Odetta, Gordon Lightfoot, and myriad other folk-based performers. Before working on Leeds's film, he had scored two movies directed by Peter Fonda, *The Hired Hand* (1971) and *Idaho Transfer* (1973). The only music not provided by Langhorne for *Shoot the Sun Down* was an original song by singer-songwriter Kinky Friedman, an unusual character who has written twenty-three novels, run for governor of Texas (in 2006), and led a country band called The Texas Jewboys.

While *Shoot the Sun Down* may have been great fun for all involved, director Leeds had a hard time finding a distributor for it. Once he managed to do that, he was asked to re-edit his movie, tightening up its 130 minutes. He agreed and started the re-editing, but before he could finish, the distributor went out of business, leaving Leeds with a half-recut film. Eventually a new distributor put up the money to finish it, but the re-editing meant that a new score would be needed. In an interview conducted more than twenty-five years later, the director looked back on his movie's music:

> The original version had a largely acoustic and slide guitar score by Bruce Langhorne, who had done Peter Fonda's film *The Hired Hand*, a movie I admired with a score I loved. There was also a wonderful end-title ballad by Kinky Friedman. He wrote the song for the movie, and it was terrific. I wish it were still in, along with most of the original score, in retrospect. Although I would have added some of the percussive, Spaghetti Western effects as well. While I liked both the original score and song, we had decided that the film needed a more aggressive score to propel the narrative, so I went for a very Kurosawaesque, more percussive feeling—with a little Spaghetti thrown in. Actually, some of the percussive stuff was a direct reference to Kurosawa—I had the composer watch *Seven Samurai* and *Yojimbo*.

The new music was provided by Ed Bogas (credited as "Bogus") and Judy Munsen, who were primarily known for their work in animation: Bogas, a member of the short-lived (1967–68) yet influential experimental/progressive/psychedelic band the United States of America, had composed the scores for Ralph Bakshi's animated features

Fritz the Cat (1972) and *Heavy Traffic* (1973). And he and Munsen, as a team, took over scoring the many Charlie Brown animated TV movies produced after the 1976 death of composer/jazz pianist Vince Guaraldi, who had given the first crop of Charlie Brown movies their easily identifiable light-jazz sound.

Bogas and Munsen's propulsive, percussive score for *Shoot the Sun Down* is a good example of why composers shouldn't be pigeonholed by genre (animation, in their case). Their music, delivered on a shoestring budget, still holds up well today. Unfortunately, David Leeds's movie never received wide distribution. Its theatrical distributor released it only in the Southeast and Southwest. So, except by those who happened to stumble across its fairly obscure VHS tape release, the movie remains largely unseen (and its score, of course, largely unheard). Its memory is preserved primarily by Christopher Walken fans, who cherish the picture.

As more and more directors tried to make their mark in the 1970s, the market became saturated with small (usually low-budget) independent pictures that, like *Shoot the Sun Down*, often weren't released until years after their production. A fun example is *Invisible Strangler* (1976), a tale of a convict who learns how to become invisible, enabling him to take revenge on those who sent him to prison. The film is best known for featuring Sue Lyon, of *Lolita* (1962) fame, in an unusual role (one of her last, since she retired in 1980). It had to wait eight years (until 1984) to get released—with, by then, a new title and new score, thanks to extensive re-edits. The picture currently haunts the low-budget independent movie scene in two versions: *Invisible Strangler* and *The Astral Factor*, each of which has its own score. The original version was scored by Bill Marx, son of Harpo; Richard Hieronymous and Alan Oldfield scored the re-edit.

■ Casey's Shadow (1978)

Original composer: **Elmer Bernstein**
Replacement composer: **Patrick Williams**

Casey's Shadow, based on John McPhee's short story "Ruidoso" and starring Walter Matthau, is a feel-good, happy-ending movie about a hard-drinking, down-on-his-luck Louisiana horse trainer, a young boy (Casey), and his horse (Casey's Shadow). Director Martin Ritt, whose previous credits included such now-classic films as *Paris Blues* (1961), *Hud* (1963), *The Spy Who Came in from the Cold* (1965), and *Hombre* (1967), hired *Hud*'s composer, the legendary Elmer Bernstein, to score it.

Bernstein approached *Casey's Shadow* with the same kind of folk-oriented ideas that characterized his fairly minimal *Hud* score, which was written for four guitars. For *Casey's Shadow* he wrote a main theme for accordion accompanied by a strummed guitar. The horse's maturing was mirrored by the music, which grew more fully orchestrated with each passing cue, all leading up to a great Americana-style closing piece. In addition to his underscore, Bernstein penned an original song, "A Chance to Grow and Watch the World Unfold" (with lyrics by Harlan Goodman), a lovely little piece about the role of home, sharing, and discovering the world. This splendid children's song was written to accompany a montage paralleling the horse's growth and Casey's maturing.

Director Ritt seemed pleased with the score—unlike producer Ray Stark, who decided not to use it and eventually hired Patrick Williams to rescore the movie. Williams was expected to bring to the movie the lively sound that had made him one of the most sought-after names in television scoring (with credits that included *The Streets of San Francisco*, *The Mary Tyler Moore Show*, *The Bob Newhart Show*, and numerous made-for-TV movies). The backbone of Williams's underscore is the horse's simple guitar theme, which is heard during most of the animal's antics. (The best version of this theme is found in the cue "Shadow Grows.") Yet the score also contains some strangely out-of-place elements, the most distracting of which are the funky licks (resembling very distant relatives of *Shaft*) underscoring some of the racing scenes.

From the producer's point of view, however, the movie's songs were primary. Of these, only the main song, "Just Let Me Go till I'm Gone," was penned by Williams (with lyrics written by Will Jennings). Sung by Dobie Gray (best known for his chart-topping "The 'In' Crowd" in 1965 and "Drift Away" in 1973), it seems to have been written to hit the pop charts rather than fit snugly into the movie. To give the Louisiana setting some local color, New Orleans fixture Dr. John provided the film's other songs—"Coonass," which he wrote, and the Cajun classic "Jolie Blonde."

A considerable chunk of Williams's score was released on a Columbia LP but hasn't been reissued on CD. Sadly, a recording of Bernstein's score for *Casey's Shadow*, like his music from *Hud*, has never been released.

■ **Dawn of the Dead/Zombi** (1978)

Composers for international version: **Goblin**
Music for American version: **De Wolfe Music Library**

Ten years after striking gold with his 1968 hit zombie flick *Night of the Living Dead*, Pittsburgh's homegrown horror-movie writer-director-producer George A. Romero set out to make its sequel, *Dawn of the Dead*. But in spite of *Night of the Living Dead*'s success, he was having trouble finding funding for his new project, because his last picture, the quirky vampire movie *Martin* (1977), had been a financial failure. (Interestingly, the darkly moody, low-key *Martin* is reported to be Romero's favorite of his own movies.) Seeking an investor-distributor for *Dawn of the Dead*, he sent its script all over the world. A copy landed on the table of Italian horror-movie writer-director-producer Dario Argento, who liked it and set up a meeting with Romero at the U.S. premiere of Argento's *Profondo rosso*. The two became friends, and Argento invited the American filmmaker to Italy to finish his script and rewrite certain sections based on the Italian director's ideas.

Once the script was finished, the film's production budget was secured—Argento came up with $250,000 and Romero's investors contributed the same. In return for his investment, Argento acquired the picture's international distribution and, importantly, the right to re-edit it for the international market if he so desired.

With cost-efficiency high on his priority list, Romero decided that instead of commissioning an original score for *Dawn of the Dead,* he'd use the services of De Wolfe Music, a production music library and licensing company from which he could select music in almost any style and license it for a reasonable price, as he had done on *Night of the Living Dead.* Interestingly, Romero not only selected cues from De Wolfe's horror section but also licensed some comedic tracks that would turn out to be some of the most memorable musical moments in *Dawn of the Dead*'s score. The best-known of these cues is Herbert Chappell's "The Gonk," a comic polka-like number that's heard accompanied by zombie growling during the end credits. In addition to De Wolfe's music, *Dawn of the Dead*'s big montage scene used the song "Cause I'm a Man" (written by Cliff Twemlow using the pen name Peter Reno and performed by Pretty Things, a popular mid-sixties British rock band, on their LP *Electric Banana*).

Dario Argento didn't like the De Wolfe music. He had other ideas about both the film's editing and its music. Romero looks back on the Italian's changes: "I don't agree with the montage done by Argento on the European version of the movie.... Taking away one hour of the film, Dario reduced it to a 'splatter' video clip.... In the end he didn't care about the story of the movie, which, according to me, is wonderful."

Argento insisted that his cut have an original score. Using Romero's library music as a template, Argento's international version—retitled *Zombi*—was supplied with new music. He hired his regular collaborators the Italian rock band Goblin to rescore his new, shorter cut of the movie (adding to their material a few classical-sounding bits of stock music from his own sources). Goblin had previously provided great scores—with great soundtrack album sales—for Argento's *Profondo rosso* (1975) and *Suspiria* (1977). Their score for *Dawn of the Dead/Zombi* would turn out to be the last stint with their most famous lineup: Claudio Simonetti (keyboards), Massimo Morante (guitars), Fabio Pignatelli (bass guitar), Agostino Marangolo (drums) and Tony Tartarini (vocals).

Goblin managed to produce one of its most entertaining scores for *Zombi.* The band had a field day composing cues ranging in style from the burlesque-like "Torte in faccia" to the disco-influenced "Zaratozom." The music's signature track is the eerie "L'Alba dei morti viventi," which utilizes a spooky-sounding keyboard part. With this film, Argento expanded on his producer-distributor-editor roles, giving himself a music credit too, although his only real music contributions had been the instructions and inspiration he gave the band. (Local distributors throughout the world would later jump on the rescoring bandwagon; for example, a Japanese-dubbed version that premiered on television used music from Goblin's *Suspiria* score.)

Romero was reluctant to use any of Goblin's music; in his "extended version" prepared for screening at Cannes, he relied on the De Wolfe music, utilizing more than sixty cues from the company's vault. He relented when an American theatrical version was prepared, however, using three Goblin cues. (In a related note, when Dario Argento went on to pick up European distribution of Romero's *Martin*, he would retitle the picture *Wampyr* and replaced its original Donald Rubinstein score with one by—who else?—Goblin.)

When Goblin's soundtrack for *Dawn of the Dead/Zombi* was released on CD in 1998 to commemorate the film's twentieth anniversary, it was chock-full of additional tracks. These included various arrangements of the main themes—which further highlighted the band's stylistic versatility—and a collection of zombie growls. And with the eventual release of all of Romero's zombie movies on DVD, fans could conveniently compare the differences in their major versions. They could also see a new one: The thirtieth-anniversary DVD of *Night of the Living Dead* actually removed old footage and music, replacing it with new scenes and a new score by Scott Vladimir Licina. Like his zombies, Romero doesn't seem to rest...

■ **Patrick** (1978)

Composer for Australian version: **Brian May**
Composers for European version: **Goblin**

Patrick is a strange little stylishly directed horror movie from Down Under director Richard Franklin, whose early career was marked by such lowbrow sexploitation comedies as *The True Story of Eskimo Nell* (1975) and *Fantasm* (1976), and his mature career by more mainstream and critically applauded films such as *Psycho II* (1983) and *Hotel Sorrento* (1995). *Patrick* is the story of a young man who falls into a coma after murdering his mother and her lover. While comatose, he unleashes murder and mayhem via highly developed psychokinetic powers.

The film was scored by composer Brian May (who is not to be confused with the guitarist from the band Queen). Today, May is best known for his scores for *Mad Max* (1979), for which he won the Australian Film Institute Award for Best Score, and *Mad Max 2* (also known in the United States as *The Road Warrior*, 1981); he had worked previously with director Franklin on *Eskimo Nell*. For *Patrick*, May delivered a deliciously dark and twisted score that opened with a heavenly main title before moving into suspenseful cues that leaned heavily on strings and shimmering percussion. May even delivered a touch of feel-good romantic pop music, with "Kathy's Theme."

The movie was picked up for European distribution by Dino De Laurentiis, who chose, of course, to replace its score. His problem with the music wasn't so much a matter of disliking it; he simply felt it didn't have hit potential (at the time, May was barely known outside Australia). So the producer-distributor had the movie rescored by the popular Italian band Goblin, hoping for another hit soundtrack record that, like Goblin's *Profondo rosso* or *Zombi*, would help bolster the film's box-office revenues. De Laurentiis also had a much more down-to-earth reason for the score replacement: To speed up *Patrick*'s pacing, he had the movie cut from 112 minutes to 96 for its foreign run. Thanks to this bit of trimming, a new score was all but unavoidable.

Patrick was one of the weaker film scores from Goblin, which now consisted of Carlo Pennisi, Maurizio Guarini (replacing longtime keyboardist Claudio Simonetti), Agostino Marangolo, and Antonio Marangolo. As the band's personnel changed, its sound was altered. This score represented the beginning of Goblin's final period, during which their recordings gained a new synth-pop sound that competed with the likes of Tangerine Dream. Perhaps the biggest flaw in the band's *Patrick* score is the main theme, which seems fine on the soundtrack album but isn't a particularly good fit in the context of the movie; its sound just doesn't click with the picture.

Patrick's official DVD release presents the original uncut Australian version of the film with Brian May's original score (which has also been released on as a soundtrack CD). Before this DVD, the uncut movie was hard to track down, but now it's Goblin's version that has become a curiosity.

■ **Agatha** (1979)

Original composer: **Howard Blake**
Replacement composer: **Johnny Mandel**

Agatha, starring Vanessa Redgrave and Dustin Hoffman, was directed by Michael Apted. It was a speculative account of famed British crime novelist Agatha Christie's mysterious disappearance in 1926. Distraught after her husband requested a divorce, Christie disappeared from her home, setting off a countrywide manhunt and wild rumors in the press. Eleven days later she turned up at a spa, where she had registered under the name of her husband's girlfriend. To this day, her missing days remain a mystery. Throughout her life, Christie pleaded amnesia as the cause of her disappearance, but this film offers an alternate explanation more in keeping with the intricate plots of her novels.

Producer David Puttnam, whose previous credits included Ken Russell's *Mahler* (1974) and *Lisztomania* (1975), Apted's *Stardust* (1974), and Alan Parker's *Bugsy Malone* (1976) and *Midnight Express* (1978), hired British composer Howard Blake to provide *Agatha*'s music. The previous year, Blake had scored Puttnam's production of Ridley Scott's directorial debut, *The Duellists*.

For *Agatha*, Blake wrote a traditional British romantic score. He also arranged and composed a number pieces of period source music, which he recorded before shooting began so that dance sequences and other onscreen bits could be synched to them. Among them was "Yes, Sir, That's My Baby" (Walter Donaldson and Gus Kahn's 1925 standard), "They Didn't Believe Me" (a classic Jerome Kern song from 1914), "My Wonderful One" (a Paul Whiteman and Ferde Grofé tune from 1922), and a Gilbert & Sullivan medley. Blake even made a cameo appearance in the movie as a pianist.

After completing the film's orchestral score, the composer recorded it at CTS Studios. But all was not well with *Agatha*, as Blake recalls:

> In the aftermath of a troubled shoot I was asked by David [Puttnam, the producer] and Michael [Apted, the director] to write a big symphonic score in the thirties tradition of Max Steiner, "in the hope that it might keep the action and interest moving and make it more exciting." This is never a good idea, but I went ahead and both scored and recorded the complete picture. However, at this moment David resigned as producer, and the incoming producer decided to stage a preview at BAFTA [British Academy of Film and Television Arts], the exit questionnaire of which seemed to suggest that a larger percentage liked the music rather more than the film generally, and this made me uneasy. Also, the music had perhaps been dubbed at too high a level and certainly was a pretty up-front element in the completed film. These and other factors resulted in my entire score being scrapped.

When his score was perceived to be overpowering the movie, and new producers Gavrik Losey and Jarvis Astaire came onboard to replace Puttnam, Blake left the project. Composer Johnny Mandel, whose previous credits included such popular and acclaimed films as *Point Blank* (1967), *M*A*S*H* (1970), and *The Last Detail* (1973), was hired to replace him. Mandel delivered a more contemporary-sounding score, which featured his original song "Close Enough for Love," with lyrics by Paul Williams. (This song would subsequently be recorded by a long list of singers, including Peggy Lee, Tony Bennett, Shirley Horn, Lena Horne, and Andy Williams.)

Interestingly, all of Blake's source music was retained in the finished picture. While his original underscore was never released on record, a suite from it was recorded in 1995 at Carl Davis's Forgotten Film Music concert series.

Blake reunited with producer Puttnam in 1999 and helped him rescore the picture *My Life So Far*, which originally had a Colin Matthews score largely made up of Beethoven adaptations. Blake would even go on to replace himself: In 1982 he worked on Franc Roddam's *The Lords of Discipline*, for which he did both source music (arrangements of "The Dipsy-Doodle" and "Bonnie Blue Flag") and an underscore that was recorded in London. After the picture was ostensibly finished, the director, the editor, and the composer were called to Hollywood with orders to shoot a new ending and write a new score. For this, Blake was given only one instruction: Make it "all-American." He wrote the new music while staying at the famous Sunset Strip hotel Chateau Marmont. Both versions of the movie eventually reached screens, but since both scores came from the same composer, few people noticed that they were not the same.

■ **The China Syndrome** (1979)

Original composer: **Michael Small**
Replacement music: **Nothing**

With the auteur theory in high regard among the ranks of 1960s and 1970s Hollywood filmmakers, radical new film music and film sound explorations occurred frequently. For example, the scores composed for Arthur Penn's *Bonnie and Clyde* (1967) and William Friedkin's *The French Connection* (1971) were dissected, moved about, and placed wherever the directors felt the music would work best.

Adventuresome filmmakers were using music cues sparingly, and only when absolutely necessary. Some of the greatest movies of the period—including many of director Sidney Lumet's movies, e.g., *12 Angry Men* (1957), *Fail-Safe* (1964), and *Dog Day Afternoon* (1975), and producer-director Alan J. Pakula's *All the President's Men* (1976)—had no music at all or only a few of minutes of it.

In 1979, two strong movies—*The China Syndrome* and *Kramer vs. Kramer*—were stripped of their original scores, which were then replaced with almost nothing. *The China Syndrome*, starring Jack Lemmon and Jane Fonda, was one of the better conspiracy thrillers of its decade. As first conceived, the picture had music—a score by Michael Small, whose previous credits included *Klute* (1971), *The Parallax View* (1974), and *Marathon Man* (1976). Small's highly regarded score for John Schlesinger's *Marathon Man* perfectly highlights the composer's forte—music that underscores particularly heavy psychological suspense. Hired by *The China Syndrome*'s producer Michael Douglas, the composer penned a score with effective ambient cues that nicely complemented the film's innovative sound-effects design. Unfortunately, the music started to disappear at director James Bridges' insistence, until finally it was decided that each and every scene would work better without music. The only important piece remaining in *The China Syndrome* is the light pop song heard during the movie's opening, "Somewhere In Between," written and performed by Stephen Bishop.

Another big picture that dropped its original score was writer-director Robert Benton's divorce drama *Kramer vs. Kramer*. Unlike *The China Syndrome*, this finished picture had a small amount of music—short adaptations of Antonio Vivaldi and Henry Purcell pieces. What's not commonly known is that, apart from adapting its classical music, John Kander (a four-time Tony-winning composer who, with lyricist Fred Ebb, was responsible for such Broadway hits as *Cabaret*, *Funny Lady*, and *Chicago*) wrote a full original score for the picture. Harsh and urban-sounding, it was ultimately tossed out because it was considered too up-front.

Judging by the critical acclaim and awards bestowed on both *The China Syndrome* and *Kramer vs. Kramer*, the lack of original scores had no negative effects on the pictures' critical and popular receptions. A recording of the unused music for *Kramer vs. Kramer* will most likely never be released, but Small's unused material for *The China Syndrome* appeared on the Intrada label.

■ Apocalypse Now (1979)

Original composer: **David Shire**
Replacement composer: **Carmine Coppola**

Director Francis Ford Coppola spent a hellish year-and-a-half in the Philippine jungles filming a story loosely based on Joseph Conrad's novella *Heart of Darkness.* In Coppola's adaptation, *Apocalypse Now,* Conrad's story is moved from central Africa in the 19th century to wartime Vietnam, in 1969. The movie follows the physical and psychological journey of Captain Willard, who has been sent upriver into the jungles of Cambodia on a secret mission—to assassinate rogue Green Beret Colonel Kurtz, who, in the fashion of an insane king, commands his own army of natives. Not unlike Dante's descent into hell, Willard's journey takes him into regions and situations of ever greater madness and violence.

Apocalypse Now is one of the few motion pictures whose making-of story is almost as exciting as the movie itself. While amassing its 200 hours of footage, the production was beset by many hardships, including a typhoon that destroyed the set, star Martin Sheen's heart attack, and the extravagantly paid Marlon Brando's (who played Kurtz) showing up too overweight to properly play his part. The movie's problems, which were heavily covered in the press, are well documented in a book by Eleanor Coppola (the director's wife), *Notes on the Making of "Apocalypse Now,"* as well as an award-winning documentary, *Hearts of Darkness: A Filmmaker's Apocalypse.*

After principal shooting ended, Francis Ford Coppola, together with editing and sound-design wizard Walter Murch, spent three years completing *Apocalypse Now* in his studio, American Zoetrope (with one return trip to the Philippines to film the movie's ending). Slowly, meticulously, the director honed his extraordinarily vast footage into a poetic depiction of personal and societal madness.

The film's earliest musical journey was detailed by synthesizer inventor Bob Moog in *Contemporary Keyboard* magazine's "The Synthesizer Soundtrack." Moog recalls:

> In the beginning, Coppola waffled between the use of contemporary rock music with traditional symphonic music to highlight the battle. He dropped the second element the moment he realized the possibilities of employing a synthesized score with which he could avoid a big problem in the final mix. For decades, music had been competing with sound effects, but Coppola came up with a way to incorporate these elements and turn the sounds of war (machine-gun ricochet, helicopter propellers) into musical elements. In order to get the best possible achievement, the director consulted with Japanese synthesizer-music pioneer Isao Tomita about providing the score, but business came in the way. Tomita was contracted to RCA Records, whereas Coppola insisted on using the Doors' "The End" in the picture, which put him in a contractual deadlock. One of the conditions of using that piece was the handing of the soundtrack's release to Elektra, a contractual point which canceled Tomita's possible involvement.

Unable to work with his first-choice composer, Coppola turned to his brother-in-law, composer David Shire (husband of Coppola's sister, Talia). The two had collaborated on *The Conversation*, for which the composer wrote and performed a compelling solo piano score augmented with a few disturbing electronic effects for the hero's nightmarish descent into madness. Shire's music for *Apocalypse Now*, however, just didn't click with Coppola, so the director changed horses in midstream and hired his father, Carmine Coppola, a highly capable composer who had proved himself in the film world with his music for the *Godfather* movies.

But the elder Coppola had one major problem in providing the electronic music his son wanted: He had no experience with synthesizers. Legendary record producer David Rubison was called in to act as a music producer, to help Carmine Coppola realize his musical ideas electronically. Rubison recruited two additional helpers, Bernie Krause, electronic music popularizer and member of the 1960s synthesizer duo Beaver & Krause, and the multitalented Shirley Walker. (This was the first film music gig for Walker, who would become an A-list film music composer-arranger-conductor and break much ground for women in the field.)

In addition, three synthesizer composer-players—Patrick Gleeson, founder of San Francisco's Different Fur recording studio; Don Preston, a longtime collaborator with Frank Zappa; and Nyle Steiner, inventor of the EWI (Electronic Wind Instrument) and the EVI (Electronic Valve Instrument)—were hired to augment the other musicians. All of these artists worked closely on the film's music. They brought in their own material, too, contingent on Francis Ford Coppola's approval. While Carmine Coppola is the film's officially credited composer, *Apocalypse Now* would have sounded quite different without the input of this group of extraordinarily talented electronic musicians.

■ **Stalker** (1979)

Composer of two scores: **Eduard Artemyev**

Influential Russian director Andrei Tarkovsky's *Stalker* is a symbolic story in which the main character—the Stalker—guides those who hire him in and out of "the Zone," a territory closed by the government. Once in the Zone, he leads people to "the Room," a mysterious place where one's deepest desires become reality. Like *Apocalypse Now*, the production was beset by many problems: Hundreds of feet of film (shot over a year's time) were ruined, and the director and his cinematographer had a falling out. Worst of all—though this tragic problem would not manifest until a few years later—the shooting of the movie next to a river into which an Estonian chemical plant was dumping massive amounts of toxic waste would eventually result in several cast and crew members' dying of cancer and other illnesses. These included the director himself.

To score *Stalker*, Tarkovsky hired Russian composer Eduard Artemyev, who had worked previously with the director on *Solyaris* (*Solaris*, 1972) and *Zerkalo* (*The Mirror*, 1975), both of which provided the composer with an opportunity to write a type of experimental music he couldn't have written for other Soviet directors. In this respect, *Zerkalo*—which combined synthesizer ambiences and acoustic instruments electronically processed to reflect the distorted memories of the hero—was especially noteworthy.

But in the middle of the scoring process on *Stalker*, the director changed his mind about Artemyev's musical approach. Artemyev recalls rewriting his music to reflect Tarkovsky's wishes:

> There were actually two versions of the score for *Stalker*. The first one was done with an orchestra alone—no synthesizer—but Tarkovsky rejected it, which surprised me, because he loved the idea of live music-making. The second version, which he accepted, was basically created on the Synthi-100 synthesizer [made by EMS in London], along with solo acoustic instruments that were extensively manipulated using various sound processors. At that time, Tarkovsky was very interested in Zen Buddhism and wanted the music to reflect certain contemplative elements that are part of Eastern religion and philosophy. To achieve this quality, I borrowed from the Indian classical tradition of using a single basic tonality, whose rhythmic patterns are slowly and constantly changing, creating a background over which the melody of a solo instrument can soar.

■ The Black Stallion (1979)

Original composer: **Carmine Coppola**
Additional composer: **Shirley Walker**

The Black Stallion, director Carroll Ballard's film adaptation of Walter Farley's children's novel of the same name, is the story of a boy's friendship with a wild Arabian stallion. The two endure a shipwreck and eventually, after their rescue, successfully train together as jockey and racehorse.

Ballard had trouble finding the right composer for this picture. By the time it was completed, he would replace his first composer's music, then augment his second composer's music with that of a third. (Four years later, on another animal-themed picture, his adaptation of Farley Mowat's memoir *Never Cry Wolf*, he would go through music by Robert Hughes and Jerry Neff before settling on an electronic score by Mark Isham.)

The multitalented Shirley Walker, arranger-conductor-cocomposer of *The Black Stallion*'s final score, remembers the first composer's work:

> Carroll had hired a composer who was in academia.... This man had his own notation system. I looked at it and thought, he isn't going to put this in front of a studio orchestra in Los Angeles and have it come out the way he thinks it's going to come out. He had this whole smoke-and-mirrors number because he was having trouble interfacing with the commercial work. And, in fact, the music of his that Carroll Ballard had heard and loved, when I heard it, I realized was stuff that a harmonica player had improvised. Maybe we shouldn't remember this guy's name. So, he was out. Who was next? Oh, God, I wish I could remember the names.... But ultimately, Carmine [Coppola] got the job.

The Black Stallion's producer, Francis Ford Coppola, proposed that his father, Carmine, take the reins as the film's composer. The elder Coppola had by 1979 composed the score for *Apocalypse Now* and worked extensively on the first two films in the *Godfather* trilogy.

But Carmine Coppola brought with him one drawback: He hadn't refined his film-specific techniques. Despite the beauty of his melodies and set pieces, his music often needed tailoring to fit tightly with the onscreen action. Shirley Walker (who had worked with him in this capacity on *Apocalypse Now*) was brought onboard *The Black Stallion* to help with this tailoring. She put together a tight score based on Coppola's themes, but in doing so had to leave out a good deal of the music he had written.

Unfortunately, someone would have to break the news to Coppola that his material wasn't going to be used as he had intended. Walker remembers:

> I wasn't going to be a patsy and call him up and say, "Oh, Carmine, I'm throwing out everything you did for the island." So we had to go to Carroll and say, "Look, somebody's got to tell him." And Carroll went to Francis [Coppola], who was the producer, and said, "Somebody's got to tell your father." And Francis said, "Okay, he's my dad, I'll take care of it." Well, the dynamics in that family were such that it never got taken care of. And, to my horror and deep regret, Carmine found out from an old friend, a flute player who'd been hired to do the session, that we were rerecording pivotal moments of the score with a huge orchestra. Of course, Carmine was explosively furious and called us all up. He was gonna blow up cars; he was gonna break legs.

The story ended sadly: Walker and the elder Coppola never managed to patch up their friendship before his death in 1991.

A sequel, *The Black Stallion Returns*, directed in 1983 by Robert Dalva (editor of *The Black Stallion*), was scored by French composer Georges Delerue. Prometheus Records released a CD of Coppola's heavily revised music paired with Delerue's score for the sequel. Luckily, all the beautiful music Coppola created for *The Black Stallion* has survived on an Intrada release, a three-CD set that includes both the revised and the original cues (including alternate takes and unused music).

■ **Zombi Holocaust/Doctor Butcher M.D. (Medical Deviate)** (1980)

Composer for Italian version (1980): **Nico Fidenco**
Composer for American version (1982): **Walter E. Sear**

The treatment/mistreatment of Italian horror movies and their scores by American International Pictures (AIP) is well documented. However, several other American distributors seemed to take pride in their modifications of foreign titles as well. Italian horror movie director Marino Girolami's *Zombi Holocaust* ended up being sliced and diced by its U.S. distributor, Terry Levene's Aquarius Releasing, which specialized in the American distribution of Italian and Japanese movies.

Levene's company took liberties with many films, editing out scenes from *Buio Omega* (1979; aka *The Final Darkness* and *Beyond the Darkness*), for example, as well as removing key footage—the first ten minutes and both opening and ending credits—from Umberto Lenzi's crime drama *Roma a mano armata* (1976, aka *Assault with a Deadly Weapon*). Aquarius even reshot several scenes from the latter film in order to remove all Italian references (e.g., Rome's youth center became the Manhattan club "Fascination" with the help of a new establishing shot). Naming himself the picture's producer, Levene also supplied *Assault with a Deadly Weapon* with new credits with fake American names.

But the changes to *Roma a mano armata* seem minor in comparison with what was done to *Zombi Holocaust*, retitled *Doctor Butcher M.D.(Medical Deviate)* for American distribution. *Zombi Holocaust* is the tale of an expedition to the Moluccas Islands that is beset by both cannibals and zombies, the latter created by a mad local doctor. Under Aquarius's stewardship, footage was removed and other footage inserted: For starters, the picture received a new opening, showing a zombie rising from its grave—even though the zombie had nothing to do with this particular movie but was instead taken from writer-producer-director Roy Frumkes' unfinished *Tales That'll Tear Your Heart Out*. A five-minute sequence of the heroes falling into and escaping from a trap was added. Not mention the fact that the whole movie's focus was shifted to the mad doctor.

To complement Aquarius's version, a new score was commissioned from Walter E. Sear, who was also responsible for the movie's new sound design. Sear, a tubist–composer–electrical engineer–tinkerer, was a longtime friend and advisor to synthesizer designer Robert Moog. He was also the owner/founder of Sear Sound recording studios in New York City. His film score credits prior to *Doctor Butcher* were few, namely, *Cherry Hill High* (1977) and *Disco Beaver from Outer Space* (1978).

Sear's *Doctor Butcher* music was performed on a Moog synthesizer. It's a wild and comedic underscore that shifts the film's focus from its gore and terror to its hammy acting and over-the-top plot. Some of it features drum sounds, to establish the island setting, but much of it is, in the best sense, simply strange noise—something that might be playing inside a medical deviate's brain.

Zombi Holocaust's original Italian score, composed by Nico Fidenco, was surprisingly serious, particularly in view of the movie's cheesiness. One of its key components was disco music, a seemingly obligatory element in most Italian zombie/cannibal/gore movies of the era. But the great majority of its cues were straightforward, with only a hint of ambient electronics. The main theme, "Make Love on the Wing," is a pleasant romantic piece featuring a haunting, wordless choral part. The score also offers "native chanting" for the cannibals and a lot of dark Gothic music featuring organ and Medieval-style vocalizing. While it never reaches the level of the ingenious Fabio Frizzi scores for Lucio Fulci's pictures (e.g., *City of the Living Dead* and *The Beyond*), it is a worthy addition to the catalogue of such genre scores.

■ **The Shining** (1980)

Original composer: **Wendy Carlos**
Additional composers: **Preexisting compositions by Béla Bartók, Krzysztof Penderecki, György Ligeti, and others**

The Shining, based on Stephen King's best-selling novel, is one of director Stanley Kubrick's most analyzed (perhaps overanalyzed) pictures. As in Kubrick's adaptation of Arthur C. Clarke's *2001: A Space Odyssey* (1968) and Anthony Burgess's *A Clockwork Orange* (1972), much of *The Shining*'s literary source material was altered to fit the director's cinematic vision (in fact, King criticized Kubrick's movie and later wrote his own screen adaptation of the book for a television miniseries).

The Shining is a one-of-a-kind experience in the horror genre. Its use of strange shots and edgy contemporary concert music from a variety of sources imbues the whole picture with an aura of eeriness. The music paints a vivid picture of the unraveling of the main character's mind.

As Kubrick repeatedly said in interviews, he never understood the need for original movie scores when there was so much great classical music to choose from. In *A Clockwork Orange* he had drawn primarily from Purcell, Rossini, Elgar, and Beethoven, as well as original music by Wendy Carlos. (For that picture, Carlos had written a number of cues that would be replaced by pieces from the director's temp track; for example, Rimsky-Korsakov's *Scheherazade* replaced her "Biblical Daydreams," and her "Orange Minuet" was dropped in favor of Terry Tucker's "Overture to the Sun.") For *Barry Lyndon* (1975), Kubrick had employed the services of composer Leonard Rosenman to write a score based largely on such classic melodies as "The British Grenadiers" (a seventeenth-century march) and Handel's "Sarabande." In the film *2001: A Space Odyssey*, he made use of music by Richard Strauss, Johann Strauss, Khachaturian, and György Ligeti.

Regardless of his predilection for constructing scores from existing classical works, Kubrick hired Wendy Carlos to score *The Shining*. In the late 1960s and early 1970s, Wendy Carlos (known then as Walter Carlos) had been one of the most famous proponents and popularizers of the Moog synthesizer. Her 1968 *Switched-On Bach* album for Columbia Records—J. S. Bach works played on the Moog—won three Grammy awards, charted on *Billboard*'s Top 40 list, and sold half a million copies. Carlos quickly followed with another album, *The Well-Tempered Synthesizer*, Moog performances of Monteverdi, Handel, Bach, and Scarlatti.

For *The Shining*, Carlos and her partner/producer, vocalist Rachel Elkind, began by composing a large amount of preliminary music based solely on King's novel, allowing Kubrick to start selecting what he liked. One of the pieces was based on "Dies Irae" ("Day of Wrath," a part of the Roman Catholic Church's Requiem Mass), a plainchant melody that has been frequently quoted in both classical and film scores (including Carlos's own *A Clockwork Orange*). Its use in *The Shining* was based on Hector Berlioz's use of it in his popular *Symphonie fantastique*. Motivated by Kubrick's enthusiasm for this theme, Carlos produced numerous variations, ranging from incredibly frightening to melancholic and romantic. But Kubrick disliked these arrangements and started exploring other classical works, while Carlos and Elkind continued to work on score ideas.

Although the film's final score retains Carlos's title music and some of her other cues, a minimal amount of her material was used. Instead, Kubrick built a score from existing recordings of contemporary classical pieces, primarily by Bartók (Music for Strings, Percussion and Celesta), Krzysztof Penderecki (*Utrenja*, *The Awakening of Jacob*, *De Natura Sonoris*, and *Polymorphia*), and Ligeti (*Lontano*). The overall sound of *The Shining* is really attributable to the work of these composers and Kubrick, who spotted the movie with these sometimes challenging pieces, often editing and manipulating them to his liking. In some scenes, he even layered multiple pieces on top of each other to create a uniquely disturbing effect.

On two CDs titled *Rediscovering Lost Scores*, Wendy Carlos has made available close to an hour's worth of her music that never found its way into *The Shining*. Some tracks were based solely on the composer's reading of the novel and were recorded as a sort of preliminary or suggested score. But many events in the novel—and the music meant to accompany them—never made it to the screen; Carlos's powerful track "Colorado," for instance, couldn't be used because it aimed to underline the majesty of the Rocky Mountains, something the director chose not to highlight. Some Carlos cues feature a chamber ensemble put together by composer John Morris, while others are purely synthesizer textures performed by Carlos herself. Of all the cues appearing on the CDs, only a track called "Clockworks (Bloody Elevators)" was used—but only in the movie's trailer.

■ **Used Cars** (1980)

Original composer: **Ernest Gold**
Replacement composer: **Patrick Williams**

Countless motion pictures have been doomed by test screenings held in front of unresponsive audiences. Negative audience feedback on any aspect of a movie can result in serious changes, very often in the music department. Writer-director Robert Zemeckis's comedy *Used Cars*, starring Kurt Russell and Jack Warden, may be one of the only movies ruined by *positive* audience response.

After Columbia Pictures received wildly enthusiastic feedback on its forthcoming *Used Cars*, the story of a state senate candidate's involvement with feuding used car lots, the studio moved up the picture's release by a month-and-a-half, to a date when it would face less box-office competition. But everything has its price, and in this case the marketing department wasn't able to react in time. As a result, the trailer was barely finished by the time of the premiere, and the premiere itself wasn't particularly glorious. The picture failed to live up to expectations, and box-office returns were slim.

When one hears the name of composer Ernest Gold, perhaps the first score that comes to mind is his Oscar-winning *Exodus* (1960), with its heartbreaking main title theme. There's also his Oscar-nominated *On the Beach* (1959), or *It's a Mad, Mad,*

Mad, Mad World, Stanley Kramer's 1963 "supercomedy." It's likely that Gold's association with *Used Cars*—one of the aging composer's last works before retirement—came about because it too was viewed as a "supercomedy," this time with a used-car theme.

But the composer's work on *Used Cars* is shrouded in mystery, since most of his music wasn't used and hasn't been released on CD, despite the fact that the tapes survive. It's only thanks to Gold's late orchestrator, composer Angela Morley, that the existence of this score even came to light.

For *Used Cars,* Gold provided both source music and dramatic underscore. His writing had the feeling of an old "serious comedy" score, mixing poignancy with a couple of clever comedic ideas, such as quoting the "Dies Irae" melody in connection with a rival used car dealer. The meat of the score is in the film's final half-hour, underscoring the mad dash to the used car lot with the type of "land rush" music one would expect to hear in a Western.

But as good as it was, almost all of Gold's music got replaced, with the exception of such source cues as the bar music, some guitar playing, and arrangements of "Hail to the Chief." The only surviving fragment of the dramatic underscore is the track "Eulogy," which plays during the car funeral.

So what happened to Gold's music? It seems that when Columbia made the suicidal decision to release the movie early, they also decided that Gold's score was too old-fashioned. Patrick Williams, a prolific (primarily television) composer whose previous credits included music for the comedy series *The Mary Tyler Moore Show* and *The Bob Newhart Show,* was hired to write a more upbeat and contemporary score. Williams's dramatic underscore included a complete makeover of the car-chase music. His music for the extended race sequence was the lively cue "Hooked on Americana," showing his great aptitude for both comedy and action. Capitalizing on the period's theme song craze, Williams, with lyricist Norman Gimbel, wrote the song "Used Cars," which was performed by country singer Bobby Bare (who had early-sixties hits with "Detroit City" and "500 Miles away from Hone") during the end credits. But like *Used Cars* the movie, "Used Cars" the song failed to rock the nation.

Since the film performed abysmally at the box office, there was no soundtrack release for *Used Cars*; even Bobby Bare's song quickly became a disposable commodity.

■ **The Hunter** (1980)

Composer for American version: **Michel Legrand**
Composer for European version: **Charles Bernstein**

Director Buzz Kulik's *The Hunter,* based on the life story of modern-day bounty hunter Ralph "Papa" Thorson, was Steve McQueen's last movie. Sadly, it wasn't a great swansong to a great career.

Once the finished movie was turned over to Paramount, Kulik's opera-fan concept received mixed reactions. The studio felt that opera music was simply out of place in a contemporary Chicago crime drama. As a result, Charles Bernstein was hired to provide a more predictable urban jazz score with lots of low, masculine instruments. This replacement music is much more aggressive and significantly changes the movie's tone. Following in the footsteps of such recent action/crime classics as *The French Connection* (1971), the spotting for *The Hunter* was relatively sparse and only featured dramatic underscore during key action scenes. In accordance with the change of mood, the music playing on Thorson's car stereo was switched to jazz and lounge styles, which would now make up a significant portion of the score.

Kulik, however, didn't easily accept the infringement on his musical vision and worked out a compromise with the studio. Bernstein recalls:

> The compromise was that the release in the United States had "Music by Michel Legrand" as the main title and "Additional Music by Charles Bernstein" in the end credits. They used my music for the more urban sections, like the chase on the rooftop, and used Michel's music in the more love-oriented areas. In Europe and the rest of the world, my score was used in its entirety and the credits read "Music by Charles Bernstein."

Since Kulik insisted on having Legrand's music in the U.S.-distributed print, Bernstein's score was relegated to the European market, where American crime movies with compelling jazz-based scores had proved very successful. In turn, Legrand's score, with a bit of help from Bernstein, worked well for the American audience.

Among currently available DVDs, the film's Region 1 release (primarily North America) has the American version of the score, but its Region 2 release (primarily Western Europe and the Middle East) allows viewers a choice—the English-language tracks retain Legrand's music, while all the other channels, such as German and French, have Bernstein's music—so the two scores can be compared with the click of the remote. Legrand's score has also been released on CD by Universal France.

■ **Captain Future** (1980)

Original composers: **Yuji Ono and Etsuko Yamakawa**
Replacement composer for German version: **Christian Bruhn**

In 1978, the Japanese studio Toei Animation produced fifty-three episodes of *Captain Future*, an anime television series based on a character created by American pulp sci-fi and comic-book writer Edmond Hamilton. The series' positive messages, such as advocating brains over brawn, appealed to a global audience. Its jazzy theme song by Yuji Ono and Etsuko Yamakawa, which sounded a bit like an American sitcom theme from the 1970s, even became a chart topper in some European countries. Jazz pianist-composer Yuji Ono, who has led trios featuring such world-renowned players as Miroslav Vitous and Lenny White, is also widely known for his music for the anime series *Lupin III*.

In Germany, however, television network ZDF (Zweites Deutsches Fernsehen) couldn't get the picture with isolated music, effects, and dialogue tracks, so their edited and dubbed version required a new soundtrack. And they hired composer Christian Bruhn to provide it with a new disco-like theme song and a new underscore.

Most replacements of this sort end up falling short of the mark, but Bruhn's *Captain Future* music is an exception. The largely synthesized new music, with an ethereal vocal overlay by Bruhn's wife, Erika Götz, was closer to the European music vernacular than the original Japanese score and, as such, became an important factor in *Captain Future*'s immense popularity in Germany. The show's theme became a widely covered hit. The soundtrack's CD release in 1995 was a great success, and a remix of it produced by Phil Fuldner titled *The Final* entered the Top 10 singles charts in both Germany and Switzerland. (The original Japanese music wouldn't make it to CD until 2001.)

Several new scores have been brought about by similar technical impasses, including Ernst Brandner's music for the German version of the 1985 miniseries *Christopher Columbus*. (*Note*: See this book's entry on Alfred Hitchcock's 1958 film *Saboteur* for an account of similar problems befalling the German version of that film.)

■ **Flash Gordon** (1980)

Original composer: **Paul Buckmaster and Queen**
Replacement composer: **Howard Blake**

When producer Dino De Laurentiis decided to make a *Flash Gordon* movie, based on the eponymous hero who battled Ming the Merciless on the planet Mongo in comic books and 1930s movie serials, he hoped to boost his picture's popularity by signing the British rock band Queen to supply music for it. Queen had recorded a string of mega-hits by this time, including "Bohemian Rhapsody," "We Will Rock You," and "We Are the Champions."

The band, however, was not well versed in scoring pictures; nor, of course, could they write an orchestral score that would support an entire movie. But they knew someone who could: cellist-arranger-composer Paul Buckmaster, who had penned arrangements for Elton John, David Bowie, Miles Davis, and many other popular performers. Buckmaster was hired for *Flash Gordon*, to adapt Queen's themes into an orchestral score. But he didn't fare too well: The eighty-five-piece Royal Philharmonic had already been booked for a week when the producer discovered that Buckmaster had completed only about a minute's worth of music.

De Laurentiis immediately sought a replacement, finding British composer Howard Blake (who previously had scored Ridley Scott's directorial debut, *The Duellists*) through the recommendation of CTS recording studios engineer John Richards. Wanting to make use of the already booked and rapidly approaching orchestral session, the producer asked Blake to write a score in less than a week and bring it in to record on the following Monday. Blake remembers:

> I said: "It'll take till Monday to actually even do the music cue, to work out where the music cues are." Finally, I said at least three weeks or a month. So they said: "Well, we will pay you a lot of money," so finally I agreed on three weeks. And I had to take what

Queen had written and incorporate it in the score. I really nearly literally died on this film, because I started writing, and I was writing a full score for large orchestra. And eventually, it was something like an hour and ten minutes of music needed. I started, and at the end of the first hour I had written about a minute, and I then realized that I would have to write at an incredible speed. So I actually just worked, and finally, the last four days I didn't sleep, and I thought it was dead easy and I wrote a 500-page score in fifteen days. After that I just slept for three days, and my wife at that time got a doctor in, and they couldn't wake me up. He chocked me full of drugs, and he said that if he'd not done that I would probably never have woken up.

Howard Blake delivered his score on time and recorded it in the presence of Queen and De Laurentiis. Those recording sessions seemed to give the band a real taste for movie scoring, and they started to explore the prospect of writing actual cues they could play themselves. They found encouragement in the producer's belief that having Queen score the entire movie would be innovative—and might result in a best-selling soundtrack. In the final version of the film, Queen's music is heard for thirty-five minutes while Blake's contributions occupy less than twenty; about ten more minutes are given to Blake's arrangements of Queen's motifs.

Blake's *Flash Gordon* experience led him to take only a limited number of film jobs in the following decades. He would focus instead on his concert music, which met with great success.

Four years after *Flash Gordon*, De Laurentiis produced David Lynch's adaptation of Frank Herbert's popular classic sci-fi novel *Dune*. Once again, the producer wanted to use a popular band for the score, but he had trouble deciding which one to choose. After learning that De Laurentiis liked their work, the progressive British band Jade Warrior sent him a fifteen-minute demo, an ethereal suite titled "Images of Dune." But despite their submitting multiple copies of the tape, the music never reached him, and he settled on the easy-on-the-ears American rock band Toto to do the score. (Jade Warrior eventually released the demo suite on the album *Horizen*.)

■ L'Ultimo squalo/Great White (1981)

Composers for Italian version: **Guido and Maurizio De Angelis**
Composer for American version: **Morton Stevens**

L'Ultimo squalo (which literally translates as "the last jaws") is a low-budget Italian ripoff of Steven Spielberg's 1975 blockbuster *Jaws*. Starring James Franciscus and Vic Morrow, *L'Ultimo squalo*'s plot was so directly reminiscent of *Jaws* that it's surprising it managed to get distribution in several countries.

The Italian production was scored by the prolific composing duo of brothers Guido and Maurizio De Angelis, who provided a synth-pop sound. Their score opens with Yvonne Wilkins singing the bouncy English-language pop song "Hollywood Big Time"—which has a tacked-on feel, since it has nothing to do with either sharks or the surfer seen under the opening titles. The De Angelis brothers offered dissonant synth textures for the underwater sequences, driving disco-style cues for the numerous shark attacks, and even a little romance theme. Most of all, their music aligned perfectly with the film's distinct B-movie feel.

When the people at Film Ventures International picked up the picture for release in the United States, they had serious issues with its musical score, which didn't match their idea of what a theatrically released picture should sound like. In addition to dubbing the movie into English and retitling it *Great White,* FVI hired veteran television composer Morton Stevens (perhaps most famous for his *Hawaii Five-O* theme) to write a new score. To avoid interference from Universal Pictures, owners of the *Jaws* movie franchise, Stevens had to be careful that his own compelling shark score did not reference John Williams's famous *Jaws* theme. Stevens's score ended up quite lighthearted and lots of fun, with just the right amount of musical winking to highlight the picture's camp aspects. Instead of relying heavily on strings, as Williams had done, Stevens's scary shark-attack music utilizes brass and percussion. He also wrote a great, slightly Italian-sounding main theme that he developed throughout the picture—from the angst-ridden opening titles to the heartbreaking "Coma" and relaxed "Aftermath" cues.

Great White opened in theaters with more than $4 million in marketing money from FVI to support it. But the picture's life was cut short by a successful lawsuit from Universal, which not only considered the movie too derivative of the Spielberg film, but noted that its Spanish distributors had even taken the liberty of presenting it as the third installment in the *Jaws* series! The Italian title itself—"The Last Jaws"—was another serious concern for Universal, which certainly wasn't ready to share its finned franchise. In fact, the studio was busy developing its own third movie, so it was inclined to take all cinematic shark tales from other entities very seriously. The result was that *Great White* disappeared from the face of the Earth. (The film's home video release, called *The Last Shark,* is not *Great White*; it is just an English-language-dubbed version of the Italian movie, complete with the De Angelis brothers' score.)

Morton Stevens's music for *Great White* was released on a CD in 1991, together with another Stevens score, *Act of Piracy* (1990). (During the writing of the latter picture, Stevens had been so ill that his score had to be completed by his composer friend Ken Thorne, who adapted Stevens's themes for the film's last two reels. As if this wasn't enough misfortune, Stevens's "Main Titles" cue was replaced in the film with a more hip composition by Michael Linn.) In 2008, Buysoundtrax released Stevens's music to *The One Man Jury* (1978), and as a special promotion, the first 100 purchasers were treated to a copy of *Tiburon* (Spanish for "shark")—an eighteen-minute orchestral work in three movements that Stevens wrote after *Great White* was pulled from circulation.

■ Clash of the Titans (1981)

Original composer: **John Barry**
Replacement composer: **Laurence Rosenthal**

Ray Harryhausen, a genius of magical and fantastical stop-motion animation, was one of the few special-effects artists whose name alone could sell a movie. Harryhausen's work was first noticed in the 1953 production *The Beast from 20,000 Fathoms*, a monster movie inspired by the 1952 rerelease of 1933's *King Kong*. (*King Kong*'s original release had inspired a young Harryhausen to begin experimenting with stop-motion animation in his family's garage.) Harryhausen deigned and animated *The Beast from 20,000 Fathoms*' creature—a rhedosaurus—for the low-budget production company Mutual Movies, which struck gold when it struck a distribution deal for the movie with Warner Bros.

Mutual Movies' tight budget had purchased a tinny-sounding score by Ukrainian-born composer Michel Michelet, whose work Harryhausen described as "horrible." But Warner Bros. had the movie rescored by David Buttolph, who ended up producing one of the most influential monster-movie scores.

Almost three decades after *The Beast from 20,000 Fathoms*, Harryhausen was still at the top of his game, although new technologies were beginning to challenge the techniques with which he had created his classic creatures. For the Greek myth–based *Clash of the Titans*, the story of Perseus overcoming numerous challenges as he rescues Andromeda from the clutches of Calibos, Harryhausen created an array of stop-motion characters that included Pegasus, Medusa, Calibos, and the Kraken (actually a Scandinavian monster). This film, which he also coproduced, would be Harryhausen's last before retirement.

Key to any phantasmagoric film is its music, and Ray Harryhausen's films and creatures had a prestigious musical history, featuring underscores by composers Bernard Herrmann (*The Seventh Voyage of Sinbad*, *The Three Worlds of Gulliver*, and *Jason and the Argonauts*), Jerome Moross (*The Valley of Gwangi*), Miklós Rózsa (*The Golden Voyage of Sinbad*), and Roy Budd (*Sinbad and the Eye of the Tiger*). Harryhausen believed music would be a crucial aspect of *Clash of the Titans*, and the legendary British composer John Barry was hired to score it.

But, as good as it was, Barry's music didn't feel right to Harryhausen. In the following interview excerpt, the animation master discusses Barry's score:

> John Barry did submit scenes he had scored for *Clash of the Titans* and, although Mr. Barry is a very good composer, we didn't feel his music was quite right. One of the main reasons we had considered him was because we were very impressed by his score for *The Lion in Winter*. That was of a classical nature, but, unfortunately, it didn't work out, and then the advance posters came out before the whole thing was consummated. That problem was solved when we got Laurence Rosenthal, who I thought did a magnificent job.

Rosenthal's previous work included scores for such film classics as *A Raisin in the Sun* (1961), *The Miracle Worker* (1962), *Requiem for a Heavyweight* (1962) and *Becket* (1964). His score, like Herrmann's scores for Harryhausen's projects, provided each mythical creature with its own musical insignia: Pegasus' floating theme, the Kraken's evil-sounding descending motif, and Medusa's disturbing orchestral stew, all of which work exceptionally well. While Rosenthal's soundtrack wasn't an instant classic, it greatly enhanced this fun movie.

Wolfen (1981)

Original composer: **Craig Safan**
Replacement composer: **James Horner**

A brand-new crop of cinema werewolves lit up theater screens in 1981: Joe Dante's *The Howling*, John Landis's *An American Werewolf in London*, and Michael Wadleigh's *Wolfen*. With its Native American spin on the creature, *Wolfen* flopped at the box office, though it would eventually find a cult following, and the same can be said of its score—or scores.

The original composer, Craig Safan, was urged by Wadleigh (whose sole previous feature credit as director was the famous documentary *Woodstock*, from 1970) to write music as innovative as John Corigliano's 1980 score for *Altered States*. And indeed, Safan penned a most unusual score. There was a lot of atonality in it, and his use of odd sounds and unusual orchestrations recalled Jerry Goldsmith at his experimental best. It contained no main theme for the Wolfen or any other character, and the lack of identifiable themes plus the score's exceptionally cold sounds perfectly captured the director's wishes.

But Wadleigh found himself in trouble—well behind schedule and working with an overly long director's cut—and the film was taken away from him. He was replaced at first by producer Robert Hitzig, who directed a number of the film's reshoots, and then by John Hancock, who came onboard to fulfill Directors Guild regulations. (Wadleigh would never direct another feature film.) Composer Safan recalls the change of command:

> Eventually they hired a new director, who basically let me go through the motions and record the entire score. He then threw the whole thing out the next day. I have no idea what he didn't like about the score, as all the executives had heard it over the several weeks it was being recorded and seemed really pleased. I can only assume that he wanted to bring on his own team to the picture, but, because of Orion's commitment to me, he couldn't get rid of me until he was firmly in power, but that's showbiz.

With the new occupant in the director's chair, Safan's score was dropped. The new director, looking for a different musical approach, hired composer James Horner, who had just finished working on another horror film, Oliver Stone's *The Hand* (1981).

Though he was somewhat mired in the low-budget sci-fi and horror genre, this was a very inventive period for Horner, who tried something new with each score. (For many fans, his early 1980s period is his best.) He took an experimental approach to the music for *Wolfen*: It was less theme-based than most of his scores, and the lack of immediately noticeable motifs helped generate a haunting atmosphere—the Wolfen's presence is everywhere. The composer talked about his soundscape for the monster:

> I wanted to create a sound world for the Wolfen which was alien, yet which wasn't just a lot of effects. It had to be very driving and very primitive, yet in a way that, hopefully, had not been done before, and I think I was fairly successful. On the alien vision scenes, I knew that everything was very highly stylized, and very subjective, and I created a kind of driving rhythm which was, basically, the Wolfen's music. There's no melody—there's a trumpet figure that keeps reoccurring, but basically I wanted to create a very driving type of feeling for the film.

Wolfen proved to be a foundation for later Horner sci-fi scores. Its trumpet figure, for example, would pop up in the "Combat Drop" cue of his 1986 *Aliens* music. But like many of the composer's genre efforts from the early 1980s, *Wolfen*'s soundtrack recording hasn't been released. Safan's unused score, on the other hand, fared a bit better in the soundtrack market: In 1997, Intrada's Douglass Fake got the rights to press a promotional CD containing about fifty-five minutes of it.

■ **Le Professionnel** (1981)

Original composer: **Ennio Morricone**
Replacement music: **Ennio Morricone's preexisting work "Chi mai"**

The espionage film *Le Professionnel*, a vehicle for the iconic French actor Jean-Paul Belmondo, features what is often regarded as one of the best (or best-known) scores of Italian composer Ennio Morricone. Any discussion of the film's music, however, must start about ten years before the picture's release.

In 1970, Ennio Morricone wrote and recorded the piece "Chi mai" for the obscure Italian film *Maddalena* (1971). It appeared almost simultaneously in that movie and on an unrelated LP. While the picture all but vanished, the tune became an instant hit with the help of Italian actress-singer Lisa Gastoni, who recorded it with lyrics in French, English, and Italian. A so-called disco version followed (it actually had little to do with disco but was merely a streamlined rendition of the tune), and after that an extended version in the same vein found its way into the soundtrack of the 1981 BBC drama serial *The Life and Times of David Lloyd George*.

Through these various appearances, "Chi mai" became a real trans-European success, climbing the pop charts at different times in different countries. Eventually it caught the ear of Jean-Paul Belmondo, who persuaded director Georges Lautner to hire Morricone to score their next film, *Le Professionnel*.

For *Le Professionnel*, Morricone penned a score with three memorable melodies. The main theme, "Il Vento, il grido" ("The Wind, the Scream"), was a close relative of the "Chi mai" melody; the composer wrote and recorded more than a dozen versions of it, some sounding like carbon copies of "Chi Mai" and others deviating from it in various ways. "Bach" was a gradually building suspense piece. "Dall'Africa" painted a musical picture of the film's militaristic regime.

Morricone's recorded score amounted to more than fifty minutes of music, primarily variations on "Il Vento, il grido" and a few alternate takes of the secondary themes. However, with the exception of the cue "Titoli di testa" (an "Il Vento, il grido" variation), little else of his material ended up in the picture. All told, there is very little music in *Le Professionnel*, and almost every time any music is heard, it turns out to be the same old late-1970s recording of "Chi mai."

Le Professionnel was a great success, and "Chi mai" was immediately associated with it—this despite the fact that it had been written for *Maddalena* and was successful well before the Lautner/Belmondo picture's release. Capitalizing on the music's popularity, even *Le Professionnel*'s poster was redesigned to emphasize Morricone's involvement and remind moviegoers that it featured "Chi mai." (Cashing in on his tune's newfound popularity, Morricone even licensed it for a dog food commercial. As a bonus, the score he composed for *Le Professionnel* would eventually find its way into an original and, later, an expanded soundtrack recording.)

While Morricone never complained about his score for *Le Professionnel* being replaced by (his own) "Chi mai," other composers have raised their voices as a result of similar treatment. For example, Dutch composer Loek Dikker went to court over his music for *Het Bittere Kruid* (1985), which was savagely cut by the picture's producer, who basically extracted a single theme from the complete score and repeated it in almost every emotional scene. Dikker felt not only that his work had been mistreated, but that the repetition of the single theme made him appear incapable of developing his material. He went as far as to try to pull the film from theaters, but since the producer had the final say, Dikker's efforts to block the picture or collect damages was doomed to fail.

■ **Neighbors** (1981)

Original composer: **Tom Scott**
Replacement composer: **Bill Conti**

Directed by John G. Avildsen, *Neighbors* is a black comedy about an average suburban couple and the crazy new neighbors who turn their lives upside down. It was the last film starring the late John Belushi, who, with co-star Dan Aykroyd, was the creative driving force behind it. To punch up the movie, Avildsen employed many camera tricks, weird angles, and various in-jokes and homages to the likes of George

A. Romero and Alfred Hitchcock. The actors, however, became critical of Avildsen's direction, and relationships on the set became strained.

At Belushi's request, saxophonist-composer Tom Scott, a founding member of the Blues Brothers band, was hired to score the picture. Scott had had a distinguished career in television, scoring such shows as *Baretta, The Streets of San Francisco,* and *Starsky and Hutch* (for which he also penned the theme). His best-known feature film score was *Conquest of the Planet of the Apes* (1972), the fourth entry in the simian mayhem series. Another Belushi request was that the punk rock group Fear write and perform an end credits song.

However, after disastrous test screenings, both Scott's score and Fear's song were tossed out. (Fear, however, ended up with a guest spot on *Saturday Night Live,* where it did $20,000 in damage to the set.) For a new score, director Avildsen turned to his friend composer Bill Conti, with whom he had worked on his previous three pictures: the Oscar-winning *Rocky* (1976), *Slow Dancing in the Big City* (1978), and *The Formula* (1980). It wasn't the first time Conti had been asked to quickly replace a score: In 1978, actor Alan Alda called on him to supply new music for *The Seduction of Joe Tynan,* a film written by and starring Alda, who felt that Michael Small's original score wasn't right for the character he played.

With only a few days left to write the score for *Neighbors,* Avildsen made a simple request of his new composer: Be endlessly frantic and manic, and punch up the comedy with funny musical quotes. (Since the comedy itself contained few laughs, it would be up to the score to provide them.) And that's just what Conti did; everything from bird tweets to whipping sounds can be found in his hilarious though somewhat overbearing music, one of the maddest scores ever composed. His "Main Title" alone contains Indian drums, a comic march that sounds like the beginning of "We're Off to See the Wizard," a Theremin knockoff, random slide whistles, and a lullaby! As a listening experience on its own, it's like a Warner Bros. cartoon, in no small part due to the appearance of the familiar zany "That's All Folks!" melody.

This hyperactive music was originally knocked by the press—along with the movie, of course. Even Conti was frank about the replacement job, labeling himself an "embalmer," as in one who's hired to make a dead body look good (but it's still a dead body). It contrasted sharply with Tom Scott's rejected music for *Neighbors,* which didn't sound particularly like a comedy score. Instead of underlining every joke with a cartoonish musical reference, Scott presented a moody take on the main character's frustration with his suburban life, with a strong Herrmannesque main theme and only occasional leavening with comic highlights. Suburban paranoia shines through the several nervous passages that often venture into thriller territory, and a good portion of the score is heavy with melancholic string work that's reminiscent of steamy Golden Age film-noir romance music.

Both Scott's and Conti's scores can be heard on a Varèse Sarabande CD.

■ **Lucifer Rising** (1981)

Original composer: **Jimmy Page**
Replacement composer: **Bobby Beausoleil**

Kenneth Anger, a cult art-film director and the author of *Hollywood Babylon* (an infamous book of scandalous celebrity gossip published in 1965), worked for two decades on *Lucifer Rising*, a thirty-minute film that paid homage—in a uniquely surreal fashion—to writer and occult philosopher Aleister Crowley's Thelema religion/philosophy. Anger started working on *Lucifer Rising* in the early 1960s and, for musical inspiration turned to Bobby Beausoleil and his 1966 psychedelic rock band the Orkustra. The filmmaker got so involved with Beausoleil that he offered the musician a starring role, an offer Beausoleil accepted on the provision that his band would do the picture's music. About a year later, however, the Orkustra disbanded, and Beausoleil put together a new band, the Magick Powerhouse of Oz, to record the film's music. Not long after that, Anger had a falling out with his composer, whom the director accused of stealing most of his footage. From the remaining footage, Anger made the eleven-minute *Invocation of My Demon Brother* (1969), with a soundtrack by Mick Jagger.

In the meantime, Bobby Beausoleil got involved (at first musically, then criminally) with another—this time much, much darker—underground figure, Charles Manson, becoming part of Manson's inner circle. In 1969, Beausoleil tortured and murdered musician and drug dealer Gary Hinman, a crime for which he was quickly arrested, convicted, and sentenced to death (a sentence commuted to life in prison when the California Supreme Court ruled the death penalty unconstitutional in 1972).

Anger next hooked up with Led Zeppelin's legendary guitarist, Jimmy Page, who shared his interest in Crowley's teachings. Not only did Page own one of the largest collections of the author's work, he owned Boleskine House, a former Crowley residences that overlooked Loch Ness. At first it seemed that Anger had found a simpatico partner for his film, but the collaboration came to a nasty end: As Anger assembled his film from seventeen hours of footage in one of Page's mansions, using equipment the guitarist had installed to edit his band's concert footage, Page's then-girlfriend threw him out of the house and forbade him to return. This led to a creative break between the filmmaker and the guitarist; Anger dropped the musician from the project, despite the fact that Page had already completed more than twenty minutes of music (which now circulate on the bootleg recording market).

Anger claimed that Page had been strung out and as a result worked too slowly. And his unkind remarks didn't end there. The diatribe continued:

> The way he's been behaving is totally contradictory to the teachings of Aleister Crowley and totally contradictory to the ethos of the film. Lucifer is the angel of light and beauty. But the vibes that come off Jimmy are totally alien to that—and to human contact. It's like a bleak lunar landscape. By comparison, Lucifer is like a field full of beautiful

> flowers—although there may be a few bumble bees waiting to sting you if you are not careful. I'm beginning to think Jimmy's dried up as a musician. He's got no themes, no inspiration, no melodies to offer. I'm sure he doesn't have another "Stairway to Heaven," which is his most Luciferian song. *Presence* was very much a downer album. In the first place his commitment to Lucifer seemed to be totally serious, and he was very enthusiastic about the project. On the one hand he's very into enterprise and hard work. But on the other hand he has this problem dragging him down. He's been acting like Jekyll and Hyde, and I have to have someone who's 100-percent. This film is my life's work.

Lucifer Rising would sit on the director's shelves for another ten years before it was completed. In the course of that time, Anger would receive musical help from an unexpected place: California's Tracy State Prison. Bobby Beausoleil, serving his life sentence there, assembled a band within the prison, the Freedom Orchestra, and recorded demos for Anger's film. With the help of a cooperative warden, Beausoleil eventually set up a recording studio where, in 1979, he recorded his experimental rock score (almost forty-five minutes of music) on a nonexistent budget. The music actually benefits from its simple surroundings, projecting a powerful rawness that might have been lost with fancier production and more sophisticated equipment. It was officially released on CD in 2004 with lots of additional material, including Beausoleil's 1967 music for *Lucifer Rising*, performed by the Magick Powerhouse of Oz.

■ **Author! Author!** (1982)

Original composer: **Johnny Mandel**
Replacement composer: **Dave Grusin**

Starring Al Pacino as a rundown Broadway playwright, *Author! Author!* is a bittersweet film written by famed playwright Israel Horovitz and directed by Arthur Hiller, whose previous credits included *The Out of Towners* (1970), *Love Story* (1970), *Plaza Suite* (1971), and *The Man in the Glass Booth* (1975).

Author! Author! is the story of a writer's creative and family problems: His wife is leaving him, his play needs endless rewrites, his girlfriend won't move in with him because of his children from his wife's previous marriage. Treading a fine line between comedy and drama, the film often relies on its music to nudge the viewer into the appropriate mood for each scene.

Its score by composer-pianist Dave Grusin—whose previous credits included such notable films as *The Heart Is a Lonely Hunter* (1968), *The Friends of Eddie Coyle* (1973), *Three Days of the Condor* (1975), and *On Golden Pond* (1981)—found the right tone for the movie. His *Author! Author!* music, featuring saxophone and synthesizer, provides the perfect lighthearted sound, especially as a backdrop to Pacino's energetic performance. Grusin also penned a song for the film, the Razzie-nominated "Comin' Home to You (Is Like Comin' Home to Milk And Cookies)," with lyrics by Marilyn and Alan Bergman.

In 2007, the Varèse Sarabande record label dug into studio archives in search of the tapes of Grusin's *Author! Author!* score, for release in its long-running CD Club series. But there they found another *Author! Author!* recording as well, one that nobody remembered. Thus, Johnny Mandel's original score for the movie serendipitously came to light, and also found its way onto Varèse Sarabande's release. (Mandel's previous scoring credits included such notable films as *The Americanization of Emily*, *M*A*S*H*, *The Last Detail*, and *Being There*.)

Unlike Grusin's score, Mandel's played down the movie's fun in favor of a serious, even dramatic, tone. The main theme is a melancholic piano piece that almost cries out for lyrics; introspective scenes play against a backdrop of slow-moving, contemplative jazz. As the movie progresses and the fictional writer's life picks up pace, more contemporary and comedic music begins to appear, featuring 1970s-style guitar licks, madcap xylophone lines, and some synth work that sounds like Amiga computer music! Finally, toward the score's end, comes a surprise: the third (presto) movement of "Summer" from Antonio Vivaldi's *The Four Seasons*.

Unfortunately, there's no surviving documentation regarding the placement of Mandel's cues, so they were simply sequenced on the recording based on their reel numbers. Though *Author! Author!* is not a great picture, listening to its two scores back-to-back on the same CD is a revelatory experience, a chance to hear a score change that makes obvious sense.

■ **Jinxed!** (1982)

Original composer: **Lalo Schifrin**
Replacement composer: **Miles Goodman**

In this creatively bankrupt comedy, Bette Midler plays the wife of a gambler who follows around a jinxed blackjack dealer against whom he can't lose. Eventually, the gambler's wife falls for the dealer, and the two plot her husband's demise. On the set, there were personal problems between Midler and co-star Ken Wahl, who played her love interest. Moreover, there was no onscreen chemistry between the two. The *Jinxed!* shoot became such a nightmare for director Don Siegel (who had directed such classics as 1949's *The Big Steal* and the 1956 *Invasion of the Body Snatchers*) that it literally gave him a heart attack and he had to abandon the project, which would turn out to be his last movie. The picture would be finished by director Sam Peckinpah, who went uncredited.

Siegel had hired Lalo Schifrin to score *Jinxed!*. They had worked on five earlier films together: *Coogan's Bluff* (1968), *Dirty Harry* (1971), *The Beguiled* (1971), *Charley Varrick* (1973), and *Telefon* (1977). But when Peckinpah replaced Siegel, the composer left the project (although Schifrin would work with Peckinpah in 1983 on the director's next—and last—movie, *The Osterman Weekend*).

Composer Miles Goodman, Johnny Mandel's cousin, was hired as Schifrin's replacement. Relatively new to the business, Goodman could claim only a few film and television credits, among them the critically praised *James at 15*. For *Jinxed!* he provided a bouncy comedic score; alas, it was not enough to save the jinxed picture.

For a long time, the only notice given to Schifrin's contribution to *Jinxed!* was an essay by fellow composer Richard Shores. It lamented the fate of great unused scores and cited Schifrin's *Jinxed!* as a "clever" example. Schifrin was a little less flattering of his own brief involvement in the project: He has said that he can't recall anything specific about his score that would merit such a compliment.

It's interesting to note that just a year prior to working on the last movies of both Don Siegel and Sam Peckinpah, Schifrin was involved in the swan song of the great director Billy Wilder. This was the Walter Matthau and Jack Lemmon vehicle *Buddy Buddy* (1981), a remake of the French black comedy *L'Emmerdeur* (1973), about a hitman and his annoying, suicidal neighbor. For Schifrin the film posed a music-replacement problem, albeit different from the one in *Jinxed!*. He had been hired to provide its comedic underscore not knowing that his friend composer Pete Rugolo had already written a score for it (which had been rejected as too old-fashioned). Schifrin later said he wouldn't have taken the assignment had he known of Rugolo's involvement. Such negative reactions to replacing a friend or respected colleague's music are one reason that studios like to keep silent about unused scores.

An arrangement of "Cecilia" by Rugolo made it into the final cut of *Buddy Buddy*, but the rest of the music is Schifrin's.

■ **Five Days One Summer** (1982)

Original composer: **Carl Davis**
Replacement composer: **Elmer Bernstein**

Five Days One Summer, starring Sean Connery and Betsy Brantley, was the last picture by legendary director Fred Zinnemann. Zinnemann's impressive list of credits spans more than fifty years and includes such highly acclaimed films as *High Noon, From Here to Eternity, Oklahoma!, The Nun's Story, A Man for All Seasons*, and *Julia*. Set in the Swiss Alps and based on a story by Kay Boyle, *Five Days One Summer* tells of a taboo May-December relationship between a middle-aged doctor and his niece, a young woman who has loved him since she was a child. Unfortunately, this beautifully photographed movie struck most viewers (including critics) as emotionally cold and sluggishly paced.

Initially, it was scored by Carl Davis, a prolific composer for numerous BBC series and movies, who may be best known in film music circles for the modern scores he has provided for many silent movie classics, as well as his work as a conductor of film music concerts with programs that range from blockbuster James Bond music to resurrected forgotten (and rejected) film scores. Davis's most famous feature film music at the time Zinnemann hired him was for Karel Reisz's *The French Lieutenant's Woman* (1981); that was the score that led Zinnemann to take him on for *Five Days One Summer.*

Signs of trouble appeared early on. Zinnemann had asked Davis for an intimate and introverted score, only to encounter, at the start of the recording sessions, an orchestra he considered too large for the intimate feel he was after. Still, he let Davis go ahead and record his music.

A version of the film with Davis's music attached was taken out for test screenings, which it failed abysmally. Zinnemann blamed the failure on the only element not directly under his control, the music, which he found overpowering, focused more on the grandeur of the beautiful mountain setting than on its main characters' strange relationship. Davis recalls his work with Zinnemann:

> It was very odd, because Fred Zinnemann was a very respected director who made some wonderful films, but it seemed I could not really attach myself to this film or understand his way of working, what he needed. What's quite interesting is when my score was replaced, I actually heard some of it and thought that composer had the same problem. We didn't really know what to do to help this film. It was a very flawed picture, it was purported to be a romance, but he had a very uninteresting leading lady and it paralleled his own life. It was really tough, it was really sad. He was a most sophisticated and amazing man, but I couldn't satisfy him. It was very hard, very sad, because I really admired him.

On the prowl for a new composer, Zinnemann turned to Elmer Bernstein, whom he admired. By this point, Bernstein had written scores for many popular and acclaimed films, including *The Man with the Golden Arm, The Ten Commandments, Sweet Smell of Success, The Magnificent Seven, To Kill a Mockingbird, Walk on the Wild Side,* and *Hud.* The director's favorite Bernstein work was his 1962 score for John Frankenheimer's *Birdman of Alcatraz,* which he felt was exactly the sort of music he was looking for—a fairly intimate sound that stressed the movie's characters rather than their setting.

To achieve this effect for *Five Days One Summer,* Bernstein would make use of a chamber orchestra for which he wrote an intimate style of music that featured solo instruments. Much of the score's emotional burden was carried by an otherworldly sounding electronic instrument, the ondes Martenot. Invented in 1928, this instrument with a disembodied sound reminiscent of that of the Theremin had appeared in scores by many classical composers, including Olivier Messiaen, Edgard Varèse, Arthur Honneger, Darius Milhaud, Giacinto Scelsi, and Pierre Boulez, and had graced film scores by Dmitri Shostakovich and Maurice Jarre.) Bernstein had first used the ondes Martenot the previous year, in his score for *Heavy Metal* (1981); he saw *Five Days One Summer* as his chance to give the instrument a more substantial role.

In the final analysis, Zinnemann's change of composer was probably unnecessary, as not even Bernstein's replacement score could save the picture. Shortly before its release, the director even considered having a third score written by Georges Delerue, with whom he had worked on *A Man for All Seasons* (1966), *The Day of the Jackal* (1973), and *Julia* (1977). But Zinnemann simply couldn't find a way to arrange for a third score commission.

Five Days One Summer, an undistinguished closing chapter to Zinnemann's most distinguished career, quickly disappeared from theaters. Perhaps the most accurate assessment of the movie's shortcomings came from critic Janet Maslin, who wrote in her 1982 *New York Times* review: "Most of the movie is simply about mountain climbing, something that is undoubtedly more thrilling to attempt than it is to watch."

Fantasia (Rerecorded Version, 1982)

Conductor of original score (1940): **Leopold Stokowski**
Conductor of rerecorded score: **Irwin Kostal**

On November 13, 1940, the Broadway Theatre in New York City premiered an animated picture that was meant to revolutionize the film industry: Walt Disney's *Fantasia*, a unique experiment in using popular classical music as inspiration for a series of animated adventures. The film employed a revolutionary multichannel recording process and "Fantasound," a specially developed early form of stereophonic playback. Theaters where it would play needed to be equipped with this new playback system, a drawback that caused the movie's initial release (1940–41) to play at only twelve U.S. theaters.

Although film critics and those among the public who were fortunate enough to see it generally gave it rave reviews, some classical-music purists were outraged by the editing liberties the picture took with revered music. Aside from its extremely limited release, also hindering the movie's turning a profit was a higher-than-normal ticket price; the fact that the film was more than two hours long and featured a fifteen-minute intermission and a printed program couldn't distract from the fact that America was just coming out of the Great Depression. Though a great cinematic and technical achievement, *Fantasia* was a box-office failure, and Disney shelved plans for an immediate sequel.

The music in *Fantasia*, introduced with narrations by music critic Deems Taylor, included excerpts from J. S. Bach's Toccata and Fugue in D Minor, Tchaikovsky's *The Nutcracker*, Paul Dukas's *The Sorcerer's Apprentice* (the movie's most memorable segment features Dukas's tone poem acted out by Mickey Mouse), Stravinsky's *The Rite of Spring*, Beethoven's Symphony No. 6 (*Pastoral*), Amilcare Ponchielli's *La Gioconda*, Mussorgsky's *Night on Bald Mountain*, and Schubert's "Ave Maria." These musical selections were compiled by Disney and Leopold Stokowski, one of the most famous conductors of his day, who assembled, edited, arranged, orchestrated, and conducted their recording with his renowned Philadelphia Orchestra, one of America's "Big Five" orchestras. Stokowski even took an active part in the mixing process.

Among *Fantasia*'s technical firsts was the use of a click track, allowing for the new-fangled process of synchronized overdubs. Overall, the care taken with the music's preparation and recording is evident from its $400,000 music budget, which was spent mostly on new equipment to record and then play back the soundtrack in theaters. Indeed, the cost of this new technology was one of several reasons *Fantasia* didn't turn a profit in its initial run.

During the next five decades, the picture would enjoy many rereleases: In 1942, RKO released a version shortened from 133 minutes to 82, leaving out Bach's music and some of the live action sequences. This version had a mono soundtrack that could be played in any theater. The film was released again in 1946, this time with the Bach restored but still a mono soundtrack. In 1956, the picture came out with a stereo soundtrack, as most theaters could now handle that format.

In 1969, zeroing in on a new audience of youth who found it "trippy," *Fantasia* finally turned a profit for Disney, in a version from which the racially stereotyped character Sunflower from the Beethoven *Pastoral Symphony* section had been removed. Yet another rerelease occurred in 1977, a dupe of the original print and soundtrack, but by this point the soundtrack's quality had so degraded that the decision was made to produce a brand-new one. Thus, in 1982, *Fantasia* reappeared with a fresh digital rerecording of the same musical selections and narrations.

The new soundtrack was arranged and conducted by Irwin Kostal, who made several changes, most noticeably using Mussorgsky's original orchestration of *Night on Bald Mountain*, which is fiercer than Stokowski's version. But the newly recorded music generated controversy: Fans of the film were attached to the original Stokowski performance, which they considered an essential part of the real *Fantasia* experience, and anything else seemed blasphemous. Moreover, some analog sound purists simply objected to its digital recording.

Within ten years, the alternate soundtrack would be retired and replaced with a sonically restored version of Stokowski's original recording. Making use of new digital restoration technologies and Stokowski's original detailed mix notes, recording engineer Terry Potter created an accurate, pristine, and vivid restoration of the great conductor's performance, rescuing it for future generations. The new soundtrack was transferred to the six-channel, 70mm format for theatrical presentation. Though the restoration was expensive, it proved to be money well spent, breathing new life into one of Disney's most important cinematic achievements.

■ Slapstick (of Another Kind) (1982)

Composer for European version: **Michel Legrand**
Composer for American version (1984): **Morton Stevens**

Slapstick, a surreal novel by Kurt Vonnegut Jr., inspired *Slapstick (of Another Kind),* a film written, produced, and directed by Steven Paul, a talent agent who moonlights as actor-writer-producer-director. The film tells the futuristic story of a rich celebrity couple (played by Jerry Lewis and Madeline Kahn) who give birth to twins (also played by Lewis and Kahn) that are deemed mentally retarded but turn out to be—when they put their minds together—wildly superintelligent alien beings. Directors Sam Fuller and Orson Welles appear in cameo roles.

Having previously worked with Steven Paul on *Falling in Love Again* (1980), prolific French composer Michel Legrand (famous for such scores as *The Umbrellas of Cherbourg, The Thomas Crown Affair,* and *Summer of '42*) provided a lightweight comedic score that contained a number of surprises, including a nice fanfare that would later be used in the opening of his James Bond song "Never Say Never Again." Legrand also penned two songs for the movie: "Two Heads are Better than One" (featured in the title and end credits) and "Lonesome No More" (an important slogan in the novel)—the latter with lyrics by Vonnegut himself. Distributed only in Europe, the film experienced a quick box-office death in each country it visited.

As years passed without an American premiere, *Slapstick (of Another Kind)*'s chances for a domestic theatrical run all but fizzled out. When an American distributor did finally pick it up, it was altered to fit their demands and then offered for only a nominal run at selected theaters before ending up on TV. Primarily, it was re-edited to look more like a sci-fi adventure than a comedy (considering the low number of laughs to be had, switching genres wasn't too difficult). It was given a new, more sci-fi–oriented score by Morton Stevens of *Hawaii Five-O* theme fame. Stevens's music utilized a smaller orchestra than Legrand's but added a "sci-fi layer"—synthesizers that, alas, never quite clicked with the rest of his music. Unsurprisingly, the score did not save the picture, which quickly sank into obscurity.

For some reason—other than the movie's degree of popularity—a soundtrack recording was issued, with selections from both Legrand's and Stevens's scores. This LP marked the first time in soundtrack history that two scores for the same movie were released on the same disc. As with any soundtrack recording that presents more than one score, it's fascinating to note how a different score alters one's perception of a movie.

■ **Tender Mercies** (1983)

Original composer: **George Dreyfus**
Replacement music: **The silence of the prairie...**

Along with George Miller (of *Mad Max* fame), Bruce Beresford (noted for his 1980 film *Breaker Morant*) became one of Australian cinema's greatest exports in the 1980s, directing such Academy Award favorites as *Tender Mercies*, his first American film, and *Driving Miss Daisy* (1989).

Written by Horton Foote (the playwright-screenwriter who penned *To Kill a Mockingbird; Baby, the Rain Must Fall;* and *The Trip to Bountiful*), *Tender Mercies* is the tale of a recovering alcoholic country singer (played by Robert Duvall) who tries to turn his life around with the help of a young widow in rural Texas.

When it came time to consider a musical underscore for the film, apart from the songs that appeared in it, Beresford contacted the German-born Australian composer George Dreyfus, on the recommendation of producer Phillip Adams. Although the director felt that his movie needed a score unrelated to the songs sung by its main character, he was skeptical about introducing scene-dependent scoring. To avoid that problem, he asked Dreyfus to write a main title and end-credits music, as well as several cues of a rather generic nature.

(*Note*: Beresford had always had an ambivalent relationship with movie scores, which he felt could badly date his films. He consciously avoided original music in his early movies; in fact, only a handful of his films even used source music. The closest he came to using a score in his early pictures was dubbing a Leos Janácek piano work into the end credits of *Don's Party*, 1976).

For *Tender Mercies*, Dreyfus spent five weeks in New York writing "night scenes," "tension," and other cues that were recorded with moonlighting musicians from the New York Philharmonic and the Metropolitan Opera Orchestra. His music captured the film's Western feel, specifically its beautiful long shots of the Texas landscape, and it had a great Americana sound. That might seem strange coming from a foreign composer, until one remembers that the man who helped define Hollywood's Western sound with his classic scores for *Duel in the Sun, Red River, High Noon, The Big Sky*, and *Rio Bravo* was composer Dimitri Tiomkin, a Russian.

After completing the recording, Dreyfus returned to Australia. He didn't participate in the dubbing process, but Beresford phoned him frequently, letting him know that this and that sequence would be left without music. Finally, the director decided to scrap the whole score:

> When I put the score up against the film I didn't like it. There was nothing wrong with the music. It was just that because these people were living out in Texas in a very remote area, out on a prairie, you really needed to get the feeling of where they were and the sort of space around them. The music, which was emotional, seemed to take that away from the film rather than add to it. So at the last minute, over a lot of producer objections, I

> dropped the score entirely. I used only a couple of simple country and western songs in a couple of places. Horton Foote was such a great writer. I just felt that putting music [into the film] seemed almost to falsify the expression in the text.

Dreyfus released his unused *Tender Mercies* score in 2002 on the compilation *The Film Music of George Dreyfus, Vol. 2,* and recorded his main titles music with various brass bands; in fact, this music became a popular piece for Australian brass bands. Dreyfus also conducted a performance of it arranged for horns and strings in St. Petersburg, Russia, in 2003. Unfortunately, the only person who couldn't do anything with the music was the director.

Despite his initial reservations, Bruce Beresford eventually got over his fear of original scores. But his musical indecision would still prevail sometimes, resulting in a number of replaced and half-replaced scores. For instance, a large portion of Mario Lavista's original score for Beresford's *A Good Man in Africa* (1994) was replaced, as a result of bad test screenings, with more comedic music by John Du Prez. In 2003, Beresford directed the fascinating HBO movie *And Starring Pancho Villa as Himself...*, a strange but true story about the Mexican rebel leader asking Hollywood producer Frank Thayer to capture his heroics on celluloid. Beresford's picture originally had a score by Stephen Endelman, but most of the music used in the final cut was by Joseph Vitarelli.

While the score to *Tender Mercies* went by the wayside because of his convictions, Beresford faced studio interference regarding the music for his Pancho Villa film, as he noted in a 2006 lecture:

> I said to my composer, Stephen Endelman, I wanted a score that summed up the relationship between Frank Thayer and Villa. Because Frank Thayer was only twenty-two when he went to Mexico, he saw Pancho Villa as a romantic revolutionary. He worshiped his idealism and his patriotism. I wanted the music to reflect this. Later, as he learns more about Pancho Villa, he starts to question a lot about him. The themes can then be varied to express Thayer's disillusionment. In the end, Endelman's score for Pancho Villa was ditched, and I don't think the replacement captured the spirit of the film at all. A surprising number of film scores, even those by celebrated composers, are replaced by the studio executives. I suppose they're right some of the time, but mostly I suspect they're making a mistake.

■ Something Wicked This Way Comes (1983)

Original composer: **Georges Delerue**
Replacement composer: **James Horner**

Written by Ray Bradbury and based on his own novel, *Something Wicked This Way Comes* was one of Walt Disney Studios' attempts to create a dark fantasy picture that was unique in both look and sound. The subject is the many facets of temptation. It tells the tale of a small, placid Midwest town that is visited by Dark's Pandemonium Carnival, a mysterious, evil, magical carnival that barters souls for the fulfillment of ambitions and desires. Looking back on the finished work years later, Bradbury would describe it as "not a great film, no, but a decently nice one."

British director Jack Clayton (noted for such literary movies as *Room at the Top, The Innocents, The Pumpkin Eater,* and *Our Mother's House*) brought on his regular musical collaborator, French composer Georges Delerue, whose long list of acclaimed films includes *Jules and Jim, A Man for All Seasons, Anne of a Thousand Days, Women in Love,* and *The Conformist.* The composer and director had previously worked together on *The Pumpkin Eater* (1964) and *Our Mother's House* (1967). To give Delerue an idea of the sort of music he wanted for *Something Wicked,* Clayton provided a tape of musical selections that included classical compositions by Prokofiev, Richard Strauss's *Death and Transfiguration,* and pieces from the soundtrack of *The Shining.*

Delerue's resulting underscore, characterized by a strange combination of beauty and darkness, was about an hour long. One of its highlights was a lovely flute melody that would become one of Clayton's favorite pieces of music; in fact, it would be played as the main theme for the British Academy of Film and Television Arts (BAFTA) tribute to the director after his death. There was also a devilish six-note descending melody for the carnival and some chilling choral chanting. In addition to his underscore, Delerue recorded a good deal of carnival source music featuring drums, trumpet fanfares, and glitzy merry-go-round tunes. The pairing of traditionally happy music with more sinister material created a dissonance befitting a festival of evil.

Unfortunately, some of the decision makers at Disney just didn't like Delerue's score. Tom Wilhite, head of production at the studio, summed up the objections to it, stating that it was "a nice score, but for the wrong picture." The music wasn't Disney's only problem with the movie, however: They had more basic concerns about whether to should risk their wholesome reputation by moving away from overtly family-oriented films. So, after a bad test screening, the company reached into its pockets and pulled out an additional $5 million to re-edit the picture, reshoot some key sequences, record a new narration to help clarify the story, and obtain a new score. (The reshoots made much of the original score irrelevant anyway; for example, the opening statement of the carnival's theme wouldn't have worked without the creepy materialization of the circus as it was originally shot.)

Although director Clayton was very much a fan of Delerue's score and was sorry he hadn't been able to defend the composer's case more energetically, he agreed to the score replacement provided he could break the news to his friend personally. This he did. Meanwhile, Walt Disney Productions contacted composer Jerry Goldsmith, but he was unavailable. Ultimately, the studio turned to composer James Horner for the movie's new score. Horner recalls stepping into the project:

> I never saw Clayton's cut and I never read the book or the screenplay. Tom Wilhite told me what he perceived as mistakes of the previous score; they didn't want it too dark, dismal, or slow It had to have a lot of energy. At the same time, Jack Clayton was trying to give me a cassette of Delerue's music. I didn't want to hear it and didn't want to discuss concepts. The film had already been overbaked with concepts. I finally told everyone,

"I don't want to hear about what you want. Just give me the film without any preconceived notions."

1983 was Horner's busiest year, with five additional movies coming out, but the heavy workload isn't evident in *Something Wicked This Way Comes*, one of his best early-period works. His score, which contains a lot of quirky material that might surprise his casual fans, shocks us right from the start with a Wagnerian main title, and then turns to idyllic suburban themes. The music gets darker with the approach of the carnival, then finally, after the nefarious Mr. Dark is killed, reverts again to a peaceful mood. Whereas Delerue had provided a relatively sparse underscore, Horner wrote well over an hour of music for a sixty-piece orchestra and female choir.

Something Wicked This Way Comes lost millions of dollars for Disney, which behaved dismissively toward both the movie and its music. Music from Delerue's unused score, however, has been released on CD, including material on a six-disc tribute set, a suite conducted by the composer on the *London Sessions* series, and several cues arranged by Robert Lafond on a disc honoring Clayton-Delerue collaborations. Most of the film's original recordings were released by Universal France in 2011.

■ Yor, the Hunter from the Future (1983)

Original composer: **John Scott**
Replacement composers: **Guido and Maurizio De Angelis**

Starring the muscle-bound American actor Reb Brown in its title role, *Yor, the Hunter from the Future* is a classic no-budget Italian postapocalyptic fantasy. A weird blend of futuristic and prehistoric elements, it achieved cult status both through sheer awfulness and a strange score that combined orchestral and sleazy pop music.

British composer John Scott (whose previous credits included *North Dallas Forty*, *The Final Countdown*, *To the Ends of the Earth*, and a number of Jacques Cousteau's documentaries) was hired by the film's distributor, Columbia Pictures, to score it. Scott wrote and recorded his score in Italy (and later recalled his stay there as one of the happiest times of his life). Although *Yor* was an admitted piece of trash with the kind of low production values certain Italian genre movies were famous for, it offered Scott the opportunity to write an epic score—and do so in a beautiful setting. The only problem he encountered was the recording itself: Because of the large number of musicians required, the union insisted on including some students, as a form of practice for them. Scott recalls the recording: "The producer and the director attended the sessions, which were recorded in Rome. They were happy with the music.... I was not happy with the Italian musicians, in fact it is the only time I walked off the recording stage and had them do some practice. I would love to record that score again with a decent orchestra. Maybe one day I will."

Italian postapocalypse movies had their own musical vocabulary, characterized by the sound of synthesizers and the inclusion of ridiculous pop songs. *Yor*'s producers decided that it didn't sound enough like its cinema siblings, so they hired veteran Italian B-movie composers Guido and Maurizio De Angelis to add some songs.

The De Angelis brothers showcased their zany pop sensibilities in *Yor* via a series of comical tunes climaxing in the humorously stupid theme "Yor's World"; the rest of their contributions were cast in a similar campy mold. And yet the final movie retained some of Scott's underscore and displayed his credit prominently. This confused a number of his fans, some of whom even phoned him to ask whether he had written the synth music and the silly song. The truth was, he had not, but that didn't spare him the honor of being considered for a Razzie Award the next year—one of three nominations for Yor, in the actor, score, and song categories.

Most of the music by all three composers can be found on various soundtrack recordings. The original LP featured material by the De Angelis brothers and portions of Scott's. Later, Label X released a CD containing all of Scott's score. A half-hour compilation, *Yor's Salon de Refuses,* focuses exclusively on the movie's rejected music, containing cues that pay tongue-in-cheek homage to "Joy to the World" and the "Imperial March." In 2011, Buysoundtrax Records released both scores on one CD, cutting up the lengthy suite on *Yor's Salon de Refuses* and debuting the De Angelises' music in digital format.

■ **Manimal** (Television Series Pilot, 1983)

Original composer: **Stu Phillips**
Replacement composer: **Paul Chihara**

Throughout the 1970s and 1980s, television producer-mogul Glen Larson and composer Stu Phillips were a nearly inseparable team, working together on *Quincy, M.E.*; *Battlestar Galactica*; *Buck Rogers in the 25th Century*; *The Fall Guy*; *Knight Rider*; and other projects.

Larson spent most of 1983 trying to launch a new television series, *Manimal,* about the adventures of a college professor who has the uncanny ability to transform into any animal he chooses. Once the show was green-lighted, Phillips departed from the series *Knight Rider* and *The Fall Guy* and followed Larson to *Manimal,* where he wrote the series' theme and its pilot episode's score. Relying heavily on synthesizers, as he had on *Knight Rider,* the composer strove to create a synth-sound world that would be immediately associated with the show and its main character.

The pilot wasn't well received, but the network gave Larson a second chance to improve it. The alterations he chose included recutting the pilot, reshooting several scenes, and replacing its music. Composer Paul Chihara (whose previous credits included Sidney Lumet's *Prince of the City* and numerous TV movies) was hired to give the show a new theme.

But after scoring eight episodes, Chihara moved on. The rest of the show's episodes were scored by Alan Silvestri (whose previous credits included *The Doberman Gang* and the TV series *ChiPs*) and, once again, Stu Phillips, who was invited back to help the fledging series. After the production of only eight episodes, however, *Manimal* was canceled in midseason. For its creators, this may have come as a heavy blow, but for the network (NBC), the show was just an insignificant bit of sand in the vast television desert, where the dropping of pilots (and their scores) is an everyday occurrence.

Two of a Kind (1983)

Original composer: **Bill Conti**
Replacement composer: **Patrick Williams**

If proof was ever needed that a soundtrack can make more money than the actual picture, *Two of a Kind* provides it. This silly preapocalyptic romantic comedy reunited Olivia Newton-John and John Travolta as a pair of crooks who hold the world's fate in their hands. The hope was to repeat their incredible success with *Grease* (1978), but the only thing this box-office bomb did was set both stars' careers back a decade.

The picture's official soundtrack, on the other hand, went platinum. Two of its hit songs were performed by Newton-John—the Grammy-nominated "Twist of Fate" (by Peter Beckett and Stephen Kipner), which reached number 5 on the pop charts, and "Livin' in Desperate Times" (by Barry Alfonso and Tom Snow), which reached number 31. A third—"Take a Chance," by David Foster, Steve Lukather, and Newton-John—featured her and Travolta in a duet. But although the songs boosted the soundtrack album to new heights of popularity, score collectors got left out in the cold: The CD listed Bill Conti as the picture's composer, but none of his music appeared on it (nor did it make it into the final movie)!

For Conti, 1983 was a hectic year. He had replaced John Barry on Philip Kaufman's *The Right Stuff* after Barry delivered themes that just didn't work for the director. But the fact that Kaufman hadn't wanted Conti in the first place and insisted on constant rewrites made for an arduous scoring process. For example, Conti was asked to provide a reasonable facsimile of one of the temp-track cues, the "Mars" movement of Gustav Holst's popular orchestral suite *The Planets*. After three rejected versions of this cue, what he finally turned in was a near-replica of the Holst. Luckily, Conti's toil on this picture was amply rewarded: He won an Academy Award for it.

Compared with *The Right Stuff*, the *Two of a Kind* job was simple, and Conti wrote a good score for it. But the movie was neck-deep in problems, and in a marketing maneuver, Conti's music got tossed out in favor of what seemed likely to be the film's only potentially profitable elements—Olivia Newton-John's songs. (Since the soundtrack recording hit record stores before the movie's release, the producers had advance evidence of the songs' profitability.)

Replacing Conti's score were various instrumental reworkings of "Twist of Fate." The picture's other songs were also given more prominent roles, and composer Patrick Williams was brought in to provide whatever further touches of underscore were needed. Williams (whose previous credits included numerous episodes of the TV series *The Streets of San Francisco, The Mary Tyler Moore Show,* and *The Bob Newhart Show*) didn't have to strain himself on this movie; his credit actually reads "music adapted by."

Primarily song-based scores became more and more fashionable in the 1980s, as adding hit songs to movies proved to be one way filmmakers could improve the visibility of their productions. A noteworthy example is 1987's *Some Kind of Wonderful.* Finding the right musical voice for the teen romance proved problematic, and producer John Hughes originally hired composer Ira Newborn, with whom he had worked in the past. But as Newborn started working on an orchestral underscore, composer/songwriter Stephen Hague also started working on the film's songs. By the time the movie arrived in theaters, *Some Kind of Wonderful* had jettisoned Newborn's brief score and instead featured Hague's songs throughout.

■ The Mack (1983)

Composer for original 1973 theatrical release and present-day DVD: **Willie Hutch**
Composer for 1983 home video reissue: **Alan Silvestri**

Michael Campus's 1973 film *The Mack* tells the tale of Goldie, an ex-con who becomes Pimp of the Year in Oakland, California. To maintain his title, Goldie must fend off corrupt cops, other pimps, a crime kingpin, and even his own brother, a black nationalist (reportedly based on Huey Newton). The picture starred Max Julien, as well as the highly popular and acclaimed social-commentary comedian Richard Pryor (who also contributed to its script) in the scene-stealing supporting role of Slim; actual Oakland pimps featured in some cameo roles. *Entertainment Weekly* proclaimed this blaxploitation gem one of the top twenty cult films of all time, and *The Mack* has been reverently referenced in the work of numerous rappers, including Snoop Dogg, Jay-Z, and OutKast.

The Mack's famous musical score was composed by legendary Motown singer-songwriter-arranger-producer Willie Hutch, who would do the *Foxy Brown* soundtrack a year later. Hutch had started his career writing and arranging for the Fifth Dimension in 1967, then went on to cowrite the Jackson 5's early hit "I'll Be There." After that came work in various capacities with such artists as Smokey Robinson, Marvin Gaye, Diana Ross, Michael Jackson, and Aretha Franklin, as well as producing his own recordings.

Hutch's score for *The Mack* aimed to paint the pimping scene in music. It featured a strangely fitting solemn theme for the main character, and set the film's chase sequences to guitar licks with "walk-a-chicken" wah-wah effects. Several tracks featured vocals by Hutch himself, while the song "Mother's Theme (Mama)" was performed by R&B star Millie Jackson. Motown assembled the soundtrack into a strong, popular album.

Ten years after *The Mack* was released, Richard Pryor, popular with multiracial audiences since the mid-1960s as a comedian, had become a big box-office draw, thanks to his roles in such films as *Uptown Saturday Night* (1974), *Car Wash* (1976), *Which Way Is Up?* (1977), *Blue Collar* (1978), *Superman III* (1983), and, with Gene Wilder, *Silver Streak* (1976) and *Stir Crazy* (1980). *The Mack*'s 1983 video reissue attempted to capitalize on Pryor's broad popularity, prominently displaying his name on its advertisements. Essentially the same movie, it had undergone many small edits and one big change: a new score.

Although shedding Hutch's popular score almost guaranteed the reissue's failure, the rescoring had a certain commercial logic to it. By 1983, the style of Hutch's score had become very familiar to moviegoers; many similar scores accompanied the 1970s wave of blaxploitation films (from *Shaft* and *Super Fly* through *Dolemite* and *Disco Godfather*), and the sound was almost an object of nostalgia. In the hope of making the reissue of *The Mack* feel more contemporary, Alan Silvestri was hired to write an alternate score with a newer funk/disco feel. (Interestingly, the composer would soon become known for his big, lush orchestral scores.) Silvestri's biggest credit up to that point was the television cop series *CHiPs*, and his music for *The Mack* is somewhat reminiscent of his *CHiPs* scores. He also penned two songs for the movie, "In the Beginning" and "Party Time," with lyrics by noted singer-songwriter Eugene McDaniels (composer of such hits as "Compared to What" and "Feel Like Makin' Love").

Silvestri's music for *The Mack* was his earliest film score to be released on LP. The material may seem odd to those expecting something along the lines of his scores for *Predator* (1987) or *Back to the Future* (1985), but for those who enjoy the *CHiPs* work, it is a welcome extension of that sound.

Though Silvestri's score still lacks a CD release, Willie Hutch's classic soundtrack remains available (and still popular) in that format. It has even found a new life in the music of the many contemporary artists who've sampled it, including Biggie Smalls, Lil' Kim, Dr. Dre, Moby, the Chemical Brothers, and UGK.

■ **Mike's Murder** (1984)

Original composer: **Joe Jackson**
Replacement composer: **John Barry**

Writer-director James Bridges (whose credits include *The Paper Chase, The China Syndrome*, and *Urban Cowboy*) filmed *Mike's Murder* in 1982. It starred Debra Winger, who had received her first big feature film break in Bridges' *Urban Cowboy* (1980) and had just finished shooting Taylor Hackford's *An Officer and a Gentleman* (1982).

An exercise in neo-noir, *Mike's Murder* is a thriller about a lonely young bank teller whose mysterious occasional lover is murdered. Driven to find out what happened to him, she wanders into a shadowy, unsavory side of LA's entertainment industry, only to discover that her lover was a ne'er-do-well hustler and amateur drug dealer killed for ripping off a bigger dealer. To tell the story, Bridges employed reverse chronology, an out-of-the-ordinary narrative technique that was a novelty at the time but would be used successfully in many subsequent films, such as *Betrayal* (1983), *Memento* (2000), and *Irréversible* (2002).

For his unusual picture's music, Bridges hired recording artist Joe Jackson, a singer-songwriter known for helping to introduce the British New Wave sound to America (in particular with his 1978 hit "Is She Really Going Out with Him?"). But while writing a movie score seemed a good way for the musician to expand his horizons, his initial experience proved problematic and unlucky. Under the pressure of a tight deadline, he produced a series of songs and instrumental pieces he wasn't fully satisfied with. In an interview promoting his *Mike's Murder* album, Jackson describes working on the picture:

> I saw the movie, I did the music very, very quickly, under incredible stress—I was on the road at the time. I recorded the album in ten days and then went back on the road. Then sometime later I heard that the release of the movie had been postponed, then I heard that they were recutting parts of it, then I heard it was postponed again, then I heard they were reshooting parts of it. Then it was postponed again.

Bridges' movie was finished by 1983, but Warner Bros. shelved it after a disastrous initial screening. The studio had it extensively re-edited, rearranging the scenes into a straightforward chronological narrative. This meant the music had to be changed, to fit what was essentially a new picture. Replacement music was composed by the legendary British composer John Barry, who provided a sultry, jazzy score not unlike his music for another neo-noir thriller, Lawrence Kasden's 1981 *Body Heat*. The film's final cut also retained three of Jackson's songs.

Mike's Murder was finally released in 1984, with the hope that it might ride the coattails of Debra Winger's critically acclaimed turn in *Terms of Endearment* (1983). It didn't.

A&M Records issued Jackson's score in 1983—almost a year before the movie reached theaters. The label knew it would have a hard time publicizing the LP as a soundtrack to an unreleased picture, but it rushed ahead with the release so as not to interfere with Jackson's next album, *Body and Soul*, which was already in the works. Even stripped of its movie tie-in, the LP reached number 64 on the Billboard 200 chart. As Jackson has made clear, however, the *Mike's Murder* album is neither his best nor his favorite:

> Half of it are songs that I was working on, or had half-finished, which I pressed into service. And half of it was written purely for the movie. I had a video on board the tour bus, and was just watching it, making notes. And in my hotel room I had a portable keyboard that I would go back to and makes notes on. I feel that because it was all done very quickly, and revolved around a movie, that it was kind of a side-step from what I am

doing. I feel rather unfulfilled about it. I feel that it is half an album. It isn't good enough to be a Joe Jackson album. But at the same time it isn't so bad it shouldn't have come out. All I can hope for is that people who're curious will pick it up and enjoy it for what it is.

John Barry's music was released in 2009 by Prometheus Records.

■ Greystoke: The Legend of Tarzan, Lord of the Apes (1984)

Original score: **Classical selections conducted by Norman Del Mar**
Replacement composer: **John Scott**

In 1981, British director Hugh Hudson struck cinematic gold with his multiple-Oscar-winning *Chariots of Fire*, which made him a hot property. His next movie, *Greystoke: The Legend of Tarzan, Lord of the Apes*, with a script by Robert Towne (who hoped to direct it), would not fare so well, though the script itself would be nominated for an Oscar.

Loosely based on Edgar Rice Burroughs' novel *Tarzan of the Apes*, *Greystoke* is a variation in which John (the name Tarzan is not used in the film), son of Lord and Lady Greystoke, is found in the African jungle, where he has been raised by apes. He's transported back to England to assume his inheritance and lead an aristocrat's life. But British life doesn't agree with him; he longs for the jungle, to which he eventually returns, leaving his love, Jane, in England.

Hudson originally wanted to hire classical composer John Corigliano, whose strikingly unusual modernist music for Ken Russell's *Altered States* had not only brought the composer an Academy Award but also made his music a point of reference and model for several future film scores (Craig Safan's unused *Wolfen* score being a prime example). Unfortunately, Corigliano was busy working on his opera *The Ghosts of Versailles* for New York's Metropolitan Opera and couldn't devote any time to this project. Hudson and Corigliano would agree to work together on Hudson's next feature, but the deal would prove unlucky for both men: Corigliano wouldn't complete his opera until 1991, and *Revolution* (1985), the picture they eventually worked on together, ended up a failure and nearly a career-killer for several crewmembers.

Unable to secure his first choice, Hudson hired composer-performer Vangelis, who had provided the Oscar-winning music for *Chariots of Fire* and a popular and influential score for Ridley Scott's *Blade Runner* (1982). But after being attached to Hudson's project for almost a year, Vangelis resumed work on his own albums, leaving *Greystoke* uncompleted.

At this point, the director decided to weave a score out of classical compositions selected by his brother, a London music critic. The selections included works by Ravel, Holst, Elgar, Varèse, and Charles Koechlin. Once he had determined which scenes the pieces would accompany, Hudson commissioned new recordings of them by the

Royal Philharmonic Orchestra. The conductor was Norman Del Mar, a specialist in late Romantic period music, particularly that of Mahler, Richard Strauss, and Elgar.

As if seeing into the future, the conductor requested a clause in his contract that provided him with screen credit even if his work was not used. And that is exactly what happened: Although *Greystoke*'s first trailers featured Del Mar's recording of Holst's "Mars" (from *The Planets*), the producers didn't like the director's classical-music concept and insisted that the film be given an original score. British composer John Scott, who had worked with Hudson on a number of commercials, took the assignment, though it posed special challenges, as he recalls:

> My reaction was that music pulled me away from the film rather than drawing me into it. Hugh had very specific ideas; he saw the film as an opera, a tragedy—*Tristan and Isolde*. He'd send me music to listen to, such as Nino Rota's *The Leopard* and music by Wagner. It seemed he was secure with me, since we could communicate, while at the same time he was insecure about what I was going to do. I was forced to do certain things—Hudson insisted on the [Beethoven] Grosse Fugue when Tarzan is suffering anguish at Greystoke and is riding his horse wildly. I felt that the sound effects, Tarzan shouting, plus that music...it all didn't work. I told Hugh I'd record those scenes two ways, first with the fugue and then with music I'd written for the scene. You see what he ended up with. I wrote a lot of music that wasn't used; in fact there was a lot of the film itself that wasn't used. Hugh insisted I use Elgar and I wasn't happy about that. I don't think it works very well.

Though forced to keep his music fairly close to what was on the temp tracks, Scott wasn't unhappy with *Greystoke*. But he certainly believed he could have done a better job if given a freer hand. The score, however, would prove to be one of his most popular works. He even recorded a special suite from it, which was released on one of his compilations.

To clear up some longstanding confusion: The Elgar music that remained in the film is credited as "additional music conducted by Norman Del Mar," but in fact Del Mar's performance didn't make the final cut. The Elgar was conducted by Scott, who made timing adjustments in his interpretation to synch with the onscreen action, in contrast with Del Mar's recording, which was done without reference to the film.

Although John Scott's score gained widespread critical attention, it was unavailable for a long time, until La-La Land Records gave it an official CD debut in 2010.

■ **Misunderstood** (1984)

Original composer: **Maurice Gibb**
Replacement composer: **Michael Hoppé**

Misunderstood, directed by Jerry Schatzberg (whose earlier films included *Panic in Needle Park*, *Scarecrow*, and *The Seduction of Joe Tynan*), was an American remake of the 1966 Italian movie *Incompreso*. This story of a father unable to connect with his son after the mother's death was a real crowd-pleaser in its Italian incarnation, and was remade there as both a television movie and a miniseries. The American version, however, so worried its producers before its release that they let it sit for two years before sending it out to theaters, where it quickly died. The lucky few who managed to see this movie enjoyed a touching performance by Gene Hackman, playing a more emotional role than we have come to expect from him. And for composer and record producer Michael Hoppé, the movie represented his big break, as he recalls:

> In 1984, I was working as VP of A&R at PolyGram based in New York. I had been with the record company for fourteen years and had always wanted to score films. And then, as sometimes happens in life, opportunity occurred.... When pitching PolyGram artists to Peter Guber in Los Angeles, a producer of the intended PolyGram picture *Flashdance 2* (which was subsequently never made), I also played him one of my piano themes on a cassette I happened to have with me. As would happen that very day, the producers of *Misunderstood* had been looking for suitable music for their recently edited film, and had contacted Peter Guber for his assistance. He contacted the *Misunderstood* producers, and suggested they should hear my music. This event changed my life, because I not only scored my first film, but subsequently left PolyGram and moved to Los Angeles with my wife· It got me started on my composing career, which I have been doing ever since.

Hoppé's melodic score was understated and romantic, and quite appropriate for the picture. Oddly, he didn't write again for the movies for twenty years. In the interim, however, he wrote and released numerous recordings of his soft-spoken New Age–tinged chamber music, and his pieces have been used in a number of television shows and short films.

Before Hoppé got the job, *Misunderstood*'s producers had made the rounds in pursuit of a suitable composer. After an unsuccessful attempt to get Marvin Hamlisch (whose previous credits included *The Way We Were, The Sting, The Spy Who Loved Me, Sophie's Choice,* and numerous others), the producers requested a demo tape from Maurice Gibb, a member of the pop singing group the Bee Gees (which had a huge success with their songs for the film *Saturday Night Fever*). Unlike most demonstration scores today, which often are a selection of synth mockups, Gibb's demo utilized the orchestration talents of Jimmie Haskell, a veteran composer who worked primarily on television movies in the 1980s. It was fully fleshed-out music. Haskell was one of the few people who got to hear what Gibb could have done had his film scoring career been longer:

> I orchestrated a "demo audition score" for only a couple of scenes of *Misunderstood*, and I conducted a simple recording of a very small band just to get the musical concept heard by the producer and director. The composer was Maurice Gibb of the Bee Gees. We had no instructions or guidance from the director or producer. Based on what we submitted to them, the "demo-audition" was not accepted, and neither one of us actually "scored" the film. Maurice was a brilliant new composer. Had he lived [Gibb died in 2003], he would have developed into a greatly in-demand film composer. He composed an excellent score for *A Breed Apart*, for which he captured and enhanced the mood which each scene required.

This wouldn't be Gibb's only unused score. He spent the first half of 1985 working on a score for *The Supernaturals,* a low-budget horror flick about a present-day army platoon facing zombie Civil War soldiers. His score was even dubbed into the picture, but, as luck would have it, the movie's release was postponed. And by the time *The Supernaturals* premiered at the Cannes Film Market in 1986, the music had been changed to a more aggressive horror score, courtesy of composer Robert O. Ragland. However, a run of the home-video copies of this film was inexplicably made from a print with Gibb's score still intact, and these items are now prized collectibles for Bee Gees fans.

■ V: The Final Battle (1984)

Original composers: **Barry De Vorzon and Joseph Conlan**
Replacement composer: **Dennis McCarthy**

V: The Final Battle, a three-part television miniseries, was the sequel and intended conclusion of writer-producer Kenneth Johnson's two-part miniseries *V,* which aired in 1983. Based very loosely on Sinclair Lewis's 1935 antifascist novel *It Can't Happen Here, V* told the story of a dystopian future in which seemingly friendly aliens, the Visitors, are welcomed to earth, but soon show their true colors as tyrants bent on exploiting the planet's resources. (Johnson's previous credits included the TV series *The Six Million Dollar Man, The Bionic Woman,* and *The Incredible Hulk.*)

The original *V* miniseries had a superb orchestral score composed by Joe Harnell. In the 1950s and 1960s, Harnell had been music director–pianist–composer–arranger for such popular singers as Peggy Lee, Marlene Dietrich, and Robert Goulet. In the 1970s he turned to TV scoring, writing music for many of Kenneth Johnson's shows (most notably *The Incredible Hulk,* with its touching "Lonely Man" theme).

But during the production of *V: The Final Battle,* Johnson developed creative differences with producing studio Warner Bros. over the series' format, and he left the show before it aired. Composer Harnell also departed the franchise, so this second miniseries received an all-electronic score by the composing team of Barry De Vorzon and Joseph Conlan, who wrote a new main theme as well. (This pair, which had scored more than 100 episodes of the early-1980s series *Simon & Simon,* as well as a number of other projects, would split up shortly after their *V: The Final Battle* assignment. Their last team score was for the 1985 movie *Stick,* replacing a score by renowned jazz composer-arranger-pianist-bandleader Bob Florence.)

De Vorzon and Conlan's all-electronic score was a dramatic departure from Harnell's orchestral music. But the miniseries' fans—and its producers—had grown to expect the latter, so the producers switched composers in the middle of episode two's production. Dennis McCarthy, future composer for the various and numerous *Star Trek* television series, was hired to step in quickly (he was given nine days to write one hour and six minutes of music for a sixty-piece orchestra) and supply an orchestral score to replace much of the De Vorzon–Conlan material.

The result was that the first episode of *V: The Final Battle* retained its De Vorzon and Conlan music, the second episode contained music by them plus McCarthy, and the third was scored exclusively by McCarthy.

Even though he received no screen credit on *V: The Final Battle*, McCarthy was subsequently hired to score all nineteen episodes of the miniseries spinoff, *V: The Series*. Miniseries creator Kenneth Johnson didn't approve of this new franchise, but he was no longer making the calls. In hindsight, his judgment appears to be validated: Despite the popularity of its miniseries parents, the weekly series' ratings declined rapidly, and after one season, *V: The Series* was canceled.

■ **Streets of Fire** (1984)

Original composer: **James Horner**
Replacement composer: **Ry Cooder**

Director-writer Walter Hill planned *Streets of Fire* as the first installment of a film trilogy about futuristic mercenary Tom Cody. Set in a dark and violent urban landscape, a city ruled by gangs and corrupt cops in some unspecified time—sort of a 1950s-meets-a-dysfunctional-future world—it tells the tale of a female rock singer who's kidnapped by a biker gang and then rescued by her ex-boyfriend. Paul McCartney was offered the opportunity to play the kidnapped singer (before the part was rewritten for a woman), but the former Beatle said no, choosing to devote his time to his screenplay for *Give My Regards to Broad Street* (1984). Another hoped-for star for the picture was Bruce Springsteen, whose song "Streets of Fire," from his 1978 album *Darkness on the Edge of Town* gave the movie its title. That song was meant to be one of the hits for the film's soundtrack, but when Springsteen learned that someone else would rerecord it, he refused to permit its inclusion.

With such big talents orbiting the project (though none were ever actually involved), its underscore seemed to be the least pressing of its director's worries. Eventually James Horner, still near the beginning of the career, was given the job. (His prior credits included *Wolfen, Star Trek: The Wrath of Khan, 48 Hrs., Something Wicked This Way Comes, Gorky Park,* and *The Dresser.*) He was asked to bring his then-fresh, percussive action-movie sound, à la his 1982 score for *48 Hrs.* (also directed by Hill), to the picture. He did so, but his music was deemed unsuitable in view of the film's newly acquired songs, which, in turn, influenced the film's overall feel. Horner remembers:

> The score that I wrote for *Streets of Fire* was a very percussive, propulsive score. It used a lot of varied, different, exotic instrumentation. They decided to take it, that feeling, out. They wanted something a little more traditional, and they went with fifties rock 'n' roll. I tried something very risky in *Streets of Fire*. I thought it worked terrifically, and so did everybody, actually. But after about a week of living with it, thinking about it, the director started to feel perhaps I had gone too far. Now there's a difference between perhaps going too far and reverting back to fifties rock 'n' roll!

Although his score was replaced for this Walter Hill film, Horner would go on to provide music for two of the director's future projects: *Red Heat* (1988) and *Another 48 Hrs.* (1990).

For a new score, composer-guitarist-producer Ry Cooder was brought on. The musician already had a history with Hill, having scored the director's *The Long Riders* (1980) and *Southern Comfort* (1981). The enjoyable, fitting score Cooder wrote for *Streets of Fire* (which he performed with the Ry Cooder Band, a group of heavyweight session players) was in the style of 1950s instrumental rock music.

Set in a world of rock clubs, the film also needed songs, and music by Bob Seger, Jim Steinman, Tom Petty, Link Wray, Duane Eddy, Lee Hazlewood, Stevie Nicks, Lieber & Stoller, Ry Cooder, and Dan Hartman was used. Performers included the Blasters, the Fixx, Fire Inc. (which included legendary rock guitarist Rick Derringer), and others. The songs most important to the film's narrative were Jim Steinman's Wagnerian rock tunes as performed by Fire Inc. and Holly Sherwood, "Nowhere Fast" and "Tonight Is What It Means to Be Young." However, the best-selling song on the *Streets of Fire* soundtrack was Dan Hartmann's "I Can Dream About You," which reached number 6 on the Billboard Hot 100 chart.

Interestingly, it had been a rejected score that got Ry Cooder the *Streets of Fire* job in the first place: Cooder had scored the movie *Stroker Ace* (1983), one of many lighthearted action films that put Burt Reynolds behind the wheel of a car, with Southern-funk-rockabilly music that its director rejected the moment he heard it. (The movie eventually was scored by Al Capps, who contributed music to such other Reynolds-in-a-car flicks as *The Cannonball Run* and *Cannonball Run II*.) Cooder, however, didn't let the material he wrote for *Stroker Ace* go to waste. He played it for Walter Hill, who was enthusiastic about it and immediately asked him to score *Streets of Fire* in a similar vein.

A look at Hill's subsequent movies establishes Cooder, with whom he has worked ten more times, as essentially his in-house composer. A variation in the pattern occurred when a scheduling conflict left Cooder unable to score Hill's *Extreme Prejudice* (1987), resulting in the task going to Jerry Goldsmith. However, Cooder produced the recordings of Mexican songs that served as source music in the film.

A dozen years after *Streets of Fire*, Cooder would again replace another composer's score—Elmer Bernstein's rejected music for Hill's *Last Man Standing* (1996).

■ **1984** (1984)

Original composer: **Dominic Muldowney**
Replacement composers: **Eurythmics**

1984 was a nicely timed and well-executed adaptation of George Orwell's classic 1948 novel of the same name (the book that gave us such terms as "Big Brother," "thoughtcrime," "newspeak," and "Thought Police"). Scripted and directed by Michael Radford (who would go on to make *White Mischief* and *Il Postino*) and starring John Hurt, Suzanna Hamilton, and Richard Burton (in his last film), it tells the story of an everyman living in a grim, dystopian future. His country, Oceania, is ruled by the Party, which uses harsh, invasive methods to indoctrinate, subjugate, and control the masses. The protagonist and his girlfriend rebel against the Party and end up imprisoned, re-educated, and condemned.

Radford hired British composer Dominic Muldowney (whose previous credits included scores for *Betrayal*, *The Ploughman's Lunch*, and the BBC's 1982 production of *The Merry Wives of Windsor*) to provide an original score for the picture. Muldowney's music was a colorful mixture of various themes. The main one, which appears in the cue "Aria," is a powerful, optimistic anthem for Oceania. A more militaristic theme, which appears in the cue "Big Brother Fanfare," is developed and softened over the course of the score. The protagonist's theme is introspective. The rest of the score blends orchestra with interesting, subtle electronics, including the ondes Martenot (performed by virtuoso Cynthia Millar), that enhance the film's surrealistic setting—which is sort of 1984 via 1948. Muldowney also wrote three songs for the picture: the country's anthem, "Oceania, 'Tis for Thee," "The Washer Women's Song" (based on Orwell's text), and "The Hiking Song," which is performed by a boy's choir.

While Muldowney was still busy writing his score, the film's production studio, Virgin, started hunting for a different sound, one that might capture a young audience's ears, conquer the pop charts, and make money. An early consideration was pop icon David Bowie, whose 1974 album *Diamond Dogs* had been inspired by Orwell's novel. When Bowie turned out to be too expensive, the producers turned to Eurythmics, the highly popular duo of Annie Lennox and David A. Stewart, who had landed a big hit the previous year with their song "Sweet Dreams (Are Made of This)." Eurythmics started working on their *1984* music without knowing about the orchestral underscore that was in the works. Muldowney, however, knew about the band's involvement—he was told in the middle of his recording sessions that his music very likely would not be used!

When the studio exercised its right to make the picture's final cut, it replaced most of Muldowney's music with Eurythmics compositions. The only Muldowney music retained with any frequency was "Oceania, 'Tis for Thee." Michael Radford, extremely disappointed with the studio's edit and the new music, aimed several attacks at Virgin, claiming that the Eurythmics music had been "foisted" on his film. In his acceptance speech at the Evening Standard British Film Awards, where *1984* won Best Film, he condemned the company's changes and publicly disowned its version of the movie, which he referred to as "the Virgin cut." To further show his displeasure with the released version, Radford withdrew it from consideration for the BAFTA (British Academy of Film and Television Arts) Awards, which meant that this strong contender couldn't even be nominated.

In 2003, MGM Home Entertainment released a Region 1 (primarily North America) DVD of the movie's so-called director's cut. It had two notable differences from the Virgin cut: (1) the film's color was reset to a normal saturation level, as opposed to

Virgin's washed-out colors, and (2) Eurythmics' music was removed and replaced with Muldowney's (although the opening credits still listed the joint music credit). Radford's cut sometimes appeared on the UK's Channel 4 network in the late 1980s, but, interestingly, the 2004 Region 2 (primarily Western Europe and the Middle East) DVD contained Virgin's desaturated colors and the combined Eurythmics-Muldowney score on its English- and French-language audio tracks; however, its German tracks had Muldowney's music.

The Eurythmics music was released on the Virgin label. Muldowney released a limited-pressing CD of his *1984* music through the Airstrip One Company. (*Note*: Airstrip One is the name of the Oceania province in which *1984*'s protagonist lived.)

■ 2010: The Year We Make Contact (1984)

Original composer: **Tony Banks**
Replacement composer: **David Shire**

Director Peter Hyams's *2010: The Year We Make Contact*, based on Arthur C. Clarke's best-selling novel *2010: Odyssey Two*, was a sequel to Stanley Kubrick's groundbreaking 1968 film *2001: A Space Odyssey*. Starring Roy Scheider, John Lithgow, Helen Mirren, Bob Balaban, and Keir Dullea (reprising his role as Dave in *2001*), it's the story of a joint U.S.-Soviet space mission sent to find out what happened to the spacecraft *Discovery One*, its computer (the infamous HAL 9000), and its missing crewmember, Dave Bowman, whose last transmission was the enigmatic "My God, it's full of stars." Another aim of the mission was to investigate the monolith that was orbiting Jupiter.

Tony Banks, keyboardist for the progressive rock band Genesis, had been seeking a film scoring job for some time when he came into contact with Hyams, whose previous films included *Capricorn One* and *Outland* (both scored by Jerry Goldsmith). Banks's pop background, and the fact he was well versed in synthesizers and electronic music, interested Hyams, who knew his music for the film *The Shout* (1978). He hired Banks for *2010*. However, as Banks has noted, their initial exchanges of musical ideas were not promising:

> Peter Hyams really didn't like what I gave him from the word "go." I thought it strange since he was the one who contacted me, based on having heard what I had done on *The Shout*. The first tape I sent him included something that I thought was great, but he came back and said he thought it was really bad. So I thought, "This is crazy. Here I consider these to be the most appropriate things, and he doesn't like them." I don't know why he got ahold of me. Anyway, I thought, "We'll fight on." So I did a couple of other tapes, and we managed to end up with something he seemed fairly enthusiastic about.

Banks continued his work on the project for six months, producing eighteen pieces of music. But the director and composer never arrived at a meeting of the minds. Banks later called this scoring experience "a blow to his confidence," yet he didn't give up his film composing career: He went on to contribute music to the abysmal, incomprehensible British sci-fi flick *Starship* (aka *Lorca and the Outlaws*, 1985), for which he reworked one of his *2010* pieces into the "Redwing Suite." He reworked another *2010* piece into a movement called "The Gateway" for his *Seven: A Suite for Orchestra*, which was recorded by the London Philharmonic Orchestra and released on CD by Naxos in 2004.

After parting with Banks, Hyams contacted David Shire, a composer whose film-related experiments with electronic music had earned him both respect (*The Conversation*) and rejection (*Apocalypse Now*). Among Shire's many previous credits were *The Taking of Pelham One Two Three* and *Norma Rae*. Shire recalls getting involved:

> I was on vacation when I got a call from my agents telling me to hurry back to town since director Peter Hyams was changing composers on *2010* and had asked about my availability. I had mixed feelings about doing it, even at the beginning. It was supposed to be a "big movie," but I'm a little suspicious when another composer has worked for six months and it hasn't worked out. Also, doing a sequel to a classic film with a classic score is something to be wary of. However, I felt I should at least go and talk to Peter. So I met with him and he told me how he'd worked with Banks for a long time and when some actual cues came in they were not what he wanted. That's all I know about Tony Banks's involvement.

The director requested an electronic score that was orchestral, by which he meant that he didn't want experimental-sounding music but, rather, something along the lines of composer-performer Vangelis's work. (Vangelis had scored *Chariots of Fire*, *Blade Runner*, and other films.) The director felt electronic music would lend an otherworldly quality to his picture, and Shire, working with synthesizer programmer Craig Huxley, turned in an eerie, sometimes atmospheric, sometimes pulsing music that featured sounds from a Synclavier (a popular and revolutionary synthesizer that combined sampling with FM synthesis). His main theme music, which changed character as it developed, was both wistfully melancholy and strongly forward-looking.

When released as an album, the soundtrack recording contained a curious addition: a disco version of Strauss's *Also Sprach Zarathustra* by Andy Summers (of the band the Police), which hadn't appeared in the picture. The rest—Shire's electronic score—is highly recommended.

■ **Ordeal by Innocence** (1984)

Original composer: **Pino Donaggio**
Replacement composer: **Dave Brubeck**

Ordeal by Innocence, directed by Desmond Davis (best known for his 1981 film *Clash of the Titans*) and starring Donald Sutherland, Faye Dunaway, Christopher Plummer, and Sarah Miles, is one of the lesser-known Agatha Christie film adaptations. Set in Britain in the 1950s, it's the story of a wrongfully convicted man hanged for murdering his mother. Confirmation of the man's alibi does not come to light until a few years after his death, when an American paleontologist appears out of the blue with new evidence for the man's family. Based on this evidence, the family become murder suspects themselves, and the American proceeds to investigate the case. Overall, the motion picture was beautifully photographed but weighed down a bit by its abundant dialogue.

Italian composer Pino Donaggio (whose previous credits included the Brian de Palma films *Carrie, Dressed to Kill, Blow Out,* and *Body Double*) was chosen to score the project, based on his past association with Cannon Films (owned by *Ordeal by Innocence* executive producers Menahem Golan and Yoran Globus), for which he had written several bombastic action-movie scores, including the company's recent *Hercules* (1983). The dialogue-based *Ordeal by Innocence* contrasted sharply with many of the Cannon films Donaggio had written for in the past.

His score was recorded in Forum Studios Rome by conductor Sergio Marcotulli and the Orchestra Sinfonica Unione Musicisti di Roma. It has a beautiful main theme and roots in traditional Romanticism, and relies heavily on the string section. The film's dialogue scenes, however, were often accompanied by simple, melodic piano music. While it doesn't strictly reflect the movie's 1950s setting, the music seems stylistically appropriate, and probably would have made a powerful impact when paired with the film's images of the English countryside.

But this just was not destined to be Donaggio's film. The aforementioned CD's liner notes claim that his music was dropped because a scheduling conflict left him with too little time to adjust and rewrite his music to match a new cut of the picture. However, producer Jenny Craven later said she hadn't been satisfied with the score in the first place, and that she and star Donald Sutherland had tried something new, creating a temp track with jazz compositions. They found they liked the results, so, to get a sound similar to what they had achieved with their temp-music track, they went straight to the source of their inspiration—jazz legend composer-pianist Dave Brubeck—and asked him to score their film. Brubeck at first declined the offer because it allowed him only one month in which to write the music. But when told that all he had to do was improvise on his existing pieces, he accepted the job.

To get him started, Brubeck was sent a detailed description of the film's story, including information on the significance of its various clues and profiles of all its characters (who was who, what their main characteristics were, and what motivated them). Some profiles were highly detailed, while others were only a few lines long. The aim of the score was stated outright: The music should project the main character's "Americanism bustling through this cloistered, classical setting." Brubeck also received a copy of the movie, which he watched many times, making careful notes on which pieces he should use for each scene. The spotting notes contained instructions on what the cues should sound like, including references to specific music he had written and recorded in the past. For the first reel (the opening ferry ride), for example, Brubeck received the following:

1M1 Theme of optimism and innocence in the vein of TAKE FIVE. Setting the period and driving the movie forward through the title sequence. Blending into... 1M2 Picking up the sound of the ringing bell and continuing under the boat crossing (low for the dialogue) picking up again as the dialogue finishes and CALGARY steps off the boat with that oblique sense of menace that the percussion provides going up the driveway through the woods... PHILIP at the lodge window, picked out by the saxophone...incorporating an instrumental phrase for KIRSTEN as she opens the house door... MUSIC OUT as Calgary puts the address book in his pocket. NOTES: PHILIP & MARY—impotence, boredom, inadequacy. Malice and slyness—always on the watch.

Brubeck prepared the list of pieces that he would use. It included "Take Five," "Lost Waltz," "Blue Rondo à la Turk," and other tunes. The score became leitmotif-driven—with each leitmotif a jazz tune! The recording session with his quartet (Brubeck on piano, Bill Smith on reeds, his son Chris Brubeck on bass and trombone, and Randy Jones on drums) was held in San Francisco under the supervision of Donald Sutherland.

Although a score by Brubeck was an interesting enticement for some of the jazz world's relatively small fan base, the movie flopped at the box office. Even so, many reviews (including some that panned the picture) lauded the score, describing it as "rich and varied" (*Los Angeles Times*) and "another point in its [the movie's] favor" (*The Guardian*). In later years, some of the enthusiasm for the music would cool, with one critic even calling it "amazingly inappropriate" (*Film Score Monthly*).

The interaction of Brubeck's music with the picture ended up problematic in three respects. First, it was mixed too loudly, sometimes causing the dialogue to be nearly incomprehensible. Second, it appeared too frequently—i.e., many scenes that would have worked well without music feel too noisy with it. And finally, though appropriate to the 1950s time frame, jazz of any stripe feels a bit out of place in a chatty film set in the English countryside.

Perhaps because of *Ordeal by Innocence*'s failure, a much-discussed Brubeck soundtrack release never materialized. Donaggio's music, on the other hand, had a few releases: The first was on a Donaggio compilation, where portions of his unused score were edited into his *Suite for a Dying Venice*. His unused score had a more complete release in 2011 on Kritzerland.

■ **The New Kids** (1985)

Original composer: **Harry Manfredini**
Replacement composers: **Michel Rubini, Lalo Schifrin**

In 1980, Sean S. Cunningham opened a can of worms with *Friday the 13th*. After its release, horror films about teenagers would start to feature more gore and nudity, to attract a target audience of teens who were just a bit younger than the actors on the screen.

Cunningham's 1985 movie *The New Kids* was a little more restrained. It was a simple chiller about a teenage brother and sister who move to a small town, where a local gang harasses them until the siblings dispatch its members one by one in a gory sequence.

But the target viewers were used to ultraviolent movies by then, and when the flick was test-screened for them, its relatively tame bloodshed didn't resonate. Reacting to the negative response, the studio looked for a way to make the film seem more hip. One logical means of doing that was to get a new soundtrack.

The film's original orchestral score had been provided by Harry Manfredini, who had worked with Cunningham on four movies, including *Friday the 13th*. (They would collaborate on a number of later movies as well.)

To provide more teen appeal in the music department, the studio decided it needed hit songs, which often played an important role in marketing such movies. The "hits" it acquired included "Stand Up" (by Bill Wray) and "Making a Move" (by Brock Walsh and Steve Nelson), neither of which managed to leave any impression outside the picture. Another step in the hipping-up of the music was to commission an electronic score by Michel Rubini (who had done *The Hunger*, starring Catherine Deneuve and David Bowie, in 1983) to replace Manfredini's orchestral one. Rubini also contributed two songs to the project, "Edge of Survival" (with lyrics by Jess Harnell) and "Over and Over and Over Again" (with lyrics by Miriam Cutler).

But while electronic scores like Rubini's were demonstrably popular in the 1980s, *The New Kids* wouldn't end up with one. Test screenings of the new version, with the new songs and score in place, showed no improvement; apparently pop songs and a synthesized score were not enough to cure what ailed *The New Kids*. The test audience's problems were with the movie itself, of course, not the music. Even so, yet another composer was brought on board.

The final score for *The New Kids* was provided by Lalo Schifrin, who had a hard time coming up with something novel. When he first screened the movie, he didn't find any problems in the music it already had. But the studio asked for another score anyway, though without offering any suggestions as to what changes the composer should make. After consulting with the film's editor, Schifrin wrote a score that was fairly close to Manfredini's original one. It was accepted and used in the finished version of the movie, along with the four songs mentioned above.

The next year, Schifrin would write a replacement score for another strange vigilante movie—*The Ladies Club* (originally titled *Take Back the Night*)—in which a raped policewoman organizes a gang of other rape victims, who abduct and castrate rapists who have escaped punishment due to legal technicalities. Director Janet Greek originally hired composer Shirley Walker not only because she was a great composer, but also because as a woman, Walker had had a hard time breaking into Hollywood's composing circles, where she was often pigeonholed as simply a great orchestrator and conductor. Walker worked closely with the director, and they agreed upon a spare, haunting sound for the picture. Her score avoided 1980s clichés and kept up with the excitement of this fast-paced thriller.

Before its release, however, the movie was re-edited. The strong anti-rape message was dropped, in favor of concentrating on shots of chicks kicking butts. It was retitled somewhat exploitatively as *The Ladies Club* and given a new score by Lalo Schifrin that was anything but subtle or sublime. (Schifrin would provide several campy scores of this ilk in the mid-1980s.) Both director Greek—who assumed an alias in the film's credits—and Shirley Walker were disappointed with the finished picture, which certainly wasn't what they had in mind. Like Cunningham's *The New Kids, The Ladies Club* became another sensibility-numbing video for B-movie enthusiasts in the 1980s, an era in which Hollywood celebrated the weak overcoming their oppressors in the most gruesome ways possible.

■ Doctor Who: "The Mark of the Rani" (1985)

Original composer: **John Lewis**
Replacement composer: **Jonathan Gibbs**

The BBC's *Doctor Who* was one of television's longest-running series. It lasted twenty-six continuous seasons (1963–89) before its temporary cancellation. Focusing on the adventures of its titular Time Lord, who travels in time and space with his companions, it enjoyed unmatched popularity in Britain and was later aired by television stations around the globe.

By the show's twenty-second season (1985), producer John Nathan-Turner (who produced 171 of its episodes, 1971–89) felt it needed fresh blood. He brought in some new writers, directors, and composers to see what they could come up with. Some of their innovations worked and led to great episodes; others didn't.

Usually, the series' music was created by members of the BBC Radiophonic Workshop (providers of innovative sound effects and music for BBC radio and TV programs from 1958 through 1998). Its members in the mid-1980s included Dick Mills, Brian Hodgson, Peter Howell, and a few other composers whose quality electronic music aligned with *Doctor Who*'s traditions. (The show's theme, written by Ron Grainer and realized as a piece of musique concrète by Delia Derbyshire, would be used with only minor modifications throughout its forty-year run.)

As part of his fresh-blood campaign, Nathan-Turner also brought in composers from outside the BBC's regular crew. In 1985 he hired Canadian electronic music composer John Lewis, who had performed on the 1979 hit song "Pop Muzik." Lewis was recommended by Workshop regular Brian Hodgson, with whom he ran the commercial electronic music studio Electrophon. In the mid-1970s, the two had also collaborated on two albums of electronic music for the Polydor label, under the band name Wavemaker.

"The Mark of the Rani" was the two-installment episode of *Doctor Who* that introduced the character Rani, a female Time Lord and evil scientific genius. Lewis scored and recorded a score for the episode's first part, but before he could get to the second he fell seriously ill and couldn't proceed. He died during the show's production, and Hodgson turned to Workshop composer Jonathan Gibbs to write a new score for both parts of the episode.

When the first installment of this episode appeared on DVD in 2006, it did so with both scores—an isolated track of Gibbs's music and a version with Lewis's music (taken from tapes owned by his estate). This presentation of the two scores side by side allows film music fans a fascinating opportunity to compare the work of two composers facing the same challenges—principally, in this case, finding a way to accommodate both the Industrial Revolution historical setting and the story's science-fiction elements, which become more dominant as the story progresses. Lewis's score didn't break with the established synthesized *Doctor Who* sound, but it was much more aggressive and nostalgic than Gibbs's.

■ **Heaven Help Us** (1985)

Composer of multiple scores: **James Horner**

Heaven Help Us is a coming-of-age comedy set in 1965. It tells the story of a teenage boy from Boston who, after being orphaned, moves in with Brooklyn relatives and attends St. Basil's Catholic Boys School. This fairly juvenile romp—wild teens versus the brutal brothers on the faculty—was the second film directed by former singer/songwriter Michael Dinner. It stars Donald Sutherland, John Heard, Andrew McCarthy, Kevin Dillon, and Wallace Shawn. James Horner was hired to provide its score, a job that turned into three scores, one right after another. (The behind-the-scenes trials that led to Horner's multiple scores were well chronicled by David Kraft in a 1985 article for *CinemaScore* magazine.)

Horner's first *Heaven Help Us* score, only nine cues, explored and exploited Irish music (as would several of his later scores) in an attempt to knit together key elements of the picture: Irishness, Catholicism, the film's Brooklyn setting, and perhaps the protagonist's Boston background. Recorded in October 1984, it featured several musicians from England and Ireland playing traditional instruments such as tinwhistle, *bodhran* drum, hammered dulcimer, bagpipes, and mandolin, all augmented by such well-known LA studio musicians as guitarist Tommy Tedesco, harpist Dorothy Remsen, and percussionist Emil Richards. Film music critic David Kraft wrote that the music resembled that of the popular Irish music group the Chieftans.

Both the director and the composer were delighted with the score and how it worked with the film. TriStar Pictures, however, wasn't so enthusiastic, and immediately asked Horner to rescore the movie. The studio wanted him to dump the Irish references and take more of a classical-music approach; in fact, they suggested that he look to Mozart for inspiration.

Horner's second effort, based largely on the overture to Mozart's opera *The Magic Flute,* also included moments from J. S. Bach's *Brandenburg Concerto No. 2,* as well as a number of original classical-style pieces by Horner. It was recorded with a moderate-sized orchestra on Paramount's scoring stage in the middle of November.

But neither the director nor the composer liked this new score, and they lobbied the studio to reconsider their original Irish music approach. At nearly the last moment, the two parties struck a compromise, allowing the use of the Irish-influenced music, but rescored and rearranged for a more traditional studio orchestra. As a result, music that had originally been played by fifes and tinwhistles was now played by saxophones and other instruments less identified with folk music.

Most of this third score made it into the movie. However, to establish the story's mid-sixties period, as well as perk up soundtrack record sales, many vintage songs of the 1960s (and even the late 1950s) were added to the picture. These included music by Junior Walker ("Shotgun"), Otis Redding ("I've Been Loving You Too Long"), Sam the Sham ("Wooly Bully"), The Singing Nun ("Dominique"), Bobby Vinton ("Blue Velvet"), the Temptations ("My Girl"), the Supremes, Marvin Gaye, Smokey Robinson, and others. One of these songs even replaced one of Horner's cues, and the eventual soundtrack LP contained none of his music. A bootleg record containing material from several Horner sessions, including the classical selections from his second *Heaven Help Us* score and some raw rehearsals, is now the only way to hear his score apart from in the picture.

■ **Lifeforce** (1985)

Original composer: **Henry Mancini**
Additional composer for American version: **Michael Kamen**

Combining a balletic space journey (à la Kubrick's *2001: A Space Odyssey*) with life-draining horror (à la Ridley Scott's *Alien*), director Tobe Hooper's *Lifeforce* is one strange animal. (Horror/slashmeister Hooper's earlier films included the notably popular *The Texas Chainsaw Massacre* and *Poltergeist.*) Based on Colin Wilson's 1976 novel *The Space Vampires* and adapted for the screen by *Alien* writer Dan O'Bannon, *Lifeforce* is the story of a space shuttle mission to Halley's Comet that brings back extraterrestrial vampires who suck out people's "lifeforce," creating havoc-wreaking zombies that terrorize London.

Labeled the most expensive B movie ever made, this space-horror adventure bought itself a touch of class when it hired composer Henry Mancini, whose previous credits included such classics as *Touch of Evil* (1958), *The Days of Wine and Roses* (1962), *The Pink Panther* (1963), and *Charade* (1963) but basically no music for science fiction or horror films. The movie gave him the opportunity to be as experimental as he pleased, with strong support from director Hooper.

Mancini's score for *Lifeforce* proved impressive and exciting. It stood apart from the then-current fad of synthesizer-driven film music, particularly for sci-fi and horror flicks (although he did utilize voices recorded into a Fairlight sampler). A pulsating rhythmic figure played into the meaning of the title cue—"Lifeforce"—and the London Symphony Orchestra's performance certainly doesn't disappoint. Mancini also provided some strong boo moments, and his Fairlight-generated choirs had an epic quality.

The picture's producing entity, London-Cannon Films/Golan-Globus Productions, found the director's cut overlong at 128 minutes. To make it more commercially appealing and allow theaters an extra showing each day, they cut it to less than two hours, sacrificing most of the space shuttle's journey (one of the longest cinematic space treks this side of *2001*). For this part of the film, Mancini had written a sixteen-minute tone poem or outer-space ballet, "The Discovery," recorded in five sections. After the movie was chopped up, he was asked to rewrite this cue, but he was already busy with his next project, *Santa Claus: The Movie* (1985). Thanks to the picture's new re-editing, Cannon had little of Mancini's music to worry about.

But even with the picture down to 116 minutes, the U.S. codistributor, TriStar Pictures, requested further changes for the American market (who apparently might be disturbed by naked space vampires and extreme violence). TriStar's *re*-re-edit of the American theatrical release made changes in about twenty scenes. In the process, it managed to compromise the movie's plot, tossing out much of the explanation behind the space vampires. Now a new composer was needed, to help pull together the entire patchwork. The choice was someone who had been approached even before Mancini was hired: Michael Kamen, whose previous credits included *Venom* (1981), *The Dead Zone* (1983), and *Brazil* (1985). Kamen recalls his first contact with *Lifeforce*:

> The producers felt Mancini's score wasn't "scary" enough, so they got me to write some scary music. The irony is that I was asked before Mancini to score the film but was doing *Brazil*, so I turned it down. I loved *Poltergeist* and admired director Tobe Hooper who directed it. So I was flattered to be asked to work with him on *Lifeforce*, but I was too busy at the time. They had originally hired James Horner, but there were problems and he left. When they called me I was not only busy but I felt uncomfortable about stepping into someone else's shoes. They then hired Mancini.

To rework the original score and add an extra level of scariness to the music, Kamen and his friend recording engineer and record producer James Guthrie (known for his work with the band Pink Floyd) provided additional dark textures. Kamen recalls his busy schedule and his work on *Lifeforce*:

> Well, they came back to me later after it was felt his [Mancini's] score lacked terror. I was then busy with an episode of *Amazing Stories* ["Mirror, Mirror"] for Martin Scorsese; so I recommended they hire James Guthrie, who is a great mixer, and have him take some of

> the tapes I have of various techniques and orchestral things and have him mix them into the soundtrack with his weird machines and black boxes. They agreed. Scorsese called me and said he needed to push our recordings dates back, so I told Cannon Films I now could do *Lifeforce*. James Guthrie and I played around in the studio, and I wrote a little bit of orchestral music for the beginning of the film to set things up. The film's credits read "Music by Henry Mancini. Additional music by Michael Kamen with James Guthrie." I feel my contribution made the opening scarier and the sounds we created were confusing enough to be worrying to the audience.

In some cases, Kamen's work literally overlapped or shrouded Mancini's, with both playing simultaneously. But the most heavily re-edited scenes required new music; the opening, for instance, dropped Mancini's "space ballet" approach and utilized Kamen's creepy, atmospheric synth textures instead. Kamen also provided suspense music for scenes that originally had not been scored at all.

All the music written for the picture by both composers is available on a limited-edition CD released by BSX Records. For a striking comparison of scores, listen to the cue "Rescue Mission," which accompanies the shuttle crew's saving of the vampires. While both scores achieve the same results, Mancini establishes his tension with low strings while Kamen emulates the disturbing sounds Jerry Goldsmith used in his *Alien* score. Needless to say, the musical meddling on *Lifeforce* left Mancini disappointed—he has stated that he never watched the movie after finishing his work on it.

■ Crimewave (1985)

Original composer: **Arlon Ober**
Additional composer: **Joseph LoDuca**

Crimewave combined many young talents. It was directed by Sam Raimi, who had one previous feature credit, the popular horror film *The Evil Dead* (1981); written by the Coen brothers, Joel and Ethan, who also had only one previous feature credit, the stylish neo-noir *Blood Simple* (1984); and coproduced by Robert Tapert and actor Bruce Campbell (one of Raimi's childhood friends). Blending Three Stooges–inspired slapstick comedy with neo-noirish elements and just plain old over-the-top acting, *Crimewave* was the story of a pair of bumbling, cartoonish exterminators-turned-hitmen on a misguided rampage, as told through a series of flashbacks by a falsely convicted man about to be executed in the electric chair.

Crimewave quickly became a problematic production, in no small part due to numerous creative intrusions by Embassy Pictures, which financed it. Embassy overruled the filmmakers' decisions in almost every area, from casting to editing to music. One major problem (and one that's common to many, many B movies) was an inadequate budget. Reportedly, the young filmmakers' lack of budgeting experience, combined with the studio's casting changes, left the picture underfunded and at the studio's mercy.

For *Crimewave*'s music, Raimi hired fellow Michiganian Joseph LoDuca, a former jazz guitarist who had scored *The Evil Dead* (and would work with Raimi again in the future). The composer joined the movie during preproduction, to supply music for a choreographed scene. For this he provided the cue "Rialto," which was performed by jazz musicians in Detroit, where the scene was shot. (LoDuca's wife choreographed the number, and the two of them appear onscreen in cameos, with the composer as a trumpet player and his wife as a hatcheck lady.)

While Raimi hoped LoDuca would score the entire movie, Embassy had other plans. It simultaneously fired Raimi's editor, Kaye Davis, and hired its own composer, Arlon Ober, whose previous credits included the black comedy *Eating Raoul* (1982) and the sci-fi anime TV series *Robotech* (1985). *Crimewave* gave Ober a chance to try his hand at a fast-paced, kaleidoscopic swirl of genres, but his broadly comic score—a musical pastiche that embraced faux classical music, horror-movie organ, musical pratfalls, and wild jazz numbers—conflicted with Raimi's philosophy of using music as the "straight man" in comedies. There's so much going on in it that it sometimes sounds unfocused, often underscoring dark, sarcastic humor with inappropriately light music (a good way to stab a joke in the back).

Before its release, Raimi was allowed to rehire LoDuca to rescore the picture's last few reels, saving the climax from Ober's inappropriately comic touches. Thus, the film ended up with a score that combined the work of two composers with quite different takes on the project. Even so, LoDuca is listed in the picture's end credits only as music consultant and the composer of "Rialto."

■ **The Journey of Natty Gann** (1985)

Original composer: **Elmer Bernstein**
Replacement composer: **James Horner**

In 1985, composer Elmer Bernstein took not one but two assignments from Disney: the animated *The Black Cauldron* and *The Journey of Natty Gann*. Set in 1935, *The Journey of Natty Gann* follows a girl's backroad trek from Chicago to the state of Washington, searching for a father who left her behind when he set out to find work in Washington's timber industry. Young Natty has many adventures along the way, including repeated escapes from unsavory Depression Era types, falling in love with a young boy who's also on the road, and befriending a wolf that accompanies her on much of her trip.

For Bernstein, the movie was about the girl's journey, and the music he provided was a sonic depiction of the beautiful and wild landscapes she encounters. The cornerstones of his score were a set of bold Americana-style fanfares and a *Magnificent Seven*–like adventure theme. But after his initial presentation of his work, the studio asked Bernstein to make major changes. They wanted music embodying action, excitement, and drama, focusing more on the main character's escapades than on the breathtaking landscape.

The composer was shocked. He had put much thought into his score and generally was not keen on rewriting cues. But, in an effort to save his music, Bernstein vigorously applied himself to a series of rewrites, sometimes delivering multiple versions of the same cue for director Jeremy Kagan's consideration. (The soundtrack release of Bernstein's version of *The Journey of Natty Gann* contains no less than fifteen alternate cues. And that represents only a fraction of his rewrites and rerecordings, as he diligently conducted hundreds of takes, and reinterpreted his work until it seemed to hit the right chords with the filmmakers.) To assist him in such a trying project, Bernstein hired his son Peter to orchestrate and to help him keep up with the rapid rewrites requested of him. Bernstein was never sure what behind-the-scenes decisions caused his *Natty Gann* score finally to be rejected:

> I don't know what happened on *Natty Gann*. They were worried about the film, they kept changing things. We did the score, we made some changes, they said they loved the changes, then the next thing I know, James [Horner] was engaged to do the score. I think that the director was not feeling well, he must have been going through some sort of crisis. James is very good friends with Jeffrey Katzenberg, who basically runs the studio [Disney], and I think that, as a last attempt to deal with the director, he had James do it. I spoke with James before he undertook it and I warned him about the director, and that time, I really don't know how he got on.

Apparently not too well—Horner reportedly left the recording sessions at one point, fuming over the director's indecisiveness. We can assume that he had to rewrite his music numerous times as well. Amid the musical confusion, two brief Bernstein cues made it into the picture: his music for the hotel escape and the cue that followed the driver's attack on Natty and the wolf.

Horner's replacement score is built around a main theme that may be familiar even to those who haven't seen the movie: his song "If We Hold On Together," which he would reuse (sung by Diana Ross) three years later in the animated dinosaur adventure *The Land Before Time*. Horner's *Natty Gann* score, like Bernstein's, embraced an Americana style but was more playful and lighthearted than Bernstein's. Its most prominently featured instruments are strings and woodwinds, lending it an idyllic feel. And, of course, there's the *shakuhachi* (a Japanese bamboo flute), since no Horner score is complete without it.

Horner's replacement music hasn't been released yet, but Varèse Sarabande issued Bernstein's rejected score in 2008. Interestingly, Disney used Bernstein's *Natty Gann* trailer music in the teasers for both *The Journey of Natty Gann* and *Benji the Hunted* (1987). Varèse Sarabande issued Bernstein's rejected score in 2008. Intrada released Horner's score in 2009, so both scores are now available for comparison.

■ Moonlighting: "The Lady in the Iron Mask" (1985)

Original composer: **Richard Lewis Warren**
Replacement composer: **Alf Clausen**

Moonlighting (1985–89) was an ABC comedy-drama-detective series starring Cybil Shepherd and Bruce Willis as mismatched, lightheartedly ever-bickering partners in a private-eye agency. The series was created by Glenn Gordon Caron, writer and producer for the very similarly themed NBC series *Remington Steele* (1982–87), which starred Stephanie Zimbalist and Pierce Brosnan. *Moonlighting*'s popular theme song was written by Lee Holdridge, with lyrics by Al Jarreau, who also sang it. Musically, the show was known for its frequent use of famous tunes often performed by stars Shepherd and Willis.

Initially, three composers worked on the show: Lee Holdridge (whose many previous composing credits included the theme song for TV's *Eight Is Enough* and scores for the features *American Pop*, *Mr. Mom*, and *Splash*), Alf Clausen (whose scoring credits included a few episodes of TV's *Fame* and a handful of TV movies), and Richard Lewis Warren (whose scoring credits included episodes of TV's *Remington Steele*, *Rhoda*, and *Dallas*).

Holdridge scored *Moonlighting*'s pilot and some of its early episodes, and hired his friend Alf Clausen to orchestrate. But Holdridge soon moved on to other projects, recommending Clausen as his replacement. Impressed with Clausen's work, Caron hired him to be one of the show's two composers, along with Richard Lewis Warren. Warren, however, would drop out soon after the start of season two and return to his work on *Remington Steele*. His *Moonlighting* fate was sealed by the episode "The Lady in the Iron Mask," the tale of a disfigured woman who seeks vengeance on the man who ruined her, a show that's recognized as one of the series' best.

Warren's score for this episode was distractingly aggressive; his music under the opening shower shots was dramatically over-the-top. His score also placed an inappropriate emphasis on the Lady's seductiveness, with sultry strains that failed to convey her underlying vulnerability. Caron didn't care for the score and asked Clausen to quickly rewrite it, giving the Lady an aura of mystique rather than seduction.

Clausen gave Caron exactly the music he wanted, and more: Among Clausen's notable cues for this episode is a climactic chase scene set to Rossini's *William Tell Overture*. (*Note*: The *William Tell Overture*, an oft-quoted, eternally popular bit of music, is well known even by those who shun classical music because of its innumerable appearances in popular media: It has appeared in many cartoons, game shows, commercials, Kubrick's *A Clockwork Orange*, and most famously as the theme music for *The Lone Ranger* radio and television shows. Due to its infectiously jaunty nature, it's often used comedically, as in the aforementioned cartoons and as part of Spike Jones's and Victor Borge's routines.)

Following the success of his score for "The Lady in the Iron Mask," *Moonlighting* kept Clausen busy as composer, music director, and principal arranger until 1989, when he took over scoring duties on *The Simpsons.*

Fans of "The Lady in the Iron Mask" were in for a sad surprise when Lions Gate released the series' seasons one and two on DVD: Clausen's score and the *William Tell Overture* were gone, replaced by music that was not from the aired show. What happened? When all the episodes were remastered for release on DVD in 2005, Lions Gate utilized the show's original video and music tapes. In the process of pulling the old tapes from the studio's archives, this episode's original score by Warren (the one rejected by Caron) was accidentally selected. Despite this blunder, this two-season DVD set remains in circulation. So the only way to see "The Lady in the Iron Mask" with Clausen's music is in rerun.

■ **Legend** (1985)

Composer for European version: **Jerry Goldsmith**
Composer for American version: **Tangerine Dream**

Director Ridley Scott is known for placing great emphasis on the role of music in his films. He's also known to occasionally have a bit of difficulty making his desires clear to composers. In 1979, for example, he hired Jerry Goldsmith to score his highly influential sci-fi film *Alien.* Scott based many of his ideas for this film's music on a temp score assembled by editor Terry Rawlings, who primarily used excerpts from Goldsmith's extensive discography. During production, however, Scott made so many changes in his approach to the music that Goldsmith ended up writing two or three alternates for many cues, as well as penning a brand-new main title. Despite all of Goldsmith's work, the director still reverted to using some of the temp tracks to replace parts of the composer's original score. These tracks included cues from Goldsmith's *Freud* (1962) score and an excerpt from Howard Hanson's Symphony No. 2 (the *Romantic*), which is heard under the end credits.

Though horrified by this scoring experience, the composer would bury the hatchet and reunite with Scott for his 1985 fantasy picture, *Legend*, starring Tom Cruise. A simple tale of good versus evil, daylight versus the darkness of night, *Legend* portrays a "once upon a time" world populated by fairies, unicorns, goblins, and demons. Goldsmith remembers working on the film:

> Ridley was somewhat surprised when they called me to do *Legend.* I flipped over the script, and you know the pity is the writer [William Hjortsberg] is taking such a rap on this picture. They're all blaming him, and he wrote a beautiful script. I wanted to do it because of the script. I told Ridley that working on *Alien* was one of the most miserable experiences I've ever had in this profession. Personally, it was a really trying time for me. And he said, "What was the problem?" I said, "Ridley, you can't communicate. I was on the picture for four months and I talked to you three times. All during the recording you

> didn't say a word to me, and I need some feedback." So on *Legend* we communicated like crazy, and the score went right out the window.

Goldsmith's work on *Legend* began before the shooting started: He had to write songs for Princess Lili to sing onscreen ("My True Love's Eyes" and "Living River," lyrics by John Bettis), as well as two pieces for onscreen dance numbers choreographed by Arlene Phillips. The composer moved to London for three months to pen the movie's eighty-plus minutes of music, which he recorded with the National Philharmonic Orchestra at CBS Studios.

Goldsmith's beautiful, lyrical score, influenced by French impressionist music, particularly Maurice Ravel's *Daphnis and Chloé*, was stylistically in the tradition of great fantasy and adventure scores. It also drew on musical ideas from Celtic folk music to present a bucolic vision of the woods, and its lovely melodies often featured evocative vocalizations by the Ambrosian Singers. Yet Goldsmith also included a good deal of strange-sounding music, which nicely introduces disturbing elements into *Legend*'s forest world. These intrusions of atonality into an otherwise tonal score often made use of the six synthesizers with which Goldsmith represented the Lord of Darkness and his evil Goblins. The combination of all these musical ideas provided a rich aural atmosphere for Ridley Scott's visuals.

Scott, however, had a hard time coming up with a final version of *Legend*. He edited the initial 140 minutes to 113 minutes and declared this the director's cut, but, unfortunately, both of the picture's main distributors—20th Century Fox for Europe and Universal Pictures for the United States—requested further changes. Fox, specifically, wanted its version chopped down to 94 minutes! To accommodate that request, the director resorted to "innovative" music-editing techniques, meaning, Scott and editor Terry Rawlings brought together all the music that Goldsmith had written for the film and then sprinkled it throughout the movie as they saw fit. The cue "Darkness Fails," for instance, was dragged into five different scenes preceding its intended place. One particularly problematic scene, the kitchen fight, had originally been left unscored by agreement between the composer and the director. But when re-editing, Scott decided the scene needed music after all, so he borrowed material from his old temp track—a combination of Goldsmith's "The Cellar"/"Main Title" from *Psycho II* (1983) and library music by British composer Tim Souster (which would be used again with the main titles of 1987's *Amazon Women on the Moon*).

For the American market, things were a bit different. Sid Sheinberg (president and chief operating officer of MCA, Universal's parent company) arranged a test screening of the film in San Diego, to see whether the company's target audience would connect with it. The test didn't go well: The audience not only didn't get the fairy tale, but they laughed at the movie. Despite the fact, noted in the "making of" documentary on *Legend*'s DVD, that many of the teenagers attending the screening were stoned, their opinions still convinced Sheinberg that changes were called for. Universal ran a trailer for *Legend* (featuring Goldsmith's score) in American theaters in the summer of 1985 but in fact decided to push back the U.S. release to April 1986, to allow for a major overhaul. (*Legend* was released in Europe in the fall of 1985.)

Universal had many concerns, among them that Tom Cruise couldn't be taken seriously with long hair. The company further believed a new musical score was needed to reach the young target audience. Scott accepted the delayed American release and set himself to obliging the distributor's requests with a vengeance, fearing that if he refused he'd lose all control over his movie. He made numerous cuts and switched scenes around. One of the more outrageous alterations involved moving a kiss between Jack and Lili from the end of the film to the beginning, implying that the couple has sex!

The new version's many cuts and overall difference in approach necessitated a new score. Scott recalls:

> I got totally paranoid. I started to hack away at the movie. A gentleman at Universal literally tried to physically stop me. As opposed to him saying, "We've got to cut this film," it was me.... I figured that maybe we'd been too adventurous with our expectations of a full-blown fairy story, and therefore, maybe the combination of the score and the visual was actually too sweet. So, with only three weeks to redo a score, I went to Berlin and did the score with Tangerine Dream. In three weeks they did an incredible job, but it was completely different. It was a driving, more modern way to go, and given what they did in the time, I thought they did a fantastic job....

Tangerine Dream, a popular German synthesizer-based progressive-rock band founded in 1967 by Edgar Froese, was a pioneer in the genre pejoratively known as "krautrock," which was characterized by a mechanized-sounding beat and an ambient-music aesthetic; the band was also a pioneer in the electronic branch of New Age music. They had provided music for a number of films, including *Firestarter* (1983), *Flashpoint* (1984), and *Forbidden* (1984), and their pop-influenced synth scores were popular on the soundtrack market. Edgar Froese recalls getting the *Legend* job:

> The first time we saw the film it still had the Goldsmith score. There was sort of a misunderstanding, or whatever, between Universal and 20th Century Fox. Fox wanted to release it over here and in Europe with the Goldsmith score because they were already under pressure to have it at the Venice Festival, some other releases in France and elsewhere. But Universal, who had the right to release the film in the States, Japan, and Australia, were not under so much pressure because they had no specific deadlines. Universal didn't like the music, so they asked for someone who could do a more or less "extraordinary" score, whatever they thought "extraordinary" should be. Someone came up with the name Tangerine Dream, and Ridley Scott already had the experience of working with electronics by using Vangelis on *Blade Runner*, so he went to our agent in LA, and that's how it came all about.

Stylistically, Tangerine Dream's New Ageish score delivered what the band was asked to do, but it worked quite differently than Goldsmith's score, and perhaps not always advantageously so: The band gave the Western fairy tale an underscore influenced by

Eastern harmonies and orchestrations. The Lord of Darkness, for example, was represented by a faux-ethnic music utilizing sampled sitars and Asian winds (à la Tibetan horns), unintentionally evoking the old Cold War stereotype of evil having Eastern origins. Overall, the score was synth-heavy, as one would expect: Tangerine Dream brought in thirty-five different machines, from sequencers to samplers (with extensive sound libraries), to provide music that some believe stands out inappropriately from the picture. By standing out, however, the music fulfilled Tangerine Dream's declared purpose of never compromising stylistic identity for the sake of a film's nature.

Yet, even before Universal's version of the film hit theaters, Tangerine Dream's music was changed: Lyrics were added to their final cue ("Loved by the Sun") and sung by Jon Anderson, a former member of the progressive-rock band Yes, and the film's end credits received a new song ("Is Your Love Strong Enough") by Brian Ferry, former lead singer for the band Roxy Music. And all without Tangerine Dream's knowledge or cooperation.

Neither Fox's nor Universal's version of *Legend* received favorable reviews during the film's theatrical run. However, the movie was rediscovered in 2002, when Ridley Scott's 113-minute director's cut was finally released on DVD. With this version, many of the other versions' unexplained plot gaps were accounted for, and Jerry Goldsmith's entire score was restored for the American audience. Though many of the restored sequences featured the music department's cut-and-paste job, the expanded movie offered fans a chance to compare the two scores.

Opinions about which of *Legend*'s scores is preferable seem to be tied to a sort of musical imprinting, by which fans tend to prefer the score they originally heard (or the soundtrack they originally bought). Thus, American and European fans of the movie are divided in their appreciation of its music. Yet it's hard to imagine a more beautiful opening to a movie than the European version, a superbly photographed blue-tinted night, with a deer and a bear running free in the wild while a haunting theme plays against the night's sounds (wind, owl hoots, etc.). If all of *Legend* had lived up to this opening, it would have become a true classic.

■ **The Clan of the Cave Bear** (1986)

Original composer: **John Scott**
Replacement composer: **Alan Silvestri**

In the mid-1980s, British composer John Scott tried to establish himself in Hollywood. The only movie that he had previously scored and recorded in the United States was *North Dallas Forty* (1979), a football picture starring Nick Nolte. Scott hoped that relocation to Los Angeles would change that. So, in 1984 he rented a house in the Hollywood Hills, just a couple of blocks from Miklós Rózsa's home. One of his early jobs as an LA resident was on an ill-conceived television movie starring Brooke Shields and Burgess Meredith, *Wet Gold* (1984), a deep-sea treasure-hunt adventure loosely based on the classic 1948 film *The Treasure of the Sierra Madre*. As unlikely as it may seem, even a simple television movie like this can generate complicated musical controversies. Scott recalls his troubled work on it:

> The producer told me he wanted a *Key Largo*–type sultry score. They gave me two weeks to write forty minutes of music. I used a full orchestra with some synthesizer and some strange sounds. I barely got five seconds into recording the first cue when the producers were telling me things like, "John, when the jellyfish comes in we want a little 'warble,'" and, "John, it sounds too big," and a list of things like that. I just think they saw things differently than I did and I was the wrong composer for them. I never finished recording the score after going into a lot of overtime and rewriting. Sylvester Levay had literally hours to come up with a scorer, since the film had a definite airday on the network. He did it all in about three days and did the best he could. Sylvester is a very good friend, and he told me he almost killed himself trying to do it so fast.

The resulting synth-based score by Hungarian-born composer Sylvester Levay (whose previous credits included a half-dozen TV movies and the theme and score for the TV series *Airwolf*) certainly didn't affect *Wet Gold* any more negatively than its pitiful script.

In the meantime, John Scott found another project, *The Clan of the Cave Bear*. Its script, based on the best-selling first novel by Jean M. Auel, told the story of an orphaned Cro-Magnon girl who is adopted and raised by a Neanderthal tribe. The film provided a unique opportunity for a composer: Set in prehistoric times, it had no recognizable dialogue, just grunts and a form of sign language that was translated for audiences via subtitles. However, the movie did have one big problem, namely, too many producers who could never agree on what it needed musically. Although Scott wrote several demos for them in the spring of 1985, he didn't end up scoring the picture. He reflects on his work on the project:

> *The Clan of the Cave Bear* had eight producers working on it and, when I was called in, they were very undecided about the way their film should go. The film had already been shot, but they were constantly editing and re-editing it. They had a showing to which we all went along, but they would get into arguments and start changing the film again. They never resolved it and, in the end, I had to leave them because I had another project starting. I did demos for them, but I can't really describe it, it was very long ago. The themes I did were on a synthesized demo—one of the producers actually demanded that I did a demo and, up to that point, I never had to do that with synthesizers. I'd always try to play the themes to them on the piano, which I much prefer to do because when you produce a synthesized score, it locks you down. They get to like it too much and won't let you change anything on it, while I prefer to have my music grow with the film.

The task of scoring *The Clan of the Cave Bear* fell to Alan Silvestri, who had just scored the immensely popular *Back to the Future* (1985). Although Silvestri's unusual *Cave Bear* score contains orchestral elements, its electronic parts are far more noticeable and memorable. In addition to sampled percussion, the score benefits from strange synth-vocals that represent the tribal life of the cavemen. Otherwise, the constant synth-beats provide a Vangelis-like aura. Unfortunately, the picture was a celebrated box-office bomb, making back little more than a tenth of its estimated $15 million budget.

■ No Retreat, No Surrender (1986)

Original composer: **Frank Harris**
Replacement composer: **Paul Gilreath**

Belgian action star Jean-Claude Van Damme's first movie, *No Retreat, No Surrender,* was a *Karate Kid*–like martial arts movie that revisited the triumphant-underdog theme (ground that had been covered so much better ten years earlier by *Rocky* and more recently by *The Karate Kid*). Set in Seattle and directed by Hong Kong filmmaker Corey Yuen, *No Retreat* is the story of a young martial arts student who prays to the ghost of Bruce Lee before taking on the local crime syndicate, to avenge his father's rough handling by the gang's intimidating Russian enforcer (Van Damme). The movie found a cult following because of an inspirational plot and lots of karate-training montages.

Composer Frank Harris supplied the picture with a total of eighty-eight music cues, including a few songs written with Joe Mortensen. Among these were the film's title credits song "Hold On to the Vision," sung by Kevin Chalfant and featuring guitarist Joe Satriani, and "Ask Me to Stay."

In the mid-1980s, New World Pictures modified quite a few of the films it distributed for the American market. (This was no longer the New World founded by filmmaker Roger Corman, a studio for which such directors as Francis Ford Coppola, John Sayles, Martin Scorsese, Jonathan Demme, James Cameron, and Peter Bogdanovich had made some of their earliest films. In 1983, Corman sold New World to an investment group that soon took it public.)

When New World Pictures got its hands on *No Retreat, No Surrender,* the company edited it and then commissioned Paul Gilreath to provide a new score on a severely limited budget. Gilreath made use of a Kurzweil 250 sampler keyboard, which allowed him access to a good selection of samples of instruments (pan pipes, unusual and traditional percussion, etc.) while adhering to a minimal budget. In addition to writing a new score, he wrote a new song for the movie, "Stand On Your Own," and came up with an original trailer piece.

Eventually, recordings of both Harris's and Gilreath's *No Retreat, No Surrender* scores were released on CD. Gilreath's music came out in 1995, when Silva Screen explored Van Damme film soundtracks through a series of compilations and individual releases. Harris's music was released digitally in 2008, followed by a Perseverance Records CD release in 2010, with the composer presenting his original tracks alongside a couple of remixes and improved performances, including four versions of "Hold On to the Vision" and at least two versions of each additional song. To get the rights to release this music, the composer himself had to track down Seasonal Films and strike a deal with the company to make the music available through CDBaby.

The new New World Pictures treatment of *No Retreat, No Surrender* was certainly not an exceptional case. One of the studio's best-known chop jobs was the American version of *Godzilla 1985*. This film (originally titled *Gojira* by its Japanese production company, Toho, for which it was the sixteenth in a series of Godzilla movies) was rendered almost incomprehensible by New World's edits, which included the addition of footage of Raymond Burr reprising his role from the 1956 film *Godzilla, King of the Monsters*! *Godzilla 1985* was also rescored with various Christopher Young cues from earlier New World projects.

New World made interesting modifications as well with the Canadian action-comedy *Highpoint* (1982), for which composer John Addison, known for his scores for such high-class films as *Tom Jones* (1963), *Sleuth* (1972), and *A Bridge Too Far* (1977), had written the music. The company came to believe that the picture would be better served by music in the style of Bernard Herrmann's *North by Northwest*, to emphasize the adventure elements rather than the comedy. To accomplish this, New World's in-house composer Christopher Young penned a new score to replace Addison's.

Yet another foreign picture run through New World's mill was German director Roland Emmerich's *Joey*, a Steven Spielberg homage. After cutting its 110 minutes down to 78 and retitling it *Making Contact*, New World asked composer Paul Gilreath to replace the original score by composer–sound designer Hubert Bartholomae. (Both the original and New World's edited and rescored versions of *Joey* were released together on a double DVD.)

■ **Invaders from Mars** (1986)

Original composer: **Christopher Young**
Additional composer: **David Storrs**

The musical history of *Invaders from Mars*, a campy remake of the 1953 classic sci-fi film (and classic of 1950s paranoia) of the same name, revisits an old issue regarding horror movie scores: While the genre can offer lots of opportunity for experimentation with modern and avant-garde music techniques—and isn't afraid to use what is often described as "ugly music"—many horror-film directors and producers opt for musical familiarity and safety instead. Director Tobe Hooper had chosen to replace huge portions of Henry Mancini's score for the American release of his previous movie, *Lifeforce* (1985), with more experimental-sounding electronic music by Michael Kamen, but he took the opposite path with *Invaders from Mars*. Christopher Young, celebrated for his wild horror-film scores, wrote a fairly far-out and complex sample-based electronic score for this alien invasion picture, but it apparently crossed the director's line of acceptability. Young remembers his *Invaders* music:

> Tobe Hooper was in a three-picture deal, and this picture was the center of the three. He and I didn't get to work together on it. We spotted the film, and then he had to leave to start shooting the next film. His only words to me were, "Chris, I want it to be different. I want you to feel free to be as experimental as you like." I decided Chris is going to be really experimental. My electronic background had been more in the analog domain, but the whole sampling thing fascinated me. I decided that I was going to have a session in which I brought in a bunch of different instruments, primarily percussion instruments, recorded them, and then manipulated them via electronics. The sampling scene at that time was pretty limited—I think the maximum amount of time you could sample was about three seconds—so I sort of stuck to manipulating acoustic tapes. I put together the thing that was really out of this world. And it was thrown out. I learned an incredible lesson through all that.

In fact, not all of it was thrown out. In addition to his score's experimental music, Young also provided fourteen minutes of orchestral music that included some bucolic cues for the movie's most touching scenes, a rousing Goldsmith-like main/action theme, and even some overly sweet material that sounds a lot like the end credits of *Jaws*. His score's action parts, based on *First Blood*'s score, are well written, well performed, and worthy of recognition. (Interestingly, his main title theme was replaced with his cue "Marines Enter Tunnel," originally written for a later scene.) All things considered, his orchestral score is, in fact, rather good.

To provide music for areas of the film that had been stripped of Young's experimental offerings, composer and electronic music specialist David Storrs was called in. His material is easy to distinguish, with the electronic replacement music being considerably more traditional and tonal than Young's. And fans of the B-movie genre will certainly be entertained by Storr's score's boo moments, which are filled with electronic suspense and mickey-mousing.

Alas, Storr's synthesized music and Young's orchestral score blend like oil and water. Moreover, although Storrs contributed more than forty minutes of music to the film, he received only an "additional music" mention in the end credits. Young is the only composer credited in the main titles.

In later years, Young himself would supervise the production of several editions of his unused experimental score for this movie. He would even assemble a suite titled "Musique Concrète" that reworked five of his rejected *Invaders* cues with some Gregorian chant and layers of piano music. In 2008, the Intrada label released this, together with all the music ever written for the picture (fourteen minutes of Young's orchestral music, forty-five of Young's electronic music, and forty-one minutes of Storr's electronic replacement score).

The experimental and uniquely inventive side that Young showed in his unused *Invaders from Mars* material was often suppressed in the years immediately following it. In 1988, the composer worked on *The Telephone*, a sorry comedy remake of Alfred Hitchcock's 1954 classic *Rear Window*. This ill-conceived comedy, written by Harry Nilssen and Terry Southern and directed by Rip Torn, starred Whoopie Goldberg.

Expanding on a concept derived from Franz Waxman's *Rear Window* music, Young initially scored *The Telephone* using only jazz source-music cues. However, he also wrote some additional music exclusively for inclusion only on an Intrada compilation CD his music.

■ The Golden Child (1986)

Original composer: **John Barry**
Replacement music: **Michel Colombier**

The Golden Child is an odd tale about a street-wise, self-styled private detective (played by Eddie Murphy) who must find a Tibetan holy child who is possessed of special powers (the Golden Child) and has been kidnapped by the forces of hell. This fantasy-comedy struggles mightily to find its identity: Is it a comedy? A fantasy? A detective film? Or just an Eddie Murphy vehicle? Much of the movie's humor seems to have been forced into the script once Murphy was signed for the lead. Much also seems to be the product of the actor's strong personal charisma and well-tuned improvisational techniques. Perhaps the film would have been more tightly controlled had not director Michael Ritchie, whose previous credits included *Fletch* (1985), *The Bad News Bears* (1977), and *The Candidate* (1972), been away in London during most of *The Golden Child*'s critical postproduction, during which time new material was shot and cut into it.

The film's score was written by John Barry, who was having a bad year—1986 also saw the release of his career's low point, *Howard the Duck*, whose music combined late Barry romanticism and rehashed action material from the 007 movie *A View to a Kill* (1985). Barry's score for *The Golden Child* was much more satisfying. (Interestingly, one of its themes was based on demo material submitted for the 1985 comedy *Once Bitten*.)

Barry's *Golden Child* music was recorded during five sessions, but director Ritchie could only attend three of them. While the score was successful in lushly setting up the movie's sense of adventure and its Asian overtones, it clashed with Eddie Murphy's hip urban screen character. The producers felt that the composer approached the movie too much like an Indiana Jones adventure when he should have been establishing Murphy's comic-action persona. So French composer Michel Colombier was hired to produce a new score in two weeks. Colombier's replacement music, a more contemporary-sounding score, was primarily performed on synthesizers, with added Eastern instruments (particularly flutes and percussion) to refer to the Golden Child's origins.

The final theatrically released movie contained music from both Colombier and Barry. Barry's had been largely removed, but a few of his compositions were retained, including his song "The Best Man in the World" performed by Ann Wilson, which sounds nothing like Barry's usual work. In fact, the song was produced with an edgy rock sound to make it a better fit with the rest of the movie's songs. Other scenes that retained Barry's score include the dance of a tin can man, Eddie Murphy's dream sequence, the lengthy repeat of the love theme after the detective completes a dangerous acrobatic stunt, and a five- minute stinger in the last reel of the film. Unfortunately, the two scores clashed quite noticeably.

The original soundtrack album by Capitol Records focused on songs "from and inspired by" the picture and contained very little of the underscore. It contained some Colombier cues and one of the few Barry cues retained in the film, "Wisdom of the Ages." The flipside of the seven-inch single release of the song "The Best Man in the World" also contained a suite of two cues that were neither in the picture nor on the soundtrack release. La-La Land Records issued the definitive edition of *The Golden Child*'s soundtrack in 2011. It contained both Barry's and Colombier's scores as well as the film's songs.

■ **Class of Nuke 'Em High** (1986)

Original composer: **Michael Perilstein**
Replacement music: **Ethan Hurt and Michael Latlanzi**

Class of Nuke 'Em High is one of the great bad movies of the 1980s. It's the story of the hideously mutating student body at Tromaville High School, which sits right next door to a nuclear power plant that leaks radioactive waste (in New Jersey, of course). Catching the eye of B-movie cultists, it spawned two sequels: *Class of Nuke 'Em High 2: Subhumanoid Meltdown* and *Class of Nuke 'Em High 3: The Good, the Bad and the Subhumanoid*. It was codirected and coproduced by Lloyd Kaufman and Michael Herz, founders of Troma Films, a low-budget shock-exploitation studio and distributor known for such tongue-in-cheek–titled sub-Bs as *The Toxic Avenger, Surf Nazis Must Die, Terror Firmer, Ferocious Female Freedom Fighters, Redneck Zombies, Tromeo & Juliet, Killer Condom*, and *Tales from the Crapper* (Troma's slogan: "Movies of the Future!").

After principle photography was completed for *Class of Nuke 'Em High*, Troma sensed the film still wasn't quite up to their standards, so Richard W. Haines (whose one previous feature credit was 1984's *Splatter University*) was hired to write, direct, and edit-in some new segments. While this was happening, the project's composer, Michael Perilstein, was spinning his wheels, trying to score an unlocked (and unfinished!) film.

A New Jersey–based composer whose previous credits included *The Deadly Spawn* (1983), Perilstein was known for producing fairly effective scores at bargain-basement prices. He wrote and recorded ninety minutes of music based on early cuts of the movie. However, coproducer/directors Kaufman and Herz's inability to "lock the picture" (complete a final edit) was accompanied by a failure to communicate with the composer. More importantly for Perilstein, it resulted in their failure to pay him for the use of his music. He withdrew it, but since *Class of Nuke 'Em High* had been completely revamped since Perilstein had written his score, this wasn't an issue for Troma anymore. A new score was commissioned from Ethan Hurt and Michael Latlanzi (whose music for *Class of Nuke 'Em High* remains both composers' only theatrically released movie credit).

In 1985, Perilstein's score for *The Deadly Spawn* was released as an LP on the Deadly Records label. However, right after signing the Deadly contract, Perilstein was contacted by indie producer Tom Timony of Ralph Records (home label of the Residents), who was interested in releasing the same music. Since that score was already spoken for, the composer offered Ralph Records the chance to release his next score—music to *The Class Of Nuke 'Em High.*

Once Troma walked away from his *Nuke 'Em* scoring deal, Perilstein was stuck with a score without a film. So he transformed the music into a concept album. Not wanting any references to *Class of Nuke 'Em High* that might work as free publicity for the film, Perilstein suggested that his record be titled *Godzilla vs. Your Mother.* In 1986, Ralph released *Godzilla vs. Your Mother,* one of the strangest soundtrack memorabilia items around, right down to its track titles, which are all palindromes (e.g., "Never Even," "No, It Is Open or Prime Position," "We Nab Anew," "A Hero-Monster Frets No More, Ha!"). Perilstein eventually reused this music, with the addition of two new pieces, for the contemporary horror movie *Winterbeast* (1991). That soundtrack (essentially an extended edition of *Godzilla vs. Your Mother*) was released in 2008.

Platoon (1986)

Original composer: **Georges Delerue**
Replacement music: **Samuel Barber's *Adagio for Strings***

When producers and directors fall in love with classical selections (often from their temp tracks), film composers usually face an uphill battle to keep their underscores intact. Stanley Kubrick, as noted earlier in this book, was a great lover of classical music, which he used lavishly in his temp tracks and in his final films as well (e.g., *2001: A Space Odyssey* and *The Shining*). Another director prone to employing more classical music than original score is Terrence Malick: In *Days of Heaven* (1978), he replaced most of Ennio Morricone's music with "The Aquarium" from Camille Saint-Saëns' popular orchestra suite *The Carnival of the Animals.* His *The Thin Red Line* (1998) featured music by Charles Ives (*The Unanswered Question*), Gabriel Fauré, and Arvo Pärt alongside an underscore by Hans Zimmer. In *The New World,* Malick utilized music by Wagner and Mozart along with an underscore by James Horner.

To this category of directors we can add Oliver Stone, specifically with his film *Platoon.* In 1986, French composer Georges Delerue collaborated on two powerful pictures with Stone. His work on *Salvador* combined percussive action music and romantic guitar material to capture El Salvador's fiery political climate, aflame with revolution. But his involvement with the multiple-Oscar-winning (including Best Picture and Best Director) *Platoon*, a story about a young recruit's loss of innocence and the horrors of the Vietnam War (and, inevitably, all war), based on writer-director Stone's own combat experiences, would be less fulfilling.

To establish the 1960s time frame, a number of songs—including the Doors' "Hello, I Love You" and the Jefferson Airplane's "White Rabbit"—served as musical counterpoint to the witnessed tragedies. But the movie also required an orchestral score, to provide a different emotional slant on the same events. Delerue composed almost twenty-five minutes of stirring underscore, which he recorded with the Vancouver Symphony Orchestra. It contained some of his most heart-wrenching, tragic-romantic material. There was only one problem: While working on his movie, Stone fell in love with one of the temp tracks, American composer Samuel Barber's elegiac, intensely beautiful, yet intensely sorrowful *Adagio for Strings*. This highly popular classical work, a string orchestra arrangement of the second movement of the composer's string quartet, premiered in 1938 in a radio broadcast by Arturo Toscanini and the NBC Symphony Orchestra and has subsequently become standard repertoire for orchestras around the world. Its sense of noble mourning caused it to be used as background to the radio announcement of President Franklin Delano Roosevelt's death, as well as at the funerals of Albert Einstein and Princess Grace of Monaco. It has been featured in a number of movies, forcing film composers to either embrace it, as did John Barry in *The Scarlet Letter* (1995), or write something remarkably similar, as did Bill Conti for *Murderers Among Us: The Simon Wiesenthal Story* (1989). Barber's Adagio also appeared in *The Elephant Man* (1980), *El Norte* (1983), *Lorenzo's Oil* (1992), *Amélie* (2001), *Sicko* (2007), and many other films and television shows.

As Delerue wrote his *Platoon* score, Stone asked him to make his music as much like Barber's as he could allow himself to. But ultimately, Stone simply decided to use the Barber work (as arranged and conducted by Delerue) to replace almost all the French composer's original score. Of the seven cues Delerue wrote for the film, only one, "Bunker to Village," was used in its entirety. (Incidentally, this is the Delerue track whose combination of percussive sounds and ethnic flutes makes it most distinct from Barber's work.) The meat of Delerue's score, including most instances of his main theme, was deleted.

Delerue's rejected *Platoon* score was released, twice, as a soundtrack recording by the Belgian label Prometheus Records. The second version contains a correction of a major sound issue, thus it is the recommended version.

■ Predator (1987)

Original composer: **Patrick Moraz**
Replacement composer: **Alan Silvestri**

Is the practice of temp-tracking useful, or harmful to creativity? What is a temp track? Why is it used?

During postproduction, a film's editor and/or its director temporarily cut existing music into a film-in-progress for a number of reasons: to make a scene easier to watch (especially for studio executives who may have difficulty sitting through musicless footage), to lend a sense of rhythm to a scene's edits, and/or to see how a particular type of music works with the film. Very often, this musical collage is made up of cues from existing film score recordings, and if a composer's past work is prominently featured in this mix, he may have a good chance of being asked to score the finished project.

The chief downside to temp-tracking is that a director may become so enamored of a certain piece of music in a certain context in his film that he may try to force the hired composer to imitate it. Of course, a director also has the option of simply licensing a preexisting piece from a temp track and using it in the finished movie.

While 99.9 percent of temp tracks are cobbled together from existing recordings, on very rare occasions a filmmaker will hire a composer to provide temp cues of newly composed music. Such an assignment might be frustrating for a composer—knowing that his music will only be used temporarily and probably is destined to be replaced by a bigger-name composer's score. But if the temp composer is very, very lucky, the director will fall in love with the temp music and give him a shot at scoring the finished film.

Swiss musician Patrick Moraz, a classically trained pianist who was keyboardist for the progressive rock bands Yes (1974–76) and The Moody Blues (1978–91), also maintained a career as a film composer. Among his early feature film scores were *La Salamandre* (1971), *L'Invitation* (1973), and *Le Milieu du monde* (1974). His best-known American film score was for the thriller *The Stepfather* (1987). In that same year, he was hired to provide an original temp track for one of the year's top action pictures, *Predator*.

This sci-fi–action hybrid, directed by John McTiernan (who would go on to direct *Die Hard*, *The Hunt for Red October*, and *Last Action Hero*), starred Arnold Schwarzenegger and Carl Weathers. It told the convoluted tale of an elite American combat squad sent to a fictional Central American country to rescue hostages held by a guerrilla group. While there, the hunters become the hunted as a brutal alien being (through whose eyes the audience sees portions of the movie) stalks and, one by one, kills the squad's members. In the end, only Schwarzenegger's character is left to do battle with the creature. The film was critically panned at its release (a *Los Angeles Times* film critic wrote: "arguably one of the emptiest, feeblest, most derivative scripts ever made as a major studio movie"), but it found an audience anyway, grossing $60 million at the US box office and spawning the sequel *Predator 2* (1990).

With regard to *Predator*, temp composer Moraz had two things going for him: As a progressive rock keyboardist, he was quite familiar with synthesizers (the era's favored instrument for sci-fi and action movies), and he was knowledgeable about Brazilian music, which the filmmakers felt could stand in for the music of a fictional Central American nation. However, producing studio 20th Century Fox decided that Alan Silvestri (whose previous credits included *Romancing the Stone*, *The Clan of the Cave Bear*, and *Back to the Future*) should write the picture's final score, not only because he was a big-name composer, but also because he was well versed in integrating synthesizers with full orchestra. Silvestri came up with a big, bold, dramatically pulsing synth and orchestra score that no doubt contributed to the film's success. (Silvestri's *Predator* score would become one of the most expensive soundtrack albums on the secondhand market, not only because of its sheer power, but also because it had been released in a limited edition of 3,000 copies.)

Moraz's *Predator* gig failed to give his movie-scoring career a boost, and after providing similar temporary music for the Brazilian-themed *Wild Orchid* (1990), he gave up film scoring and embarked on a solo jazz-fusion keyboard career.

Today, few original temp scores are written, and only a couple of directors devote their time (and money) to this sort of venture. One director who likes original temp cues is Oliver Stone, who used them while working on his 1997 feature *U Turn*. Editor Hank Corwin started to temp the picture with preexisting music by composer Paul Kelly (a composer who is also a film editor for commercials and music videos). As work on *U Turn* progressed, Stone grew attached to some of Kelly's temp pieces, and he had the composer do minor rewrites for several scenes. But TriStar Pictures decided that the film needed an original score by Ennio Morricone, so the final *U Turn* doesn't include any of Kelly's temp contributions. His fill-in work was rewarded nonetheless: He got to know Stone, who went on to use Kelly's music in both *Any Given Sunday* (1999) and *Comandante* (2003).

Another director who likes specially composed temp music is Michael Mann. While working on his picture *Heat* in 1995, Mann commissioned several temp pieces from guitarist-composer Michael Brook (who would go on to score *Affliction*, *An Inconvenient Truth*, and *Into the Wild*). But Mann utilized only one of Brook's cues in the final film. Elliot Goldenthal (whose previous credits included *Pet Sematary* and *Interview with a Vampire*, and who would go on to score *Michael Collins* and *Frida*) wrote *Heat*'s score.

Sometimes Mann likes to have several composers on a project, offering him a variety of music from which he can pick and choose. To provide an original temp score for his film *The Insider* (1999), he hired three composers—Craig Armstrong (who would go on to score *Moulin Rouge!* and *The Incredible Hulk*), Lisa Gerrard (a founding member of the group Dead Can Dance, who would go on to collaborate on film music with Hans Zimmer, Ennio Morricone, Jeff Rona, and others), and Graeme Revell (whose previous credits included *The Hand that Rocks the Cradle* and *The Crow*). Along with music editor Curt Sobel, Mann then carefully assembled the film's final music—a patchwork of cues by all three composers. Several interesting cues were also left on the cutting-room floor.

■ A Prayer for the Dying (1987)

Original composer: **John Scott**
Replacement composer: **Bill Conti**

In 1972, ten years after *El Cid*'s production wrapped in Spain, Charlton Heston returned to that country to direct and star in a new adaptation of Shakespeare's *Antony and Cleopatra*. According to the terms of the coproduction deal (similar to the one that plagued *El Cid*), *Antony and Cleopatra* producer Peter Snell was contractually obliged to hire a Spanish composer. He hired Augusto Algueró Jr. , a popular Spanish composer, songwriter, and orchestra leader known for his easy-listening pop sound—what might be called "lounge music" today—with more than seventy-five previous film score credits and numerous LPs. Unfortunately, Heston didn't like Algueró's score, so while Algueró remained on the production for contractual reasons, and some of his source cues were utilized in the finished film, Snell hired British composer John Scott (whose previous credits included *Greystoke* and *The Shooting Party*) to pen a new score for the picture. This was Scott's first chance to write an epic score, and even though the film didn't do well at the box office, it represented some of his best work. Subsequently, he was often invited to participate in other Snell productions, namely, *Hennessy* (1975), *The Hostage Tower* (1980), and 1987's *A Prayer for the Dying*.

Another troubled coproduction, *A Prayer for the Dying* starred Mickey Rourke, Bob Hoskins, and Alan Bates and was directed by Mike Hodges, whose previous credits included *Get Carter* (1971), *The Terminal Man* (1974), and *Flash Gordon* (1980). It is the story of an IRA terrorist who, after accidentally blowing up a bus full of schoolchildren, becomes disgusted with his world of violence and wants to leave the movement. But he is too deeply enmeshed to escape. Hunted by both the British and the IRA, he moves to London, where he is forced into an alliance with a local crime boss.

Due to some horrible miscommunication between coproducing partners, *A Prayer for the Dying* was scored twice. To musically realize his vision of the story, British producer Peter Snell hired his friend John Scott, who delivered a very unusual score for a small string ensemble supplemented by a few additional instruments. The music is surprisingly contemporary, with rock-style guitar often taking the lead role and percussion providing an underlying rhythm for most cues. Any Irish flavor in Scott's score is very modest—subtle local color is provided by a harp in some of the gentler tracks. He also provided the picture with a couple of source cues that show off his rarely heard funky side, as well as the song "Rest Eternal," which was to have accompanied the end credits.

But even while Scott was at work on his score in London, with Snell and Hodges, the film's American coproducers were busy changing the picture. After a private screening, Samuel Goldwyn Jr. had the movie recut to feature more action. He also commissioned a score from composer Bill Conti, whose previous credits included *Rocky, That Championship Season, The Right Stuff,* and *The Karate Kid.*

Conti's *A Prayer for the Dying* music approached the film's subject matter in more typical Hollywood fashion: In the main title we hear one of Ireland's most recognizable musical calling cards, a fiddle. (A film critic for *The Washington Post* commented that "Conti's lilty Irish score brings to mind Irish Spring soap commercials.") The score is largely a pairing of fiddle solos with powerful string orchestra passages that dramatically propel the action. A third component is suspense music that glistens with a hint of electronics—a most identifiable Conti sound.

Regardless of its action-oriented plot and Hollywood-style score, *A Prayer for the Dying* barely registered at the box office, even failing to make back its roughly £6 million budget. Even worse, both director Hodges and star Rourke publicly disowned the Goldwyn version that went out to theaters.

Snell and Scott would work together again on two great TV movies: the 1990 historical epic *Blood Royal: William the Conqueror* and an adaptation of Alistair MacLean's *Night Watch* (1995). Scott eventually released his music for *A Prayer for the Dying* on his own JOS Records label, together with his intimate *Winter People* (1989) score. Conti's score for *A Prayer for the Dying* has never been officially released.

■ **Hellraiser** (1987)

Original composer: **Coil**
Replacement composer: **Christopher Young**

Hellraiser, written and directed by Clive Barker, based on his own novella *The Hellbound Heart,* ramped up the presence of dark malevolence and sadomasochistic violence in mainstream contemporary horror films. It is a tale about the purchaser of an antique puzzle box that calls forth hideous pain- and pleasure-seeking demons. These beings, the Cenobites, are led by a character known as Pinhead, and once released, they tear apart the box's owner and haul him away to a sort of hell, from which he attempts to reconstitute his flesh with the blood of others (particularly those within the house where his transformation took place). The movie was Barker's debut as a feature film director.

Working on *Hellraiser*'s music very early in the project's development were John Balance and Peter Christopherson, the founding and primary members of the British industrial-experimental band Coil, and also friends of Clive Barker's. The duo's previous film work included the score for Derek Jarman's *The Angelic Conversation* (1985), and they also contributed music to Jarman's 1983 film, *Blue.* As John Balance recalls, their involvement with *Hellraiser* extended beyond just providing music: "The thing is we were in right at the very beginning of the project. Clive Barker was writing a screenplay, and he came to our house and took away a load of piercing magazines and things—which is where they got all the Pinhead stuff from."

While Coil was known for taking abrasive sound to an extreme, their work for *Hellraiser* was strangely in line with other contemporary horror scores. Their prime themes (as presented on their score's LP) are all quite exciting: Their main theme is a sinister synth motif that gradually builds terror, as is the "box theme." The movie's puzzle is treated with a light music-box melody that metamorphoses into shrieking horror sounds.

But as appropriate for the picture as their music might have been, when Hollywood showed interest in the movie, it quickly became apparent that Coil wasn't going to remain on board. Again, Balance recalls:

> We saw some original footage, which we unfortunately didn't keep, but it was really heavy and good, like a sort of twisted English horror film. And then when the Americans saw this footage they thought it was too extreme, and they also gave Clive ten times the original money. So then Clive sort of felt, because it was his first film and with Hollywood being involved, it was his gateway to the stars. So they changed the location to America, dubbed all the actors over, and took out a lot of the explicit sex.
>
> It would have been brilliant, but we wouldn't have carried on, because they were changing everything and they weren't being very nice to us, the actual film people. They were keeping us in the dark a lot. We said we'd had enough.... They just wanted normal film music. They didn't want anything too scary, which is sad and ridiculous for a horror film.

Once the film was Americanized (recut and dubbed), Christopher Young was hired to provide its music. And his orchestral score certainly didn't disappoint horror fans—in fact, it attracted a cult following and helped to propel Young's career. (He would go on to pen the score for the first of the movie's seven sequels, too.) Young's Gothic approach to *Hellraiser* became so influential that its presence was felt not only in the sequels, but also in numerous other horror-film scores as well. The tension between the score's "reality" melodies and its disturbing noises from hell make it instantly recognizable.

A recording of Coil's *Hellraiser* work was released on cassette, 10-inch EP, and CD under the title *The Unreleased Themes for Hellraiser (The Consequences of Raising Hell)* by Solar Lodge (COIL 1). It also appeared on the compilation album *Unnatural History II (Smiling in the Face of Perversity)*. Many loyal Coil fans have continued to celebrate the band's thwarted involvement with the movie, keeping the memory of its unused score alive by sometimes handing it to Clive Barker during autograph sessions, even decades after the film's release.

■ **The Belly of an Architect** (1987)

Original composer: **Glenn Branca**
Replacement composer: **Wim Mertens**

In *The Belly of an Architect,* a highly symbolic tale by filmmaker Peter Greenaway, an American architect named Kracklite (played by Brian Dennehy) becomes obsessed with mortality when he travels to Rome to construct an exhibition dedicated to the work of the visionary eighteenth-century French architect Étienne-Louis Boullée. Kracklite's intense dedication to the project and the ridicule he faces from his Italian colleagues while in Rome leave both his health and his marriage in ruins. As his life falls apart, he becomes obsessed with the Roman emperor Caesar Augustus, who was rumored to have been poisoned by his wife, and gets the notion that he, too, is being poisoned by his wife. Like most of Greenaway's films, the movie's images are often spectacular and painterly.

Musically, Greenaway has frequently been drawn to the work of contemporary concert composers. So much so, in fact, that in 1983 he directed the four-part, four-hour documentary *Four American Composers,* which uniquely presented performances and commentary by and about Robert Ashley, John Cage, Philip Glass, and Meredith Monk. In 1999, Greenaway provided the scenario and libretto for and filmed a television version of Dutch composer Louis Andriessen's opera *Rosa, a Horse Drama* (number six out of Greenaway's ten-libretto *Death of a Composer* series).

During the 1980s, Greenaway's most frequent and well-known musical collaborator was Michael Nyman, a musicologist and critic turned composer. As a musicologist, Nyman cultivated a special interest in Baroque music (the period's motor rhythms and harmonic progressions, particularly those of Henry Purcell, have haunted his own compositions) and contemporary postexperimental music. In 1968, he was one of the first critics to apply the term "minimalism" to music, and in 1974 he authored the first wide-ranging book on experimental music, *Experimental Music: Cage and Beyond.*

Nyman's own music—he is the composer of seven operas, much chamber music, music for his often raucous-sounding Michael Nyman Band, and a good number of film scores—is generally steeped in minimalism, particularly of the pulsing, repeating-cell variety. As a film composer, he is perhaps best known for his music for director Jane Campion's *The Piano* (which went multiplatinum as a soundtrack recording). Nyman has provided music for numerous Greenaway films, including *The Falls* (1980); *The Draughtsman's Contract* (1982); *A Zed & Two Noughts* (1985); *Drowning by Numbers* (1988); *The Cook, the Thief, His Wife, and Her Lover* (1989); and *Prospero's Books* (1991).

When it was time to score *The Belly of an Architect,* however, Nyman was unavailable because he was busy at work on his opera *Noises, Sounds & Sweet Airs.* On his recommendation, Greenaway hired American avant-garde composer Glenn Branca, who is best known for his extremely loud, long-form microtonal compositions (most often based on the harmonic series) for large ensembles made up primarily of electric guitars. (His largest massing of electric guitars was 100, for his 2001 Symphony No. 13, *Hallucination City*.) Since the late 1980s, he has also written a number of long-form orchestral works as well.

Branca spent a week with *The Belly of an Architect*'s film crew in Rome, collecting ideas for its score, which he wrote for string orchestra. Although he composed almost an hour's worth of music for the picture, he recorded only about twenty minutes of it with a forty-eight-piece group from The London Sinfonietta. Of this material, only nine minutes were used in the movie. This dark, slow-moving music is made up of a series of gradually changing sonic monoliths.

But Greenaway was apparently looking for music with Nyman's lively, pulsating sound, so he turned to Belgian concert composer Wim Mertens. Although Mertens had a dozen recordings out by 1986, *The Belly of an Architect* was his first feature film score. Like Nyman, Mertens was best known for his minimalist-style pieces. (He also authored one of the major books on the movement, *American Minimal Music*.) Since his compositional voice was not too distant from Nyman's, his music was a more obvious fit for Greenaway's work.

When Greenaway first heard Mertens' music, he was immediately taken by it and selected some of the composer's existing works to be featured in the picture. There was still money in the music budget after Branca's score was aborted, so the rest was devoted to recording new versions of Mertens' *Close Cover*, *Struggle for Pleasure* (one of his better-known works) and *4 Mains*, as well as some new pieces. All things considered, Mertens' music works admirably within the picture.

The film's soundtrack CD opens with "Augustus," a Branca cue that is used five times in the movie (and has been licensed several times for other projects). Then the majority of the disc is given to Mertens' music, after which comes Branca's finale, rounding out the album in a slightly disturbing fashion. Despite Branca's taking a backseat in the movie itself, many reviewers believe that the edgy heart of the album is Branca's contribution. Sadly, this project wasn't followed by many more Branca film scores. Mertens, on the other hand, went on to score a number of movies, including *Between the Devil and the Deep Blue Sea* (1995), *Fiesta* (1995), and *Der Lebensversicherer* (2006).

■ Witchfinder General/The Conqueror Worm (VHS, 1987)

Original composer (1968): **Paul Ferris**
Additional composer (1968): **Kenneth V. Jones**
Replacement composer for video release (1987): **Kendall Roclord Schmidt**

Advertised as the most violent film of 1968, *Witchfinder General*, a vividly photographed picture starring Vincent Price, quickly found a cult following. Set in seventeenth-century England during the war between Cromwell's Roundheads (the Parliamentarians) and King Charles's Cavaliers (the Royalists), it is the tale of a sadistic petty official who travels from town to town, fulfilling the locals' bloodlust by wrenching confessions—for a fee—from peasant "witches."

When this British-made movie, cofinanced and distributed by American International Pictures (AIP), was prepared for America's screens, changes were inevitable. With popular horror-movie villain Vincent Price in the title role, AIP hoped the film would be perceived as part of their successful Edgar Allan Poe–inspired series, which also featured Price. (AIP's Poe series included *The Raven, The Fall of the House of Usher, The Pit and the Pendulum, The Oblong Box, Murders in the Rue Morgue, Masque of the Red Death,* and *The Tomb of Ligeia.*) Although the story had nothing to do with Poe, the distributor renamed the movie *The Conqueror Worm,* the title of one of Poe's poems. It also added opening and closing narrations from the poem and trimmed out some of the film's nudity. However, AIP stopped short of subjecting the movie to the full re-creation treatment—they didn't hire Les Baxter to rescore it.

Witchfinder General's music was written by British composer Paul Ferris, who even acted in the movie under the pseudonym Morris Jar (a tip of his hat to French film composer Maurice Jarre). Ferris was an actor who took composing jobs on the side. Among his credits at this time were *She Beast* (1966), *The Sorcerers* (1967), and *The Vampire-Beast Craves Blood* (1968). In 1967, he scored the spy spoof *Maroc 7,* but only his main theme and a piece of "party music" were used; the rest was replaced by British composer Kenneth V. Jones, whose earlier credits included *The Horse's Mouth* (1958), *There Was a Crooked Man* (1960), and *The Tomb of Ligeia* (1964).

When it turned out that Ferris wrote too little music for *Witchfinder General,* Jones was brought in to write additional cues. But his contributions—a couple of chase and tavern cues—are not particularly prominent in the final movie. Interestingly, Jones never even saw the picture; he wrote his music based solely on the timing notes he was given. The movie's final Ferris-Jones score (which has never been released on CD) was quite short.

Now, advance the clock by sixteen years. In 1984, Orion Pictures acquired AIP's film library for home-video release. However, since the original composers' contracts had been drawn up before the dawn of the lucrative home-video market, they didn't grant the studio/distributor home-video rights. Therefore, the agreements for each film had to be renegotiated before the movies could be distributed as home videotapes.

In clearing the necessary music rights, Orion's legal department faced three primary challenges: First, some of the composers were already dead, which meant that their estates had to be tracked down (often not an easy task, and sometimes simply not possible). Next, several of the movies were foreign productions with music by foreign composers, and communication with those overseas composers was often extremely difficult. Finally, some of the original composers had become celebrities who now commanded exorbitant fees. Vangelis, for example, had won an Oscar for his *Chariots of Fire* (1981) score, which meant that using his *Crime and Passion* (1976) music on a video release would cost quite a bit of money. Another big name was James Brown, who reportedly wanted a million dollars to permit his score (a collaboration with longtime musical associate Fred Wesley) to be used in the video release of *Slaughter's Big Rip-Off* (1973). Frustrated by the daunting task at hand, Orion's legal department quickly took care of the easy cases, and then contacted composers to provide new music for the problematic ones.

Enter composer-pianist Kendall Roclord Schmidt, who had scored more than fifty trailers. His first two Orion rescoring jobs, *Slaughter's Big Rip-Off* and *Unholy Rollers* (1972), were recorded with live players, but his replacement-score workload soon grew so big that he switched to providing synthesizer scores for the remaining films. This not only cut back the music budget, but it gave the composer enough time to actually finish his large number of commissions from Orion. Schmidt's best-known rescorings included *Witchfinder General* and *Scream and Scream Again* (1970, original score by David Whitaker), with each score written and recorded within three weeks.

Since Schmidt answered only to the studio's lawyers, not its producers, he was allowed great creative freedom in his work. Over two years of rescoring Orion's videos, he produced both music that stylistically mimicked the original scores (e.g., *Scream and Scream Again*) and music that was completely different (e.g., *Crime and Passion*). He also quickly became adept at cutting corners by using the same cue in different scenes within the same movie, although he never reused one film's material in a different film. Schmidt recalls his Orion work:

> Technically it was interesting, because the budgets were so low, if the movie needed forty-five minutes of music, I could only actually afford to do about twenty-five, and so with many of the cues I would have two or three different scenes in mind, and I would time the cues according to where they would fit for three scenes, rather than just one. It was a real education in film scoring, because it's hard enough for a lot of people to just figure out one timing, let alone make the same piece of music fit three completely different scenes. I pretty much had to do everything myself, make my own timing notes, and figure out where my music was necessary and where I could get away without music.

Additional Schmidt rescorings were *Planet of the Vampires* (1965, original score by Gino Marinuzzi Jr.), *Curse of the Crimson Altar* (1968, original score by Peter Knight), *War Italian Style* (1966, original score by Piero Umiliani), and *Winterhawk* (1975, original score by Nicholas Flagello and William Goldstein). Schmidt also provided new end credits music for the VHS versions of *Madhouse* (1974, original score by Douglas Gamley) and *Journey to the Seventh Planet* (1962, original score by Ib Glindemann). Most of these film's original composers never learned about his replacement music.

Orion's rescoring commissions make up the largest part of Schmidt's filmography. Oddly, he gave up composing in the mid-1990s and reinvented himself as a portrait photographer!

By the end of the 1980s, the practice of rescoring home-video releases pretty much died out, although isolated instances occur to this day. With the decline of the VHS format, Schmidt's rescored movies are difficult to find—the DVD versions of the same movies usually utilize the films' original scores.

■ **The Serpent and the Rainbow** (1988)

Original composer: **Charles Bernstein**
Replacement composer: **Brad Fiedel**

The Serpent and the Rainbow, a zombie film that craftily zips in and out of hallucination scenes, was inspired by anthropologist-ethnobotanist Wade Davis's best-selling nonfiction book of the same title. It was directed by horror specialist Wes Craven, best known at this time for writing and directing the highly successful *A Nightmare on Elm Street* (1984). Set in a Haiti aflame with revolution, it's the story of an anthropologist-ethnobotanist who, in the pay of a pharmaceutical company, goes to Haiti to explore voodoo culture and find the zombie drug. There he runs afoul of a Tontons Macoutes (secret police) captain who is also an evil voodoo priest bent on thwarting his quest and driving him out of the country. Eventually, after enduring horrible tortures at the hands of this sadistic man, the researcher is turned into a zombie and buried alive. Escaping his grave just as dictator "Baby Doc" Duvalier's government collapses, he battles the evil captain-priest, whom he dispatches to hell.

To provide the score for *The Serpent and the Rainbow*, the filmmakers made a bold choice, at least by Hollywood standards: They opted to have largely improvised music provided by the great Nigerian-born, American-educated drummer Babatunde Olatunji, a Columbia Records artist whose greatest hit among his numerous albums was 1959's *Drums of Passion*, and who had worked and recorded with many notable jazz and pop musicians, including John Coltrane, Pharoah Sanders, Max Roach, Abbey Lincoln, Quincy Jones, Horace Silver, Randy Weston, Stevie Wonder, Carlos Santana, and Mickey Hart. (The drummer also was a social activist and an educator, marching with Martin Luther King Jr., founding Harlem's Olatunji Center for African Culture, and writing a number of books on percussion technique.)

The material Olatunji recorded for the movie, however, simply didn't work out as hoped. So a more typical Hollywood score was commissioned from the composing team of Jeff Koz and Jesse Frederick, whose previous credits included *The Last Horror Film* (1982) and *The Mission...Kill* (1987). But that score didn't work out either.

The filmmakers' musical thinking then turned in yet another direction, and composer Charles Bernstein, who had enjoyed a good working relationship with director Craven on *A Nightmare on Elm Street*, entered the scene. (Bernstein's previous credits included *Mr. Majestyk* and many, many television movies.) His score for *The Serpent* contains some of his most intense, though largely synthesized, action-scene writing.

But, remarkably, this score didn't quite do it either. And although his name still appears in the film's trailer (which, incidentally, was scored with Tangerine Dream's music from the film *Sorcerer*), Bernstein's score was replaced. As he recalls, the production proved to be one of the worst gigs of his long and prolific career:

> It was just a hodgepodge of different people wanting different kinds of music. It turned out to be a very confusing and very unsatisfactory environment for a composer to work

> in. It was a simulated orchestral score, which I did in a synthesized manner. One of the enemies of this kind of moment is the preview, and they were using parts of the score that were not complete. They needed some music even when I wasn't ready, but they said it was only wanted for the test screening, but it wasn't properly mixed at all. My score wasn't too dissimilar in style to Brad Fiedel's replacement music, nor was it too different from Olatunji's music. There were elements from each earlier score that were carried on into the later ones.

The Serpent and the Rainbow's final score was written by Brad Fiedel, whose previous credits included *The Terminator* (1984) and *The Big Easy* (1986). His music for the film combined the electronic soundscapes he is known for with tribal-sounding rhythms, exotic ethnic instruments, and sound effects that evoked the jungle (from deep blasts of wind to snake hisses). The film's cold nightscapes and inherent zombie tragedies were occasionally warmed by heartfelt woodwind performances.

The CD of Fiedel's *Serpent* score has become one of the most expensive soundtrack CDs on the used market. When it was issued in 1988, the CD format was still an experimental medium for the Varèse Sarabande label, so apart from the standard run of cassette and LP copies, the label pressed only about 200 compact discs. The minuscule pressing makes original CDs of *The Serpent and the Rainbow* incredibly rare: A near-mint copy can be yours for just $550!

■ A Night in the Life of Jimmy Reardon / Aren't You Even Gonna Kiss Me Goodbye? (1988)

Original composer: **Elmer Bernstein**
Replacement composer: **Bill Conti**

A Night in the Life of Jimmy Reardon started its life as an independent production written and directed by William Richert, who based the movie on his semiautobiographical novel, *Aren't You Even Gonna Kiss Me Goodbye?*, which he wrote at the age of nineteen. His original version of the film, which carried the same title as his novel, was produced in 1986 by Russell Schwartz's Island Pictures and starred some of the nation's hottest stars of the time, including River Phoenix, Matthew Perry, Ione Skye, and Ann Magnuson. A coming-of-age tale set in suburban Chicago in 1962, it tracked the sometimes comic, sometimes sad misadventures of its hero, Jimmy Reardon, a poetry-writing, wild-oats-sowing kid who, just out of high school, is desperately trying to avoid his father's workaday fate.

But Richert's original movie would prove quite different from what was eventually released. It featured a narration by Richert (as the voice of Jimmy Reardon's older self remembering his teenaged days), which added a nice perspective to the story. And it had an original jazz-influenced score by Elmer Bernstein (whose recent prior credits included *¡Three Amigos!*, *Spies Like Us*, and *Ghost Busters*). The wistful, touching, sometimes quite dark music was recorded with the London Philharmonic. Under the titles was a song by Bernstein and lyricist Don Black, "I'm Not Afraid to Say Goodbye," performed by Johnny Mathis. In addition, River Phoenix wrote and performed a jaunty song that played under the end credits.

When 20th Century Fox picked up the movie for distribution, its president, Leonard Goldberg, felt it needed some drastic changes. After showing it to their marketing and publicity department, the studio decided to change it in both tone and content, hoping to make it more suitable for River Phoenix's avid fan base of teenaged girls. Among the many changes that Fox ordered: The older Jimmy's narration had to go, as did Bernstein's score, which the studio felt was too heavy and old-fashioned for a teen-targeted picture.

While certainly not crazy about these alterations, Richert went along with them just to get his movie released. The changes took about a year to complete and affected almost every portion of the film. A line containing the word "fuck," for example, was edited out on the insistence of Phoenix's parents, hoping to lighten the picture for a young audience.

Fox replaced the Bernstein-Black song for Johnny Mathis with the Motown classic "Shop Around," performed by Smokey Robinson and the Miracles. And period songs by Bo Diddley, Booker T. and the MG's, Bobby Bland, John Lee Hooker, LaVerne Baker, and others were squeezed into various scenes. This selection of vintage songs was then given a wild counterpoint—a new underscore of odd, synth-heavy music by Bill Conti.

Although writer-director Richert had been very happy with what he considered a perfect score by Bernstein, he met several times with Conti, hoping to help the replacement composer find an appropriate sound. But Fox stepped in and assembled a temp score to give Conti an idea of what the execs wanted to hear. When the studio held a crew screening of the movie with this temp score, Richert was dismayed and angered. (The only parts of this music that the director felt worked at all turned out to be some cues by Conti.)

Conti attempted to be as classical as he could in his replacement score, although most of it is heavily laden with 1980s synth sounds that place the movie in the wrong decade. The two themes that serve as the score's basis are simple and hummable, and lend a wide-eyed innocence to the story's romance. Typical of Conti's 1980s work, his score is plagued by disco beats and rock effects, and even instruments that could have been played live (such as the pan flute on the track "Hawaiian Dreams") were synthesized instead. (A couple of Bernstein's source cues were retained, but he received no proper credit for them.)

Richert and Fox eventually agreed on a score so that the movie could finally be released, but the new music, not to mention the new version of the picture itself, was so far from Richert's vision that he never made his peace with it. In early 1988, Fox released the completely revamped film to theaters. But the strange saga of *A Night in the Life of Jimmy Reardon* doesn't end there: The copies of the film sold to Europe and Japan turned out to be made from a version of its workprint that still carried Bernstein's score!

In a deal with Fox, Richert got permission to release his own cut of the movie five years after the studio's version premiered. This, however, was easier said than done, and the director had to wait almost twenty years to get his version released. In 2007, he launched the director's cut along with an open letter to the Chicago Film Critics Association, detailing his film's troubled history. Richert's version, retitled *Aren't You Even Gonna Kiss Me Goodbye?,* not only reinstated the scenes that Fox had chopped out, but also reinstated Bernstein's score, including the Johnny Mathis and River Phoenix songs. With only one print available, the movie slowly made the rounds of independent theaters and then was released on a DVD that is available from the writer-director's official website. Thanks to this DVD, a very good Elmer Bernstein score survived a trip to the scrap heap.

■ **Stars and Bars** (1988)

Original composer: **Elmer Bernstein**
Replacement composer: **Stanley Myers**

Stars and Bars, a fish-out-of-water comedy of manners written by Ghana-born, British-educated novelist and screenwriter William Boyd (based on his 1984 novel of the same title), chronicles the strange adventures and misadventures of a young, innocent, upper-middle-class Brit in America. An expert on eighteenth-century art who works for a second-rate New York City auction house owned by his fiancée's father, he's given the task of traveling to the Deep South to find and purchase a Renoir painting held by a private collector. But everyone he meets in the South (and in New York, for that matter) is wildly eccentric and broadly comic. In his travels, the young man's straitlaced demeanor begins to wither, and he becomes slightly Americanized.

Directed by Pat O'Connor, an Irish filmmaker whose previous credits included *Cal* (1984) and *A Month in the Country* (1987), the picture starred Daniel Day-Lewis, hot off his lead role in *The Unbearable Lightness of Being* and featured roles in *A Room with a View* and *My Beautiful Laundrette.* Playing some of the film's many strange characters are Harry Dean Stanton, Spalding Gray, Martha Plimpton, Maury Chaykin, and Joan Cusack.

Elmer Bernstein (whose recent prior credits included *Da, Funny Farm, ¡Three Amigos!,* and *Ghost Busters*) was hired to provide the movie's score. His main theme, which frames the film, contains hints of Gershwin's *Rhapsody in Blue.* The movie's offbeat characters are musically treated in traditional referential fashion: The music for the innocent Brit is full of pomp and Elgarisms, while the Southerners' music has a hint of the blues. Generally, this Americana-tinged score plays the part of the straight man during most of *Stars and Bars*' comedic moments, but it also contains such overtly comedic gestures as over-the-top fanfares and quotations from a number of songs, including "When You Wish Upon a Star," and Bernstein's own music for *Airplane!*. Some passages feature electronic sounds, including those from Bernstein's favorite electronic instrument, the ondes Martenot, which plays the movie's love theme.

Unfortunately, the mysterious powers-that-be decided to replace Bernstein's music. Just why has never been fully discussed in print, no doubt due to the movie's obscurity. A new score was commissioned from British composer Stanley Myers, whose prior credits included *Sammy and Rosie Get Laid* (1987), *Wish You Were Here* (1987), *The Deer Hunter* (1978), *No Way to Treat a Lady* (1968), and the Nicholas Roeg films *Castaway* (1986) and *Insignificance* (1985). (Myers would eventually score a total of seven Roeg-directed films.) Myers's music had a more restrained, British edge to it than Bernstein's, yet it also projected the wide-eyed enthusiasm a young Englishman might feel on his first visit to New York. Being English himself, Myers may have reflected more of the fish-out-of-water perspective with his music.

In 1991, Varèse Sarabande issued Bernstein's score as its CD club's eighth release, which was limited to 1,000 numbered copies. Due to a lack of original documentation, the CD's tracks weren't given titles. However, the fact that Bernstein picked it as one of the earliest of the series' releases suggests that the rejected score retained a special place in the maestro's heart.

■ The Big Blue/Le Grand bleu (1988)

Composer for European version: **Eric Serra**
Composer for American version: **Bill Conti**

French writer-director Luc Besson's *Le Grand bleu*, his first English-language film, tells the story of two freedivers (undersea divers who rely on extreme breath control rather than scuba gear) who eventually face off in a deadly diving competition off the coast of Italy. In Europe, this beautifully photographed meditation on the sea and those who are drawn to it, starring Jean-Marc Barr, Jean Reno, and Rosanna Arquette, was a smashing success. Besson's previous credits included *Le Dernier Combat* (1983) and *Subway* (1985), and he would go on to direct such films as *La Femme Nikita* (1990), *The Professional* (1994), and *The Fifth Element* (1997). Although he is known particularly for his stylized action films, *The Big Blue* was a perfect vehicle for him, since both of his parents were scuba instructors and he grew up dreaming of becoming a marine biologist.

Eric Serra, a French composer who has since scored all but one of Besson's directorial efforts (as well as the Bond film *GoldenEye*), was hired to provide its score. His ambient, often haunting music was rich with real and imagined underwater sounds, such as crashing waves, dolphin calls, etc. A strange and enchanting, primarily electronic score, it became both a critical and a commercial success, selling more than three million copies. Built from Serra's sample library (home to such trademark sounds as his electronically modified tympani and various synth-percussion effects), it featured soulful performances of its main themes on many instruments, from guitars to saxophones. The composer recalls preparing for his work on the film:

> At the start, Luc wanted a symphonic music for *The Big Blue*, this was his first idea because it was the current trend...big orchestral scores. Then, for the three years preceding this film, I drowned myself in symphonic music, I listened to a lot, assiduously.... I wanted to understand how that worked...such works as *Daphnis and Chloé* by Ravel or *Petrushka* by Stravinsky, but also Debussy and Bartók, it was those that I appreciated the most. As soon as I heard an unbelievable color, I looked into [the] sheet music [to see] how it was done, but I could not read them, since I have no musical culture, I did not learn the solfeggio but I tried to decipher although poorly. For three years I did that.... [Then,] while speaking with Luc, we changed our minds to do something more corresponding to our culture. Therefore I did not write any symphonic music, but the ones I listened to enriched considerably my culture.

Shortly after *Le Grand bleu* became a hit in European theaters, producer Jerry Weintraub (whose previous credits included *Nashville*, *Diner*, and *The Karate Kid*) picked up its American distribution rights through his Weintraub Entertainment Group. The movie's success on the continent gave him the confidence to aim for a late summer release, but he had quite a few problems with the original film. He cut its 132 minutes down to 118, removing its nudity and violence to earn a PG rating, and saddled it with a happy ending. In view of all these changes, especially its revised ending, a new score—one that reflected the picture's newfound optimism—became inevitable.

Among Weintraub's gripes about the original score was its lack of a memorable, whistleable theme, which he felt would be essential to the movie's US success. So he called in his old friend Bill Conti, with whom he had worked on the first two *Karate Kid* movies (and would go on to work on the third and fourth as well). Conti recalls when the two of them sat together and decided on the score's changes:

> When Jerry Weintraub bought *The Big Blue* for America, he did not like Eric Serra's score. He called me to watch the movie. After the screening, he said to me, "What do you think?" "I think the score is fun!" "I don't like it: I want you to do a new score!" I said, "OK!" It is very simple, because he has the money to distribute the film in America. But my score is really different from Serra's score. It is not the same approach. The CD is not available because the film was a flop in the USA. No success, no CD!

There is no official CD release for Conti's score, but his melody still haunts those who saw the film's American version. If Weintraub wanted an easily recognizable theme, he couldn't have any complaints about Conti's work on *The Big Blue*. The composer created a memorable and magical theme, played by flutes, that captured the heart of those few people who saw the movie in U.S. theaters. (Imagine their disappointment when they ran out to record stores to grab the soundtrack, only to find that Conti's theme was not on it. It was a CD of Serra's music!)

Eric Serra reflects on *The Big Blue*'s changes:

> The Americans put up a lot of money for the promo of this film. They believed a lot in it, but at the last moment they were afraid, for there were essentially French actors. They wanted to release the film as a blockbuster, then it was necessary for them to get American names. And when the film is finished, the only thing that one can change [at] the last minute...is the music. Having seen the success of the music over the world, this was almost a gag. The funniest is that the music of Bill Conti, who replaced me, was close [to] mine, in the same spirit. He had only three weeks to do it, it was not his usual universe, then the editing of the film and the end were changed. Finally, this was an artistic as well as a financial disaster. But I have nonetheless sold discs in the United States without the people seeing the film with this music.

(*Note*: American audiences can now see the full picture with Serra's music on DVD. Sony Pictures Home Entertainment has released a 168-minute director's cut that restores Serra's music.)

■ **Cocktail** (1988)

Original composer: **Maurice Jarre**
Replacement composer: **J. Peter Robinson**

Cocktail, a celebration of 1980s pop-culture kitsch and fads, is a silly fairy-tale-meets-soap-opera starring Tom Cruise as a womanizing, bottle-juggling celebrity bartender who dreams of getting rich, and Elizabeth Shue as his love interest. Set in New York City's club scene and Jamaica's tropical bars and beaches, it's a featherweight love-triangle story (young guy, young gal, older woman) directed by Australian-born New Zealander Roger Donaldson, whose previous credits included *Smash Palace* (1981), *The Bounty* (1984), and *No Way Out* (1987).

Musically, *Cocktail* was notable for an eclectic song collection that gathered both Grammy and Golden Globe nominations. It included songs performed by Bobby McFerrin, Jimmy Cliff, Starship, Little Richard, the Everly Brothers, and the Beach Boys, whose *Kokomo*, with its steel drums and Caribbean-celebrating lyrics, set much of the film's musical tone.

To provide the picture's dramatic underscore, director Donaldson turned to French maestro Maurice Jarre, who had scored his *No Way Out*. Along with director Peter Weir, Donaldson was one of the filmmakers who encouraged Jarre to experiment with synthesizer-based music. Thus the composer who had once penned symphonic masterpieces for *Lawrence of Arabia* (1962) and *Doctor Zhivago* (1965) seemed to specialize in the 1980s in intimate electronic scores, such as *The Year of Living Dangerously* (1982), *Witness* (1985), and *Apology* (1986).

Synthesized scores were popular with some producers, who felt they spoke to and attracted teenaged audiences. For the producers at Touchstone Pictures (a division of Walt Disney Pictures), the studio behind *Cocktail*, an electronic score usually meant contemporary, pop-influenced music that could easily be interwoven with a variety of songs. Tangerine Dream's music exemplified this sort of approach; synthesizer scores such as the band provided for *Risky Business* (1983) proved popular with both moviegoers and filmmakers (and sold a lot of soundtrack albums).

An electronic score by Maurice Jarre, however, was quite a different case. His electronic work struck *Cocktail*'s filmmakers as a bit heavy-handed. They felt that their movie's music should be lighter, and reflect both its exotic setting and the numerous pop songs interspersed throughout. Particularly troubled by one of Jarre's cues, they called on British composer J. Peter Robinson to fix it. The classically trained composer-pianist had worked with Eric Clapton, Phil Collins, David Bowie, Al Jarreau, and other pop icons; his previous film music credits included *The Wraith* (1986), *The Gate* (1987), *The Believers* (1987), and a few TV movies and TV series episodes.

Robinson picks up the story of *Cocktail*'s score:

> Roger Donaldson and I had a meeting at Disney regarding the music for the film, which already had a score by another composer. One cue in particular was not working and I was brought in to replace that cue. Once Roger had heard where I was going with the replacement, he asked if I could do the rest of the score. All this was happening on a Friday. I was starting another film on the following Monday and told Roger that I was going to be unavailable. "We're print-mastering on Monday, mate!" Roger said. So from that point on I stayed up writing the score and delivered it on Monday morning at around five in the morning. Needless to say, I slept for a while after that one.

The longest weekend of J. Peter Robinson's life resulted in a mildly entertaining if not particularly spectacular pop-oriented score. What he achieved was an instrumental score that matched the style of the movie's songs: heavily rhythmic in style for the New York City scenes and Caribbean-sounding for the Jamaica scenes. Robinson received an ASCAP award for his work, but in an odd twist of fate, the composer change came so late that Jarre's name was already on *Cocktail*'s posters, so many respectable film books still attribute the film's score to the French composer.

■ Young Guns (1988)

Original composer: **James Horner**
Replacement composer: **Anthony Marinelli**

Young Guns, directed by Christopher Cain—whose previous credits included *The Principal* (1987), *That Was Then... This Is Now* (1985), and *The Stone Boy* (1984)—is a youth-oriented "Brat Pack" Western that starred teen heartthrobs Emilio Estevez, Charlie Sheen, and Kiefer Sutherland, playing vigilantes bent on avenging the murder of their beloved employer and benefactor. Its plot was based on New Mexico's notorious Lincoln County War and the legend of its most famous participant, Billy the Kid.

For music, the director turned to James Horner, with whom he had worked on *The Stone Boy* and *Where the River Runs Black* (1986). Among Horner's recent previous credits were *Red Heat* (1988), *Willow* (1988), *An American Tail* (1986), *The Name of the Rose* (1986), and *Aliens* (1986). The composer's previous work with Cain allowed him an opportunity to experiment and stretch his musical muscles (e.g., *Where the River Runs Black* was Horner's first all-electronic score). For *Young Guns* he prepared something quite unusual, a wild Western ride with lots of driving, restless themes, and a hint of Celtic flavor.

Having just finished Ron Howard's *Willow*—a movie with a luxuriant music budget—Horner reassembled a number of the same musicians for *Young Guns*. They included multi-instrumentalists (and masters of many unusual instruments from around the globe) Tony Hinnigan, Mike Taylor, Forbes Henderson, Claudia Figueroa, the late Tommy McCarthy, David Lindley, Ian Underwood, and Ralph Grierson. Most of the score's synth material was performed by the composer himself.

Recording at London's AIR Studios went on for three-and-a-half weeks. The players would get together at nine o'clock each morning and record until seven or eight o'clock in the evening. With few of Horner's cues set in stone, he encouraged the unique gathering of musicians to experiment with all aspects of the music. There was a lot of improvisation, and the musicians worked hard to find just the right "color" for each track, a task that can eat up a lot of studio time. The sessions were upbeat and fun for all involved. Tony Hinnigan relates two session anecdotes:

> James [Horner] hadn't thought, initially, to have a bagpiper on the score but, a few days into the recording, realized that he needed one and asked Mike [Taylor] and I if we could find him someone. We asked Tommy [McCarthy], and he came down to the studio and performed his slow airs most beautifully. When he had finished, James asked us how much Tommy was being paid. Mike told him and he said, "Double it.".... David Lindley started each day with a session of tai chi in the studio. He then went down to the Burger King on Oxford Circus and bought a triple-Whopper-burger-with-extra-bacon-and-cheese, which he brought back to the studio and ate for breakfast. Every day. When we finally asked him how someone who practiced meditation and tai chi could eat something so heinous for breakfast so regularly, he replied, "It's biomass, man."

On completing the recording, Horner and the group were pleased, feeling that they had done a very good job. But the producing studio (Morgan Creek Productions, distributed by 20th Century Fox) thought otherwise.

Horner's music certainly wasn't a traditional Western score: In fact, it featured several instruments that the studio considered just plain out-of-place. These included bagpipe and pennywhistle, which were felt to be too Irish. Originally designed to portray the Wild West's great outdoors while also representing the story's Irish-American and English characters, Horner's score was nonetheless deemed unsuitable and possibly even offputting for its targeted young audience.

This, of course, made no sense. Since the film featured a collection of Hollywood's hottest young actors—who by themselves would attract the target audience—why not indulge in an unusual and evocative soundtrack instead of an everyday dramatic score? But art didn't triumph over commerce this time, and the filmmakers hired replacement composer Anthony Marinelli.

Composer-keyboardist Marinelli's previous screen credits included *Rigged* (1986), *Nice Girls Don't Explode* (1987), *Pinocchio and the Emperor of the Night* (1987), and sixty-five episodes of the animated TV series *Ghostbusters* (1986–87). Interestingly, Marinelli's score was not traditional Western music either. No doubt well aware of the film's target audience, he provided a pop-oriented 1980s-sounding electronic music score. It combined strange sounds, including ambient noise, heartbeat effects, and drum loops, with synthesizers. His end credits cue, which features a rock guitar power anthem with percussion and honky-tonk piano, provides the ultimate example of his score's pop style.

Even though it was never officially released, Marinelli's soundtrack turned out to be a hot item for soundtrack collectors. For a sample of Horner's unused music, check out the album *Camera: Reflections on Film Music*, by Tony Hinnigan and Mike Taylor's world-music/film-music group Incantation (True North Records).

■ **Alien Nation** (1988)

Original composer: **Jerry Goldsmith**
Replacement composer: **Curt Sobel**

Set in Los Angeles in the then-near-future of 1991, *Alien Nation* is a sci-fi cop-buddy movie that addresses the theme of racial discrimination. It involves a race of human-looking aliens, the Newcomers, who fled their native planet, where they were slaves, and came to Southern California, hoping to integrate themselves into human society. The "buddies" in this tale are a streetwise racist cop (played by James Caan) and the first Newcomer cop (played by Mandy Patinkin), who fight a Newcomer underworld boss (played by Terence Stamp). It was directed by Graham Baker, whose previous directing credits included *Omen III: The Final Conflict* (1981), *Impulse* (1984), and a few TV series episodes. Fairly popular at the box office, *Alien Nation* spawned a television series and five TV movies.

Hired to score the picture was Jerry Goldsmith, whose recent previous credits included *Rambo III* (1988), *Rent-a-Cop* (1987), *Innerspace* (1987), and *Hoosiers* (1986). Goldsmith and director Baker had worked together previously on *Omen III*. The composer took on *Alien Nation* primarily because it afforded him an opportunity to experiment with an all-electronic score. Like his music for *Runaway* (1984), *Alien Nation*'s entire score was performed by Goldsmith, using only his synth equipment. Generally speaking, for him, synths simply stood in for standard acoustic musical instruments, and one of his electronic-music predilections that's evident in this score is a reliance on stock synth patches and samples (instead of creating his own).

Goldsmith's synthesizer timbres for *Alien Nation* provided a good contemporary sound that reflected the film's near-future setting. It's the music of a place and time where almost everything looks, feels, and sounds like 1980s Los Angeles. For this score's key theme, he reappropriated a melody he had first sketched out the previous year for *Wall Street*—the sole theme he would write for a film he worked on for only one week before resigning due to creative differences with the filmmakers. In *Alien Nation*, the theme appears prominently in the cue "The Wedding."

(When this same theme was performed two years later by Branford Marsalis in Goldsmith's score for *The Russia House*, it became one of the composer's best-loved tunes. There's nothing unusual about such "wandering" themes in film music: For instance, in 1973, Goldsmith had reused the main theme he wrote for the seldom-seen 1971 television movie *Crosscurrent*, turning it into the main title theme for *Escape from the Planet of the Apes*.)

In addition to this addictive melody, Goldsmith's *Alien Nation* score contained many of the composer's traditional musical figures. And, much like the aliens in *Close Encounters of the Third Kind* (1977), Goldsmith gave *Alien Nation*'s Newcomers a musical calling card—a separate theme consisting of three notes, as opposed to John Williams's *Close Encounter*'s alien theme, which had five.

Like all of Goldsmith's electronic scores, *Alien Nation* offered carefully crafted synth orchestrations, including detailed imitations of acoustic instruments. The strange and funky aliens' sounds, which included faux-saxophones and faux-percussion, are a lot like sounds he came up with for his score *Explorers* (1985).

But as he worked on *Alien Nation* at Los Angeles' Record Plant studio, Goldsmith seems to have been unaware of the movie's many problems. By the time he finished recording in May 1988, the second half of the picture had been extensively recut, and his music had to be reworked to make it fit. Partway into the rewrite, his busy composing schedule intervened, and he simply had no more time to spend on the picture.

At this point, his whole score was dropped (making it Goldsmith's first rejected score!), and a new one was commissioned from music editor-composer Curt Sobel, whose one previous film-scoring credit was *The Flamingo Kid* (1984). Sobel was asked to keep the original music's essential style, but lose most of the freaky alien sounds and make it a bit more contemporary sounding. His electronic score mixes jazz elements with bursts of acoustic guitar, sometimes slipping into a slow, mellow, tonal feel. His overall approach isn't radically different from Goldsmith's, but it lacks the other composer's memorable theme. Furthermore, Sobel's action music is less violent, more in touch with a lighter urban-pop sensibility.

While Goldsmith's rejected score was released as a CD in 2005, Sobel's score hasn't had an official release, even though it would have been interesting to hear it alongside the film's original music.

The Accidental Tourist (1988)

Original composer: **Bruce Broughton**
Replacement composer: **John Williams**

After having worked with composer Bruce Broughton on *Silverado* (1985) and *Cross My Heart* (1987), writer-director Lawrence Kasdan hired him to score his bittersweet romance *The Accidental Tourist*. Broughton's involvement with *The Accidental Tourist* was long viewed by film score fans as a sort of urban legend, until the Film Score Monthly label uncovered some long-buried paperwork while producing a CD of John Williams's final soundtrack for the picture. According to these papers, Broughton had recorded adaptations of a few J. S. Bach works with a chamber orchestra on July 25, 1988. These were temp tracks for the picture, and he never got a chance to write an original score, as he explains:

> The original plan on this picture was to score the film with Bach transcriptions. The idea was originally Kasdan's and I agreed to try it. Selecting the right music from Bach for the scenes proved to be very difficult, so we had a session in which I recorded several Bach pieces for inclusion into the film as a sort of temp track for screenings. During a couple of screenings, as I talked to Kasdan, it became obvious that we didn't see the film in the same way at all. We didn't have a musical problem on the film; we had a disagreement on what the film was about. It was really a creative difference, but not one that had to do with either music or personalities.

Replacement composer John Williams was hired four days after Broughton was let go. He, too, didn't have a particularly easy time writing for *The Accidental Tourist*: Kasdan asked him to rewrite his main title and establish a new main melody in his thematic score (the discarded melody would find a home in the picture's wedding sequence). His rewritten main titles work well, with none of the thematic inconsistency that often plagues such rewrites.

Williams's music for the film is of a piece with the intimate emotional scores written during the latter part of his career. The sound of the smallish orchestra he used on *The Accidental Tourist* is enhanced by subtle electronics that emphasize the emotional detachment of the movie's main characters. The score, a sensitive and introspective portrayal of the film's unusual relationships, was nominated for an Academy Award.

Broughton, one of Hollywood's most reliable composers, has been involved in penning a couple of rescue/replacement scores himself. One of these was written just a couple of months after he was let go from *The Accidental Tourist*, when he stepped in to replace the original score for director David Jones's acclaimed post-Vietnam drama *Jacknife*. The movie's original composer, Mark Isham (whose previous credits included *The Moderns, The Hitcher, Mrs. Soffel*, and *Never Cry Wolf*), provided a jazzy underscore that didn't meet the filmmakers' expectations. Broughton was shown parts of the movie with its original score in place, without being given any specific instructions for its replacement, so he had to figure out a new approach on his own. What he came up with was a sort of mournful trumpet theme (not altogether unlike Goldsmith's for *First Blood*) with an overlay of urban beats.

Broughton's superb *Jacknife* music hasn't been released on CD yet. But given the great number of Broughton scores that have been issued by such specialty labels as Film Score Monthly and Intrada, a release may not be far off. As for Isham's rejected score, he later turned it into a concert piece.

■ Apartment Zero (1988)

Original music: **Astor Piazzola**
Replacement composer: **Elia Cmiral**

It seemed like a match made in heaven when Argentinean-born director Martin Donovan managed to get the legendary tango composer and bandoneón virtuoso Astor Piazzola (an internationally famous, classically trained musician who had scored dozens of films) to pen the music for *Apartment Zero*, an oddball political thriller starring Colin Firth. Donovan thought he wanted an authentic Argentinean-sounding, tango-based score for his American production set in Argentina, but once he heard the music Piazzola wrote for him, he changed his mind. It turned out that the director only wanted a tango-*flavored* score—not the real thing. So he hired Czech composer Elia Cmiral, who was living in Los Angeles and, at the time, had only one other feature scoring credit, the Swedish film *A Matter of Life and Death* (1986).

Although Cmiral had no intimate knowledge of tango music, he liked the film and readily accepted the job. Within the ten days he was given to score the film, he wrote and recorded twenty minutes of tango-tinged music for a small orchestra, which he supplemented with twenty-five minutes of music that he improvised on synths, piano, and percussion—all of which suited the director's musical needs well.

> I first came to the United States in 1987 to study at the well-known USC Scoring Program. After I finished USC, I secured a record deal in Sweden. Before I left, I was hanging around LA, and I got *Apartment Zero*. The movie was shot in Argentina, and they wanted an Argentinean tango. The Argentinean Tango King (Astor Piazzola) was hired to do the film, and wrote part of the score. The director and producer went to Buenos Aires to listen to it and didn't like it. They called the movie's sound-designer (who is friend of mine) to tell him that the music didn't work. What could they do? So my friend called me next day and screened the movie for me. It was an interesting film, but I didn't know anything about Argentinean tangos! So the director and producer came that afternoon, and asked me if I could write an Argentinean tango. "Of course! No problem!" They wanted to know if I could write it in ten days. "Of course! No problem!" [laughs] So I had forty-five minutes of music to write in ten days in a musical style I had no experience with! Twenty minutes for a small orchestra was all I could write in that time. Remember, I was young, fresh, and just finished USC Scoring. I had no idea about musicians, orchestrators, nothing! I didn't know who to call, so I called a composer I knew from a USC seminar, a real composer. He came over to my house, listened to the music, gave his advice, put me in

contact with his contractor, and helped me get to the point where we could record in studio. The remaining twenty-five minutes of the score I improvised with rented synthesizers, piano, and percussions directly in studio.

■ **Alienator** (1989)

Original composer: **Chuck Cirino**
Replacement composers: **John Bigham and Michael Bishop**

From the 1980s on, the ready availability of low-priced polyphonic synthesizers made many composers' work easier, especially for low-budget features. Most cheap horror, sci-fi, and action movies dispensed with scores performed by live players, and their composers wrote, produced, and performed their own synth scores—sometimes within a matter of days. One of the most notable names in this game is composer Chuck Cirino, whose vast output is primarily concentrated in the horror and sci-fi categories. A jack-of-all-low-budget-movie-trades, Cirino has also worked as a cinematographer, director, actor, producer, writer, and editor.

In 1989, Cirino, whose previous composing credits included *Chopping Mall* (1986), *Big Bad Mama II* (1987), and *Transylvania Twist* (1989), was hired to score *Alienator*, a film by Fred Olen Ray. (Ray boasts having written, produced, and directed more than 100 features. Prior to *Alienator*, his directing credits included *The Brain Leeches*, *Evil Spawn*, and *Hollywood Chainsaw Hookers*.) *Alienator* is the outlandish tale of an intergalactic prison escapee who lands on Earth and takes up with a group of college kids on a camping trip. This space criminal is hunted by Alienator (think Alien plus Terminator)—an ultraviolent, sexily clad female android.

Cirino shares the story of his *Alienator* score's treatment:

> The movie was shot in about five days. I also scored it in about five days. Fred [Olen Ray] and Jeff [producer Jeffrey C. Hogue] were very happy with the score when it was done. Later, Fred was the one who told me the distributors were replacing it, but he didn't seem to know the reason. My score was melodically unique but electronic in its execution and style—yet I have reused cues in one of my own productions, http://www.weirdtv.com, so it couldn't have been that bad.
>
> I do not know who they hired to rescore it. All I know is what is evident: The new composer must have had three hours to redo the whole thing. The distributors didn't even have the decency to change the opening title credits—that would have cost them more money. Fred told me he would have been happier with the original score—but it was not his choice. If anyone would like to take the credit for scoring this film, please step forward and claim your right. For God's sake, you deserve it.

In fact, the movie was rescored by John Bigham and Michael Bishop, neither of whom was credited and who were only identified much later. (Bigham is a multi-instrumentalist who has recorded with Miles Davis, Fishbone, and Bruce Hornsby. His only film scoring credit is *A Single Rose*. Bishop is a singer-songwriter-composer whose previous scoring credits included *Duet for One* and *A Night at the Magic Castle*.) A likely reason for the rescoring may have been rights ownership. By having new music written for the picture as "work-for-hire" (meaning the employer becomes the legal owner of all rights to the work), the producers could own it outright and collect its royalties from such performing rights societies as BMI and ASCAP when the film showed on North American TV or in overseas theaters.

Similarly, rights ownership may have been the issue in 1988 when Harvey Cohen wrote his first feature film score for the horror flick *Ghost Town*, a production of Empire Pictures, headed by producer Charles Band. Although Cohen's music was used for the film's initial screening at Los Angeles' Beverly Center mall, when it made its way to theaters nationwide around Halloween, it was refitted (with the exception of a few cues) with preexisting music by the producer's brother, Empire's in-house composer, Richard Band. Band's previous credits included *Re-Animator* (1985), *Ghoulies* (1985), *Troll* (1986), and *The Caller* (1987).

■ **Cyborg** (1989)

Original composers: **James Saad and Anthony Riparetti**
Replacement composer: **Kevin Bassinson**

This fairly early Jean-Claude van Damme vehicle set in a postapocalyptic world was directed by Albert Pyun, a specialist in low-budget martial arts and horror movies, especially sequels to such films as *Nemesis* and *Kickboxer*.

Music was intended to play a big part in *Cyborg*'s plot—hence its characters' names Gibson Rickenbacker, Nady Simmons, Fender Tremolo, Marshall Strat, and Pearl Prophet (all derived from names of musical instruments and their manufacturers). The director originally conceived the movie, the most artistic of his career, as an electronic action-opera without dialogue. Needless to say, Cannon Films (which had filed for bankruptcy in 1987) wasn't crazy about that idea, so the picture became a simple van Damme actioner shot on sets built for the studio's aborted *Masters of the Universe* sequel.

Composers Anthony Riparetti and James Saad, both of whom had worked for Pyun on his previous picture, *Alien from L.A.* (1988), were hired to provide *Cyborg*'s score. (And they would go on to work with the director on two dozen more movies.) Although their music can't be called operatic by any means, it was still quite accomplished electronic material that fit the then-current style of Italian postapocalyptic film scores. Their action music was pretty standard stuff—percussive sounds versus guitar riffs—but their emotional music (yes, there is such a thing in *Cyborg*) had some truly moving, tender moments that probably would have worked a lot better if they had been scored for acoustic instruments. The Riparetti-Saad score also contained a number of odd elements, including emulated/processed whispering and extended rock-guitar solos.

But none of that made it into the movie after its extensive re-edit, and the composing team's score was replaced with one by Kevin Bassinson, making his feature film scoring debut. (Bassinson would go on to score a few more features, including *Eight Days a Week* and *100 Girls*, but his primary gig in Hollywood has been music editor, working on many episodes of such TV series as *Nash Bridges*, *The West Wing*, and *Burn Notice*.)

Bassinson's *Cyborg* score is irritatingly synth-based. Its highlights are a couple of thematic ideas, one of which—the emulated horn motif—almost becomes the score's calling card. Otherwise, with the exception of some Eastern-sounding melodies (in the cue "Music at the Mall"), his postapocalyptic music is simply generic and uninteresting.

A suite drawn from *Cyborg*'s rejected Riparetti-Saad score was released on a Silva Screen compilation CD celebrating the music of Jean-Claude van Damme movies in 1991. Howlin' Wolf Records issued the complete Riparetti-Saad score in 2011. Bassinson's work was also released on the Silva Screen label. The movie itself is now available in two versions as well, with director Pyun's original cut carrying the Riparetti-Saad score.

■ Say Anything... (1989)

Original composer: **Anne Dudley**
Replacement composer: **Richard Gibbs**

Ever since the memorable scene in *Say Anything...* when Lloyd (played by John Cusack) holds up a stereo to play Peter Gabriel's "In Your Eyes" for his special girl (played by Ione Skye), director Cameron Crowe has made something of a career out of directing movies set to catchy songs. This song-heavy approach climaxed for Crowe with *Almost Famous* (2000), a semiautobiographical film about a boy who follows his favorite band and writes about them for *Rolling Stone* magazine.

Say Anything..., a well-written, character-driven, romantic comedy-drama in which a pair of teens—seeming opposites—find each other, was writer-director-producer Crowe's directorial debut. (He's gone on to make such films as *Singles*, *Jerry McGuire*, *Vanilla Sky*, and *Elizabethtown*.) The many songs featured in *Say Anything...* are performed by such popular bands as Cheap Trick, the Red Hot Chili Peppers, Depeche Mode, Fishbone, Steely Dan, Aerosmith, and others.

Although Crowe's films often feature only marginal underscores, often by his wife, singer-songwriter Nancy Wilson (a founding member of the rock band Heart), he shows painstaking care in selecting and approving underscore cues. To provide music for *Say Anything...*, he hired Anne Dudley, a classically trained British composer-performer-arranger and record producer (and former member of the 1980s synth-band Art of Noise), who had previously scored the films *Hiding Out* (1987), *Buster* (1988), and *The Mighty Quinn* (1989). But as the director, trying to satisfy his musical vision for the film, requested rewrite after rewrite, Dudley finally reached the point where she had had enough.

Brought in to replace her was composer Richard Gibbs, whose one previous film scoring credit was *Sweet Hearts Dance* (1988). Gibbs recalls his work on *Say Anything...*:

> They had already hired Anne Dudley to score it, and apparently Cameron wanted to keep trying different things, and was asking Anne to rescore and rescore. She got fed up and literally hopped back on a plane to England. The music department at Fox came to me and asked me to help Cameron, who was monkeying around with the music. I tried a bunch of different little things, and Cameron liked what I was doing, so he asked me to look at a scene in which John Mahoney gives Ione Skye a ring that once belonged to her mom. So we're in a recording studio, Cameron is out in the control room, and I'm sitting at a piano, watching a TV monitor, and ad-libbing while watching the scene for the first time. It's not very long, maybe a 30- or 40-second cue. I finish playing and Cameron says, "Great." I asked him if he liked it, and he just said, "Great." And I said, "Well, let me think about it while we're recording and I'll practice it some more." Cameron interjected and said, "No, you don't understand, we recorded that!" And that's what ended up in the film, my initial playing.

Gibbs continued working on the score with Crowe in a similar vein, and his finished score is quite effective. Incidentally, both Gibbs and Dudley are credited with the movie's score, because the director wanted to somehow honor the composer whom he had driven mad. While this crediting suggests a collaboration, the two composers never met on the project, although Gibbs did use some of Dudley melodies to round out his score.

Say Anything... is essentially Crowe's only movie in which the score does more than pad out the empty spaces between songs, and yet none of the underscore cues made it to the film's official soundtrack CD.

■ **The Seinfeld Chronicles** (1989)

Original composer: **Jep Epstein**
Replacement composer: **Jonathan Wolff**

On July 5, 1989, NBC made television history when it aired *The Seinfeld Chronicles*, the pilot episode of what would become the sitcom series *Seinfeld*, about New York comedian Jerry Seinfeld, just minding his everyday business onscreen. After this debut, NBC had faith in the show and put up the money to shoot more episodes (creating what would become one of television's most popular and beloved shows, running for nine seasons).

There were several differences between the pilot and the subsequent episodes, one of the most noticeable being the music. The pilot was scored by Jep Epstein, who wrote contemporary-sounding music for it. The problem was, even though his music fit the show's spirit, it tended to clash with the dialogue. So, once the show was picked up, veteran screen composer Jonathan Wolff (who would go on to score such popular TV comedies *Will & Grace, King of Queens,* and *Married with Children*) was called in. He immediately saw the problem with the pilot's music and came up with a way to solve it:

> Jerry called me directly and said, "George Wallace said you're my man," and showed me what some other composers had tried for him. I recognized that it wasn't a musical problem, rather a sound-design problem. At the time, the pilot was called *The Seinfeld Chronicles*, and the opening titles had Jerry doing stand-up material—with every week being a different monologue. Jerry wanted music that was signature and unique and quirky—identifiable. Remember, this was the late 1980s: Signature, identifiable TV music meant melody. Thematic melody. [But] you can't have melody while he's trying to do monologue—they butt heads. So the sound-design problem I saw was that the opening title already had its melody—it's Jerry! So I built the music around him. And instead of using standard instruments like drums and clarinets, because of the human nature of the melody—his voice, I went with the organic sounds of the finger snaps, mouth pops, lip smacks, and tongue noise. ... For the pacing, I watched some of his HBO special and noticed that he has a rhythmic, musical pacing to the way he delivers his monologue. I clocked a tempo for it—about 110—and built the music around him at that tempo. The bass mainly hangs out in a frequency range that doesn't interfere with his voice, below him—it supports him as a bass does with a melody.... And that's how I built this theme for Seinfeld to adapt to different monologues, the music is completely modular. And it worked—it was quirky and fun and identifiable and signature.

Wolff's music—with its immediately recognizable slap-bass sound—worked so well with the program that not only was he contracted to do the whole show, but he also was asked to rescore the pilot, which was later integrated into the syndicated series under the title "Good News, Bad News." The series' Season 1 DVD includes both the original and the rescored pilot for comparison. Wolff's sound doesn't need introduction, but Epstein's music might surprise some people, as it is quite unlike what one has grown to expect from the show.

It takes a long time for any comedy show to find its proper sound, and there are quite a few examples like *Seinfeld*, where first tries didn't work out. For example, in 2005 comedian Rodney Carrington launched an ABC series titled *Rodney*, which was somewhat similar to *Seinfeld* but set in Tulsa, Oklahoma, rather than New York City. *Rodney*'s creators contacted several composers, including *Seinfeld*'s Jonathan Wolff, to provide the show with musical ideas. The challenge for *Rodney* was finding a bluesy sound that didn't lean on harmonica or saxophone or other human voice-range instruments, which might conflict with the dialogue. The pilot's score, written by Eric Hester (whose previous credits included episodes of *The Pretender, Nash Bridges,* and *Flatland*), utilized a pop-ish blues sound. It was accepted by the show's creators, but his work on the show stopped there due to a professional disagreement between him and a contracted cocomposer. Because of this dustup, ABC hired composer Steve Dorff (whose previous credits included episodes of *Murder, She Wrote; Alien Nation;*

Growing Pains; and *Murphy Brown*) to redo the pilot and provide music for the show's future episodes.

Even when scores play only nominal roles, as they often do in sitcoms, their composers have to establish a program's sound within a matter of seconds, which is never an easy task.

■ Koneko monogatari/The Adventures of Milo and Otis (1989)

Composer for Japanese version (1986): **Ryuichi Sakamoto**
Original composer for American version: **Joe Raposo, David McHugh**
Replacement composer for American version: **Michael Boddicker**

When Columbia Pictures picked up the American rights to *Koneko monogatari* (literal translation: *A Kitten's Tale*), an adorable Japanese family movie about the friendship of a cat and dog, the studio had problems with several aspects of the original picture. Among them were the philosophical nature of the story's narration and the poems by acclaimed contemporary Japanese poet Shuntaro Tanikawa that were interspersed through it. For the American version, rewritten by Mark Saltzman, Columbia substituted a new, decidedly less philosophical narration performed by Dudley Moore. This version, renamed *The Adventures of Milo and Otis*, was also significantly cut, ending up a mere seventy-six minutes long. This was done not only to make it more child-friendly (in the short-attention-span sense), but also to remove scenes that the studio deemed too intense for children.

The final change was in the picture's music. The Japanese version's score, an orchestral work with some interesting synth overlays, had been done by Ryuichi Sakamoto, a popular composer-performer (founding member of the electropop group Yellow Magic Orchestra) who had scored such films as *Merry Christmas, Mr. Lawrence* (1983) and *The Last Emperor* (1987). Columbia, however, didn't like Sakamoto's approach, which it felt was as highbrow as the Japanese narrations.

The American version's first score was the work of screenwriter Saltzman penning lyrics to music by his frequent collaborator Joe Raposo (the two had worked together on *Sesame Street* and *The Great Muppet Caper*). Eventually, however, the powers that be decided to ditch these songs entirely and take the film's music in a different direction.

Composer David McHugh, whose previous scoring credits included *Moscow on the Hudson* (1984) and *Mystic Pizza* (1988), was then called in by Columbia's production consultant Gareth Wigan to discuss a new, synthesizer-based score that kids would like. But, based on the composer's suggestion, Wigan agreed to fund an orchestral score, and after hearing samples from McHugh, he greenlighted its recording. Unfortunately, due to a gall bladder operation, Wigan couldn't attend the recording sessions, so he didn't hear the final score until it was already committed to tape. On finally seeing the movie with McHugh's music, Wigan found the score to be too soft—he felt it wouldn't grab a child's attention. McHugh's music, orchestrated on a *Peter and the Wolf*–type premise, assigned instruments to specific characters (e.g., castanets for crabs) and humanized the movie's little critters with memorable tunes. Alas, as wonderful and creative as McHugh's approach was, the studio ultimately wanted something different.

Returning to the synthesizer-score idea, Wigan hired a new composer, his son-in-law Michael Boddicker, a well-known composer-performer. As an in-demand session player, Boddicker has performed synthesizer parts on numerous albums by such top stars as Michael Jackson and played on countless film scores. As a composer, his previous film scoring credits included *Get Crazy* (1983) and *The Adventures of Buckaroo Banzai* (1984).

Boddicker provided *The Adventures of Milo and Otis* with a kid-friendly adventure score with dashes of humor and an abundance of musical quotations, including classical works by Grieg, Schumann, and Schubert and such traditional American folk tunes as "Turkey in the Straw." Rounding things out is the bouncy, country-tinged children's song "Walk Outside," written by Dick Tarrier and performed by Dan Crow.

Of all the different scores, only Ryuichi Sakamoto's *Koneko monogatari* score is available on CD.

■ **Trust Me** (1989)

Original composer: **Elmer Bernstein**
Replacement composer: **Pray for Rain**

In the late 1980s, after years of scoring more than his fair share of comedies (e.g., *Airplane, Airplane II: The Sequel, Ghost Busters, Spies Like Us, ¡Three Amigos!, Funny Farm*, etc.), composer Elmer Bernstein, in search of some more experimental ventures, took on strange little movies that had no major studio backing. One of these was *Trust Me*, starring the British singer Adam Ant (of the New Wave band Adam and the Ants), who plays an art dealer out to maximize his investments by killing a painter he represents, to increase the value of his collection of the artist's works.

Why would Bernstein take this picture? For one thing, he had grown fascinated with the expressive sound of the ondes Martenot. Having used it to at least some small degree in many of his scores, he was always on the lookout for a picture in which he could work extensively with the instrument. (Invented in 1928, this electronic instrument with a disembodied sound reminiscent of the Theremin had been used in scores by many classical composers, including Oliver Messiaen, Edgar Varèse, Arthur Honneger, Darius Milhaud, Giacinto Scelsi, and Pierre Boulez, and had graced film scores by Dmitri Shostakovich and Maurice Jarre. Bernstein first used it in his 1981 score for *Heavy Metal*.) In 1986, he was set to write an ondes Martenot–heavy score for *Night of the Creeps*, but the deal fell through. So, three years later, when *Trust Me*'s writer-director, Robert Houston (whose previous writing-directing credits included *Growing Pains* and *Shogun Assassin*), gave him an absolutely free hand, out came the ondes Martenot.

But Bernstein's unusual score, which used the instrument exclusively, didn't please Houston, who went looking for a new composer. After consulting with music supervisor Peter Afterman, the director listened to a couple of demos by the San Francisco–based band Pray for Rain, which had previously scored Alex Cox's films *Sid & Nancy* (1986) and *Straight to Hell* (1987). Houston liked the band's work, and after scoring a few scenes for him, they were hired. Like Bernstein, Pray for Rain received no instructions about what to write. What they came up with was a modern jazz-based score that successfully supports the movie.

An odd twist of fate: In 1990, Bernstein scored the television movie *Murder in Mississippi*, directed by Roger Young (with whom the composer had worked on the 1985 TV movie *Gulag*). It was the story of the same incident—the infamous 1964 Ku Klux Klan killing of three civil rights workers—that inspired the 1989 film *Mississippi Burning*, but told from a different perspective. But whereas Bernstein's music for *Trust Me* had been considered too experimental, his music for *Murder in Mississippi* was deemed too old-fashioned and short on Southern flavor. His score (with the exception of one cue) was dropped, and a new, blues-tinged score was commissioned from composer Mason Daring, whose previous credits included the John Sayles pictures *Return of the Secaucus 7* (1979), *The Brother from Another Planet* (1984), *Matewan* (1987), and *Eight Men Out* (1988).

■ **Tremors** (1990)

Original composer: **Ernest Troost**
Additional composer: **Robert Folk**

When it was released in 1990, *Tremors*, a tribute to campy monster movies, was both a critical and a commercial success. Starring Kevin Bacon and Fred Ward, it's the story of a tiny dead-end town—Perfection, Nevada—under siege by giant wormlike creatures that live under the desert sand. Called "graboids" by the locals, these sandworms feed on whatever they can swallow, whether it's animals, humans, or houses.

Almost every aspect of *Tremors*, from the acting to the special monster effects to the musical score, received praise from newspaper reviewers. A writer for *Daily Variety* compared the score to John Williams's *Jaws* music in the sense that it was "enough to evoke images of a fin knifing through the desert sand." *The Hollywood Reporter*'s Duane Bygre complimented the music similarly: "[R]ousing, Western-style sounds smartly fit both the film's geography and its thematic points of horror and comedy."

But who should receive the praise for the score? Let's go back to the beginning of the story.

Composer Ernest Troost is best known for the touches of country music in many of his scores. This is probably why he was hired for *Tremors*—to lend its vast desert landscape a proper Western aura. His score features banjo, harmonica, piano, and percussion, The appearance of the graboids is mostly highlighted in traditional horror-music fashion, i.e., with a *Jaws*-like string section accented with metallic percussion. Yet even this horror material has a certain chilled-out country vibe to it.

The film's executive producer, Gale Anne Hurd (whose previous producer credits included *Terminator*, *Aliens*, and *The Abyss*), found Troost's music too laid-back for a picture crawling with flesh-eating monsters. Feeling it wasn't aggressive or propulsive enough, she pulled the plug on it. Replacement composer Robert Folk (whose previous scoring credits included six *Police Academy* films) recalls being brought onto *Tremors* with its premiere date looming:

> I was brought in to replace the entire score on *Tremors*. Then all of a sudden, Universal changed the release date to be much earlier than planned. Having only about two and a half weeks with the new schedule, it was decided to replace only the biggest and most important cues in the score. I was living in Malibu at the time, and the producer, Gale Anne Hurd, asked me to come over to her Malibu beach house. We went through the entire film, while Gale gave me her comments about the original score. In each scene she wanted a larger, more aggressive, more energetic approach to the music. The only thing she liked about the original score were a few scenes with grooves and harmonica. As I had very little time, I worked alone with no supervision from director Ron Underwood, or from anyone else on the film. I gave no demos to anyone. There were no listening sessions, and no themes were asked to be reviewed. This is a process that would be unheard of in today's film-scoring world. My very short schedule required me to use a number of people to help with the orchestration.
>
> We recorded the new score at Sony Pictures scoring stage in Los Angeles with 98 of LA's very finest musicians. The orchestra was fantastic. The music was very complex, and they "ate it for breakfast." Nothing was too difficult for them. We had limited recording time because of the new release schedule, and because the studio had already spent a considerable amount on the first score. Gale felt that the original score was too small, too lethargic, and that it was lacking in both style and content. I was asked to compose a score that was "bigger, better, more thematic, more action-adventure oriented," and to do it in a very short time.

Tremors' large orchestral cues, including those in the last twenty minutes of the picture, are Folk's cues. Writing roughly forty minutes of music, he gave the movie its requisite fill of complex action-music. One telling example of the differences between the two scores can be found when Kevin Bacon's character runs to fetch a vehicle during a fierce graboid attack. The only way he can survive when the creatures approach is to stop moving so that they can't feel his presence. In Troost's suspenseful cue ("Val's Run"), the music stops when the character stops, but in Folk's replacement cue, the music remains relentless despite the fact that the character is standing still.

Although he did an incredible job on the movie, Folk declined a credit on the picture based on his agent's advice. Therefore, to this day, many people believe that Ernest Troost was the only composer involved. While Folk released only a seventeen-minute suite drawn from his *Tremors* score on the soundtrack compilation CD *Robert Folk—Selected Suites*, Troost's complete score (most of it unused in the picture) was released by the Intrada label. Of course, the fact that Troost's CD doesn't contain the movie's memorable energetic music confused many fans of the film.

■ **White Fang** (1991)

Original composer: **Basil Poledouris**
Additional composer: **Hans Zimmer**
Additional additional composers: **Fiachra Trench, Shirley Walker**

White Fang is based on Jack London's popular 1906 novel of the same name. Set during the late-nineteenth-century Klondike River gold rush, it tells the story of a wolf-dog that befriends and is tamed by a young gold hunter. (The tale, which has appeared on the screen a number of times, was first filmed in 1925.) Produced by Walt Disney Pictures, the film was one of the studio's last attempts at serious live-action movies before its center stage was overtaken by animated musicals. For director Randal Kleiser, whose previous credits included *Big Top Pee-wee* (1988), *Grandview, U.S.A.* (1984), and *Grease* (1978), *White Fang* offered the opportunity to reunite with composer Basil Poledouris. Although Kleiser had worked with several other composers in the preceding few years, among his favorite musical experiences were two films he did with Poledouris: *The Blue Lagoon* (1980) and *Summer Lovers* (1982). Unfortunately, the duo's third collaboration was not destined to go as smoothly.

Disney was all over the place in its *White Fang* music requests, which seemed to Poledouris to boil down to an epic score done on a minimal budget. The composer remembers:

> It was a very interesting exercise in how to spend a lot of money on a film which was reported to have had a minimal budget. I think there was a strong desire to keep the production costs minimal on the score. On the other hand, there was the conflicting directive which requested in general the score should be very melodic, and the example was "like *Lawrence of Arabia*," which as a composer I interpret to mean very large orchestra. There was a strong desire on the part of the music personnel over there to keep the cost down. I was instructed to think in terms of real ethnic kinds of music, after which I did some research about Eskimo music. It's not terribly rich, Eskimo music. In fact, it's essentially chanting. And even the instruments themselves (and I suspect because trees are scarce) are primarily percussive. There are very few, if any, melodic kinds of instruments involved. So what this essentially led to was a small group consisting of about six musicians: flutes and drums and synthesizer, because I knew that I would need some dramatic sense in a few of the scenes. That represented about one quarter of the score,

that size group, and I proceeded scoring. And the rest of it was not exactly giant orchestra, but I think it was around sixty, or sixty-five musicians.

In an attempt to satisfy all the confusing directives he received, Poledouris devised a score that had Eskimo chants, colorful orchestral sounds, and musical fireworks as well. Unfortunately for the composer, the movie's beginning contained mostly atmospheric synth and percussion music (largely consisting, with the exception of the main title, of indigenous-sounding flutes accompanied by various rattles), which gave the studio powers-that-be, who initially watched only its first six reels, an inaccurate impression of the entire score. While the more adventurous second half of the film contained most of the composer's epic music, with warm melodies and even some action cues, the Disney brass was shocked by the music they heard in the film's first half.

Fearing that the whole score would have the same exotic sound, Disney CEO Jeffrey Katzenberg hired composer Hans Zimmer (whose recent previous scoring credits included *Pacific Heights* and *Driving Miss Daisy*) to do an alternate score. Zimmer had to write eighty minutes of music in sixteen days while being "sick as a dog." To help him finish this immense workload, two other composers joined his team: One was Irish composer and orchestrator Fiachra Trench, a regular collaborator of Zimmer's mentor, Stanley Myers. While working as an orchestrator on *White Fang*, Trench also composed a number of uncredited cues. (He and Zimmer would later work together on the composer's similarly introverted scores for *The House of the Spirits* and *Beyond Rangoon*.) The other composer-orchestrator was Shirley Walker, a big Zimmer supporter and the orchestrator-conductor of his breakthrough action score, *Black Rain* (1989).

Zimmer's alternate score was recorded in London at the same time that Poledouris was still working on his own score. Poledouris recalls:

> I finished mine, knowing that Hans was writing another. Hans finished his, having no idea I was in fact still at work. I must say that it is a really underhanded thing to do to a composer, to both composers. You should fire one, and let the other one do a score. It just really markedly shows they had no idea what the hell they were looking for, so they're going to try potluck. Now the director was always on my side because it was Randal, and I had worked with Randal; he knows I sort of have an understanding. So they brought in the [exec in charge], they showed him the first reel with my score, and then they showed him reel one with Hans' score, and Fiachra and Shirley. And then he would choose. He'd say, "Oh I like that, and that, and that."

In conclusion, we can't say anybody was actually rejected on this picture, because the producers hand-picked cues from each composer who worked on it. More than eighty percent of the score that accompanied the finished movie was Poledouris's, and he received the main composer credit. Poledouris estimates that the other composers had the following portions of the score's screen time: Zimmer, 14 percent; Walker, 1.2 percent; Trench, 3.6 percent. Interestingly, the credits don't mention Hans Zimmer at all. They do list Trench as a composer of "additional music," and give Walker credit for writing the cue "The Bear."

The final patchwork score is not as much of a mixed bag of music as one might expect. *White Fang* stands as a memorable film with a memorable score, both of which are miles ahead of Disney's more recent live-action offerings.

■ **New Jack City** (1991)

Original composer: **Wally Badarou**
Replacement composer: **Michel Colombier**

New Jack City is a crime thriller set in New York City during the 1980s crack cocaine epidemic. It is a cop-versus-drug-lord story accompanied by a "New Jack Swing" soundtrack (an R&B subgenre characterized by R&B-style vocals sung over hip-hop rhythms and samples) featuring such well-known performers as Ice-T, Keith Sweat, Christopher Williams, 2 Live Crew, Queen Latifah, Johnny Gill, and Essence. Starring Wesley Snipes and Ice-T, it marked the feature film directorial debut of actor Mario Van Peebles (son of filmmaker Melvin Van Peebles). Well received both critically and at the box office, *New Jack City* became the highest grossing independent film of 1991. (And its album of songs featured in the movie reached No. 1 on Billboard's Top R&B/Hip-Hop Albums chart.)

French-born composer-performer-producer Wally Badarou (who had recorded with Miriam Makeba, Level 42, Grace Jones, Robert Palmer, Jimmy Cliff, Black Uhuru, Power Station, Talking Heads, and Sly & Robbie and also released three solo albums) had only a few previous film scoring credits—*Countryman* (1982), *They Call It an Accident* (1982), and "additional score" for *Kiss of the Spider Woman* (1985)—prior to being hired to score *New Jack City*. But Badarou's work was already an important part of the movie before he was hired: His piece "Mambo" (from his solo album *Echoes*) was used as temp music for the film's action sequences. During his six-month stay on the picture, Badarou developed and recorded a five-minute piece that he intended to use as the basis of the rest of his score. The filmmakers okayed this music, but the picture kept changing, and a number of scenes were reshot, leaving the composer without a locked picture to work from. After six months, he had to leave the project and return to France for tax-related reasons.

His replacement was French composer-conductor Michel Colombier, a musician with strong backgrounds in classical, jazz, and pop music, whose previous scoring credits included *Ruthless People* (1986), *The Couch Trip* (1988), and *Impulse* (1990). Colombier was one of Hollywood's urban-action music specialists, and his *New Jack City* score had all the right grooves. Unfortunately, his music for the film has never been released on CD. Badarou's music, which also hasn't been released, is too good to be missed and seems bound to appear in some of his future projects.

In the Heat of the Night: "No Other Road" (1991)

Original composer: **Larry Blank**
Replacement music: **Stock music by David Bell and Nan Schwartz**

The 1967 film *In the Heat of the Night* was an acclaimed landmark production that won five Oscars, including Best Picture. Directed by Norman Jewison from a script by Stirling Silliphant, it starred Sidney Poitier and Rod Steiger and featured a score by Quincy Jones, whose popular bluesy theme song for it was performed by Ray Charles. The film is about a sophisticated, well-educated black police detective from Philadelphia, Virgil Tibbs (Poitier), who is arrested for murder while he's passing through a tiny Mississippi town. He quickly proves his own innocence and then slowly befriends the town's arrogant, redneck chief of police (Steiger), who gets Tibbs to hang around and help him and his staff of ne'er-do-wells solve the murder. Woven throughout the story is the townfolk's intense racial hatred of blacks. Among the movie's memorable moments are Tibbs's returning the slap he receives from a wealthy white aristocrat, and his response when the police chief asks him what he's called in Philadelphia: "They call me *Mister* Tibbs!" (which is No. 16 on the American Film Institute's list of the top 100 movie lines).

The film led to two feature-film sequels—neither of which lived up to the original—and a popular late-1980s/early-1990s television series that ran for five seasons on NBC and two on CBS, and spawned four made-for-TV movies. The series premise was that Detective Tibbs has returned to Mississippi to become the small town's head police detective and again work with the ill-mannered local police chief. Of course, the story is updated by more than twenty years, which dampens some of the poignancy and timeliness of the original film's sizzling portrayal of Southern racial tensions.

The TV series *In the Heat of the Night* didn't need a lot of underscore, but what music appeared on screen was immediately recognizable, transmitting a sense of local color through its bluesy guitar- and synthesizer-heavy cues. The show's music was handled at one time or another by a half-dozen composers, but the two whose music predominated were Nan Schwartz, who scored fifty-one episodes, and David Bell, who scored thirty-one. Handling a few episodes each were Joseph Harnell, Dick DeBenedictis, and Larry Blank.

Larry Blank, an orchestrator who was just getting his feet wet as a television composer, first wrote for the series' 1990 episode "Quick Fix." This episode, about an abandoned infant, allowed Blank to add a bit more emotional weight to his music than was the series' usual practice. He used the show's regular orchestra, but with an augmented string section and additional woodwinds (a recorder and a baritone oboe), and he had session guitarist Mac Dougherty scat along with his guitar lines, adding another interesting musical color. Blank's out-of-the-ordinary underscore did not go unnoticed by the show's line producer, Walton Dornisch, who liked it quite a bit and hired Blank to score another episode, "No Other Road," a follow-up to the "Quick Fix" story.

Trusting Blank fully, Dornisch didn't attend the score's recording sessions. They were, however, visited by prominent fellow composers Artie Kane and Morton Stevens, both of whom liked the score. Once he had finished recording the episode's music, Blank flew to London and didn't arrive back in the United States until after it had aired. At that time, Artie Kane told him that although his name was in the credits, the music didn't sound like Blank's. And Kane was right: When Dornisch saw the finished episode with Blank's score, he decided it was too far afield from the show's tried-and-true sound, and he replaced it with stock cues from earlier episodes.

Raiding the stock-cue vault is common practice on television series. As a series runs, its stock of previously used music grows, and later episodes often make use of this wealth of preexisting music, especially if a composer delivers a score that deviates too far from the show's established sound.

■ **Regarding Henry** (1991)

Original composer: **Georges Delerue**
Replacement composer: **Hans Zimmer**

Director Mike Nichols's film *Regarding Henry* is about a wealthy, driven, unpleasant lawyer who, after being shot in the head during a robbery, loses his memory of his personal life as well as his abilities to speak and walk. As he goes through rehab therapy, regaining his motor skills and trying to put his life back together again, he must depend heavily on his wife and daughter. His demeanor and attitudes become childlike, and he grows into a nice, kind person.

Musically balancing the picture's tragedy with its bittersweet humor was going to be a tough job. Nichols hired a composer he had worked with three times in the past (in *The Day of the Dolphin* in 1973, *Silkwood* in 1983, and *Biloxi Blues* in 1988), Georges Delerue, among whose recent previous scoring credits were also *Mr. Johnson* (1990), *Steel Magnolias* (1989), and *Twins* (1988).

Delerue's music for *Regarding Henry* leaned toward the story's tragic side and was organized around a heartbreaking violin solo. A couple of weeks after recording his score, the composer received a warmly congratulatory letter about it from Nichols. However, that letter was followed by one that told him his music wasn't going to be used. It seems that Nichols, unsure about Delerue's approach, let Paramount Pictures persuade him to try someone else—Hans Zimmer, whose recent credits included *Thelma & Louise* (1991), *Backdraft* (1991), *Driving Miss Daisy* (1989), and *Rain Man* (1988). (It may have been Zimmer's score for *Rain Man*, a film that explored certain similar themes, that got him the job.)

Zimmer's score for *Regarding Henry*, which works very well with the picture, balances the film's comedy and drama with a hybrid New Ageish synth score that prominently features piano, sampled instruments, and vocals by Bobby McFerrin. Zimmer's music, especially his memorable "Walkin' Talkin' Man" theme, is more upbeat than Delerue's work. Another important difference between the scores is their sound: Compared with Delerue's romantic, orchestral music, Zimmer's largely synthesized sound lends the movie a whole new tone. Few replacement scores differ so radically from the scores they replace and change a picture's complexion so much.

Despite having replaced Delerue on *Regarding Henry*, Zimmer was a supporter of Delerue's score, suggesting in vain that his music appear on the film's official soundtrack LP. In 2011, however, Universal France issued Delerue's music on CD.

■ The People Under the Stairs (1991)

Original composer: **Graeme Revell**
Replacement composer: **Don Peake**

The People Under the Stairs, from popular horror-movie writer-director Wes Craven, is the tale of a thirteen-year-old boy who tries to rescue a cellar full of kidnapped children who've been gruesomely brutalized by an insane, ghoulish slumlord couple who happen to be brother and sister. (Among Craven's previous horror successes were *The Last House on the Left*, *The Hills Have Eyes*, and *A Nightmare on Elm Street*.)

To score *The People Under the Stairs*, Craven hired New Zealand–born composer Graeme Revell, whose previous credits included *Dead Calm* (1989), the made-for-TV movie *Psycho IV: The Beginning* (1990), and Wim Wenders' *Until the End of the World* (1991). Revell's score for Craven's movie consisted primarily of well-worn bits of orchestral mayhem that would stop now and then to allow some of the composer's nice, original ideas to be heard. Scattered among the music's scary moments, which were heavily laden with traditional horror-score brass bursts, were some clever twists, such as a theme played by raindrop-sounding percussion instruments that is picked up and then carried by the piano. Revell also created some heavy-breathing effects that lent an unearthly sonic aura to the house itself.

Unfortunately, his demanding orchestral score was quite a drain the production's music budget. Revell explains:

> [The] *People Under the Stairs* by Wes Craven is, I think, one of the movies where I didn't really hit it properly. I agreed to do it with not enough resources, and I wasn't happy with the work I did on that film. There was a certain amount of money, and then when I saw the movie, I realized it needed a lot more orchestra than I'd judged. One of the things we have to do is budget the score as well, and that was one I underbudgeted.

To provide a more budget-conscious soundtrack, composer Don Peake (whose previous credits included *The Hills Have Eyes*, *The Orkly Kid*, and seventy-two episodes of TV's *Knight Rider*) was hired. He used cost-effective synthesizers and samplers to create a musical landscape similar to Revell's. His purely electronic music aptly supports the picture, and proved to be the right solution for such a tightly budgeted production.

But although Peake's music is the movie's dominant sound, it is supplemented by excerpts from Revell's score (Revell received an "additional composer" credit). An excerpt from Krysztof Penderecki's famous 1960 string orchestra piece, *Threnody for the Victims of Hiroshima*, found its way into the movie as well.

The Bay Cities record label released a soundtrack recording that contained music for the film by both composers. Revell's contributions were presented as two suites, and Peake's as a single piece. In 2009, Hitchcock Media released Don Peake's entire score, together with the original audition material he wrote to get the job.

■ K2 (1991)

Composer for European version: **Hans Zimmer**
Composer for American version: **Chaz Jankel**

Adapted by Patrick Meyers from his own Broadway play, *K2* is the story of a party of climbers out to conquer the second-highest peak in the world—K2, in the Himalayas. This breathtakingly photographed though dramatically clichéd picture about the heroics of mountain climbing was directed by Franc Roddam, whose previous directing credits included *Quadrophenia* (1979), *The Lords of Discipline* (1983), *The Bride* (1985), and *War Party* (1988).

The filmmakers had one musical agenda for the film: to get a great, edgy rock score that emphasized the characters and the mountain. At one point rock legend Peter Gabriel was attached to the project, but nothing came of it. The director then hired his friend composer Chaz Jankel, a founding member (with Ian Dury) of the 1970s British New Wave band the Blockheads. Jankel had a few previous scoring credits, including *D.O.A.* (1988), the *Rachel Papers* (1989), Roddam's *War Party* (1988), and episodes of the UK television show *The Secret Diaries of Adrian Mole, Aged 13¾* (1985). Jankel recalls his *K2* score's bumpy path:

> I originally recorded it while living in Los Angeles.... We had problems with the synchronization of our tape, and the Dolby setup was another challenge. Eventually the score was finished, but a few months later I was informed that the movie had been edited and the producers didn't like the music, but a few months later still when the top dog from Miramax heard the new score he didn't like it. There was already a schedule to release it on video...so they left Hans Zimmer's score with "bits" of mine in it.... [T]o be honest it put me off movie scores for years, in particular "disaster" movies.

To please producing studio Miramax's powers-that-be, Roddam asked his friend composer Hans Zimmer to write and record a brand-new score. Zimmer's new music wasn't radically different in style and orchestration from Jankel's, though it was more bombastic and thematically driven. This synth-based score featured solo electronic guitar played by Pete Haycock (a founding member of the British group Climax Blues Band and, later, a session player popular with film composers) and several ethnic instruments performed by noted composer–multi-instrumentalist Richard Harvey.

Zimmer also used a strange electronic effect that he had previously employed in his score for *Pacific Heights* (1990). Hans Zimmer talks about his *K2* work:

> I was in England for a holiday and I ran into Franc, and he said, "Look, before it [*K2*] comes out in Europe, do you think you could just change a couple of things?" He gave me two weeks. I said, "Sure, I'll write you a score." So I wrote him a score. Then what happened was they recut the whole film for America. There are three versions of this film now: The Japanese version with Chaz's original score, the European version with my score, and the American version with...I think it's a different score, because my stuff just wouldn't cut.... After they recut the thing, they asked me if I wanted to go and sort out my score. There was just no way. I was doing something else. It's just like, "Leave it alone guys." I just went, "I don't want to have anything to do with it." So I think they went back to Chaz.

Interestingly, the edits on *K2* are not as drastic as the composer change might lead one to expect. The American version certainly cuts out a few minutes of footage, but most of its edits involve unscored sequences. While both versions of the movie start with the same song, "I Need Ya," by Zahid Tarag, the main titles only credit Chaz Jankel with the movie's score. Zimmer isn't even mentioned in the version of the film that bears his score.

In 1991, Varèse Sarabande released a CD of Zimmer's score, even though it was not part of the film's American version. Here, his cues were assembled into two suites by record producer Robert Townson. The first, "The Ascent," covers the score until the climbing team reaches K2's peak. The second suite, "The Descent," focuses on the movie's climatic ending—in which getting down from the mountain proves harder than conquering it. This second suite is more dramatic than the first, and includes a powerful reprise of the main themes along with the end credits guitar solo.

Interestingly, Zimmer's *K2* music is more enjoyable when experienced as a CD, outside the context of the movie. With the picture, it sometimes feels overbearing, more powerful than the onscreen action: Each time somebody climbs a few yards on the mountain, a powerful rock anthem (occasionally colored with Eastern percussion to highlight the Himalayan setting) breaks in. Divorced from the picture, however, the music comes across as a strong tribute to the forces of nature.

■ The Prince of Tides (1991)

Original composer: **John Barry**
Replacement composer: **James Newton Howard**

In *The Prince of Tides*, a New York psychiatrist (Barbra Streisand), treating a poet who attempted suicide, invites the writer's twin brother (Nick Nolte), a football coach who lives in the South, to come north to help with his sister's care. Over the course of the movie, the coach reveals his and his sister's repressed, troubled childhoods and begins a friendship and an affair with the psychiatrist, who is going through a crisis of her own. Based on Pat Conroy's novel of the same title, the film was directed by Streisand, who had directed only one previous film, the musical drama *Yentl* (1983), in which she also starred.

To provide a score that would give her film a strong emotional backing, Streisand hired British composer John Barry, whose recent previous credits included *Dances with Wolves* (1990), *Masquerade* (1988), *Peggy Sue Got Married* (1986), and *Out of Africa* (1985). Streisand was known as a tough taskmaster, particularly when it came to music, so Barry didn't expect an easy ride, and he didn't get one. When the very first theme he wrote for the picture was deemed unsuitable—his lush, romantic music was too big for the movie, which needed a more intimate sound—his work on the film came to an end. (In 1995, he would use his rejected *Prince of Tides* theme in the Imax film *Across the Sea of Time*.)

But one man's bad luck is sometimes another's good fortune. For composer James Newton Howard, an unused cue he had written for *Pretty Woman* (1990) became his ticket into *The Prince of Tides*:

> My biggest problem was on *Pretty Woman*, where I actually wrote a pretty theme that nobody ever heard. I gave a DAT of that theme to an editor named Don Zimmermann, who is a friend of mine. He was trying to get me the job on *The Prince of Tides*. So he cut the opening scene to the *Pretty Woman* love theme. The whole thing, all three and half minutes, was a voice-over. And it was outstanding! It was so much better in that movie than in *Pretty Woman*. It had a tremendous emotional quality to it.

Howard's music for *The Prince of Tides* allowed him to show off his emotional side. It also proved to Hollywood, once and for all, that he was capable of writing lush orchestral scores, not just synthesizer-based music, as his scores for such films as *Russkies* (1987) and *Flatliners* (1990) had led some to believe. The same busy year, 1991, would see Howard scores for films ranging from the comedies *King Ralph* and *My Girl* to the dramas *Grand Canyon*, *The Man in the Moon*, and *Guilty by Suspicion*. Thereafter, he readily found projects that built on his orchestral writing strengths, and the fact that he was ready to produce music to meet the tastes of the pickiest directors perhaps explains why he subsequently hasn't been replaced on any project except *Hearts in Atlantis* (2001).

■ **Gladiator** (1992)

Original composer: **Jerry Goldsmith**
Replacement composer: **Brad Fiedel**

In 1992's *Gladiator*, James Marshall and Cuba Gooding Jr. play two boxers caught up in the brutally violent world of illegal boxing. Directed by Rowdy Herrington, whose two previous features were *Jack's Back* (1982) and *Road House* (1988), the movie originally had an interesting Jerry Goldsmith score. In an online interview arranged by AOL, Goldsmith cited *Gladiator* as his most unpleasant experience.

The composer was not unfamiliar with sports movies: In the same year he worked on *Gladiator*, he wrote music for *Mr. Baseball*, and in 1986 he had scored the popular basketball movie *Hoosiers*. In fact, the sound world he created for *Gladiator* is not dissimilar from that of his Academy Award–nominated *Hoosiers* score. (Perhaps that's why one of the bootleg releases of his rejected *Gladiator* music paired it with the basketball picture's score.) And while the electronic sound palette he draws on for *Gladiator* is definitely old-fashioned—often sounding like a combination of 1970s cop drama and 1980s workout video—he integrates acoustic instruments well with those sounds. The score's actually quite fun in a testosterone-filled way, and its most satisfying aspects are the engaging masculine themes written for the numerous fight scenes.

Why did Goldsmith take on *Gladiator*? Starting in the early 1980s, the composer hand-picked his assignments, often tackling subpar projects submitted by former collaborators, like Graham Baker's *Alien Nation* (1988), from which his score was rejected. Another of these, George P. Cosmatos's mediocre underwater horror flick *Leviathan* (1989), caused the composer to reconsider how he was picking his jobs. Armed with a new agent in the early 1990s, Goldsmith set out to work on projects directed by those who seemed to be Hollywood's most promising up-and-coming talents, e.g., Steve Miner's *Forever Young* (1992) and Rowdy Herrington's *Gladiator*.

But due to bad communication between the filmmakers and the composer, as mentioned in his AOL interview, Goldsmith was dismissed from *Gladiator*. Hired as his replacement was Brad Fiedel, whose previous scoring credits included *Terminator* (1984), *The Big Easy* (1986), *Blue Steel* (1989), and *Terminator 2* (1991). Fiedel's primarily electronic score wasn't radically different in style from Goldsmith's, but his palette of electronic sounds was certainly more up-to-date, more 1990s-sounding.

(*Note*: Goldsmith's rejected score's intimate musical moments—yes, it had some—were put to use the following year in his score for *The Vanishing*.)

■ **Split Second** (1992)

Original composer: **Wendy Carlos**
Replacement composers: **Francis Haines and Stephen W. Parsons**

Split Second, directed by Tony Maylam (whose previous directing credits included the features *The Burning* and *Riddle of the Sands*, as well as the documentaries *Genesis in Concert* and *Hero*), is set in the then-near-future year 2008. A mishmash of clichés borrowed from a long list of monster, slasher, and renegade-cop movies, it's the story of a tough cop (played by Rutger Hauer) battling a mysterious flesh-eating creature that haunts a flooded, post-eco-disaster London. Wendy Carlos was hired to provide its score.

As a film composer, the synthesizer pioneer and popularizer Wendy Carlos was best known at the time for her work on Stanley Kubrick's films *A Clockwork Orange* (1971) and *The Shining* (1980), and Disney's *Tron* (1982). Prior to her film work, Carlos had made a big splash with her triple-Grammy-winning 1968 album *Switched-On Bach,* which made her (as Walter Carlos) a household name and made the Moog brand synonymous with the synthesizer. (It's a little-known fact that, right on the heels of *Switched-On Bach,* she was asked to provide an electronic score for director John Sturges's 1969 space adventure, *Marooned,* starring Gregory Peck. But during post-production, Sturges decided that, although he liked Carlos's music, his movie would be most effective without any music, just sound effects, so the composer was let go.)

For *Split Second,* Carlos created a lot of strange and interesting music that never saw the light of day, with the exception of two cues (dark electronic textures amounting to just over four minutes) that she eventually put out on the compilation CD *Rediscovering Lost Scores Volume 2.* In her notes to that release she described her work on the film:

> In mid-1991 I was approached by two independent filmmakers to score a British horror movie. The project began well, and some memorable music resulted. Long story short, someone else gained control of the film, and I was dropped midstream. Infuriating. These two completed cues ["Visit to a Morgue" and "Return to the Morgue"], shelved until now, score very intense scenes, with red-herring twists and scares. Note the elastic way the music sneaks forward, hesitates, then picks up again, and in [track] #17 ["Return to the Morgue"] those two shattering fortissimos. It's written for orchestra, realized with my LSI instrumental replicas. [Carlos's LSI Philharmonic was a 500-voice library that she created for the GDS/Synergy digital synthesizer. All of the voices were purely synth-derived and did not involve sampling.] The numerous "deliciously nasty" metallic effects are added via HD audio.

Hired to do a low-cost new score for *Split Second* was the composer team of Francis Haines (on his first film-scoring assignment) and Stephen W. Parsons, who had previously scored *Howling II* (1985) and *Food of the Gods II* (1989). The duo's *Split Second* score, realized primarily with an array of synthesizers, was released on a CD by the Milan label, possibly to capitalize on the soundtrack's cover of the old Moody Blues hit "Nights in White Satin."

■ CrissCross (1992)

Original composer: **Michael Convertino**
Replacement composer: **Trevor Jones**

Critically applauded for being both touching and tough-minded, *CrissCross* tells the story of a twelve-year-old boy and his mother (played by Goldie Hawn) living on their own in 1969 Florida. Staying in a seedy hotel, both mother and son work multiple jobs, scrimping and saving to get free of the hotel and buy a little place of their own. Once the boy learns that his mother has begun moonlighting as a stripper after her daytime waitressing job, he's determined to bring in enough money so that she can quit. But one of his part-time jobs leads him into the drug trade. The film was directed by Chris Menges, a British cinematographer who had won two Oscars (for *The Killing Fields* and *The Mission*). Prior to *CrissCross*, Menges had directed two films: the feature *A World Apart* (1988) and *East 103rd Street* (1981), a documentary about Spanish Harlem.

To provide the music for *CrissCross*, Menges hired Michael Convertino, a composer known for scoring intimate dramas. Among Convertino's previous scoring credits were *Children of a Lesser God* (1986), *Bull Durham* (1988), *Queen of Hearts* (1989), *The Doctor* (1991), and *The Waterdance* (1992). The composer moved to London to write and record his *CrissCross* score. The job proved challenging, due to the film's long dialogue scenes, which limited what could happen musically. In style, Convertino's writing was similar to his soothing music for *Queen of Hearts*. *CrissCross*'s tranquil moments were mostly scored with a theme played on piano (augmented with synth textures) and string melodies, which were recorded by the London Chamber Orchestra, featuring violinist Christopher Warren-Green and cellist Caroline Dale, at All Saints Church, a space favored by a number of classical ensembles because of its good acoustics.

The music was supervised by director Menges and editor Tony Lawson (who had previously edited ten of Nicolas Roeg's films). The pair checked out Convertino's work on a couple of occasions, and Lawson made several suggestions while Menges seemed to be happy with the material as it was. After the recording sessions, the score was dubbed into the movie at Twickenham Studios—and then never heard again.

Convertino's score was dropped shortly before the movie's premiere, and Trevor Jones was hired to write a new one in only one week's time. Jones's prior scoring credits included *Dominick and Eugene* (1988), *Mississippi Burning* (1988), *Sea of Love* (1989), and *True Colors* (1991). The material he composed for *CrissCross* is quite sparse, yet it brings out just the right emotions. Its main theme is played mostly on guitar (performed by virtuoso John Williams), and its effective use of saxophone (performed by Andy Sheppard) lends certain other cues a jazzy feel. Since the movie was dialogue-heavy, the score is very gentle, and a couple of scenes that had been scored by Convertino are left without music in Jones's version.

Intrada Records released a recording of Jones's score, but Convertino's has been sadly forgotten.

■ **Encino Man** (1992)

Original composer: **Jonathan Sheffer**
Replacement composer: **J. Peter Robinson**

Devised as a vehicle for comedian Pauly Shore, *Encino Man* is a fish-out-of-water tale about a caveman who was frozen during the ice age and gets thawed out in late twentieth-century California The movie is made particularly likable by the appearance of actor Brendan Fraser, who perfectly captures the confused caveman's demeanor and obviously had fun filming his mad antics. Unfortunately, a lot of the film is taken up by Shore's Valley-talk shtick, which grows increasingly irritating as the movie progresses.

Jonathan Sheffer was hired to score *Encino Man*. Among his previous credits were *In a Shallow Grave* (1988), *Pure Luck* (1991), and a half-dozen television movies, including *The Omen IV: The Awakening* (in which several of the key scenes were tracked with Jerry Goldsmith cues from the first three *Omen* installments), as well as some additional music for *Darkman*. Also an adept conductor, Sheffer had conducted Danny Elfman's *Batman Returns* score. He recalls his *Encino Man* experience:

> I created the score on a Synclavier in a small studio in North Hollywood, planning to sweeten the tracks with orchestra. The director seemed excited by my concept of John Williams–type of symphonic music for the prehistoric beginning of the movie, and for an adjustment to comedic music flavored by synthesized bamboo flutes and African instruments. All seemed to progress well until a screening in, ironically, Encino, where the producers encountered a wide range of comments from indifference to praise. One comment card said that the music sounded "old," a reference that was never really clarified. The next day I was paid the balance of my fee and told that another composer was being brought in. A few weeks later, when the film was at the dub stage, I received word that the director was requesting permission to use several of my cues, because he preferred them to the second composer's work.

Encino Man's second composer was J. Peter Robinson, whose score for *Wayne's World* (1992) made him an obvious choice for filmmakers doing teen-oriented comedies. Among his other scoring credits were *Cocktail* (1988), *Blind Fury* (1989), and *Cadillac Man* (1990). Robinson created a score with more rock elements than Sheffer's, perhaps a better match for the many pop songs that peppered the movie's soundtrack. (Among the artists who performed them were Def Leppard, Cheap Trick, Queen, Steve Vai, Right Said Fred, the Smithereens, the Jesus and Mary Chain, and Alice Cooper.)

The film's final score, however, amalgamated both composers' work. Sheffer's "old" music stayed in the picture during many of its dramatic scenes set in prehistoric times, while Robinson's music covered most scenes set in the present. Neither composer's score has been released as a soundtrack recording, though one cue from Robinson's music was released on a promotional compilation CD.

■ **Honeymoon in Vegas** (1992)

Original composer: **Marc Shaiman**
Replacement composer: **David Newman**

Writer-director Andrew Bergman's *Honeymoon in Vegas* is the comic story of private eye Jack Singer (played by Nicolas Cage), who, although he has serious marriage commitment issues, goes to Las Vegas to get hitched to his girlfriend,

Betsy (Sarah Jessica Parker). But before the couple is married, con man and gambler Tommy Korman (James Caan) notices Betsy, who reminds him of his dead wife. With his sights set on her, he pulls Jack into a poker game and fleeces him to the tune of $65,000, which Jack doesn't have. Tommy then proposes that he'll forgive Jack's debt if Betsy will spend the weekend with him. And off the story goes. As a mayhem-adding backdrop, Vegas happens to be hosting a convention of Elvis impersonators at the same time!

With this in mind, it's only natural that the movie's underscore would take a back-seat to a healthy selection of songs made famous by Elvis Presley. Probably trying to appeal to a young audience, its soundtrack includes both original Elvis recordings and covers of songs he made famous performed by such popular contemporary singers as Bruce Springsteen, Billy Joel, Brian Ferry, John Mellencamp, Dwight Yoakam, Travis Tritt, and Willie Nelson. To provide underscore between Elvis tunes, the filmmakers hired composer Marc Shaiman, whose previous credits included *The Addams Family* (1991), *City Slickers* (1991), and *Misery* (1990). But, due to an unfavorable reaction by a test screening audience (a sad story we've certainly heard before in this book), Shaiman's music was dropped. The composer recalls this rejection:

> The movie sorta sucked, and they blamed my music at a screening that didn't go well. It was the first final mix I was not part of, and I myself was HORRIFIED when I heard it at the screening. A terrible mix, a real lesson in how a bad mix affects a film. I had a billion notes which were moot after they decided to rescore. I went to see the film when it opened, figuring it would be a fantastic lesson, getting to see how someone else approached a movie I knew frame-by-frame. Unfortunately, the score sounded just like what I had done (stylistically speaking), and I didn't learn anything except that it all means nothing!

While Shaiman quipped that he contemplated taking out an ad in *Variety* to announce that *Honeymoon*'s filmmakers had "popped his cherry," his agent, Richard Kraft, felt his client's rejection simply pointed up how inconsequential composer replacements had become in Hollywood. In a discussion with *Film Score Monthly*, Kraft shared the story of another picture's young star, who demanded that her boy-friend's composer buddy be hired or else she'd decline to market the movie (the names associated with this Hollywood horror story were not revealed). The movie's previous composer was replaced.

David Newman was hired to provide *Honeymoon*'s replacement score. Among his previous credits were *Other People's Money* (1991), *Don't Tell Mom the Babysitter's Dead* (1991), *Mr. Destiny* (1990), and *The War of the Roses* (1989), and he and director Bergman had worked together previously on *The Freshman* (1990). Newman's guidelines for finding the right sound were Shaiman's score—illustrating what to avoid—and the film's temp score, which was loaded with Elmer Bernstein's music from *The Grifters*—suggesting what to aim for. The replacement score's main theme is a playful comic waltz, but its most distinguishing features are the rock 'n' roll licks clearly influenced by the film's many songs. As it should, the score coexists well with those songs.

Considering that Shaiman's music has not been released on CD, it's hard to make a fair comparison between it and the score that replaced it.

■ A River Runs Through It (1992)

Original composer: **Elmer Bernstein**
Replacement composer: **Mark Isham**

Based on Norman Maclean's popular semiautobiographical book of the same name, *A River Runs Through It* is a lushly photographed movie in which the art-craft-hobby of fly-fishing serves as a metaphor for life. Directed by Robert Redford (whose two previous directorial outings were *Ordinary People* and *The Milagro Beanfield War*), this parable-like tale contrasts the lives of two close yet dissimilar brothers coming of age in Montana in the first half of the twentieth century (between the teens and the 1930s), as told from the perspective of the older, more conservative brother. The fairly slow-paced, charming film contains much narration pulled directly from Maclean's book and read by director Redford, which leads the audience in and out of episodes from the brothers' lives.

Redford hired Elmer Bernstein (who had recently scored *Rambling Rose, The Grifters,* and *My Left Foot*) to score his picture. But Redford and the composer discovered that they had quite different musical visions for it. Bernstein felt it needed lyrical music highlighted with a bit of Americana—perhaps something in the vein of his (replaced) score for *The Journey of Natty Gann* (1985). The composer describes how he and the director differed about the picture:

> Robert Redford and I saw the film in totally different ways. I thought it was a good film. To me, the film was a very poetic film, and I had done some themes which were sort of abstract because I perceived the film as a very poetic film. He did not, he perceived the film as more sort of down-to-earth, a folktale, and he wanted a much simpler approach in the music than I was interested in doing. Eventually, he ended up with Mark Isham at the last minute. I think Robert Redford, as a director, has a great deal of difficulty making up his mind; he is not certain.

Replacement composer Mark Isham (who had recently scored *A Midnight Clear, Billy Bathgate, Little Man Tate,* and *Reversal of Fortune*) worked closely with Redford as he prepared his score, studying the film's temporary music as well as other recordings that the director gave him. In an interview, Isham talked about how the movie's temp track influenced the music that became its signature sound:

> For *A River Runs Through It,* I only had three weeks to do the score. First I heard a temp score, most of which was unmemorable. But there was one thing in it that validated exactly what I had been thinking. I was sitting there, watching the work-print, and about halfway through the film, I was saying to myself, "I know what this needs. I know what I

can do for this. And the last thing in the temp score was exactly that—a Celtic song. And I thought, "I'm right. I need to write five or six beautiful folk songs in the Celtic vibe, and choose one for the theme."

Isham's finished work provided a Celtic flavor for the film's main characters, the Maclean brothers, and the music also resonated nicely with the central role played by the river. Isham recalls Redford's deep concern and involvement with his Oscar-nominated score:

> Robert is a really fastidious director. He's a perfectionist and an incredibly bright guy who knows how to communicate well about what he wants. He already had a score on that picture that he decided wasn't working. He knew a fair amount of what the movie needed and what didn't work in it. Also, there was this area where it hadn't been done quite right yet. He was very involved. He would come over to the house and bring some CDs and things. He worked very closely with me on demos. At one point, he had to be on the East Coast, so I would send demos to him via messenger, and he would call me while listening to the demos in his car. He really wanted to get it right and I think it all paid off. The score worked really well and people responded really well to it.

■ **The Public Eye** (1992)

Original composer: **Jerry Goldsmith**
Replacement composer: **Mark Isham**

The Public Eye was written and directed by Howard Franklin, who had only one previous directing credit, *Quick Change* (1990), but had written the scripts for *The Name of the Rose* (1986) and *Someone to Watch Over Me* (1987). It's a bit of fiction heavily based on real-life photographer Arthur "Weegee" Fellig (usually simply known as Weegee), a highly regarded New York City photojournalist famous for his hard-hitting black-and-white street photography, particularly of grisly crime and accident scenes. (When Weegee was most active, in the 1930s and 1940s, his car was equipped with both a police radio and a darkroom, and he was known for his uncannily quick arrivals at crime scenes. Interestingly, producer Mark Hellinger's film *The Naked City* was inspired by Weegee's 1945 photo book *Naked City*.)

Writer-director Franklin, unable to secure the rights to the autobiography *Weegee on Weegee*, barely disguised his film's protagonist as Leon "Bernzy" Bernstein, a photojournalist who gets the first and best shots of the most gruesome crime scenes and eventually becomes entangled in a crime case himself. Joe Pesci, hot off his Oscar-winning performance in *Goodfellas* (1990), played Bernzy.

Having shot the film as a neo-noir, the director wanted music that would pay homage to noir scores but also have a contemporary twist. So it made perfect sense to commission *The Public Eye*'s music from Jerry Goldsmith (whose recent credits included *Basic Instinct, Sleeping with the Enemy*, and *Total Recall*), composer of perhaps the most famous neo-noir score, *Chinatown* (1974). Goldsmith's music for *The Public Eye* is certainly a nod in the direction of his *Chinatown* work but is much darker. It has more contemporary touches, provided by electronic effects and sampled drums (meant to underscore the harshness of Bernzy's world) that at times seem intrusive. This score, again like *Chinatown*'s, often presents its main theme via trumpet and piano.

But Goldsmith's material didn't resonate with the filmmakers, and late in the game it was dropped. Hired to replace it was composer-trumpeter Mark Isham, whose recent scoring credits included *A River Runs Through It* (1992), *A Midnight Clear* (1992), *Cool World* (1991), and *Billy Bathgate* (1991).

Isham's approach, a moody neo-noir score rooted in jazz, was not altogether unlike Goldsmith's, but its contemporary elements were certainly more refined. Had the movie itself been a success, which it wasn't, Isham's score—one of the best noir-ish soundtracks of the 1990s—would probably be widely known. Its overall dark ambience plays very well on the undeniable darkness shrouding Bernzy's world, and its short piano and trumpet phrases and jazz percussion lend the film a palpable tension. To give the jazz cues the right feel, noted jazz trumpeter and arranger Shorty Rogers was brought on to contribute four arrangements and one piece; also, among the music's soloists are a few well-known jazz studio musicians, including pianist Gerald Wiggins and tenor saxophonist Plas Johnson.

■ **Jennifer 8** (1992)

Original composer: **Maurice Jarre**
Replacement composer: **Christopher Young**

Actor-turned-writer/director Bruce Robinson (who had written the script for *The Killing Fields* and written and directed *Withnail and I* and *How to Get Ahead in Advertising*) had a hard time finding the right music for his thriller *Jennifer 8*. It was a movie about a burned-out Los Angeles cop (played by Andy Garcia) who moves to a small town, where he investigates an unsolved serial murder case and becomes involved with the girl he expects will be the killer's eighth victim (Uma Thurman).

The production studio, Paramount Pictures, lobbied Robinson to hire a big-name composer, even though the director, based on the soundtrack CD from *The Fly II* (1989) wanted to hire Christopher Young, whose recent previous credits also included *The Vagrant* (1992) and *Bat 21* (1988). Paramount insisted Robinson hire Maurice Jarre, who had recently scored *Jacob's Ladder* (1990), *Ghost* (1990), and *Dead Poets Society* (1989). Young recalls this situation:

> Bruce Robinson wanted me, but the producer insisted on a composer with the stature of Maurice Jarre. Well, you know why these things happen. Usually composers will try their best. My experience has been that scores get thrown out because there's no communication between the director or whoever's in charge, and the composer. In this instance, Bruce did not want Maurice Jarre, so I'm sure he had trouble communicating to Maurice about what he wanted.

Robinson's collaboration with Jarre didn't go well. Hearing and liking Young's music for *The Fly II* had set the director on a track from which he couldn't be derailed, and he set a number of guidelines for *Jennifer 8*'s music that, due to miscommunication, Jarre failed to meet. In an unusual turn of events, the director's will won out over the studio's: Jarre's music was dropped, and Young was hired to replace it.

But the project was not all smooth sailing for Young either. First of all, he had to pay attention to pieces already integrated into key scenes in the movie, such as the humming chorus from Puccini's opera *Madame Butterfly* and such standards as "Silent Night." Another difficulty was nailing down an approved main theme. Young's first demo was rejected, but on his second try he hit the mark with a simple piano melody that he came up with while driving home one day. It became the cornerstone of the score that would turn around his career: Through *Jennifer 8*, Young finally broke out of the horror genre and established himself as a solid composer for somewhat less gory thrillers as well.

Although Jarre's unused score still hasn't been released, its haunting main title theme is available on the 2010 collection *Le Cinéma de Maurice Jarre*, released by Emarcy/Universal Music.

■ **Trespass** (1992)

Original composer: **John Zorn**
Replacement composer: **Ry Cooder**

Directed by Walter Hill (whose directing credits included *48 Hours*, *Streets of Fire*, and *Extreme Prejudice*) and written by Robert Zemeckis and Bob Gale (who cowrote the 1985 hit *Back to the Future*), *Trespass* is about two firemen who, following a map they took from a dying man, find a cache of stolen gold artifacts in an abandoned building in East St. Louis's slums. While retrieving the loot they witness a street-gang murder. This means serious trouble for the two, trapped in the building, and the movie's testosterone-fueled action commences.

Originally called *Looters*, the movie was scheduled for a July 1992 release, but it was postponed due to racial turmoil in Los Angeles a couple of months earlier. (*Note*: Several days of rioting—looting, arson, and assault—occurred in Los Angeles at the end of April and beginning of May 1992. The result of myriad social injustices, including high unemployment, urban decay, racism, police brutality, and economic despair, the unrest's flashpoint was the acquittal of four LA policemen who were on trial for beating African-American motorist Rodney King, in an incident that had been videotaped by a passerby and widely distributed through the media.) Socially insensitive in many respects, *Looters* depicted African-Americans as gangsters and was replete with racial slurs. Universal Pictures was nervous about rekindling the city's smoldering tensions and postponed the film's release until December. In the meantime, the movie underwent several alterations: Its title was changed to *Trespass* to avoid any connection to LA's riots, a new ending was added, and its music was replaced.

Because of the delayed release, the filmmakers had time to reevaluate the original score, by avant-garde/experimental composer and saxophonist John Zorn. As a concert composer, Zorn writes eclectic chamber and orchestra works; as an improviser, he plays both jazz-based and enigmatically personal music. Prior to *Trespass*, his feature-film scoring credits included *The Golden Boat* (1990), *Distributing Lead* (1988), and *She Must Be Seeing Things* (1987). His fascinating and strange *Trespass* score was dark and moody and perhaps even a bit introverted. Its unusual instrumentation included, in the hands of a number of notable musicians, Brazilian percussion (Cyro Baptista), didgeridoo (Andy Haas), prepared piano (Anthony Coleman), guitar and banjo (Marc Ribot), and even turntables and samplers (David Shea). Had the music been retained in the film, a broad spectrum of moviegoers would have been introduced to Zorn's surreal musical vision. (A CD of his *Trespass* music was released in 1996 on the composer's own Tzadik label, as *Film Works II: Music for an Untitled Film by Walter Hill.*)

But it was not to be. As replacement composer, Hill brought in his most frequent musical collaborator, guitarist and composer Ry Cooder. Cooder, famous for his own albums as well as for performances with legendary musicians in various genres, had scored six previous Hill-directed films (including *Crossroads, Southern Comfort,* and *The Long Riders*) as well as Wim Wenders's 1984 *Paris, Texas*, perhaps his best-known score. The composer remembers his work on the film:

> The movie was taken out of its release schedule after the LA riots, which opened the door for me to come in and write a score that would go in a new direction. Walter [Hill] wanted something that was spooky and weird, and I got some experimental instruments together and improvised in the studio with [drummer-percussionist] Jim Keltner and [trumpeter] Jon Hassell. Scoring *Trespass* wasn't nearly as complicated as *Last Man Standing* [a Hill-directed film that Cooder would score in 1996], but it was still difficult for me to musically relate to a film that mostly took place indoors. *Trespass*'s environment hardly changed, and it was interesting for me to solve the problems that brought up.

Although Cooder's score for *Trespass* has strange and exotic aspects, it is much more traditional than Zorn's. Performed by Cooder, Hassell, and Keltner, the music is built essentially on the sound of only a few instruments (most prominently a giant slide guitar, which the soundtrack album notes call "Floor Slide"). Cooder's haunting electric slide-guitar solos give it an otherworldly, hyperblues flavor. *Trespass*'s soundtrack also includes several rap songs, one of which is a duet by the film's costars Ice-T and Ice Cube.

Although Zorn's and Cooder's approaches were not night-and-day different in basic mood or overall thrust, and Zorn's work offered an effective if sometimes rather esoteric soundscape, Cooder's music was a nice, tight fit with the movie's songs and action. A recording of it is available on a Sire/Warner Bros. CD.

■ **McLintock!** (Public Domain Version, 1993)

Original composer (1963): **Frank De Vol**
Composer for unauthorized home-video release of public domain version (1993): **John Ottman**

McLintock!, starring John Wayne and Maureen O'Hara, was a popular comedic Western produced by Wayne's own Batjac Productions and directed by Andrew V. McLaglen (veteran director of such TV Western series as *Rawhide*, *Gunsmoke*, and *Have Gun—Will Travel*). In it, Wayne plays a blustery, rough-hewn cattle baron who is perpetually at odds with his wife and just about everyone else he encounters. It was scored by Frank De Vol, whose feature scoring credits included *Kiss Me Deadly* (1955), *Pillow Talk* (1959), and *Under the Yum-Yum Tree* (1963).

In 1993, Batjac Productions, run by Wayne's son Michael, forgot to renew the picture's copyright, allowing *McLintock!* to enter the public domain. (At that time, U.S. copyright law protected a work for twenty-eight years, which could be extended for an additional twenty-eight if the copyright owner filed a renewal with the Copyright Office in a timely fashion.)

The idea behind the exploitation of a public domain movie is simple: Find a popular film that has slipped into the public domain, copy it, and then pay nothing but manufacturing costs to produce a video version, which can, in turn, be sold for a bargain-basement price. Accordingly, shortly after the rights to *McLintock!* slipped out of private hands, a number of companies capitalized on it as a video release, including UAV Entertainment, GoodTimes Entertainment, and Gemstone Entertainment. Maljack Productions Inc. (MPI) also released a Batjac-authorized video version of the film around this same time.

Batjac and MPI worked hard to recapture the film's copyright, suing UAV, GoodTimes, and Gemstone over the film's various elements and related properties. They filed copyright suits based on the unpublished underlying script, but lost when the court ruled that the script was a component part of the film and thus its copyright had expired with the film's copyright. They sued regarding music synchronization and lost again, with the court ruling that Batjac's music synch rights were also a component part of the film and expired with the movie's copyright. And they sued regarding their own pan-and-scan version of the widescreen film, which the intruding video companies had simply copied. On this last count they finally won: The court declared their pan-and-scan version to be a legitimate and protected derivative work. (UAV circumvented this obstacle by simply creating its own pan-and-scan version.)

With *McLintock!* in the public domain, its musical score became the property of composer Frank De Vol's estate, meaning that if a company wanted to release the movie they would have to license the music from the composer's family, considerably raising their video production costs. Of course, the music could easily have been taken out and replaced, if the video companies had access to the film's original tracks containing the music, sound effects, and dialogue as separate elements. But Batjac and Maljack certainly had no reason to allow them access to those elements. So one of the video companies took the long way around: It hired a young composer to do an all-synthesizer score as cheaply as he could, replaced the movie's sound effects, and dubbed in new dialogue! That young composer was John Ottman (a man of many hats—composer, film editor, orchestrator, director, producer—with only one feature scoring credit at the time, director Bryan Singer's *Public Access*, a film he also edited), who shares his tale of working on this strange project:

> In the lull period between being fired from my day job and *Usual Suspects* [which Ottman edited and scored in 1995] taking off, I was hired to rescore an old John Wayne film, *McLintock!* A company had bought the rights to the film to release as a video to be sold in department stores. What they didn't get the rights to, however, was the original score. Therefore they needed it replaced with a new one. One catch: all the dialog and sound effects were married to Frank De Vol's original music. So, they went through an extremely elaborate process of replacing all the actors' voices (including Wayne's, Maureen O'Hara's and Jerry Van Dyke's) as well as all the effects, Indian and group walla—everything. The hilarious part of it is that the association looking at the actors speaking was so strong, that you would never imagine in a thousand years they were not real. All in all I wrote about 110 minutes of music, including source, all synthesized and desperately trying to sound real. It would be fun to record parts of that score with a real orchestra someday as well. It was kind of a goofy western score with some big-brawl action music as well as some saloon music.

Ottman has said that the version he scored never made it to video shops because another video company finally invested a little in *McLintock!* and paid the De Vol estate to use the original music. As a result, the budget releases with Ottman's music are obscure curiosities now. Selections from his *McLintock!* music have been issued on a promotional CD; De Vol's score was released on LP in 1963. It's worth noting that high-quality authorized versions of the film, such as the recently issued Paramount Home Video DVD, which features excellent picture and sound, bear the inscription "John Wayne Estate Authorized Edition."

Note: A similar copyright situation was responsible for Frank Capra's 1946 film *It's a Wonderful Life*'s becoming a much-loved Christmas classic. When originally released, the movie was a box-office flop, but since entering the public domain in 1974 due to Republic Picture's failure to renew its copyright, it has received seemingly endless television airings, catapulting it to great popularity. Interestingly, the studio recaptured the movie's copyright via some of its underlying music—such as an instrumental version of Irving Berlin's tune "This Is the Army, Mr. Jones"—for which copyright had not expired.

Homeward Bound: The Incredible Journey (1993)

Original composer: **David Shire**
Replacement composer: **Bruce Broughton**

Homeward Bound, a remake of Disney's classic 1963 kid-flick *The Incredible Journey,* tells the story of three pets (a wise old golden retriever, a pesky bulldog pup, and a fussy Himalayan cat) who believe that the three children who are their masters have left them behind. The animals—speaking to one another with the voices of Don Ameche, Michael J. Fox, and Sally Field—embark on a long, treacherous trip through the Sierras to find the children, who've moved temporarily to San Francisco.

To provide the music, Walt Disney Pictures hired composer David Shire, who had scored such noted films as *2010* (1984); *Norma Rae* (1979); *All the President's Men* (1976); *Farewell, My Lovely* (1975); and *The Taking of Pelham One Two Three* (1974) but had since the mid-1980s been mired in scoring made-for-TV movies (an area he would remain in through most of the 1990s). For Shire, *Homeward Bound* was a great opportunity to return to the big screen with a solid Disney picture. He reflects on his experiences on the movie:

> I worked with the director [Duwayne Dunham] on this picture for three months.... I came up with all the themes, one by one—he loved them all and as we got to work on them I met with him every Monday for week after week. I went to Germany to record the score, but the orchestra there was not good enough, so we scrapped those sessions and then I re-recorded them in LA. Then [Jeffrey] Katzenberg [Disney's CEO] wanted to hear a cut of the picture with the score on it and the voices for the animals—and I remember going over to his house and we sat there while he watched it. He smiled and shook my hand and said, "Fine, fine," and by the time I got home there was a call from my agent saying he scrapped my score and wanted a new one. He also fired the three people who were the principal voices of the animals, and he almost fired the director....
>
> It was just a totally disappointing experience because that was the last score I thought was going to get me back in the loop. It was a big, romantic, fun picture with the Disney stamp on it and that was a huge disappointment.... Frankly, it was so painful I never went back and even listened to it. But we'd have to get the master tapes and mix it because we never finished it. I have a tape of it somewhere. If somebody wanted to put it out and thought it was good enough to put out, I'd have no objections.

The original cut of *Homeward Bound* was a completely different picture from the one we now know. The movie had a slightly depressing tone, so it was re-edited to give it a happier feel. Strong performances from its new voice actors (Ameche, Fox, and Field had not been the original cast) also greatly improved it. While Shire could have easily written a new score or rewritten his existing one to accommodate the film's changes, the studio opted to take the music back to square one, hiring a new composer, Bruce Broughton, whose recent scoring credits included *The Rescuers Down Under* (1990), *Narrow Margin* (1990), and *The Presidio* (1988).

Broughton came up with a soaring melody that could be juxtaposed against individual character themes. On this framework he hung a lush, though sometimes comedic, Americana-flavored score that spoke to the animals' wilderness adventures. For example, much of the movie's comedy is provided by the bulldog pup, whose antics are underscored in many ways, including big-band circuslike music for his escape from a pound. Overall, Broughton's music elevated the picture above standard kiddie fare and lent it the warmth of familiarity. His great versatility is on display throughout the film.

■ **Point of No Return** (1993)

Original composer: **Gary Chang**
Replacement composer: **Hans Zimmer**

Director John Badham's *Point of No Return*, an American remake of French writer-director Luc Besson's *La Femme Nikita* (1990), tried so hard to repackage the heart of the original picture that it even duplicated some of the original's dialogue and camera angles, leading some reviewers to question why it was made at all. It's the tale of a beautiful young female junkie, Maggie (played by Bridget Fonda), who commits a murder for which she is sentenced to death. But just before her execution is to be carried out, she's offered the option of taking on a new identity and becoming a trained government assassin. She takes the deal, undergoes extensive training, and then is sent off on her deadly tasks. As the movie progresses, romance and other things get in the way of her duties.

For its music, *Point of No Return*'s filmmakers sought a blend of preexisting songs and underscore that would reflect Maggie's love of the music of jazz singer-songwriter Nina Simone. For the underscore, director Badham hired Hans Zimmer, with whom he'd worked on *Bird on a Wire* (1990). But Zimmer soon had to bow out because of a scheduling conflict. With him unavailable, the production contacted Gary Chang, whose scoring credits included *Under Siege* (1992), *Miami Blues* (1990), and *A Shock to the System* (1990). Chang spent weeks on the project, doing synthesized demos of the entire score and even recording a few cues with an orchestra.

But the producing studio, Warner Bros., felt that Chang's music wasn't melodic enough, and that it didn't work seamlessly with the Simone songs they were using. By this time, Zimmer found he had a bit more time, so he offered to write a couple of themes that Chang could adapt to fit the picture. This, however, didn't turn out to be an acceptable way of working, and Chang exited the production, leaving the music fully in Zimmer's hands. The replacement score, which had to be done quickly, was recorded in Zimmer's Santa Monica studio at night. It successfully blended original cues with Simone's songs, with the two nicely interlacing to create a melodic, yet disturbingly dark sonic atmosphere that reflected the assassin's inner torments.

Interestingly, in 1993, Hans Zimmer and Mark Mancina were hired to pen additional music for another movie that had been scored by Gary Chang, *Sniper*. The director's cut was very violent, and when some of the violence was tamed for its theatrical release, Zimmer and Mancina provided the cues needed to smooth out the alterations. Also interesting are the mixing changes that Chang's remaining score underwent from one version to the next, clearly showing that a score can be given a radical makeover simply by remixing it.

Three of Hearts (1993)

Original composer: **Richard Gibbs**
Replacement composer: **Joe Jackson**

Three of Hearts is a romantic comedy about an unusual threesome entangled in a complex and humorous web of homosexual, heterosexual, and bisexual relationships. It wasn't destined to be New Line Cinema's big picture of the year. In fact, its music budget was so small that its composer, Richard Gibbs (whose credits included *Once Upon a Crime* and the TV movies *Sins of the Mother* and *A Killing in a Small Town*), had to perform all of the score's parts himself, with the exception of the guitar. Regardless of its budget constraints, almost everyone involved with the project considered Gibbs's quirky little score, which featured a fetching guitar theme, a perfect match for the offbeat comedy. Director Yurek Bogayevicz (whose one previous directing credit was 1987's *Anna*) was especially enthusiastic about the music.

But then, just when everyone seemed happy with the finished picture, New Line shelved it. By the time *Three of Hearts* was dusted off for its 1993 release, most of the principal people involved in its production, with the exception of New Line executive Toby Emmerich, had moved on to other pictures.

With *Three of Hearts* finally on track for release, Emmerich chose to replace its score. So he contacted composers agent Richard Kraft to see if he had any clients who could provide a new score for it. Since Kraft represented original composer Gibbs, Gibbs was contacted to write a second score for the picture. The composer dutifully did this without being given specific directives on what he should change relative to his first score. But when the real impetus for a new score was revealed—screenwriter Mitch Glazer—Gibbs bid the project farewell.

Mitch Glazer (whose writing credits included *Scrooged* and *Off and Running*) thought that singer-songwriter-composer Joe Jackson (whose previous scoring credits included *Tucker: The Man and His Dream* and *Queens Logic*) should score the movie. Although he had harbored this idea throughout the production, he hadn't been in a position to hire Jackson. However, after a long negotiation that also involved the studio's marketing department, Glazer managed to sign Jackson on (Glazer even covered the rescoring costs himself). Jackson's music didn't differ greatly from Gibbs's, and Jackson ended up disappointed with the project when one of what he felt were his best cues was replaced with a song licensed earlier by the production. In an interesting twist, the picture's European prints retained Gibbs's music—the result of a music track mixup.

La Belle et la bête/Beauty and the Beast (Opera, 1994)

Original composer (1946): **Georges Auric**
Composer for opera version (1994): **Philip Glass**

French poet-novelist-playwright-illustrator-filmmaker Jean Cocteau's *Beauty and the Beast* was a transcendently beautiful cinematic telling of the popular fairy tale. The wonderful film, which he both wrote and directed (his one previous outing as a film director had been the 1930 classic *The Blood of a Poet*), was made even more remarkable by the fact that it was shot for very little money, and at a time (right at the end of World War II) when film stock was in very short supply and Cocteau was so ill that he had to bow out of postproduction to be hospitalized.

The film's haunting and lovely score was written by French concert composer Georges Auric, who was no newcomer to cinematic music, having penned three dozen film scores before *Beauty and the Beast*, including *Caesar and Cleopatra* (1945), *Dead of Night* (1945), *Paris at Midnight* (1942), and *The Curtain Rises* (1938). Since he had to write and record his complex score quickly, Auric chose not to synchronize his music with the picture frame-by-frame. Instead, he wrote his cues based on each scene's mood (and this is a very moody picture), without "hitting" specific moments of onscreen action. The resulting material is impressionistic, with each scene's mood exquisitely painted with music.

Despite Auric's very prolific film composing career in both France and Britain, most of the scores he wrote are available only as rerecorded excerpts, instead of complete music soundtracks. One of his few film scores available in its complete form is *La Belle et la bête*, a recording that owes its existence to Swiss film music champion Adriano, who reconstructed and conducted all twenty-four of its cues.

In the 1990s, composer Philip Glass paid tribute to Jean Cocteau with a trilogy of pieces based on Cocteau's work as a writer and filmmaker. The second of these, *Beauty and the Beast* (1994), is in Glass's words a "music-theater work with film." In it, Cocteau's 1946 film serves as inspiration, template, and actual theatrical backdrop for a wholly original musical work by Glass. Thus, this is neither a replacement score for the film nor a pointed act of art reappropriation (such as Marcel Duchamp's *L.H.O.O.Q.*, a work in which the artist painted a mustache and goatee on a cheap reproduction of da Vinci's *Mona Lisa*).

In creating his piece, Glass analyzed the film and derived from it an underlying allegory in which the transformation of the beast to a human represents an average human's turning into a noble artist. Approaching the project as an opera, he incorporated every line of the film's dialogue into a libretto that, when sung, could be matched perfectly to the picture. The piece premiered in June 1994, in Gibellina, Italy, performed by the Philip Glass Ensemble, conducted by Michael Riesman. The singers performed their parts while a restored print of the picture (with subtitles) played behind them.

Glass discusses some of the project's details:

> The very idea of the project is the vision: "I'm going to take *La Belle et la bête*, eliminate the soundtrack, write a new fully operatic score, and synchronize it with the film." You know, someone has to synchronize the film with the music, and also someone has to do the programming—in this production that someone is the musical director Michael Riesman. And the sound designer Kurt Munkacsi (also the record producer) must translate that into a finished musical result, which must then be brought to the stage by Jedediah Wheeler. People might think we're some kind of technicranks who are just fiddling around with a masterpiece using calculators and computers. In one or two interviews I have talked about how I took the film and put a time code on it, timed every line in it, wrote down the libretto (which is not the same as the published one, since I wanted the words that were in the film), I timed every word, I placed it mathematically in the score...and then when I got done, Michael Riesman and I recorded it and put it up against the film and discovered it wasn't accurate enough. So we began using computers to move the vocal line around until it synched with the lips, and then I had to rewrite the music in order to achieve a better synchronization. Then Michael had to teach it all to the singers and they had to learn to do it live.

The work toured in Europe with great success, and the score was eventually released both on CD and as an alternate musical score on Criterion's *Beauty and the Beast* DVD, which, of course, has the Auric score as the film's first-choice music option.

Traveling a somewhat different, though not altogether unrelated avenue, Universal Pictures hired Glass in 1999 to provide an original score for its DVD release of Tod Browning's 1931 horror classic *Dracula*, starring Béla Lugosi. The movie, shot right at the changeover from silents to talkies, originally didn't have an underscore, with the exception of an excerpt from Tchaikovsky's *Swan Lake* that played under its main titles. Aiming for a nineteenth-century feel, Glass wrote his score for string quartet. His wall-to-wall score was performed by new-music champions the Kronos Quartet (an ensemble that had also recorded Glass's music for Paul Schrader's 1985 film *Mishima*). As strange as a wall-to-wall score may seem to us today, it may be viewed as keeping with the early sound film tradition of providing a movie with either no score or nearly continuous music from beginning to the end.

■ **I Love Trouble** (1994)

Original composer: **Elmer Bernstein**
Replacement composer: **David Newman**

Cowritten by Nancy Meyers and her husband at the time, Charles Shyer (who together had written *Private Benjamin*, *Baby Boom*, and *Father of the Bride*), *I Love Trouble* was a modern-day take on the classic romantic comedies that featured the fast-paced bickering of Katherine Hepburn and Spencer Tracy, such as *Adam's Rib* (1949), *Pat and Mike* (1952), and *Desk Set* (1957). Directed by Shyer and starring

Julia Roberts and Nick Nolte, *I Love Trouble* mixed action and comedy in a tale about rival reporters—one old and crusty, one young and ambitious—who form a partnership to break a big story. As they work together, their professional relationship turns amorous.

Hired to score this deliberately old-fashioned picture was Elmer Bernstein, whose recent scoring credits included *The Good Son* (1993), *The Age of Innocence* (1993), *Lost in Yonkers* (1993), and *Mad Dog and Glory* (1993). Bernstein clearly understood *I Love Trouble*'s mix of genres, and his music acknowledged all aspects of its story. His score—which deftly moved from orchestral mayhem to madcap jazz within a matter of seconds—is a good showcase of the composer's great versatility. Underscoring the chemistry between the two main characters is a seductive, jazzy tune often played on saxophone. Bernstein's eclectic blend of music for the film's action and comedy scenes, however, took a distinctly different path, and he often wrote overtly serious cues as a counterpoint to some of the movie's uninspired action sequences.

However, the composer developed a strained relationship with Meyers and Shyer from the word go. There are reports of a recording session where Bernstein allegedly said, "Either she goes or he does," reflecting his frustration with what he saw as undue interference. Since he didn't work well with either one of them, they pulled the plug on his score about two weeks before its deadline.

With the film's release date looming, David Newman, whose recent scoring credits included *The Cowboy Way* (1934), *Undercover Blues* (1993), *The Sandlot* (1993), and *The Mighty Ducks* (1992), was hired to replace Bernstein's score. To meet the project's deadline, Newman brought on a number of other composers to help with additional music cues. Among them were Chris Boardman, William Kidd, Mark McKenzie, and Peter Tomashek. He later described the process as his most nightmarish; he literally composed many cues while on the scoring stage with the orchestra. Surprisingly, despite the numerous helping hands, the replacement music is more homogenous in style than Bernstein's, although it's also less inspired. The score is sweet, with a soft saxophone melody that's given the task of making an emotional connection with the audience. It also contains its fair share of comedy score clichés. The official soundtrack recording contains about half the film's underscore. Unfortunately, a legitimate recording of Bernstein's original version has never been released, even though it's among the most interesting of his later comedy scores.

■ **The River Wild** (1994)

Original composer: **Maurice Jarre**
Replacement composer: **Jerry Goldsmith**

In *The River Wild*, director Curtis Hanson, who directed *The Hand that Rocks the Cradle* (1992), revisits the idea of an average family terrorized by strangers. Starring Meryl Streep, Kevin Bacon, David Strathairn, and John C. Reilly, *The River Wild* is the beautifully photographed story of a family on a whitewater rafting trip that goes bad when they're taken hostage by armed robbers fleeing the police. Perils both manmade and natural ensue, as the group travels down the dangerous river together.

The early 1990s was a transitional period in the world of film scoring. It saw numerous clashes between the use of synthesizer-based scores so popular in the 1980s and the return to favor of traditional orchestral scores. The change in composers for *The River Wild* may be a prime example of this conflict.

Maurice Jarre, whose recent scoring credits included *Fearless* (1993), *Mr. Jones* (1993), *Jacob's Ladder* (1990), and *Ghost* (1990), was hired to write *The River Wild*'s music. For this wet and wild adventure, he revisited the electronic styles used in his scores for the popular films *Witness* (1985) and *No Way Out* (1987). He painted the river with streams of ambient music, while the film's action scenes were powered by harsh ostinatos. Jarre recalls his work on *The River Wild* (a brief suite from which is available on the collection *Le Cinéma de Maurice Jarre*):

> I worked with the director, Curtis Hanson, and producers Larry Turman and David Foster. They always came to the recording sessions and everybody was very happy. We mixed the music and everything was fine and we did the record and the people from RCA went to see the movie with the music and they liked it. Curtis Hanson had even written liner notes for the CD booklet. But the preview was disastrous and the head of the studio at Universal, Sidney Sheinberg, didn't like the movie. He ordered Hanson to change the music. [Hanson] was really surprised, but Sheinberg was the boss. The next morning, they called Jerry Goldsmith. So, fine. I was paid. In the end Sheinberg wanted to change Goldsmith's music also, again because he didn't like the music.

After tossing out Jarre's score, Sheinberg hired Jerry Goldsmith on the advice of Hanson. Goldsmith's recent scoring credits included *Six Degrees of Separation* (1993), *Rudy* (1993), *The Vanishing* (1993), and *Basic Instinct* (1992). No doubt due to a short scoring schedule, his music for *The River Wild* turned out to be fairly predictable Goldsmith. Its warm, family-outing material is made up of variations on the well-known traditional folk song "The Water Is Wide" (which is also featured in the film in a version performed by the alternative country-rock band Cowboy Junkies). His pounding action music and the revelatory trumpet solo that appears at the end revisit familiar moments from some of his other scores. Interestingly, this would become the composer's best-documented score: The documentary *Film Music Masters: Jerry Goldsmith* (1995) extensively covers the composer's work on *The River Wild*, including a good bit of footage of him conducting its recording sessions. (Director Hanson would hire Goldsmith to score his very next film, the 1997 *L.A. Confidential*.)

Sadly, Jarre's experience on *The River Wild* proved to be one of the first steps in his gradual retirement from movies. The next year, he collaborated with director James Foley on the sentimental coming-of-age film *Two Bits*, but after Miramax acquired the movie for distribution, it was recut and Jarre's score was replaced. Miramax head Harvey Weinstein disliked Jarre's largely monothematic approach; he wanted a more playful music that reflected the perspective of the film's young protagonist. Carter Burwell was hired to write a replacement score, and director Foley grew to like his music so much that he went on to work with him on three more pictures: *Fear* (1996), *The Chamber* (1996), and *The Corruption* (1999).

■ **Sirens** (1994)

Original composer: **Geoffrey Burgon**
Replacement composer: **Rachel Portman**

Based loosely on the life of early twentieth-century Australian artist and writer Norman Lindsay, whose nudes (drawings, paintings, and sculptures) were at one time deemed controversial, writer-director John Duigan's lively romantic comedy *Sirens* is about temptation with a capital T. Starring Sam Neill as the artist, it's the story of a straitlaced Anglican priest and his wife (Hugh Grant and Tara Fitzgerald) who are sent by the local church to ask the artist to withdraw a controversial piece, *Crucified Venus*, from a forthcoming art show. But the minister's wife soon falls under the spell of the artist and his liberated household, which includes his wife, a housekeeper, and various female models.

For this Australian-English production, coproducer Sarah Radclyffe contracted composer Geoffrey Burgon, with whom she had worked on the 1991 made-for-TV movie *Robin Hood*, to provide its music. The composer, receiving only a few instructions for his score, wrote detailed sketches that he previewed for the filmmakers on the piano. The director reacted enthusiastically, and became even more excited when the recording sessions started and he heard the music with a full orchestra. Burgon's light score perfectly captured the artist's strange, carefree world of sensuality and playfulness, his good-natured immersion in the pleasures of life.

The composer, however, had one minor clash with the director. Duigan insisted on using a specific Ralph Vaughan Williams piece, *March Past of the Kitchen Utensils* (a playful, jaunty piece written in 1909 as part of the incidental music for a Cambridge University presentation of Aristophanes' comedy *The Wasps*) under his film's main titles, which run over a scene in which two ministers walk through a museum filled with scandalous art. Burgon opposed the idea and composed his own march.

At this point, Australian coproducer Sue Milliken voiced her objections to what Burgon came up with. A long negotiation between the two coproducers boiled her problems with the music down to bare essentials: The question was whether certain specific scenes needed Burgon's score at all. The result was that, unbeknownst to the composer, three-quarters of his music was thrown out, leaving only about fifteen minutes' worth, in fleeting appearances throughout the movie.

The final obstacle for Burgon's score came when Miramax, the film's American distributor, saw the picture. Miramax's head, Harvey Weinstein, found the lack of music puzzling, but instead of restoring the excised portions of Burgon's material, he commissioned a brand-new score from English composer Rachel Portman. Like the film's first score, Portman's is both playful and romantic. With its lush string music shaded with lovely woodwind solos, it works admirably with the picture and is an enjoyable listening experience in itself. (It also includes the Vaughan Williams music that the director was so keen on.)

Milan Records released a recording of Portman's score in 1994. Burgon's version didn't altogether disappear: He released eight cues from it on a promotional CD, and an extensive suite drawn from it was premiered in 1995 on Carl Davis's Forgotten Film Music concert series.

■ **Interview with the Vampire** (1994)

Original composer: **George Fenton**
Replacement composer: **Elliot Goldenthal**

Based on Ann Rice's best-selling novel of the same title, *Interview with the Vampire* is an epic film that chronicles 200 years of dark escapades—particularly those of the vampires Lestat, Louis, and Claudia—on two continents. Featuring a highly bankable cast that included Tom Cruise (Lestat), Brad Pitt (Louis), Kirsten Dunst (Claudia), Antonio Banderas, Stephen Rea, and Christian Slater, the production was helmed by Irish director Neil Jordan, whose directing credits included *The Company of Wolves* (1984), *Mona Lisa* (1986), *The Miracle* (1991), and *The Crying Game* (1992). The movie fared moderately well with critics and was a box-office hit.

To score *Interview with the Vampire,* director Jordan hired George Fenton, a composer with whom he had worked on three previous films: *The Company of Wolves, High Spirits* (1988), and *We're No Angels* (1989). Fenton wrote a romantic score with dark, sweeping melodies to underscore the vampires' personal tragedies. Among its most memorable moments are vocal passages of strangely ethereal beauty. Fenton was also responsible for adapting excerpts from a few pieces by Handel, Haydn, Chopin, and Soler that served as the film's source music.

But all was not well in Vampireland: Unbeknownst to Fenton, the movie's producers were dissatisfied with his score, which they found too slow and not hip enough. So, even while Fenton's score was being recorded, they hired Elliot Goldenthal to compose a replacement score more to their liking. (Among Goldenthal's previous scoring credits were *Pet Sematary, Drugstore Cowboy,* and *Alien^3*.) The two composers' scores were at one point actually being recorded on the same day, with Fenton finishing his last cues in the morning and Goldenthal's sessions starting that afternoon.

Goldenthal wrote his *Interview* score to reflect the story's centuries of "time travel," gradually following it from Baroque to rock music. It also progressively darkens as the film unfolds, and employs avant-garde instrumental techniques to twist the orchestra's sound as the tale descends into madness. As Goldenthal remembers, the swiftness with which his score had to be written kept the studio's meddling to a minimum:

> Everyone was working twenty hours a day, and I'd play something and the director might or might not like it. So it didn't seem like there would be time to second-guess, but there was. I think what happened was a combination of a few things: First off, I locked into a concept pretty fast that the music would go in a chronological development. From arcane sounding music with viola da gamba and boy soprano singing Latin and stuff like that, to the harpsichord, to the modern piano, and the nineteenth-century orchestra, to sort of the Polish avant-garde, and finally to "Sympathy for the Devil" [a Rolling Stones song covered for the movie by Guns & Roses]. So, having that kind of "up the ladder" of the chronology of music was something that Neil Jordan and I felt comfortable with. The other thing was that there wasn't much time for other folks (editors, the studios) to second-guess it.

Goldenthal's Oscar-nominated score was a big success, and he went on to score four more of Jordan's films: *Michael Collins* (1996), *The Butcher Boy* (1997), *In Dreams* (1999), and *The Good Thief* (2002).

Music from Fenton's *Interview* score was eventually assembled into a suite called "The Vampire" and premiered in London by conductor Nicholas Cleobury. It may not have won the producers' hearts, but it's a great piece of concert music in its own right.

■ **Picture Bride** (1995)

Original composer: **Cliff Eidelman**
Replacement composer: **Mark Adler**

In the early twentieth-century more than 20,000 young women, often fleeing poverty, came to Hawaii as "picture brides" of Japanese immigrants who worked in its cane fields. These marriages between strangers were arranged through an exchange of photographs and letters, both of which were often misleading about the actual circumstances in which the women would find themselves upon their arrival.

Picture Bride, written and directed by Kayo Hatta, is the tale of a sixteen-year-old orphan who encounters a harsh reality in Hawaii, as the picture bride of a man in his forties who has sent her outdated photos of himself and described life in Hawaii in terms more wishful than real. Saddened and terrified by marriage, the girl works hard and saves her money with the hope, at first, of buying passage back to Japan. Over time, though, she comes to accept and appreciate her new life.

The picture would inspire two heartfelt and emotional scores. The first was by Cliff Eidelman, whose scoring credits included *Untamed Heart* (1993), *Star Trek VI: The Undiscovered Country* (1991), and *Triumph of the Spirit* (1989). He delivered a melancholic, romantic score that he recorded in Seattle. Eidelman's fairly traditional orchestra material had strong, well-developed themes and slight hints of Asian music (through his use of bamboo flutes). The movie premiered at the 1994 Cannes Film Festival with his music attached.

However, Harvey Weinstein of Miramax, the film's production studio and distributor, didn't feel that Eidelman's music had enough of an Asian feel to it. Director Hatta also had reservations about the score, feeling that it portrayed the film's young protagonist in an overly tragic light and led the audience to empathize with her too much. So Weinstein and Hatta set out to find a replacement composer. Director Wayne Wang recommended Mark Adler to them, with whom he'd worked on two films: *Eat a Bowl of Tea* (1989) and *Life Is Cheap...But Toilet Paper Is Expensive* (1989). Adler's other previous scores included *The Unbearable Lightness of Being* (1988) and a number of documentaries. The new composer spotted *Picture Bride* with Weinstein.

Although Adler had been hired months before the movie was to be released, an advance screening of it scheduled for the Sundance Film Festival meant that he had only about two weeks to write, orchestrate, and record forty-five minutes of music. The deadline was so short that Miramax even dropped its usual cue-by-cue approval process and greenlighted Adler's score after just the first few cues were demonstrated.

The new material had a decidedly stronger Japanese flavor than Eidelman's. Even so, the studio asked Adler to highlight that aspect even further, and he had to struggle to keep it from becoming overbearing. The score's guitar and flute solos were prerecorded in Adler's home studio, and its strings and brass were added in a larger facility. The composer was so exhausted by this point in the process that he actually fell asleep during one recording session. He recalls how he went about combining American and Japanese influences:

> As the writing progressed, I began to think of the emerging score as having a "Pacific rim" sound, where American idioms and Japanese ones interpenetrate one another. Flutist Jim Walker arrived at my studio with a sack of bamboo flutes. I had notated parts for him in detail, including pitch-bends. (As I'm a keyboard player, I had composed much of that music by improvising it on a Yamaha VL-1 synthesizer, which has a breath-controller and wheels for pitch bend and vibrato. I then manually transcribed those improvisations.) Jim really made the music his own, often suggesting where he could add shakuhachi-like sounds. Sometimes we would simplify phrases to allow more space for expressive inflection. My old friend Peter Maunu played acoustic guitar. Although there are a few koto samples in the score, they're often playing along with Peter's guitar work—it was a way of suggesting the koto, but bending it towards the west.

Regardless of how hard Adler had to work to write and prepare so much music in so little time, he later described the experience as one of the happiest of his career.

At the time of the movie's release, both composers' scores were released on CD: Eidelman's on his regular label, Varèse Sarabande, and Adler's on Virgin Records. Both recordings sold well.

■ **Johnny Mnemonic** (1995)

Original composer: **Mychael Danna**
Replacement composer: **Brad Fiedel**

Johnny Mnemonic is a film loosely based on a 1981 short story by William Gibson (inventor of the sci-fi subgenre term "cyberpunk"), who also wrote its screenplay. It stars Keanu Reeves and Dolph Lundgren and was directed by artist Robert Longo (his only outing as a feature film director, though he had previously directed a few music videos for such bands as R.E.M. and New Order). Set in a dystopic future world, the movie tells the story of a man implanted with a digital storage device, who works as a courier of sensitive digital data. In the form in which the picture was finally released (see below), it failed both critically and commercially.

To provide music for the film's dark world, Longo hired the relatively obscure industrial rock band Black Rain, which delivered about a dozen songs specifically written for the project (which can be heard on the band's album *Black Rain 1.0*). The picture's eclectic electronic underscore was provided by Canadian composer Mychael Danna, whose scoring credits included *Dance Me Outside* (1994), *Exotica* (1994), and *Ordinary Magic* (1993).

But neither Black Rain's nor Danna's work would make it into the finished picture. In the course of a torturous postproduction period, control of the film was taken away from Longo and his team by its production studio-distributor, Columbia TriStar Pictures (owned by Sony). The studio dramatically recut the picture, excising a significant amount of footage and altering its overall comprehensibility and impact in an effort to make it safer and friendlier for the mainstream moviegoer. According to director Longo, "TriStar insisted on making Johnny–Keanu Reeves likable."

According to William Gibson:

> Nobody got to see the film that Robert Longo shot. Longo shot the script I wrote, which I was happy with. The tragedy with *Johnny Mnemonic* is that we shot an ironic, broadly comic action film that at some level was supposed to be about bad science-fiction movies. We were not trying to make a blockbuster mainstream adventure film starring Keanu Reeves. When we started shooting that film Keanu wasn't a movie star. Speed came out while we were shooting. As soon as it was a hit we had guys from the studio coming out of the woodwork telling us that we shouldn't shoot a funny movie, where's the bus? It just got worse from there. We kept doing what we wanted to do. Keanu and Dolph were both doing exactly what we told them to do. Sony cut ninety percent of Dolph's role because they said it would offend the religious right. He doesn't even have a character in the movie they put out. He's just this insane caveman who comes rushing in and flinging people around. It doesn't make any sense. In the film we shot you get his backstory where he is preaching stark naked to churches full of women who're afflicted with the weird disease in the movie. He completely got into doing this comic villain and it just ended up making him look like an idiot. I personally felt very bad about that because he was doing what he was told to do.

Although no one seems to know specifically why, the studio replaced Black Rain's songs during postproduction with songs from a variety of well- and not-so-well-known performers, including Bono, The Edge, Henry Rollins, Helmet, Orbital, Stabbing Westward, and Cop Shoot Cop. It's hard to tell whether the original songs would have served the movie better: While Black Rain's work is thematically and stylistically more homogenous than what it was replaced with, the new selections work well within the movie.

Due to the picture's re-editing, Mychael Danna's score also had to change. But by this time, Danna was unavailable to make alterations to it: "As far as *JM* goes, after I finished the film (the 'long' version), I left the country (to India where I taught English in a small village in Bengal). Meanwhile, they decided to cut the film significantly, and therefore, the music no longer fit, hence the hiring of Brad Fiedel."

Danna's music was retained in one market, Japan. The Japanese distributor preferred one of the movie's early longer versions, which had more scenes with popular Japanese actor Takeshi Kitano (a cut that's also perhaps closer to the director's original vision), and this version happened to still have Danna's score attached to it.

Replacement composer Brad Fiedel, whose recent scoring credits included *True Lies* (1994), *Blink* (1994), and *Striking Distance* (1993), provided a new electronic score for *Johnny Mnemonic*. It's hard to compare Fiedel's and Danna's work, though, because the film's songs got the greatest emphasis, pushing both composers' scores toward the background. While both were synthesizer-based, Danna's incorporated a couple of Asian acoustic instruments as well, providing an exotic touch that Fiedel's lacked. Also, having been written for the longer version of the film, which provided him with a broader canvas on which to develop his ideas, Danna's work had a better chance to establish its presence.

Johnny Mnemonic represented one of the last big films for Brad Fiedel, who would soon all but disappear from scoring theatrically released features. The man who had composed some of the defining scores of the 1980s, including the first two *Terminator* pictures (in 1984 and 1991), and saved many troubled productions with quick score replacements, exited the business with two unfinished works. First, he was announced as replacement composer for *Money Train* (1995), but one month later the film's original composer, Mark Mancina, was back on board. Shortly after that, Fiedel started work on *Sgt. Bilko* (1996) when Alan Silvestri seemed to have scheduling conflicts. But Silvestri's schedule soon opened up, and he ended up scoring the entire picture. Since that time, Fiedel has primarily worked on made-for-TV movies.

■ **The Indian in the Cupboard** (1995)

Original composer: **Miles Goodman**
Replacement composer: **Randy Edelman**

In addition to being a director, Frank Oz is an actor and a puppeteer. He has worked with the Muppets—operating and voicing such characters as Bert, Grover, Cookie Monster, and Miss Piggy—since the early 1960s. In *The Indian in the Cupboard* he lent his magical touch to a feature intended to entertain adults and children alike. Based on a popular children's book by Lynne Reid Banks, adapted for the screen by Melissa Mathison (who wrote the script for *E.T.*), the film tells the story of a boy who receives an old cupboard and a plastic toy Indian for his ninth birthday. He soon discovers that the cupboard is magical and can bring his toy figures to life as tiny humans snatched from history. Through this bit of wizardry he learns about the importance of responsibility and the dangers of playing God.

The obvious choice for the film's composer seemed to be Miles Goodman, with whom Oz had worked on four previous films: *Little Shop of Horrors* (1986), *Dirty Rotten Scoundrels* (1988), *What About Bob?* (1991), and *HouseSitter* (1992). But at first the director was reluctant to hire him. Oz recalls the situation:

> It was a situation where I was hesitant hiring my good friend to do something that I had not seen him do before, and Bud [Miles Goodman] and I had a talk about it. He said, "You just don't want to hire me because you're concerned about having to fire a friend." I said, "That's true." He said, "Well, give me an opportunity," and I said, "Okay," because I thought he was brilliantly talented. So he had the score, and the producers and the writer didn't think the score was that successful. And in the long run, I had to agree with them—it wasn't happening. So I had to say to Bud, "Sorry, Bud, we have to go with somebody else," and Randy [Edelman] came in and finished it and did a very good job.... But Bud went in as an adult with his eyes open.... Fortunately, thank God, before he passed away (which is one of the mortal blows in my life, because he was a good and dear friend) I asked Bud to do the music for *In & Out*. So he knew everything was fine with us, and he did a great job.

Goodman's score, one of his last completed works before his untimely death, was essentially based around a little Indian flute, for which he wrote his main theme. In an interview with *Film Score Monthly* conducted in December 1994, Goodman went into some detail about his score, talking about how he wanted to combine a big orchestra with Native American music. The material he wrote and recorded was playful without being too emotional, but it apparently wasn't magical enough and didn't have enough of the Hollywood adventure-movie feel to it.

The replacement score by Randy Edelman, whose recent scoring credits included *While You Were Sleeping* (1995), *Billy Madison* (1995), *The Mask* (1994), and *Angels in the Outfield* (1994), was family-friendly, balancing a distinctly Western flavor with a pop sensibility. While the main instrument in his score, like Goodman's, was a flute, Edelman's music was more aggressive and more steeped in musical Americana. Nine minutes of Goodman's unused *The Indian in the Cupboard* work survives on his *Film Music Vol. 3* promotional CD.

Despite not fully connecting with the right audience on its initial release, *The Indian in the Cupboard* has grown in popularity ever since.

■ Waterworld (1995)

Original composer: **Mark Isham**
Replacement composer: **James Newton Howard**

In a postapocalyptic future world that's flooded due to the melting of the polar ice caps, the most sought-after item is a rumored patch of dry land called, simply, Dryland. Mankind's remnants, which include both humans as we know them and genetically mutated humanlike beings with gills, live on floating settlements and are the occasional prey of vicious pirates. This is the underlying premise of *Waterworld*, which starred Kevin Costner (who was also one of its producers and would step in as the uncredited director responsible for finishing the picture), Dennis Hopper, and Jeanne Tripplehorn.

Directed by Kevin Reynolds (whose directing credits included *The Beast of War*, *Robin Hood: Prince of Thieves*, and *Rapa Nui*), *Waterworld* was notorious before it was even released: Due to numerous filming problems, the picture's costs had skyrocketed, earning it the dubious honor of being the most expensive movie ever made. In fact, it became such an unwieldy mess that director Reynolds eventually left the project and Costner stepped in to finish it, reworking and reshaping much of what Reynolds had done.

Hired to score the film was Mark Isham, whose recent credits included *Nell* (1994), *Quiz Show* (1994), *Mrs. Parker and the Vicious Circle* (1994), and *Romeo Is Bleeding* (1993). Reynolds and the composer had worked together once before, on *The Beast of War* (1988). Isham's interesting thematic approach to *Waterworld* centered on a music box melody that played an integral role in the movie as one of the last pieces of music to survive on Earth. In this capacity it was part of the picture's source music: The music box played onscreen, and film's characters hummed its tune.

But after the departure of director Reynolds, things did not go smoothly for Isham. Costner had a sweeping, swashbuckling action score in mind, and he didn't hear this concept in Isham's work. On the other hand, the composer was confused by the filmmakers' temporary score that was both bleak and impressionistic. Thus the composer's fate was sealed, as he recalls:

> What went wrong was that the film politically exploded at the end. Kevin Reynolds quit the film, which left me working for Kevin Costner, who listened to what I had written and wanted a completely different point of view. He basically made a completely different film—he recut the entire film, and in his meeting with me he expressed that he wanted a completely different approach to the score. And I said, "Oh, let me demonstrate that I can give that to you," so I presented him with a demo of my approach to his approach, and he rejected that and fired me. What I find a lot in these big films, because the production schedules are so insane, is that the directors have very little time to actually concentrate on the music.

Reflecting on this rejected score, Isham offers some advice to fellow film composers:

> On a personal level, you've got to just roll with the punches. This is part of the business. That particular scenario was so understandable because of the politics. I was low man on the totem pole. There were a lot of dead bodies on that picture, and I was one of many, so it wasn't exactly a mystery as to what happened there. It only gets personally upsetting when you can't understand it, and so I just always get as much information as I can from the producers...so I really do understand why these things are going on. And then it's really just part of the game that you're playing if you're in this business.... One of the things that I do in scoring is I try to find a unique sound for each film. I believe that, at least to me, is the most artistic way to approach it. I'm not a formula composer. So here, in this case, Costner I think just didn't want to put in the time. He wanted to give someone the assignment, go away, and come back in six weeks' time and it would be exactly what he wanted. Because he had a long working relationship with James Newton Howard, he knew he could do that with him, and he knew he couldn't do that with me because he'd have to work with me, he'd have to come and listen and respond and we would have to shape this score. That's my interpretation of what happened.

The replacement score was written by James Newton Howard, whose recent scoring credits included *French Kiss* (1995), *Outbreak* (1995), *Just Cause* (1995), and another film that starred and was produced by Kevin Costner, *Wyatt Earp* (1994). Howard had only a few weeks to come up with an epic adventure score for *Waterworld*, a movie that was well over two hours long in its "short" version and roughly three hours long in its director's cut. His replacement music, which was more thematic than Isham's, featured memorable tunes for Costner's character and to represent the desire to find Dryland. Adding a futuristic tint was composer-performer Steve Porcaro (a founding member of the rock band Toto), who provided it with some of its sci-fi sounds and electronic percussion.

■ **Assassins** (1995)

Original composer: **Michael Kamen**
Replacement composer: **Mark Mancina**

Starring Sylvester Stallone, Antonio Banderas, and Julianne Moore, director Richard Donner's *Assassins* is a preposterous action-thriller about rival freelance hit men—a tired and disillusioned old pro and an ambitious up-and-comer—who end up in a deadly cat-and-mouse game with one another.

Donner (whose directing credits included *The Omen*, *Superman*, *Maverick*, and the *Lethal Weapon* series) hired Michael Kamen to score *Assassins*. He and the director had a history of successful collaborations, with *Lethal Weapon* (1987), *Lethal Weapon 2* (1989), and *Lethal Weapon 3* (1992). Among Kamen's more recent scoring credits were *Don Juan DeMarco* (1994), *The Three Musketeers* (1993), and *Last Action Hero* (1993).

But 1995 was not a good year for Kamen. He had scored Kathryn Bigelow's *Strange Days*, only to have his score (which he was enthusiastic about) replaced by a more electronic one by Graeme Revell. He then scored *Die Hard: With a Vengeance*, but the bulk of his score was replaced with music adapted from the first *Die Hard*. Then came two Joel Silver productions, *Fair Game* and *Assassins*. Apparently, having written little for *Fair Game*, Kamen shifted from it to work on *Assassins*. But in the end, both pictures would be scored by Mark Mancina. Kamen's *Assassins* score was deemed too heavy and was rejected, though reports differ on who—Sylvester Stallone or Richard Donner—actually pulled the plug on it. In any case, only Kamen's song "La Muerta" (performed by Danielle Wiener) remained in the film; the rest of his music was replaced by Mancina, who wrote a more modern-sounding action score in only thirteen days. Mancina's recent previous scoring credits included *Bad Boys* and *Speed*.

In spite of the *Assassins* rejection, Kamen would go on to work again with Donner on *Lethal Weapon 4* (1998). Sadly, he would die of a heart attack at age 55 in 2003. He is a much-missed composer known for his generosity: In 1996, he created The Mr. Holland's Opus Foundation, a charity that supports music education through the donation of musical instruments to underprivileged schools, music programs, and individual students.

■ **The Scarlet Letter** (1995)

Original composer: **Ennio Morricone**
Replacement composer no. 1: **Elmer Bernstein**
Replacement composer no. 2: **John Barry**

Few screen adaptations of famous literary works have taken as much criticism as director Roland Joffé's version of Nathaniel Hawthorne's *The Scarlet Letter*. The director took many, many liberties with his source material. Some of them—such as the expansion of the novel's background story—worked, but most (including the Hollywood-style upbeat ending) didn't. All questions of fidelity to the original story apart, the script was simply sluggish.

The first composer on the project was Ennio Morricone, who had written an Oscar-nominated score for Joffé's powerful film *The Mission* (1986). But the music he came up with for *The Scarlet Letter* (partially based on his *Mission* music, which had been used as a temp track) was a disappointment to all involved, so Joffé called on the services of another composer.

Next in line was Elmer Bernstein, who proceeded to write and record a complete score for the picture. Whereas Morricone's work had been deemed heavy-handed, Bernstein's was a bit lighter and more historical in its approach. His score, about ninety minutes of music recorded in Dublin, Ireland, conveys the idea of a joyous celebration of life with such cues as "Lovemaking," and its finale transmits a sense of redemption for Hester Prynne.

But the filmmakers were still not altogether happy with the picture's music. Demi Moore (who played Hester Prynne) recommended a third composer, John Barry, who had provided music for her *Indecent Proposal* (1993). In hopes he would supply something on the emotional level of his Academy Award–winning scores for *Out of Africa* (1985) and *Dances with Wolves* (1990), Barry became composer number three. He recalls the project's turmoil:

> Morricone was Roland's first choice because he had done that wonderful movie with De Niro, *The Mission*. I don't know what went wrong, but suddenly Elmer Bernstein came on it. I don't think Morricone had written a complete score; he may have written certain things. But Elmer did do a full score. I had lunch with Elmer in London when he was doing it. Then, when I got back here, I got a call from the producer, saying that, for whatever reasons, they had to change the score, and asking if I was available to do it in only five weeks including recording time.

Barry wrote his score on a tight schedule:

> The two other composers on this movie are two gentlemen that I respect totally. But this became an emergency. The movie was already booked into theaters, and the posters are out—with other composers' names on them! It's like, "We need something else," for whatever reason. So I said, "Okay, send me the video." The video came through and I liked it. As I said this morning, having not read the book, I didn't have...I mean, if it was Charles Dickens and somebody'd changed the end of it, I'd say "pass." It wasn't that. I think Joffé did an incredible job. I said, "Okay, I'll go to work, let's get on with it now...." I played them the music, they liked it very much, and then I had literally four weeks to do the score. It's an awfully pressured kind of a situation, but there's a kind of excitement about that kind of thing in movies. I've had it before and it sometimes brings out the best in you. I didn't have any problems when I saw the movie; this deep, psychological thing in the movie...it seemed to me a wonderful narrative story, which is the kind of story I like very much.

The scoring's short (five-week) schedule took a bit of a toll on Barry's music. Sticking with mostly safe strategies, it was essentially a collection of the composer's favorite romantic melodies enmeshed with a sound that referred back to *Dances with Wolves*. And, like *Dances with Wolves*, *The Scarlet Letter* also utilized the talents of Peter Buffett, an expert in Native American music, who contributed heavily to the score's main title and many of its livelier moments. Barry's score is a lot heavier than Bernstein's version, and even its happiest moments seem to contain the seeds of sorrow. To add yet another tragic element, the filmmakers augmented Barry's score with a choral version of Samuel Barber's well-worn Adagio for Strings. (This piece's impact on film music is discussed earlier in this book with regard to its use in *Platoon*.)

Although critics quickly savaged it, the picture did a moderate business at the box office. But it's fair to say that *The Scarlet Letter*, an American literary classic, still lacks an adequate film adaptation. CDs of both Bernstein's and Barry's scores have been released.

■ **Silver Strand** (1995)

Original composer: **Bruce Rowland**
Replacement composer: **Joseph Conlan**

Before their work on the television movie *Silver Strand*, a story about the rigorous training of U.S. Navy SEALs, Australian composer Bruce Rowland and Scottish-born Australian director George Miller (not to be confused with another Australian George Miller, the writer-director-producer-physician perhaps best known for his *Mad Max* movies) had worked together on nine productions in both Australia and America, including *The Man from Snowy River* (1982) and *Gross Misconduct* (1993).

But a successful Miller-Rowland collaboration on *Silver Strand* was apparently not in the cards. The film's producer, without much explanation, decided that a composer of his own choosing should replace Rowland's work. But the producer's composer also turned in an unsuccessful score that, in turn, had to be replaced. This replacement was done by television-music veteran Joseph Conlan (whose credits included the TV movie *Menendez: A Killing in Beverly Hills*, 58 episodes of the series *Tour of Duty*, and 111 episodes of *Simon & Simon*).

Fortunately, this replacement experience had no noticeable effect on the relationship between Miller and Rowland, who have worked together on four subsequent movies. Nor was *Silver Strand* Rowland's only score replacement; another unfortunate experience involved the 2002 Australian fantasy *The Inside Story*. Its writer-director-producer, Robert Sutherland (for which this movie is his only credit in all three areas), worked closely with Rowland on the music, only to suddenly realize during its mixing sessions that he didn't like it. He commissioned a replacement score from Australian composer Robert Clarke (whose only scoring credit is this film).

For Rowland, however, score replacement has not always been a one-way street: In 1987, he replaced a score-gone-wrong for one of his pal George Miller's movies, *Les Patterson Saves the World*, a silly farce starring Barry Humphries, playing both of his popular comedic stage alter egos, Sir Les Patterson and Dame Edna Everage. Tim Finn, a New Zealand pop musician (and founding member of the rock band Split Enz), had provided the picture's score, but once his music was on the mixing stage, it proved a problem and was rejected. Miller called in Rowland to replace the score's troublesome bits (more than two-thirds of it!). With little time and little money, the composer flew to Sidney with his own equipment and quickly recorded a replacement synthesizer score.

■ **Cutthroat Island** (1995)

Original composer: **David Arnold**
Replacement composer: **John Debney**

Cutthroat Island was a megabudget pirate movie that, failing to score big at the box office, contributed to the bankruptcy of its production company, Carolco Pictures.

Directed by Renny Harlin (whose previous directing credits included *Cliffhanger*, *The Adventures of Ford Fairlane*, and *Die Hard 2*) and starring his then-wife, Geena Davis, and Matthew Modine, the film was a mostly predictable exercise in the swashbuckling pirate genre, about a search for missing pieces of a treasure map and the eventual discovery of the loot. Its one departure from the standard formula was to make its lead pirate a hard-drinking, hard-fighting woman.

Hired to pen the picture's score was British composer David Arnold, who at the time had only two feature scoring credits: *Stargate* (1994) and *The Young Americans* (1993). The only instruction he was given was to write a theme that would "make the hair on the audience's head stand up."

Arnold looks back on his experience from the perspective of 2007:

> It's the weirdest thing that has ever happened to me. I was asked to do *Cutthroat Island* by [executive producer and Carolco co-founder] Mario Kassar and [producer] Joel Michaels whilst we were recording *Stargate*. At that point, Michael Douglas was cast with Geena Davis, but by the time they finished shooting, Douglas wasn't in the film anymore. It was a Geena Davis movie with Matthew Modine. Renny Harlin had quite some unusual working practices, which involved not showing me the film. He asked me to write themes, and I wrote a couple of themes which I thought were pretty good and he thought the same. I was there for a week in the Chateau Marmont [a famous hotel in West Hollywood, CA], waiting to see a scene and for some reason, I couldn't see anything. He wanted to hear the theme first. He invited me to his office to play it for him and once he heard it, he said, "Okay, let me show you a scene." He showed me a couple of scenes which looked very impressive and he told me how he accomplished that take. He gave me a couple of scenes to write music for using that theme. I went back to my room and did two short one-minute scenes. He came over to my room to hear these scenes, he pulled a few funny faces and that was pretty much the last I've heard of him.

Arnold wrote about five minutes of music and then was bounced off the project before he recorded anything. (He later used a couple of the themes he developed for *Cutthroat Island* in his score for 1996's *Independence Day*).

John Debney, whose recent scoring credits included *Sudden Death* (1995), *Houseguest* (1995), *Little Giants* (1994), and *Hocus Pocus* (1993), was hired as the replacement composer. For *Cutthroat Island*, he succeeded in fashioning a score in the style of classic Hollywood pirate pictures, stylistically in the vein of something Erich Wolfgang Korngold might have written. His excellent, delightful music for this ill-fated movie was recorded with the London Symphony and the choral group London Voices. Further enhancing the score was the picture's fine sound mix, which provided the music with sufficient sonic space to allow it to soar—a true rarity among action and adventure movies.

Debney's score is perhaps the best music ever written for a Renny Harlin picture. Interestingly, Debney's other highly celebrated score—*The Passion of the Christ* (2004)—was a similar rescue job.

■ White Squall (1996)

Original composer: **Maurice Jarre**
Replacement composer: **Jeff Rona**

White Squall is a nautical adventure movie based on a true story, the 1961 sinking of the sailing ship *Albatross* off the Florida coast during a sudden and unexpected squall. The *Albatross,* which had an interestingly storied history, was owned at the time by a sailing academy that used it for hands-on training. When the ship went down, two of its teaching crew and half of its dozen teenage student sailors were drowned.

While working on *White Squall,* director Ridley Scott (whose directing credits included *1492, Thelma & Louise, Black Rain, Blade Runner,* and *Alien*) assembled an eclectic temp score that included all sorts of film music. It included some Vangelis synthesizer excursions, John Barry's sweeping *Out of Africa* (1985) orchestra music, and Maurice Jarre's electroacoustic score for *Dead Poets Society* and his electronic *Witness* music. This latter score was what persuaded Scott to hire Jarre, with whom he hadn't worked before, to score *White Squall.*

Unfortunately, their first collaboration would be their last. Jarre's music would be rejected for a most unusual reason: He followed the temp tracks too closely! Jarre, shares his thoughts about the experience:

> When he [Ridley Scott] asked me to score *White Squall,* I was curious why he asked me. He had used music from *Witness* and *Dead Poets Society* as temp-track. He wanted me to write music in the same mood as for those two films. It was partly electronics and there was a little choir and an orchestra. We decided to start recording the electronics first. So we did one session with electronics and he came in late and I told him what I was doing and he asked me to continue. Before the second session started, the producer told me Ridley didn't want me to continue the music. He had changed his mind. He didn't want to have the mood of *Dead Poets.* He would have liked to have more time to cut the film. Everything was ready, all the musicians were booked, the choir was booked and I said: "Let me at least record what I wrote, because no matter what, you are going to have to pay these people and we have three full days of recording ahead." The producer had no idea what it is like to work with musicians. You have to pay the musicians and the recording studio. But they decided to just stop after one session. I couldn't believe it. I called Ridley and he told me he had made a mistake to have the same mood as *Dead Poets.* The real problem was that they realized the film was bad and Ridley wanted to have some time to recut the film. Actually they wanted me to wait until February (this was in December of last year) and then write a second score for the same money. In the end they had to pay the full three days: an orchestra of eighty people for two days, five men for the electronics plus the choir, plus the studio. They could at least have recorded the music.

After tossing out Jarre's score, Scott turned to his frequent collaborator Hans Zimmer, who suggested that he hire composer Jeff Rona (whose scoring credits included episodes of the TV series *Homicide: Life on the Streets* and *Chicago Hope*). Rona and the director agreed that *White Squall* needed at least one whistleable theme and that its temp tracks shouldn't be aped too closely. Rona's music for the picture leaned heavily on the pennywhistle, not because of the movie's seafaring setting, but simply because of the Celtic instrument's haunting quality. The composer, who happened to collect flutes, also used a number of other interesting ethnic wind instruments in his score, including one of the most basic of them all, the conch shell. Unfortunately, the picture was neither a great box-office success nor a big breakout for the composer, although Rona still feels it's one of his most important works and dedicates a whole chapter to it in his book *The Reel World: Scoring for Pictures.*

A rumor that Vangelis worked on *White Squall* is widespread, but while he was considered as a possible composer for the film, he couldn't take on the project because he was in the middle of completing his 1996 album *Oceanic*. The fact that his CD contained a strangely nautical theme probably helped fuel the misunderstanding.

■ **Mission: Impossible** (1996)

Original composer: **Alan Silvestri**
Replacement composer: **Danny Elfman**

Back when the Cold War was a hot issue, television aired a popular series that played on this conflict, *Mission: Impossible*, which ran from 1966 to 1973. The idea of turning the series' basic concept into a big feature film had been kicking around Hollywood for years, but it wasn't until it caught the attention of Tom Cruise that it became a reality. With Cruise as the star, director Brian De Palma (whose directing credits included *The Untouchables, Body Double, Scarface,* and *Dressed to Kill*) signed on. Among the rest of the cast were Jon Voight, Emmanuelle Béart, Jean Reno, Ving Rhames, and Vanessa Redgrave.

In the original TV series, clever trickery rather than action drove most plots. But the movie version's convoluted plot was action-driven. De Palma's *Mission: Impossible* never quite decides whether it wants to pay homage to the original series or be a James Bond–style action vehicle for Tom Cruise. Wisely, the TV show's famous and popular theme music, composed by Lalo Schifrin, was retained as *MI* made its leap from the small to the big screen.

Alan Silvestri (whose recent scoring credits included *The Quick and the Dead, Judge Dredd, Blown Away,* and *Forrest Gump*) was hired to provide the film's music. He wrote a score in the vein of his synth-heavy music for *Romancing the Stone* (1984). For *Mission: Impossible*'s action scenes, his music was propelled by relentless rhythms, over which the orchestra played his main melodies. Acknowledging that Cruise's character, Ethan Hunt, was a new addition to the Impossible Missions Force as it had been presented on TV, Silvestri developed a separate theme for Hunt. This melody first appeared as the crew is killed off, but it was not heard in a full-blown version until the film's big train scene. Other interesting uses of it were when Hunt breaks through a restaurant glass window and when he leaves the organization, the latter featuring a big, frenetically orchestrated fragment of the theme.

Unfortunately for Silvestri, the filmmakers didn't buy his musical ideas. De Palma:

> We began recording it, but five days later, he [Silvestri] had to rewrite half of his cues. It wasn't working. I did not have the time to supervise what he had written. He came in with his score and right away went to record it in the studio, without taking any notice of my suggestions. It was not what we were looking for, it was too melodic. There always was something too excessive in his music, no matter what we would change. Yet, we kept on doing modifications, but after four sessions, I said to my editor, Paul Hirsch: "This is not going to work, Tom won't love this music."

Replacement composer Danny Elfman was brought to Cruise's attention by Cruise's wife, Nicole Kidman. Elfman had just scored her latest movie, director Gus Van Sant's dark comedy *To Die For*. In that film, her character's crazy personality had benefited a lot from Elfman's evocative and schizophrenic score, which mixed 1950s television tunes with crazy guitar licks and haunting female vocals. (At the time he was hired for *Mission: Impossible*, Elfman's recent scoring credits included *Dead Presidents, Dolores Claiborne, Black Beauty*, and *The Nightmare Before Christmas*.)

Elfman talks about his work on the film, and its previous score:

> I heard a few of Alan's cues and they sounded really nice. I just think he went for a different tone, really. And now Brian [De Palma] wanted a fresh take, so I purposely never really listened to anything but a few temp cues. I wanted to see the film cold. It was a real down and dirty, quick thing, but very intense. It was not an easy task, having Lalo's theme to work with. Even though it wasn't used that many times, it actually made it much more difficult, because I had to always keep it alive. I still had to develop fresh themes that would come back and play the different scenes, but there was always this past reflection that had to be referred to, so it never completely went away.... In fairness to Alan, anybody coming in second has a huge advantage in understanding what the director doesn't want—at the expense of a lot of work already put in. I knew that they wanted energy, they wanted something a little more operatic and theatrical. Just seeing the movie without a score, I had an idea and I told them what I thought. A unique thing about coming into a project with very little time left is that you have to jump right in—there's no time for experimentation. I actually really enjoy that, because I go right for my instincts. There's an entire part of the process, experimenting with all sorts of different shapes and sizes, which you just don't get to do then.

Elfman's score not only featured Schifrin's famous *Mission: Impossible* theme in three key sequences, but it also included subtle references to Schifrin's secondary theme for the TV show, "The Plot." Elfman's music for this film would also herald a change in his sound: It marked his first extensive use of a percussive and somewhat experimental sound in a big-profile project (he had taken a stab at this approach previously, but in lower-profile projects).

Ironically, the biggest hit from the whole *Mission: Impossible* music package would turn out to be the "Mission Impossible Theme" as arranged and performed by Adam

Clayton and Larry Mullen of the rock band U2. As for Alan Silvestri's Ethan Hunt theme, it would later find a home in the composer's score for *Eraser* (1996).

■ The Island of Dr. Moreau (1996)

Original composer: **Zbigniew Preisner**
Replacement composer: **Gary Chang**

New Line Cinema's *The Island of Dr. Moreau*, starring an absurdly dressed and made-up, scenery-chewing Marlon Brando as the doctor, was a sad production in which the conflict of many artistic visions resulted in an outrageous failure. Before 1996, two previous movies had been based on H. G. Wells's popular 1896 novel: the classic 1932 version called *Island of Lost Souls*, starring Charles Laughton as Moreau, and the so-so-at-best 1977 *The Island of Dr. Moreau*, which starred Burt Lancaster in the same role. The Wells story is about a shipwreck survivor rescued at sea by Moreau's assistant, who takes the man to a remote island where the genius-gone-mad vivisectionist Moreau uses horrible experimental surgery to make creatures that are half man and half animal. The 1996 film version updates things by changing the shipwreck to a plane crash, and the doctor's research is now in genetics—but it still yields horrible hybrid creatures.

The 1996 version started out as the baby of South African writer-director Richard Stanley, whose two previous features as a director were *Dust Devil* (1993) and *Hardware* (1990). However, artistic disagreements led the studio to fire Stanley after only four days of shooting, and New Line hired legendary director John Frankenheimer to replace him. Although he had been directing a lot of television movies in the 1990s, such as *Andersonville* (1996) and *The Burning Season* (1994), Frankenheimer's fame rested primarily on the string of strong, highly praised films that he had directed in the 1960s, including *Birdman of Alcatraz* (1962), *The Manchurian Candidate* (1962), *Seven Days in May* (1964), and *Seconds* (1966). New Line also replaced Stanley's script with a new one by Ron Hutchinson, who had previously scripted two TV movies directed by Frankenheimer. (Although he is credited with cowriting the film's screenplay, almost nothing from Stanley's original script remained in the new version.)

Stanley had engaged Polish composer Zbigniew Preisner during the film's preproduction phase to write some pieces of music that could serve as onscreen source material (requiring prerecording before shooting started). And at this same time, the two discussed the film's final score that would unite these pieces and the underscore in a single Stanley-Preisner musical vision. Preisner was primarily known at this time for his scores for director Krzysztof Kieslowski *Three Colors* series of films: *Red* (1994), *White* (1994) and *Blue* (1993). Stanley sought out the Polish composer because he really liked Preisner's score to *The Double Life of Veronique* (1991), and he stuck by his choice even when the studio objected.

In his telling of the story, Stanley imagined Moreau as a complex man concerned with educating the beasts he had created. One of his educational ventures would involve them with music, and Stanley and Preisner envisioned a piece of chamber music that would be performed by the beasts as part of an onscreen recital. Moreau was to be deeply involved with music himself, partially fueled by memories of his ex-wife, who, like the doctor, was a pianist. Their piano theme (to be performed onscreen) was to represent a link to his past. Finally, as Stanley and Preisner envisioned it, the central theme of the score would be a choral setting of Charles Baudelaire's poem "A Voyage to Cythera" (from *Les Fleurs du mal*). This piece was to be performed onscreen by a choir of beasts.

Unfortunately, all the planning fell apart at this stage, even as the composer was preparing his source music. Once Stanley was fired, several project members, including Preisner, left the picture. The shooting of the new version quickly turned into a disaster for all involved, as cast and crew and studio continued to butt heads throughout the production.

Once Frankenheimer took over the movie, he brought on composer Gary Chang, with whom he had worked on five previous films (and would go on to work on two more after *Moreau*). Chang's scoring credits included the features *Miami Blues* (1990), *A Shock to the System* (1990), and *Dead Bang* (1989), and, starting in the early 1990s, numerous made-for-TV movies. His largely electronic, atmospheric score for *The Island of Dr. Moreau* successfully focused on Moreau's demented creatures and did an all-around great job for the picture. It's unfortunate that the composer's most accessible music is linked to this much-maligned production.

■ **Last Man Standing** (1996)

Original composer: **Elmer Bernstein**
Replacement composer: **Ry Cooder**

Written and directed by Walter Hill, *Last Man Standing* is an adaptation of *Yojimbo*, Akira Kurosawa's 1961 samurai film that starred Toshiro Mifune. (Kurosawa's movie is often said to be based on Dashiell Hammett's novels *Red Harvest* and *The Glass Key*, and the 1942 film of the latter book, as well as John Ford's body of Westerns, a strong influence that Kurosawa was quick to cite for many of his films.) Hill's movie was *Yojimbo*'s second acknowledged remake, the first being director Sergio Leone's spaghetti Western *A Fistful of Dollars* (1964), a film that greatly boosted the career of its star, Clint Eastwood.

In Hill's version of the tale, set in the nearly deserted corrupt West Texas town of Jericho sometime during Prohibition, Bruce Willis plays the man with no name (actually John Smith), who uses his wits to manipulate two rival bootlegging gangs (one Italian, one Irish) into mutual slaughter. Deliberately anachronistic in some of its production design, Hill's film is strikingly stylized, somewhat surreal, and generally forbidding, with everything appearing as if seen through a yellow-brown haze (which is not altogether inappropriate for a dusty, decaying, out-of-the-way town in West Texas).

In many ways *Last Man Standing* is a textbook example of style's victory over substance. The dark film did not fare well with either audiences or critics. Popular *Chicago Sun-Times* critic Roger Ebert called it "a desperately cheerless film."

Selected to score the movie was Elmer Bernstein, whose most recent previous scoring credits included *Devil in a Blue Dress* (1995) and *Frankie Starlight* (1995). The picture provided the composer an opportunity to pen a significant action-Western score, something he hadn't been doing lately. Based on the style of his own classic Western music, Bernstein's big, traditional orchestra score for *Last Man Standing* was built on a single theme that was most fulfillingly presented at the film's beginning and as a glorious finale for Bruce Willis's character. The rest of the score had reflective moments as well as standard action music, with the film's violence propelled by all kinds of wild percussion. (And a citing of the "Dies Irae" theme is heard in the cue "Hijacking.")

Although Bernstein's musical choices seem quite appropriate in the abstract, his score felt light when set against the movie's over-the-top violence, particularly the wild gunfights that stylistically fall somewhere between those of directors Sam Peckinpah and John Woo. Most importantly, Bernstein's great late score simply didn't fit Hill's cinematic vision. The director felt the music was too traditional, too old-fashioned; he wanted something stranger, something more in tune with his stylized visuals.

New Line liked Bernstein's score, but the director chose to switch composers, hiring his old cohort Ry Cooder, with whom he had worked on eight previous films, including *The Long Riders* (1980), *Crossroads* (1986), and *Extreme Prejudice* (1987). *Last Man Standing* wasn't the first time Hill had called on him as a replacement composer: Cooder replaced James Horner on Hill's *Streets of Fire* (1984) and John Zorn on *Trespass* (1992).

Cooder remembers getting started on *Last Man Standing*:

> *Last Man Standing* is a totally surreal film, and I needed to search for the right musical approach. This movie is based on *Yojimbo*, which had a brilliant score [by Masaru Satô]. I could try to describe it as post-atomic Japanese new-wave music, which is a pretty amazing genre. Post-war Japan was so turned on its head that the film music could sound like anything, and the composers of that time were orchestrating cacophony they must have been hearing. When Walter Hill turned to me and asked if I could write a score like *Yojimbo* for *Last Man Standing*, all I could say was "Jesus!" I didn't have the social context of post-war Japan to fall back on! I could only hope to update *Yojimbo*'s sound without having the time to really think about it. That's because I was really thrown into the water with this one.... I saw *Last Man Standing* on Friday and I was scoring on Monday.

Cooder's quirky and ominous score matched the film's exaggerated, almost operatic scenes of violence and eclectic production design. Featuring the composer on guitars and keyboards, his son Joachim on percussion, Rick Cox on bass saxophone, synths, and samplers, and a few other players (on exotic flutes and percussion), it mixed haunting, drifting electroacoustic textures with various flavors of old-time blues, a pinch of Southwestern music, and a strangely twisted but infectious bit of blues-funk.

A recording of Cooder's score is available on the Verve label. A recording of Bernstein's rejected score was released on the Varèse Sarabande label.

■ **The Winner** (1996)

Original composer: **Pray for Rain**
Replacement composer: **Daniel Licht**

The Winner is a dark, moody comedy about an oddly naive fellow named Philip (played by Vincent D'Onofrio), who hits a winning streak in Las Vegas, attracting the attention of all sorts of sleazy lowlifes and thugs, including a lounge singer (Rebecca De Mornay), her boyfriend (Billy Bob Thornton), and Philip's own homicidal brother (Michael Madsen). Alex Cox, known for his edgy aesthetic, directed it.

To score the picture, Cox hired the San Francisco–based film-music band Pray for Rain, which had previously scored Cox's *Sid & Nancy* (1986), *Straight to Hell* (1987), and *Death and the Compass* (1992). The score they did for *The Winner* was somewhat experimental and incorporated processed casino sounds (slot machines, roulette tables, etc.) into the music. Also providing music was Zander Schloss, a musician who had been a member of the group the Circle Jerks, the Weirdos, and Thelonious Monster, and had contributed music to a half-dozen of Cox's films.

Dan Wool from Pray for Rain remembers the score:

> The original score for *The Winner* was carefully and deliberately designed to play to the characters and to the comically metaphysical sub-plot. In doing so we organically created counterpoint to the visuals that framed the natural vulgarity of Las Vegas. Much of the original score was heavily synthetic and atmospheric. Extremely processed and overbaked sonically. Tangerine Dream with a hangover. Atypical for a noir-y, Vegas-y film. The rest of the music was guitar-based with both Zander and I often abusing the instrument to generate the desired tone. The guitar-based parts that did have melodic content we left as raw as possible. Nothing sounded remotely the way a Hollywood film, even an "indie," would be scored. In no way did we attempt to cater to the norms of what the genre called for. While the score was hardly on the frontier of sonic innovation, it at least didn't sound like any film we were aware of.

But all was not well with *The Winner*. While director Cox was off in Mexico, the film's producers recut it and, out of sync with the director's musical vision, replaced its Pray for Rain score with a sort of pop-jazz–tinged lounge music that they felt was more in the spirit of the movie's setting. (Incidentally, much of Schloss's music survived the picture's changes.) Cox tells of his film's sad postproduction saga:

> In 1995 I was asked to direct a film based on *A Darker Purpose*, a stage play by Wendy Riss. I did so, in Las Vegas and Los Angeles. I made the acquaintance of some very

nice actors and crewpersons. Unfortunately, the film was re-edited by the producers, and its ironic score by Dan Wool and Pray For Rain—sometimes synthetic, sometimes sad, sometimes demented, often lyrical—was completely stripped out and replaced with fake jazz of the kind producers buy by the yard for pornos.

All this went on behind my back, while I was in Mexico working on *Death and the Compass*. And the resultant mess—ironically titled *The Winner*—went straight to cable. Sadly, it is not my movie. It's an Alan Smithee film. [*Note*: "Alan Smithee" is the traditional credit for a film from which the director has withdrawn his name.]

(In Japan, the distributors Cable Hogue and GAGA insisted on showing a version which partially resembled my original cut; and the Pray For Rain score was preserved.)

To provide the movie's replacement score, the producers hired composer Daniel Licht, best known for his earlier work on the *Children of the Corn* and *Amityville* horror franchises. With *The Winner*, one of his most unusual scoring assignments, Licht branched out into the world of Vegas-style lounge music. Since Alex Cox, who opposed the score change, was unavailable for consultation, Licht worked with executive producer Mark Damon, who gave him a fairly free hand. With help from orchestrator-conductor Pete Anthony, Licht worked under a tight deadline. He recalls the experience:

This is one score that's completely different from anything I've done. It's almost go-go music, it's bluesy, it's a synthesis of South Indian drones with pop. It's a song-oriented score. Everything happens in song form—there are no five bars of this, no odd-metered stuff. Everything happens in eight-bar phrases, a bridge, and then eight more bars. It had its own internal rhythm, and, for some reason, it seemed to fit just right. The film was all cut in master shots—there was no intercutting, a scene was all one long setup. There were scenes that were three, four minutes long. The score had to have its own life as well.

Two cuts of *The Winner* exist. Its American distributor, Live Entertainment, handles the recut, rescored version, while its Japanese distributors, Cable Hogue and GAGA, handle what they call the "director's cut" (though director Cox takes exception to this), with the film's original score intact. Toho Music Co./Couer Records released a CD of Pray for Rain's score in Japan.

■ 2 Days in the Valley (1996)

Original composer: **Jerry Goldsmith**
Replacement composer: **Anthony Marinelli**

Featuring an all-star cast, *2 Days in the Valley* is a cleverly plotted crime thriller with darkly comic overtones set in Los Angeles' San Fernando Valley. In the way it weaves together myriad intersecting storylines and quirky characters in its forty-eight-hour time frame, it may be said to be in debt to such films as Jim Jarmusch's *Mystery Train* (1989), Robert Altman's *Short Cuts* (1993), and Quentin Tarantino's *Pulp Fiction* (1994). Written and directed by John Herzfeld (whose previous writing-directing credits included the feature *Two of a Kind* and the TV movies *The Preppie Murder* and *Casualties of Love: The Long Island Lolita Story*), the movie lets fate and coincidence draw together a disparate cast of also-rans and lowlifes in a series of crisscrossing crimes and betrayals. Among them are a kindhearted hit man (Danny Aiello), a sadistic hit man (James Spader), the sadist's girlfriend (Charlize Theron), a murderous wife (Teri Hatcher), a suicidal writer-director (Paul Mazursky), a nurse (Marsha Mason), an obnoxious art dealer and his verbally abused assistant (Greg Cruttwell and Glenne Headley), two second-rate vice cops (Eric Stoltz and Jeff Daniels), and a homicide detective (Keith Carradine).

2 Days in the Valley was a small movie that came to composer Jerry Goldsmith through its producer Herb Nanas, with whom Goldsmith had worked on *First Blood* in 1982. (Among Goldsmith recent scoring credits were *Executive Decision, City Hall, Powder,* and *First Knight.*) The film's complex storyline, with its plot twists and dark humor, intrigued the composer, who wrote a forty-five-minute score made up primarily of stylized and colorful little musical vignettes produced for individual scenes.

The most important "character" represented musically in the score is the Valley itself, for which Goldsmith provided dark, synthesizer textures. Riding atop these is the movie's main theme, an homage to his own *Chinatown* theme, with a sultry trumpet solo that later develops into a more contemplative piece. Generally, synth sounds underscore the picture's darker scenes, and ostinatos propel such scenes as the shootout and the death of the hitman's girlfriend. The kinder hit man's Italian heritage is underlined with a faux Nino Rota piece for mandolin and strings, echoing traditional Italian melodies à la "The Godfather Waltz." The murderous wife's theme seems to foreshadow the composer's "Willa's Theme" from *Fierce Creatures* (1997).

Goldsmith's music provided a smooth, dark sonic world for the movie, but the filmmakers obviously saw and heard things differently. Director John Herzfeld hired a replacement composer who would not only score the movie but also write some songs for it, Anthony Marinelli, whose recent scoring credits included *Underworld* (1996), *One Tough Bastard* (1996), and *Payback* (1995). Marinelli's score is made up mostly of steamy jazz- and blues-based tracks that utilize guitar and saxophone. His instrumental score was more marginal than Goldsmith's because, in the replacement soundtrack, many of the movie's key scenes are accompanied by songs performed by such blues-based artists as Junior Wells, Wilson Picket, and Taj Mahal. (The kindhearted hit man's Italian heritage is now underlined by Donizetti and Bellini opera excerpts.)

■ **Ransom** (1996)

Original composer: **Howard Shore**
Replacement composer: **James Horner**

Ron Howard's popular thriller *Ransom*, starring Mel Gibson, was a loose remake of *Ransom!*, a 1956 film that starred Glenn Ford, which was in turn an adaptation of the television play *Fearful Decision*, presented on the anthology drama series *The United States Steel Hour*. Although details differ from version to version, a simple storyline is common to them all: A wealthy man's son is kidnapped, and a ransom is demanded for his safe return. Harboring doubts that his son will ever be returned, regardless of whether the ransom is paid, the man turns the table on the kidnappers. He goes on TV and announces that he will not pay the ransom; instead, he will take the same amount of money and place it as a bounty on the kidnappers' heads unless his son is quickly returned safe and sound. Until the plot is resolved, the man is tortured by doubts about whether he made the right decision or simply signed his son's death warrant.

To pen his film's music, director Ron Howard hired Howard Shore, a composer known for edgy and unusual scores, particularly for films by David Cronenberg. (By 1996, Shore had scored eight Cronenberg features and subsequently would score four more.) Prior to *Ransom*, Shore's recent scoring credits included *Striptease* (1996), *Crash* (1996), *Before and After* (1996), *Looking for Richard* (1996), and *Se7en* (1995). The composer was enthusiastic about working on *Ransom* and seemed to have a good rapport with Ron Howard.

For his superb book *The Score*, composer Michael Schelle interviewed Shore during *Ransom*'s final recording sessions. The composer described his relationship with the director:

> We actually discuss things. He sees what you're doing, and he likes it, but then he might want to give you his ideas, too. He wants both things—he wants the traditional and he enjoys the more experimental approaches, too. A lot of the *Ransom* score pays attention to the genre and the kinds of things you'd expect, but I'm also trying to keep it edgy and contemporary—paying respect to the genre, but not locked into predictability or cliché. On *Se7en*, the director didn't want me to pay attention to the drama, he was just interested in sounds. Occasionally, I would slip something in, like a little mickey-mousing or an operatic thing or a little genre referencing, and he would go, "Oh, really? Well, okay." But he didn't want me to do too much of that. Ron Howard wants more of a balance, more respect for the drama of the picture. That's just the type of person he is.

Two weeks later, Schelle learned that Shore's score had been replaced, so he phoned him and asked about the rejection. The composer was not sure what was behind it:

> Well, these things happen—all the time. It's frustrating because you spend so much time and so much energy. I aged about ten years in those two weeks...! All I can figure out is that he [Ron Howard] came into the picture wearing a black leather jacket and left wearing a white sport coat. I think he got nervous—the music was probably too contemporary or too experimental in the long run.

The large orchestra Shore employed was treated to some complex counterpoint and contemporary techniques that are somewhat uncommon in the average film score. These include aggressive dissonances, clusters, sound-mass techniques, reverse articulations, and industrial/grunge effects. Although he stated at that time that he'd never be able to use any of these cues in other projects since they were so deeply rooted in the movie they'd been written for, Shore later referred to some of his *Ransom* music in his magnum opus, *The Lord of the Rings* trilogy (2001–2003).

For a replacement score, Howard called on composer James Horner, with whom he had worked on *Cocoon* (1985), *Willow* (1988), and *Apollo 13* (1995). (After *Ransom*, they would work together on another three films, including *Missing* and *A Beautiful Mind*.) For *Ransom*'s quickly written replacement score, Horner pulled out an array of his favorite suspense ideas, building on music he had written for a number of previous movies, including *Clear and Present Danger* (1994), *The Pelican Brief* (1993), and *Sneakers* (1992). The movie (and its official soundtrack CD) also contained quite a few songs by Billy Corgan, a founding member of the popular grunge-rock band Smashing Pumpkins. These were used as source music.

The chief difference in *Ransom*'s two scores was that Horner's always kept the movie's happy ending in sight, while the original one remained bleak and overwhelming until the end.

■ **Mariette in Ecstasy** (1996)

Original composer: **Leonard Rosenman**
Replacement composer: **Christopher Klatman**

Mariette in Ecstasy is an unusual picture that unfortunately has never been released theatrically or on home video. It was cinematographer John Bailey's third directorial effort. (Among his many cinematography credits were *American Gigolo*, *The Pope of Greenwich Village*, *Silverado*, *Mishima: A Life in Four Chapters*, and *The Accidental Tourist*; his two previous directing credits were *China Moon* and *The Search for Intelligent Life in the Universe*.)

Starring Geraldine O'Rawe and Eva Marie Saint, *Mariette in Ecstasy* was based on a novel by popular author Ron Hansen, who adapted his own work for the screen. It is the story of a passionately religious young girl who enters a cloistered Catholic nunnery and soon experiences a mystical transformation: As she's in the midst of a divine ecstasy, the stigmata (marks of Christ's wounds when he was crucified) appear on her hands. Is she a saint? Is she a fake? These questions, and the notoriety her stigmata generate outside the convent, upset and divide the nuns with whom she lives.

Director Bailey originally wanted to hire British composer George Fenton, but by the time the picture was finished, Fenton wasn't available. His next choice was Leonard Rosenman, who had begun his music career as a New York modernist concert composer but was soon lured into film work by his friend James Dean. Among Rosenman's earliest scores were two movies that helped define Dean's screen persona—Elia Kazan's *East of Eden* (1955) and Nicholas Ray's *Rebel Without a Cause* (1955). (Rosenman would go on to write many more film scores, two of which, *Bound for Glory* and *Barry Lyndon*, would win him Academy Awards.) *Mariette in Ecstasy* became one of his last completed film projects, due to both failing health and a lack of compelling projects sent his way.

When Rosenman was hired for *Mariette,* he was fresh off a strange and unsatisfying experience on writer-director Ernest Thompson's *The West Side Waltz* (1995), a made-for-television movie about an aging musician. Thompson had wanted Rosenman's music to complement the classical selections played onscreen by the film's characters. While writing his score, Rosenman got hooked on a single theme, and for the music's recording session in Salt Lake City, he prepared only that theme. Thompson wanted to save the day by having the assembled musicians record variations on the theme, but the film's producer nixed that idea and ended the session on the spot. The movie was eventually scored by composer Patrick Williams, a TV-movie specialist who had worked with Thompson on *The Lies Boys Tell* (1994).

Rosenman's haunting music for *Mariette in Ecstasy* fell victim to the movie's many unresolved problems: Shortly after it was completed, director Bailey left the project and one of its producers took over. At this point, concerns about Rosenman's music were raised, and the producer hired composer Christopher Klatman to write a replacement score. (Klatman's previous work, which had mostly been in television, included numerous episodes of such series as *Knots Landing, Guns of Paradise,* and *Bodies of Evidence.*) The new composer came up with material meant to address the producer's impression of a lack of warmth in Rosenman's music. Klatman's small, intimate chamber score sought to establish a strong connection between the audience and Mariette.

But the picture's release was axed soon after his music was completed. After a few test screenings, *Mariette in Ecstasy*'s financiers backed out of the project, and the completed film was unable to find a distributor. With no distribution, the picture disappeared, and neither it nor its two scores have ever resurfaced.

■ **Rosewood** (1997)

Original composer: **Wynton Marsalis**
Replacement composer: **John Williams**

Rosewood was a small, predominantly black town on Florida's Gulf Coast. In 1923, white residents from the neighboring town of Sumner went on a racist rampage, burning and razing Rosewood and killing a number of its residents. This incident, now known as the Rosewood Massacre, remained something of a secret to most Americans until newspaper and television reporters brought it to light in the 1980s and the state of Florida awarded damages to Rosewood's survivors in the 1990s.

Director John Singleton, whose previous directing credits included *Boyz n the Hood* (1991), *Poetic Justice* (1993), and *Higher Learning* (1995), filmed a cinematically powerful story of the Rosewood tragedy featuring actors Ving Rhames, Don Cheadle, and Jon Voight. For the *Los Angeles Times,* Singleton spoke of his motivation for the project: "I had a very deep—I wouldn't call it fear—but a deep contempt for the South because I felt that so much of the horror and evil that black people have faced in this country is rooted here.... So in some ways this is my way of dealing with the whole thing." Although *Rosewood* was not a great success at the box office, it was generally well received by critics. Author and critic Stanley Crouch wrote in *The New York Times*, "Never in the history of American film had Southern racist hysteria been shown so clearly. Color, class, and sex were woven together on a level that Faulkner would have appreciated."

To score his film, Singleton hired acclaimed trumpeter, composer, and self-styled jazz scholar Wynton Marsalis, whose film scoring credits included *Tune in Tomorrow...* (1990) and the TV drama *Shannon's Deal* (1989). The music that Marsalis wrote for the movie (and often performed too) was very much in touch with the picture's 1923 Florida setting, combining older jazz styles (and a few more modern ones) with rural blues and folk music. It featured quite a few noted performers, including Cassandra Wilson, Shirley Caesar, and Mark O'Connor.

Marsalis reflects on his score:

> What this score represents is...the opportunity to use musicians of various generations and sensibilities to give the listener an accurate rendering of the variety of human experiences one has when the worlds of the young and the old interact. To have the emotions of a giant like Claude "Fiddler" Williams, a majestic woman like Cassandra Wilson, and all of the other musicians to give their substance to your music is truly a blessing. It is one equal to having grown up where I did and when I did. And that is the full meaning of the score for *Rosewood*.

John Singleton, however, was not satisfied with Marsalis's music, which didn't mesh well with his vision of the film. Apparently, the director wanted something a bit bigger, less period-bound, and more traditionally cinematic. Having admitted that undertaking *Rosewood* was to some degree inspired by Steven Spielberg's *Schindler's List* (1993), Singleton turned to that film's composer, John Williams, whose recent credits included *Sleepers* (1996) and *Nixon* (1995). While replacing Marsalis with Williams on this particular picture might seem a strange move, it should be noted that Williams had some legitimate background in black gospel music: In the early 1960s, he had worked as accompanist, arranger, and orchestrator on some of the music that gospel great Mahalia Jackson recorded.

Singleton and Williams respotted *Rosewood* and discussed how to remain true to the film's context without leaning too heavily on period musical styles. Williams's solution resulted in one of his most unusual scores. It's not big on the monumental themes with which he is so often associated, yet it does have a few fairly sweeping melodies that sit alongside with or are accompanied by little fiddle, harmonica, and jaw harp moments. The score also features some very moving gospel pieces. (A few of Marsalis's source cues were retained in the picture as well.) In some ways, Williams's replacement score can be viewed as a prelude to his work on another picture that depicted an African-American tragedy, *Amistad* (1997). A recording of Williams's *Rosewood* soundtrack is available from Sony Records.

When Singleton released Marsalis from his scoring duties, the composer got back the rights to the material he had composed for *Rosewood*. This he released on his 1999 Sony CD *Reeltime*. In 2004, some of it also appeared in filmmaker Ken Burns's documentary *Unforgivable Blackness: The Rise and Fall of Jack Johnson*, the story of the legendary boxer.

Welcome to Woop Woop (1997)

Original composer: **Stewart Copeland**
Replacement composer: **Guy Gross**

Stewart Copeland, perhaps best known as a founding member of and the drummer for the popular rock band the Police, is one of few musicians to have made highly successful transitions from rock music to film scoring. Still, his prolific film career includes a few rejected scores. In 1997, the Kraft-Benjamin Agency released a promotional CD of Copeland's film music titled *From Rumble Fish to Gridlock'd*, which featured cues from some of the composer's best work, including excerpts from a couple of scores that had been rejected. It contains two cues, "Ice Pick Love" and "Bootleg Montage," from *Mobsters* (1990), a film whose original director, Luis Mandoki, was replaced by Michael Karbelnikoff, and for which Copeland's music was replaced by Michael Small's. Another surprise on this promotional disc is the cue "Slithered," from director Phillip Noyce's thriller *Sliver* (1993), which was eventually scored by Howard Shore (except for its re-edited finale, which had music by Christopher Young).

In 1997, Copeland faced another rejected score, for *Welcome to Woop Woop*, a little-seen curiosity of Australian cinema. Writer-director Stephan Elliott, whose two previous directorial credits were *Frauds* (1993) and *The Adventures of Priscilla, Queen of the Desert* (1994), made the dark and broad comedy *Welcome to Woop Woop* as a quasi-sequel to his popular *Priscilla*. Based on Doug Kennedy's novel *The Dead Heart*, *Welcome to Woop Woop* is the tale of a New York City con artist and rare-bird dealer (played by Jonathon Schaech) who, fleeing trouble in the United States, travels to Australia, where he's kidnapped by a sex-crazed girl. She takes him to the off-the-map, asbestos-polluted Outback village of Woop Woop, where her father, known as Daddy-O (Rod Taylor), rules its inbred population with an iron fist. The town's only entertainments are recordings and films of Rodgers and Hammerstein musicals, particularly *The Sound of Music* and *South Pacific*.

Stewart Copeland provided a score for the film, but the movie took years to complete, going through several versions before it arrived in theaters around the globe in 1998. Elliott screened an unfinished work print at the 1997 Cannes film festival with Copeland's music, and then continued editing (removing twenty minutes of footage, based on the feedback he received at Cannes).

Although the picture's American distributor, Goldwyn Films, allowed the director a relatively free hand in shaping the picture, they did ask for a new score. Elliott called on the services of his old friend the Australian composer Guy Gross, who had scored both of Elliott's previous films.

Gross's replacement work involved writing the picture's underscore and providing song arrangements in a variety of styles. As with *Priscilla*, *Welcome to Woop Woop*'s instrumental underscore played a small part in the movie's overall sound, whereas such classic Rodgers and Hammerstein songs as "Climb Ev'ry Mountain" are at its core.

■ **Breakdown** (1997)

Composer with multiple scores: **Basil Poledouris**
Additional composer: **Richard Marvin**

Breakdown, starring Kurt Russell, is a well-made thriller about a couple whose cross-country drive is interrupted by their car's breakdown on a desolate stretch of Southwestern desert highway, where they are terrorized and preyed on by a trucker and some creepy locals. It may sound a bit like Steven Spielberg's *Duel* (1971), but it turns out to be considerably more like George Sluizer's 1988 Dutch thriller *The Vanishing*. Writer-director Jonathan Mostow's financial backing for the movie came from legendary producer Dino De Laurentiis.

Mostow wanted his friend composer Richard Marvin, with whom he had worked on the 1991 television movie *Flight of Black Angel*, to score the picture, but Marvin's lack of notable credits made the producers reluctant to hire him (his resumé included *Interceptor*, *3 Ninjas*, and a half-dozen made-for-TV movies). De Laurentiis suggested that Mostow go with composer Basil Poledouris, who had previously worked with the producer on the *Conan* movies.

Mostow's screenplay fascinated Poledouris, and after reading through it he immediately took the job:

> *Breakdown* was an incredible script, I think it was the quickest read I've ever had, a real page-turner. It was kind of a gestalt in the way it read, very clean, very clear, it wasn't burdened with all kinds of camera directions and scene descriptions and blocking and things like that. Jonathan Mostow took it and gave it a real style quite different from the way I thought it would be.... [The final film] was much sparser than I'd imagined. It would be the difference between *The Wild Bunch* and...well, *Breakdown*! *The Wild Bunch* was very epic, full of grandeur, and *Breakdown* is more internal. I thought originally *Breakdown* would have a fuller sound with a larger orchestra representing the heroic kinds of things, whereas in fact it's about a guy who is not a fighter; he's not a cop, he's just a guy, an Everyman who finds the strength to overcome that terror to save his life. But he doesn't do it with trumpets and French horns!

The first score Mostow got was grandiose, epic Poledouris: great themes played on brass aided by minimal synth work. Guitar also had an important role, playing a simple, often-recurring theme that slowly deconstructed, like the hero. Yet this was not what Mostow had in mind. He wanted something more modern-sounding, with synth textures and a hint of Italian Western music. Unfortunately, he only made up his mind about the music's direction once Poledouris's entire score had been recorded. Realizing this was a mistake on his part, Mostow gave the composer a second chance to do a completely different score, as Poledouris explains:

> I wrote three scores—well, two and a half. Jonathan Mostow and I talked a lot about the style of music he was looking for, and it came around to Bernard Herrmann. Dino De Laurentiis, whom I hadn't worked with in twenty years, since *Conan*, wanted a strong "tema"—theme. So the first time around, I came up with this idea of using guitars (because it takes place in the Southwest) and orchestra—and came up with this main theme which was...well, I wouldn't say that it was as much Bernard Herrmann as *Kimberly* was Georges Delerue. [*Note*: *Kimberly* was a 1999 film directed by Frederic Golcham. Following the director's desires, Poledouris wrote a theme for it that resembled one that Delerue might have written.] It was a pretty large orchestra. We came back, and Jonathan decided that it wasn't really what the film needed. So he decided that it should be more like Ennio Morricone than Bernard Herrmann. So we explored that approach, and that wasn't it either. From there it became very deconstructionist. We utilized a lot of synthesizers. Eric Colvin played the synths, Judd Miller played the EWI [Electronic Wind Instrument] (and got a lot of strange effects), and Steve Forman did the percussion. We ended up with those three instruments on the score—a drastically different approach. At first it really bothered me that Jonathan could be so flip about it, but in the end I think he really got a score that best represented the film's ideas.

Once the second score was recorded, Mostow still wanted to make a few last-minute music changes, but Poledouris had already moved on to scoring Paul Verhoeven's *Starship Troopers* (1997). So Mostow had Richard Marvin compose some additional music—more than twenty minutes of material for the first chase scene, the bank scene, and the entire showdown.

In the finished picture, the director mainly used Poledouris's second score, filling any holes in it with bits of Poledouris's first score and Marvin's additions. (Marvin would go on to score three more of Mostow's movies, including *U-571* and *Surrogates*.)

In 2011, La-La Land Records released a three-CD set of the music for *Breakdown*. It contains all of Poledouris's music (both the used and the unused cues) along with alternate takes and additional music by Richard Marvin and others.

■ **Air Force One** (1997)

Original composer: **Randy Newman**
Replacement composer: **Jerry Goldsmith**
Additional composer: **Joel McNeely**

Director's Wolfgang Petersen's *Air Force One* puts America's President (played by Harrison Ford) in the middle of a Russian terrorist attack in which he must take on the role of action hero.

Hired to provide its music was Randy Newman. Best known for his Disney and Pixar scores, Newman might seem an unlikely choice for such an action movie, whose makers wanted a big patriotic score with action music à la James Horner or Jerry Goldsmith—exciting percussive music for fights and threatening mood pieces for less physical confrontations. At the time, Newman's recent credits included *James and the Giant Peach* (1996), *Toy Story* (1995), and *Maverick* (1994).

Once Newman's busy action score (which was heavily "mickey-moused," acknowledging almost every onscreen punch and gunshot) was completed, the filmmakers found fault with the way it depicted the movie's villains as comic foils rather than serious evildoers. Yet it was its musical depiction of the President that finally led to its rejection.

In action flicks, it is important to keep the music "straight." This is because the acting, the visuals, and the effects are often so far over the top that introducing exaggerated elements into the music can disturb the comedy-drama balance, and cause audiences to chuckle at inappropriate times. Petersen felt that Newman's pumped-up main theme—which borrowed a few bars from Beethoven's Ninth Symphony—did just that. Feeling that it was making fun of the picture's basic concept, the filmmakers discarded Newman's otherwise excellent score. A new one was commissioned from Jerry Goldsmith, a composer who could write a straight patriotic score in his sleep. Goldsmith's recent credits included *L.A. Confidential* (1997), *Fierce Creatures* (1997), and *The Ghost and the Darkness* (1996).

With only two weeks to pen and record his score, Goldsmith called on composer Joel McNeely (whose recent credits included *Vegas Vacation* and *Squanto)* for some additional music.

For *Air Force One,* Goldsmith pulled some poignant and patriotic material out of his hat. For the movie's main theme, he reworked some of his noble music from *Star Trek: First Contact* (1996). But the film's most inspired and memorable music is a Slavic choral motif that underscores the Russian terrorists toward the movie's end. (Accompanying cinema Russians with choral music has been almost compulsory since Basil Poledouris's influential *The Hunt for Red October* score in 1990.)

Although the Goldsmith music was an apt, if perhaps not inspired, replacement, Newman's unused score would be one of the few rejected works to get the industry talking about the score-replacement phenomenon. *Troy*, for which James Horner wrote a score to replace Gabriel Yared's, would create a similar stir in 2004.

Randy Newman's unused score clearly showed that he could write excellent material outside his usual and/or favored genres, and other Hollywood composers complimented him on it. The following comment by Hans Zimmer reveals a lot about the current state of music in Hollywood (and provides the likeliest reason why Newman's score was rejected):

> I heard it [Randy Newman's rejected score] and said, "I have never written an action cue as good as this. And I'm supposed to be good at action stuff." Jerry Goldsmith did the replacement score. But when I saw the movie, I kept howling with laughter throughout the film.... It was all that overdone patriotism. I just thought it was hilarious. And I know that as a cynic, Randy's patriotic themes reflected a twinkle in the corner his eye. But I think they caught him at it. And the one thing you can't do when you're being cynical or satirical is get caught at it. I should know. I got caught at it big-time in *Broken Arrow*. But I wanted to be caught. I didn't think we could sell an audience this bill of goods as a serious movie.

■ **Drive** (1997)

Original composer: **David C. Williams**
Replacement composer: **Walter Werzowa**

The martial arts movie has been a popular genre in China since the late 1940s, when a long stream of Cantonese-language films featuring the character Wong Fei Hong began to be produced. In the 1960s, Hong Kong became the center of martial arts filmmaking with a new style of special-effects-laden Mandarin-language films. And in the 1970s, martial arts star Bruce Lee's popularity in such movies as *Enter the Dragon* (1973) brought the genre international prominence. Elements from martial arts films began to creep into American independent features in the late 1960s and early 1970s in such popular youth-oriented fare as *The Born Losers* (1967) and *Billy Jack* (1971), which starred Tom Laughlin, and such popular blaxploitation films as *Three the Hard Way* (1974) and *Black Belt Jones* (1974), which starred Jim Kelly. In the 1980s, Hong Kong–based martial arts star Jackie Chan both revitalized and altered the genre, adding a good bit of humor and further broadening its international audience. The popularity of the 1984 family movie *The Karate Kid* gave martial arts films mainstream legitimacy.

In 1998, Jackie Chan paired up with Chris Tucker to make *Rush Hour*, a comedic martial arts buddy movie that did very well at the box office but was a far cry from the real Hong Kong martial arts movie in spirit. However, one year before *Rush Hour*, Steve Wang had directed *Drive*, a comedic buddy picture that many aficionados of the genre consider true to the spirit of the Asian martial arts film. The picture teams up a bionically enhanced martial artist with a wisecracking sidekick; together, the pair flee a small army of hit men. But as interesting as it was within its genre, *Drive* went directly to video without a theatrical release, except in a few Asian markets.

Drive's director commissioned an exciting orchestral adventure score from composer David C. Williams, whose recent credits included *No Way Back* (1995), *The Prophecy* (1995), and *American Yakuza* (1993). Its heavily percussive action music was colored with electronic effects and a harmonica that lent a Southern feel to some scenes. Unfortunately, the picture was deemed too long, so, against Wang's wishes, several scenes were cut. Not surprisingly, the dropped footage was mostly character-building material, and its removal rendered much of *Drive*'s plot senseless.

Along with this major edit came a request from the producers for a new score; they believed the movie would do better with a harder rock-music sound that featured techno elements. In the face of opposition from Wang, they asked Williams to write a new score along these lines. But he declined, believing that Wang had the right idea about what the picture needed musically.

When the picture was released as a DVD in 1998, a year after its completion, a score by Walter Werzowa had been added. Werzowa's previous credits included *Countdown* (produced in 1996 by Overseas Film Group, the company behind *Drive*), three episodes of the TV show *Tales from the Crypt*, and Intel's famous five-note "Bong" jingle. Werzowa's score for *Drive* was loud and busy, matching the newly concentrated action material. However, it didn't convey the emotional qualities of Williams's music, and its straight-to-video, action-fodder style detracted from the movie's martial arts sensibility.

By the time *Drive* arrived in video shops, *Rush Hour* was in theaters, making *Drive* seem like a *Rush Hour* knockoff, despite the fact that it had been completed a year before the other film. Today one can enjoy a *Drive* director's cut DVD in which all the tampering has been reversed, not only reinserting the movie's lost twenty minutes but also reinstating Williams's score. (A suite from this score can also be heard at the composer's website.)

In 2000, David C. Williams once again had a score replaced. The movie was *Civility*, the story of a boy seeking his rightful inheritance by avenging his father's death in a small Arizona town. Williams played to the film's setting with music that had an Americana vibe, but when the producers couldn't find a distributor for the film, they replaced the score with one that had a pop and hip-hop sound, by Brad Segal and Nic. tenBroek.

■ The Disappearance of Garcia Lorca (aka **Death in Granada**) (1997)

Original composer: **Ángel "Cucco" Peña**
Replacement composer: **Mark McKenzie**

Puerto Rican director Marcos Zurinaga's *The Disappearance of Garcia Lorca*, based on books by Ian Gibson (*The Assassination of Garcia Lorca* and *Federico Garcia*

Lorca: A Life), is the fictional and speculative tale of an exiled Spanish journalist (played by Esai Morales) who returns to Spain in 1954 (while it is still ruled by fascist dictator Francisco Franco) to investigate the 1936 disappearance and death of Spain's revered poet and dramatist Federico Garcia Lorca (Andy Garcia). Although it is known that thirty-eight-year-old Garcia Lorca was murdered by right-wing forces very shortly after the outbreak of the Spanish Civil War, the exact details of his death remain a mystery today.

Zurinaga's previous directing credits included the features *Tango Bar* (1988) and *La gran fiesta* (1985) and a number of documentaries. A Spanish- and Latin-tinged score was provided for *Garcia Lorca* by the scorer of *La gran fiesta*, Zurinaga's friend Ángel "Cucco" Peña. Peña is a noted Puerto Rican composer–arranger–music director who has worked with many popular Latin music stars, including Willie Colón, Celia Cruz, Jóse Feliciano, Ricky Martin, and Gloria Estefan.

With its fascinating subject matter and the use of some well-known American actors, Zurinaga's little independent English-language movie caught the attention of American distributor Triumph Films. But as the picture (which premiered in England in 1996 but did not get its worldwide release until 1997) received growing acclaim, Zurinaga was persuaded to part with his friend's score, which some felt didn't have enough emotional bite to underscore the tragic story. Thus composer Mark McKenzie, who had worked as an orchestrator for Bruce Broughton, Marc Shaiman, Randy Edelman, and Danny Elfman, came to the project. Among McKenzie's scoring credits were *Dr. Jekyll and Ms. Hyde* (1995), *My Family* (1995), and *Frank & Jesse* (1995).

McKenzie recalls starting the project:

> It was a very special project and it was also painful in some ways. They had thrown out the score by a dear friend of the director and had used up all their money and time. When they asked me, I had an immediate liking for the director because he had artistic vision, passion, and a really big heart. It was painful for me to have to say, "No, I will not do it given these parameters, because it will not be what the film deserves." The director, who also was the producer, had to make some difficult monetary decisions. Fortunately, he believed strongly in me and insisted that he wanted me to compose the score. I was very happy that he was able to come up with enough money to produce the score properly. It was so painful for both of us to have to put each other through this. Once I began composing, I knew that every penny being spent on the music was personal hard-earned money, so there was a special sense of responsibility to make it great.

McKenzie delivered a high-quality, theme-based score that featured flamenco singer Manolo Segura, whose vocal performance lent the score a Spanish touch. McKenzie's music worked well for Zurinaga's movie, and the director was grateful for the composer's help. (*Note*: Some of Peña's score was retained in the picture, used mostly as source music.)

A somewhat similar instance of the replacement of a director's friend's score is Roland Emmerich's *Moon 44* (1990). When the production moved from Germany to

America, composer Joel Goldsmith was hired, despite the fact that Emmerich's friend Kuno Schmid had already completed twenty minutes of music for the film.

■ **Kiss the Girls** (1997)

Original composer: **Carter Burwell**
Replacement composer: **Mark Isham**

Kiss the Girls, starring Morgan Freeman and Ashley Judd, is a thriller based on the second in James Patterson's series of novels featuring the character Alex Cross, a forensic psychologist. In this story, Cross (Freeman), working with the Washington, DC, police, is on the trail of a serial kidnapper-rapist-murderer known as Casanova. The movie was directed by Gary Fleder, whose one previous theatrical feature was *Things to Do in Denver When You're Dead* (1995).

Carter Burwell, an expert in providing interesting scores for small films, was hired to furnish the music. Among Burwell's recent scoring credits were *Conspiracy Theory* (1997), *Assassin(s)* (1997), *Fear* (1996), and *Fargo* (1996). With the filmmakers having already licensed a number of songs for the movie performed by such big-name artists as John Lee Hooker, James Brown, and Little Richard, *Kiss the Girls*' small music budget was already a bit stretched before Burwell came aboard. So Burwell was asked to write and perform a synthesizer score. The composer, however, wanted to include live players in the music, and did so. But his musical efforts fell on unreceptive ears, as he recalls:

> Originally all they wanted was a synthesizer score, one person playing a synthesizer—they had a very small budget—and I got them to broaden it to be enough for a string quintet and a few other players. So it ended up being a string quintet, piano, heavily processed electric guitar, Bulgarian bagpipes, Bulgarian flute, and percussion. And it actually came together really well. I was really proud, and I guess in the end it was just a little too strange for Paramount Pictures, or for the director. And the director had liked it all; when we were recording it, he was present and was enjoying it, but a few weeks after we recorded it he came by and asked me if I could do a more conventional score for him.... I think he felt the movie as made and with that music was just going to appeal to a smaller audience; it was going to be looked on as a kind of arty psychological thriller. Whether it was him or Paramount Pictures, I could never say who was driving a decision like this.

A replacement score was commissioned from Mark Isham, whose recent scoring credits included *Afterglow* (1997), *Night Falls on Manhattan* (1997), *Fly Away Home* (1996), and *Home for the Holidays* (1995). But after paying for Burwell's score, little money remained for Isham to work with. So he wrote his music to rely heavily on synthesizers and samplers, which provided dark textures and percussive bursts of sound, and only a few acoustic instruments, to highlight the story's human elements.

Particularly noteworthy in this respect is the cue "Casanova," which underscores the killer's deranged mind with a creepy violin solo.

While *Kiss the Girls* is one of Isham's lesser achievements due to time and budget constraints, it works well on an atmospheric level, providing the picture with the necessary eerie sonic support.

■ The House of Yes (1997)

Original composer: **Jeff Rona**
Replacement composer: **Rolfe Kent**

When Jeff Rona published his book about film scoring, *The Reel World*, he made sure to include a couple of horror stories about the business's downside. His score-replacement story concerns "Arnold" (not his real name), a composer who spoke with Rona shortly after being fired from a film. Arnold's story isn't particularly unusual—it involves a composer who finds that the filmmakers he's working for want his score to mimic their temp track. As a creative person (and an honorer of other composers' copyrights), Arnold fights against aping the temp track too closely, and after months of artistic tug-of-war he is fired. The rejection leaves him questioning the viability of his career and even his own abilities. In his commentary on this tale, Rona points out that most score replacements have nothing to do with the quality of the music. Having faced score rejection himself, he speaks from firsthand knowledge. *The House of Yes* was one such experience.

First-time director Mark Waters' cleverly twisted comedy of dark family secrets is the story of a college student who brings his fiancée (Tori Spelling) home for Thanksgiving, where she is confronted by his dysfunctional and demented family: his just-out-of-the-institution twin sister (Parker Posey), who calls (and fancies) herself Jackie O and harbors some troubling secrets; his sullen younger brother (Freddie Prinze Jr.), and his thoroughly goofy mother (Genevieve Bujold). When Waters contacted Rona about scoring the film, it had just been accepted for screening at the Sundance Film Festival. The composer, meanwhile, was on a midseason break from his television work. (His scoring credits included numerous episodes of the popular television series *Chicago Hope*, *Profiler*, *Homicide: Life on the Street*, and the feature *White Squall*.)

Right at the start of their collaboration, Waters and Rona discovered that they had conceptual differences: Waters favored a lot of very short (five to ten seconds), transitionlike music cues, while Rona favored longer cues that allowed the music to add to and comment on scenes rather than simply plugging holes. But they soon seemed to find common ground on this issue, and Rona started composing. The director didn't want a typical comedy score, so Rona focused on the maniacal Jackie O character with a theme he described as a "twisted chromatic tango" played on a nylon-string guitar. For the main title cue (which played under quite a bit of dialogue), this theme was carried by soprano saxophone and flute as well. Rona discusses working under the filmmakers' close supervision:

> I had the producer and the director over to my studio during the entire time I was writing. Because of the compressed schedule I had them over every other day to approve cues and give notes. Fortunately, things were going well so far, and I started to get a number of cues signed off, meaning everyone agreed that they were accepted and finished. After cues are signed off, they are ready to record and mix. As cues were signed off, I gave MIDI files and DAT tapes of my demos to my orchestrator, who began preparing parts for the small ensemble of players I was using. Some cues had to go through two or three revisions before I came up with the goods that they would accept, but some cues got nailed on the first or second shot, so I was keeping up with the deadline more or less.

Rona's work was completed in only ten days—just in time for Sundance. But since he happened to be too ill to attend the final mixing sessions, the first time he saw the movie with its final mix was at the festival. He found his score disadvantaged by both the lack of a real music editor and, more importantly, the filmmakers' decision to push it into the background. Regardless of those problems, the movie was a hit at the festival, where it collected an award and was picked up for wide distribution by Miramax.

However, after holding a test screening for the film in New York, Miramax decided it needed some changes, and replacing its score was one of the cheapest ways to reinvent it without reshooting a single scene. It turned out that although Rona's music for *The House of Yes* had been approved by one of its producers, director Waters apparently had never been completely behind it. So, with Miramax's help, the project hired a new composer, Rolfe Kent, whose scoring credits included *Citizen Ruth* (1996), *Mercy* (1995), and *Dead Connection* (1994). (Kent had just begun a long collaboration with director Alexander Payne, which would turn him into an expert at scoring quirky comedies; after *Citizen Ruth*, Payne and Kent would work together on *Election*, *About Schmidt*, and *Sideways*.)

The House of Yes was a winner for Kent, whose score was based around an eccentric waltz that appeared in fairly short cues throughout the film. He would later write scores for four more Waters-directed films: *Freaky Friday* (2003), *Mean Girls* (2004), *Just Like Heaven* (2005), and *Ghosts of Girlfriends Past* (2009). For Jeff Rona, on the other hand, this score-rejection experience would become a cautionary tale that he could pass on to young composers. Four cues from it are presented on his website.

■ **The Gambler/A játékos** (1997)

Original composer: **Gerard Schurmann**
Replacement composer: **Brian Lock**

Hungarian director Károly Makk's *The Gambler* is an interesting tale about Russian novelist Fyodor Dostoyevsky's (played by Michael Gambon) addiction to roulette, based on his semiautobiographical novella that bears the same title. It was a European coproduction involving an array of producers and coproducers.

One of the producers, Marc Vlessing, contracted fellow Dutchman Gerard Schurmann to do the picture's music. Schurmann's scoring credits included *The Bedford Incident* (1965), *The Ceremony* (1963), and *The Third Key* (1956), but he had practically retired from film work following his score for the 1968 Hammer picture *The Lost Continent*. Since then, he had successfully pursued a concert music career, with the exception of two brief returns to film scoring in 1984. In the first one, he was informally hired to pen a score for director Richard Donner's *Ladyhawke*, a medieval fantasy picture that Schurmann worked on for a mere ten days (without a contract) before being replaced by composer Andrew Powell, who would provide a hilariously anachronistic pop score. After being bumped from *Ladyhawke*, Schurmann had made one more venture into film scoring, for the Italian movie *Claretta* (1984), which turned out to be a somewhat frustrating experience for him. So it took some persuading to get the septuagenarian to sign on to his final film assignment, *The Gambler*, thirteen years later. Schurmann recalls that troubled production:

> There were simply too many cooks and that was the trouble, because they all wanted to put their own things into it. When I got to Holland to do the picture and discuss the music with Károly, there was one producer there I didn't like. I said to Károly, "I don't want to do this film if I have to deal with this producer." He said, "Don't worry, I'll deal with the producers, you'll deal with me." Between him and me, we decided how the score should go. The trouble was they put a temp track into the movie and then the producers couldn't agree on the music!

After recording his score with the London Session Orchestra and the Crouch End Festival Chorus, Schurmann was surprised to learn that it wasn't going to be used. To rescore the film, its British producers turned to young British composer Brian Lock, whose two previous scoring credits were *Foreign Moon* (1996) and *Lagodna* (1995), a Polish film that, like *The Gambler*, was based on a Dostoyevsky work.

Lock recorded his score with the Prague City Philharmonic Orchestra, conducted by Stepán Konícek. But with all those cooks still in the kitchen, *The Gambler* arrived in theaters with a hodgepodge hybrid score that mostly utilized Lock's work but also retained a few of Schurmann's cues.

The film's titles credit both composers, and *The Gambler*'s soundtrack CD (on the Virgin Classics label) contains both scores. Taken side by side, it's easy to hear a distinct difference in the two composers' approaches: Schurmann's score takes a somewhat modern tack, while Lock's is unabashedly romantic, with a heavy reliance on piano solos.

With producer-heavy coproductions so frequent, it's only natural that the too-many-cooks problem manifests itself repeatedly in replacement scores. For example, director Paul Cox's *Molokai: The Story of Father Damien* (1999) was a Belgian, Dutch, and Australian coproduction that ended up with two scores because of the coproducing parties' differing musical visions. First, Belgian concert composer Wim Mertens wrote an essentially minimalist score that he recorded with his own ensemble. But Mertens's music was replaced with more traditional and lyrical music by Australian composer Paul Grabowsky. Both composers' scores are available on CD, although not on the same disc.

■ **The Wings of the Dove** (1997)

Original composer: **Edward Shearmur**
Alternate composer: **Gabriel Yared**

The Academy Awards can have a huge impact on a composer's career, but that impact is not always purely positive. Gabriel Yared's win for *The English Patient*, for instance, pigeonholed him in the romantic drama genre, and led to his unfulfilling experience on the romantic drama *The Wings of the Dove* the following year.

Starring Helena Bonham Carter, *The Wings of the Dove* was a beautifully photographed and well-acted film by English director Iain Softley, whose previous credits included *Backbeat* (1994) and *Hackers* (1995). Based on Henry James's 1902 novel of the same title, it's a fairly complicated story about a dying wealthy woman and the strange, morally corrupt love triangle into which she's drawn. This James tale had been adapted for film a number of times in the past: As a teleplay it appeared on the series *Studio One in Hollywood* (1952) and *Playhouse 90* (1952), and in England in two BBC versions (1965 and 1979); a French feature film version starred Isabelle Huppert and was directed by Benoît Jacquot in 1981. Softley's critically acclaimed rendition would garner four Oscar nominations, five BAFTA nominations and two wins, and award attention from numerous other organizations, including the Golden Globes, the Screen Actors Guild, and the Writers Guild.

Hired to score the film was up-and-coming British composer Ed Shearmur, whose scoring credits included *The Leading Man* (1996), *Demon Knight* (1995), and *The Cement Garden* (1993). But Harvey Weinstein, head of Miramax, the movie's distributor, wanted to punch up *The Wings of the Dove* with a replacement score by recent Oscar winner Gabriel Yared, a Lebanese-born composer whose previous credits included *Map of the Human Heart* (1993), *Vincent & Theo* (1990), and *Betty Blue* (1986). Yared recalls his involvement:

> The distributor of *The English Patient* [Harvey Weinstein/Miramax] was so impressed by my score that he proposed my name to the director of *The Wings of the Dove*, Iain Softley, to replace the composer already on board, who had composed almost the whole score. The producer felt that the film needed more emotional themes...so I met with the director, I listened to the music already recorded by Ed Shearmur and I found it very interesting and I said to the director, "Listen, this music is good, what more do you want me to do?" He told me then that this was neither his wish, nor his choice. So I was in a very awkward situation. I have never ever—and I will never ever—replace anybody. This

> was my only and first and last experience in replacing a composer. I found it very difficult, very unethical, actually, to replace a score that I believe is good—jump on a project at the last minute and replace a good composer, but yet, I didn't know a lot about the Hollywood business; I had only composed for French and European films. So I accepted to do this job and I did my best to compose the music.

Yared wrote a chamber orchestra score that was exotically tinted with Asian percussion. But, perhaps on the director's insistence, the tables turned again, and Shearmur ended up as the picture's final composer after all. His impressionistic music worked very well. Yared:

> In the end the director went back to his previous composer and I was so relieved and happy that he got in the end what he had wanted since the beginning, because, in a way it's completely insane to try to replace a composer, especially if he already had a long and good relationship with the director. You know, a director spends time with a composer, he spots his film, he explains to him how he wants things to go, and he is happy with his composer; what's the point of replacing him? So this was my only, first and last, experience in replacing anybody's work and, in the end, my score was replaced by Ed Shearmur's score. I was just like—happy. Relieved and happy. My first and last experience in replacing, but not in being rejected. Actually I can say that the score Ed Shearmur did for *The Wings of the Dove* was excellent. I did my job and, although I had composed, I think, a good score, I was really happy. Deep in my heart, happy and relieved to know that the previous composer was again onboard.

In 2000, musical indecision would again cause Miramax to waffle between composers. For *Chocolat*, the distributor alternated between using music by Rachel Portman and Luis Enriquez Bacalov before finally opting to go with the former composer.

■ **Below Utopia** (aka **Body Count)** (1997)

Original composer: **Ice-T**
Replacement composer: **Joseph Williams**

In the 1990s, a number of rappers and DJs known for their songwriting and producing skills tried their hand at movie scoring. In most of these ventures the artist's score was tied to his or her on-screen performance in the picture.

Well-known rapper and actor Ice-T wrote a score for *Below Utopia* (retitled *Body Count* for its home video release), a little thriller directed by Kurt Voss, whose directing credits included *Baja* (1996), *Horseplayer* (1990), and *Border Radio* (1987). With Ice-T as one of its stars, the picture told the story of a young man and his girlfriend who must hide from and fend off a gang of murderous home-invasion thieves who've just killed his family.

Although Ice-T had frequently produced songs for movies he appeared in, such as *Ricochet* (1991), *Below Utopia* was his first attempt at a full film score, and he came up with a surprisingly moody ambient electronic score for it. (This music can be heard on his album *Below Utopia: The Lost Score.*) But the filmmakers eventually opted to take a different musical path, hiring Joseph Williams (son of film composer John Williams) to replace Ice-T's score. Williams was a member of the rock band Toto; his scoring credits included *Phat Beach* (1996), *The Legend of Gator Face* (1996), and *Last Gasp* (1995).

A number of other rap artists have involved themselves in writing movie music: RZA, for example, wrote an effective score for Jim Jarmusch's *Ghost Dog: The Way of the Samurai* (1999), but he would have less success on several later projects, including *Derailed* (2005) and *Freedom Writers* (2007), neither of which ended up with an RZA underscore. Among DJs, the one who made the transition to film scoring with the greatest ease was Brian Transeau (aka BT), who has written scores for such critically acclaimed movies as *Go* (1999) and *Monster* (2003), as well as mindless entertainments like *The Fast and the Furious* (2001).

■ **Babylon 5: "The Gathering"** (Special Edition, 1998)

Original composer: **Stewart Copeland**
Composer for Special Edition: **Christopher Franke**

Created by writer J. Michael Straczynski, television's popular sci-fi series *Babylon 5* got its start in February 1993 with the airing of its pilot show, "The Gathering." The series' first season began airing almost a year later, in January 1994, after which the show ran for five seasons.

Stewart Copeland, drummer for the rock band the Police and a prolific composer of movie and television music, scored the pilot. (Among his credits were the late-1980s films *Wall Street, Talk Radio,* and *See No Evil, Hear No Evil.*) The most memorable aspect of his score for "The Gathering" was its propulsive main theme, despite the fact that much of it was drowned out by an introductory voiceover. The music spotting for the pilot was sparse compared with that of the series installments that would follow, all 110 episodes of which would be scored by Christopher Franke. (Franke had been a member of the German synth band Tangerine Dream from 1971 through 1988. His scoring credits included numerous made-for-TV movies and episodes of such series as *Raven* and *M.A.N.T.I.S.*, while among Tangerine Dream's many credits were *Risky Business, Wavelength,* and *Firestarter.*)

Before Franke was hired as the series' composer, Copeland was offered the job, but he turned it down, not wanting to deal with a series' day-to-day concerns. This decision has generated speculation about what caused Copeland's music to disappear from the show's pilot in 1998, when TNT aired a new version of "The Gathering" that had been modified to improve its pacing and make it conform to the series' format. Attempting to retroactively make a show's pilot more like the episodes that followed it is not a new practice (see this book's entry on *Seinfeld*'s pilot). On his message board, writer Straczynski detailed some of the ways in which the revamped pilot differed from its original incarnation:

> While there were some areas we couldn't get into because of the complexity in redoing the mix, virtually every scene got tinkered with to one degree or another, and most important, the roughly fourteen minutes of footage left out of the original version is now back in. The whole thing is tighter and faster, and there's more recent CGI, we'll have [sic] Chris Franke rescore it, and it's just in general a lot better. (Some parts of it even make more sense now.) One additional change: because of the desire on PTEN's [Prime Time Entertainment Network, a short-lived (1993–97) TV network] part to have as many commercial breaks as possible, the six-act script was jerry-rigged and broken down into nine acts. One side effect of this is that nine acts wear on you, and wear you out, more than the standard six. You start to get a feeling of being led up to things too often, and there isn't time to dwell on the act you're in. I was finally able, with this re-edit, to move scenes back around again to what I originally wanted in a six-act structure (you'll see a number of scenes juxtaposed from their original order).

The reshaped pilot's new score provided a unique opportunity for Franke to spread his series themes and sound designs, including excerpts from existing series cues, into the pilot. With this accomplished, the whole show had a unified voice.

On CD, Franke's music for *Babylon 5* is one of the most fully represented television series scores of all times. With dozens of its episodes' scores available, it's surprising that his music from "The Gathering" hasn't been released.

Generally speaking, television pilots have been rescored for a variety of reasons. In 2008, for example, the pilot episode of TV's *Terminator: The Sarah Conner Chronicles* underwent corrective surgery in the editing room to remove a school shooting scene that might remind viewers of the April 2007 Virginia Tech massacre, which had occurred between the time when the pilot was filmed (January–February 2007) and its initial airing (January 2008). After undergoing content changes, the pilot lost its score by Blake Neely, replaced by one by Bear McCreary, who would score all of the series' other episodes. (*Note*: Brad Fiedel penned the show's theme music.)

■ **Les Misérables** (1998)

Original composer: **Gabriel Yared**
Replacement composer: **Basil Poledouris**

If cinema history is any indicator, French author Victor Hugo's classic, sprawling 1862 novel *Les Misérables* is a story well worth revisiting and reinterpreting. It has been adapted for film and television more than forty times. It also has been adapted for radio (by Orson Welles) and stage, including the musical stage, where it was made into one of the world's most successful musicals. Hugo's panoramic story of the power of mercy and redemption, set in the first half of the nineteenth century, in the roughly twenty years immediately following the Napoleonic Wars, provided commentary on society, politics, justice, and morality.

The 1998 American production, helmed by Danish director Bille August (whose directing credits included *Smilla's Sense of Snow*, *House of the Spirits*, *Best Intentions*, and *Pelle the Conqueror*), retained the most of the novel's key themes and characters within its 135-minute running time. But despite a stellar cast that included Liam Neeson, Geoffrey Rush, Uma Thurman, and Claire Danes, the movie flew below most moviegoers' radar.

August hired composer Gabriel Yared, a recent Oscar winner for *The English Patient* (1996), to score the picture. (Among the composer's other recent scoring credits were *Tonka*, *Wings of Courage*, and *Map of the Human Heart*.) Yared recalls his work on the project:

> Bille August called me just after the Oscars night and said, "We are starting to shoot in Prague, come to see us on the set." So I came to Prague and I looked at some images in the editing room. I went to see the editor and went to see the actors because this is what I like, also—to go on the set, to meet the actors, the actresses, visit the editor, and start to "smell the flavor" of the film before it gets to be finished. And I started composing, and slowly I discovered that this director had not a real interest in music—he was probably not sensitive to music. He was anchored in his musical habits, and his habits were not my cup of tea. He didn't know a lot about the effect of music on a picture and what he was expecting from me was just to be kind of like wallpaper. So, when I started composing and I found out I had no deep relationship with him on this musical level, I started to wonder how this is going to end up, and I remembered being in Abbey Road Studios in London, with a huge, large orchestra of a hundred pieces, and the director saying not a word about the music, not having any reaction, any feedback, any comment, and I understood while I was recording that, well, this was an insane relationship. It was like a doomed relationship.

Yared wrote and recorded his score despite his reservations about the director's musical sensibilities. He wrote epic music, aiming to capture the scope of Hugo's novel. The score had themes that were easily adapted into both powerful action music and deeply lyrical passages, which sought to capture the story's essence, the theme of redemption.

However, Yared feared from the start that his music might not make it to the finished film, and he was right:

> When I learned that I was fired, I was not at all surprised, I knew it—I understood—working with a director is a kind of marriage. This marriage was doomed. We were not able to share anything. Let's say there was nothing between him, probably, and music. So what he was expecting from me was just to, you know, paint here and there some colors and especially not to be personal—especially not to be empathic or lyrical. He just wanted drones and basses playing along one single note and holding it forever and I remember my last chance was when I had two or three sessions with a large orchestra and he told me, "Just play one note," so I would tell the orchestra to play "F"—all the

> double basses, all the celli, all the horns—and he said, "I am happy with that." I said, "Okay, well...let's hope that this will stop somewhere," and it stopped—I was fired, and I was really happy to be fired. Happy...Yeah, it's terrible, but it's true! When it goes this way, when it looks useless, what can you do? I tried and tried to stick with him, tried to explain—to widen his range of interests, but if there is no more communication, well, the best thing is to split and go. And I was happy when he said, "Okay, I am moving to another composer." Actually, the reason he came to me was probably wrong, some reason related to the success of *The English Patient*, but he didn't come to me for artistic reasons, for my music.

The new composer was Basil Poledouris, no stranger to epic scores (e.g., *Conan the Barbarian* and *Flesh + Blood*). Poledouris's recent scoring credits included *Starship Troopers* (1997), *Switchback* (1997), and *The War at Home* (1996). After the project's composer change, production company TriStar Pictures became more directly involved with the music, to ensure there would be no further problems. The producers wanted a score with lots of action, and the director asked Poledouris to give the music a sense of repression, which he did by incorporating a muted quality into the darkest passages. August also asked Poledouris to try to remain faithful to the era while not becoming too technically historical. The composer readily embraced this request:

> I wanted to keep the score in the period of the film, if anything, in the style of Berlioz. I tried not to become any more complicated harmonically or melodically than would have been relevant for that era. It just seems that if an art director and costumer and director of photography and director work hard to create a moment in time, why shouldn't a composer? There is a reason why we don't see jet planes or cell phones in 1700 [sic] France. Why should we be subjected to the same kind of intrusions musically? Romanticism wasn't around yet, which may feel as if the melody doesn't soar, nor were Bizet or Wagner with their grand orchestration. One of the goals of the music was to provide a restless urgency or undercurrent to represent the ever-threatened Jean Valjean by Javert. The other requirement was to keep the temperature medium to cool. This was a directive by Bille [August], and what he was asking was that by not letting the music become overly passionate or romantic that a tension would be created. As if this guilt of Valjean's was just below the surface and he needed to keep himself in check and not let his emotions betray his feelings.

Les Misérables proved to be one of Basil Poledouris's best scores.

■ The Horse Whisperer (1998)

Original composer: **John Barry**
Replacement composer: **Thomas Newman**

The Horse Whisperer, based on the best-selling novel by Nick Evans, marked actor-director Robert Redford's first time as star of a movie that he also directed. Redford's previous directing credits included *Quiz Show* (1994), *A River Runs Through*

It (1992), and *The Milagro Beanfield War* (1988). *The Horse Whisperer* tells the story of a physically and emotionally scarred girl and her injured horse, both of whom are healed by a horse whisperer (a horse trainer who uses kindness as his primary tool), who also strikes up a romantic relationship with the girl's mother.

Brought in to score the picture was film music legend John Barry, whose recent credits included *Swept from the Sea* (1997), *Across the Sea of Time* (1995), and *Cry, the Beloved Country* (1995). He also had scored three films that starred Robert Redford: *The Chase* (1966), *Out of Africa* (1985), and *Indecent Proposal* (1993). Barry's elegantly sweeping music for *The Horse Whisperer* captured the beauty of the picture's Montana setting and the exhilaration of horseback riding, but it perhaps failed to reflect the story's inner world—particularly its darker moments and the girl's troubled mind. Redford did not completely buy the composer's musical take on his film, and Barry was not keen on revisions and rewrites. (In his later years Barry became quite uncompromising and was notorious for sticking to his musical vision. The same year he worked on *The Horse Whisperer* he also scored *Mercury Rising*, a failed Bruce Willis action movie for which he refused to revise any of his cues. Consequently, Carter Burwell penned most of the film's action material.)

Redford turned to composer Thomas Newman, whose score for *The Shawshank Redemption* (1994) had featured prominently in *The Horse Whisperer*'s temp tracks. Among Newman's recent scoring credits were *Oscar and Lucinda* (1997), *The People vs. Larry Flynt* (1996), and *Phenomenon* (1996).

The general tone of Newman's score for *The Horse Whisperer* was more reflective than that of Barry's work. Although it also had some beautiful, lush orchestral passages, much of Newman's varied and colorful score was intimate: sometimes folk-influenced, featuring fiddle, guitar, and mandolin, and sometimes wistful and moody, featuring unusual and complex sample-based textures over which simple piano music often drifted. It also contained a few lovely little chamber music cues. Overall, the score captured the film's rustic landscape with a gentle Americana sound that ventured in and out of rich orchestral writing. It also commented on the characters' psychological states with its moody, floating textures.

As for John Barry's unused score, his 1998 concert work and concept album, *The Beyondness of Things*, is rumored to contain material from it, though just which of the suite's twelve tracks may be based on his *The Horse Whisperer* music has never been disclosed. The movement "The Day the Earth Fell Silent" is said to have been inspired by the assassination of John F. Kennedy, and "Childhood Memory" looks back to the day Barry's grade school was bombed during World War II. "Meadow of Delight and Sadness," on the other hand, is said to have been inspired by the Montana landscape, making it a likely candidate for music from *The Horse Whisperer*.

■ **Halloween H20: 20 Years Later** (1998)

Original composer: **John Ottman**
Additional music composer: **Marco Beltrami**

When *Halloween H20: 20 Years Later* (simply *H20* to its fans) was released, it was the seventh and last stand for a staggering franchise. The original 1978 *Halloween*, which was written, directed, and scored by John Carpenter and marked the screen debut of actress Jamie Lee Curtis, was a low-budget movie that paid off big at the box office. Its story of psychopathic killer Michael Myers (ever stalking heroine Laurie Strode) popularized and helped define the "slasher film" horror subgenre. Over a period of twenty years, it would spawn seven inferior (and sometimes downright abysmal) sequels. (The seemingly immortal Michael Myers reappeared yet again in 2007, when heavy metal musician and filmmaker Rob Zombie directed a remake of the original *Halloween*—followed two years later by a sequel to his remake!)

Halloween H20 resurrected the Laurie Strode character (and even brought back Jamie Lee Curtis), to give her one final showdown with Michael Myers. Its director, Steve Miner, previously had helmed the second and third installments of another popular horror franchise, *Friday the 13th.*

Assisting in Michael Myers *H20* resurrection was up-and-coming composer (and highly accomplished film editor) John Ottman, who had recently visited the horror genre with his score for the chilling *Snow White: A Tale of Terror* (1997). Ottman's non-horror scores included *The Usual Suspects* (1995), *The Cable Guy* (1996), and *Incognito* (1997).

Synthesizer scores had characterized *Halloween* and its sequels, so hiring Ottman to pen an orchestral score—including an orchestral arrangement of John Carpenter's popular and addictive little 5/4 synth theme—for the franchise's last installment marked quite a departure. The composer reflects on his own horror story as *H20*'s composer:

> I was hired to bump up the film to a slightly higher plane. The philosophy was to provide a Hitchcockian score that would be a little more intelligent than the expected horror score. So that's what I did. My goal was to make the film believable so that it would be scarier. I created a new theme for Laurie Strode that developed along with her throughout the film, because she is the real element that pulls the audience along. I also played a lot with "-isms" of Carpenter's themes throughout but in a new orchestral way. That's largely non-evident now.
>
> Everything was approved musically by the director and editor, and I was excited because it would be a great opportunity to show what can happen with a horror film if you use a thoughtful scoring approach, and make the effort. But the bomb went off when we started mixing the movie. Miramax wanted the music to be more like the obvious music in the temp score, which was very parody-like. We were in a rushed situation where Miramax [H20's production company, Dimension Films, was run by Miramax's co-chair Bob Weinstein] had a movie with super-high test scores temp tracked with obvious

> horror music. They didn't have time to test it with my score, of course, so the baby was thrown out with the bathwater. Director Steve Miner was shooting another film, and the editor was left to anticipate what the higher-ups would want by hiring a barrage of music editors to slice, dice, and rearrange the cues. After a while things were being shuffled for the sake of shuffling. Then "other" music [excerpts from Marco Beltrami's scores for *Scream* and *Mimic*] was brought in to supplement or replace my cues. To smooth out the edits between the *Scream* and *Mimic* music and my score, they flew Marco Beltrami up to provide synthesized effects, and the score became a mish-mash. So that's the story, in a nutshell.

Wes Craven's *Scream* (1996) and Guillermo del Toro's *Mimic* (1997) were highly successful horror films that would generate a number of sequels. And Beltrami's music for *Scream* had a huge impact on subsequent horror genre scoring: This sound became the musical calling card of Dimension Films, which produced *Scream, Mimic,* and *H20*. Beltrami recalls his *H20* assignment:

> I was called up to do this Halloween project, and was excited by it. I knew they had used *Scream* and *Mimic* in it, and it would be hard to make it match with another score. I don't know what the story was with John Ottman's score, but the movie tested well with the temp score, and my job was to come up there and make the *Scream* and *Mimic* score work with the music that had been composed and the original *Halloween* theme. I also had to make the *Scream* and *Mimic* stuff more to the nature of *Halloween*—take out some things that would identify it as *Scream* or *Mimic* music. That was my primary task. I feel bad for John [Ottman], that he had his score removed from the movie—I don't know what to say, but it happens. I guess it wasn't what the producers were looking for—I was just up there doing my job.

Not counting its source cues, the finished picture's music is two-thirds Ottman's work (heavily sliced and diced, as noted above) and one-third Beltrami's. And about half of Beltrami's contributions are actually tracks from his earlier scores for *Scream, Scream 2,* and *Mimic*.

Ottman released his *H20* work on a CD titled *Portrait of Terror*, which presented his score as it was originally written. While the CD's notes made no direct mention of the music's connection with *H20*, they did say that the disc was "a soundtrack of horror by the composer of *The Usual Suspects, Apt Pupil,* and *Halloween H20*" (*Touché,* Michael Myers!).

■ The Avengers (1998)

Original composer: **Michael Kamen**
Replacement composer: **Joel McNeely**

Composer Michael Kamen was unlucky in the mid-1990s, suffering a series of rejections (see, for example, this book's entry on his 1995 rejected score for *Assassins*). In 1998, rejection struck again by way of *The Avengers*.

The Avengers was a feature film based on the popular 1960s British television series of the same name, which aired around the world from 1961 through 1969. One of a wave of 1960s Cold War spy series, the show was unique in that it celebrated being fantasy-based rather than true-to-life, featuring wildly fanciful escapades by a pair of eccentric, quick-witted British spies: John Steed (played by Patrick Macnee) and Emma Peel (played by a few different actresses, but most famously by Diana Rigg). For its first few years, the series sported a jazz theme by British jazz saxophonist and composer John Dankworth. This was replaced in 1964 by a lighter, campier, longer, yet still jazz-based theme by British film and TV composer Laurie Johnson. It is the memorable Johnson theme that most people associate with the show.

The film version of Steed and Peel's adventures starred Ralph Fiennes and Uma Thurman and was directed by Jeremiah Chechik, whose directing credits included *Benny & June* (1993) and *Diabolique* (1996), the latter a sequel to Henri-Georges Clouzot's classic 1955 film of the same title. Hired to pen *The Avengers'* music was Michael Kamen, whose recent scoring credits included *The Winter Guest* (1997), *Event Horizon* (1997), and *Inventing the Abbotts* (1997).

Kamen began work on his score in the autumn of 1997, delivering his first demos in December. He was asked to incorporate the television series' popular Laurie Johnson theme into his score, which was certainly a valid and logical request, but the 1960s material ended up sounding anachronistic alongside Kamen's new music. To try to make the old theme work, Kamen reorchestrated it; however, he was reluctant to use it heavily.

Soon—well before the movie had a finished edit and a finished score—the studio began holding test screenings, utilizing very rough footage and Kamen's unfinished music. The feedback was negative, and the studio had a panic attack. More test screenings were held, with equally bad results. Kamen:

> The sneak previews, always the sneak previews! First, in the States, the producers showed some dailies to a targeted audience: it went wrong, the movie was not working. There was maybe one hour's worth of footage, with the broad lines of my score played by an American orchestra. That's when the producers freaked out and decided to come to England to do the real test. It occurred in mid-March, in London. There, the previews went even worse: they were disastrous!

The Avengers had serious problems in all areas, but editing and music were the two that its producers could most quickly and easily revamp late in the game. (Once a picture is shot and deep into its postproduction phase, roles can't be recast even though some scenes can be reshot. But editing and music are always seen as disposable and infinitely variable!) In the picture's first round of studio-driven changes, it was cut from two hours to ninety minutes, leaving gaping plot holes. Dozens of sequences were removed, the opening changed completely, and the final battle was shortened, giving Steed (who many felt was miscast) the upper hand in it. As for the music, it had to be rewritten to fit this radically new edit. Kamen recalls the ensuing chaos:

> From that point, all things were rushed. I had to cancel all the concerts I had scheduled mid-March at Carnegie Hall in New York to rescore the picture. Jeremiah [Chechik] now wanted a closer identification to the original Laurie Johnson music, and to the TV series, but I was not particularly interested in doing that. *The Avengers'* score...turned into a James Bond movie score, see? In the Bond movies, I was always able to predict when the Monty Norman theme would play, because the musical and scriptwriting approach was so obvious. On *License to Kill,* I tried to play that tongue-in-cheek, but, again, they did not like it and made me change it. [Kamen scored *License to Kill* in 1989] On *The Avengers,* what they wanted was some Michael Kamen, then the Laurie Johnson theme, then some more Michael Kamen...there was no room for identity, and certainly no room for playing it tongue-in-cheek. Yet I managed to rewrite my score, for a new cut of the movie, which was faster and drier. Unofficial recording sessions took place here in London, then we came back during April. Then, the clash. Nobody understood my approach, or should I say nobody tried to understand it....

After Kamen had spent an incredible amount of time and energy on the movie's score, he and the filmmakers finally parted ways. As it happened, he already had another commitment awaiting him, scoring Richard Donner's *Lethal Weapon 4.*

After Kamen's departure, producer Jerry Weintraub hired composer Joel McNeely, who was working on the producer's simultaneous production, *Soldier* (1998). McNeely's recent credits included *Buffalo Soldiers* (1997), *Wild America* (1997)—for which he had been the replacement composer—and *Vegas Vacation* (1997), a film that also was produced by Weintraub. However, McNeely's score, which would be celebrated by some film music fans, was unable to save *The Avengers,* a sorry picture that was spurned by critics and the public alike.

■ **Head On** (1998)

Original composer: **Philip Brophy**
Replacement composer: **Ollie Olsen**

Directed by Australian Ana Kokkinos, *Head On* is the story of Ari, a young, gay Greek-Australian man living in Melbourne. Alienated from both his conservative family and society at large, he searchers for his own identity in a gritty subculture that thrives on drugs, ambiguous sexuality, and techno music.

Head On's music was meant to underscore Ari's inherent duality—his Greek heritage and his newfound gay lifestyle. This idea was marvelously rendered into music by Australian composer-filmmaker Philip Brophy, who had previously worked with Kokkinos on her 1994 hourlong film about a Greek-Australian lesbian teen, *Only the Brave.* (Brophy's one previous feature scoring credit was for the 1993 film *Body Melt,* which he also wrote and directed.) In his *Head On* score, Brophy cleverly combined traditional Greek instruments with techno music elements in an unusual mix of source music and underscore:

> The work period on this film was quite detailed and covered a lot of territory in pre-production. This comprised extensive meetings with Ana [Kokkinos] and the supervisor for all the Greek music in the film, Irine Vela, a local expert, performer, and composer with a passionate interest in Greek music. Irine's band appears in the film, and Irine organized all the Greek-music musicians for the songs in the film. I engineered and produced all those recordings, which was great to do. I then reworked elements—individual fragments from the multi-track recording—into my composed score to produce a schizophrenic aural meld of traditional Greek instrumentation and harmony with viscerally electronic and digital manipulations of those elements. This was to symbolize the main character being caught between two worlds—one of his Greek parents' home and the other of his hedonistic gay nightclub realm.

But apparently director Kokkinos had a change of heart about the appropriateness of Brophy's music in her film. She replaced it with a score by Australian electronic music composer Ollie Olsen, whose previous work ran the gamut from experimental to pop and included music for the TV series *Raw FM* (*Head On* was his first feature score). Olsen's score was not as prominent in the film as Brophy's had been, and Vela's Greek songs often upstaged it. Nonetheless, it was nominated for the Australian Film Institute's award for Best Music Score.

Not all was lost for Brophy: His own Sound Punch record company released his *Head On* score on a CD titled *Filmmusic Vol. 1.*

■ Bram Stoker's Shadowbuilder (1998)

Original composer: **Guy Zerafa**
Replacement composer: **Eckart Seeber**

Shadowbuilder is an obscure horror movie about a priest who pursues a shadow-dwelling demon to a small town, where it sucks the souls out of unlucky locals while planning the sacrifice of a stigmata-bearing child during an upcoming solar eclipse. The flick was the directing debut of Jamie Dixon, a visual effects supervisor-producer-animator, and it merits mention here chiefly due to a couple of articles that Roman Deppe wrote about its music for *Film Score Daily*, an online arm of the magazine *Film Score Monthly*.

Deppe saw a preview screening of the unfinished film accompanied by its temp music tracks at the Fantasy Film Festival in Germany. Screened this way, *Shadowbuilder* provided an interesting look into temp scoring. The selection of tracks included excerpts from Christopher Young's *Hellraiser* (1987) and *Species* (1995), plus choral music from Jerry Goldsmith's *The Omen* (1976) and Patrick Doyle's *Needful Things* (1993). Oddly, even though *Shadowbuilder* didn't have an original score yet, Canadian composer Guy Zerafa (whose recent scoring work included the films *Redline*, *Vivid*, and *Sabotage*) was already listed in its credits. By the time the movie reached theaters, though, his score had been written, recorded...and replaced.

The new score came from Austrian-born Canadian Eckart Seeber, who was hired by *Shadowbuilder*'s executive producer Ash R. Shah of Imperial Entertainment. Seeber's previous scoring credits were *Island of Fire* (1990), *Legend of the Red Dragon* (1994), and *To the Ends of Time* (1996), the last of these also produced by Shah. His new wall-to-wall orchestra and chorus music was big and energetic and contained elements reminiscent of both contemporary and classic horror scores.

Seeber reflects on his work on the film:

> The producers, upon receiving Guy Zerafa's score, did not feel that his music was appropriate for the film and they rejected the soundtrack in its entirety. The film was co-produced by Imperial Entertainment of Los Angeles and Apple Creek Productions of Toronto. Apple Creek hired the original composer.... The medium that this composer works in is probably electronic and, I guess, no one really anticipated that the score could turn out to be at odds with what the producers wanted. I was told that the producers did not hear the score until it was already completely finished. Under the circumstances it was deemed necessary to replace the music, and since I have done a lot of orchestral work and my take on the film and work practice seemed to mesh well with what the producers wanted, I was hired to do the job.... I read the script first and already had a notion of what kind and style of music the film needed. The fact that the temp music was very close to what I already envisioned was reassuring and certainly made it possible to go right into the music creation process more swiftly. To some degree I accept the temp score as a helpful element in the way that it provides a ready guideline to what the producer/director is looking for.... I was fortunate to have been able to collaborate with both the producer and the director on this film.... After the score seemed basically agreeable with the producers and director, I would commence the orchestration process and record the material.

Eckart Seeber was originally given only three weeks to do his score—from writing to mixing—because the producers wanted to get the movie to the Cannes Film Festival. But he managed to get this expanded to a more reasonable seven weeks, and the idea of a Cannes screening was abandoned. The extended deadline also gave him the opportunity to work with the orchestra of his choice, the Ukrainian State Radio Orchestra and Chorus, conducted by Vladymir Sirenko, who spent a week recording the score. (The Sonovide Entertainment label released a CD of Seeber's score.)

Contrary to some claims, Zerafa's score wasn't electronic, it was orchestral. Furthermore, there were no quality issues with his music, which had been supervised and approved by the director. According to Zerafa, despite everybody's agreeing on the finished score, the music was dropped for a most curious reason: The film's CGI (computer-generated imagery) hadn't been completed on time, and to avoid blaming the digital effects company for the delay, the score was deemed unacceptable and in need of replacement. Thus the film's overall deadline could be pushed back without suggesting that the unfinished CGI was the cause.

■ The Eighteenth Angel (1998)

Original composer: **Simon Boswell**
Replacement composers: **Starr Parodi and Jeff Eden Fair**

Written by David Seltzer, who had penned scripts for *The Omen* (1976) and *The Hellstrom Chronicle* (1971), *The Eighteenth Angel* is the story of a Satanic sect of Etruscan monks led by a Father Simeon (played by Maximilian Schell), who seek the last of the eighteen children needed to bring about Lucifer's incarnation on Earth.

Hired to score the flick was British composer Simon Boswell, whose recent scoring credits included *American Perfekt* (1997), *Photographing Fairies* (1997), and *Perdita Durango* (1997). For *The Eighteenth Angel*, he completed a sinister, Gothic-sounding score that featured choral music. But before recording it, he quit the project for a number of reasons.

After being trotted out for test screenings, the picture was completely reimagined and revamped and turned into a gorefest. Even if Boswell had wanted to stay involved, the many reshoots caused such a delay that recording his score would have created schedule conflicts with the next three pictures he was committed to. Boswell discusses *The Eighteenth Angel*'s changes:

> I spent six weeks in Los Angeles working on the film with the director, William Bindley, during the course of which they had a test screening for a bunch of fourteen- to seventeen-year-olds. The script was quite interesting...it was kind of a supernatural thriller—but after this test-screening, all the kids who watched it wrote down a load of really helpful comments like "Didn't f****** scare me!" so they [the filmmakers] went away and re-shot a load of scenes. So before, people had simply fallen down some stairs, but now they fell and they were impaled on something. I really did not want to do another horror movie. It was a spooky film before, but it wasn't in any way gory, and they turned it into that, and I just thought, "I don't want to get involved in this," so I left.

After Boswell left the thriller-turned-slasher flick, the husband-and-wife composing team of Starr Parodi and Jeff Eden Fair took over its music. (Specialists in music for movie trailers, Parodi and Fair had scored many trailers for such popular films as *Species*, *Mulholland Falls*, and *GoldenEye*. They also had scored such TV movies as *Little Girls in Pretty Boxes* and *A Nightmare Come True*.) The duo's music for *The Eighteenth Angel* made extensive and effective use of a boys choir in a score built on horror-movie traditions. At the time, it was their most important feature work, and Parodi and Fair remain proud of it, more than once stating that it is among their favorite scores.

■ **What Dreams May Come** (1998)

Original composer: **Ennio Morricone**
Replacement composer: **Michael Kamen**

What Dreams May Come is a sentimental fantasy film based on a novel by Richard Matheson, a noted sci-fi and horror novelist-screenwriter who penned thirteen episodes of the classic *Twilight Zone* series and whose novel *I Am Legend* has been filmed three times under three different titles. It was directed by New Zealander Vincent Ward, whose directing credits included *Map of the Human Heart* (1993) and *The Navigator: A Medieval Odyssey* (1988). Filmed by cinematographer Eduard Serra and featuring Oscar-winning special effects, *What Dreams May Come* is a magnificent-looking movie (shot on Fuji Velvia, a film stock known for its vivid color and high resolution) that tells a supernatural tale about a couple, Chris and Annie (played by Robin Williams and Annabella Sciorra), who experience overwhelming tragedies and end up at afterlife's opposite ends—Chris in heaven and Annie (a suicide) in hell. With obvious references to Orpheus's underworld quest for Eurydice and Dante's *Inferno*, Chris travels to hell to rescue Annie.

Hired to score the picture was famed Italian film composer Ennio Morricone, whose recent scoring credits included *Bulworth* (1998), *Lolita* (1997), and *U Turn* (1997). For it, he wrote one of his most heartfelt and satisfying later scores, which featured great thematic development as well as revisiting a theme he had originally composed for the little-seen Italian picture *L'Assoluto naturale*. Its dark opening string textures recall Morricone's music for the reissue of the 1912 silent film *The Life and Death of Richard III* (the oldest surviving American feature film), while other string passages bring to mind his music for *Bulworth*. Due in part to the voice of Edda Dell'Orso, whose wordless vocals have graced many of Morricone's most famous scores, his music for *What Dreams May Come* felt religiously charged. And as the movie's focus turned to heaven, the composer added further—and not too subtle—religious references via extensive choral writing.

But while Morricone worked on his score, the picture kept changing, and by the time he completed it, many crucial scenes had been altered. Worse, once the music was recorded and paired with the film's powerful images, its heavy religious overtones struck the filmmakers as over-the-top. The score was tossed out. This rejection affected the composer greatly, and at a Los Angeles seminar held not long afterward, he said that he should have been given a second chance to satisfy the film's producers.

Replacing Morricone was Michael Kamen, whose recent scoring credits included *Lethal Weapon 4* (1998) and *The Winter Guest* (1997). Kamen:

> The main theme was taken from a song that I had written in the 1970s while in the New York Rock & Roll Ensemble. It was co-written with my best friend and fellow band member and oboist now known as Mark Snow [born Martin Fulterman]. The song was called "Beside You," and my wife suggested using it the first time we viewed the film. As

you probably know, the film had a complete score by one of our finest composers that the producers and Vincent Ward decided to replace. Additionally, there were also some lingering doubts about the final edit of the film—but not the release date.

Kamen took pride in the simplicity of the music he wrote for the picture:

> *What Dreams May Come* was indeed an accelerated schedule compared to most films, but I have inflicted myself with a reputation for doing things quickly (but never in a hurry)! *Robin Hood,* for instance, was over two hours of music written in roughly three weeks, although I had a good period of time (approximately twenty-five years!!!) to create the various themes. In a way, a film as dense and complicated in story and texture as *What Dreams May Come* actually benefits from a score that isn't dense and complicated. The "straight lines" that the music draws can make a film easier to comprehend, and the lack of time to question myself and try different approaches resulted in a feeling of "immediacy" and simplicity.

In America, the movie received a lukewarm reception from both critics and the public, bringing in about $55 million at the box office (against its estimated $85 million production costs). But it was better received internationally, breaking the opening-weekend box-office record in Italy at that time. An amusing assessment of the film appeared in an interview with writer Richard Matheson, who said, "I will not comment on *What Dreams May Come* except to say that a major producer in Hollywood said to me, 'They should have shot your book.' Amen."

■ **Practical Magic** (1998)

Original composer: **Michael Nyman**
Replacement composer: **Alan Silvestri**

If you've listened to enough rejected scores and their replacements, you might notice that in many cases the differences in approach from score to score are minimal, and rejections actually seem to stem from either huge egos or deaf filmmakers. Not so with *Practical Magic,* where the difference between its two scores was dramatic, and the replacement turned an edgy dark comedy into something sweeter and more commercial.

Practical Magic is a romantic comedy in which Sandra Bullock and Nicole Kidman play sisters who are witches descended from a long line of witches. All the witches in the family, however, carry a curse: The men who fall in love with them suffer untimely and gruesome deaths. Directed by actor-turned-director Griffin Dunne, whose two previous directorial outings were *Duke of Groove* (1996) and *Addicted to Love* (1997), the movie was described by a *The New York Times* critic as "Barbie joins a coven."

However, Dunne originally designed his movie to be a bit offbeat, a step beyond standard romantic-comedy fare, and, in keeping with this concept he hired British composer Michael Nyman to do the music. Among Nyman's recent scores at the time were *Gattaca* (1997), *Der Unhold* (1996), and *Carrington* (1995).

Practical Magic also featured quite a few easy-on-the-ears pop songs by such well-known artists as Elvis Presley, Stevie Nicks, and Faith Hill. While Nyman wasn't required to write around these fluffy songs per se, his score's more outré cues may have worked against them. Confident, however, that his fairly eclectic material was what the director wanted, and proud of the fact that it wasn't a typical "Hollywood soundtrack," Nyman recorded it at Abbey Road Studios in London.

But somewhere along the line, the composer's and the filmmakers' musical visions diverged, and Nyman's music was thrown out. In a lengthy interview with *SoundtrackNet*, he expressed his anger over the treatment he and his score had received:

> What happened with *Practical Magic* was that I wrote the best score I think I've ever written for a film that engaged me not at all. It's a miracle how my relationship with Griffin Dunne and his encouragement to write a particular kind of score brought out a score from me that did all of the things I wanted it to do. It had the new Nyman lyricism, and had some very wild Greenaway kind of stuff. [*Note*: Nyman had written music that embraced a sort of raucous minimalism for seven features by British director Peter Greenaway, including *The Draughtsman's Contract*; *The Cook, the Thief, His Wife, and Her Lover;* and *Prospero's Books*, as well as numerous shorter films.] It had lots of irony, it was very sexy, it was humorous, it had some sleazy music, and it had some scary music. In terms of range, it was very diverse. In terms of quality, it was very high-quality. But when it was shown to the head honcho at Warner Bros., the film had a lot of problems as a film—the narrative didn't make sense, and Lorenzo di Bonaventura [President of Worldwide Production for Warner Bros. Pictures] took one look at it and said, "This score has got to go," not realizing, of course, that I had six weeks to work on the score—and they had two years to work on the film. So I was the whipping boy.

In an odd twist of fate, the movie's soundtrack CD was put together before Nyman's score was rejected, so in addition to the popular songs that made up the bulk of it, the disc's initial pressing contained two Nyman tracks: "Convening the Coven," wild Greenawayesque music from the end of the picture, and "Maria Owens," romantic music from the movie's beginning. (The first of these tracks was also released on the Virgin Records two-CD set *The Very Best of Michael Nyman: Film Music 1980–2001*.) Nyman:

> The soundtrack album was obviously recorded before my score was dumped, and I regret the fact that those cues are on the album because I think they're remarkable pieces of music—and they have no use whatsoever, except to sit in the archive of the people who have the CD. It did, at least, prove that I was involved in the project. I'm not saying that the score I wrote was in any sense a difficult score, but it's a totally different take than what an American would do. I've learned lessons from that, but I've not learned anything from them. I keep doing things my way, and if it works, it works. And if it doesn't, it doesn't.

Practical Magic's replacement score was done by Alan Silvestri, who engaged in a streak of lighthearted projects in 1998: *The Odd Couple II*, *The Parent Trap*, and *Holy Man*. His replacement score, a nice but not-too-challenging entry in his overall body of work, was composed in just twelve days, a period he described as his most demanding schedule ever. It avoided the eccentric emotional extremes of the rejected score and was considerably more a part of the Hollywood mainstream than Nyman's music. Tied together by a simple melody that undergoes a variety of treatments, it was upbeat and romantic and devoid of the dark features that Nyman had aimed for.

When a corrected soundtrack CD was issued, Nyman's two tracks were replaced by two of Silvestri's—"Practical Magic" and "Amas Veritas"—which displayed his romantic main theme and lush orchestra writing.

■ Playing by Heart (1998)

Original composer: **John Barry**
Additional composer: **Christopher Young**

Written and directed by Willard Carroll, *Playing by Heart* is an earnest yet lighthearted romantic comedy-drama performed by an attractive all-star cast. Structurally, it cuts back and forth among a half-dozen parallel love and relationship stories that eventually converge at the end.

Revisiting his jazz roots, John Barry provided the picture with a jazz-based score that employed trumpeter Chris Botti in a tribute to the popular, ever-melancholic trumpeter and singer Chet Baker (1929–1988), one of the most recognizable figures on the West Coast cool-jazz scene of the 1950s. In the spirit of many of Baker's recordings, Barry's bittersweet and sensuous score generally floated a trumpet playing sultry jazz lines (often aided by a piano trio) on a sea of lush strings. The score was somewhat reminiscent of (though more elegiac than) Barry's music for Lawrence Kasdan's 1981 neo-noir film *Body Heat.*

But as the film reached its final form, Barry's heartfelt score found itself pushed into the sonic background by a variety of songs performed by such popular artists as Bonnie Raitt, Moby, Morcheeba, P. J. Harvey, and Neneh Cherry, as well as some older music performed by such popular-in-their-day folk as Ray Anthony, Les Baxter, Laurindo Almeida, and even Chet Baker. (The film uses four Baker performances, including one of the 1940 tune "Everything Happens to Me," a song that Baker may very well have seen as autobiographical.) And, while Barry's name remained in the film's opening credits, a further portion of his score was also replaced by film composer Christopher Young, whose five cues garnered him a spot in the closing credits. The differences between Barry's sound and Young's—with its more improvised feel—is evident as one watches the movie.

Young remembers his involvement:

> The reason why I got involved with *Playing by Heart* was because I'd just finished working on *Rounders* for Miramax, and I was the "hot guy" over there at that time. What happened on *Rounders,* as you may or may not have heard, is that I wrote one score for it, and then I had to come back and rewrite another one very quickly. It didn't veer too

> far away from the original one, but they wanted it to be "beefed up" at certain moments. They were thrilled that I was able to get what Harvey Weinstein was looking for at such short notice, so when they were having problems with Barry's score I came in to salvage things. I hated doing it—you know how it is—but if I hadn't done it someone else would have, and I've had it done to mine. It's an unfortunate situation to be in. But the one thing I did do was save that score from being ditched entirely.... So there was this one camp who wanted to have it thrown out entirely, and there was another camp who wanted to retain as much as they possibly could. They knew they were going to have to get rid of some of the Barry score, but out of respect for Barry they wanted to hold on to as much as they could. So Miramax looked to me to be the doctor who was going to diagnose what was right and what was wrong. If I had said, "Well, I think the whole score is not working," they would have gone ahead and replaced the whole thing. What they wanted was something more contemporary. As great as Barry's stuff is, it's fifties jazz rather than nineties jazz. And Harvey hates jazz to begin with! But he had no choice.

Only two pieces from Barry's score ("Remembering Chet" and "End Game") made it onto the film's official Capitol Records soundtrack CD, which was otherwise packed with the current popular songs from the movie. However, Decca later released Barry's complete score on the CD *Playing by Heart*, an album whose cover (which features photos of Barry, Botti, and Baker) makes no reference to the movie, apart from the title (although Jon Burlingame's liner notes do). In addition to Barry's work, this CD features old recordings of Chet Baker performing three jazz classics that are not used in the movie: "Tenderly," "You Go to My Head," and "These Foolish Things (Remind Me of You)."

Although director Willard Carroll wanted to work with John Barry again on *Tom's Midnight Garden* (1999), the collaboration never moved beyond some informal contact, and Debbie Wiseman would end up scoring the film.

Barry again suffered a score replacement in 1999, when he worked with director Roland Joffé on the dark and steamy thriller-comedy *Goodbye Lover*. Once the film with Barry's score was put before a test audience, the filmmakers decided that the music was too straight; it didn't sufficiently emphasize the film's funny bits. They hired John Ottman to replace it with more lighthearted material, and in fact, some of the comedic ideas in Ottman's version—including extensive use of the classic tune "My Favorite Things" from *The Sound of Music*—are far from subtle. But it apparently communicated the filmmakers' message successfully, and Ottman ranks it as one of his best scores.

Barry's music for *Goodbye Lover* has never been released on CD.

■ Stepmom (1998)

Original composer: **Patrick Doyle**
Replacement composer: **John Williams**

Director Chris Columbus's *Stepmom* could illustrate the word "tearjerker" in a dictionary. Starring Julia Roberts and Susan Sarandon, it's the story of a broken family, told in an unabashedly manipulative way through a series of clichés (younger stepmom, biased children, natural mother diagnosed with terminal cancer). This emotionally pumped-up picture reached a sizable audience yet collected only mixed reviews.

The score was penned by Scottish actor-turned-composer Patrick Doyle, who has been—from *Henry V* in 1989 through *Thor* in 2011—a frequent collaborator on films directed by his friend Kenneth Branagh (ten of them, in fact). He has also scored films by many other notable directors, including Brian De Palma and Régis Wargnier; at the time of his work on *Stepmom*, his recent scoring credits included *Donnie Brasco* (1997), *Hamlet* (1996), and *Sense and Sensibility* (1995).

For *Stepmom*, Doyle delivered a beautiful score designed to open tear ducts. In a strange twist of fate, he wrote his music for this tale of a woman who falls ill with cancer while recovering from treatments for acute myeloid leukemia, with which he had been diagnosed in 1997. (During his four months of treatment, he scored the animated feature *Quest for Camelot*.)

But, for one reason or another—and there exist conflicting stories about this—Doyle's music was eventually dropped from *Stepmom* and John Williams, who had scored two previous Chris Columbus films (*Home Alone* and *Home Alone 2*) was hired to replace it. (Williams had recently scored *Saving Private Ryan* and *Amistad*, among other films.) Williams delivered a simple and restrained romantic score that played down the film's in-your-face treatment of its tragedy. Like a number of other low-key romantic works from this point in the composer's career, it featured a renowned performer, in this case guitarist Christopher Parkening, whose performances are among the score's most notable moments.

■ Cruel Intentions (1999)

Original composer: **John Ottman**
Replacement composer: **Edward Shearmur**

Roger Kumble's directing debut, *Cruel Intentions*, was a Generation X version of *Les Liaisons dangereuses*, the oft-adapted eighteenth-century French novel about malice, seduction, betrayal, and revenge. (The tale had been filmed three times before: in 1959 by Roger Vadim, in 1988 by Stephen Frears, and in 1989 by Milos Forman. It also had inspired two French TV movies and two operas.) Relying heavily on the box-office draw of its young stars—Sarah Michelle Gellar (as Kathryn), Ryan Phillippe

(Sebastian), Reese Witherspoon (Annette), and Selma Blair (Cecile)—the sexy though creatively bankrupt movie did well at the box office and even managed to spawn two direct-to-DVD sequels. Aiding its fame and commercial buzz was its notorious (and MTV Award–winning) onscreen "lesbian kiss" between Gellar and Blair. As a film critic for *LA Weekly* put it, "the only reason this film was made was to allow viewers to ogle pretty young things behaving badly."

As for the movie's music, it was evident from the start that *Cruel Intentions* would keep its teen audience happy by featuring a good number of popular songs. But it also needed a dramatic underscore (or connecting material between the songs). To provide this, the filmmakers hired composer John Ottman, known for his brooding orchestral works and unusual intimate scores, from *The Usual Suspects* (1995) to *Apt Pupil* (1998). The picture's producers, however, felt that to speak to the movie's young target audience his music should sound like "instrumental pop music." Ottman thought otherwise:

> As a filmmaker and composer I thought the film's score needed to live up to the gutsiness of the film, yet supplying emotional depth I thought the film desperately lacked to be successful. So I combined the "alternative sound" the producers wanted with a strange blend of classical sound, a featured string trio and a woman's voice: I used a female singer as a sound to haunt Sebastian. Sometimes it reflects his obsession and guilt about Annette, but other times it represents the other woman in his life, Kathryn. The lines were often blurred to represent Sebastian's torment. The score was designed to be dark yet emotional, reflecting the purgatory of these vampire-like characters and the love Sebastian found to inspire himself to tear away from that life. I believed a more sophisticated and dense approach would make more of the film and would offer a great juxtaposition of all the source music throughout. I also wanted there to be delicious moments as well to go along with the sordid decadence of the siblings, especially Kathryn. It all worked great—believe me! Anyway, at the last minute some test-screening scores dipped (after they changed a few songs as well) and none other than the score was thought to have been a likely suspect. Love those valuable test-screenings and the wisdom they inspire!

During early test screenings, *Cruel Intentions* was shown accompanied by a temp track that included popular songs the production could never afford to license. (Since temp music use doesn't require contracts and fees, the filmmakers could select anything they wanted.) This would cause Ottman and his score some trouble:

> The nail in the coffin for my score was one arbitrary test-screening. It was a song-driven film, and their first test featured hugely popular songs they could never afford. But the object is to test as high as possible. The musical score was merely a thread between these well-known songs. One of the focus-group questions is to rate the music—as if the kids are commenting on the score with that question. It's their favorite songs they're commenting on. So naturally this question tested high on the screening. Later they had a screening with most of these songs stripped out in lieu of lesser-known ones they could afford. By this time, a synth mock-up of my score was included. The test scores dropped

a bit, as did the ratings of the music question. What a surprise. Then everyone panics, and babies get thrown out with the bathwater. I was one of the babies.

For a replacement score, the producers turned to British composer Edward Shearmur, who had well-established credentials in the pop-music world (having worked with many popular artists) and whose recent scoring credits included *The Very Thought of You* (1998), *The Governess* (1998), and *Wings of the Dove* (1997). Shearmur's score, which incorporated pop music elements and sounded like a natural extension of the licensed songs, was considerably more lighthearted and comedic than Ottman's. Yet many of the film's most effective musical moments came from the actual songs, such as the Verve's "Bitter Sweet Symphony," which appears in the finale. (Among the many other artists and bands who perform songs used in the film are Fatboy Slim, Counting Crows, Aimee Mann, Marcy Playground, and Blur.)

As for Ottman's unused *Cruel Intentions* score, ten tracks from it were released on Varèse Sarabande's CD *Music Inspired by the Film* Cruel Intentions*: Suites and Themes from the Scores of John Ottman*, which also included a selection of tracks from Ottman's scores for *Fantasy Island, Halloween H20, Lake Placid, Snow White: A Tale of Terror, Incognito*, and *Apt Pupil*.

■ **A Midsummer Night's Dream** (1999)

Original composer: **Wojciech Kilar**
Replacement composer: **Simon Boswell**

When director Michael Hoffman adapted one of William Shakespeare's most famous comedies into a movie starring Kevin Kline, Michelle Pfeiffer, and Stanley Tucci, he moved its ancient Greek setting to nineteenth-century Tuscany and devised a two-part approach to its musical landscape.

On one hand, he used famous nineteenth-century Italian opera excerpts, including music by Verdi, Rossini, Mascagni, Donizetti, Puccini, and Bellini, performed by such popular stars as Renée Fleming and Luciano Pavarotti. And (of course) he employed excerpts from Mendelssohn's incidental music for *A Midsummer Night's Dream*, including its Overture and Wedding March.

On the other hand, a score made up solely of adapted classical music excerpts would not have fulfilled Hoffman's cinematic vision—he wanted unique original music to underscore the play's fairy world. For this, he contacted Polish composer Wojciech Kilar, a master of dark fantasy music.

Kilar was one of Poland's most prolific film composers in 1992 when he was hired to score his biggest Hollywood film, Francis Ford Coppola's *Bram Stoker's Dracula*. His *Dracula* score, parts of which found their way into several Hollywood movies' temp scores, immediately made Kilar a sought-after composer for films dealing with otherworldly matters. But he was reluctant to hire orchestrators, and only took on projects that he liked and that suited his composing time frame and working methods, which differed from Hollywood's current film-scoring practices. Such artistic idiosyncrasies may have ultimately led to the rejection of his music for *A Midsummer Night's Dream*: Instead of writing actual demos for director Hoffman, Kilar sent him recordings of piano sketches, which apparently proved insufficient for the director's purposes.

Kilar was let go, and British composer Simon Boswell was hired to replace him. Boswell's recent scoring credits included *This Year's Love* (1999), *The War Zone* (1999), and *Cousin Bette* (1998), and he had started his scoring career with a dark fantasy picture, Dario Argento's *Phenomena* (aka *Creepers*, 1985).

Boswell had first been contacted by Hoffman around the same time that Kilar was hired, but he didn't sign on to the picture until considerably later. He recalls:

> The producers first approached me about doing it [*A Midsummer Night's Dream*] back in the summer of 1998, but they had also approached Wojciech Kilar, and I believe they actually started working with him. My agent in America, Vasi, who is very tenacious, kept an eye on the project, because he knew they were having a few problems. To cut a long story short, I eventually got a call asking me to fly over to Skywalker Ranch, where they were editing, at just a few hours' notice, to talk about doing the music, and they gave me the job. I remember seeing lots of vultures circling around the grounds of the ranch, and I speculated with Michael Hoffman that that was where Wojciech was buried. (laughs)....
>
> The thing Michael [Hoffman] was concerned about the most was finding some kind of voice for the fairy world, and especially the music that the fairy band would play. That was really the key thing.

Boswell created a "pan-world sound," utilizing instruments from many cultures, for Hoffman's fairy realm:

> There were some medieval instruments, like shawms, bombards (Renaissance oboes), dulcians (bassoons), chalumeau (clarinet), Russian lur (cornett), and flageolets. The guy that played all these instruments, Keith Thompson, came round with a big bag and we sat downstairs in my studio and just experimented with the sounds. I then wrote parts for them—providing he could tell me what the range was! There were also Arabic instruments, and ancient Persian percussion, and many other things. It was a lot of fun. I approached it in the same way that other people approach sampling records these days. You take interesting sounds, and write from a textural point of view. I work like that a lot, especially when I'm doing electronic scores....
>
> I was very happy with it.... It doesn't really sound much like anything else I've done, but I guess it depends how much of my stuff you have heard. I try to do different things with almost every film, which, from a career point of view, is sometimes not to my advantage. But it was a departure, I had a big budget, and it felt like a major studio project.

Boswell also had the strange and difficult challenge of writing source music that had to match the movements of actors playing musical instruments in existing footage.

Regardless of his *A Midsummer Night's Dream* experience, Kilar remained his own man. During the latter part of his career, after Hollywood had noticed him, he received a number of interesting offers, but he turned down several great movies for a variety of reasons. Kilar:

I turned down the proposition to compose music for *Femme Fatale* [2002] directed by Brian De Palma and I regret it very much, because I wanted to write music for this film. Unfortunately, during that time I was writing music to Polanski's *The Pianist*. For a completely different reason I turned down Barbet Schroeder's proposition to write music to the film *Desperate Measures* [1998]. I had been honest with him and said that I did not feel this kind of film genre. This film was not meant for me. Another time, I was turned down. I am talking about *Lord of the Rings* [2001]. However, I believe it was a fortunate circumstance, otherwise this job would have killed me, and I would not have been able to take such pressure, such load of work. I would not have been up to such a challenge, such projects require a whole team of coworkers. I, on the other hand, always work alone. It was doomed to failure. And I honestly think it was God's finger.

■ **Mystery Men** (1999)

Original composer: **Stephen Warbeck**
Additional composer: **Shirley Walker**

Based on characters that appeared in Bob Burden's *Flaming Carrot Comics*, *Mystery Men* is a superhero-movie parody in which blue-collar superheroes with unimposing powers battle equally odd forces of evil. The one and only feature film outing for award-winning commercials director Kinka Usher, it featured an all-star cast led by William H. Macy (as the Shoveler), Ben Stiller (Mr. Furious), Hank Azaria (the Blue Raja), Janeane Garofalo (the Bowler), Greg Kinnear (Captain Amazing), and a host of other well-known actors in cameo roles, doing battle against Casanova Frankenstein (Geoffrey Rush), Dr. Leek (Lena Olin), and the Disco Boys (led by Eddie Izzard). Regardless of its notable cast, the uneven picture fared poorly at the box office and is perhaps best summed up by Shoveler's line "We're on a blind date with Destiny, and it looks like she ordered the lobster."

To score this twisted comedy, the filmmakers hired recent Academy Award–winning British composer Stephen Warbeck, whose scoring credits included *Shakespeare in Love* (1998), *Her Majesty, Mrs. Brown* (1997), and the first five seasons of the popular British TV series *Prime Suspect*.

While working on *Mystery Men*, Warbeck discussed coming onto the project shortly after his Oscar win for *Shakespeare in Love*:

> For some reason, people are more interested in meeting somebody who's won something than somebody who hasn't, although the person is actually exactly the same.... I still write music the way I wrote it before I won the Oscar, so that hasn't changed. I think on a personal level it hasn't made a dramatic difference, but I think that perhaps it opens the door to some projects which wouldn't have come my way if it wasn't for the Oscar.

Warbeck's *Mystery Men* music utilized a number of out-of-the-ordinary (for Hollywood, that is) instruments, including the Hungarian tárogató (a single-reed woodwind instrument), played by Martin Robertson, and the Greek bouzouki (a long-necked, mandolinlike instrument), played by John Parricelli. Because he had only twenty-eight days in which to compose his score, Warbeck brought in additional orchestrators to help him finish the job.

Like many of the best action-comedy scores, the music takes itself seriously as it underscores ludicrous adventures with a strong sense of heroism. But although Warbeck initially was very enthusiastic about the movie, some of his enthusiasm seemed to wear off as the filmmakers, reacting to test screenings and seemingly unsure of their own minds, reinvented it. Warbeck:

> Initially the film seemed a good idea, the freshness of something different, very eccentric with less of a stupid superheroes side, so I felt like I could have a lot of fun in doing something very different to what I had done before. I remember that the original film had a huge amount of scenes with Geoffrey Rush and Lena Olin, some very good ones indeed. And then they did a test preview in California to a younger audience and they started to cut some of the weirdest parts. So two months before the film was released, I saw it and it still was very mad and then they just tried to make it a more straight comedy type of film, so finally the original formula evolved into a strange animal.

After he recorded his score and returned to England, the picture was heavily re-edited, drastically changing many of its sequences. (In addition to a complete revamp of its opening, more than eighty special-effects shots were added.) Because of this, many parts of Warbeck's score no longer fit the picture. When the composer couldn't travel back to the United States to make the necessary adjustments, noted composer, orchestrator, conductor, and ghost writer Shirley Walker was called on to rewrite quite a few of his cues as well as compose additional music. Among Walker's recent scoring credits were *Turbulence* (1997), *Escape from L.A.* (1996), and the animated TV series *The New Batman Adventures* (1997–1999).

Although she was on a tight schedule, Walker had a lot of fun with her additional material, for which she was pretty much left to her own devices. The rules were simple: She should grab the audience at the movie's beginning and then focus her rewrite efforts on only the key cues, where the re-edited picture's clashes with the original score would be most noticeable. Her rewritten cues included most of the movie's action sequences as well as the opening party-crashing scene. In her work, she was aided by orchestrators Peter Tomashek and Kristopher Carter (in charge of the electronic music), composer Mark Mothersbaugh (writer of "The Mystery Man Mantra"), and legendary orchestrator-conductor Bruce Babcock.

According to producer Lloyd Levine, the final cut of the picture used about eighty percent of Warbeck's score. However, *Mystery Men* is a good example of an additional-music composer making a significant change in a movie's tone.

In the last few years the hiring of additional-music composers has become an increasingly frequent practice. Depending on contractual negotiations, such a composer might get a mention in a movie's opening credits, as in *Halloween H20*, or end credits, as in *Invaders from Mars*. Or she may get no mention at all, as in *Tremors*.

■ **The 13th Warrior** (1999)

Original composer: **Graeme Revell**
Replacement composer: **Jerry Goldsmith**

The 13th Warrior was a big, expensive action film based on Michael Crichton's best-selling novel *Eaters of the Dead,* which itself was based on the real-life adventures of Arab poet Ahmed Ibn Fahdlan and the classic Anglo-Saxon tale *Beowulf.* This violent movie (which included dialogue in English, Swedish, Danish, Norwegian, Latin, and Arabic), told the tale of a tenth-century Arab poet (played by Antonio Banderas) who is sent by the Caliph of Baghdad to be ambassador to the Vikings. Once among them, he's recruited to be part of a thirteen-man force sent to find and destroy a cannibalistic neighboring tribe. Directed by John McTiernan, whose most recent credits included *Die Hard: With a Vengeance* (1995) and *Last Action Hero* (1993), the initial 127-minute version of the movie did not fare well at test screenings held in 1998, and was shelved for a while.

The music for this version of the film was penned by Graeme Revell, whose recent scoring credits included *Suicide Kings* (1997), *Chinese Box* (1997), and *Killer: A Journal of a Murder* (1996). His score, which utilized instruments from a number of cultures, featured the unique vocal talents of musician-singer-composer Lisa Gerrard, a founding member of the band Dead Can Dance, who had turned her attention to film scoring, both on her own and in collaboration with such well-known composers as Hans Zimmer.

Some time after *The 13th Warrior*'s shelving, Michael Crichton took a more active hand in it. The author was no stranger to the film business: More than a dozen movies (including *The Andromeda Strain* and *Jurassic Park*) had been based on his novels, and he had even written and directed some movies himself, including *Westworld* (1973) and *Coma* (1978). Hoping to turn *The 13th Warrior* into an audience pleaser and, at the same time, bring it more in line with his own literary-cinematic vision, Crichton re-edited the picture, cutting out almost a half-hour of footage, and shot some new sequences. (At this point, director John McTiernan was already busy setting up his remake of *The Thomas Crown Affair.*) Crichton also chose to replace the original score, as Revell recalls:

> What happened was John McTiernan, the director, who I had not been working closely with, didn't get involved in the music very much, and pretty much removed himself from the movie during post production. Michael Crichton took it over, and I don't think he even listened to my score. When he took it over, I think he just decided his friend Jerry Goldsmith should be the composer and that was the end of that. I never really counted that as a rejection, and I don't think there was anything inferior about that score, and I'm quite happy to still own it. Goldsmith's score was good, it was a bit different, more old-fashioned than mine. I didn't think the movie did either of us justice, but that was my final impression.... I still really like that score. It was very odd—I'm always astonished at how a production can spend that much money recording something, and then not even

listen to it, simply because the new director or producer has a prior relationship that he wanted to go with. To be honest, I don't think it made any difference either way for that particular film. Jerry did a good job, but certainly I think there was a structural problem with the film—there was no action on the screen for the first six reels. There was a lot of reporting of action—someone would come on screen and say, "It was terrible!" Well, why don't we just see glimpses of it? That would be the way to do it. But I was proud of the music, and I hope to use it again.

After dropping Revell's score, Crichton called on his old friend Jerry Goldsmith for a new score for a revamped picture. The composer, whose recent credits included *The Mummy* (1999) and *Star Trek: Insurrection* (1998), had enjoyed a long relationship with Crichton, having scored four of the writer's earlier directorial outings.

Recorded in London, *The 13th Warrior*'s replacement score—with its strong mix of ethnic-flavored music and relentless action music—became one of Goldsmith's more celebrated late-period works.

The key to *The 13th Warrior*'s score replacement is found in Crichton's liner notes for its Goldsmith soundtrack CD (on the Varèse Sarabande label):

> Musically, the movie presented some difficult challenges. First of all, the film required an old-fashioned heroic theme of the kind not often heard in contemporary movies. In addition, because *The 13th Warrior* was about the clash of two cultures—Arab and Viking—both would have to be represented musically in varying moods. Although there is a rich tradition of Arab music, we know nothing about what Viking music was like, which meant Jerry would have to invent it. To the extent that the audience would bring an expectation about the music based on well-loved old films about Vikings, Jerry would have to meet those expectations, while also revising them. I blithely assumed he'd have no trouble with all this. And I was right.

■ Operation Condor 2: The Armour of the Gods (aka **Long xiong hu di**) (1999)

Original composer (1987): **Michael Lai Siu-tin**
Replacement composer: **Michael Wandmacher**

Hong Kong martial artist and actor Jackie Chan is recognized around the world today for his unique blend of death-defying stunts, acrobatic combat, and comedy, but this wasn't always the case. Until the mid-1990s, his audience outside of Hong Kong was small, made up primarily of Asian martial-arts films devotees. But after Chan scored big-time American market successes with *Rush Hour* (1998), a cop-buddy movie costarring Chris Tucker, and *Shanghai Noon* (2000), with Owen Wilson and Lucy Liu, he was catapulted to stardom, and his old movies were dusted off for discovery by a newfound audience. Among the most successful of Chan's older pictures was 1987's *Long xiong hu di* (*Armour of God*), which eventually would be retitled *Operation Condor 2: The Armour of the Gods*, in which Chan played Indiana Jones–style adventurer Asian Hawk. *Long xiong hu di* was followed by a sequel in 1991, *Fei ying gai wak* (*Armour of God II*).

Miramax, inspired by New Line Cinema's success in distributing Chan's *Rumble in the Bronx* (an edited and dubbed version of the 1995 film *Hung fan kui*, with a new score by J. Peter Robinson) in 1996 and Dimension Films' similar success with his *Supercop* (aka *Police Story 3*, an edited and dubbed version of the 1992 film *Ging chat goo si 3: Chiu kup ging chat* with a new score by Joel McNeely) that same year, picked up American theatrical distribution rights for *Fei ying gai wak* in 1997.

Miramax then changed *Fei ying gai wak*'s title from *Armour of God II* to *Operation Condor* (omitting "II" so as not to scare off prospective viewers who hadn't seen the film to which it was a sequel). After removing some footage to pick up the picture's pace and dubbing it into English, the distributor hired Stephen Endelman to replace its music.

Confused? Wait—the real confusion is yet to come.

After seeing that Chan was indeed a successful brand, Miramax and other companies quickly revamped and released a number of his other old films for the U.S. home-video market. As had become common practice, these titles were dubbed and altered in numerous other ways to appeal to Chan's new audience. Of these many new-old releases, *Long xiong hu di* (*Armour of God*), distributed by Dimension Films/ Dimension Home Video, would become one of the most popular. To link it to its already-released sequel, the Miramax-distributed *Operation Condor*, it was positioned as *Operation Condor*'s sequel (!) by retitling it *Operation Condor 2: The Armour of the Gods*.

Dimension hired composer Michael Wandmacher, who is reported to hold a black belt in karate, to rescore their catalogue of Asian martial-arts films with modern action music that retained some Asian sounds. These new scores were designed not only to hide American-version edits but also to provide a unified soundscape in line with the U.S. market's tastes. In the case of *Operation Condor 2*, Wandmacher replaced a score by award-winning actor and composer Michael Lai Siu-tin (aka Siu-tin Lei and Hugo Lai).

In addition to *Operation Condor 2*, Wandmacher rescored a number of other Chan movies for Dimension, including *Supercop 2* (*Chao ji ji hua*), *The Legend of the Drunken Master* (*Jui kuen II*), *Twin Dragons* (*Shuang long hui*), and *The Accidental Spy* (*Dak miu mai shing*).

It's important to note that most of Dimension's Jackie Chan movies not only contain cuts and replacement scores that significantly alter the tone of the original films (*The Accidental Spy* being the most telling example), but their DVD releases rarely contain the original films for comparison. Purists may want to seek out the originals, but for casual viewers who simply want to be entertained by Chan's gravity-defying antics, Wandmacher's scores provide a satisfying accompaniment.

■ La lengua de las mariposas (aka **Butterfly/Butterfly's Tongue/Butterfly Tongues**) (1999)

Original composer: **Ángel Illarramendi**
Replacement composer: **Alejandro Amenábar**

Spanish director José Luis Cuerda's *La lengua de las mariposas,* which was released in North America as *Butterfly* (and elsewhere in the world as *Butterfly's Tongue* or *Butterfly Tongues*), is a beautifully photographed coming-of-age story set in 1936, during the onset of the Spanish Civil War. Its young protagonist, Moncho, full of curiosity and confusion, is befriended by the kindly, freethinking local schoolteacher Don Gregorio (played by famed Spanish actor Fernando Fernan Gómez), a supporter of the new republic. But when fascist forces rise up against the republic and round up the town's republican sympathizers, Moncho, swayed by his family's fear for their own lives, betrays his beloved teacher.

Spanish composer Ángel Illarramendi was hired to score the film. (Among his previous scoring credits were *Twice Upon a Yesterday* and *El último viaje de Robert Rylands.*) But Illarramendi and the director failed to communicate well. When Illarramendi played his themes on the piano for Cuerda, the director couldn't picture how they would sound when adapted for orchestra and, similarly, couldn't imagine how they would fit with his film. So Illarramendi was let go and replacement composer Alejandro Amenábar was hired. This was an unusual job for the multitalented Amenábar—also a director and writer—who had previously scored only films that he had both written and directed, such as his highly regarded *Open Your Eyes* (1997) and *Tesis* (1996).

Amenábar discussed the lack of communication between Illarramendi and Cuerda:

> The other day, I met Ángel [Illarramendi] and I told him that I think his music for the *La Lengua de las Mariposas* was wonderful, very moving. The only problem was that José Luis Cuerda doubted that the music would match the scenes of the movie. When he proposed this, I told him that I would compose for him worse music, of course, and that my piece of work would not be so consistent, but maybe it would meet his expectations much more, because basically the problem was due to the lack of communication. When Ángel showed him the themes for the piano, José Luis was not aware how the final orchestration was going to be, and at that moment they lost each other. I explored the other side. José Luis told me that the instruments had to be worthy but ignoble, I had to go the other way around. Lucio [Lucio Godoy, Amenábar's orchestrator] also intervened at this point and suggested a reduced number of instruments...and introduced the flute, by which it sounded old, like coming from a small town.

Amenábar's affectionate, nostalgic, heavily emotional score for Cuerda's picture featured beautiful, evocative woodwind and string writing. And it remained hauntingly melodic even during the film's most disturbing scenes, unlike Illarramendi's score.

The JMB label released Amenábar's score. The same label also released a recording of Illarramendi's rejected score under the title *Una historia reciente.* On this album, one can hear how his themes fragmented and grew militaristic-sounding as the fascists took power. His idyllic theme "Primavera" self-destructs—it morphs and disappears into the story's increasing violence. Illarramendi explains his approach to this melody:

> The music of the "Primavera" summarizes a child's experiences gained through his teacher. The child discovers the world, the actual world of nature, and also other more human things by the teacher. When the war breaks out, the child realizes that he is surrounded by people who shout at the teacher to be a murderer. And he, pushed by his family, finally does the very same thing. When he is doing so, the music reminds us of the experiences they shared and the happiness of the past as a counterpoint of the scene we are watching. It was a way to illustrate the way the child had changed. It was also a very opera-like ending—that is how we made it.

■ Godzilla 2000/Gojira ni-sen mireniamu (1999)

Original composer: **Takayuki Hattori**
Additional composer for American version: **J. Peter Robinson**

Ever since the first Godzilla picture, *Gojira,* was produced in Japan in 1954, the monster has endured one rough trip after another across the Pacific Ocean to American screens. His first adventure was significantly modified: It was re-edited, dubbed into English, Americanized by the addition of new footage featuring actor Raymond Burr, and retitled *Godzilla, King of the Monsters!.* And (of course) its musical score was pumped up with several stock/library cues from Universal's old horror films.

Japan's 1984 Godzilla movie, *Reijiro Korohu* (for which the monster suddenly grew from his long-established 167 feet to 267 feet), had a similarly rocky voyage to America: After it was picked up by U.S. distributor New Line Cinema, it was retitled *Godzilla 1985,* controversially edited, and then shored up with music excerpted from Christopher Young's score for New Line's *Def-Con 4.* Even director Roland Emmerich's American-produced 1998 *Godzilla* (which was not directly tied to the Japanese series) faced music troubles: Composer David Arnold had to redo several of its cues in order to turn the monster from "scary" to "magnificent."

The often dubious process of Americanizing Godzilla, which had affected many of the monster's twenty-two previous screen appearances in the United States, continued with the trans-Pacific trek of *Godzilla 2000,* Toho Films' official relaunch of the monster's franchise. In this tale, Godzilla stomps around in a wonderfully campy-looking Tokyo as he battles the evil, shape-shifting, flying rock-turned-UFO-turned-monster Orga. It's Godzilla the good guy, saving Earth from alien invaders.

Godzilla 2000's American distributor, TriStar Pictures, implemented several changes to its version. Eight minutes of footage were removed, to pick up the movie's pace and make it more serious (omitting shots in which victims of Godzilla's thrashing survived in comical ways). And new sound effects and music were added—the latter job handled by J. Peter Robinson.

One reason Robinson was selected was that he was no stranger to rescoring Asian pictures. He had done a lot of work for New Line in the mid- through late 1990s, including rescoring its Americanized—i.e., edited and dubbed—Jackie Chan movies, starting in 1995 with *Rumble in the Bronx* (*Hung fan kui*).

TriStar's version of *Godzilla 2000* ended up with a score that was roughly fifty percent Robinson (about thirty minutes of music) and fifty percent original score by Takayuki Hattori. The differences between the two composers' music are quite noticeable: Hattori made use of Akira Ifukube's original *Godzilla* themes from 1954 and was orchestral in its approach. Robinson's music, mostly scored for synthesizers, consisted primarily of short connecting cues, though he provided a couple of powerful action sequences as well. TriStar apparently deemed Hattori's action music too Japanese, whereas Robinson's replacement action music was right in line with the synth-heavy American action-movie scores then in vogue.

■ **Supernova** (2000)

Original composer: **Burkhard von Dallwitz**
Replacement composer: **David C. Williams**

One of the first movies to be dumped on cinemas in January 2000 was *Supernova*, a dark, post-*Alien* sci-fi movie set aboard the medical rescue vehicle *Nightingale 229*, cruising deep space in the twenty-second century. Starring James Spader and Angela Bassett, it boasted few of the cosmic explosions its title hints at. Instead, it featured a mutant psycho-killer on the loose within the space ship's confines. Its director was the pseudonymous Thomas Lee.

(*Note*: The Directors Guild of America had just retired the use of "Alan Smithee" as its official pseudonym for a director who, for one reason or another, wished to remove his or her name from a film. The name had been in regular use since 1969, when Don Siegel used it to hide his contribution to the film *Death of a Gunfighter*. Its demise was brought about by the release of Arthur Hiller's 1997 dud comedy, *An Alan Smithee Film: Burn Hollywood Burn*, which alerted the filmgoing public to the name's meaning. *Supernova*'s "Thomas Lee" stood in for Walter Hill, Jack Sholder, and Francis Ford Coppola.)

Originally and primarily directed by Hill, *Supernova* was shelved for a while by its production studio, MGM/UA, and then handed off to director Sholder and eventually to Francis Ford Coppola, who greatly re-edited and re-envisioned it. As he had done on his previous film, *The Rainmaker* (1997), Coppola whittled away at *Supernova*, creating numerous editions/versions of it, each one (it was hoped) better than the last.

The project's original composer was Burkhard von Dallwitz, whose most notable scoring job to date had been Peter Weir's 1998 film *The Truman Show* (which also used excerpts from Philip Glass's scores for the films *Powaqqatsi*, *Anima Mundi*, and *Mishima*)—no mean feat, since the music had to comment on the goings-on in both the movie itself and the movie-within-the-movie. Dallwitz's *Supernova* score was of an electronic-ambient nature.

But once the movie was in Jack Sholder's control, he chose to give it a more orchestral score, by composer David C. Williams, whose recent scoring credits included *Wishmaster 2* (1999), *Phantoms* (1998), and *The Prophecy II* (1998). Before his *Supernova* work was finished, however, Williams would be collaborating with Coppola on a score that seemed to pay homage to the outer-space music of John Williams, although it was of a streamlined, simpler nature.

Supernova was a massive failure at the box office. It also collected generally scathing reviews: A critic for *The New York Times* wrote that the film was "light on originality and low on suspense though high on design and special effects." Dallwitz received an "additional music" credit on the picture; some of his music can still be heard in the movie, as well as in the twenty minutes of deleted scenes added as "bonus" elements to the DVD. In early 2010 the Intrada label released both scores on a two-CD set, with Williams's music on disc 1 and Dallwitz's music on disc 2.

■ **My Dog Skip** (2000)

Original composer: **Van Dyke Parks**
Replacement composer: **William Ross**

Loosely based on Willie Morris's best-selling autobiographical tale of growing up in Yazoo City, Mississippi, in the 1940s, *My Dog Skip* is a film about an awkward boy and the dog that helped him overcome his shyness. Directed by Jay Russell (whose one previous directorial outing was 1987's *End of the Line*), it starred Frankie Muniz, Luke Wilson, Kevin Bacon, and Diane Lane, and featured narration by Harry Connick Jr. Making back almost six times its budget, *My Dog Skip* was a sleeper hit that received the Broadcast Film Critics Award for Best Family Film.

To score it, Russell hired composer Van Dyke Parks, who was also born and raised in Mississippi. (Among Parks's recent scoring credits were *Shadrack*, *Private Parts*, and *Bastard out of Carolina*.) Using his childhood as inspiration, Parks wrote a wonderfully Southern-flavored score that worked well with the picture and pleased all who were involved with the project.

But then, for one reason or another, the "finished" picture underwent a massive re-editing, rendering large portions of the score unusable. Tied up with other projects, Parks was unavailable to revamp his material.

At this point, composer William Ross (Alan Silvestri's regular orchestrator) was hired to compose music in a similar vein. (Among Ross's recent scoring credits were

My Fellow Americans, The Evening Star, and *Tin Cup.*) A good portion of Parks's score had been retained (for which Parks received an "additional music" credit), and it was up to Ross to maintain a cohesive voice with the original score. This he did well, and he and director Russell would work together again on *Tuck Everlasting* (2002) and *Ladder 49* (2004).

In addition to the underscore by Ross and Parks, *My Dog Skip* utilized a good bit of period source music performed by such popular artists as Gene Krupa, Louis Jordan, Harry James, the Andrews Sisters, and Louis Prima.

■ The Kid (aka Disney's The Kid) (2000)

Original composer: **Jerry Goldsmith**
Replacement composer: **Marc Shaiman**

In the latter half of his career, Jerry Goldsmith had to endure a number of score replacements. One of the lesser-known ones involved *Babe* (1995), director Chris Noonan's popular film about a talking pig. Goldsmith's music became the victim of a struggle between Noonan and producer George Miller over the character of the picture. One wanted a darker approach and the other something more kid-friendly, and when the latter concept won out, Goldsmith's music—written for the darker vision—became unnecessary. Composer Nigel Westlake was hired to replace it.

A couple of years later, Goldsmith would face a similar problem on *The Kid*, a fantasy parable that teetered between melodrama and comedy, leaving it to the music to determine its genre. (The picture is also known as *Disney's The Kid*; perhaps Disney appended its name out of concern that the public might confuse it with Charlie Chaplin's classic *The Kid* from 1921.)

Directed by Jon Turteltaub (whose recent credits included *Instinct, Phenomenon,* and *While You Were Sleeping*), *The Kid* was one of Disney's better offerings at the time. It was a character-driven family film about a rude, cynical, angry fortysomething image consultant who magically meets his eight-year-old self, who teaches him about life and love.

Goldsmith, whose recent scoring credits included *The Haunting* (1999), *The 13th Warrior* (1999), and *The Mummy* (1999), was hired to pen its music. (His most recent Disney score had been the 1998 animated feature *Mulan.*) He immediately started working on a low-key dramatic score, presenting the director with elaborate synth mockups even before shooting started. Guitar, envisioned to be performed by classic guitar virtuoso John Williams, was the music's central instrument.

Turteltaub took extreme care with the movie's postproduction, becoming unusually involved in its music. He experimented with placing Goldsmith's mockups in different contexts within the film, using them as emotional templates since they were not attached to specific scenes. But after a while he realized that the music was not what he was looking for—it didn't work the way he wanted it to—so he had to let

Goldsmith go. (The composer would reuse this score's love theme in 2003 in his score for *Timeline*—which was also rejected.)

With only about two weeks in which to come up with another score, Turteltaub hired Marc Shaiman as replacement composer. (Among Shaiman's recent scoring credits were *The Story of Us, South Park: Bigger, Longer & Uncut*, and *Patch Adams*. His previous work for Disney was 1997's *George of the Jungle*.) Shaiman wrote a lighthearted score filled with the big comedic flourishes and playful orchestrations that have been his lighter music's trademarks. With this new music, *The Kid* lost some of its edge and became a more typical family movie. Shaiman's upbeat material also helped steer a potential melodrama into the realm of comedy.

But Goldsmith's string of bad luck didn't end with *The Kid*. Just a year later, he met with another rejection, this time while working on director Harold Becker's thriller *Domestic Disturbance* (2001). Although Goldsmith and Becker must have had some ability to communicate with each other, since they had successfully collaborated on two movies in the mid-1990s (*Malice* and *City Hall*), Goldsmith was asked to leave *Domestic Disturbance* before he even finished recording his score. His material was deemed too "thematic" and "upfront," problems that the replacement music by Mark Mancina took care of. (Interestingly, early advertisements for a CD of Mancina's score compared it to Goldsmith's 1992 *Basic Instinct* score.)

■ **Highlander: Endgame** (2000)

Original composer: **Nick Glennie-Smith**
Additional composer: **Stephen Graziano**

Highlander: Endgame is an odd fantasy picture that combines characters, plot elements, and stars from a series of successful feature films (it's the fourth *Highlander* film) with those from a successful television series (*Highlander: The Series*, which aired for six seasons, 1992–1998). In this final installment of the film series, two members of the Scottish MacLeod clan who were born in the sixteenth century—Connor (hero of the film series) and Duncan (TV's hero)—are "Immortals" who battle others of their kind through the centuries and around the globe. (Via numerous flashbacks, this globe- and time-hopping takes moviegoers through 450-plus years and a number of locales, ending up in New York City.) Almost needless to say, this is a film with a lot of violence and swordplay: An Immortal can take on another Immortal's life force by beheading him, for example. In *Highlander: Endgame*, the franchise's presumed final outing, Connor and Duncan combine their powers to behead their archenemy, the mega-evil Immortal Jacob Kell, although only Duncan remains standing at the end.

Hired to provide the movie's music was British-born composer Nick Glennie-Smith, whose recent scoring credits included *The Lion King II: Simba's Pride* (1998), *The Man in the Iron Mask* (1998), and *Home Alone 3* (1997). But just as the slaying of

Kell called for the power of two MacLeods, the movie apparently needed the talent of two composers to score it, and the producers employed Stephen Graziano to write a replacement score. (Among his recent scoring credits were the movie *Nice Guys Sleep Alone* and episodes of the television series *Dawson's Creek* and *Party of Five*.) Graziano:

> Nick Glennie-Smith, (whom I've never met, but would like to some day) scored *Highlander: Endgame*. The producers didn't like his score. The editor, Michael Knue, said he knew someone who could do a great job, and I was hired to replace Nick's score. I was only given two weeks (ideally, a composer gets five weeks to score a film), so it was decided that they'd keep half of Nick's score and I'd replace the other half, mainly the action cues (though some of Nick's action cues stayed). If you have the CD, you can kind of see the breakdown.... I felt bad that I never contacted Nick (kind of rude on my part!), but I was so busy, then I went on to another film and just forgot about it. I hope he wasn't offended. There's one cue ["Heather Cuts Her Hair"] that indicates that we wrote it together, but, in fact, they gave me his track and asked me to add a female voice to it, so we both got credit.

With a wealth of music—two whole scores—at their disposal, *Highlander: Endgame*'s producers, handpicking music cues one by one, incorporated both composers' work into the movie's final music soundtrack. (GNP Crescendo released a soundtrack CD containing cues by both Glennie-Smith and Graziano.)

In the most general terms, both composers explored Celtic influences in their melodies and selection of solo instruments. However, Glennie-Smith's music had a more Media Ventures feeling (Hans Zimmer's film music company, of which Glennie-Smith had been a member a few years earlier). Graziano's arrangement of the traditional Scottish tune "Bonny Portmore" (sung by Jennifer McNeil accompanied by uilleann pipes) is one of the score's highlights.

■ **Chinese Coffee** (2000)

Original composer: **Howard Shore**
Replacement composer: **Elmer Bernstein**

Chinese Coffee, an adaptation of a play by Ira Lewis, is a small-scale, intimate drama directed by Al Pacino. Pacino also plays the role of Harry, an unsuccessful writer who, having lost his job as a doorman, goes to his friend Jake (played by Jerry Orbach) to collect an old debt. Jake doesn't have the money, but the two chat through the night about art and the ups and downs of their lives.

The film, which premiered at the Telluride Film Festival in 2000, never received regular theatrical distribution, going unseen by the general public until it was released in 2007 on the DVD boxed set *Pacino: An Actor's Vision*, which also contained two other out-of-the-ordinary Pacino films: *Looking for Richard* (1996) and *The Local Stigmatic* (1990).

Chinese Coffee was scored by Elmer Bernstein, whose recent scoring credits included *Keeping the Faith* (2000) and *Bringing Out the Dead* (1999). His music for Pacino's film was as spare and intimate as the movie itself. Bernstein comments:

> It's a really interesting film about the artistic endeavor. Because it comes from a play, it is static. He loved the score. But he never wanted to do anything further. That was two, three years ago. I don't think Al intends for it to be released. It was fun doing the work. I thought we had it made.

But Elmer Bernstein wasn't the only composer who worked on the project. Before him, Howard Shore tried his hand at writing music for it. (At the time, Shore's recent credits included *High Fidelity* and *Dogma*.) This wasn't the first Shore-Pacino collaboration, as the composer had worked on the two other Pacino-directed movies mentioned above. *The Local Stigmatic* is an odd little one-hour film that Pacino codirected with David H. Wheeler. In it, Pacino and Paul Guilfoyle play two British ne'er-do-well lowlife sociopaths who one day meet a famous actor in a pub and, for no discernible reason, beat him severely. After premiering in 1990 at New York's Museum of Modern Art, it sat in the museum's archives until it was resurrected as part of the *An Actor's Vision* DVD set. The other Shore-Pacino collaboration was the fairly well publicized and well-distributed documentary *Looking for Richard*, a film that offered myriad perspectives on Shakespeare's *Richard III* by combining performance and rehearsal excerpts with interviews and commentary by actors (including John Gielgud and Kenneth Branagh), Shakespeare scholars, and others. Shore wrote a score that lent this documentary the feel of a drama.

For his reunion with Pacino on *Chinese Coffee*, Shore wrote and recorded (with the London Philharmonic Orchestra and harmonica virtuoso Adam Glasser at CTS, Wembly) a fairly textural score that he later said, "may have been considered somewhat controversial. It's interesting that in film music it's not good to be too controversial, yet for new music compositions, to have people discuss and debate them is welcomed."

Unfortunately, neither Bernstein's nor Shore's *Chinese Coffee* music has appeared on CD.

■ Into the Arms of Strangers: Stories of the Kindertransport (2000)

Original composer: **Michael Kamen**
Replacement composer: **Lee Holdridge**

Traditionally, documentary filmmakers tend to establish longstanding relationships with particular composers, so rejected scores in this generally low-budget field are a rarity. The earliest recorded case of a rejected documentary score comes from 1936, when *The Future's in the Air*, the British aviation film scripted by famed novelist Graham Greene, became the first film credit for composer William Alwyn, whose music replaced a score by Raymond Bennell. (During World War II, Alwyn was a prolific composer for documentaries. He later scored such noted films as *Odd Man Out, The Fallen Idol,* and *The Crimson Pirate.*)

After documentarian Mark Jonathan Harris's *The Long Way Home* (1997), a film about the post–World War II plight of Jews liberated from in Nazi concentration camps and the founding of the state of Israel, won an Academy Award, he received strong backing for his *Into the Arms of Strangers: Stories of the Kindertransport.* The movie told the story of the 10,000 Jewish children of Nazi-controlled Germany, Austria, and Czechoslovakia whose parents sent them away to find safety and new lives in England. Along with studio support for this film came the suggestion from the head of the Warner Bros. music department that Harris hire Michael Kamen to write its music. Kamen's recent scoring credits included *The Iron Giant* (1999), *Frequency* (2000), and the film he was working on at the time, *X-Men,* which turned out to be a terribly stressful assignment. Kamen liked Harris's film and, even though he was still dealing with *X-Men* headaches, wrote several sketches for its music. But Harris and his producers were disappointed by the sketches; they felt that Kamen's opening theme, in particular, didn't have the emotional quality they were looking for. So Harris returned to the composer who scored *The Long Way Home*—Lee Holdridge, whose recent credits included the TV movies *Anya's Bell* (1999) and *By Dawn's Early Light* (2000) and the documentary *Kings of the Ring: Four Legends of Heavyweight Boxing* (2000).

Holdridge, who deliberately avoided listening to Kamen's music, completed his replacement score in only three weeks. It definitely contributed to the success of *Into the Arms of Strangers,* which won an Oscar.

■ Harrison's Flowers (2000)

Composer for French version: **Bruno Coulais**
Composer for American version: **Cliff Eidelman**

Harrison's Flowers is an emotional and moving motion picture about a determined woman, Sarah (played by Andie MacDowell), who throws herself into the middle of the early-1990s Balkan civil war's horrors to search for her photojournalist husband, Harrison, who has disappeared while on assignment there. Writer-director Elie Chouraqui helmed this French production, which was shot in English and featured a largely American cast.

The film's French print carried a score by Bruno Coulais, best known at that time for his work on the hit documentary *Microcosmos* (1996). Coulais's music for *Harrison's Flowers* presents beautiful piano and small string ensemble themes that float among dark yet vivid ambient textures and haunting background sounds. His score also includes the love song "You Disappear," performed by French-Israeli singer

Yael Naim. Although Coulais's music worked admirably in the picture, the internationally distributed version was rescored.

In the United States, where it was distributed by Universal Pictures, the movie received a new score by Cliff Eidelman, whose recent credits included *Witness Protection* (1999), *One True Thing* (1998), and *Montana* (1998). Relying primarily on strings and piano (which he played himself), his *Harrison's Flowers* music is restrained—forgoing overly dramatic high points and clashing crescendos—and finds just the right balance between romance and tragedy. It often focuses quietly on Sarah's personal tragedy, her grief over her missing husband, and her experiences in the war zone.

The two scores for *Harrison's Flowers* don't differ in any extreme ways, and both support the film well. A recording of Coulais's music was released by EMI (France), and Varèse Sarabande released Eidelman's music.

■ **All the Pretty Horses** (2000)

Original composer: **Daniel Lanois**
Replacement composer: **Marty Stuart**

All the Pretty Horses, directed by actor Billy Bob Thornton, is based on Cormac McCarthy's best-selling, National Book Award–winning novel of the same name, a dark and elegiac Western story set in the mid-twentieth century. This rites-of-passage film starring Matt Damon, Henry Thomas, Lucas Black, and Penélope Cruz follows three teenage cowboys on a series of sometimes harrowing adventures in Texas and Mexico. But while the film utilized direct passages from McCarthy's highly stylized prose in its dialogue, it lost much of the book's philosophical underpinning and disquieting atmosphere—a loss that may be the result of Miramax's demand that Thornton toss out almost half his nearly four hours of footage.

To provide *All the Pretty Horses* with music, Thornton hired Daniel Lanois, with whom he'd worked on one of his earlier directorial outings, *Sling Blade* (1996). Lanois, a Canadian musician, singer, composer, and record producer, had produced albums by Bob Dylan, Peter Gabriel, Emmylou Harris, Willie Nelson, Jon Hassell, and many other well-known artists, as well as his own records, and had coproduced with Brian Eno many of U2's albums (including *The Joshua Tree*, *Achtung Baby*, and *All That You Can't Leave Behind*). In collaboration with Eno and Hassell, Lanois had also recently done the music for director Wim Wenders' film *The Million Dollar Hotel* (2000).

Lanois's hauntingly lovely score for the four-hour version of *All the Pretty Horses* was quite sparse and minimalist. Mainly utilizing guitar, Lanois provided both underscore and source music (and even appeared in a cameo role in the picture). But Miramax wasn't buying the artistic path Lanois had chosen—the studio wanted more, something bigger, as Thornton recalls:

> Miramax said, you know, "We don't want Daniel's music in the movie." They thought it was too sparse. In other words, you know when you're making a big movie, it's like people

> vote for movies that have big music and thousands of extras, I guess, or something, so they want bigger music. So they need an orchestra. Well, Daniel did this amazing score to the movie.

After it was decided that Lanois's music had to go, Thornton turned to country musician-singer-songwriter-composer Marty Stuart for a less sparse, more traditional-sounding score. Stuart, in collaboration with Nashville musicians (and husband and wife) Kristin Wilkinson and Larry Paxton, wrote a very capable and moving Western score that featured Stuart's guitar playing with orchestra accompaniment. (With Wilkinson and Paxton, he would also go on to score Thornton's 2001 writing-directing effort *Daddy & Them*. And that same year, Stuart would produce and perform on Thornton's debut as a singer-songwriter, an album called *Private Radio*.)

The loss of Lanois's music had further-reaching implications than might have been imagined in 2000: It led to a halt in Thornton's plans to release the director's cut of his picture on DVD. The director explains the situation:

> [Lanois's score] is beautiful and perfect for the movie, so when they said we could do the DVD, I called Daniel and said, "Look, they wanna put out a Director's Cut, isn't that swell?" And Daniel said, "Well, it's not so swell because they didn't want my music in the movie in the theaters. I don't know that I want to give it to them for a DVD, because that's my music and I can use it." Because he retained the rights to it, he can use it for other things, and maybe he will have it in a big movie in a theater someday, and I said, "I'm on your side. You're my friend. I agree with you. I wouldn't give them the music either." So, as a result, because I'm on Daniel Lanois's side, I don't want to put the movie out because I would want his music in it. So that's a long-winded explanation for "No. There's not gonna be [a director's cut DVD]."

One can hear both composers' work (though only a taste of Lanois) on the official Sony soundtrack CD, which includes two Lanois cues—a gentle waltz for guitar and a Mexican-flavored ballad performed by Raúl Malo (lead singer of the alternative country band the Mavericks).

■ **Pollock** (2000)

Original composers: **Donald Rubinstein, Zbigniew Preisner**
Replacement composer: **Jeff Beal**

Directed by and starring Ed Harris in its title role, *Pollock* is a biographical film about the turbulent, self-destructive life of renowned American abstract expressionist painter Jackson Pollock, the most famous (and perhaps first) "action painter."

The first composer on the project was Donald Rubinstein. This eclectic composer-performer-songwriter rarely writes film music, but when he does, something unusual usually results. His best-known film music was written for three of director George A. Romero's pictures: *Martin* (1977), *Knightriders* (1981), which starred Ed Harris, and *Bruiser* (2000).

After many discussions with Harris, Rubinstein wrote an impressionistic yet jazzy score, which he recorded at Cello Studios, Los Angeles, with some interesting soloists: multi-instrumentalist–composer–improviser Vinny Golia (who started his creative life as a painter), drummer John Densmore from the Doors, and legendary percussion wizard Emil Richards. Rubinstein's music, however, didn't work for Harris and his shifting musical vision for *Pollock*. So Zbigniew Preisner (best known for his work on Krzysztof Kieslowski's *Three Colors* trilogy in the mid-1990s) was called in.

But Preisner also failed to find exactly what Harris was looking for. So, on the recommendation of composer Mark Isham, Harris contacted Jeff Beal, an eclectic composer with a jazz background whose recent film/TV scoring credits included *Mambo Café* (2000), *Harlem Aria* (1999), *The Passion of Ayn Rand* (1999), and numerous episodes of the popular television series *Monk* (2002–2009). For *Pollock*, Beal wrote a rhythmically exciting score in which one can hear hints of both Steve Reich's music—with its overlaying streams of repeating musical cells—and Aaron Copland's Americana sound. Beal:

> I went over to Ed's to meet him after I had seen a tape. Although this was just supposed to be a meeting, we had a great conversation about a lot of issues: Pollock's work and what we felt the film needed. Ed had such a rich understanding of the subject matter that really jived with my own feelings. I guess we hit it off pretty well because we ended spotting the film that same afternoon....
>
> Ed told me he thought the story was a tough one, but he wanted the score to really celebrate his [Pollock's] painting, i.e., the vibrancy and originality of his work stand in bitter contrast to his personal life, and ultimate surrender to alcoholism.... Because the painting themes are very much about movement and gesture, the sad stuff also has motion and repetition. But it's almost a caricature of the more frenetic material, playing so slowly. For me, it was as if this guy's mind was always churning about something....
>
> Some of my structures were modeled on the minimalist composers, like John Adams and Steve Reich, whose work I enjoy. Pollock was ahead of minimalist music in the sense that he used a very repetitive visual rhythm in his paintings in the '40s and '50s. He was also influenced by folk art, and painted his most distinctive works on the floor of his Long Island barn. To this end, I tried to use some of the Americana dialect with a more modern spin. Like the banjo plays this frantic ostinato in 7/4, etc. Maybe frantic is the wrong word; maybe it's graceful. This is one of the things that fascinated me about Ed's performance of him, these incredible extremes of grace, intelligence, and pure energy, and, of course, anger.

CDs of both Beal's and Rubinstein's scores have been released to great acclaim. In 2008, Harris, Beal, and Rubinstein were reunited on Harris's next directorial effort, the Western *Appaloosa*, for which Rubinstein wrote the song "Ain't Nothin' like a Friend" and Beal provided the film's underscore.

■ **Crossfire Trail** (2001)

Original composer: **David Shire**
Replacement composer: **Eric Colvin**

Crossfire Trail, based on a novel by Louis L'Amour, is built on a traditional Western premise: The hero (played by Tom Selleck) must keep a promise to a dying friend. In the case of this made-for-television movie, that oath is to look after the friend's widow and Wyoming ranch, both of which—it just so happens—are in jeopardy.

Crossfire Trail was directed by Australian Simon Wincer, whose credits at the time included *Lonesome Dove* (1989), *Harley Davidson and the Marlboro Man* (1991), *Free Willy* (1993), a few episodes of the TV series *The Young Indiana Jones Chronicles* (1992–1993), and *The Phantom* (1996). For music, he most frequently turned to Basil Poledouris, who had scored five of his films.

Crossfire Trail was the second in a series of TNT-produced Westerns starring Tom Selleck. The first, *Last Stand at Saber River* (1997), featured a successful score by David Shire, so when *Crossfire Trail* went into production, TNT naturally invited Shire to score it. Shire's work from the early 1990s onward had been limited to television movies (e.g., just before *Crossfire Trail* he scored *Thin Air*, *Sarah, Plain and Tall: Writer's End*, and *Spenser: Small Vices*), despite the fact that throughout the 1970s he had written celebrated scores for such highly regarded movies as *The Conversation*; *The Taking of Pelham One Two Three*; *Farewell, My Lovely*; *The Hindenburg*; and *Norma Rae*.

Director Wincer, respecting TNT's instincts, didn't listen to Shire's *Crossfire Trail* score while it was being written and recorded. But as soon as he heard the music on the dubbing stage, he realized it wasn't what he wanted. He felt that it was "an outdated approach, and dramatically over the top." So, buying three more weeks to have a replacement score written, he contacted Poledouris protégé composer Eric Colvin, with whom he had worked on the 1998 television movie *Escape: Human Cargo*. (Colvin's most recent scoring credits included the TV movies *Model Behavior* and *Life-Size*.)

Colvin's replacement score was more understated and romantic than Shire's and functioned like Poledouris's music for *Lonesome Dove*. Its broad Americana sound, calling to mind the West's vast open spaces, is surprisingly lush for a television production. After *Crossfire Trail*, Wincer directed another made-for-television Western starring Tom Selleck: *Monte Walsh* (2003). For this movie, the director again turned to Colvin, who wrote an excellent score for it. A recording of Colvin's music for both Wincer-directed Westerns has been commercially released together on La-La Land Records.

■ Town & Country (2001)

Original composer: **John Altman**
Replacement composer: **Rolfe Kent**

British director Peter Chelsom's muddled comedy of manners *Town & Country* was such a major box-office failure that it came close to jeopardizing the future of its production company, New Line Pictures. The project started in 1998 with a moderate budget, but the star-studded film's costs grew out of hand in the three years it took to complete, during which time its script underwent numerous changes and its busy actors (including Warren Beatty, Diane Keaton, Andie MacDowell, Nastassja Kinski, Charlton Heston, Goldie Hawn, and Garry Shandling) were always coming and going to fulfill other obligations, making shooting almost impossible. The picture eventually cost more than $100 million, a feasible budget for a summer blockbuster but not for a small, quirky ensemble comedy. Its box-office returns amounted to only a tenth of its budget, ranking it alongside such other notorious financial disasters as *Cutthroat Island* (1995), *Ishtar* (1987), and *Heaven's Gate* (1980). *Town & Country*'s lengthy post-production naturally allowed for some musical second thoughts as well.

The idea behind *Town & Country*'s first score was to utilize and adapt existing musical works. This sort of approach can seem a good idea for several reasons: Depending on the material one chooses, it can sometimes be less expensive than commissioning an original score. And the use of well-known tunes (either popular standards or classical pieces) can play to an audience's nostalgia and lend a comfy air of familiarity. Hired to do the job was composer-arranger-orchestrator John Altman (a musician with a strong background in arranging for and performing with top rock, pop, and jazz artists), whose recent scoring credits included *Beautiful Joe* (2001) and *RKO 281* (1999). Although he is a highly capable composer in his own right, Altman may be best known for some of his arrangement work for movies: He adapted the "James Bond Theme" for *GoldenEye*'s (1995) tank-chase sequence (replacing Eric Serra's work), and he arranged the period music for *Titanic* (1997). For *Town & Country*, Altman worked with tunes from the 1930s through the 1960s. But, as could be expected from a movie suffering a topsy-turvy search for its tone and voice, Altman was replaced in late 2000, when the film's producers decided an original score written especially for the picture might help the struggling production.

Hired as replacement composer was Rolfe Kent, who had recently scored New Line's *Happy Campers* (2001). Among Kent's other recent scoring credits were *Someone Like You* (2001) and *Nurse Betty* (2000). Based upon something heard in Kent's demo reel, the filmmakers had him feature the tuba as a frequent comedic voice—a deliverer of musical punch lines—in his score. In many ways, Kent's eclectic and colorful music, with its definite 1960s and 1970s comedy-movie throwback (almost Manciniesque) vibe, was used as a narrative aid, underlining the picture's humor. Interspersed with Kent's cues are recordings of a number of familiar old tunes performed by such greats as Django Reinhardt, Fats Waller, Louis Armstrong, and Patsy Cline. (A few of Altman's arrangements were also retained in the film, and he received an "additional music" credit.)

New Line eventually released Kent's score on CD, accompanied by five of the movie's old songs.

What's the Worst That Could Happen? (2001)

Original composer: **Marc Shaiman**
Replacement composer: **Tyler Bates**

What's the Worst That Could Happen?, a weak and flawed comedy with a title that offered critics an easy target, was directed by George Weisman, whose recent directing credits included *The Out-of-Towners* (1999) and *George of the Jungle* (1997). It's about a cat burglar (played by Martin Lawrence) who breaks into a millionaire's (Danny DeVito) home, but the heist goes awry and the burglar is caught by the homeowner, who steals his lucky ring. Most of the rest of the movie involves the thief's attempts to get his ring back.

Hired to provide its music was seasoned comedy-score veteran Marc Shaiman, whose recent scoring credits included *One Night at McCool's* (2001) and *When Harry Met Sally* (2001), as well as director Weisman's two previous movies (*George of the Jungle* and *The Out-of-Towners*), both comedies.

Shaiman wrote a score that leaned on both hip-hop and classic blaxploitation music influences. He mixed turntable effects with funky rhythm-guitar wah-wah effects (à la *Shaft*) and myriad vintage soul and funk sounds and grooves to give his score a particularly fun and twisted retro character.

Unfortunately, the film just wasn't all that funny, so the filmmakers decided that Shaiman's score should take a backseat to a lengthy slate of R&B and hip-hop songs. In this context, Shaiman's stylish score became a distraction, and while a couple of his cues were kept in the movie (providing him with an "additional music" credit), most of his music was replaced.

What's the Worst That Could Happen? was pumped up with quickly produced and/or licensed hip-hop and R&B numbers from a broad variety of artists—including James Brown, Marvin Gaye, Queen Latifah, Snoop Dogg, and Jo Dojo—and its soundtrack was then marketed as a collection of hits. (It would chart respectably on a couple of *Billboard*'s lists.) Tyler Bates, a film composer with a strong rock and pop background whose recent scoring credits included *Kingdom Come* (2001) and *Get Carter* (2000), was then hired to fill the sonic holes between songs with some hip comedic cues in just a few weeks. But his efforts, no matter how successful, were doomed to play second banana to the film's songs. His nominal contributions would later become popular among editors, however, who used them in temp tracks for other comedies.

Shaiman would later claim in a *Playbill.com* article that *What's the Worst That Could Happen?* was the worst job he ever had. Yet he was and would continue to be no stranger to score replacements: His whimsical work on *Inspector Gadget* (1999) was replaced by John Debney, who wrote a more straightforward action score with only hints of comedy. In 2000, Shaiman completed only about two-thirds of his score for the animated movie *The Emperor's New Groove* before he was replaced by John Debney once again. *The Cat in the Hat* (2003) turned into a torturous experience after Shaiman was asked to rewrite two of its songs endlessly—until he finally backed out and was replaced by David Newman. And then there was *Team America: World Police* (2004), which will be discussed later in this book.

■ **Lara Croft: Tomb Raider** (aka **Tomb Raider)** (2001)

Original composers: **Greg Hale Jones, Michael Kamen**
Replacement composer: **Graeme Revell**

Lara Croft: Tomb Raider, a film adaptation of the video game Tomb Raider, stars Angelina Jolie as British archaeologist Lady Lara Croft, daughter of another tomb-raiding archaeologist (played by Jon Voight), who was lost on the job. In this logic-defying movie, Lara must follow her father's clues to find and put together an ancient gold object—the Triangle of Light—that gives its possessor godlike power, including the control of time, during a once-every-5,000-years planetary alignment, which happens to be imminent. But in this adventure that takes her to Italy, Cambodia, and Siberia, Lara is in competition for the Triangle with the Illuminati, an evil secret society. Simon West, whose two previous directorial outings were *The General's Daughter* (1999) and *Con Air* (1997), directed this commercially successful but critically slammed action-fantasy-thriller.

Getting the right music for a film version of a video game shouldn't be a hard task—just fill it with a bevy of songs by hot recording artists. Among the artists whose music appears in *Lara Croft: Tomb Raider* are U2, Fluke, Outkast, Moby, Fatboy Slim, Nelly Furtado, Nine Inch Nails, and The Chemical Brothers. But what about the music that will fill the gaps—be the sonic connective tissue—between the songs? That's the hard part.

After deciding not to hire the Tomb Raider video-game series' composer, Nathan McCree (who had only one feature film score under his belt, the 2000 Chinese thriller *A Lingering Face*), director Simon West hired Greg Hale Jones, a composer known for his music for the original MTV animated logos and similar work for The Disney Channel. West had worked with Jones on *The General's Daughter*, a film for which Jones created entrancing arrangements of a cappella American folk song recordings from the Library of Congress collection by editing or recomposing the original vocal tracks and adding accompaniment. Now Jones's job was to work a score around *Lara*

Croft's licensed songs. To this end, he wrote roughly forty-five minutes of music that featured Russian folk songs and exotic percussion.

Not completely sold on Jones's score, the production team, acting on the recommendation of executive producer Stuart Baird, hired composer Michael Kamen to replace it. As a highly regarded action-film veteran, Kamen certainly seemed to be the right composer for *Tomb Raider*, but his most recent work in this genre had been either replaced, as happened to his music for *The Avengers* (1998), or partially rewritten by others, as in *X-Men* (2000). To show the producers his musical vision for the film, Kamen assembled a demo of themes for their review. Garnering no adverse reaction, he proceeded to write more of the score. Then, after submitting a second set of demos, he finally got a reply—a negative one. Remembering his humiliating *Avengers* experience, Kamen decided he wanted no part in this nightmare and departed the project. (Shortly after leaving, he began work on the epic television miniseries *Band of Brothers*, for which he wrote ten hours of superb music.)

With *Tomb Raider*'s premiere looming, the producers quickly hired composer Graeme Revell, whose recent scoring credits included *Human Nature* (2001) and *Blow* (2001). Revell wrote his score for sixty-five-piece orchestra, fifty-voice choir, and a bank of synthesizers in just ten days. Since he had to work fast, the writing and the recording took an unusual route: Revell composed in Los Angeles while his team of orchestrators and copyists worked in England, where the recording would take place. The recorded tracks, however, were to be mixed in Los Angeles, so the London studio was hooked up with a high-speed Internet connection to aid the transcontinental work.

Apart from writing and recording the score, Revell also had to rush out a soundtrack recording, which, due to the haste with which it was put together, was marred by bad edits, incorrect mixing, and misspelled track titles (for which the composer actually issued a public apology).

Interestingly, the second *Tomb Raider* film, *Lara Croft Tomb Raider 2: Cradle of Life* (2003), underwent a composer change as well. Craig Armstrong wrote and recorded about forty-five minutes of music for it, but the finished film used only his lab scene cue. The film's producers wanted a score bigger than Armstrong's, a more traditional action score, so they hired Alan Silvestri, fresh off *Pirates of the Caribbean: The Curse of the Black Pearl* (2003). Silvestri delivered just what the studio wanted: a wall-to-wall score (with holes for the songs, of course) with loud orchestral fireworks.

■ **Scary Movie 2** (2001)

Original composer: **George S. Clinton**
Replacement composers: **Marco Beltrami and friends and more**

Scary Movie—the Wayans Bros.' spoof of the slasher-movie genre, especially *Scream* and *I Know What You Did Last Summer*—was a big hit in 2000. Its first sequel, *Scary Movie 2*, a weak gross-out comedy, took its inspiration from a mix of horror movies and bits of recent pop culture: Beginning with a spoof of *The Exorcist*, it included parodies of and references to *Poltergeist, The Legend of Hell House, Suspiria, A Nightmare on Elm Street, What Lies Beneath, Hannibal, Hollow Man, Charlie's Angels, Mission: Impossible II*, and many other films, as well as a Nike commercial and even TV's *The Weakest Link*. Its primary story—a college professor bribes a group of students to spend a weekend in a haunted house—was possibly based on the 1963 horror classic *The Haunting* (or more likely its 1999 remake). Although *Scary Movie 2* was a terribly uneven and fragmented movie that was roughed up by most critics, it did fairly good business at the box office.

The movie was plagued with innumerable reshoots and other changes, and its score also became a hodgepodge. The first composer involved was George S. Clinton, whose recent credits included *3,000 Miles to Graceland* (2001) and *Austin Powers: The Spy Who Shagged Me* (1999). He remembers his work on the project:

> I met the director [Keenan Ivory Wayans] and we seemed to be on the same page, that the movie was continuously developing. Even the ideas the director talked to me about initially began to change as well. The Weinsteins were producing it, and they decided on many of the changes. I was already gone down the road to writing a score which was an orchestral horror score that didn't try to be jokey. I wanted the music to be scary—the fun part was that you realized that the jokes are funny. They are not scary, they are funny, but the music is communicating something else. The attitude changed and they decided they didn't want the music to be scary—in fact they wanted it to be funny. Rather than giving me the opportunity to make that adjustment, they decided to go with other people. In fact, what they were temping the score with was Randy Newman's *Meet the Parents*. That's a very light comedy score, but they decided that's what they wanted.

As new gags appeared and the picture changed, the director requested new cues, so additional composers were brought in to replace a considerable amount of Clinton's music with funnier cues that had stylistic similarities to the pictures they spoofed. Composer Danny Lux wrote six big cues (about twenty minutes' worth of music), but all but one of his cues went unused. Soon, more composers got involved, writing and rewriting cues for the same sequences. Composer Marco Beltrami was hired to write replacement music and wrote a number of cues. But when Clinton's entire score was scrapped, the job grew too big for Beltrami, who was still busy on *Angel Eyes* and other commitments.

Many composers (often Beltrami cohorts) were brought in on the project through either Beltrami (who would get a "score coordinator" credit) or the producers. These "additional music" composers included guitarist and synth programmer Buck Sanders, orchestrator Ceiri Torjussen, Kevin Kliesch, Benoit Grey, Rossano Galente, Michael McCuistion (an orchestrator on Elliot Goldenthal's *Batman & Robin* and *Batman Forever* scores as well as the animated *Batman* TV series and Shirley Walker's score for *Batman: Mask of Phantasm*), Kevin Manthei (of *Invader ZIM* and *Xiaolin Showdown* fame), Christopher Guardino, and Tom Hiel. As a result of the large number of contributors, the music ended up just like the movie—a series of individually funny moments with no overarching concept or structure.

■ **Rat Race** (2001)

Original composer: **Elmer Bernstein**
Replacement composer: **John Powell**

Producer-director Jerry Zucker's *Rat Race,* essentially a variation on Stanley Kramer's zany star-studded comedy *It's a Mad, Mad, Mad, Mad World* (1963), was about a motley group of people who set off on a treasure-seeking race from Las Vegas, Nevada, to Silver City, New Mexico. It was yet another in Zucker's long line of broad comedies, which included *Airplane!* (1980), *Top Secret!* (1984), and *The Naked Gun: From the Files of Police Squad!* (1986). With the exception of a couple of amusing sequences, though, *Rat Race* wasn't very good. To score it, Zucker first approached composer Jerry Goldsmith, with whom he'd worked on *First Knight* (1995), but an appendectomy left Goldsmith out of the running. So Zucker hired Elmer Bernstein, with whom he had worked on *Airplane!*. (Bernstein's most recent scoring credits were *Chinese Coffee, Keeping the Faith,* and *Bringing Out the Dead.*)

Sadly, the music that Bernstein wrote and recorded for *Rat Race* was rejected. In fact, the score's very existence seemed to get swept under the rug: The composer never came forward with the full story about it, only mentioning the score in an interview conducted right after he finished recording it. Moreover, when Bernstein's catalogue of works was initially published by his estate, it was easy for film music fans and scholars to overlook the existence of this rejected score because, as a simple listing, it was easily confused with Bernstein's music for director Robert Mulligan's romantic comedy *The Rat Race* (1960). A more detailed catalogue later revealed that USC's Bernstein Collection houses material from both *Rat Race* and *The Rat Race.*

John Powell, whose recent scoring credits included *Evolution* (2001) and *Shrek* (2001), became *Rat Race*'s replacement composer. His score is a collection of colorful vignettes that range from deranged dance pieces to overblown circus music. When compared with Bernstein's somewhat serious approach, Powell's music, with its more overtly funny cues (particularly those featuring the steroid-pumped circus music and the quiet choir), tied into the movie's madcap scenes more effectively, while also highlighting the no-holds-barred race's "epic" quality.

■ **Behind Enemy Lines** (2001)

Original composer: **Paul Haslinger**
Replacement composer: **Don Davis**

Behind Enemy Lines, a war-action movie starring Owen Wilson and Gene Hackman, was Irish director John Moore's feature film debut. Set in the final months of the 1990s Bosnian War, it's the story of a US Navy pilot on a recon mission who, after photographing a mass grave and illegal Serb troop activity in a demilitarized zone, is shot down behind Serbian lines. Once on the ground, the pilot must stay alive, awaiting rescue, by outwitting and eluding the tracker that the Serb commander sent to find and kill him.

The film's original vision of war-torn Bosnia was considerably darker than what finally made it to theater screens. Austrian composer Paul Haslinger, a former member of the innovative and influential synth group Tangerine Dream, was hired to score it in its original dark form. (Haslinger's recent scoring credits included *Picture Claire* and *Crazy/Beautiful*.) His idea was to create, right from the start, an unsettling mood with music that combined electronic and orchestral forces. To help him achieve some of the score's unusual textures, Haslinger worked on processed samples and electronic sounds with ambient-music composer, performer, and sound designer Robert Rich. In an interview given while he was working on the movie, Haslinger said that his score (in which he utilized ReCycle! software, a sample looping program) "combines traditional war movie music with current up-to-date structures and sound, including loops.... Due to the nature of the film, much of the material is rhythmic." To evoke the movie's Eastern European setting, Haslinger made use of a *duduk*, an ancient Armenian double-reed instrument of the oboe family.

While Haslinger was writing his score, the film's producers decided that the picture needed more action and less ambiguity in its characterizations. To shift its emphasis toward action and a broader audience, some of its darkest material—e.g., some mass grave images, a death squad scene, etc.—was edited out (a director's cut containing much of this is available on DVD). And by the time the producers' new vision of the film had been finalized, a new composer was on the job: Don Davis, whose recent scoring credits included *The Matrix* (1999) and *The Unsaid* (2001).

Davis's highly eclectic score was more action-oriented than Haslinger's and featured military marches, driving technopop-oriented music, and splashy orchestral cues. It bookends the movie with "Ustao," a hymn with lyrics by director Moore.

The picture was a success and spawned two direct-to-video sequels—sequels only in the sense that they were tales of soldiers caught behind enemy lines (*Behind Enemy Lines II: Axis of Evil*, set in North Korea, and *Behind Enemy Lines: Colombia*)—that did not draw on the original movie's' creative talents.

■ Texas Rangers (2001)

Original composer: **Marco Beltrami**
Replacement composer: **Trevor Rabin**

Texas Rangers, directed by Steve Miner (whose credits included *Lake Placid* and *Halloween H20*), was designed to be an old-fashioned oater that followed the casting lead of 1988's successful *Young Guns*. It starred a group of young teen heartthrobs, including James Van Der Beek, Rachael Leigh Cook, Ashton Kutcher, and Dylan McDermott, in a story loosely based on the exploits of Texas Ranger Leander McNelly's battle with rustler-gunslinger John King Fisher along the Texas-Mexico border in the 1870s. Unlike *Young Guns*, it would turn out to be an utter disaster at the box office.

For one reason or another, *Texas Rangers* lounged on Miramax's shelves for two years after its production wrapped. During this time, the movie lost much of its commercial appeal as its young stars aged. It also lost its music, by Marco Beltrami, a composer who had scored a number Miramax's horror films and whose work with director Miner on *Halloween H20: 20 Years Later* (1998) apparently led to the *Texas Rangers* gig. (Among Beltrami's other recent scores were *The Minus Man*, *The Faculty*, and *54*.)

Beltrami wrote what he considered one of his best works—a contemporary Western score that blends traditional Western movie music elements with modern orchestrations. For instance, his action cues' propulsive percussion was given a Western flavor with harmonica and trumpet solos (though, stepping completely outside the Western movie tradition, the score also included a "Dies Irae" quotation). The wailing vocals he used for such tragic cues as "Palo Alto Massacre" and "Burial" were also very effective, and he would make use of this color again in his *Dracula 2000* score.

But problems arose for Beltrami's score at a test screening that featured his temporary demo music, produced in his own studio. It's a fact that demo music often doesn't convey the vibrancy that a final score will have once it is recorded by an orchestra, and after the screening, Beltrami's music was deemed too old-fashioned for the youth market the film hoped to reach.

For a replacement score the picture's producers turned to Trevor Rabin, a former member (from 1983 to 1994) of the British progressive-rock band Yes. Rabin's recent scoring credits included *Gone in 60 Seconds* (2000), *Remember the Titans* (2000), and *The 6th Day* (2000). For *Texas Rangers* he wrote music that featured rock power anthems with a Western flavor—in other words, a genre score modified to fit the target audience's rock-music tastes. Rabin rates the score high in his filmography, and interestingly, he would very soon score another revisionist Western featuring another hot young cast, *American Outlaws* (2001). But, like *Texas Rangers*, it would also turn out to be a box-office disaster.

Marco Beltrami dealt with another half-finished scoring job in 2007, when he worked on the animated resurrection of the Teenage Mutant Ninja Turtles franchise, *TMNT*. The movie's early versions were a lot darker in tone than what finally made it to theater screens, and Beltrami's score played to this darkness with evocative action writing along the lines of his music for *Blade II* (2002). But *TMNT*'s great alteration in mood sealed his score's fate before it was even recorded (it exists only in the form of synth-sampler demo cues). A new score was provided by German composer Klaus Badelt, whose music was more lighthearted than Beltrami's and incorporated elements of Oriental music to highlight the turtles' ninja skills.

■ **The Mothman Prophecies** (2002)

Original composer: **tomandandy**
Additional music composer: **Jeff Rona**

The Mothman, West Virginia's answer to the Loch Ness Monster and the Yeti, was a large red-eyed, winged creature supposedly seen in the mid-1960s in a little town along the Ohio River. Noted ufologist John Keel wrote a book about it, *The Mothman Prophecies*, which became the basis for a film of the same name starring Richard Gere. Being about a paranormal phenomenon, it was fitting that the movie should have an atmospheric score. To provide this, director Mark Pellington turned to his favorite musicmakers, tomandandy, the duo of composers Tom Hajdu and Andy Milburn. Tomandandy had previously worked with Pellington on the documentary *United States of Poetry* (1995), the comedy *Going All the Way* (1997), the paranoid thriller *Arlington Road* (1999), and a few smaller projects. On *Arlington Road*, they had to collaborate with composer Angelo Badalamenti, David Lynch's regular composer, because the film's producers didn't fully trust the duo of relative newcomers. Badalamenti and tomandandy soon found an interesting way to work together, and the final score was a perfect atmospheric accompaniment for the film. The duo remember this collaboration:

> There were some concerns from the producers that we could do a proper score. Their concern manifested itself in the hiring of Badalamenti for the primary score. Pellington was always interested in using us on the project, and I think he just had a hard time selling that, frankly. The great news was that Angelo had a really collaborative mind, and we learned a lot by working under him on that job.... We worked primarily in modules. We would do one chunk and he would do another chunk. Then we later started to smear those boundaries by smearing our stuff underneath and around some of the work that Angelo did. Angelo worked on a lot of the themes, then we helped to sort of expand on that.

By the time *The Mothman Prophecies* project came around, there was enough confidence in tomandandy's talents that the studio didn't insist on hiring a name composer to work with them. Yet the duo once again found themselves in an unusual collaboration, this time due to music that was part of the film's temp tracks. Highly regarded sound designer Claude Letessier (in the mid-1990s a member of the sound design department at Media Ventures) created some memorable atmospheric textures for the film using music by composer Jeff Rona. This music, featured in the temp score, soon became a part of the film's final musical vision. Rona remembers his unorthodox involvement with the movie for which he never wrote a note:

> Some of my music had made it into the temp. Claude Letessier, a friend of mine, was the sound designer on the film, and he had a very heavy role in the overall architecture of the soundtrack, sound effects, and music. Everything to do with the sound passed through him in a really unusual way, with him integrating music and effects together

> and manipulating everything rather abstractly. Pellington had really responded to some of these pieces that I had written and licensed them into the score. In the end, they used around eighteen cues of mine in the film, including the opening title music and the whole ending sequence of the movie. Actually, tomandandy took a whack at replacing some of my music, and they just couldn't, because their approach is somewhat different from mine. There's a couple of their cues in the movie that quote my pieces, if you know what I mean. I think they did a terrific job on the score.

The strange backstory of *The Mothman Prophecies* soundscape wasn't known at the time of the movie's release, so after Jeff Rona's credit for additional music appeared, some film score fans conjectured that he had penned a rejected score for the film. But that was not the case.

■ The Bourne Identity (2002)

Original composer: **Carter Burwell**
Replacement composer: **John Powell**

The Bourne Identity, a movie based on the first novel in Robert Ludlum's popular Bourne trilogy, told the story of Jason Bourne (played by Matt Damon), a spy suffering from amnesia who, against a backdrop of dangerous internal intrigue at the CIA, tries to discover his identity. It was directed by Doug Liman, whose previous directing credits included *Swingers* (1996) and *Go* (1999).

Hired to score it was Carter Burwell, a composer who had scored all but one of the Coen Brothers movies and whose recent credits included *A Knight's Tale* (2001) and *Before Night Falls* (2000).

Although Liman's hit *Go* had a soundtrack made up mostly of songs compiled by popular music producer, engineer, composer and songwriter BT (Brian Transeau), when the director got together with Burwell, the two set out to redefine Hollywood's spy music genre with a melodramatic score that would reflect the profession's loneliness. Lending the picture an unusual soundscape, Burwell wrote a percussive score that featured lots of electronics, which he felt perfectly fit the tone of the film's protagonist. Liman, however, wasn't very communicative regarding the music and never gave Burwell completely clear indications of what he liked and disliked.

Burwell finished writing the score, produced synth-sampler demos of it, and had recorded about one-third of it when real-life events suddenly interceded. Learning that his wife was expecting, he flew back to his home in New York. The 9/11 attacks occurred the very next day, and not only did that New York tragedy affect Hollywood by bringing all motion picture production to an immediate halt, but *The Bourne Identity*'s subject matter, political assassination, suddenly became especially touchy. The movie was put on a hold for half a year while its producers figured out whether anything in it needed to be modified to accommodate America's changed political climate. During this extended postproduction period, Burwell was in an uneasy situation: His scoring assignment, which had been put on hold, was scheduled to resume around the time when his wife would most need him by her side. Although he liked the picture, he chose his family over *Bourne*'s.

Around this time, composer John Powell, whose recent credits included *I Am Sam* (2001) and *Rat Race* (2001), was actively shopping for future projects, particularly with the director Liman, as he recalls:

> The year before I got that job [*The Bourne Identity*], I was standing in a video store with my agent, we were walking around—I think we were just killing time—and we were looking at the shelves of films and I was pointing out filmmakers that I thought were great, and my agent said wouldn't it be great if I could work with this guy and this guy. I was looking at *Go* by Doug Liman, and I had just seen it, and I said, "This is an incredible film, you know, this guy is really good. Could we find out what he is doing at the moment?" And of course the next day she called and she said he's doing this film called *The Bourne Identity* but they've already got a composer, so I didn't think anything of it, but a year later, the film had been delayed and it had gone through a bit of a rough exogenesis. It had been a bit tough for everybody, but that's the way Doug works.

Hired to write a new score for *The Bourne Identity*, Powell succeeded in coming up with the sound Liman was looking for. To do this, he spent the first four weeks experimenting—putting all kinds of electronic, percussive, and classical cues against the picture to determine which sorts of music worked and which didn't. The central idea he arrived at, which would come to define the Bourne sonic identity, was powerful drumming enhanced by sampled and synthesized sounds. While this concept certainly wasn't groundbreaking, the way Powell combined restless, driving rhythms with his mystery-laden orchestral themes made the "Bourne sound" the "in" sound for several years. Just as the Bond scores defined spy movie music in the 1960s, the popular and influential Bourne scores would define the sound of spy and assassin movies at the dawn of the twenty-first century.

Most composers toil away through to the final recording day before their music is thrown out, but Burwell seems to have the good luck (or good sense) to exit projects that he senses aren't working out for him at an early stage. In addition to *The Bourne Identity*, two other unfinished Burwell scores are worth noting. One was for the notoriously unfunny comedy *Gigli* (2003), for which Burwell had barely finished recording a quarter of his score when the first negative reactions arrived from the film's test screenings. The picture then went through extensive recutting that threw off the composer's schedule, so Burwell departed the project before finishing his score's recording. Once again, John Powell stepped in to provide new music for the production. Another unfinished Burwell score worth mentioning was for director Joss Whedon's *Serenity* (2005), for which the composer wrote only about five demo pieces before he and the director realized they had different pictures in mind.

One Hour Photo (2002)

Original composer: **Trent Reznor**
Replacement composers: **Reinhold Heil and Johnny Klimek**

When the popular rock band R.E.M. announced that it was writing a song for the 1998 drama *A Cool, Dry Place,* the band's bassist, Mike Mills, was also named as the picture's composer. However, a combination of scheduling problems and a lack of familiarity with the medium resulted in Mills's being replaced on the project by composer and music editor Curt Sobel. Whether anything from Mills's unused music for this picture was later utilized by R.E.M. is still a subject of conjecture among the band's fans. But his unused *A Cool, Dry Place* music is not as hot a topic as the score that industrial rock band Nine Inch Nails (NIN) founder and leader Trent Reznor supposedly wrote for *One Hour Photo.*

Before his feature film debut with the psychological thriller *One Hour Photo,* writer-director Mark Romanek had directed music videos for NIN and R.E.M., as well as for Johnny Cash and Madonna; his credits included NIN's "Closer" and "The Perfect Drug" videos, and Cash's cover of NIN's "Hurt."

One Hour Photo, starring Robin Williams, relates a twisted tale of a lonely film developer working in a discount department store's photo department. As the story progresses, this obsessive and obsessed protagonist grows more and more mentally unhinged. During the film's production, Romanek reportedly used instrumental tracks from NIN's *The Fragile* album to put the actors in the right mood for shooting. Word of this caused some NIN fans to speculate that Trent Reznor might actually write the movie's score. And apparently Reznor did write a couple of cues: When the NIN CD *Still* was released, its instrumental tracks "Gone, Still" and "The Persistence of Loss" were said to have been composed for the movie. But for some reason those cues didn't work out, so Reznor never wrote a complete score.

Hired to score *One Hour Photo* was the composing team of Reinhold Heil and Johnny Klimek, whose scoring credits included German director Tom Tykwer's *Winter Sleepers* (1997), his highly influential *Run Lola Run* (1998), and his *The Princess and the Warrior* (2000). Heil analyzes an inherent problem with the director's original musical vision for the project:

> Mark [Romanek] had an idea of something very ambient, and the problem with that is if you have a film that starts off very slowly and you have a lot of ambient music there, it doesn't propel the story. So our efforts went in this direction. Luckily, they did a screening and there was a budget crunch and a hiatus—there were all sorts of limitations—and I think he really made the most of that. Instead of taking a focus group or doing a screening he just did internal screenings for the crew, and those are very informative because you see what's not working immediately. He absolutely admitted the first approach wasn't working and took responsibility for that. We changed direction, started over, and tried something where the music propels the story. It was very hard with a lot of long nights,

> but the director gave us a lot of guidance. He's very detail-oriented and very precise, and we like a dialogue with the director.

The film's very effective Heil-Klimek score was quite different from what Reznor's music probably would have been like. It features a simple music-box-like tune that degenerates along with the lonely protagonist's mental state. By the second half of the movie, growing dissonance signals the disintegration of his friendly personality. This gradual dissolution of the music aided the story's development instead of just setting its mood.

It's interesting to note that while this early score wasn't such a success for Reznor, he and other former members of NIN managed to launch successful film music careers. Charlie Clouser, for instance, became the in-house composer for the *Saw* series of films, and Reznor won an Academy Award for his score for *The Social Network* (2010).

■ Till Human Voices Wake Us (2002)

Composer for Australian version: **Dale Cornelius**
Composer for international version: **Amotz Plessner**

Writer-director Michael Petroni took the title (and perhaps some of the plot) of his debut feature film, a sentimental supernatural romance, from the final lines of T. S. Eliot's poem "The Love Song of J. Alfred Prufrock": "We have lingered in the chambers of the sea / By sea-girls wreathed with seaweed red and brown / Till human voices wake us, and we drown."

It told the story of two youths, the fifteen-year-old boy Sam and a crippled, poetry-loving girl named Silvy, who fall in love during a summer break from school. One night, the two go for a dip in a nearby lake, and when Sam releases his hold on Silvy to point out a falling star, she disappears beneath the water and drowns. The story then jumps ahead twenty years. Sam (played by Guy Pearce), now a psychology teacher, is troubled by the guilt he feels over Silvy's death. On a train home to attend his father's funeral, he meets Ruby (Helena Bonham Carter), a woman whom he later saves from drowning when she she throws herself from a bridge. After thwarting her attempted suicide, although she now suffers from amnesia and an inability to walk, he builds a relationship with her. The question is, is Ruby the returned spirit of Silvy?

To score his picture, Petroni hired Australian Dale Cornelius for what would be the composer's first feature film gig. Cornelius remembers.

> I was asked by Michael Petroni to write the music for his film after he had heard some of my string quartet compositions. I didn't have much time to write, record, and mix the score after pic lock-off (approx four weeks), so I got copies of the rough cuts and improvised collectively around forty minutes of music on piano as a guide to where I felt emotionally the tone of the picture was centered and also from discussions with Michael Petroni. Michael came over and listened to these improvisations, pictured them within

> the film as it was basically an assembly at this stage and liked the romanticism and exoticness of the ideas. There turned out to be a lot more music upon spotting the film than they (director and producers) originally thought. Once we reached the recording stage I knew we had tremendous amounts of music to get through per call. Most of the cues were recorded without overdubs, so it was really important for me to get the orchestration and arrangement right beforehand and create a flow to the recording process—which I think helped in this case with me conducting.

Cornelius's chamber score worked wonderfully with the director's cut of the movie. However, once Paramount Classics picked up the picture for the American market, everything started to change. The distributor was troubled by the fact that the film's famous leads—Pearce and Carter—didn't appear until almost forty minutes into it. To remedy this, the picture was recut, and its first act—the story of teens Sam and Silvy—was spread throughout the movie as a series of flashbacks set into the story of adults Sam and Ruby. After that, composer Amotz Plessner (whose recent credits included *After Sex* and *Escape to Grizzly Mountain*) was hired to mock up a temp score that would fit the new cut. Seeing the updated version accompanied by Plessner's temp music persuaded the distributor to have Plessner write and record a new orchestral score for it. Plessner remembers:

> Then they gave me the job of scoring the movie. This was an executive decision, it wasn't the director's choice. Michael was in Australia and we started talking about the score over the phone. We got on very well and I actually traveled to Australia to record the music. The original Australian score is an ensemble score, and we recorded my score with a bigger orchestra, a bit more Hollywood-like. I believe they thought that the small chamber orchestra would not sell in America.

The movie opened in 2004 on only five screens in North America, where its reception was lukewarm. Re-editing *Till Human Voices Wake Us* for the American market made the film a wholly different experience—its story, now directly paralleling the characters' lives as children (via flashbacks) and as adults, became too obvious. Currently, the American version is the one commonly available worldwide; however, the movie's original cut is available in Australia on a Region 4 DVD with Cornelius's score intact. His score is also available on CD, released by Mana Music Productions. Plessner's music hasn't been released.

■ **The Tuxedo** (2002)

Original composer: **Christophe Beck**
Additional composer: **John Debney**

First-time feature film director Kevin Donovan's spy spoof *The Tuxedo* is an action-comedy in which a master spy's chauffeur (played by Jackie Chan) slips into his injured boss's magic biotech tuxedo, enabling him to, among other strange and silly powers, walk up walls, sing and dance like James Brown (who puts in a cameo appearance as himself), and camouflage himself, not to mention granting him martial arts expertise. The chauffeur uses it to thwart a mad bottled-water magnate's plot to poison the country's water supply.

The picture was scored by Canadian composer Christophe Beck, who had penned music for quite a few small comedy features (including the recent films *Bring It On, Broken Hearts Club, Slap Her...She's French, Big Fat Liar,* and *Stealing Harvard*) and a good number of television shows, including fifty-eight episodes of *Buffy the Vampire Slayer*. He wrote an updated and slightly electronic James Bond spoof score, but the filmmakers, for one reason or another, chose to hire another composer as well. That second choice, John Debney, had previously written faux spy music for *Inspector Gadget* and *Cats & Dogs*. (Among his other recent comedies were *Liar Liar, My Favorite Martian, Dick, See Spot Run, Jimmy Neutron: Boy Genius, Spy Kids,* and *Spy Kids 2*.)

The Tuxedo's final score utilized both composers' work. However, it's hard to say that any one of its cues has a signature musical identity that would distinguish it as the specific work of one composer or the other. This is likely due to the limitations imposed on the music by both the genre and the picture. Also, both composers employed the same ensemble, the Hollywood Studio Symphony (a loose grouping of Los Angeles studio musicians formed in 2002 to draw more scoring business back to LA), and even used similar electronic samples to underscore Jackie Chan's spy antics. Both Beck's and Debney's music is represented on the film's official soundtrack CD, which even includes both composers' cues for some of the same scenes, e.g., "The Rope".

The Tuxedo wasn't the first or the last time that either Beck or Debney was called on to help out comedies that already had scores: Beck provided music-doctoring services for such features as *Dog Park* (1998), replacing Craig Northey's score, and *Fred Claus* (2007), replacing Rolfe Kent's score. Debney's resumé of replacement music for comedies includes *Carpool* (1996), replacing Bill Conti's score, *The Adventures of Elmo in Grouchland* (1999), replacing Graeme Revell, and *Inspector Gadget* (1999) and *The Emperor's New Groove* (2000), replacing scores by Marc Shaiman.

Some film composers tend to specialize in writing for comedies, either by choice or as the result of musical typecasting. And Hollywood's inclination to typecast composers by film genre, often asking them for the same musical solutions over and over again, can lead to an unfortunate homogenization of film music.

■ Hellraiser: Hellseeker (2002)

Original composer: **Raz Mesinai**
Replacement composer: **Stephen Edwards**

The first *Hellraiser* movie was discussed earlier in this book. Now it's time for one of its sequels to feel the wrath of filmmaking's Cenobites. The series' sixth installment (i.e., fifth sequel), *Hellraiser: Hellseeker*, picked up the story of Kirsty Cotton, the heroine of the first two *Hellraiser* movies.

Not altogether unlike the band Coil, which wrote a replaced score for the first *Hellraiser*, its sixth installment's original composer—Israeli-born New York composer-performer Raz Mesinai—is best known for his musical experimentation. He was chosen to score the movie after its director heard his album *The Heretic of Ether*, an excursion into Middle Eastern–flavored music featuring masterful hand drumming, in a Los Angeles record shop. Although he had never scored a movie before (music of his had, however, been used in the soundtracks to Ridley Scott's *Black Hawk Down* and Jonathan Demme's *The Truth About Charlie*), Mesinai accepted the job because he was a fan of *Hellraiser*'s creator, author-director Clive Barker. (Even if, by this point in the franchise's life, Barker was no longer directly involved with the movies.)

Mesinai faced two obstacles in writing his score: First, he was situated in New York while the production was based in Los Angeles, so communications were conducted by phone. Second, this being his first film-scoring job, his personal studio didn't have the necessary equipment to synchronize picture and music, so this gear had to be rented and learned. Regardless of these technical handicaps, Mesinai put together a very effective dark, textural score for voices, violin, viola, double bass, piano, harpsichord, and percussion that contained some of the scariest sounds he could create, including top-of-one's-lungs screaming. But when he presented his music to the film's producers, it was rejected as being "too scary"—a most unusual problem for a horror score!

Despite the fact that *Hellraiser*'s sequels were scored by various composers (including Randy Miller and Daniel Licht), they all followed a similar orchestral approach and sometimes even referenced Christopher Young's themes from the first movie. (Young also scored the film's first sequel.) Mesinai's music, however, was from a sound world that was completely new to the franchise. To replace it, the filmmakers hired Stephen Edwards, whose recent scoring credits included *No Sleep 'til Madison* (2002) and *Children of the Corn: Revelation* (2001). Edwards' score revisited the more orchestral *Hellraiser* sound, although it seems a bit pale when compared to the series' previous scores.

But Mesinai's discarded music would not rest quietly: It rose from the grave and began a new life of its own when Messina released it as an album titled *The Unspeakable*. This recording does not present the actual score in cue-by-cue fashion; instead it is a remixed and resequenced program with a few new pieces added to make for a better listening experience. As an album it is one of the scariest recordings you may ever hear. Like Coil's release of its unused music for the first *Hellraiser*, Mesinai's unused score for the sixth installment became a fairly popular recording.

■ Gangs of New York (2002)

Original composer: **Elmer Bernstein**
Replacement composer: **Howard Shore**

Gangs of New York was a project Martin Scorsese had been planning for more than twenty-five years. The story concerned nineteenth-century New York City's gang wars among various immigrant groups, particularly focusing on the Irish (which made up a quarter of the city's population at that time) and their opposition by a gang of native-born Americans. It was a big undertaking that covered a lot of history, including the dealings of the infamously corrupt local politician "Boss" Tweed and the violent 1863 New York Draft Riot (a revolt against Civil War draft laws that favored the well-to-do over the poor and the working class, and that turned into an anti-black race riot).

This colorful and strange epic, produced by Harvey Weinstein of Miramax Films, was filmed on an enormous set built at Cinecittà Studios in Rome and featured an all-star cast headlined by Leonardo DiCaprio and Daniel Day-Lewis. Three hours long after its initial edit, the movie ran considerably over budget. For various reasons, its premiere was pushed back by a year, during which time it was honed down to two hours and forty minutes. During this postponement, the movie's musical landscape also was altered.

The first composer on the project was Elmer Bernstein, who had a history with Scorsese, having worked on the director's 1991 remake of *Cape Fear* (for which Bernstein adapted and arranged Bernard Herrmann's score from the original 1960 film) and then scored Scorsese's *The Age of Innocence* (1993) and *Bringing Out the Dead* (1999). Although Bernstein worked on *Gangs of New York*'s music for almost a year before recording it with the Royal Philharmonic Orchestra in London's Abbey Road Studio, the movie's score had been in a state of flux from the outset because the director and the composer didn't fully agree on the best approach. Bernstein recalls:

> Marty [Scorsese] and I started talking about it over a year ago. He wasn't that sure what he really wanted, but he got really married to the idea of ethnic music—a lot of this film is about Irish immigrants coming to the U.S. He got very hung up on the ethnic aspects of the music, too much so in my opinion, so we were never really able to get to grips with it. I wrote a whole bunch of stuff, but Marty ultimately did something that he very often does, which is to construct a score from various sources. So, there's a lot of my music and a lot of ethnic music, but not a score as we would conceive a score.... I felt that the film was very exotic, but didn't have any obvious heroes and was without a strong love story. Marty and I had conversations about this—I said that the language of the music should be a language that concerns the audience with the film. But Scorsese was more concerned with street authenticity, and wanted to use Irish music because it was authentic. If you hear a lot of nineteenth-century Irish music, is that going to connect you with the film? I don't know. It's a judgment call on his part.

Bernstein penned a score that combined traditional Irish-sounding melodies with big, propulsive historical-epic music that favored the orchestra's brass, lower strings, and percussion. For the love interest and more poignant cues, he favored woodwinds. (For those who keep a tally of such things, the tumultuous cue "Battle" quoted the famous "Dies Irae" melody.) Regardless of how exciting the music was, in the end, Bernstein's penultimate film score went unused.

The final movie's music was culled from a broad variety of sources. In total, *Gangs of New York* utilized eighty-six different pieces of music, ranging from fife and drum music to hymns to Irish, British, and African-American folk music (some pulled from the famous Alan Lomax collection of recordings), to a Chinese opera excerpt to songs by famous pop artists U2 (providing the Oscar-nominated "The Hands that Built America") and Peter Gabriel. This diverse selection of music was bookended by three Howard Shore cues (the three-part "Brooklyn Heights") that each present a different view of more or less the same thematic material, hinting at Irish melodies and instrumentation and featuring some haunting solo vocals. (Shore had first worked with Scorsese in 1985 on *After Hours*, and he would go on to work on the director's films *The Aviator* and *The Departed*.)

As for Bernstein's massive rejected score, the composer wanted very much to get its recording released, but that project fell into limbo when he died in 2004. However, Varèse Sarabande released it in 2008 in a boxed set of CDs that also included Bernstein's unused music for *The Journey of Natty Gann* (1985) and *The Scarlet Letter* (1995).

The Hours (2002)

Original composer: **Stephen Warbeck**
Replacement composer: **Michael Nyman**
Replacement composer of replacement composer: **Philip Glass**

Based on the Pulitzer Prize–winning novel by Michael Cunningham and adapted for the screen by playwright David Hare, *The Hours* is a triptych of tales about three solitary women from different generations and places: the influential British modernist author Virginia Woolf in the mid-1920s (played by Nicole Kidman), a housewife in early-1950s Los Angeles (Julianne Moore), and a present-day New York book editor (Meryl Streep). A number of themes, including depression, death, and Woolf's novel *Mrs. Dalloway*, connect the women's lives.

Creating a score for such a complex picture was not an easy task, so director Stephen Daldry (whose one previous feature film was *Billy Elliot*) constructed a temp score to test how music might hold together the movie's various times, places, and people. Excerpts from the works of popular concert and film composer Philip Glass, noted for his readily identifiable minimalist style, dominated this temp score. But, unaware that Glass might be interested in such an assignment, the filmmakers turned to British composer Stephen Warbeck to score the film. Warbeck, whose recent scoring credits included *Captain Corelli's Mandolin* (2001) and *Quills* (2000), had won an Academy Award for his *Shakespeare in Love* (1998) music; he also scored director Daldry's *Billy Elliot* (2000). Warbeck first discussed *The Hours* with its producer Scott Rudin, who championed a minimalist-style approach to the music. However, as the movie moved toward its final shape, Warbeck and the director decided that the score needn't adhere to a minimalist style after all. But the producer was sold on the idea of Glass-like music, so a new composer was brought on to the project.

This was Michael Nyman, a British film and concert music composer noted for his own very recognizable brand of musical minimalism. (Interestingly, Nyman is generally credited with being the first to apply the term "minimalism" to music, which he did in a 1968 article about composer Cornelius Cardew for the *The Spectator* magazine.) Among Nyman's recent scoring credits were Michael Winterbottom's *The Claim* and Neil Jordan's *The End of the Affair*. Like Warbeck, Nyman had to battle the filmmakers' predisposition to the temp score of Glass's works. And likewise, it was a battle he couldn't win: Nyman was dropped from the project after delivering a complete demo score recorded with eleven players, anticipating that a final recording would take a similarly intimate chamber-music approach.

At this point, the filmmakers finally got in touch with the composer whose work had spoken so directly to them as they put the picture together. To their surprise, Glass eagerly accepted the job. (Among his recent scoring credits were *The Baroness and the Pig* and *Naqoyqatsi*.) Looking back on *The Hours*, Glass commented:

> They were looking for my style of music, but they didn't think I would be interested in film. But, as you know, I've done a lot of work in films. They contacted me and showed me the film, and I was very impressed with it. I connected right away and knew that this is something I could do. I knew exactly what to do. We got along very well. Everything was terrific. You don't get to have that much fun in movies every time you go to bat.... I was looking for intimacy, and there is certainly something about intimacy with the piano for me. It's the thing you can have in your home. I contrasted it with the string section to give it depth and variety, but it's basically about the piano. I thought about what instrument would be playing in the room, which might be a strange question in a way, but it sometimes leads to interesting answers.

For *The Hours*, Glass wrote an insistent, lyrical, vaguely romantic score for string orchestra, string quartet, and piano. This subtle minimalist music stood as its own character ("a bold presence," as Glass put it), movingly commenting on the three stories' pervasive sadness while also acting as a common thread stitching together their different times, places, and characters. The score's effectiveness might be best measured by the large number of film reviewers who chose to comment on its emotional impact.

■ **Confessions of a Dangerous Mind** (2002)

Original composer: **David Holmes**
Replacement composer: **Alex Wurman**

George Clooney's directorial debut was a fanciful film about the supposed secret life of eccentric 1960s and 1970s television personality Chuck Barris (producer of such popular lowbrow TV fare as *The Dating Game, The Newlywed Game*, and *The Gong Show*), based on the autobiography in which Barris claimed to have been a globe-hopping CIA assassin. The movie starred Sam Rockwell, Drew Barrymore, Julia Roberts, and Clooney, and its style—its narratives twists and camera work, and even its original composer—owed a lot to its executive producer, Clooney's friend writer-director-producer Steven Soderbergh. (Clooney had starred in Soderbergh's *Out of Sight, Solaris*, and *Ocean's Eleven* and would go on to work on many later Soderbergh films.)

Irish DJ-turned-film-composer David Holmes was hired to score *Confessions of a Dangerous Mind*. Holmes had made his first splash in film music with his music for Soderbergh's *Out of Sight* (1998), a gig he got after the director heard his album *Let's Get Killed*. Following that, he scored Soderbergh's remake *of Ocean's Eleven* (2001) and its two sequels. (Soderbergh's primary composer, however, has been Cliff Martinez, who scored his *Sex, Lies, and Videotape*; *Traffic*; *Solaris*; and a half-dozen other films.)

The funky score that Holmes provided for *Confessions*, however, apparently wasn't exactly what Clooney was looking for, so he replaced him with composer Alex Wurman, whose recent scoring credits included *Thirteen Conversations About One Thing* (2001) and *Sleep Easy, Hutch Rimes* (2000). Holmes recalls getting hired and working on the picture:

> I have a friend named Stephen Mirrione, who cut Doug Liman's first movie, which I scored. He went on to cut Doug's next movie, *Swingers*, and they didn't offer it to me because they didn't have enough money and thought I wouldn't want to do it! I was kicking myself for a long time because, when I saw the screening, before Miramax bought it, I thought it was a very cool movie—I would have loved to do it! Stephen is a fantastic editor. Steven Soderbergh saw *Swingers*, hired Stephen to cut *Traffic*, and he got the Academy Award—but he's still a friend! So Stephen then cut *Thirteen Conversations About One Thing*, which, thanks to him, I scored. It was such a joy!.... Then Stephen was cutting *Confessions* and director-actor George Clooney was working with a different composer and he wanted to go in a different musical direction. Stephen suggested bringing me in to write some cues, and I was hired to score the film.... Clooney was very pleased because he had struggled to get something that he thought was working, and then they gave me one shot at it, and I got it right the first time. So it was smooth sailing for both of us! He is a great guy, too.

Wurman didn't have to write a lot of music for *Confessions of a Dangerous Mind*—the picture contains only about twenty minutes of his 1960s-flavored underscore, the rest of its sonic landscape being filled with easily identifiable songs of the era (including Freddy Cannon's 1963 hit "Palisades Park," which Chuck Barris wrote). Among the odd melange of oldies used in the picture were songs by the Moonglows, Link Wray, Donovan, Esquivel, Yma Sumac, Vikki Carr, the Who, and Peter, Paul and Mary. The film's official soundtrack CD focuses on its songs but also contains three cues penned by Wurman. However, a promotional release of Wurman's score shows off his music's honestly touching moments.

Confessions of a Dangerous Mind was not David Holmes's first rejected film work: In 2000, he worked on director Thaddeus O'Sullivan's *Ordinary Decent Criminal*, based on the life of the infamous Dublin criminal Martin Cahill (played by Kevin Spacey), who was active from the late 1960s until his murder in 1994. (The film's title is the Irish police term used to distinguish criminals out for financial gain from those with terrorist intentions. Interestingly, it was the third film on Cahill produced within a span of two years, the best-known being John Boorman's *The General*, starring Brendan Gleeson.)

Holmes apparently worked too hard on the score for O'Sullivan's film, reportedly spending four weeks perfecting one particular sound for it, so the director, having neither the time nor the money to wait for such slowly progressing music, parted ways with him. English singer-songwriter (and member of the alternative pop band Blur) Damon Albarn was called upon at the last minute to write the film's score, and his music provided *Ordinary Decent Criminal* with outstanding momentum. A CD of the film's music was released, but, as is often the case with soundtrack recordings, it was filled with unrelated songs and put little emphasis on Albarn's score.

■ **Phone Booth** (2002)

Original composer: **Nathan Larson**
Replacement composer: **Harry Gregson-Williams**

After his 1997 big-budget debacle, *Batman and Robin*, director Joel Schumacher came back with a series of interesting, dark, and often disturbing films, including *8mm* (1999), *Flawless* (1999), *Tigerland* (2000), and *Bad Company* (2002). *Phone Booth*, another of these small, dark films, starred Colin Farrell as Stu, a hustling, duplicitous, small-time New York publicist (not altogether unlike Sidney Falco, the character played by Tony Curtis in *Sweet Smell of Success*), who finds himself caught between the proverbial rock and a hard place. Answering a phone in a Times Square phone booth, he immediately finds himself in a nightmare: On the other end of the line is a sadistic, moralizing sniper (the voice of Kiefer Sutherland) who has him in his sights (in more ways than one) and, after implicating him in a murder in front of the booth, will not let him hang up the phone. Once the police (led by Forest Whitaker) arrive, Stu's damned if he leaves the booth and damned if he doesn't. The film, a sleeper hit, was fairly well received by critics, some of whom claimed it had Hitchcockian elements.

To score *Phone Booth*, Schumacher turned to Nathan Larson, a film composer with one foot firmly in the popular music world, who had provided the music for his gritty *Tigerland*, about army recruits training for the Vietnam War in 1971, when the war was clearly lost. (Among Larson's other recent scoring credits were *Prozac Nation* and *Boys Don't Cry*.) Larson's score for *Phone Booth*, in keeping with the nature of the project, was primarily tension music. Due to a well-publicized real sniper incident in Washington, DC, the movie's release was pushed back for almost a year, allowing for studio executives and the director to indulge in a lot of postproduction tinkering, which also involved the score. Larson recalls this tiring period, and the hiring of a new composer by the powers-that-were:

> The studio wanted to have themselves a [Jerry] Bruckheimer-style action thriller, which is tricky to pull off considering you're dealing with one guy in a phone booth the whole time, but it seems they managed. And I think that's totally their prerogative, of course—it's their money after all; and it's appropriate for the film. As for Joel [Schumacher], I think it was a combination of feeling that he wanted to be in more familiar, more traditional territory.... What I was doing (which was what I was initially instructed to do) was this weird minimalist electronic stuff, most of which was less bombastic than that bit I have on my CD. Another factor was fatigue: the post-production for that film dragged on for over a year, as Joel was off on other projects, so it was sort of start and stop and I think gave executives and director alike time to ponder what the score was doing for the movie, which really was a much more internal thing, 'cause that's sort of what I do, less to the action than just to general mood and emotion, etc. So I reckon they did the right thing, and I don't feel weird about it in the least.

Larson's replacement was Harry Gregson-Williams, a composer particularly noted for his comedy and animation scores. Among his recent scoring credits were *Spy Kids* (2001), *Shrek* (2000, with cocomposer John Powell), and *The Tigger Movie* (2000). Gregson-Williams recalls his work on the film:

> When I was over in Dublin on the set of *Veronica Guerin*, Schumacher asked me if I could look at a little experimental movie they'd already completed and scored and everything. He wanted to know if I felt that there was something that could be improved on with the music. I really enjoyed working on that one—so we've worked on two films now.... I hadn't done a purely electronic score before, and that's why it appealed to me. It was a lot of fun to leave the orchestra behind. I never saw it as a major musical work, but it does support the picture. I created a library of sounds, of the street around the phone booth. The idea was for the score to be part of the general atmosphere of New York—it was fairly liberating, actually! I'm constantly looking for these kinds of movies to score—things that are not ostentatious.

The new composer had two primary restrictions on his work: First, it was to be an electronic suspense score. There are few ways to approach such a claustrophobic thriller—and suspenseful electronic music is a good avenue if you ensure that the score won't intrude upon the film's psychological intensity. Secondly, Gregson-Williams had to follow the lead of Larson's score, because the producers still wanted to use portions of Larson's original music. In some senses, *Phone Booth* proved an important project for Gregson-Williams, leading, along with *Veronica Guerin* (2003), to more work with Schumacher—*The Number 23* (2007) and *Twelve* (2010)—and helping the composer stay out of a comedy-animation pigeonhole.

Following the movie's release, Nathan Larson, who received an "additional music" credit, checked its cue sheet to verify how much of his work had been used. According to the document, more than half of the film was still scored with his material, but after seeing the picture he claims he recognized little of it. His compilation CD *FilmMusik* contains a single cue ("Operator") from his score.

■ **Hulk** (2003)

Original composer: **Mychael Danna**
Replacement composer: **Danny Elfman**

Taiwan-born director Ang Lee's big-budget *Hulk*, produced by Universal Pictures, was based on Marvel Comics' Hulk, a giant green hero of superhuman strength created in 1962. (Among Lee's critically acclaimed earlier films were *Eat Drink Man Woman, Sense and Sensibility*, and *Crouching Tiger, Hidden Dragon*.) As in the comic book, the film's Hulk is the anger-triggered alter ego of mild-mannered, gamma-ray-mutated research scientist Dr. Bruce Bannon, although an additional DNA mutation backstory helps update the tale to the 2000s. Lee's vision of the protagonist (played by Eric Bana) didn't lend itself to the parameters of the traditional superhero action movie, so the director spent a good bit of screen time exploring Dr. Bannon's psyche. Lee comments:

> I mixed a lot of elements...King Kong, Frankenstein, Jekyll and Hyde, Beauty and the Beast, Faust, and a lot of Greek mythology. This is really a modern-day myth.... I don't think the Hulk is a superhero. He's the first Marvel character who is a tragic monster. Really an anti-hero. I feel that everyone has a Hulk inside, and each of our Hulks is both scary and, potentially, pleasurable. That's the scariest thing about them.

Hired to score the film was Canadian composer Mychael Danna, whose recent credits included *Antwone Fisher* (2002) and *Ararat* (2002). Before *Hulk*, Lee and Danna had worked together on *The Ice Storm* (1997), *Ride with the Devil* (1999), and the 2001 short *Chosen* (actually a long ad financed by BMW as part of a car-chase anthology film, *The Hire*, for which they commissioned five well-known directors to do shorts featuring The Driver—behind the wheel of a BMW, of course—a character portrayed by Clive Owen).

As the picture's postproduction progressed, the studio grew fearful that, in view of its character-driven plot and Lee's introspective vision of the protagonist, *Hulk* might bomb at the box office. As is so often the case in such situations, they decided to play it safe with the music. Mychael Danna recalls his brief association with the project:

> That was such an unfortunate situation. I think Ang was making a very unusual superhero movie and I was doing a very unusual score for it. We had recorded Japanese taiko, African drumming, Arabic singing, we had all this really wild music and then we were going to have a big orchestra as well, and I think the studio got very, very nervous about having something so unusual on the screen and having at the same time music so unusual. I think they just basically panicked, because again there's so much money at stake and they were thinking that if we're going to have such a weird movie we better at least have something that the audience is comfortable with, a score that we've heard a million times before, and Danny Elfman can write it.

Brought in to replace Danna was a composer long associated with the comic-book hero genre, Danny Elfman, whose recent credits included *Red Dragon* (2002) and Tim Burton's remake of *Planet of the Apes* (2001). (Among Elfman's previous comic-book-inspired scoring credits were *Dick Tracy*, *Batman Returns*, *Men in Black*, and *Spider-Man*, as well as the theme for TV's *The Flash*.)

Elfman's *Hulk* score became one of his more interesting genre works. The music featured haunting vocals by Belgian Natacha Atlas (known for fusing Arabic music and Western hip-hop and drum-and-bass music) and the Armenian double-reed instrument the duduk. While Danna never recorded a final score, some of his prerecordings of exotic instruments became elements of the new score, and he was credited for its "Mother" theme. Elfman explained how he utilized some of the preexisting material:

> There's a theme I'm only taking half credit for because it's part of an improvisation that a singer had done for the original score. They sent me all the material of all this ethnic stuff that they had recorded, because Ang really wanted to use a lot of ethnic influences, Middle Eastern and Indian, which I was totally down for because I love doing shit like that and it made it even more challenging. There was a singer named Natacha Atlas they recorded in England; her voice was really beautiful and there was one thing she sang that caught my ear called the "Mother" theme. It starts out with a melody from before that I credited to Mychael Danna, and I take it after the first four bars into another part of the theme. I liked how it started, [but] I just wanted to take it to another place at the end, so it relates to the lost mother image.

Elfman's addictive main theme, with its repeating six-note descending melody, is some of the composer's strongest thematic writing in years, especially in this genre. This motif is one of the score's four themes—from the transformation fanfare to the love theme—that explore Bannon's different aspects. Discussing the film's music on its DVD, Ang Lee said that he learned a lot from Elfman about a genre he was not familiar with.

Despite the movie's flourishing visuals, excellent CGI work, and innovative, comic-book-style editing, *Hulk* was only modestly successful at the box office, barely making back its budget domestically (although succeeding in terms of worldwide revenues).

■ **Shade** (2003)

Original composer: **Christopher Young**
Replacement composer: **James Johnzen**

Gambling movies are a popular subgenre of the crime drama. Among the most respected films in this category are *The Hustler* (1961), *The Cincinnati Kid* (1965), *The Sting* (1973), *The Gambler* (1974), *House of Games* (1987), *Casino* (1995), and *The Cooler* (2003).

Shade, a well-made gambling picture with a complicated mix of grifters and gangsters and cons and cardplay, was writer-director Damian Nieman's feature film debut, for which he assembled a large, strong ensemble cast that included Gabriel Byrne, Jamie Foxx, Sylvester Stallone, Bo Hopkins, Hal Holbrook, and Melanie Griffith. Hired to score the picture was Christopher Young, whose recent credits included *The Core* (2003), *Bandits* (2002), and *The Shipping News* (2001).

Young took his first roll of the dice on a gambling film with director John Dahl's *Rounders* (1998), a poker movie starring Matt Damon, Ed Norton, and John Malkovich. But that gig started an unusual streak of bad luck for the composer. His completed *Rounders* score was deemed unsuitable by the picture's distributor, but he was given a second chance, and his second score ended up in the movie. While it often happens that composers have to rewrite individual cues several times, it's rare that one writes two whole scores for a movie.

Although Christopher Young salvaged his *Rounders* rejection, he didn't have such luck with *Shade,* for which he penned a score that referenced 1960s- and 1970s-style jazz. After the film fared poorly at test screenings, it was re-edited, necessitating modifications in its music as well. Most of Young's work was dropped in favor of a more contemporary-sounding music composed by James Johnzen (whose only feature film credit is *Shade*).

Intrada released a CD of Young's *Shade* score in a limited edition of 1,000 copies (which quickly sold out). The composer's liner notes for this recording indicate that he at least had lots of fun working on the movie's music, regardless of its eventual displacement:

> Working on the score to *Shade* was a welcome return to a retro jazz-funk vocabulary I first explored in the film *Rounders.* Since I'm an ex–jazz drummer, it was nostalgically comforting to think again of music propelled by wood sticks on a live snare. I also happen to love the colors of vintage electric keyboards from the sixties and seventies—the Fender Rhodes, the Wurlitzer [electric] piano, the Hammond B3 organ, and the Clavinet (all used here). However my ultra-favorite keyboard from that time period is the Mellotron Mark II (used most recently in *The Core*). Boy, did the sound of that keyboard take me to magical places when I was a teenager! Most of these cues are self-contained entities. Each one has a tune of its own, and there is very little thematic repetition or development. The unity therefore comes more from a consistent sound and style. When I edited and sequenced

this CD, it was with the hope of it playing more like a seventies jazz record than a standard film score.

Following *Shade*, Young scored another gambling film in 2007, writer-director Curtis Hanson's *Lucky You*, a drama built around a Las Vegas poker tournament. The film kept the composer busy for a long time, but its final version used only a fragment of his overall work: twenty-six minutes out of the two and a half hours of music he had composed for it. (The amount of music he composed was longer than the movie itself because it included numerous alternate cues for the same scenes.) Young's breezy *Lucky You* score was a worthy successor to his previous jazz-based scores for *Rounders* and *Shade*.

■ Pirates of the Caribbean: The Curse of the Black Pearl (2003)

Original composer: **Alan Silvestri**
Replacement composer: **Klaus Badelt**

Sometimes replacement-score myths sprout up about scores that never actually existed. This happened with *Pirates of the Caribbean: The Curse of the Black Pearl*, the first installment of the comedic adventure-fantasy franchise starring Johnny Depp. Alan Silvestri was announced as composer for the film; his name even appeared on the movie's teaser posters. And when he disappeared from the project and started work on *Lara Croft Tomb Raider: Cradle of Life* instead, some film-score fans' Internet message boards invented the existence of a Silvestri score that was removed from *Pirates* under disgraceful circumstances. These patently false rumors took a long time to disappear—even after Silvestri gave an extensive interview about the situation. Silvestri, in fact, was director Gore Verbinski's first choice of composer for *Pirates*, but he never completed a score for it. Here's the scoop:

> I was brought into that project through Gore Verbinski, who I had worked with on *The Mexican* and *Mousehunt*. But it was a Jerry Bruckheimer film, which has a certain sound that has to be kept in the mix. Jerry is a very powerful producer—not just in terms of his success rate, but he's also a very creatively involved producer. I can only speak for the dynamic in this particular film, but Jerry is not the kind of producer that hires a director, and then sends him off to make the movie. Jerry is a very big part creatively of the making of the movie, with the director. So when you walk into that situation, in a sense you have two very strong entities that have to agree on a collective vision of the film. Jerry has people that he's worked with in the past, and a mode of working in the past, that has been very successful for him.

In the past, Jerry Bruckheimer had worked often with composers who were part of Hans Zimmer's film music company Media Ventures, especially Zimmer himself, who did music for the producer's *Days of Thunder* (1990), *Crimson Tide* (1995), *The Rock* (1996), *Pearl Harbor* (2001), and *Black Hawk Down* (2001). Even though Silvestri had a good relationship with *Pirates'* studio, Walt Disney Pictures, through his scores for such films as *The Parent Trap* (1998) and *Lilo & Stitch* (2002), the scoring decision for *Pirates* was made by its strongest driving force—Bruckheimer. Silvestri continues:

> What really happened was that Jerry's creative needs, and work mode, needed to be addressed as well as Gore's. In the end, I think Jerry was much more comfortable working in a way that he had worked historically, with people he had worked with historically, and it seemed the best idea for us to part our ways. But never anything acrimonious happened, and he was just fantastic. It just wasn't the right chemistry in the end, for all of the forces at work. As you know, in all of these movies there's a tremendous amount at stake and certainly it's a Jerry Bruckheimer film—it's not an Alan Silvestri film! [...] We had a really lovely chat after all of that, and there's no harm, no foul there for us.... We never recorded anything, and we really didn't get that far. But we got far enough for Jerry to feel that he wanted to change horses.... He's the man ultimately responsible to the studio for bringing that product, and having it be viable—so he has to do what he has to do to accomplish that. But he couldn't have been more respectful, and sensitive to how it all ultimately happened—and that's all one can ask!

After Silvestri was dismissed, the film's music was turned over to Hans Zimmer, a composer with whom both the producer and the director had worked in the past. Zimmer was the driving force behind some of Bruckheimer's best-known pictures (as noted above) and had worked with Verbinski on *The Ring* (2002). However, at the time when the *Pirates* job opened up, Zimmer was bound to *The Last Samurai* (2003) by a contract that specified he couldn't do other movies simultaneously. So, in the end, although Zimmer contributed a couple of themes to it, the *Pirates* score was written by a team of almost a dozen composers, who helped lead composer Klaus Badelt (who received the film's main composer credit) write and record it in about a month's time. This music was well received by the general public; however, some film score fans condemned it because it was put together by a committee and contained several themes that sounded similar to motives from *The Rock* (1996), *Gladiator* (2000), and even *Shrek* (2001, all of which were done by composers from Media Ventures. Regardless of such criticisms, the first three *Pirates of the Caribbean* movies and their scores became quite popular, with the second and third (subtitled *Dead Man's Chest* and *At the World's End*), from 2006 and 2007, respectively, featuring music by Zimmer.

■ **Open Range** (2003)

Original composer: **Basil Poledouris**
Replacement composer: **Michael Kamen**

Actor-turned-director Kevin Costner's directing career has been marked by sharp ups and downs. After directing and starring in two widely lambasted expensive dystopian sci-fi movies—*Waterworld* (1995) and *The Postman* (1997)—he had a hard time redeeming himself in an industry in which one is often judged solely on the success or failure of one's most recent project.

But redeem himself he did, with a beautifully photographed tip of the Stetson to classic Hollywood Westerns of the 1930s through 1950s, *Open Range*, a movie that, with its clearly delineated right and wrong, honored in spirit pre-Peckinpah and pre-spaghetti Westerns. Set during range wars in 1880s Montana, the film, which starred Costner, Robert Duvall, Annette Bening, and Michael Gambon, marked Costner's return to the genre in which he had achieved his great directorial success, *Dances with Wolves* (1990).

To score *Open Range*, Costner hired the composer he originally wanted for *Dances with Wolves*, Basil Poledouris, whose Emmy-winning score for television's acclaimed Western miniseries *Lonesome Dove* (1989) Costner admired. (*Note*: As discussed earlier in this book, Poledouris was replaced on *Dances* by John Barry, who won an Oscar for his work.)

Poledouris wrote a number of themes for *Open Range*, but Costner wasn't satisfied with them and replaced the composer before he wrote an actual score for the movie. Poledouris described his work on *Open Range* as merely a "brief involvement." Costner then moved on to composer Michael Kamen, whose recent credits included television's critically acclaimed ten-part miniseries *Band of Brothers* (2001) and *X-Men* (2000). Kamen recalled his work on *Open Range*:

> I think Kevin Costner was shopping around, and he found someone whose themes didn't go down with him very well. He called me because he knew my score for *Robin Hood* [a 1991 film produced by and starring Costner].... He recognized that I had a melodic temperament and asked around about me. I think John Williams recommended he use me, which was a great endorsement.... Anyway, I called him and met him in LA and we had a good meeting. I saw them working on the film, and I hired his music editor because he didn't really have much experience spotting the movie. I took my spotting basically from his temp score and put the music where his music editor knew he had been looking for music; not necessarily exactly what he'd been looking for, but I gave him music everywhere in the film where it was tracked. I told him he didn't have to use it all.... I'm sure I gave him more music than he needed—I wrote about an hour and forty-five minutes.

Kamen's music, his final score before his November 2003 death, was a success. It was a big, though not overly busy, orchestral score with Western flourishes provided by guitar and fiddle. Often leisurely paced—as was the film itself—it presented an introspective, elegiac Americana that highlighted the landscape depicted in the movie. A recording of it was released by Hollywood Records.

After *Open Range*, Poledouris had a hard time taking new assignments because of his deteriorating health. Still recovering from Costner's Western, the composer scored the television production *The Legend of Butch and Sundance* (which, although completed for a planned 2004 broadcast, did not actually air until 2006), providing a final taste of the interesting music he could create within the Western genre. His last-ever film score, it was released on CD by Movie Score Media.

■ **Timeline** (2003)

Original composer: **Jerry Goldsmith**
Replacement composer: **Brian Tyler**

Directed by Richard Donner and based on a novel by Michael Crichton, *Timeline* was the tale of an archaeology professor (played by Billy Connolly) and his students' wild shuttle between present-day America and fourteenth-century France—courtesy of a wormhole and a time machine (owned by an evil corporation, of course)—where they encounter the Hundred Years War and alter history. The movie seemed a good opportunity to reunite composer Jerry Goldsmith with Crichton (with whom the composer had worked on a half-dozen films in the 1970s–1990s, including *Coma, The Great Train Robbery*, and *The 13th Warrior*) and Donner (Goldsmith scored Donner's *The Omen* in 1976), but his *Timeline* score—his penultimate scoring job—was not fated to make it to the screen.

Starting in August 2002, Goldsmith spent nearly seven months composing music for this big, century-hopping picture, recording the first part of his score in a three-day session in December 2002 and the second part in another three-day session the following March. However, the movie found itself in serious trouble after receiving negative prerelease feedback. Following a series of reshoots, it was up to the postproduction team to improve its pacing and fill its plot holes, which seemed to grow with each new edit. One victim of this process was an opening sequence that's central to the story, detailing the excavation of the fourteenth-century French site. Goldsmith's cue for this, "The Dig," became useless once that sequence was removed. Through similar whittling-away, the movie lost more and more coherence, until the entire score had become irrelevant. Eventually, the director changed his musical vision for the film and decided that the whole score should be redone. Donner recalls:

> It was early on when I told him what I wanted, I really was very specific in the terms of the music, I wanted to stay away from action scoring and just wanted it to be a very strong orchestral piece that would carry the film. Jerry understood it totally. Little by little he played it to us, I loved it, it was just great. Then I laid it up to the picture for the first time, and I realized that I had really screwed up, that I was really hurting the picture. What I really needed was a lot of drive, a lot of action, and a lot of music that keeps you on the edge of your seat. I went back to Jerry and I said, "I really screwed up, I would appreciate it if we could talk and change this." He said, "What kind of changes are you talking about?" and I told him. He said, "Listen, Dick, I love you. If you tell me to do it, I'll do it, but I really feel what you asked for I've given you." I said, "True! It's totally one-hundred-percent true, I love what you've done." Then he said, "If you make me do it I'll do it, but I'd rather not." It was heartbreaking and he was right. He had done a phenomenal job and here I was asking him to change it, to go back and do the whole thing over again. It wasn't fair to Jerry. He bowed out, I allowed him out because I respect him so. That was very difficult because I respect him, I love him, and he did a phenomenal job

> on the piece of music that he did. I say that without reservation and it's too bad nobody will ever hear that track.

Well, not exactly: Varèse Sarabande issued a CD containing forty-five minutes of Goldsmith's score shortly after his death in 2004. This first-ever release of one of his rejected works allowed fans to hear an outstanding score that contained not only breathtaking action cues but also a simple romantic theme, elegiac music for the old French setting, and swirling melodies that underscored the time travel. Even his synthesized ram's-horn effects worked well!

Replacing Goldsmith was composer Brian Tyler, who was best known at that time for his work on the three-part TV miniseries *Children of Dune* (2003). Among his other recent scoring credits were *Bubba Ho-tep* (2002), *Vampires: Los Muertos* (2002), and *Last Call* (2002). The composer remembers how *Timeline* arrived on his doorstep:

> The *Timeline* music editor had a bunch of my scores, and after Jerry left the project, they re-temped the score with a lot of my music. And the "new" style they wanted, according to Richard Donner, was to emphasize energy, big themes, and don't use period instruments like madrigal or old-style horns. So for me, it was my Jerry Goldsmith tribute score! He was one of my very biggest influences, and I wanted to write a score in the style that he would do when he wrote those orchestral scores that would just hit you, and not hide in the corners, and not be sonic wallpaper. So the way it came about, there were some cues in *Children of Dune* that had that feeling, and they also used the "Canamar" episode of *Star Trek: Enterprise* that I had done, with the temp.

Tyler didn't listen to Goldsmith's unused material, so as not to be influenced by it, though film-score fans naturally compare Tyler's work with Goldsmith's. (Varèse Sarabande also released a CD of Tyler's replacement score.) Both scores emphasized the epic historical nature of the picture, as opposed to its science-fiction aspects, yet there were considerable differences between them: Although both were filled with themes that painted the story's various times and places, Tyler's contained more textural music than Goldsmith's. And Tyler's score emphasized the contemporary setting with techno beats and drum loops, while the rest of the music (action, romance, and suspense bits) embraced a more traditional, orchestral sound. Criticism of Tyler's work seems to have been fueled chiefly by what a few people perceived as a desecration of Goldsmith's legacy.

Goldsmith's final score, for the 2003 live-action/animated comedy *Looney Tunes: Back in Action*, was not completed by him due to his failing health. The final touches were added by John Debney, who received an "additional music" credit.

■ **Something's Gotta Give** (2003)

Original composer: **Alan Silvestri**
Replacement composer: **Hans Zimmer**

Something's Gotta Give, a romantic comedy starring Jack Nicholson and Diane Keaton, was written, produced, and directed by Nancy Meyers. To provide its underscore, she hired composer Alan Silvestri, who had scored four of her earlier films: *Father of the Bride* (1991), *Father of the Bride Part II* (1995), *The Parent Trap* (1998), and *What Women Want* (2000). But, their history of successful collaboration notwithstanding, *Something's Gotta Give* proved musically troublesome. The two simply couldn't find the right musical voice for it, a problem that apparently manifested itself in their inability to agree on a main theme. At that point, composer Hans Zimmer was drawn into the project by Sony's Lia Vollock. (Vollock is head of worldwide music for Sony Pictures Entertainment, overseeing the music for all of Sony's films, which include movies from Screen Gems and Columbia Pictures.) Zimmer explains:

> The problem apparently was that they didn't like his [Silvestri's] tune. I said, "I got a tune lying around that I've never been able to use. It's quite a nice tune, it's quite romantic. Maybe it will help him out." Initially I just wanted to help, send the tune over as a gift. Nancy got wind of this and said: "No, don't send over the tune. Maybe you should see the movie before, it might be completely wrong." So I went to see the movie and the first thing I thought of [was], "This is completely wrong." I said, "Let me just sit down. I'll spend a couple of hours sitting down and see if I come up with something." But it literally is a gift—if the other composer feels it, he could incorporate it into his score.... I knew I wanted to write a tune for Heitor Pereira and his guitar. I made this stupid mistake of phoning Lia and saying, "Oh, I think I'm getting an idea." And she said, "Oh, I'll be right over with Nancy." But I haven't finished it yet. I hate playing in front of people, and hadn't finished the thing. I actually had to sit there and play the tune on the piano. Now when you play, you couldn't see her reactions. I was playing it much too fast as I'm very nervous.... So I played this thing, I turned around and Nancy was weeping. So I'm thinking, "That's not a good sign. It looks like a disappointed moment here. I was her last hope." She said, "This is not at all what I imagined."

It turned out, however, that Nancy was weeping tears of joy, so Zimmer was hired to expand his tune into a whole score. With a deadline looming, a few of the film's musical gaps were filled by some of Zimmer's regular collaborators, including composers Ramin Djawadi, James Dooley, James S. Levine, Trevor Morris, Blake Neely, and Heitor Pereira. Composers Rolfe Kent and Christopher Young also provided additional music but had no interaction with Zimmer's team. Young's contributions "ripped off" his *Wonder Boys* (2000) music, which had been part of *Something's Gotta Give*'s temp track.

The official soundtrack CD for *Something's Gotta Give* didn't present the film's underscore. Instead, positioning itself as an album of romantic ballads (many of them classics), it contained about half the songs that were liberally sprinkled throughout the film. These included numbers performed by Louis Armstrong, the Flamingos, Astrud Gilberto, Eartha Kitt, Django Reinhardt, Stéphane Grappelli, Marvin Gaye, Paul Simon, and even Jack Nicholson, who tentatively crooned a version of Edith Piaf's signature song "La Vie en Rose." However, Hans Zimmer's theme that was so essential in the scoring process is not left out: It appears as "Remember Me," featuring guitarist Heitor Pereira.

■ The Passion of the Christ (2004)

Original composer: **Jack Lenz**
Replacement composer: **John Debney**

There was probably no more controversial movie in 2004 than actor-turned-director Mel Gibson's *The Passion of the Christ*, which presented Jesus Christ's final twenty-four hours of life in gruesome and gory detail. Interestingly, all the movie's dialogue was rendered in reconstructions of ancient languages—Aramaic, Latin, and Hebrew—accompanied by subtitles.

With worldwide religious controversy swirling around the film even before it was released, it's no surprise that its musical oddities and rumors were not a focus of attention. The first of them was the premature announcement—or a simple rumor?—that composer James Horner was associated with the project. This seemed logical, since Horner had scored both of Gibson's previous directorial efforts: *The Man Without a Face* (1993) and *Braveheart* (1995). But in fact Horner would never work on *The Passion*.

Similarly mysterious was the announced involvement of vocalist-composer Lisa Gerrard (a founding member of the band Dead Can Dance) and Irish concert composer Patrick Cassidy (who collaborated on the 2004 album *Immortal Memory*, which had songs in Gaelic, Aramaic, and Latin).

But even as all this scuttlebutt circulated, a Canadian film and television composer named Jack Lenz was busy researching and writing music for the picture. Lenz acted as the production's primary music researcher, and it seemed that the score would be built from the fruits of his research. A key to all aspects of *The Passion of the Christ* was Gibson's attempt at authenticity (which was why its dialogue was in ancient languages), and that impulse led Lenz to seek out appropriate instruments, delve into what could be pieced together about musical techniques of the era, and then write and record what he believed period- and locale-appropriate music might have sounded like. (No one, of course, knows exactly what the Middle Eastern music played during Christ's lifetime sounded like.)

But after Lenz had prepared hours of thoroughly researched, best-guess authentic music for the movie, Gibson's musical vision changed. Now he sought a more traditional orchestral score, and that is when composer John Debney, whose recent scoring credits included *Elf* (2003) and *Bruce Almighty* (2003), was hired. Debney recalls:

> A guy I grew up with, [producer] Stephen McEveety, called me in October and said they were having some problems on a movie; I didn't know what movie he was talking about. [He said] they had a composer on it for a year but Mel was concerned because this composer hadn't done a lot of scoring work—he had done a lot of research for them and gotten a lot of great ethnic samples for them, thinking that they were going to score the movie with period music. As we were talking, it dawned on me finally that he was talking about *The Passion*, and I was floored because it would be anybody's dream project to work on, but especially me being a lifelong Catholic. At that point I offered to write some pieces for free because it would be an honor just to try some things. So he showed me the movie and I spent that weekend writing four or five pieces, one of which is the trailer music.

Debney's intense, moody, haunting score employed a broad color palette that included orchestra, choir, solo voices, electric cello, synth, and a broad assortment of ethnic instruments (including *erhu*, duduk, oud, and a selection of flutes).

His music for *The Passion*, one of the most celebrated scores of the year, earned Debney an Oscar nomination. Jack Lenz's ancient music re-creations, on the other hand (some of which are still present in the movie), provided a backbone for the production's soundscape but didn't make it onto the movie's popular soundtrack album.

■ **Troy** (2004)

Original composer: **Gabriel Yared**
Replacement composer: **James Horner**

Among recent film scores, few have raised as much debate among film music fans as the two scores written for German director Wolfgang Petersen's massively expensive three-hour epic, *Troy*, a story of the ancient Trojan War centering on the exploits of Greek hero Achilles (played by Brad Pitt) and Trojan prince Hector (Eric Bana).

In early 2003, Petersen hired Lebanese-born composer Gabriel Yared to score *Troy*. Although he had written all sorts of music, Yared was known for intimate scores for such dramas as director Anthony Minghella's *The English Patient* (1996), for which he won an Oscar. That movie's success resulted in his scoring a number of similarly tragic love stories, including *Message in a Bottle* (1999) and *Autumn in New York* (2000). His work on the acclaimed movies *The Talented Mr. Ripley* (1999) and *Cold Mountain* (2003), both directed by his friend Anthony Minghella, helped provide a welcome break from a steady diet of romances.

Before working on *Troy*, Yared had penned music for only one movie of truly epic scope: director Bille August's *Les Misérables* (1998). But his score went unused in the finished picture, replaced by Basil Poledouris's music. Thus *Troy* offered Yared a perfect opportunity to show audiences a different side of his talents. Known for his attention to detail and desire to be involved with a film through its entire production, he started researching his *Troy* score before shooting began:

> I started studying the music of Greece in the ancient times. I went to the British Museum and had meetings with many teachers and musicologists, and I came up with a lot of information about this music [from the time period]. So after all of the studies through February and March [2003], I found that I had nothing to take from this. I had to reinvent some things. So I asked myself, "What is Troy, what is Greek, what is closer to that?" By studying this, I came up with the idea of something more Bulgarian and Macedonian. Then I started writing, casting choirs, and met with an orchestra. I did the first session at Abbey Road at the end of April with an orchestra made up of Celtic harps, krummhorns, all these medieval instruments, some percussion, and a big choir of Greek, Turkish, Macedonian, and Bulgarian [singers].

Much of this music was meant as source music for the movie. It included choral pieces to be used at celebrations (e.g., "Sparta") and funerals (e.g., "Mourning Women" and "Hector's Funeral"). The vocal soloist on these sessions was Macedonian singer Tanja Tzarovska, who had provided some of the haunting vocals in John Debney's score for *The Passion of the Christ*. Yared:

> Having settled on the overall ideas and concepts I then set to work writing each cue in detail and providing demos so that Wolfgang could hear what I was doing and become familiar with the themes and concepts.... I provided a very detailed, orchestrated demo with full orchestra, choir, percussion, and even vocal samples for every single cue. Wolfgang was genuinely delighted with everything we sent to him; he loved the big epic sound, powerful and yet still moving and emotional. Of course he had some comments here and there which we always endeavored to fix straight away.

Yared's score contained many memorable themes—the Greeks are equipped with aggressive melodies and the Trojans with more refined ones:

> For Achilles I wanted something very trivial, very simple...this was a glorious theme in a very obvious way. For Hector, as a noble character, as he was, I wanted something more elaborated in the thematic aspect, more noble and serious.... [B]ut where I really wanted to make a difference was between Paris's and Helena's and Achilles's and Briseis's love themes. The love theme for Achilles and Briseis comes from Achilles's [theme]. And the first four notes of his theme become the central melody for his love theme. For Paris and Helen I wanted a theme more, how can I say, much more ethnic, and that's why I wanted a beautiful, simple theme, not too exaggerated.

All seemed to be going well with Yared's score, until the movie was sent out for preview screenings accompanied by a rough and incomplete mix of it. The test audiences were very critical of the music—they found it distracting. Yared:

> 14th February [2004] and the next stage was to join my friend and engineer Peter Cobbin at Abbey Road Studios for the recording of the score. The next three weeks of recording were very tough and tiring...recording a 100-piece orchestra for two sessions a day followed by evenings of overdub sessions. It was a wonderful time, however, of creation

> and realization and much enthusiasm from Wolfgang and the producers and production team. Wolfgang was over the moon and could be heard in the corridors of Abbey Road Studios singing the main themes, he was enchanted with the music and began to wonder about the temp music he'd been using thus far for the test screenings. So it came that Wolfgang used all his charm to persuade me to allow him to use some of our unfinished monitor mixes to replace the temp music. Despite my misgivings he seemed so keen and proud of the music that I agreed.... After the test screening [in Sacramento, California] on 10th March, though, everything had changed. The focus group at the preview decided my music was "overpowering and too big, old fashioned and dated the film." Thus, in this twenty-four-hour period my score was completely rejected by director and studio, and a collaboration of one year came to an end.

Composer James Horner, who would eventually replace Yared on the picture, talks about this screening:

> They brought it to California, to preview the film, the studio insisted on a preview. Wolfgang was so sure of himself, he thought, "Oh my God, wait until you see the reactions to this movie!" Gabriel hadn't even put the choir on. The choir was doubling some of the strings dub, and it was going to make it more massive, and he also had a lot of Middle Eastern stuff. They played it for an audience in Sacramento and took the usual focus group with the cards. There were lots of comments about flaws in the movie, but everybody said the music is the worst they had ever heard. Hundred percent, take out the score. I never heard of a preview where people are so in tune to the music that they even notice it, much less demand that it ruins the movie for them. In the focus group, they got the same reaction. They all said, "It's horrible music. Who did this music?" I hadn't seen the film; this is all in hindsight, 'cause I didn't keep up with the movie. They previewed it again with the same results. Wolfgang was white, completely shaken; [he] totally lost his confidence.

After the disastrous screenings, Warner Bros., the producing studio and distributor, took matters into its own hands and contacted composer John Debney, who turned down the enormous project because of its short deadline. Then Horner, with whom Petersen had previously worked on *The Perfect Storm* (2000), was offered the job. (Among his recent scoring credits were *The Missing, House of Sand and Fog,* and *The Four Feathers.*) Having been interested in doing the music for *Troy* since he first heard about it, Horner agreed to score the picture, even though he had to work very fast to meet its May 14 premiere deadline.

Petersen had the sad task of breaking the bad news to Yared. This was Yared's biggest professional disappointment, made all the worse by what the composer perceived as Petersen's neutral behavior. Shortly after losing the job, Yared posted about a half-hour of his *Troy* score on his official website, accompanied by an open letter describing his yearlong work on the project. The final section of his letter was a passionate and subjective philippic against the studio and Petersen because they hadn't given him a chance to correct in the music whatever they felt wasn't working. Soon, Yared was contacted by the film's producers, who him told to remove the score excerpts and letter from his site.

Horner had to write almost three hours of music in nine days. In doing this, he ended up retaining certain of Yared's orchestrational elements, including the Bulgarian women's choir and vocalist Tanja Tzarovska (even using her, with singer Josh Grobin, on his score's romantic ballad "Remember").

While Horner often enjoys developing his own motifs while referencing classical pieces, he had little choice on *Troy*, whose workload was simply overwhelming. To meet the deadline, Petersen gave Horner carte blanche, the only condition being that he was contractually obliged to deliver at least seventy-five minutes of music. Horner and his orchestrators made the most of their limited time, using some of Horner's best-known motifs as the score's basis: A lot of *Troy*'s action material is similar to that which Horner developed for *Enemy at the Gates* (2001). The often-quoted fourth movement from Dmitri Shostakovich's Fifth Symphony also makes an appearance. Quotes aside, however, the theme that Horner developed for Achilles is one of the best film-score melodies written in 2004.

When Wolfgang Petersen put together Troy's director's cut (released on DVD in 2007), for which he added thirty minutes of footage (extending the battle and sex scenes, as well as the sack of Troy), he seems to have completely reimagined the picture, changing in one way or another almost every scene. This cut's music was quite a mixed bag: Horner's score was re-edited and a good number of his cues were noticeably looped. His successful Achilles theme was removed from many key sequences (including Patroclus's training and the beach attack). And music from the film's original temp score found its way back into this version: Excerpts from Basil Poledouris's *Starship Troopers* (1997) score and Edward Shearmur's *The Count of Monte Cristo* (2002) score made fleeting appearances, and the battle between Hector and Achilles now featured Danny Elfman's main theme from Tim Burton's *Planet of the Apes* (2001). Most surprisingly, some of Yared's score made it its way back into the picture: "Mourning Women" now accompanied the funeral scene, closing the book on the story of *Troy*'s music with an ironic twist.

■ **I, Robot** (2004)

Original composer: **Trevor Jones**
Replacement composer: **Marco Beltrami**

Directed by Alex Proyas, *I, Robot* was one of 2004's strongest action blockbusters. Suggested or inspired by (rather than based on) Isaac Asimov's famous and influential 1951 anthology of science-fiction stories by the same name, the movie is set in 2035 Chicago, an era in which robots are commonly employed as humans' helpers. While investigating a suspicious death at a robot manufacturing company, a police detective (played by Will Smith) discovers that the company's master computer has evolved on its own and reinterpreted the all-important Three Rules of Robotics: (1) A robot must not injure a human; (2) A robot must obey all human orders that do not conflict with the first law; (3) A robot must protect itself unless doing so conflicts with the first two laws.

For *I, Robot*'s music, director Proyas wanted to reestablish his connection with composer Trevor Jones, with whom he had worked on *Dark City* (1998), a film for which the composer stayed on board even as the picture kept changing shape and direction. (Among Jones's recent scoring credits were 2003's *The League of Extraordinary Gentlemen* and *I'll Be There*.)

But *I, Robot* was not destined to be their next collaboration. It fell through due to a not-uncommon obstacle—the schedule. Many collaborations fail to come to full fruition as the result of scheduling problems, and composers often have to (or choose to) leave projects before writing even a single note. In this case, though, Jones had extensive music discussions with the director and even wrote some material for the film, as he explains:

> I know that sometimes filmmakers do not allow musicians to do their job in a proper way, and many composers share the same problem with time restrictions or instructions which are unacceptable. I had read the Asimov story, so when Alex and I talked about scoring this film, I admit I was very enthusiastic about the project. The problem was that final orders came two months after my conversation with Alex and I was very busy scoring *Around the World in 80 Days*. I contacted the director and told him I hadn't the time needed to write a score for such a movie, the way that such an ambiguous film deserved.... I even wrote some sketches. I planned this to be a very futuristic score. I wish I had the chance to work on that project. Unfortunately, I cannot choose how to do things and I cannot do all I'm offered to do. I must respect a scheduled program and I need to concentrate fully on my work. I know that some musicians can work on two projects at the same time...I just could not.

Once Jones had to bow out of *I, Robot*, Marco Beltrami, whose recent scoring credits included *Hellboy* (2004) and eighty-five episodes of the TV drama *The Practice* (2000–2004), was hired to score it. At the time, Beltrami was best known for his work on *Scream* and similar horror flicks (including *Mimic*, *Scream 2*, *The Faculty*, *Scream 3*, *Dracula 2000*, and *Resident Evil*) and therefore not often given a chance to show his capabilities in other genres. So *I, Robot* was an exceptional opportunity for him to show what he could do for an action-heavy sci-fi story that tackled philosophical issues. Beltrami had a mere three weeks to come up with the music, which he wrote for a large orchestra, featuring brass and percussion, and choir:

> I wish all the movies I did could go as smooth. I had seventeen days to do the score, to write it, and we recorded after that. It was a short schedule and I was fortunate to start out on the right foot; everyone was happy right from the start.... [Alex Proyas] was very easy. He said he wanted a strong theme that was woven throughout the movie and would be able to [be] manipulate[d] through different cues. My first impression after seeing the movie was that it needed some electronic manipulation of acoustic sounds for the robots in conjunction with the orchestra, and he seemed to respond to that. From a conceptual standpoint, we were on the same page from the beginning.

I, Robot proved to be one of Marco Beltrami's best scores.

Wimbledon (2004)

Original composer: **Klaus Badelt**
Replacement composer: **Edward Shearmur**

Directed by Richard Loncraine, *Wimbledon* is a lighthearted British film that takes the classic sports movie formula—the underdog triumphs in the end—and combines it, as most such movies do, with a love story. It's about an aging tennis pro (played by Paul Bettany) who finds the strength to make a comeback through his love for an up-and-coming player (Kirsten Dunst). *Wimbledon* is one of very few tennis movies ever made.

Selected to score the movie was composer Klaus Badelt, fresh off 2003's successful *Pirates of the Caribbean: The Curse of the Black Pearl.* (His other scoring credits from that same year included *Beat the Drum, Basic,* and *Ned Kelly.*) Badelt started work on *Wimbledon* in early 2004. Using forty members of the London Metropolitan Orchestra, a session orchestra that specializes in film scores, he recorded detailed mockups of some of the movie's important cues, so that its American previews would be accompanied by a score of sorts while he finished writing the actual score. His recording of the picture's final score was scheduled for May of that same year.

At this same time, Warner Bros.' *Catwoman*, an expensive DC Comics adaptation starring Halle Berry, was enmeshed in a troubled postproduction and encountering numerous delays. The originally announced composers for the movie were Graeme Revell and William Orbit. But, due to scheduling conflicts caused by the film's delays, they had to withdraw from it. The studio was desperate for a composer who could do a good score quickly, so they turned to Badelt for help. For a while, he was designated as both *Wimbledon*'s and *Catwoman*'s composer, but he proved unable to focus on both projects at the same time, so he let go of *Wimbledon*. (Despite his best efforts on *Catwoman*, the movie turned out to be one of the worst big-budget pictures ever made.)

Wimbledon's scoring duties were turned over to Edward Shearmur, whose recent credits included *Laws of Attraction* (2004), *Win a Date with Tad Hamilton!* (2004), and *Charlie's Angels: Full Throttle* (2003). The London Metropolitan Orchestra recorded his *Wimbledon* score, and yet many of the movie's most important scenes were scored with preexisting music. The main title, for instance, utilized "Ghostwriter," a piece by hip-hop musician and music producer RJD2. This popular bit of music has been used in numerous TV ads and would reappear on the big screen in the 2005 romantic comedy *Prime*. Its inclusion in *Wimbledon* seems to have influenced much of the picture's underscore. Other music licensed for the film included songs performed by OK Go, David Gray, and Sugababes, and its climactic tennis match is scored with Craig Armstrong's "Ball," from his score to *Plunkett & Macleane* (1999).

■ I ♥ Huckabees (2004)

Original composer: **Stephen Endelman**
Replacement composer: **Jon Brion**

Writer-director David O. Russell is not afraid to leave his mark on his offbeat films' music. For example, in 1999, Carter Burwell scored Russell's *Three Kings*, a story about U.S. soldiers stealing gold during the war in Iraq. But during postproduction, Russell chopped many of Burwell's cues into bits and pieces and tinkered with them, sometimes intercutting them with short bits of licensed music that had appeared in the film's temp score.

Russell's *I ♥ Huckabees*, an imaginative, zany, existential comedy about a rogues' gallery of oddball characters who tackle life's most basic questions, featured an all-star cast that included Jason Schwartzman, Dustin Hoffman, Lily Tomlin, Isabelle Huppert, Jude Law, Mark Wahlberg, and Naomi Watts. For its music, Russell, whose previous directing credits also included *Flirting with Disaster* (1996) and *Spanking the Monkey* (1994), hired composer Stephen Endelman, who had scored *Flirting with Disaster*. (Endelman's recent scoring credits included *And Starring Pancho Villa as Himself*, *Evelyn*, and *I'm with Lucy*.)

Although Endelman recorded his orchestral score with the director present, Russell eventually decided that this score, influenced by the classical music Russell had used for the movie's temp track, might not be what *Huckabees* needed. Endelman's music was dropped without a great falling-out, and Russell was left with the difficult task of finding the right new sound for his picture. Singer-songwriter-composer-performer-producer Jon Brion was introduced to the director through mutual friend Paul Thomas Anderson (director of *Magnolia*). Brion had produced albums by Aimee Mann, Fiona Apple, Rufus Wainwright, Robyn Hitchcock, and Brad Mehldau and had scored the films *Eternal Sunshine of the Spotless Mind* (2004), *Punch-Drunk Love* (2002), and *Magnolia* (1999). Russell soon hired him, and the two set out to find *Huckabees*' perfect sound. Brion recalls:

> I wanted to go back to making records. But the call came, and it's like, "Oh, that's David O. Russell, so I have to look at this [film]." Initially he had a lot of classical music as a temp score, and that is where we started, with kind of traditional soundtrack music—and David said, "You know, I just want stuff with more feeling." So I went through this whole dialogue about how some directors are uncertain of emotional stuff in scores. He says, "No, f--- that, I want feeling." So I talked to him about the absence of song in American film that I have been missing. I also told him how much I hated the kind of cross-marketing that studios use to crowbar a song into the film that they hope will somehow be a big hit because it is jammed into a big scene. I talked about how I wished that soundtrack music could be more songlike and could have a feeling of just having a record playing. Then we found stuff that was perfect for the movie but didn't have a vocal on it. You know, there is all that great Henry Mancini stuff from the sixties that you hear in the movies that, if it is bittersweet, it is unapologetically bittersweet. Originally, we

> were going to do a full orchestral score.... When I saw David enjoying what I was showing him, the amount of variations I could generate, we both realized that I wasn't going to construct an orchestra score because [if we did] we would do the thing, building up to the session—and then want to move pieces around. I though it was smarter for us to keep it self-contained.

Brion's music for *I ♥ Huckabees* is what's called a "song-score"—a set of self-contained pieces (and songs) that are not written to be tightly synched to specific moments (specific scenes, yes, but not specific moments) in a film. A song-score offers a director great liberty to experiment with music placement—its pieces can be moved around like building blocks, each of which evokes a different mood. A traditionally synchronized film score, on the other hand, is made up of cues designed to be used in just one particular spot in the film, often reflecting or underscoring specific onscreen changes in mood and action.

The *Huckabees* score is made up of quirky, breezy, bouncy little pieces that overall have a lounge-music feel, plus a half-dozen generally upbeat pop songs. The instrumental music features mallet percussion and various acoustic and electronic keyboards (heavy on cheesy organ sounds), guitar, bass, and drums, all performed by the composer. Brion also employed a small chamber group (flute, euphonium, harp, and string quartet) to add color and weight to some of his pieces. His main theme, the strange waltz "Monday," had been lying around for three years before it was used in the picture. Brion:

> When David [Russell] kept talking about the feeling he wanted, and I saw—watched—the music he related to, I knew [I had] some things that might give him that response.... He walked in the studio one day, and I said, "I have a present for you. You might like it." And he was dancing around like "Oh-my-God!" He ended up using that piece of music a few places in the movie. Mind you that's after we'd been hanging out for weeks—watching the movie together, talking, having dinner, talking about everything—talking about the universe! He loves to do that and so do I. So we got on like a house on fire!

■ **Being Julia** (2004)

Original composer: **Lesley Barber**
Replacement composer: **Mychael Danna**

Being Julia was a comedic melodrama based on W. Somerset Maugham's novel *Theatre*, adapted by Ronald Harwood. Set in 1930s London, it told the story of a theater diva's midlife crisis (with hints of Joseph L. Mankiewicz's 1950 classic film about the New York theater world, *All About Eve*). Starring Annette Bening, Michael Gambon, Jeremy Irons, Shaun Evans, and Lucy Punch, the production was helmed by noted Hungarian director István Szabó, whose films included *Taking Sides* (2001), *Sunshine* (1999), and *Meeting Venus* (1991).

Szabó, who generally perceived underscore as being overtly theatrical and preferred limited reliance on it, hired Canadian composer Lesley Barber to score the movie. Barber's recent scoring credits included *Hysterical Blindness* (2002), *You Can Count on Me* (2000), *Mansfield Park* (1999), and *A Price Above Rubies* (1998). Following Szabó's directives, Barber, who worked on *Being Julia* for almost a year, wrote a score that eventually would be seen as too subtle for the film.

Hired to replace her was another Canadian composer, Mychael Danna, whose recent credits included *Vanity Fair* (2004), *The Snow Walker* (2003), and *The Shattered Glass* (2003). Danna recalls:

> I was replacing another composer. As you know, this is a very common occurrence nowadays. I've been on both sides. Nine times out of ten it wasn't incompetence or anything like that, it was misdirection, or a matter of the team figuring out what it is they don't want at the expense of the composer's job. As the incoming composer I think it's good to reach out and call the outgoing composer and try to make the best of an awkward situation. Anyway, what they had discovered is that they wanted a more dramatic score. István comes from the school of less is more, and when it comes to music, for him, way less is more. He doesn't like music that informs, or tells the audience anything that might duplicate what the actors are doing on the screen. He was still very cautious, but I think he had discovered that he had gone too far in that direction with the other composer. In fact, the film is very dramatic in the theatrical sense of the word, and quite different from any of his previous projects, so the film could, and does, successfully accept a more demonstrative score.

With the possible exception of Szabó's previous film, the historical drama *Sunshine*, which was scored by Maurice Jarre, it's hard to find a picture on the director's resumé that relies as much on its underscore to tell its story as *Being Julia* with Danna's music did.

Over the years, Lesley Barber has had to face a few other score rejections: In 2003 there was the Disney comedy *Uptown Girls*, which was directed by Boaz Yakin, with whom Barber had worked on *A Price Above Rubies*. Her score for this picture fell victim to creative differences between its director and its producer, and was replaced with inoffensive, fluffy music by frequent Disney composer Joel McNeely. In 2004, Barber's score for the drama *We Don't Live Here Anymore* was rejected. *Variety* reviewed the picture when it still carried her music and was generally favorable toward her score, but it was replaced by composer Michael Convertino. Bad luck visited again a few years later, when Barber's work on *Kit Kittredge: An American Girl* (2008) was largely replaced by Joseph Vitarelli. (Barber received an "additional music" credit for the portion of her music that was retained.)

■ **Team America: World Police** (2004)

Original composer: **Marc Shaiman**
Replacement composer: **Harry Gregson-Williams**

Team America: World Police, a feature film from Trey Parker and Matt Stone, the creators of the *South Park* animated series and movie, was a political and cultural satire starring marionettes (à la the British TV series *Thunderbirds*). Like most Parker-Stone work, it took a fairly nihilistic stance, lampooning a broad political and cultural spectrum of people. It was also, and perhaps primarily, a well-aimed parody of big-budget flag-waving action movies of the sort produced by Jerry Bruckheimer. Its wild story centered on a secret U.S. antiterrorist force (Team America) that polices the world from its headquarters inside Mount Rushmore. In the course of the movie, the Team destroys major landmarks in Paris and Egypt and battles both North Korea's Kim Jong-il (who's plotting world destruction) and a group of liberal Hollywood actors and filmmakers-turned-terrorists.

For composer Marc Shaiman (whose recent credits included *Alex and Emma*, *Down with Love*, and *One Night at McCool's*), hiring on to score *Team America* was a reunion with Parker and Stone, for whom he had penned the Oscar-nominated *South Park: Bigger Longer & Uncut* score in 1999. During *Team America*'s production, Shaiman posted his thoughts about the movie on his blog. Judging by these posts, he seemed pleased to be writing a dramatic score for an over-the-top movie, where he could throw in the kitchen sink while mimicking the so-called "Bruckheimer sound"—the big, loud, driving, percussive music featured in many of Bruckheimer's action films (particularly those scored by Hans Zimmer and Media Ventures composers such as Trevor Rabin and Harry Gregson-Williams). Shaiman also seemed to enjoy the fact that there was not a bar of comedic music in his whole score, which took six days to record with a ninety-piece orchestra conducted by Pete Anthony at Paramount Studios. Interestingly, he noted a lack of supervision from the film's director and the producers, who were busy elsewhere.

Their absence, however, would later turn out to be a problem. Shaiman:

> To make a long story short, they COMPLETELY eliminated postproduction to rush the film into theaters for the two weeks before election day.... Trey never had time to ever hear a note that I was writing because he was still editing and rewriting and reshooting(!) the movie. So, when he heard my score, he thought it was too playful...he wanted it to be even more wallpapery, like, "Just give me five minutes of battle music, five minutes of sad music, etc."

The film—almost a musical—contained a number of songs. Parker and Shaiman collaborated on only two that made it to the final picture—"Everyone Has AIDS" and "Derka Derk (Terrorist Theme)," the latter a takeoff on John Williams's "Cantina Band" music from *Star Wars*. Most of the film's other dozen songs, such as "America, Fuck Yeah," were written by Parker alone.

Less than a month before the movie's scheduled release, Paramount Pictures' Music Division president, Burt Berman, announced that the film had a new composer—Harry Gregson-Williams, whose recent scoring credits included *Shrek 2* (2004), *Man on Fire* (2004), and *The Rundown* (2003). Excerpts from a number of scores that Gregson-Williams had written or contributed to, including the Bruckheimer films *The Rock*, *Armageddon*, and *Enemy of the State*, had appeared in *Team America*'s temp tracks. With only a few weeks in which to write and record his score, the new composer got help from some other Media Ventures composers, including Stephen Barton, Toby Chu, James McKee Smith, Damien Kaiser, and Steve Jablonsky. Gregson-Williams:

> If I had wished to take six months to score *Team America* because creatively I felt I needed it, it would have made no difference...the job had to be completed within a matter of days. That was just the situation I found myself in.... Not for one moment was I to score this movie as a comedy; I had to imagine that these were not puppets but Hollywood stars acting out a hugely slick, massively budgeted, FX-laden Hollywood action movie.

The final score was wall-to-wall heavy-duty action music, but supplemented with a few comedic moments, such as stereotypical accordion music under the opening Paris scene, a mock-heroic march, and "Derka Derk (Terrorist Theme)" (one of the only remnants of Shaiman's music that made it to the screen). Gregson-Williams's score was exactly what director Parker wanted: Bruckheimer-style action music featuring wailing vocals, ethnic and electronic percussion, ethnic woodwinds, punchy brass, and even electric cello. In a strange and funny way, the score is practically a Media Ventures stock action-music sampler. (*Note*: The official soundtrack CD was rushed out with such haste that Gregson-Williams's name didn't even appear on it!)

■ Zoey 101: Episodes 2–5 (2005)

Original composer: **Eric Hester**
Replacement composer: **Michael Corcoran**

Zoey 101, a Nickelodeon TV series starring Jamie Lynn Spears (younger sister of Britney), was created by writer-producer Dan Schneider. Designed for a pre- and young-teen audience (the ten-to-fourteen crowd), the show was about a girl's adventures at an exclusive, formerly all-boys, boarding school.

When a new television series is launched, its producers work hard to define the visual and musical signatures and traditions that will connect its episodes. A defining musical aspect of *Zoey 101* was the use of preexisting pop songs, a natural choice for a series with its particular target audience. Therefore, much of the show's music was provided by alternative bands from whom the producers could license songs cheaply (because song-placement in an episode would afford the artists wide exposure to a music-hungry audience). To address the series' minimal needs for traditional underscore—the glue between the tunes—the creators first hired composer Scott Clausen (son of composer Alf Clausen, noted for scoring TV's *The Simpsons*). Clausen had scored many episodes of another Dan Schneider Nickelodeon series, *Drake & Josh* (2004–2006). But the cues he wrote for *Zoey 101*'s pilot episode didn't seem to work for the powers-that-were. So they let him go and moved on to composer Eric Hester, whose scoring credits included episodes of the TV series *Flatland, Rodney,* and *Nash Bridges.* Hester's music proved to be closer to what they were looking for, so he was hired to score the show.

The biggest problem Hester faced with *Zoey 101* was that its producers wanted the music cues immediately—even when they had only rough cuts of the episodes. Right up to premiere night, he found himself having to rescore versions of shows whose editorial changes, while often minimal, were still usually big enough to alter the spotting of his cues. (Naturally, this problem didn't really exist for the licensed songs.)

Although Hester recorded thematic scores for the first five episodes ("Pilot," "New Roomies," "Webcam," "Defending Dustin," and "Prank Week"), only the music he wrote for "Pilot" was retained. The other four episodes would be rescored by composer Michael Corcoran, another veteran of *Drake & Josh,* who would go on to compose the music for the rest of the series.

■ **Hide and Seek** (2005)

Original composer: **Christopher Young**
Replacement composer: **John Ottman**

A film called *Secret Window* (2004), a psychological thriller involving split personalities, was to be scored collaboratively by composers (and friends) Hans Zimmer and James Newton Howard. But while scheduling conflicts kept the pair from going forward with project, it would still end up as a musical collaboration, between composers Philip Glass and Geoff Zanelli. In this split-personality score, Glass provided a dark version of his usual sound while Zanelli supplied somewhat more traditionally dramatic cues.

The following year saw the release of yet another psychological thriller involving split personalities, *Hide and Seek,* starring Robert De Niro and Dakota Fanning. Its musical path led from point A all the way to point B and back again. Point A was composer John Ottman, who recalls his introduction to the project:

> I was sent the script to *Hide and Seek.* I remember how the story started conjuring up musical imagery for me as early as the first few pages. The director, John Polson, was doing pre-production in New York. It's always great to find an excuse to go there, so I flew out to meet him. A blizzard attacked the city just after I arrived, but I was able to meet him for breakfast the next morning. John's friendliness is matched equally by his intensity—extremely focused. Well, we had a good meeting. Weeks went by and a couple months later I learned I didn't get the job. I'm not sure what I said wrong! You can't get them all, I remembered.

Point B was composer Christopher Young, whose resumé (like Ottman's) had more than its fair share of horror and thriller flicks. Although Young didn't end up scoring the movie, due to a drawn-out postproduction period that created scheduling conflicts with his work on the comedy *Beauty Shop* (2005), he provided *Hide and Seek* with a lot of demo music. This material was well produced enough that it was later released on a CD as *A Child's Play*. Much of Young's proposed *Hide and Seek* score was built on a music box theme, and six of his twelve variations on this theme are presented on the CD.

John Ottman stepped back into the picture about a year after his first conversations with the director. He wrote a strong, vibrant score for the movie. Interestingly, it also featured a music box. In an interview, Ottman acknowledged Young's work on the film: "He [Young] had already written a good theme, so it was a challenge and intimidating to walk in and try to outdo it."

Soundtrack specialty labels have been putting out increasingly arcane film scores lately, so it comes as no surprise to see best-selling film composers releasing much of their obscure material as well as their well-known work. For example, in addition to his incomplete *Hide and Seek* music, Young has also released his piano sketches for *An Unfinished Life* (2005). Other unused works of his seem likely candidates for future release: For example, his unrecorded score for *Squanto: A Warrior's Tale* (1994) and the extensive amount of material he produced for Tom Shadyac's *Dragonfly* (2002) before having to leave due to a scheduling conflict. Young also did two weeks' work on Robert Towne's screen adaptation of John Fante's quintessential LA novel, *Ask the Dust* (2006). And for *The Exorcist III* (1990) he wrote a whole new, although unrecorded, orchestra score to replace Barry De Vorzon's electronic one).

■ The Magic Roundabout/Doogal (2005)

Original composer: **Mark Thomas**
Additional composer: **James L. Venable**

The Magic Roundabout was an animated children's television series (approximately 500 five-minute episodes) produced in France, where it was known as *Le manège enchanté*, from 1963 through 1971. In 1965 the series came to Britain and became extremely popular. In 2005, Pathé and various coproducing companies created a feature-length computer-animated movie based on it, titled *The Magic Roundabout* (aka *Sprung! The Magic Roundabout*). This too was a hit in England; it featured the voice talents of Kylie Minogue and Ian McKellen among others.

One year later, the film came to America via The Weinstein Company—which completely altered it. Now called *Doogal*, it was re-edited, supplied with a lot of new dialogue, and, with the exception of Minogue's and McKellen's voices, redubbed by American celebrities such as Tina Fey and Jimmy Fallon. Straying far from the spirit of the original series, which was not well known in the States, the reworked picture was pumped up with pop-culture references and even flatulence jokes aimed at a lowest-common-denominator teen audience. Not surprisingly, its music also underwent a facelift, changing some of its songs and underscore cues. The new cues were written by composer James L. Venable.

■ Miss Congeniality 2: Armed and Fabulous (2005)

Original composer: **Randy Edelman**
Additional composers: **Christophe Beck, John Van Tongeren**
Replacement music: **The temporary score**

There are countless horror stories about composers being told to ape temp tracks. Occasionally, when such demands are not met, a production will simply license some of its temp-track music and use that in lieu of original cues. This is why Ridley Scott's *Alien* (1979) contains music from the earlier Jerry Goldsmith score *Freud* (1962). It is also why some of Christopher Young's cues from *Hellraiser* (1987) appear in *Spider-Man 2* (2002), a film otherwise scored by Danny Elfman. Recently, this practice seems to have become more frequent. *Miss Congeniality 2: Armed and Fabulous* pushed the practice to an extreme—a good deal of the music we hear in the film came from its temp track.

Miss Congeniality 2: Armed and Fabulous was the lackluster sequel to the successful comedy *Miss Congeniality* (2000). The films starred and were produced by Sandra Bullock, who played the same character—FBI Agent Gracie Hart—in both. Hired to provide the sequel with music was Randy Edelman, a reliable comedy-film composer who previously scored one of Bullock's greatest hits, *While You Were Sleeping* (1995). Among his recent credits at this time were *Surviving Christmas* (2004) and *Shanghai Knights* (2003). On *Miss Congeniality 2*, he faced an all-too-common problem: The filmmakers had fallen in love with their temp tracks. He soon found himself endlessly rewriting cues in order to make them sound close enough to the temp music to satisfy the producers. After a while, the project sought the services of two additional composers: Christophe Beck (whose recent scoring credits included *Saved!* and *Under the Tuscan Sun*) worked on the movie for two weeks, scoring its first reel as well as its underwater finale. And John Van Tongeren (whose recent scoring credits included *Malibu's Most Wanted* and many episodes of the revived TV series *The Outer Limits*) was invited to work on the film by Edelman. Van Tongeren patched up numerous sonic holes, a task that included penning music for the casino chase and pirate ship sequences. Despite the three composers' best efforts, almost all their music simply disappeared, replaced by an incredible amount of material retained (and licensed) from the temp score. While some original underscore remained in the picture, the film's primary musical voice belonged to the temp cues.

Miss Congeniality 2 had been temp-tracked with a broad selection of music (from dramas, comedies, thrillers, and clay-animation adventures), including cues from other Warner Bros. films, previous Sandra Bullock movies, and temp-track staples that are popular with many editors. Sixteen tracks from this eclectic collection became part of the movie's final "score." These included music from Edward Shearmur's score for the original *Miss Congeniality*, from John Powell's *Two Weeks Notice* (2002) and *I Am Sam* (2001), Graeme Revell's *Gossip* (2000), Christopher Young's *Sweet November* (2001), George S. Clinton's *Ready to Rumble* (2000), Thomas Newman's *Pay It Forward* (2000), James Newton Howard's *My Best Friend's Wedding* (1997), and Harry Gregson-Williams' and John Powell's *Chicken Run* (2000). The result is a score with little coherence (though that problem is not overly noticeable when viewing the film). Adding to the soundscape were many licensed songs by such artists as Pink, Tyler Bates, Liza Minnelli, Ike and Tina Turner, Patti LaBelle, Thelma Houston, the Staple Singers, the Ohio Players, and Dave Alvin.

■ **Major Dundee** (Extended Version, 2005)

Composer for original version (1965): **Daniele Amfitheatrof**
Replacement composer for extended version (2005): **Christopher Caliendo**

Major Dundee (1965), set during the American Civil War, is the story of a misanthropic, glory-seeking Union cavalry officer, Dundee (played by Charlton Heston), who, after showing too much initiative in battle, is exiled to New Mexico to run a prisoner-of-war camp. There he assembles a motley personal army of Union cavalry, Confederate prisoners (including a former West Point friend/rival played by Richard Harris), and local mercenaries to vanquish a group of Apaches who've been raiding white settlements. An obsessed Dundee illegally pursues the Indians into Mexico, where he must also fight French troops loyal to Mexico's Emperor Maximilian. In short, it's Dundee against the world—the Apaches, his own men, the unruly Confederates he attempts to command, and the French army. An oft-quoted assessment of the story made by one of its actors is "*Moby-Dick* on horseback."

A troubled production, *Major Dundee* was directed by Sam Peckinpah, the famously hard-boiled, hard-drinking, maverick filmmaker known for such highly regarded movies as *Ride the High Country* (1962), *The Wild Bunch* (1969), *Straw Dogs* (1971), and *Pat Garrett and Billy the Kid* (1973)—three of which, like *Dundee*, are Westerns. Peckinpah was something of a Western specialist, directing numerous episodes of such TV series as *Gunsmoke*, *Broken Arrow*, *The Rifleman*, and *The Westerner* in the 1950s. And the fairly nihilistic Westerns he made in the 1960s helped redefine the genre.

Dundee is often regarded as Peckinpah's most flawed picture; due to studio interference, it was definitely not the movie the director envisioned. It also occasioned the first of many (often alcohol-fueled) fights with studio brass that would dog the director's career. Fearing that Peckinpah was out of control, Columbia Pictures shortened the shooting schedule by a week and took creative control of the movie away from him. Producer Jerry Bresler then took over postproduction, lending his own tastes to the project. The rough cut had been rumored to be four and a half hours long, and the first roughly polished cut ran 156 minutes. Under Bresler's control, however, that was trimmed to 122 minutes, punching holes in its plot and its pacing. The footage that ended up on the cutting room floor included most of Dundee's romance with the Mexican nurse, some of Peckinpah's signature slow-motion battle shots, and reaction shots that helped give the work emotional depth.

Once the movie was chopped to a "reasonable" length, Bresler called on the services of semiretired, Russian-born composer Daniele Amfitheatrof, with whom he had worked on a half-dozen pictures in the 1930s and 1940s. (Among Amfitheatrof's scoring credits were *Lassie Come Home, Song of the South, Another Part of the Forest, Letter from an Unknown Woman,* and *The Desert Fox.*)

In creating his competent but rather bombastic *Dundee* score, Amfitheatrof relied only on Bresler's instructions (Peckinpah being out of the equation by this point). Against images of flaming ranch buildings and a field of dead bodies, the music opened with a male chorus singing the jaunty "Major Dundee March," an obvious tribute to such John Ford cavalry movies as *She Wore a Yellow Ribbon* (1949), *The Horse Soldiers* (1959), and *Sergeant Rutledge* (1960), all of which opened with jaunty marches sung by male choruses. The lyrics for the march were by Ned Washington, who penned theme song lyrics for such classic 1950s Westerns as *3:10 to Yuma, Gunfight at the O.K. Corral,* and *High Noon.* To perform *Dundee*'s march, Bresler hired Mitch Miller's Sing-Along Gang, a popular, albeit saccharine, choral group. (Miller was an oboist-turned-record-executive-turned-TV-celebrity who had his own TV show in the early 1960s, called *Sing Along with Mitch.*)

Amfitheatrof's music covered the picture practically wall-to-wall. The composer recalled his score in a letter:

> He [Bresler] asked for an "upbeat, old-fashioned fifties-type score." At the time of the recording I was obliged to add certain textural changes in the orchestration following his objections to "the tone" of some cues. One was the cue titled "Are You El Tigre?" My original orchestration of the so-called waltz, depicting the scene of [Charlton] Heston and [Senta] Berger's copulation in the lake was dissonant, in the style of Bartók. Bresler did not approve. I rewrote the cue to his satisfaction, but it ended up sounding more like Max [Steiner] than Daniele [Amfitheatrof]. There were many other changes which were attended to on the recording stage. I had an excellent handpicked orchestra contracted by Marian Klein, including John Williams (piano), Emil Richards (percussion), and Laurindo Almeida (guitar). So it was not as difficult as it might otherwise have been on account of their cooperation.

The score was neither terribly original nor terribly effective at accompanying what Peckinpah had conceived as a fairly offbeat Western, and the director hated it. The release of an enhanced and restored version of the picture on DVD in 2005 would provide an opportunity to try and reclaim Peckinpah's concept.

For this DVD, Michael Schlesinger (head of Sony Picture's Repertory division) and Grover Crisp (vice president of Sony's Film Restoration department) constructed a new and improved version of *Major Dundee* with the hope of bringing the picture more into agreement with Peckinpah's original vision. This version restored twelve minutes of footage that producer Bresler had edited out, greatly aiding the film's development, tone, and pacing.

During *Dundee*'s restoration, Crisp also decided to have a new score written for it, to try to bring its music closer to what Peckinpah might have wanted. For this new, more fitting score he hired composer Christopher Caliendo, who had worked for Crisp once before, providing music for a reissue of the 1926 silent film *The Belle of Broadway*. Determined to write a score that would be as close as possible to Peckinpah's intent, Caliendo was advised by two Peckinpah authorities, who were also working on the *Dundee* DVD: Paul Seydor (a film editor who wrote the book *Peckinpah: The Western Film—A Reconsideration* and directed the Oscar-nominated documentary *The Wild Bunch: An Album in Montage*) and Nick Redman (the producer of four short documentaries on Peckinpah). They discussed such subjects as how Jerry Fielding, the only composer Peckinpah had worked with more than once (scoring *The Wild Bunch, Straw Dogs, Junior Bonner, Bring Me the Head of Alfredo Garcia*, and *The Killer Elite*), might have done the picture.

Due to both budget constraints and the desire to make his score as 1965-sounding as possible, Caliendo utilized a thirty-one-piece orchestra (in the mid-1960s, fifty players was considered a large group), which he recorded with an ear to achieving a period analog sound. Through his creative use of musical texture and orchestration, Caliendo made his thirty-one players sound very full and rich. Unlike Amfitheatrof's purely traditional action-Western music, the new score helped bring out the film's somber moments and internal conflicts. Caliendo discusses his Dundee theme:

> It was very clear to me that Dundee's character is prone to anger very quickly, so how do you capture the anger that quickly? It really had to be a motif, and as I grew to the score the motif became metaphysical as the film does and as Dundee's character does—it's almost Shakespearean in a way because you have a man who's a great tactician on any level ground, he can make decisions for his military, and they respect him for it throughout the picture, but they also keep their distance, they fear him and respect him at the same time. You see that kind of character in many of these men-of-action films, and Heston portrays that kind of character very well. That theme is, above all, truly organic and grows in many different directions because it has to take on the ribald quality of men in war, the tension between man and man, French and Union, Confederate, it became much more than Heston's motif, so the colorization of that changed rapidly.

In addition to Dundee, a number of other characters (and often their ethnicity or nationality) needed to be musically represented as well. Amfitheatrof never received any instructions for scoring the film's Apaches other than to make their music over-the-top. However, Caliendo employed musical specialists to help him provide rich ethnic coloring for his score, which was considerably more sensitive and diverse than the original one. An Irish sound was achieved via fiddle and accordion. An Apache sound relied, for the most part, on wooden and bone flutes, except in the case of certain specific characters: The Apache chief, a warrior, required a more strident feeling, for which Caliendo chose to use a Japanese shakuhachi flute, whereas a passive Indian was musically portrayed by the rare bass recorder.

One of the most important differences between Amfitheatrof's and Caliendo's scores was the spotting. While the Russian composer's music was nearly wall-to-wall, Caliendo placed his music more carefully and judiciously, finding just the right moments for it to enter and exit. It's worth noting that the new score's comparative sparseness makes it obvious that the original picture was missing a lot of sound effects (their lack having been hidden by Amfitheatrof's omnipresent score). Because of this, the extended version may seem a bit quiet to those who know the 1965 version.

Describing the new score, Sony's Grover Crisp said:

> If you wanted something to compare it to, and without detracting from its own uniqueness, I would say it is in the vein of similar Jerry Goldsmith or Elmer Bernstein or Alex North scores for similar pictures. Big where it needs to be, intimate where it needs to be, but really full-bodied and complex, fitting its subject perfectly. It captures the internal discord within the character of Dundee and the relationship of the other characters.... Key Peckinpah enthusiasts and film-score experts who have seen the film and heard this new soundtrack are quite ecstatic about the achievement.

The extended picture with Caliendo's music was not only released on DVD, it was also given a limited theatrical run. The Intrada label released a limited edition CD of Caliendo's soundtrack.

■ **Constantine** (2005)

Original composer: **Brian Tyler**
Additional composer: **Klaus Badelt**

Constantine was a dark metaphysical fantasy picture that marked the feature film debut of director Francis Lawrence, director of music videos for such well-known artists as Britney Spears, Black Eyed Peas, Alanis Morissette, and many others. Based on the *Hellblazer* comic book series, it was set in present-day Los Angeles (not London, as in the comic) and told the story of John Constantine (played by Keanu Reeves), an exorcist or spiritual hit man who's dying of cancer. Because of his attempted suicide when he was young, he has been barred from heaven. Now he's trying to get this ban lifted through meritorious earthly deeds, battling Satan's forces. (*Note*: In the story, earth, heaven, and hell are parallel planes between which one may hop.)

Hired to provide *Constantine*'s music was Brian Tyler, whose recent scoring credits included *The Final Cut* (2004), *Thoughtcrimes* (2003), and *Timeline* (2003); on the last of these he had replaced a Jerry Goldsmith score. In an interview with Dan Goldwasser, Tyler discussed his *Constantine* score:

> Originally I was called in to meet with Francis Lawrence and the editor. Apparently *Frailty* [a 2001 Bill Paxton film that Tyler scored] had been used to temp a few key scenes in the rough cut, and the director found it really interesting. He was new to the world of film scores, but he knew what he liked when he heard it, so we met and he showed me the film. At the time I saw it, it was a bit longer, but it still felt tight and it really knocked me out. So I gave him my vision about what I thought the score would be—something that emphasized the reality of the world, very dark, and makes the audience feel uncomfortable. That was the approach in the beginning—we took a "darker is better" direction on the score. It was still thematic, but very low-register, brooding—and unapologetic in the way that there was no "winking" with the audience.... Initially we wanted to emphasize the "Hell" in Hellblazer—it's a story about a guy who has only a few months left to live, because he's dying from cancer, and he's battling the devil, and trying to save a girl from Hell.... Our film was dark and gritty—it was shot that way, too....
>
> After I finished the score, and conducted and recorded it, it was felt that after watching it in context, it might have benefited from some humor being injected into the music to add some levity. The basic idea was that we could support some of the wisecracking in the film with music. We were all aware from the first day on the film that there were wisecracks in the film, but we didn't hit those comedy beats. To change that, we added a bit more production polish—not as much ancient instrumentation in the score. Some electronic elements were brought in to bring it a more buoyant feel, and some cues became quirky and fun, and winky.
>
> Ultimately it's the studio's film. I did what I thought was right...I addressed the new direction and wrote music that would modularly fit in with the foundation that had been laid down.

Tyler's finished score was deemed a bit too bleak, so another composer was brought in to add a new perspective to the music. This was Klaus Badelt, a Media Ventures composer whose recent scoring credits included *Catwoman* (2004), *Beat the Drum* (2003), and the highly successful *Pirates of the Caribbean: The Curse of the Black Pearl* (2003). With Tyler, he reworked a lot of *Constantine*'s music, adding new elements, including electronic overlays that made the score sound more contemporary. Badelt's past work with Hans Zimmer gave him a strong mastery of synthesized elements and a refined use of choir (one of the most noticeable technical strengths of the Media Ventures group). Tyler didn't oppose the score adjustments, and he welcomed the collaboration. He discusses working with Badelt and explains the impact of their changes:

> I have a lot of respect for Klaus. We had all talked about it and we were in agreement regarding him coming on board. I had been on the film for six months, and we only had a few weeks left. Klaus and I collaborated on the new material and really tried to come up with some key ideas to hone in on and have the greatest impact on certain spots—so that the studio would get what they wanted, and the score would still retain what we liked about the film....
>
> It was done to alter the tone of the film in a bit of a way to make it have a wider appeal. I was a fan of *Hellblazer*, as was Francis [Lawrence], and it initially was a collaboration of what everyone wanted to see on screen. To their credit, the changes weren't overly drastic—like a techno score—we kept the same approach, and after a few weeks

of writing new music, I was out on the stage conducting the new music. It was quite a whirlwind experience! I got to know Klaus, and he has his own fascinating technique of doing things. I had never collaborated with someone on any type of writing, except maybe in a band—it was a new experience, very interesting and one I'll never forget!

Constantine is but one example of why Klaus Badelt has become one of the most requested figures when troubled movies needed quick replacements of individual cues or isolated sequences. In the last couple of years, Badelt reworked small portions on Bryan Singer's *X-Men* (2000), which was scored by Michael Kamen, and larger sections of Michael Mann's *Miami Vice* (2006), which was scored by John Murphy. Both of these films exploited Badelt's electronic music prowess.

■ La marche de l'empereur/March of the Penguins (2005)

Composer for European version: **Émilie Simon**
Composer for American version: **Alex Wurman**

March of the Penguins, a French documentary written and directed by Luc Jacquet, vividly portrayed the arduous annual trek of Antarctic emperor penguins. The birds leave their home in the ocean each autumn and "march" en masse more than sixty miles inland to court, lay eggs, and tend to the eggs until they hatch (barring any misfortunes that may befall them). The film was wildly popular throughout the world and was dubbed into many languages. In the United States it was awarded an Oscar for Best Documentary Feature.

In the original French version, three voiceover actors—a man, a woman, and a child—told the penguins' saga in anthropomorphized first-person narrations. Its score was written by French singer and composer and electronic musician Émilie Simon. (Interestingly, when director Jacquet contacted her about scoring his film, she just happened to be researching musical representations of "coldness" for an album she was working on.) Her delightful and unusual *La marche* music creates a magical and strange sonic world. The largely song-based score mixes her haunting vocals (sung in English) into a bed of vivid instrumental music performed by a chamber group (about eighteen players) augmented by samplers, ondes Martenot, and even the Baschet brothers' 1952 sound-sculpture the Cristal Baschet (a unique sort of glass harmonica that a number of composers, including Luc Ferrari and Toru Takemitsu, have written for). In general, Simon's score, littered with allusions to winter (the sounds of the chilling Antarctic winds and footsteps in snow), has the sort of experimental feel one might expect from Björk. Simon:

In the studio I can make the wind in the reeds sing, as I did on "In the Lake," or I can build a beat out of the noises made by a fireplace. In *March of the Penguins*, I wanted to evoke the sound of snow being walked on, of melting ice. I was interested in things that alluded to the idea of cold, so I used atypical instruments like the Cristal Baschet, which is made of glass rods that you rub with wet fingers.

When the movie was picked up by American distributor Warner Independent Pictures, a number of changes were made to it: A few minutes showing leopard seals killing penguins were removed. The three-commentator, talking-penguin approach was abandoned in favor of a new, longer text and a single narrator (Morgan Freeman), making the movie feel more traditionally documentary-like. Lastly, Simon's score was dropped because, now that the film no longer had a talking-penguins narration, songs written from the penguins' perspectives seemed out of place. Moreover, the songs simply clashed with the new extended narration.

Deciding that a more traditional underscore would better suit the movie, WIP hired a new composer for the American version. Alex Wurman's recent scoring credits included *Anchorman: The Legend of Ron Burgundy* (2004), *Criminal* (2004), and *Hollywood Homicide* (2003). He recalls:

> I just had a chance meeting with Mark Gill, the head of Warner Independent Pictures. They needed to hire somebody. He knew of my work on a few interesting projects and offered this one to me on a hunch. I watched it and loved it. I came into the process about two to three weeks before they finalized the deal with the French—so it wasn't certain that it was going to work out. But if it was going to work out, the clock was already ticking. Even before their deal was finalized, I started working on it, and in total spent about six weeks writing, recording, and mixing the music.... I worked directly with Warner Independent and National Geographic, who bought the French version at Sundance, but they wanted to redo the elements. Collaborating with Jordan Roberts (who wrote the American script), Mark Gill, Tracy Bing (of Warner Independent Pictures), and Adam Leipzig (of National Geographic) was a pleasure. In fact, there was something cool about being in contact with the studio heads directly throughout the project.

In Wurman's orchestra score, Antarctica's desolation is represented by a lonely flute melody, heavenly vocals, and various bells. The score also has its fair share of sweepingly romantic moments, which are set off from time to time by minimalist piano and vibraphone figurations, the vibes lending a nice aura of eternal coldness. The hatching of penguin chicks, on the other hand, is scored with a comedic sense. A soaring finale accompanies the penguins as they return to the sea so that their circle of life can start over again.

Although Wurman's music did its job very well (and made for a great soundtrack CD), many American fans of the film were curious about the French version's music. So Milan Records released Simon's score in the United States under the title *March of the Empress.*

■ An Unfinished Life (2005)

Original composer: **Christopher Young**
Replacement composer: **Deborah Lurie**

A character-driven story of reconciliation and redemption set on a present-day Wyoming ranch, *An Unfinished Life* starred Robert Redford, Morgan Freeman, and Jennifer Lopez. It was the last installment in Swedish director Lasse Hallström's multipicture deal with Miramax Pictures. His previous Miramax efforts included the character-driven dramas *The Cider House Rules* (1999), *Chocolat* (2000), and *The Shipping News* (2001).

Throughout the production's life, the director's and Miramax's visions of the project were somewhat at odds—and, as such things usually go, the production company's demands (including the casting of Lopez) won out. What the movie was to look and sound like were also points of contention. Composer Christopher Young, whose recent scoring credits included *The Grudge* (2004) and *Runaway Jury* (2003), and who had previously worked with Hallström on *The Shipping News*, was hired to score *An Unfinished Life*. He recalls the Miramax-Hallström conflicts:

> They [Miramax] wanted that picture to be a big, opulent Western and it wasn't; it was never going to be that. So I got caught between two opinions. On the one hand there was Lasse [Hallström], who was looking for the film to be a slow-moving and intimate drama which was not trying to rush to the finish line. He certainly didn't want it to be a big Western. Miramax on the other hand was hoping the film was going to be as I've already described. So I was writing two scores; I wrote one for Lasse's version of the movie and then, sort of behind his back, I was told that I had to write a score for Miramax's version as well. As one can imagine, that doesn't work and it will certainly cause problems, which it did. Although Lasse was furious that I had been willing to write music for Miramax that did not follow his vision, I finished the score and in the end everyone seemed to be happy. But then the film was put on hold for two years, and when it was finally set for release, they had a last-minute change of heart and they figured there was only one chance to make the movie better, which was to change the music. I offered to rewrite it myself, but they chose to go with Deborah Lurie, who had been recommended to them by Randy Spendlove from the music department at Miramax.

Deborah Lurie's previous scoring credits included *Drop Dead Sexy* (2005) and *Imaginary Heroes* (2004). She had worked for Miramax previously and, through the years, had become a master of score-doctoring. (Just two years earlier, she rewrote a large part of Theodore Shapiro's music for the Miramax comedy *View from the Top*.) For *An Unfinished Life*, Lurie was simply instructed to "write from her heart," and her replacement score turned out to be closer to Lasse Hallström's vision than Miramax's. Her music, which wasn't radically different from Young's, seemed to fall into two main categories: country-flavored scene-setters and subtle emotional cues. While Young was understandably very disappointed to have his score replaced, he felt good that the picture provided Lurie with one of her early big projects. (*Note*: Some bit of

Young's music must still be in the film, as its credits list him as an "additional music" composer.) Young:

> In the case of Deborah Lurie, I think that she is extremely talented, not to forget that she is an ex-student of mine from USC. As hard as the situation was, I was excited for her to have the opportunity to work on a major motion picture. So this is interesting: I had an ex-student of mine replace my work and she was probably as uncomfortable in doing it as I was when I replaced John Addison's score [for *Highpoint*] all those years ago [in 1982]. I mean, she was replacing her teacher, but these things happen, and someone was going to replace my score anyway, so why shouldn't it be her? Believe me when I tell you that I haven't seen the movie with her score and I haven't heard her score either, because it was too painful at that time. However, I am sure that she did a very good job because she is extremely talented.

As soundtrack recordings, *An Unfinished Life* had a rich life. In addition to Varèse Sarabande's release of Lurie's score, the label also released Young's unused music (a 1,000-copy limited edition that was one of the company's fastest sellouts) in 2006. Interestingly, Young's disc included not only his finished orchestral score but also fourteen of his piano demos/sketches. In 2008, the BSX label released another limited-edition CD of Young's *An Unfinished Life* music—three suites (twenty-one individual pieces) of solo piano music compiled and arranged from his piano demos/sketches.

■ **Mrs. Harris** (2005)

Original composer: **John Frizzell**
Replacement composer: **Alex Wurman**

Thanks to great improvements in television production—particularly in the cable TV arena, and most notably by HBO—the line between television and theatrically presented movies has grown blurrier and blurrier. Since the early 1990s, numerous TV movies have boasted casts and crews that would be the envy of many theatrical features. So it's not surprising that quite a few good film composers regularly accept work on these movies.

One of HBO's first replaced movie scores was for *Barbarians at the Gate* (1993), the true story of the attempt by Nabisco's CEO (played by James Garner) to buy out the company. The picture's first score—primarily synthesizer music enlivened by woodwind overdubs—was written by composer Trevor Jones, whose recent scoring credits included *The Last of the Mohicans* (1992) and *Freejack* (1992). Unfortunately for Jones, his score didn't suit the producers' tastes and expectations, so they hired Richard Gibbs, a former member of the band Oingo Boingo whose recent scoring credits included *Passed Away* (1992) and *Once Upon a Crime* (1992), to replace it. Gibbs's music, completed in only two weeks, was more lighthearted and funky, with a definite comedic edge.

In 2005, HBO produced another fascinating real-life story—*Mrs. Harris*, the chronicle of Jean Harris (played by Annette Bening), a headmistress of a girls' boarding school who in 1980 murdered her fiancé, Dr. Herman Tarnower (Ben Kingsley), a famous cardiologist and author of the best-selling book *The Complete Scarsdale Medical Diet*. Hired to score the picture was John Frizzell, a composer best known for his horror movie scores, whose recent credits included *Cradle 2 the Grave* (2003) and *Gods and Generals* (2003).

Mrs. Harris had been temp-tracked with an eclectic array of music that included cuts from classical pianist Christopher O'Riley's album of pop tune arrangements *True Love Waits: Christopher O'Riley Plays Radiohead*. Following this lead, Frizzell's score featured offbeat adaptations of classical music, including a Chopin piece with saxophone and a Bach homage with percussion. Sadly for Frizzell, his score didn't win the hearts of the film's producers, who felt that it relied too much on the direction set by the temp tracks.

A new composer was hired: Alex Wurman, whose recent credits included *A Lot Like Love* (2005) and the US version of *March of the Penguins* (2005). Wurman's music was a bit more restrained than Frizzell's and even had a suburban Americana feel to it. Contrasting beauty with grim reality, it followed the dramatic arc of the title character as she gradually loses her grip on reality.

Mrs. Harris premiered at the Toronto Film Festival in 2005 and, following its TV airing in 2006, was nominated for a dozen Emmys and three Golden Globe Awards (none of which it won).

Dreamer: Inspired by a True Story (2005)

Original composer: **Jan A. P. Kaczmarek**
Replacement composer: **John Debney**

Dreamer is a sweet, optimistic movie about three generations of a Kentucky horse-breeding family (represented by stars Kris Kristofferson, Kurt Russell, and Dakota Fanning) who are brought closer together and their farm saved from foreclosure by Soñador, a seriously injured racehorse that they nurse back to health. ("Inspired by a True Story" refers to the horse Mariah's Storm, which broke a foreleg in 1993 and, against the odds, went on to win a number of races during the next two years.) Written and directed by John Gatins, the film was produced by DreamWorks SKG.

DreamWorks' choice to score the movie was Polish composer Jan A. P. Kaczmarek, who had just won an Academy Award for his *Finding Neverland* (2004) score. Kaczmarek recalls his work on *Dreamer*:

> It was right after the Oscars. It was a first-time director [Gatins], and I have to warn everybody that this is the most dangerous situation. With a first-time director and a big studio picture, you really have too much at stake in a way. So I did the music. The director was a really lovely man, a sweet man and very sensitive, and we had so many good

> moments together; he'd cry occasionally while we were playing music, which was very moving. Then we went to Prague and recorded the whole thing, and the mood was absolutely spectacular. We were really happy...we gave hugs and kisses and I went to Poland and he went to mix it here [Los Angeles]. And then the mix was finished and still the mood was really great and I got these reports from the scoring stage occasionally saying it was all great....

After Kaczmarek's score met with seemingly enthusiastic approval, the people in charge decided to pep up the picture with a love ballad. In order to find the perfect tunesmith for the job, the producers held a contest—an advance screening of the movie was arranged for a group of recording artists, who then wrote songs inspired by it. The winner was the aptly titled "Dreamer," written and performed by Bethany Dillon. With the introduction of this pop song, the movie's whole musical landscape started to change. Director Gatins also had a change of heart/ear/mind and let Kaczmarek go. To replace him, DreamWorks hired John Debney, who had just been nominated for an Oscar for his score for *The Passion of the Christ* (2004), which lost out to Kaczmarek's previously mentioned *Finding Neverland*. Kaczmarek:

> Suddenly the day came when he [Gatins] woke up, a month later, after one of the screenings with the executives, thinking that it was all too dark—that the score, my score, was too dark and needed to be replaced with something light, and they did it, you know! And he called me and he was very courageous, not many people do this, and he said, "You are being replaced." They just don't call you directly. Usually your agent gets the message and, you know, your agent is your psychotherapist who tells you how wonderful you are and it means nothing and they're a bunch of idiots.... No, this director, to his credit, he called me. I was in the middle of a forest in Poland on my cell, and he told me what had happened. I said, "I really cannot be depressed because I'm in such a beautiful place now and I'm in the middle of doing something really great, but I'm really shocked and surprised, and I think this must be a mistake, but what can I say?"

John Debney's score (one of the composer's top five picks of his own works) was an emotional effort not unlike the scores he'd been writing for years for romantic comedies and dramas. His Americana-tinged work for *Dreamer*, however, displayed a newfound maturation of his ideas. It is one of the most effective of his scores, with heartfelt themes carried by two well-known virtuosos—violinist Joshua Bell and pianist Michael Lang—who lend the weight of their own personalities to the composer's simple melodies.

A recording of Debney's score was released on a Sony CD but, unfortunately, Kaczmarek's score hasn't been released, so the two works cannot be directly compared. However, given the Polish composer's talents, one can imagine that his *Dreamer* music was quite beautiful. The experience taught Kaczmarek some important lessons, which he kindly shared:

> They replaced my score, and I believe it was a mistake, but that's my right to believe that this was a mistake, and their right is to believe it wasn't a mistake. I told you this story because you can get an Oscar on February 27th and be replaced on April 29th. And in

a way that's wonderful. And then you ask yourself how did I contribute to this? Was it necessary to score this picture? Was it, is it, my fault as well? And maybe it is, you know, and when I look at it today, I believe the score was right, but maybe I shouldn't have scored another picture about children; maybe that's unnecessary. Maybe one picture with a child as the main character is enough? Maybe I'm victim of my own kind of...I don't know what. As a man from Eastern Europe I'm always thinking that I'm being treated as a composer who cannot write music for the mainstream American box-office hit. I said, "No, no, no, I will do it!" And even if it's not the most sophisticated movie about a horse which breaks its leg and a little girl, I will try to prove I can do it. So, a certain vanity, and maybe too much ambition, was the reason that I wanted to prove something. On the other hand, I think I did it!

But that's the reality of our profession; we face incredible, unexpected events. We all go through this...this industry is being driven by incredible forces we cannot control. And my advice to myself and other people who are in my situation is to have another part of your life. I mean, in order to be a composer who is always optimistic and full of passion and always looking for the unique voice and solution, I need to have something else. I also have to write music when I'm really enjoying freedom, then I can be much better psychologically, because it's all about our feelings, yes, it's nothing else. It's our emotions, and in order to be fresh and a virgin when I enter another production, I need to be somehow repaired in the meantime. So I'm repairing myself by writing and doing other things which confirm that I'm really in control. Then I can devote myself [to] and be fully and completely curious about the next adventure.

■ **Æon Flux** (2005)

Original composer: **Theodore Shapiro**
Replacement composers: **Reinhold Heil and Johnny Klimek**
Replacement for replacement composers: **Graeme Revell**

Æon Flux was a live-action feature film adaptation of a heavily stylized MTV sci-fi-fantasy cartoon series about a tall, scantily clad, acrobatic female secret agent and assassin named Æon Flux, who lives in a dystopian near-future society. The feature starred Charlize Theron in the title role and was directed by Karyn Kusama, whose one previous directorial outing was *Girlfight* (2000). Unfortunately, the cartoon did not translate well to live action, and the movie was something of a flop.

The example of the cartoon's distinctively hyperactive music, the work of Drew Neumann (whose scoring credits included *The Wild Thornberrys* animated TV show and *The Wild Thornberrys Movie*), was not followed in its film adaptation, for which the first composer was Theodore Shapiro, whose recent scoring credits included the comedies *Dodgeball* (2004) and *13 Going on 30* (2004). For one reason or another, his work was rejected and the composing team of Reinhold Heil and Johnny Klimek, whose scoring credits included *Swimming Upstream* (2003) and episodes of the TV series *Deadwood* (2004–2006), took his place. Their work, too, was rejected, and Graeme

Revell, whose recent credits included *The Fog* (2005) and *Sin City* (2005), was hired. Revell summarized what he knew about the picture's music before he came on board:

> The director [Karyn Kusama] had a friend of hers, Teddy Shapiro, doing the music to begin with. I don't really know, of course, what went on, but I do know that Karyn was striving to make the piece as emotional as possible. Unfortunately, for one reason or another, some of the folks involved decided the approach was somewhat sentimental or overly emotional. The second two guys [Reinhold Heil and Johnny Klimek] have done fantastic work with [director] Tom Tykwer's movies—*The Princess and the Warrior* is one of my favorite movies.... I guess they moved a little more in the direction of what I wound up doing, but it's a tricky movie. You need to try and make the movie propel forward while still being feminine and telling the story, and that's tricky. I didn't hear very much of what they did, so of course I won't comment on that, but it's just unfortunate when composers get caught in that kind of a different viewpoint of what the music should be.

By the time Revell was hired, the picture's deadline loomed large. However, the composer was familiar with tight schedules—he had worked under similar circumstances when replacing Michael Kamen's score for *Lara Croft: Tomb Raider* (2001). Revell reflects on how he came to be involved in *Æon Flux*:

> I had worked with Gale Anne Hurd, the producer, and David Gale, from MTV, before on a project back in 1993. When they were having difficulty on this one, I guess they thought of me to come and help them find a direction that the movie needed. It was good to hook up with them again. I had about three weeks...and that's not a problem for me. Three weeks is a fine amount of time to write a movie score in. I have done one in ten days, so that's what I call a "crunch." It's just a matter of finding a direction in a hurry. Then, if everyone's in agreement on the direction we are going, it becomes a bit of a mechanical exercise, and there is a lot of help you can get in that world.

Revell's score utilized the Los Angeles studio ensemble known as the Hollywood Symphony Orchestra, relying heavily on its string section, which he supplemented with a great number of electronic samples, reminiscent of his *Tomb Raider* music. Its two key themes, which he passes among the instruments, are developed well. For its finale, the main theme is performed in the style of an instrumental rock anthem.

■ **King Kong** (2005)

Original composer: **Howard Shore**
Replacement composer: **James Newton Howard**

Composer Max Steiner's work for the original 1933 *King Kong*, a masterful picture on many levels, is considered the first original, full-blown American movie score; it's also considered the first film score to fully utilize leitmotifs, which would become Hollywood's musical lingua franca. In 1976, producer Dino De Laurentiis remade *King Kong* in a version directed by John Guillermin (who had directed *The Towering Inferno* two years earlier), in which Kong is shot off the top of the World Trade Center.

John Barry composed the film's romantic score, which was peppered with a strange combination of musical styles that ranged from percussive tribal music to church organ and disco beats.

In 1986, De Laurentiis and Guillermin teamed up again for the *King Kong Lives*, a sequel to their 1976 ape movie. This version has Kong kept alive—in a coma—for ten years following his nosedive off the WTC, followed by a heart transplant that allows him to resume his wild ways. The film was fairly abysmal, and composer John Scott's score far outshone it.

Kong once again climbed onto the big screen in 2005, in director Peter Jackson's remake of the original 1933 movie. For this big-budget extravaganza Jackson hired composer Howard Shore, who had scored his massive and massively successful *Lord of the Rings* trilogy (2001–2003), winning Best Original Score Oscars for the first and last of the series. But the simpatico musical vision they had enjoyed while working on the Tolkien tales simply did not carry over to the ape story, and Shore was let go before he even finished recording his orchestra score. Peter Jackson recalls:

> Howard and I came to realize that we had differing creative aspirations.... Rather than waste time arguing with a friend and trying to unify our points of view, we decided amicably to let another composer score the film.

Jackson again (from a different source):

> Howard Shore was [the] original choice for composer.... [W]e're very good friends [but] it just came to a point where it seemed like our sensibilities for the film were somewhat different. So we decided as friends that it was better not to go down that road any more for this film. James Newton Howard was a composer that we've obviously admired for a long, long time and we'd used some elements of his earlier scores in some temp tracks that we'd done, and his sensibility and feeling for the music seemed to relate really well to the pictures that we'd shot.

When Shore was asked about his *King Kong* score by online radio host Daniel Schweiger, the composer simply said that he and Jackson didn't communicate as well on *King Kong* as they had on *The Lord of the Rings* trilogy and that he was looking forward to working with the director in the future.

As *King Kong* was being made, an official website posted short videos related to its production and postproduction. One of them was about Shore's score, featuring a snippet from his recording sessions with the New Zealand Symphony Orchestra. The video disappeared from the site after Shore's music was rejected, and, unfortunately, it didn't reappear among the short bonus docs on the film's DVD, which includes two shorts about James Newton Howard.

King Kong's impressive replacement score—almost three hours of orchestra music—had to be delivered in five weeks, so Howard assembled a team to help him produce it. Among the talented and industrious composers on that team were Chris P. Bacon, Blake Neely, David Long, and Mel Wesson. Supervising orchestrator Jeff Atmajian reminisces:

> I did it by putting all of [my] life on hold and getting very little sleep! One person could never orchestrate a project like this with the time given. We had a very able crew, which I oversaw. Each day cues would be written, then the MIDI files transcribed by the hard-working and brilliant crew at JoAnn Kane Music Services. We would then orchestrate those cues. In addition to myself, the main team was Jon Kull, Pete Anthony, Brad Dechter, and Patrick Russ. We also used Bruce Babcock and Bill Liston. For the source music, we used Frank Bennett, Eddie Karem and Harvey Cohen.... [The score] was so full of wonderful and strong themes that it had the richness and power of the kind of score one might have got in the 1940s. In addition, it is so current and modern sounding. James is masterful at fusing contemporary sound design and orchestral elements into organic music.... All the music and most of the color were in the demos. Our job was to score it clearly so that the orchestra would play back just what James clearly intended. I am also amazed that with the little time he had, James was just as thorough in his demos as he always is.... You should hear them—they are often quite intimidating in their level of finesse!

While director Jackson and the film's postproduction crew worked in New Zealand, Howard and his team composed and then recorded his score in Los Angeles. The two parties communicated via a telephone-line transfer of digital images and recordings (through an ISDN connection), as noted in the short documentaries accompanying the picture's DVD.

An amusing aside: In Jackson's *King Kong,* when the ape is put on public display in a theater, the pit orchestra plays the jungle motifs from Max Steiner's score for the 1933 movie. About this, Peter Jackson said, "What was also fun with the music was finding a little opportunity to pay homage to Max Steiner. We used some of his original score." Furthermore, the onscreen conductor of this orchestra is none other than Howard Shore, filmed prior to his exit from the project. When the creature breaks free of its restraints and begins its rampage, it leaps into the orchestra pit, squashing the conductor. Talk about a composer's brutal rejection!

■ **Transamerica** (2005)

Original composer of multiple scores: **Mason Daring**
Replacement composer: **David Mansfield**

Writer-director Duncan Tucker's feature film debut, the critically acclaimed comedy-drama road picture *Transamerica,* was about a thirty-seven-year-old pre-op male-to-female transsexual. Living as a woman under the name Bree, Stanley (played by Felicity Huffmann, who was nominated for a Best Actress Oscar for the role) travels from New York City to Los Angeles with the son he never knew, a teenage hustler whom he fathered during a one-night stand in college. It's a journey of discovery and enlightenment for both parent and son, the latter of whom remains unaware throughout most of the picture that Bree is actually his father.

To provide the film's music, Tucker hired Mason Daring, a composer with a most unusual background. Before becoming a professional film composer, he had been a practicing entertainment lawyer and part-time musician. It was through his work as a lawyer that he met writer-director John Sayles, going on to score Sayles's directorial debut, *Return of the Secaucus Seven* (1979). He then became the writer-director's go-to composer, penning music for such other highly regarded Sayles films as *Matewan* (1987), *The Secret of Roan Inish* (1994), and *Lone Star* (1996).

Transamerica had been temped with a collection of simple, folksy tracks, and Daring's score remained relatively true to the example set by these selections. Once finished, though, it was deemed too simple. The problem seems to have been with the temp music, which gave the composer a misleading indication of the picture's musical needs.

Sayles, however, gave Daring a second shot at the movie's score. On that attempt, the composer wrote more complex and less folksy music that highlighted the cross-country trek while adding to the film's emotional impact. It seemed to be just what the director wanted, but a family tragedy cut short Daring's involvement—he had to leave the project before finishing the recording of his music.

For a new score, the director turned to composer and multi-instrumentalist David Mansfield, whose previous scoring credits included 1980's *Heaven's Gate* (a film in which he also appears, playing fiddle on roller skates), *The Apostle* (1997), and *Songcatcher* (2000). In addition to his film work, Mansfield is a highly regarded session player (fiddle, guitar, mandolin, pedal steel guitar) who has performed with Bob Dylan (as part of the Rolling Thunder Revue, 1975–1978), T-Bone Burnett, Johnny Cash, Sam Phillips, the Roches, Edie Brickell, Spinal Tap, Dwight Yoakam, Lucinda Williams, Loudon Wainwright III, and many others.

In 1988, one of Mansfield's favorite scores—the music he wrote for *Fresh Horses*—had been rejected and replaced with a score by Patrick Williams. So, when informed that he would be replacing another composer on *Transamerica*, he was reluctant to take on the job. However, when he learned that Daring had departed to attend to personal matters, not due to a creative disagreement, he agreed to do the picture.

Mansfield's bluegrass-flavored score—written primarily for a traditional string band (fiddle, mandolin, banjo, guitar, string bass)—was recorded in his home studio. Not only did this music, which was never heavy-handed or melodramatic, nicely underscore the story's physical and emotional journeys, it also meshed well with the many songs heard throughout the film, performed by such country and folk stars as Lucinda Williams, Dolly Parton (who wrote the Oscar-nominated "Travelin' Thru" for the picture), the Nitty Gritty Dirt Band, David Poe, and others.

The movie's official soundtrack CD favors its songs and provides only a couple of Mansfield's cues. However, his own website offers a good number of excerpts from his score.

■ Tsotsi (2005)

Original composers: **Paul Hepker and Mark Kilian**
Composer of unused alternate score: **Guy Farley**

Tsotsi is a critically acclaimed (and Oscar-winning, for Best Foreign Language Film), gritty film written and directed by South African Gavin Hood, based on renowned South African playwright Athol Fugard's novel of the same name. Set in Johannesburg's violent urban ghetto of Soweto, it covers six days in the life of Tsotsi (a local slang term meaning "thug"), the leader of a small but vicious gang of young criminals. After accidentally kidnapping an infant during a bloody carjacking, Tsotsi reflects on his own early childhood, awakening his sense of empathy and humanity as he tries to care for the child.

Chosen to score the picture were composers Paul Hepker and Mark Kilian, both of whom were born and raised in South Africa. Prior to *Tsotsi*, the two had written a number of television and film scores. (In 2007, they would reunite with writer-director Hood to score his film *Rendition*.)

The music in *Tsotsi* has two chief components: first, a dramatic underscore that incorporates various ethnic music elements; and second, Kwaito, a popular post-apartheid urban dance music that counts hip-hop and international "house" music among its primary roots. Kwaito is a culturally defining music for many young South African blacks.

Hepker and Kilian produced their dark, moody, emotive underscore, which featured the voice of legendary African singer-songwriter Vusi Mahlasela, at their Santa Monica, California, studio. Most of the film's Kwaito was written and performed by the genre's superstar singer-poet Zola, who also played the part of a rival gangleader in the film. Zola is well known for bringing a politically charged message to Kwaito, which had previously been dominated by an apolitical gangster stance and/or a lack of message altogether.

Once the Hepker-Kilian score was finished, however, the film's producers met with British composer Guy Farley in London. (Among Farley's recent scoring credits were 2004's *Wake of Death*, *Out of Season*, and *Modigliani*.) Farley, who had been considered for the job before the South African duo was hired, found the movie powerful and emotional enough with its current score. But the film's producers asked him to try a more thematic approach to its music and increase the presence of Kwaito in it. Farley wrote about twenty-eight minutes of music, but writer-director Hood wasn't involved in this and reportedly never listened to Farley's score, because he was committed to Hepker and Kilian.

Farley's material was filled with elements of native African music and, as requested, incorporated Kwaito into the score itself. When discussing the recording sessions for *Tsotsi*, Farley listed many of the outstanding soloists who took part in the recording:

> My score was led by the emotional and powerful voice of Nicola Emmanuel, whom I first heard perform in the film *Cry Freedom*, directed by Richard Attenborough.... We recorded the producer-approved rescore I had written for female voice, African flutes, African percussion, kalimba, bass ocarina, kora, marimba, and orchestral strings. I used the strings as a harmonic pad playing most of the time with mutes and without vibrato. I wanted the sound to be almost transparent, but rich in sound, as a background to the main instruments. Jan Hendrickse played the flutes and ocarina parts (beautifully, really moving), and ethnic percussion was provided by Paul Clarvis on various African drums and percussion. Where I used Kwaito music in my score I worked with South African producer Pete Martin, whose understanding of Kwaito music and programming was first-hand, having produced multi-platinum-selling albums in SA. His work was outstanding and literally shook the room.

While Farley's music was in the works, *Tsotsi* hit the film festival circuit, premiering in August 2005 at the Edinburgh Film Festival, where it won two awards. Once the awards started coming in, it was decided that the original Hepker-Kilian score was perfectly fine on its own. During the next few months, *Tsotsi* won prizes at many festivals, including the Toronto International Film Festival, the AFI Fest, the Thessaloniki Film Festival, the Denver International Film Festival, and the St. Louis International Film Festival. *Tsotsi* continued winning awards through 2006.

■ **Nacho Libre** (2006)

Original composer: **Beck**
Replacement composer: **Danny Elfman**

Writer-director Jared Hess was a fan of alternative rock singer-songwriter Beck, so he invited him to score his film *Nacho Libre*, a slapstick turn on Mexican masked wrestling, starring popular comedic actor Jack Black as a Mexican priest who secretly turns to wrestling to support the local orphanage.

Beck had only limited experience in film scoring. His biggest work in the field was for David Atkins's *Novocaine* (2001), a comedy in which Steve Martin played a dentist enmeshed in Hitchcockian intrigue. But Beck's music for that picture had been replaced with a score by Steve Bartek, former lead guitarist for Oingo Boingo, whose previous scoring credits included *Get Over It* (2001) and *The Crew* (2000). *Novocaine*'s makers originally wanted Danny Elfman to score their picture, but his busy schedule left him able to provide only a couple of themes (he is credited with writing the film's "theme music"), which meant his orchestrator, Bartek, had to do the score's heavy lifting. With *Nacho Libre*, Beck must have felt a pang of déjà vu: After he and his band recorded his score, the powers-that-be (Paramount Picture's music department in this case) decided that it should be replaced with one by Elfman.

Beck provided *Nacho Libre* with a fairly experimental-sounding, guitar-based score that utilized his usual crew of musicians—Brian Lebarton, Matt Mahaffey,

Matt Sherrod, Justin Stanley, and Ken Andrews. With him playing guitar and singing eccentric vocals, Beck's out-of-the-ordinary score focused on the film's Mexican aspects. (Even though, given the musician's penchant for creative noise, his *Nacho Libre* material seems rather restrained.)

The director was very happy with Beck's score and thought it was a perfect fit for his comedy. Paramount, however, felt the movie should have funnier music—and should be more than "just one person playing his guitar" (which, of course, it was anyway). So the studio turned to Elfman, who wrote a colorful, Latin-flavored score. But once Elfman's music had been recorded with the Hollywood Studio Symphony, it was decided to use an amalgam of both Beck's and Elfman's scores. This opened the door to a troubled composer-credit situation.

A film composer who feels his work has been slighted in one way or another can bring this to light by having his name removed from the offending picture's credits. This was famously done in 1942 by the ever-feisty Bernard Herrmann. He removed his credit from Orson Welles's *The Magnificent Ambersons* after producing studio RKO chopped up the lengthy picture, removing thirty-one minutes of Herrmann's fifty-eight-minute score, and then hired staff composer Roy Webb to write music for its new (including a newly shot, saccharine ending) and re-edited scenes. Similar situations have cropped up when pop songs overtook a soundtrack: John Barry had issues with *First Love* (1977), when most of his music was replaced with romantic tunes, and Danny Elfman reportedly considered removing his name from *Anywhere But Here* (1999) when a good deal of his music was similarly omitted in favor of sappy songs.

Although about two-thirds of Elfman's *Nacho Libre* score ended up in the picture, he felt that his work hadn't been treated well. Furthermore, he didn't want to share the composing credit (a shared credit often denotes a collaboration, which clearly wasn't the case here). After Elfman reportedly threatened to remove his name if Beck were listed as cocomposer, a deal was worked out to allow both composers' names to appear in the main titles. As part of that deal, the end credits list all of the musical cues separately—eighteen by Elfman and six by Beck, as well as almost two dozen songs, including a couple written by the film's star, Jack Black.

■ You, Me and Dupree (2006)

Original composer: **Rolfe Kent**
Replacement composer: **Theodore Shapiro**

Comedy can be one of the most treacherous fields for film composers. When a comedy fails to spark during its test screenings, filmmakers often call for a new score. Sometimes they have something more eccentric in mind (e.g., David Kitay's replacement of Graeme Revell's score for 2006's *The Darwin Awards*), while at other times they want something more tame (e.g., George S. Clinton's replacement of Richard Marvin's score for 2004's *Eulogy*). But most often a new score is ordered in the hope that overtly "funnier" music will buttress weak jokes and pratfalls and deliver laughs for a humor-shy picture.

You, Me and Dupree, directed by brothers Andrew and Joe Russo, was a lightweight comedy about a houseguest (played by Owen Wilson) who overstays his welcome with a newlywed couple (Matt Dillon and Kate Hudson). Hired to score it was comedy specialist Rolfe Kent, whose recent credits included the comedies *Failure to Launch* (2006), *Just Like Heaven* (2005), and *Thank You for Smoking* (2005), and whose earlier work included three of director Alexander Payne's comedies: *Sideways* (2004), *About Schmidt* (2002), and *Election* (1999).

You, Me and Dupree seemed to be fun while Kent worked on it. The crew of the soundtrack info and review website SoundtrackNet even attended his score's recording sessions at Sony Studios and put together a little photo essay about it (which was later moved to the site ScoringSessions.com). The photos show a session attended by both directors, who witnessed excellent performances from a large orchestra and a variety of soloists, including guitarist George Doering.

But fate was not kind to Kent's score. The positive reaction that test audiences gave the film when it was accompanied only by its temp score led to Kent's score being dropped before it was even dubbed in. Instead, a replacement score was quickly commissioned, with the instructions that its composer adhere more closely to the temp's flavor than Kent had.

The replacement composer, Theodore Shapiro, was no stranger to comedy either; among his recent scoring credits were the well-regarded comedies *The Devil Wears Prada* (2006), *Fun with Dick and Jane* (2005), and *The Baxter* (2005). But while Shapiro's replacement music may be closer to the temp score's style, it seems to leave little impression as it ducks in and out of the many preexisting songs the filmmakers stuffed into their film.

Interestingly, Kent would have a score for another comedy, *Fred Claus*, replaced the following year. Although the picture united three principals from 2005's successful *Wedding Crashers* (director David Dobkin, actor Vince Vaughn, and Kent), the movie, as Kent put it in his blog, "fell victim to some studio exec," and his score was replaced by Christophe Beck.

■ The Woods (2006)

Original composer: **Jaye Barnes Luckett**
Replacement composer: **John Frizzell**

The Woods was a well-made, moody supernatural horror film directed by Lucky McKee, a filmmaker best known for the cult film *May* (2002). It tells the story of a troubled teen who is sent off to a remote (set in the woods) girls' boarding school in New England. There she falls prey to the academy's headmistress-witch (played by Patricia Clarkson) and discovers her own latent evil powers.

On *The Woods,* McKee intended to use many of the same people he had worked with on *May,* including composer Jaye Barnes Luckett, his friend since both were students at USC. Luckett's previous scoring credits also included McKee's "Sick Girl" (2006), an episode of the TV series *Masters of Horror.* Luckett wrote *The Woods'* important choral source music, with the prospect of also writing the picture's score, which was to be developed from those pieces.

But the studio, United Artists, which had been undergoing major internal changes and had shelved McKee's film for a couple of years, had other ideas. Luckett:

> It was a case where the director wasn't allowed to use his crew. It wasn't just me, but people in other key roles as well. Really no one involved with *May* was allowed on board, even though we were willing to work for far less than they paid our counterparts. I only got so far because the music was treated like two separate jobs. I did Job One, the prerecorded choir songs, at a time when the project was in more encouraging and respectful hands at the studio. But then the administration changed before I had a chance to formally submit anything for Job Two, the full score. The demos on the CD were among about twenty different scratch tracks I made for Lucky right after he signed on to direct... rough sketches of proposed themes, for his ears only. From those, Lucky chose the two needed for the onscreen choir scenes, we knocked out the recording in lightning speed, and the music went over very well with the cast, crew, and early test audiences. I was told by the production that a separate contract would be coming for me to do a full score. However, the same changing of hands at the studio that plagued the movie otherwise over the following years threw a wrench into it. The folks who took over came in wanting an established composer. They came to Lucky with a list of composers, said, "Pick one," and that was that. So my temp score and demos never had a chance to be rejected or unused. No one listened to them, except for Lucky. Even though the choir material was already the main theme of the movie, we never had a shot to develop the demos into anything more. I unfortunately couldn't get the cooperation needed to include those choir tracks on the CD, but I'm glad people can hear the demos as well as "Bad Girl," which is actually in the film.

Luckett received screen credit for her contributions, but the movie's actual score was written by John Frizzell. No stranger to horror and thriller movies, he counted among his recent credits *Stay Alive* (2006), *The Prize Winner of Defiance, Ohio* (2005), and *Cradle 2 the Grave* (2003). His score for *The Woods* cleverly presented the titular woods as a source or mounting terror, progressing from bucolic, Americana-flavored music to claustrophobic atonal strains.

■ **Bonneville** (2006)

Original composer: **Shie Rozow**
Replacement composer: **Jeff Cardoni**

Bonneville is a sweet, leisurely paced tale about three fiftysomething Mormon women—a widow (played by Jessica Lange) and her two best friends (Kathy Bates and Joan Allen)—driving a 1966 Pontiac Bonneville convertible from Pocatello, Idaho, to Santa Barbara, California, to deliver the widow's late husband's ashes for burial next to his first wife. The women have numerous bonding experiences as they motor past scenic landscapes and encounter friendly strangers. The little independent feature, which premiered at the 2006 Toronto Film Festival, marked the directorial debut of Christopher N. Rowley.

Bonneville's score was by composer Shie Rozow, whose previous credits included a few short-lived television shows and some short films, including director Rowley's *The Remembering Movies* (2004). Rozow is also an active music editor who had previously acted in that capacity on a number of Danny Elfman projects, including *Charlie and the Chocolate Factory* (2005), *Corpse Bride* (2005), and *Big Fish* (2003).

Rozow built his score on an interesting concept: a focus on the deceased husband's job as an anthropologist. Featuring various world-music elements, it created an ethereal feeling through the use of a range of ethnic flutes and the duduk (an evocative Armenian woodwind instrument of ever-growing popularity among film composers). This score accompanied the film at the Toronto Film Festival.

But when *Bonneville* had trouble finding a distributor, producer Robert May of SenArt Films decided to recut it and equip it with a new score that would help define it more traditionally as a road movie. The replacement composer was Jeff Cardoni, whose recent scoring credits included *Just Friends* (2005) and episodes of the TV series *Entourage* (2005–2006) and *CSI: Miami* (2003–present). Cardoni's *Bonneville* score was less exotic and a bit more driving than its predecessor, replacing the world-music flavor with an Americana-style music that featured some particularly nice acoustic guitar performances.

Following its alterations, SenArt gave the movie only a limited theatrical run in 2008, after which 20th Century Fox released it on DVD.

■ **Open Season** (2006)

Original composer: **Paul Westerberg**
Replacement composer: **Ramin Djawadi**

Since the death of classic song-and-dance-filled animated movies, several studios have tried to produce edgier and hipper music-filled animated pictures. Disney itself tried to break from the traditional mold by hiring Carter Burwell to score its 1995 feature *A Goofy Movie*. Burwell, who had been an animator before becoming a professional composer, had previously scored such films as *The Hudsucker Proxy* (1994), *Kalifornia* (1993), and *Barton Fink* (1991). However, the studio's executives had second thoughts about Burwell's music and ended up hiring Don Davis to soften it, to make it fluffier. Davis, whose previous scoring credits included the animated TV series *Capitol Critters* (1992–1995), *Taz-Mania* (1993), and *Tiny Toons Adventures*

(1990–1993), rewrote some of Burwell's music and contributed additional music of his own.

This same sort of thing—producers getting cold feet about a too-nontraditional score—would happen ten years later with Sony's *Open Season.* Paul Westerberg, lead singer and guitarist with the popular 1980s alternative rock band the Replacements, was hired by Sony to pen songs for their first full-length animated feature, a computer-animated comedy about woodland creatures teaming up against hunters. Westerberg, believing he had been hired to do rock-'n'-roll tracks, started writing his tunes using pencil sketches of the animated characters and recordings of dialogue excerpts for inspiration. He wrote close to a dozen songs, many of which were recorded in variant versions to meet the studio's changing demands. His songs appear in three forms in the final film: as their original recordings, as tracks covered by other bands, and as remixes done without Westerberg's involvement. His ballad "I Belong" fell victim to the studio's rethinking:

> That was the biggest pain in the ass. I wrote it through improvising: I shut my eyes and started playing chords on the piano and saying the words. I came up with a charming, as they say, version. Then for a solid year they kept asking me to re-record it. Then they started wanting me to change the title: "This Is Where We Belong," "Is This Where We Belong?" "Is This Where I Belong?" They even got Peter Yorn to sing an alternate version, which they use in the film. On the record you get "I Belong" with me and the band, but on the vinyl version you get what I did by myself in the first place, at home. That, to me, is the one. It had lots of "waiting" chords, like I throw all these diminished things in while I'm waiting for a rhyme to pop into my head. There was an ache in that version that we couldn't seem to get back.

In addition to writing songs, Westerberg was asked to contribute to the film's underscore, which he was to write in collaboration with Ramin Djawadi, who had the scoring experience the songwriter lacked. Among Djawadi's previous scoring credits were *Ask the Dust* (2006), *Blade: Trinity* (2004), and the TV show *Blade: The Series* (2006). Although communication between the two musicians was easy, Westerberg soon grew tired of the film's steady stream of editing changes and felt that, by not including certain of his ideas, Djawadi didn't put enough humor in the music. After three years of stress working on the project, Westerberg left it with about eighty percent of its score finished and his songs recorded in several versions.

Although the officially released soundtrack recording focuses on the Westerberg songs and has nothing of Djawadi's score on it, the songwriter was disappointed with how his works were treated—he was upset that his rock-'n'-roll songs were accompanied by orchestra, resulting in a hybrid sound that took the edge off his music.

■ **The Queen** (2006)

Original composer: **Nathan Larson**
Replacement composer: **Alexandre Desplat**

The Queen, written by Peter Morgan and directed by Stephen Frears, is a fictional depiction of the behind-the-scenes aftermath of the death of Diana, Princess of Wales. It contrasts the positions taken by Queen Elizabeth II (played by Helen Mirren, who would win an Oscar for her work), Prime Minister Tony Blair, and Diana's ex-husband, Prince Charles, about handling the extraordinarily popular princess's sudden demise.

The film's production history could be said to have begun in 2003, when Frears and Morgan worked together on *The Deal*, a British television movie about the alleged pact between Gordon Brown and Tony Blair that gave Blair leadership of the Labor Party. (Michael Sheen played Blair in both movies.) The composer who provided *The Deal*'s music, Nathan Larson, had first worked with Frears on the 2002 *Dirty Pretty Things* (for which Larson replaced a large portion of Anne Dudley's score), and he was also hired to pen *The Queen*'s music. Among Larson's recent scoring credits were *Little Fish* (2005), *Palindromes* (2004), and *A Love Song for Bobby Long* (2004). For *The Queen*, he delivered elegant electronic textures skillfully mixed with a solo cello, a strange score that helped provide a disturbing portrayal of the royal family.

Knowing an Oscar contender when he saw it, Miramax Films head Harvey Weinstein picked up the production's American distribution—and requested a few changes be made to it. Nathan Larson remembers his score's rejection:

> Harvey Weinstein took one look at the film and declared Helen Mirren's performance the stuff of Oscars (he was right!) and that everything, from editing to music and I think even a reshoot or two, would be geared towards buffering her up, and making sure she was a sympathetic character. I think I was more or less history the moment that conclusion was made, but I hung in there and was very stubborn about my take on the story.... It also, alas, must be said that there was a crucial screening of the film in New York for the big cheeses in which the copy of the film they got was somehow fucked up, and the sound (particularly the music) was muffled and barely audible. This was a technical error, and as you're rushing to finish something this stuff happens. But I do think, as a result, those making the decisions never did hear what I was doing properly. Which, of course, doesn't change the fact that they made a good call on getting in somebody new, if the success of the film is any indication of these things.

Frears personally told Larson that his score would go unused. Replacing it, *The Queen* received a more classical-influenced orchestral score by French composer Alexandre Desplat, who was introduced to the project through his connection with its production company, Pathé, for whom he had written his breakthrough score *Girl with a Pearl Earring* (2003). Among Desplat's recent credits were *Syriana* (2005), *Casanova* (2005), and *Hostage* (2005).

Desplat wrote a thematically rich score for *The Queen* that contained leitmotifs for each of the three major characters and painted a more sympathetic picture of the monarch via some Elgarian strains. Among *The Queen*'s six Academy Award nominations was one for Desplat's score (which would lose to Gustavo Santaolalla's music for *Babel*).

Larson reports a curious experience following his score's rejection:

> I was in a deli here in New York and an ad came over the radio pumping up the soundtrack for *The Queen* (this was just before the Oscars) and the voice-over was something like, "Take home the magical Oscar-nominated music from the film *The Queen*." Standard stuff, except the music that was playing in the commercial, which would surge to the forefront for as much as five seconds at a time, was in fact my weird, spooky score. Anyway we figured out later that Miramax (although they never fessed up to it) must've used the music they got from an early promo cut for *The Queen*, which at that point had my score.... It bothered me for about ten minutes, and then it just seemed funny, so I just moved on. What are you gonna do?

In another amusing postscript, just before Larson signed on to *The Queen* he had worked on the comedy *The Ex* (2006), directed by his friend Jesse Peretz. The executives overseeing that film requested a comedy score in the vein of Randy Newman's music for *Meet the Parents* (2004) and *Meet the Fockers* (2000). That's what Larson delivered, even though it wasn't what he had in mind for the movie. When *The Ex* eventually ended up in a troubled postproduction phase, Larson had to leave to begin his work on *The Queen*, and *The Ex* was subsequently rescored by Edward Shearmur. The final ironic twist is that the same distribution executives were in charge of both *The Ex* and *The Queen*, and even after his two replacements at their hands, they invited Larson to work on a third film—as if nothing had happened in the past.

■ Payback: Straight Up (2006)

Composer for **Payback** *(1999):* **Chris Boardman**
Composer for **Payback: Straight Up** *(2006), the director's cut video of* **Payback***:* **Scott Stambler**

Payback, starring Mel Gibson, was the feature film directing debut of screenwriter-turned-director Brian Helgeland, whose previous screenwriting credits included *L.A. Confidential*, *Conspiracy Theory*, and *The Postman* (all 1997). It was based on Donald E. Westlake's novel *The Hunter* (as was John Boorman's 1967 classic noirish film *Point Blank*, which starred Lee Marvin as its antihero). In many aspects—from photography and color use to music—*Payback* was a stylistic tip of the hat to gritty 1970s crime dramas such as *The French Connection*, *The Taking of Pelham One Two Three*, and *Shaft*.

One of the most effective elements of this stylization was the movie's score by Chris Boardman, who got the job based on a demo he wrote after reading the script but without seeing a frame of the film. Boardman's recent credits included *Bordello of Blood*

(1996) and the TV movies *Sleeping with the Devil* (1997) and *Deep Family Secrets* (1997). His rhythmically churning, funky title music for *Payback* was written in 7/4 and featured an ominous five-note line that slowly danced over a busy percussion section and dramatic stabs of brass chords. (Some have compared it to the title music from David Shire's wonderful, funky twelve-tone score for 1974's *The Taking of Pelham One Two Three.*) Boardman's effective, jazz-tinged score highlighted electric bass, electric guitar, and organ amid a big-band-with-orchestra presence that allowed the composer to build dark, moody cues that stepped outside standard jazz scoring as the need arose.

While all concerned parties were happy with Boardman's music, the movie itself slowly began to change shape and character. At the insistence of the studio and the star, *Payback*'s criminal main character was altered in an attempt to project (and protect?) Mel Gibson's well-honed screen persona as a charmingly crazed individual (à la the *Lethal Weapon* series of movies). In general, the studio attempted to make Gibson's character lighter and more humorous. To this end, one-third of the movie was reshot in just ten days and the remainder subjected to extensive re-editing. The process left one character cut out, a new character inserted, and a voiceover track added. Although the film still carried Helgeland's credit as director, the version that went out to theaters in 1999 was no longer his baby: It had holes in its plot, a new ending, and a distinctly different tone from Helgeland's original.

A half-dozen years later, Gibson and the production company gave Helgeland a chance to revisit the movie and release his own cut straight to home video, under the title *Payback: Straight Up*. The project's very small budget didn't allow the director to shoot any new sequences; what Helgeland could do, however, was work with the existing original footage—including many shots that had gone unused—and manipulate the picture's dialogue and voiceovers.

When compared with the theatrically released cut (both versions are available on DVD), Helgeland's *Payback: Straight Up* showcases how the postproduction process (with the aid of some good unused footage lying around) can completely revamp a film, lending it an altogether different feel and sensibility. For the director's cut, Helgeland's key collaborators were editor Kevin Sitt and music-editor-turned-composer Scott Stambler, who ended up providing a new score for it. (This is Stambler's only scoring credit; his previous music editing credits included *Rumor Has It...*, *Alex and Emma*, and *Daredevil.*) Helgeland and his team wanted to use Boardman's score in the director's cut, but soon realized that it didn't match up with the movie's new version. Stambler recalls:

> I kept writing small cues, then bigger ones. When I had written the Chinese car-jacking scene, I realized that it would make a good main title. I proposed the idea to Brian, and he dug it—the music kept evolving from there. We pulled out every song except the Dean Martin track in the bedroom ["Ain't That a Kick in the Head"].... As the months went by, and we still didn't have authorization from the studio to rescore the movie I just continued to write—at some point I had written fifty-five minutes of music. It was a very challenging and terrifying experience, because I had never written a film score....

> If I didn't have Brian and Kevin's encouragement and patience, I really think I could have done some psychical damage to myself. Things just seemed to click. By the time all the music was written and approved, we kept hoping the studio would pay for a real orchestra, and they came around to that idea, but not for fifty-five minutes. So I limited the themes and ended up scoring about thirty minutes with a rhythm section, then overdubbed the rhythm section with a string section. I used many of the recordings in other cues that were designed with that in mind. In other words, I saved the budget for the "Big" cues. The "Main Title" and the last cue took up about fourteen minutes! Where I didn't have the budget for live instruments, I either played on stuff myself or brought in a few players to overdub on synth cues.

With meager financial support from Paramount, Stambler wrote and recorded a score that pleased Helgeland and fit his new/old vision of the movie. Stambler's score retains the classic 1970s sound established by Boardman's music but is a bit less melodic than Boardman's. The new score offers good support for Gibson's grittier character, who has been relieved of much of the humor inflicted upon him in the studio's cut. It is well suited to a rough-edged Gibson character whose motivations have been stripped to the core.

■ The Good German (2006)

Original composer: **David Holmes**
Replacement composer: **Thomas Newman**

Steven Soderbergh's *The Good German*, based on Joseph Kanon's novel of the same name, was a black-and-white experiment in style that featured pronounced expressionist camera angles, deep-focus photography, rear-projection backgrounds, and period archival footage in a moody-looking film shot on studio soundstages and backlots and presented in the old 1.33 (i.e., 4:3) aspect ratio (i.e., the screen image's width:height ratio). Starring George Clooney, Cate Blanchett, and Tobey McGuire, this 1940s-style noirish thriller investigated the birth of postwar moral relativism through a plot that paid homage to and echoed elements of Carol Reed's *The Third Man* (1949), Billy Wilder's *A Foreign Affair* (1948), Michael Curtiz's *Casablanca* (1942), and perhaps even Roman Polanski's neo-noir *Chinatown* (1974). Set in bombed-out Berlin shortly after VE Day, it was the story of a reporter (Clooney) sent to cover the Potsdam Conference (during which Churchill, Truman, and Stalin set out Europe's Cold War future). The newsman finds himself drawn into a dark world of intrigue in which little is as it appears, as a black market thrives and the United States and the U.S.S.R. vie for Germany's top scientists, regardless of their guilt as Nazi war criminals. While fairly successful at imitating a period style, the ambitious movie was uneven and flopped at the box office.

Although the production carefully maintained a 1940s style in almost every regard, a notable exception was its first score. For this, the director hired Irish

DJ-producer-turned-composer David Holmes. To those who know Holmes from his jazzy scores for such Soderbergh movies as *Out of Sight* (1998) and *Ocean's Eleven* (2001) and its sequels, his *The Good German* score's fusion of orchestral and electronic elements—which has been described as a "cross between David Bowie and Philip Glass"—might come as a shock. Holmes himself has said that the recording was a departure for him and sounded like a "live band playing in a strip club." It was, however, carefully modeled on the movie's initial temp track—which had turned into a disastrous combination of unusual, clashing styles by the time the picture neared completion.

Once it was determined that Holmes's strange score failed to fit the picture, the movie's musical concept was rethought, bringing it more into line with the 1940s noir style that informed its plot, production design, and photography. A new score was commissioned from Thomas Newman, with whom Soderbergh had worked on *Erin Brockovich* (2000). Among Newman's recent scoring credits were *Jarhead* (2005), *Cinderella Man* (2005), and *Lemony Snicket's A Series of Unfortunate Events* (2004). *The Good German*'s replacement score expertly and elegantly tipped its hat to such past masters of noir music as Max Steiner, Bernard Herrmann, Franz Waxman, and the composer's father, Alfred (who had scored a 1950 film about postwar Berlin, *The Big Lift*), while still retaining its own integrity. Newman's rich, complex, thematically strong, and often voluptuous orchestral score received a well-deserved Oscar nomination, and a recording of it was released on the Varèse Sarabande label.

■ **The Reaping** (2007)

Original composer: **Philip Glass**
Replacement composer: **John Frizzell**

A supernatural horror flick set in the fictional backwater Louisiana town of Haven, *The Reaping* was directed by Stephen Hopkins and starred Hilary Swank. Described by film critics at *The Guardian* as "*Exorcist* meets *The Wicker Man*" and an "*Exorcist*-meets-*Deliverance* mash-up," it's the tale of a debunker of miracles who is forced to reexamine her loss of faith when faced with a series of unexplanable events. These occurrences—a repeat of the ten plagues described in the Old Testament's Book of Exodus (blood, boils, frogs, locusts, lice, etc.)—are rumored to be divine retribution visited on a local group of Satanists.

Hired to score the picture was popular concert and film composer Philip Glass. Known for his involvement in weightier cinematic offerings, such as the documentaries *Powaqqatsi* (1988) and *Naqoyqatsi* (2002) and the highly regarded drama *The Hours* (2002), he may not be the first to come to mind in relation to horror movies. However, the versatile Glass had successfully scored the eerie and unusual Clive Barker–inspired horror flicks *Candyman* (1992) and *Candyman: Farewell to the Flesh* (1995), both also set in Louisiana. His scores for these chillers are among the more unusual ones in the genre. Shortly after recording his score for *The Reaping*, Glass discussed it and other horror film scores he'd done:

> Oh, it's more than that [another horror film]. It's about a fundamentalist religious sect in the countryside of the South, and you get to see the ten biblical plagues. Hilary Swank plays the part of an investigator that's trying to debunk the plagues, thinking everything can be explained, but over the course of it, she finds that she can't explain it. And at the end of it, literally all hell breaks loose! [...]
>
> These kinds of films are more about action instead of character, if I can put it that way. With *Notes on a Scandal* [a 2006 psychological drama scored by Glass], you're talking about interpersonal dynamics—they're very delicate, and profoundly dramatic and challenging and exhausting in a way. With *The Reaping* and *Candyman*, for that matter, you're talking about events which you can't really explain, and can't be explained by character—they have nothing to do with character! You're talking about music that works more with the surface of the action than with the depths of the character. It's a very different way of working, and I had to learn how to do it.
>
> When I was doing more abstract theater pieces, there are similarities with working on those and horror films. Wouldn't it be funny to compare doing a Beckett play and doing a slasher film? But it's true! You're working with more abstract ideas with these kinds of films. I'm putting it the way I experience working on it, and I've found that horror movies are more difficult to do. They're more challenging for me, and I find them very interesting. So I enjoyed working on *Taking Lives* [a 2004 serial-killer thriller].... It was a very interesting film to work on. I felt that was true of *The Reaping* too. It was a long process because, again, it was a film where the director really began to understand the film as they were making it. There were whole sections re-shot, people re-cast, and things were being changed all along. It was a film that was a voyage of discovery, there's no question.

With so many facets of the film in flux, it's not surprising that Glass's score got replaced. The horror genre has certain expectations, and in the minds and hands of nervous studio executives gambling with large sums of money, the safest solution is often preferred to the most original one. Glass's replacement was veteran horror-movie composer John Frizzell, whose previous work in the genre included *Alien: Resurrection* (1997), *I Still Know What You Did Last Summer* (1998), *Thir13en Ghosts* (2001), *Ghost Ship* (2002), *Primeval* (2007), and *First Born* (2007). His orchestra and choir score for *The Reaping* offered a dark, effective mingling of time-tested musical solutions and quite unusual cues. Less in-your-face than many horror scores, it featured simple piano figurations poised above strings, ominous low brass, and a good bit of electronics in its mix of eerie and religious musical strains. Frizzell reflected on his score:

> When you read some reviews, people say the score is very loud, and it just isn't.... There's a lot more emotion in it, and a lot more melody. The first conversation I had with [co-producer Joel Silver] is that "this is a different kind of film; it's different from what [the production company] Dark Castle has done before, and we're going into a different territory...." This film is very patient in taking its time to pull you in.

The Prize Winner from Defiance, Ohio [a 2005 drama scored by Frizzell] is a little film, and one of my favourites...and it's definitely one of my melodic sides, as is *Gods and Generals* [a 2003 historical drama scored by Frizzell].... It is nice to do this in a film which has some genre elements in it.... I thought, Hey, [*The Reaping*] is a great opportunity to sort of break the mold and go into more traditional film-scoring, but also towards the experimental things that I like to do.

■ Before the Devil Knows You're Dead (2007)

Original composer: **Richard Rodney Bennett**
Replacement composer: **Carter Burwell**

For famed 82-year-old director Sidney Lumet, the engaging crime drama *Before the Devil Knows You're Dead* proved that age had not diminished his creative abilities. An ensemble drama starring Philip Seymour Hoffman, Ethan Hawk, Marisa Tomei, and Albert Finney, it told the story of a pair of ne'er-do-well brothers whose supposedly victimless jewelry store robbery goes horribly wrong. Shot in high-definition video, the critically lauded picture explored a nonlinear or fractured timeline, which worked well to ramp up the movie's tensions by carefully highlighting various events before, after, and during the robbery, which was replayed several few times to provide different perspectives.

Composer Richard Rodney Bennett, who seems to have semiretired from film work after the 1990s, was hired to pen the picture's score. Bennett had previously written acclaimed music for Lumet's *Murder on the Orient Express* (1974) and *Equus* (1977). More recently, he had scored *Swann* (1996) and *Four Weddings and a Funeral* (1994).

Writing music for Lumet would seem to be a tough task, because the director is famous for making dramatically intense pictures that don't have—and don't need—musical scores (although most of them do contain some source music). Among his scoreless films are the highly regarded classics *12 Angry Men* (1957), *Fail-Safe* (1964), *Dog Day Afternoon* (1975), and *Network* (1976). For *Before the Devil Knows You're Dead,* Bennett adhered to the director's usual sparse, less-is-more approach to music spotting and wrote roughly a half-hour of chamber ensemble (nine players) underscore for the two-hour film.

But Lumet felt that Bennett's music wasn't sufficiently character driven, so he hired composer Carter Burwell to replace it. Although he has worked with many directors, Burwell is perhaps best known for scoring films by the Coen brothers, from *Blood Simple* (1984) through *Raising Arizona* (1987), *Barton Fink* (1991), *Fargo* (1996), *O Brother, Where Art Thou?* (2000), *No Country for Old Men* (2007), and a half-dozen others. Burwell recalls his work with Lumet:

I had never met Sidney Lumet before he contacted me about replacing the score to this film [*Before the Devil Knows You're Dead*]. I never heard the original score, but Sidney felt for some reason that it wasn't working and that the music needed to tell the audience

> more about the characters. I took this advice seriously because Lumet does not slather on the underscore like most American directors. Indeed, as he reminded me, many of his best films have no score, like *Network* and *Dog Day Afternoon*. In this case the film is a family melodrama wrapped in a crime drama.... There are a few good points in replacing a score, even as one must feel sympathy for the first composer. First, everyone is a step closer to knowing what works. Second, there is no time for vague exploration. In this case the music was written in about three weeks and recorded in two days—not such a terrible schedule as they go.

When compared with some other Lumet dramas, the music in *Before the Devil Knows You're Dead* was quite upfront. As he usually does, Burwell tried to express the "unsaid" in the movie, devising a clever, sympathetic theme for Philip Seymour Hoffman's character, who initiates the situation that inevitably leads to the story's tragedies. Meshing with the film's nonlinear structure, which repeatedly revisits the robbery as the hub from which the plot's many spokes radiate, the music invests this key incident with subtle differences each time it reappears, echoing the shifting views from which we witness it.

Before the Devil Knows You're Dead did not mark the first time that Lumet had replaced a score. In 1997, he replaced Wynton Marsalis's score for his crime drama *Night Falls on Manhattan* with one by Mark Isham.

■ Mr. Magorium's Wonder Emporium (2007)

Original composer: **Alexandre Desplat**
Replacement composer (unused): **Patrick Doyle**
Replacement composer (in collaboration with original composer Desplat): **Aaron Zigman**

Writer-director Zach Helm's directorial debut, the family/children's fantasy *Mr. Magorium's Wonder Emporium*, was the fanciful tale of 243-year-old Mr. Magorium (played by Dustin Hoffman) and his delightfully wild toy store, which he bequeaths to his only real employee, Molly (Natalie Portman), a terribly insecure former child-prodigy pianist. Unsure of herself ever since her nerves failed her on stage, Molly learns self-reliance once Magorium dies and she takes over the store.

Because Molly is a pianist, the picture's music needed quite a bit of advance preparation and prerecording, and the composer engaged for this during the project's preproduction phase was Alexandre Desplat, whose recent scoring credits included *The Painted Veil* (2006) and his Oscar-nominated score for *The Queen* (2006). Desplat wrote many themes for the picture and also penned Molly's piano concerto, which played a prominent part in the story.

However, few composers can afford to be tied to one project for years, and Desplat was no exception. He recalls:

> I started this movie more than two years ago.... Unfortunately the movie kept reshooting and rewriting to make it better and better... until it ended at the point where I was on another project.... I was committed to *Golden Compass* and I couldn't do this movie anymore. So it went to the hands of another composer.... and I was really depressed I could not finish it.... It was a movie I loved.

The composer hired to pick up where Desplat had left off was Patrick Doyle, whose recent scoring credits included *Eragon* (2006) and *The Last Legion* (2006). However, only a few weeks after he was announced as *Mr. Magorium*'s composer, his association with the picture ended. Replacing him in turn was Aaron Zigman, whose recent credits included *The Jane Austin Book Club* (2007) and *Bridge to Terabithia* (2007). Desplat explains the double composer switcheroo and his own role in the final score:

> It was said everywhere that he [Patrick Doyle] had replaced me, but he replaced me because I was not free anymore. So they took Patrick Doyle, but it didn't work out as well as they thought, and they came back to me. That's why Aaron Zigman came in. I thought about Aaron because I like him very much. I like his work and his talent and his personality. I called Aaron and asked him if he wanted to help me finish this movie, working from my themes, which I had written through the two years—many, many, many themes, and ideas of orchestration—and bring his craft to maybe make links, add a few themes if necessary, and make it possible. So that's what he did. We, in a way, co-composed. I was the inventor of the music, and he is the one who made it possible.

Mr. Magorium's Wonder Emporium wasn't the only 2007 film that, musically speaking, went from point A to point B and then back to A again: *Stardust* was scored by Ilan Eshkeri, with whom its director, Matthew Vaughn, had worked on *Layer Cake* (2004). However, due to studio politics, a composer with a bigger name, John Ottman, was also hired and recorded music for the picture. And yet the final movie was accompanied by Eshkeri's music only. In the same year, Dario Marianelli was announced as composer for the Arctic thriller *Far North*, directed by Asif Kapadia, with whom he had worked on two previous films. Yet within a few months composer Michael Nyman was in the studio with his Nyman Band recording a replacement score for the film. In the end, though, the picture jettisoned the Nyman score and carried only Marianelli's music.

■ **Grace Is Gone** (2007)

Original composer: **Max Richter**
Replacement composer: **Clint Eastwood**

Writer-director James C. Strouse's low-key yet emotional *Grace Is Gone* was the story of a taciturn suburban dad (played by John Cusack, who was also one of the film's producers) who is caring for two young daughters while his wife is in the military in Iraq. When he receives news of her death, he is unable to face telling his daughters about it, so he piles them into the car for a spur-of-the-moment road trip (from Minnesota to Florida) to visit a theme park. Along the way, he searches for the right time and place to tell them their mother is dead.

Grace Is Gone premiered at the 2007 Sundance Film Festival, where it won the Audience Award for Best Drama and was immediately picked up for distribution by the Weinstein Company. The company chose to replace its score, by British experimental/classical composer Max Richter, a newcomer to film music whose credits included the score to the BBC movie *Soundproof* (2006) and the use of several of his recorded pieces in such films as *Stranger Than Fiction* (2006) and *Cocaine Angel* (2006).

What spurred this score replacement? Reportedly, the simple fact that actor-director-producer-composer Clint Eastwood, quite moved by the film when he saw it at Sundance, had offered to write a new score for it. And clearly, the prospect of an Eastwood score would be too wonderful a publicity boon for the distributor to turn down.

Throughout his career, Eastwood has maintained an avid (and not always sidelines) interest in music—particularly jazz and country-western—and has contributed songs and short pieces to a number of the films he's been involved with. Starting in 2003, however, he began writing full scores for some of his pictures, including *Mystic River* (2003), *Million Dollar Baby* (2004), and *Flags of Our Fathers* (2006).

Grace Is Gone marked the first time Eastwood had written a score for someone else's movie. His spare, gentle, sentimental (and perhaps a bit emotionally manipulative), slightly jazz-tinged score featured piano and strings and fit the picture well. His title song, with lyrics by Carole Bayer Sager, was performed by young British jazz-pop singer-songwriter Jamie Cullum. Both the score and the song were nominated for Golden Globe Awards. (Interestingly, Eastwood's melancholy music generally struck the same emotional chords as Richter's. Perhaps there are but a few musical paths to follow for such a simple, heart-on-its-sleeve picture.)

Rescoring movies after they have successfully debuted at film festivals isn't a rare occurrence. For instance, *The House of Yes* (1997), which is discussed earlier in this book, was accompanied by a Jeff Rona score at its festival screenings, before Miramax Films picked it up for distribution and replaced it with music by Rolfe Kent. Similarly, the drama *The Spitfire Grill* carried a score by jazz saxophonist-arranger-composer Bennie Wallace at its Sundance premiere, but after being picked up for theatrical distribution by Columbia Pictures it acquired a new score by James Horner. The twist to such scenarios is that, whereas the initial composers for these high-class indie pictures often view them as a chance to break into a higher echelon of the business, it's the films' very same high quality that can cause those scores to be replaced once a distributor signs on.

■ Charlie Wilson's War (2007)

Original composer: **Ry Cooder**
Replacement composer: **James Newton Howard**

Charlie Wilson's War, a darkly comedic biopic about twelve-time Texas congressman Wilson (played by Tom Hanks), a notorious drinker and womanizer, was written by Aaron Sorkin (based on the book by George Crile) and directed by Mike Nichols. The story centered on Wilson's big moment on the international stage: his prominent hand in launching Operation Cyclone, the CIA's covert program to arm, train, and finance Afghan's mujahideen fighters during the Soviet war in Afghanistan in the 1980s.

This was not the first time that director Nichols tackled a political subject: In 1998 he filmed *Primary Colors*, a satirical look at recent American Presidential elections scripted by his former comedy-duo partner, Elaine May, based on Joe Klein's novel of the same name. The film's music was originally to be provided by famed singer-songwriter Carly Simon, who had scored Nichols's 1990 comedy *Postcards from the Edge*. But Simon dropped out of *Primary Colors* (a variety of reasons/rumors have been reported for this), and composer-performer Ry Cooder took over its music. With an eclectic ensemble that included his son, percussionist Joachim, and his friend trumpeter-composer Jon Hassell, he produced a score that stretched Americana-hued music from classic to warped.

Nine years later, Cooder was asked to provide the music for *Charlie Wilson's War*. For this picture, he assembled another eclectic ensemble that included Jon Hassell and Malian guitarist Vieux Farka Touré. This score had a distinctly Southern/Southwestern feel to it, underlining Charlie Wilson's Texas roots, and the way it offered space for improvisation and experimentation reportedly made the recording process fun for its performers.

At some point during the postproduction phase of *Charlie Wilson's War* it caught the fancy of the popular press, and soon it was being heralded as a Best Picture Oscar contender. The media buzz seemed to generate elevated commercial expectations, leading to inevitable changes in the movie. As a result, a new score was commissioned. While Cooder remained listed as one of the film's composers almost until its premiere, James Newton Howard, whose recent scoring credits included *I Am Legend* (2007) and *Michael Clayton* (2007), was hired to replace him shortly before the scheduled release.

Howard took a considerably different approach to the film: His orchestra score, also Americana-tinged, was much more mainstream, while featuring a variety of colorful multiethnic musical elements to underscore its specifically Afghan-related moments. One cue, "The Belly Dancer," was cowritten with singer-violinist-composer Gingger Shankar (daughter of famed Indian violinist L. Subramanian), who also sang the vocals on this small but important bit of music. The score's standout cue—"Turning the Tide," which accompanies a montage contrasting Afghan fighting and Charlie Wilson's life in America—is an imaginative eight-minute composition that features choir, lending it an almost Christmas carol sensibility.

One bit of Ry Cooder's music remained in the final film: his arrangement of the traditional song "This Little Light of Mine."

■ **The Fugitive: Second Season** (DVD, 2008)

Composers of music for original television airing (1964): **Pete Rugolo** *and others*

Composers for DVD release: **Mark Heyes** *and others*

Some television series undergo musical alterations on their way to becoming DVDs. For instance, a DVD of the highly regarded comedy series *Freaks and Geeks* (1999–2000) might feature different (perhaps lesser-known) pop songs from those that appeared in the episodes when they originally aired. The reason for such changes has nothing to do with a show's creator changing his or her mind about the music. It is pure and simple business: The rules and fees for licensing songs are different for a broadcast than for a home video release. So, to cut costs and/or avoid contractual problems, songs are frequently replaced.

Underscore replacements for TV shows issued as DVDs, on the other hand, are rare. One of these rare replacements occurred when CBS/Paramount prepared the second season of *The Fugitive*, a Quinn Martin–produced crime drama series that aired from 1963 to 1967, for DVD release. This record-breakingly popular show chronicled the adventures of ever-on-the-lam Dr. Richard Kimble (played by David Janssen), a man wrongly convicted of murdering his wife. Week after week, for 120 episodes, he eluded the police while searching for his wife's real killer—the mysterious one-armed man.

Part of the show's appeal was its original theme music (featuring a memorable four-note opening) by Pete Rugolo, one of the most sought-after television composers of the 1960s. Before turning to TV work, Rugolo had been a top jazz composer-arranger. In the postwar 1940s, he became well known for the distinctive music he wrote and arranged for the Stan Kenton Band. In the 1950s he branched out, working for such major artists as Peggy Lee, Nat King Cole, and Miles Davis, and toward the end of the decade he became director of A&R for Mercury Records. In the 1960s he turned to television, writing themes and/or episode scores for such popular series as *Richard Diamond, Private Detective*; *Thriller*; *Leave It to Beaver*; *Run for Your Life*; and *The Bold Ones*.

While *The Fugitive*'s creator, Roy Huggins, wanted his friend Rugolo involved with the show, the composer wasn't available to score its individual episodes. So an alternate solution was worked out: Rugolo composed the series' theme, as well as themes for a few of its main characters, then penned many short variations on them, creating a library of thematically appropriate music reflecting many dramatic moods that could be used in a broad variety of circumstances, such as chases, tender moments, cliffhanger situations, etc. These series-specific yet semigeneric cues (about an hour and a half of music) were recorded in England by a fifty-five-piece orchestra conducted by Harry Rabinowitz. From Rugolo's *Fugitive* library, music was selected and cut into each episode as needed.

Of course, this assortment of music could not possibly cover every scene in all 120 episodes. So, as was the practice on many television series at the time, *The Fugitive* also extensively licensed cues originally written for and appearing in various other shows. This often was music from such shows as *Gunsmoke*, *Have Gun—Will Travel*, *Perry Mason*, and *The Twilight Zone*, written by such heavyweight talents as Bernard Herrmann, Jerry Goldsmith, and Fred Steiner. Reflecting on the use of this music from the CBS Music Library, the series' postproduction supervisor, John Elizalde, once commented, "[F]or all intents and purposes, [*The Fugitive*] was a Jerry Goldsmith–Benny Herrmann show."

As the series progressed, it used more and more cues from other productions, including music from the Columbia Music Library, from Dominic Frontiere's scores for *The Outer Limits* TV series, and even such jazz standards as "I'll Never Smile Again" (by Ruth Lowe) and "I'll Remember April" (by Gene de Paul, Don Raye, and Patricia Johnston), which became associated with Dr. Kimble's wife. Regardless of the fact that most of it was not written for the series, this grab-bag of music became an integral part of the show's feel.

When Paramount released the first volume of the second season on DVD in 2008, its fifteen episodes had been given new underscores. With the exception of each episode's opening and closing credits, all of the dramatic underscore (whether by Rugolo or licensed from some other source) was replaced with music written by Mark Heyes, a composer whose credits included episodes of the television series *Grace Under Fire* (1996–1998), and *Seventh Heaven* (1997–2007), with additional music from composers Ron Komie and Sam Winans. The DVD's end credits were even digitally modified to add these replacement composers' names—and Rugolo retained a credit for only the main theme.

The series' rescoring met with an outcry from fans and had a bad effect on its DVD sales. CBS Home Entertainment offered the following rationale for the score replacements:

> Obviously we would have preferred to include all the original music in *The Fugitive* second season DVD release, but unlike season one, there were a large number of cues, the current ownership of which was not clear. We didn't want to disappoint fans by significantly delaying the release of the second season, so we chose to replace the music. We kept the original theme song, but decided it would be better to rescore full episodes to give viewers a seamless, consistent experience throughout. Taking everything into consideration, we thought this was the best solution.

According to film and television music historian extraordinaire Jon Burlingame (author of *TV's Biggest Hits: The Story of Television Themes from "Dragnet" to "Friends"* and other books), the reason CBS/Paramount ran into trouble when sorting out the ownership of the second season's music cues was that its cue sheets—which list composer, publisher, duration, and usage for every second of music in a film or TV show—were irregular, grouped by publisher, not listed cue-by-cue. In an article written for *Variety*, he offered the following explanation:

> For example, on the second-season episode "Escape Into Black," the cue sheet cites 19 uses of Rugolo music—as little as six seconds ("Fugitive Curtain No. 1") to as long as 63 seconds ("Fugitive Suspense")—and 42 instances of CBS Library music (including three by Herrmann, 13 by Goldsmith, 11 by Steiner and others by CBS stalwarts Rene Garriguenc and Nathan Scott, among others). And a single instance of Capitol Library music (39 seconds, by Nick Carras). Total music in that episode: just over 35 minutes, according to the cue sheet.
>
> Couple this with the fact that ownership of the music in the Capitol library is now in dispute.... With different parties claiming ownership, there is no easy way (perhaps no way at all) to legally clear music from the Capitol library....
>
> Now that I've seen the cue sheets, I understand their problem. Unless one knows those shows—and more specifically that music—extremely well, a novice would have a hard time separating the Rugolo from the Goldsmith from the Steiner from the generically Capitol.

Over the years, and for a variety of reasons, there have been isolated instances of similar music problems with cult TV shows. A VHS release of *Thunderbirds*, for instance, replaced all of Barry Gray's music with cheap synthesized cues. Another example involves Fred Steiner's music for the *Star Trek* episode "The City on the Edge of Forever." In this episode, written by Harlan Ellison, the crew of the *Enterprise* travels back to the era of the Great Depression; Steiner's score was largely based on the popular 1930s song "Goodnight, Sweetheart" (by Ray Noble, Jimmy Campbell, and Reg Connelly), which was used to underscore a romance between Captain Kirk and pacifist Edith Keeler (Joan Collins). When the episode was released on VHS, an unidentified composer had replaced all the music based on the song, for which home video rights were, for one reason or another, unobtainable at the time. This music change was reversed, however, when the episode later appeared on DVD. Shortly after this, CBS offered replacement discs for volume 1 of *The Fugitive Season 2*, with much of the original music restored.

■ The Mummy: Tomb of the Dragon Emperor (2008)

Original composer: **Randy Edelman**
Additional composer: **John Debney**

Every summer, American cinemas are taken over by movies that Hollywood bets its big bucks will be blockbusters. Sometimes these are expensive new bids for the filmgoer's dollar; sometimes they are sequels to well-proven, commercially successful earlier films. Into the latter group falls *The Mummy: Tomb of the Dragon Emperor,* an effects-laden third entry in the *Mummy* franchise established by writer-director Stephen Sommers (who neither wrote nor directed this installment). Sommers' *The Mummy* (1999) picked up the thread from the 1932 classic Universal horror film of the same name starring Boris Karloff and gave the monster a lavish makeover. Sommers followed this with *The Mummy Returns* (2001). His two *Mummy* pictures had bombastic action scores by Jerry Goldsmith and Alan Silvestri, respectively.

The Mummy: Tomb of the Dragon Emperor, directed by Rob Cohen, is set in 1946 and continues the adventures of explorer Rick O'Connell (played by Brendan Fraser, reprising the role he played in Sommers' two films mentioned above) and his wife, who travel to China, where they meet the recently awakened mummy of Dragon Emperor Han (Jet Li) and his legion of no-longer-slumbering warriors. Randy Edelman, one of director Cohen's frequent collaborators, was hired to score the film; his recent scoring credits included *Balls of Fury* (2007) and *The Last Time* (2006), and he had provided the music for Cohen's movies *Dragon: The Bruce Lee Story* (1993), *Dragonheart* (1996), *Daylight* (1996), *The Skulls* (2000), and *xXx* (2002). (He was also the first composer on Cohen's *Stealth,* a techno-thriller that eventually was scored by BT and Trevor Morris.)

The Mummy gave Edelman a great opportunity to show off his expertise at writing intense action material. While some of his best work belongs to the action genre, it is occasionally criticized for its simplicity and its heavy use of synthesizers. Edelman's bombastic *Mummy* score, however, supported the picture very well. Recorded with the London Symphony Orchestra, it even featured a wee bit of Oriental musical flavor, to help distinguish this *Mummy*'s Chinese setting from the previous two films' Egyptian backdrop.

After Edelman recorded his score, however, the movie underwent extensive changes before being sent out to theaters. During this postproduction reworking, some major battle sequences were altered and new FX shots were added. Consequently, several of Edelman's more intense mickey-mousing action cues no longer matched the onscreen action. Cohen wanted Edelman to adjust his music to fit the changes, but the composer had become quite ill and couldn't write new material. Therefore, John Debney, whose recent scoring credits included *Evan Almighty* (2007) and *Georgia Rule* (2006) and who had earlier done *The Scorpion King* (2002), a Sommers-scripted prequel to *The Mummy Returns,* was hired to pen music for the heavily altered scenes.

The final version of *The Mummy: Tomb of the Dragon Emperor* contained roughly an hour of Edelman's work and a half-hour of additional music by Debney. In retrospect, the decision to have new cues written for its battle scenes might seem almost unnecessary, since the music ended up barely audible in the final mix—where it was buried under very loud sound effects.

An interesting aside: John Debney was not new to rescoring when a fellow composer was hospitalized. In 2003, he provided the music for the last two reels of music of *Looney Tunes: Back in Action* when its composer, Jerry Goldsmith, fell ill and subsequently died before finishing the project.

■ Gears of War 2 (2008)

Original composer: **Kevin Riepl**
Replacement composer: **Steve Jablonsky**

The practice of score replacement has grown so pervasive in today's entertainment world that it affects not only movies and television shows but videogames as well. Until recently, it wasn't an issue for videogames, because most games were created by in-house teams, and whatever creative differences came up were settled within the company. However, as videogames became more and more elaborate and their music became more and more like Hollywood movie scores (and were sometimes written by well-known film composers), score replacements became inevitable.

The highly popular videogame *Gears of War 2*, a sequel to 2006's best-selling *Gears of War*, is one of the earliest reported examples of game-score replacement. This sci-fi/action game produced by Epic Games is set on the fictional planet Sera and involves human characters, particularly members of an elite fighting squad who are at war with "Locust" creatures bent on taking over an already ravaged world.

The original *Gears of War* game was scored by Kevin Riepl, who had provided the music for such earlier Epic games as *Unreal Tournament 2003*, *Unreal Tournament 2004*, *Unreal Championship*, and *Unreal Championship 2*, as well as some other companies' games, including *Shrek 2*, *City of Villains*, *Nancy Drew: Curse of Blackmoor Manor*, and *Nancy Drew: Danger by Design*. Riepl had also scored a number of episodes of Disney's TV cartoon *Brandy and Mr. Whiskers* (2004–2005).

The score for *Gears of War 2* was also to have been written by Riepl, who worked on it for quite a while, composing several cues. (He even let fans have a sneak listen to his work-in-progress by posting a couple of audio clips on his website.) What he didn't know at that time was that Epic was undergoing a change of heart concerning the new game's music. The company decided it needed a bigger sound, a large orchestral score, and with this in mind it contacted composer Steve Jablonsky in November 2007, having been impressed by his score for the film *Transformers* (2007). Jablonsky's other recent scoring credits included the 2007 remake of *The Hitcher*, *The Island* (2005), numerous episodes of the TV series *Desperate Housewives* (2004–present), and music for the videogames *Command & Conquer 3: Tiberium Wars* and *Transformers: The Game.*

After Epic approached him, Jablonsky played the first *Gears of War* for a few days, then accepted the job. In February 2008, Kevin Riepl removed his cue samples from his website and announced his dismissal from the project. Jablonsky's replacement of Riepl received a good bit of coverage in the videogame press. Jablonsky analyzed the reasons for his involvement for the now-defunct videogame music website *Music4Games*:

> For *Gears 2*, the guys at Epic wanted every aspect of the game to be bigger, darker, and crunchier than the original game. And I guess they had heard some of these qualities in my film scores. I love writing for orchestra and choir, but I also love experimenting with electronics and different types of percussion. I basically use anything I can get my hands on when composing a large-scale score like *Gears*. Epic gave me a blank canvas, which was really great. I experimented with a lot of hybrid organic/electronic elements, and combined them with the power of a large orchestra and choir. The one thing that we discussed keeping from *Gears 1* was the Locust riff. It's a short aggressive rhythmic phrase that works really well in the original game, and they asked for my take on it. The rest of the material and themes are all new. Mike [Larson, the project's audio director] and Cliff [Bleszinski, the project's design director] made it clear that *Gears 2* is bigger, meaner, and even more insane than the original game. So I knew I had a big task ahead of me, and the music had to match the intensity of the game.

The new score worked quite differently than that of the first episode, and in certain ways it was sometimes over-the-top. The need for a more movielike score with more movielike fidelity was deemed essential by Epic, a point made evident by the choice of recording facilities: Riepl's music for the original game had been recorded in Seattle's Bastyr University' chapel, while Jablonsky's orchestra and choir score for the sequel was recorded at George Lucas's Skywalker Ranch, a high-end professional facility that allowed for the latest in complex recording work. As with most videogame scores, the live instrumental sections were recorded with only winds and strings, and all the percussion (i.e., the electro-techno sounds that gamers expect to hear) was added electronically. *Gears of War 2* helped embed Hollywood musical traditions (including score-replacement traditions) in the videogame world.

■ ■ ■

With this, the book's final story, we've come full circle. We started at the eve of sound film's birth, went through all of cinema's ages and styles (touching briefly on work from a number of different countries), and ended with a discussion of music for an interactive media form that is growing in complexity and importance every day.

Film score replacements continue to prevail: Big-budget examples from 2010 include *The Wolfman*, *Clash of the Titans*, and *Edge of Darkness*. But many of the most recent score replacement tales are too fresh to tell just now. To do them justice, we will need the sense of perspective that only the passage of time can provide.

Sources

[**A:** audio (LP, CD, or other format). **V:** video (DVD or videotape). **B:** book. **P:** periodical. **W:** Website or blog. **C:** correspondence (unpublished letter, email, conversation, interview, etc.).]

The Most Dangerous Game (1932)
A: Morgan, John. Liner notes to *Son of Kong/The Most Dangerous Game.* Naxos 8.570813, 2000. **V:** Morgan, John. Interview about *King Kong* (2005). Special Edition DVD, 2006.

Don Quixote (1933)
A: Adriano. Liner notes to *Macbeth/Golgotha/Don Quixote.* Marco Polo 8.223287, 1990. **B:** Goss, Madeleine. *Bolero: The Life of Maurice Ravel.* NY: Henry Holt and Company, 2008, pp. 246–247. **B:** Larner, Gerald. *Maurice Ravel (20th-Century Composers).* London: Phaidon Press, 1996, pp. 213–216. **B:** Rózsa, Miklós. *Double Life.* NY: Wynwood Press, 1989, p. 120. **B:** Zank, Stephen. *Maurice Ravel: A Guide to Research.* NY: Routledge, 2004, pp. 16–18.

The Good Earth (1937)
B: Frisch, Walter. *Schoenberg and His World.* Princeton: Princeton University Press. 1999, p. 11. **B:** Huckvale, David. *Hammer Film Scores and the Musical Avant-Garde.* London: McFarland & Company, 2008, pp. 25–37. **B:** MacDonald, Malcolm. *Schoenberg.* Oxford: Oxford University Press, 2008, pp. 78, 196.

Union Pacific (1939)
B: Antheil, George. *Bad Boy of Music.* Los Angeles: Samuel French Trade, 1990, pp. 238–240. **B:** Bernstein, Elmer. *Elmer Bernstein's Film Music Notebook.* Los Angeles: The Film Music Society, 2004, p. 112. **B:** McCarty, Clifford. *Film Composers in America: A Filmography, 1911–1970.* Oxford: Oxford University Press, 2000, p. 188.

The Westerner (1940)
B: Herman, Jan. *A Talent for Trouble: The Life of Hollywood's Most Acclaimed Director, William Wyler.* NY: Da Capo Press, 1997, p. 207. **C:** Interviews with Warren Sherk, 2008.

The Thief of Bagdad (1940)
B: Palmer, Christopher. "Miklos Rozsa on *The Thief of Bagdad.*" *Elmer Bernstein's Film Music Notebook.* Los Angeles: The Film Music Society, 2004, pp. 319–322. **B:** Rózsa, Miklós. *Double Life.* NY: Wynwood Press, 1989, pp. 93–95. **P:** Bush, Richard H. "The Thief of Bagdad: The Musical?" *Pro Musica Sana,* PMS 58, Summer 2000.

Commandos Strike at Dawn (1942)
B: Joseph, Charles M. *Stravinsky Inside Out.* New Haven: Yale Universiy Press, 2001, p. 119. **B:** McCarty, Clifford. *Film Composers in America: A Filmography, 1911–1970.* Oxford: Oxford University Press. 2000, p. 105. **B:** Stravinsky, Igor, and Robert Craft. *Memories and Commentaries* (New One-Volume Edition). London: Faber & Faber, 2003, p. 223. **P:** Rosar, William H. "Stravinsky and MGM." *Film Music I.* Ed. Clifford McCarty. Los Angeles: The Film Music Society, 1989, pp. 113–114. **B:** Rózsa, Miklós. *Double Life.* NY: Wynwood Press, 1989, pp. 113–114.

Hitler's Madman (1943)
B: Fernett, Gene. *Hollywood's Poverty Row, 1930–1950.* Satellite Beach, FL: Coral Reef Publications, 1973. **B:** McCarty, Clifford. *Film Composers in America: A Filmography, 1911–1970.* Oxford: Oxford University Press. 2000, p. 284. **P:** Haberfelner, Mike. "Producers Releasing Corporation," *[re]Search My Trash* August 2005.

Since You Went Away (1944)
B: Behlmer, Rudy. *Memo from David O. Selznick : The Creation of "Gone with the Wind" and Other Motion Picture Classics, as Revealed in the Producer's Private Letters, Telegrams, Memorandums, and Autobiographical Remarks.* NY: The Modern Library, 2000. **C:** Original research at David O. Selznick Collection, Harry Ransom Center, The Univ. of Texas at Austin. Memo from David O. Selznick to Robert Johnston, 13 March 1944. Letter from Abe Mayer to Dan O'Shea, 14 April 1944.

Caesar and Cleopatra (1945)
A: Liner notes to *The Film Music of Arthur Bliss.* Chandos CHAN 9896, 2001. **A:** Liner notes to *The Film Music of Georges Auric.* Chandos CHAN 9774, 1999. **B:** Bliss, Arthur. *As I Remember.* London: Faber & Faber, 1970, pp. 166–167 **B:** Dukore, Bernard F. (ed.). *Bernard Shaw and Gabriel Pascal (Selected Correspondence of Bernard Shaw).* Toronto: University of Toronto Press, 1996, pp. 164, 175. **B:** Miklós Rózsa. *Double Life.* NY: Wynwood Press, 1989, p. 120. **B:** Pascal, Valerie. *The Disciple and His Devil.* Bloomington, IN: iUniverse, 2004.

The Naked City (1948)
B: Rózsa, Miklós. *Double Life.* NY: Wynwood Press, 1989, pp. 152–154. **P:** Mangold, Charles. "George Bassman: Rhapsody in Black." *FSM*, vol 9 no. 6, July 2004, p. 15. **C:** Email between Charles Goldman and Jim Fox.

Michurin (1948)
B: Egorova, Tatiana. *Soviet Film Music (Contemporary Music Studies).* NY: Routledge, 1997, pp. 122–123. **B:** Riley, John. "From the Factory to the Flat: Thirty Years of the Song of the Counterplan." *Soviet Music and Society Under Lenin and Stalin: The Baton and Sickle.* Ed. Neil Edmunds. NY: Routledge, 2009, pp. 67–80.

Night and the City (1950)
A: Faiola, Ray. Liner notes to *Night and the City.* Screen Archives SAECRS008, 2003. **W:** Dalkin, Gary. "Editor's Recommendation." MusicWeb (*http://www.musicweb-international.com/film/2003/Oct03/night_and_the_city.html*). October 2003. **C:** Interview with Dimitri Kennaway, 2008.

Distant Drums (1951)
B: Henderson, Sonya Shoilevska. *Alex North, Film Composer.* London: McFarland & Company, 2003, p. 43. **P:** Sherk, Warren. "Welcome to Hollywood: Alex North's Unused Score for *Distant Drums* (1951)." *The Cue Sheet* vol. 16 no. 2, April 2000, pp. 20–30.

A Place in the Sun (1951)
B: Darby, Ken. *Hollywood Holyland: The Filming and Scoring of* The Greatest Story Ever Told. Lanham, MD: Scarecrow Press, 1992. **B:** Karlin, Fred. *Listening to the Movies: A Film Lover's Guide to Film Music.* New York: Schirmer Books, 2000, p. 64. **B:** McCarty, Clifford. *Film Composers in America: A Filmography, 1911–1970.* Oxford: Oxford University Press, 2000, p. 341. **B:** Thomas, Tony. *Music for the Movies* (2nd ed.). Los Angeles: Silman-James Press, 1997, p. 75–76.

Summer with Monika / Sommaren med Monika (1955)
B: Gado, Frank. *The Passion of Ingmar Bergman.* Durham, NC: Duke University Press, 1986, pp. 152–162. **B:** Hall, Phil. *Independent Film Distribution: How to Make a Successful End Run Around the Big Guys.* Studio City, CA: Michael Wiese Press, 2006, p. 184. **B:** Steene, Birgitta. *Ingmar Bergman: A Reference Guide.* Amsterdam: Amsterdam University Press, 2006, pp. 200–204. **B:** Toop, David. *Exotica.* London: Serpent's Tail, 1999, pp. 33–48.

Storm Over the Nile (1955)
A: Phillips, James. Liner notes to *The Prisoner of Zenda. FSM* vol. 7 no. 1, 2004. **C:** Interview with Dimitri Kennaway, 2008. **B:** Korda, Michael. *Charmed Lives: A Family Romance.* NY: Harper Perennial, 2002, pp. 356, 382, 418. **C:** Private correspondence from the Benjamin Frankel Collection.

Forbidden Planet (1956)
A: Barron, Louis, and Bebe Barron. Liner notes to *Forbidden Planet.* Small Planet Records PR-D-001, 1989. **V:** Chasalow, Eric. Interview with Bebe Barron in *OHM: The Early Gurus of Electronic Music.* Ellipsis Arts DVD 3694. **B:** Wierzbicki, James. *Louis and Bebe Barron's Forbidden Planet: A Film Score Guide*, Lanham, MD: Scarecrow Press, 2005. **P:** Long, Donald J. "Forbidden Film Score." *FSM* vol. 9 no. 4, April/May 2004, pp. 23–25. **C:** Conversation and email between Barry Schrader and Jim Fox.

The Barretts of Wimpole Street (1957)
A: Faiola, Ray. Liner notes to *Night and the City.* Screen Archives SAECRS008, 2003. **B:** Miklós Rózsa. *Double Life.* NY: Wynwood Press, 1989, p. 120. **C:** Interview with Guenther Koegenbahn, 2008.

Saddle the Wind (1958)
A: Bond, Jeff, and Lukas Kendall. Liner notes to *Saddle the Wind.* FSM vol. 7 no. 15, 2004. **B:** Bernstein, Elmer. "A Conversation with John Green." *Elmer Bernstein's Film Music Notebook.* Los Angeles: The Film Music Society, 2004, pp. 456–457.

Saboteur (1958)
B: Sullivan, Jack. *Hitchcock's Music.* New Haven: Yale University Press, 2006, pp. 101–103. **C:** Comparison with German DVD release. Special Thanks to Henrik Jordan.

The Horse's Mouth (1958)
P: Baxter, Brian. "Letter. Tristram Cary." *The Guardian* 9 May 2008. **C:** Interview with Kenneth V. Jones, January 2008. **C:** Interview with Tristram Cary, 22 June 2007.

Green Mansions (1959)
A: Whitaker, Bill, and Jeff Bond. Liner Notes to *Green Mansions.* FSM vol. 8 no. 3, 2005. **B:** Rózsa, Miklós. *Double Life.* NY: Wynwood Press, 1989, p. 83. **W:** Bond, Jeff. "Morning Becomes Goldsmith." Film Score Daily (*http://www.filmscoremonthly.com/articles/1998/18_Feb---Morning_Becomes_Goldsmith_Radio_Appearance.asp*), 18 February 1998. **W:** Frey, Dean. "From Odeon to Green Mansions: Villa-Lobos at the Movies." VillaLobos.Ca (*http://www.villalobos.ca/previous/filmmus.html*), n.d.

Jack the Ripper (1959)
A: Cooke, Mervyn. Liner notes to *The Film Music of Stanley Black*. Chandos CHAN 10306, 2005. **A:** Lee, Gypsy Rose. Liner notes to *Jack the Ripper*. RCA Victor LSP 2199, 1960.

Goliath and the Barbarians / Il Terrore dei Barbari (1959)
A: Fuiano, Claudio. Liner notes to *Il Terrore dei Barbari*. Digitmovies CDDM113, 2008. **A:** Fake, Douglass, and Joe Sikoryak. Liner notes to *Master of the World /Goliath and the Barbarians*. Intrada Special Collection ISE 1029, 2009. **P:** Kraft, David, and Ronald Bohn. "A Conversation with Les Baxter." *Soundtrack!* no. 26, 1981.

Black Sunday / La Maschera del Demonio (1960)
A: Kimmel, Bruce. Liner notes to *Black Sunday*. Kritzerland KR 20018-7, 2011. **B:** Lucas, Tim. *Mario Bava: All the Colors of the Dark*. Cincinnati: Video Watchdog, 2007. **P:** Kraft, David, and Ronald Bohn. "A Conversation with Les Baxter." *Soundtrack!* no. 26, 1981.

Surprise Package (1960)
B: Silverman, Stephen M. *Dancing on the Ceiling: Stanley Donen and his Movies*. NY: Knopf, 1996. **C:** Interview with Dimitri Kennaway, 2008. **C:** Interview with Kenneth V. Jones, January 2008. **C:** Private correspondence from the Benjamin Frankel Collection.

Something Wild (1961)
A: Wilson, Peter Niklas. "Canvasses and Time Canvasses: Comments on Morton Feldman's Film Music" (liner notes to *Something Wild*). Kairos 0012292KAI, 2002. **W:** Noble, Jeremy. Interview with Aaron Copland. BBC Four (*http://www.bbc.co.uk/bbcfour/audiointerviews/profilepages/coplanda1.shtml*), 7 July 1961.

El Cid (1961)
A: DeWald, Frank K. Liner notes to *El Cid*. Tadlow Music Tadlow005, 2008. **B:** Rózsa, Miklós. *Double Life*. NY: Wynwood Press, 1989, pp. 193–195. **P:** Elley, Derek. "The Film Composer—Miklós Rózsa, Part Two." *Films and Filming* 23, no. 9, June 1977, pp. 30–34. **P:** French, Lawrence. "Ray Harryhausen, Film Music Fan." *FSM* vol. 11 no. 1, January 2006, p. 2. **P:** Fuiano, Claudio. "A Conversation with Mario Nascimbene." *Soundtrack!* no. 20, December 1986, pp. 9–10. **P:** Reali, Ezio, and James Marshall. "A Conversation with Mario Nascimbene." *Soundtrack!* no. 24, Winter 1980/81, p. 5.

Hatari! (1962)
B: Mancini, Henry. *Did They Mention the Music?* NY: Cooper Square Press, 2001, pp. 108–110. **B:** Sudhalter, Richard M. *Stardust Melody: The Life and Music of Hoagy Carmichael*. Oxford: Oxford University Press, 2003, pp. 313–314.

The Day of the Triffids (1962)
A: Schechter, David. Liner notes to *This Island Earth*. Monstrous Movie Music MMM-1954, 2006. **B:** Hunter, I. Q. *British Science Fiction Cinema*. NY: Routledge, 2002, pp. 80–81, 23–33. **C:** Conversation and emails between Michael Hyatt and Jim Fox.

I Thank a Fool (1962)
B: Cochran, Alfred W. "The Documentary Film Scores of Gail Kubik." *Film Music: Critical Approaches*. Ed. Kevin Donnelly. NY: Continuum International, 2001, pp. 117–128. **B:** Cochran, Alfred W. "The Functional Music of Gail Kubik." *Film Music 2*. Eds. Claudia Gorbman and Warren M. Sherk. Los Angeles: The Film Music Society, 2004, pp. 89–112. **C:** Interview with Gerard Schurmann, 7 December 2007.

Dr. No (1962)
A: Gleason, Alexander. "Music for James Bond: The Beginning" (liner notes to *The Essential James Bond*). Silva Screen SSCD 1034, 1993, pp. 3–4. **P:** Hedman, Tomas. "The Full Monty." *007 Magazine* no. 46, 2005, pp. 6–9. **W:** Farrington-Williams, Adam. "An Interview with Monty Norman." Universal Exports (*http://www.universalexports.net/interviews/norman.shtml*), 2006. **W:** Gross, Terry. "Interview with John Barry." Fresh Air (*http://www.npr.org/templates/story/story.php?storyId=1110572*), March 1999.

Lawrence of Arabia (1962)
A: Bremner, Tony. Liner notes to *Lawrence of Arabia*. Silva Screen FILMCD 036, 1989. **B:** Zador, Leslie T., and Gregory Rose. "A Conversation with Bernard Hermann." *Film Music I* (2nd ed.). Ed. Clifford McCarty. Los Angeles: The Film Music Society, 1998, pp. 243, 252–253. **C:** Original research at the Richard Rodgers collection, Library of Congress, 2008. **C:** Interview with Gerard Schurmann, 7 December 2007.

Contempt / Le Mépris / Il Disprezzo (1963)
A: Fuiano,Claudio. Liner notes to *Il Disprezzo*. Digitmovies CDDM 002, 2003. **V:** Lopate, Phillip. "Contempt: The Story of a Marriage." *Criterion Collection*, 2002. **B:** Brody, Richard. *Everything Is Cinema: The Working Life of Jean-Luc Godard*. NY: Metropolitan /Henry Holt and Company, 2008, pp. 157–174. **B:** Youngblood, Gene. "Jean-Luc Godard: No Difference between Life and Cinema (1968)." *Jean Luc Godard Interviews*. Ed. David Sterritt. Jackson: University Press of Mississippi, 1998, pp. 18, 25. **C:** Interview with Colette Delerue, 11 March 2008.

Seven Days in May (1964)
P: Foster, Jason. "Final Take: Director John Frankenheimer, 1930–2002." *FSM* vol 7 no. 7, September 2002, p. 17. **C:** Interview with David Amram, 3 February 2008.

The Man Who Laughs / L'Uomo che ride (1966)
A: Bender, John. Liner notes to *Kenner/More Than a Miracle*. FSM vol. 14 no. 7, 2011. **W:** Mansell, John. "Interview with Piero Piccioni." Movie Music Italiano (available at *http://www.soundtrackfan.com/livescores/other/italian/italian-interview-piero-piccioni.htm*), 2003.

Torn Curtain (1966)
B: Smith, Steven C. *A Heart at Fire's Center*. Berkeley: University of California Press, 2002, pp. 267–274. **B:** Sullivan, Jack. *Hitchcock's Music*. New Haven: Yale University Press, 2006, pp. 276–289. **B:** Zador, Leslie T., and Gregory Rose. "A Conversation with Bernard Hermann." *Film Music I* (2nd ed.). Ed. Clifford McCarty. Los Angeles: The Film Music Society, 1998, pp. 219. **P:** Bernstein, Elmer. "A Conversation with John Addison." *Elmer Bernstein's Film Music Notebook*. Los Angeles: The Film Music Society, 2004, pp. 456–457. **W:** Koegebehn, Guenther. "Talk on the Wild Side: Elmer Bernstein Remembers His Friend Bernard Herrmann." The Bernard Herrmann Society (*http://www.bernardherrmann.org/articles/interview-bernstein/*), June 2003. **W:** Luchs, Kurt. "*The 7th Voyage of Sinbad*—An Interview with Robert Townson, Part 1." The Bernard Herrmann Society (*http://www.bernardherrmann.org/articles/interview-townson/*), October 1998.

One of Our Spies Is Missing (1966)
A: Burlingame, Jon. Liner notes to *The Spy with My Face: The Man from U.N.C.L.E. Movies (1965–1968)*. FSM vol. 9 no. 18, 2006. **B:** Heitland, Jon. *The Man from U.N.C.L.E. Book: The Behind-the-Scenes Story of a Television Classic*. NY: St. Martin's Press, 1987.

Chappaqua (1966)
A: Ginibre, Jean-Louis. Liner notes to Ornette Coleman's *Chappaqua*. Columbia COL 480584 2, 1996. **A:** McKean, Gil. "A Conversation with Conrad Rooks" (liner notes to Ravi Shankar's *Chappaqua*). Columbia Records OS 3230, 1966.

After the Fox / Caccia alla volpe (1966)
B: Silov, Ed. *Mr. Strangelove: A Biography of Peter Sellers*. NY: Hyperion, 2003, pp. 253–257. **B:** Simon, Neil. *Rewrites: A Memoir*. NY: Simon & Schuster, 1998, pp. 184–222.

The Bible: In the Beginning (1966)
B: Huston, John. *An Open Book*. NY: Da Capo Press, 1994, pp. 318–329. **P:** Anile, Alberto. "Ho messo il cinema italiano in musica." *Sorrisi e Canzoni* 4 November 2003. **C:** Interviews with Didier Thunus, 2008.

Bonnie and Clyde (1967)
B: Biskind, Peter. *Easy Riders, Raging Bulls*. NY: Touchstone, 2002, pp. 15–50. **P:** Mangold, Charles. "George Bassman: Rhapsody in Black." *FSM* vol 9 no. 6, July 2004, p. 17. **C:** Interview with Charles Strouse, 16 November 2007. **C:** Email between Charles Goldman and Jim Fox.

A Time for Killing (1967)
W: Official Manos Hatjidakis website, *www.hadjidakis.gr/#*. **W:** Patten, Forrest. "Interview with Van Alexander." Robert Farnon Society (*http://www.rfsoc.org.uk/jim26.shtml*), 8 September 2004.

Bora Bora (1968)
B: Toop, David. *Exotica*. London: Serpent's Tail, 1999, pp. 33–48.

2001: A Space Odyssey (1968)
A: Burlingame, Jon, and Nick Redman. Liner notes to *2001: A Space Odyssey*. Intrada ISC 38, 2007. **A:** Mulhall, Kevin. "Alex North's Celestial Symphony: The Music for *2001*." Varèse Sarabande VSD 5400, 1993. **B:** Agel, Jerome. *The Making of Kubrick's 2001*. NY: Signet, 1970, pp. 198–199. **B:** Ciment, Michel. "Kubrick on *Barry Lyndon*." *Kubrick*. NY: Holt, Rinehart, and Winston, 1982. **B:** Henderson, Sonya Shoilevska. *Alex North, Film Composer*. London: McFarland & Company, 2003, pp. 70–73. **B:** Morgan, David. *Knowing the Score*. NY: Harper Collins, 2000, pp. 277–284. **P:** Henderson, Kirk. "Alex North's *2001* and Beyond." *Soundtrack!* vol. 13 no. 49, March 1994, pp. 30–31. **P:** Kendall, Lukas. "The Re-Making of Alex North's *2001*: An Interview with Robert Townson." *FSM* vol. 1 nos. 36–37, August/September 1993, p. 26.

The Lost Continent (1968)
A: Interview with Gerard Schurmann, GDI Records GDICD015, 2000. **B:** Huckvale, David. *Hammer Film Scores and the Musical Avant-Garde*. London: McFarland & Company, 2008, pp. 49, 89. **P:** Larson, Randall D. Interview with Gerard Schurmann, *Soundtrack!* no. 46, pp. 22–24. **C:** Interview with Dimitri Kennaway, 2008. **C:** Interview with Gerard Schurmann, 7 December 2007.

Land of the Giants: The Crash (1968)
A: Burlingame, Jon. Liner notes to *Land of the Giants.* GNP Crescendo GNPD 8048, 1996. **B:** Abbott, Jon. *Irwin Allen Television Productions, 1964–1970: A Critical History of* Voyage to the Bottom of the Sea, Lost in Space, The Time Tunnel *and* Land of the Giants. London: McFarland & Company, 2006.

Barbarella (1968)
A: Keech, Andrew. Liner notes to *Barbarella.* Harkit Records HRKCD 8004, 2002. **C:** Interview with Frank Ernould, January 2008.

Sinful Davey (1969)
C: Interview with Kenneth Thorne, 13 February 2008.

Age of Consent (1969)
B: Skinner, Graeme. *Peter Sculthorpe: The Making of an Australian Composer.* Sydney: University of New South Wales Press, 2007, pp. 499–506. **P:** Stein, Ruthe. "Michael Powell's *Age of Consent* on DVD." *San Francisco Chronicle* 11 January 2009. **W:** Plush, Vincent. "Sculthorpe in the Cinema." **C:** Interview with Peter Sculhorpe, 3 March 2008.

The Appointment (1969)
A: Kendall, Lukas. Liner notes to *The Appointment.* FSM vol. 6 no. 1, 2003. **P:** Michaud, Stéphane. "The Man Who Loves Adventure: Michel Legrand." *FSM* vol. 12 no. 3, March 2007. **B:** Phillips, Stu. *Stu Who?* Studio City, CA: Cissum Press, 2003, p. 179.

Battle of Neretva / Bitka na Neretvi (1969)
B: Smith, Steven C. *A Heart at Fire's Center.* Berkeley: University of California Press, 2002, pp. 303–304.

Battle of Britain (1969)
B: Jackson, Paul R. W. *The Life and Music of Sir Malcolm Arnold: The Brilliant and the Dark.* Aldershot (UK): Ashgate, 2003, p. 140. **B:** Thomas, Tony. *Music for the Movies.* Los Angeles: Silman-James Press, 1997, pp. 2–3. **P:** Hasan, Mark R. "The Restoration of William Walton's Battle of Britain." *Music from the Movies* no. 43, pp. 64–66. **P:** Ritchie, Christopher. "A Conversation with Ron Goodwin!" *Soundtrack!* vol. 8 no. 30, p. 26. **P:** Williams, John. "A Conversation with Ron Goodwin." *From Silents to Satellite* vol. 1 nos. 1/2, February/May 1990.

The Red Tent / Krasnaya palatka / La Tenda rossa (1969)
B: McCabe, Bob. *Sean Connery.* London: Pavilion Books, 2000, p. 39. **C:** Interview with Didier Thunus, 25 May 2008.

The Reivers (1969)
B: Einarson, John, and Gene Clark. *Mr. Tambourine Man: The Life and Legacy of The Byrds' Gene Clark.* San Francisco: Backbeat, 2005, p. 154. Interview with Bruce Broughton, 14 October 2008. **C:** Interview with Lalo Schifrin, 21 July 2008.

The Molly Maguires (1970)
B: Jackson, Carlton. *Picking Up the Tab.* Bowling Green, OH: Bowling Green University Popular Press, 1994, p. 103. **B:** Mancini, Henry. *Did They Mention the Music?* NY: Cooper Square Press, 2001, p. 159. **C:** Interview with Charles Strouse, 16 November 2007.

Cry of the Banshee (1970)
W: Reis, George. "Interview with Gordon Hessler." DVD Drive-In (*http://www.dvddrive-in.com/hessler.htm*), n.d.

Le Cercle rouge (1970)
P: Vincentelli, Elisabeth. "Take five with...Eric Demarsen." *Time Out New York* no. 552, 27 April–3 May 2006.

Love Story (1970)
A: Tackett, Fred. Liner notes to *The Moon's a Harsh Mistress: Jimmy Webb in the Seventies.* Rhino Handmade, 2004. **C:** Interview with Richie Unterberger, 30 July 2007.

The Go-Between (1970)
B: Bernstein, Elmer. "A Conversation with Richard Rodney Bennet." *Elmer Bernstein's Film Music Notebook.* Los Angeles: The Film Music Society, 2004, p. 191. **P:** Phillips, James. "A Touch of Elegance." *FSM* vol. 7 no. 2, February 2002, p. 26.

A New Leaf (1971)
B: Bazelon, Irwin. *Knowing the Score: Notes on Film Music.* NY: Arco Publishing, 1981.

See No Evil (1971)
B: Larson, Randall D. *Musique Fantastique: A Survey of Film Music in the Fantastic Cinema.* Lanham, MD: Scarecrow Press, 1984, p. 307. **P:** "Mia Farrow Movie Loses an Andre Previn Score." Friday, June 11, 1971, http://rejectedfilmscores.150m.com/info.html. **C:** Interview with David Whitaker, 5 March 2008.

Brother Sun, Sister Moon / Fratello Sole, Sorella Luna (1972)
B: Zefirelli, Franco. *Franco Zefirelli: An Autobiography.* NY: Grove Press, 1986. **C:** Interview with Ken Thorne, 11 January 2007.

Frenzy (1972)
B: Sullivan, Jack. *Hitchcock's Music.* New Haven: Yale University Press, 2006, pp. 298–307. **B:** Mancini, Henry. *Did They Mention the Music?.* NY: Cooper Square Press, 2002, pp. 155–156. **W:** Romero, Jorge Leiva. "At British Cinema's Service." FSM (*http://www.filmscoremonthly.com/articles/2001/09_May---Lost_Issue_Wednesday_Ron_Goodwin_Interview.asp*), 9 May 2001.

Sounder (1972)
B: Henderson, Sonya Shoilevska. *Alex North, Film Composer.* London: McFarland & Company, 2003, p. 83.

Columbo: The Greenhouse Jungle (1972)
A: Kendall, Lukas, and Douglas Payne. Liner notes to *Zigzag/The Supercops.* FSM vol. 9 no. 2, 2006. **C:** Interview with Paul Glass, 19 April 2008. **C:** Interview with Elizabeth Swados, 3 August 2007.

The Getaway (1972)
A: Redman, Nick. Liner notes to *The Getaway.* FSM vol. 8 no. 18, 2005. **V:** Redman, Nick. *Main Title 1M1: Jerry Fielding, Sam Peckinpah, and* The Getaway (documentary), 2007. **P:** Sam Peckinpah. Open letter to Jerry Fielding. *Daily Variety*, 17 November 1972. **C:** Interview with Nick Redman, 8 November 2007.

The Neptune Factor (1973)
C: Interview with Lalo Schifrin, 21 July 2008. **C:** Interview with Matthew McCauley, 29 January 2009. **C:** Interview with Nick Redman, 8 November 2007.

The Man Who Loved Cat Dancing (1973)
A: Eldridge, Jeff. Liner notes to *The Man Who Loved Cat Dancing.* FSM vol. 5 no. 4. **P:** Michaud, Stéphane. "The Man Who Loves Adventure: Michel Legrand" *FSM* vol. 12 no. 3, March 2007, p. 3.

Hex (1973)
C: Interview with Charles Bernstein, 19 April 2008. **W:** The Dave Grusin Archive. "Music for the Screen: Tell Them Willie Boy Is Here." GrusinNet (*http://www.grusin.net/tell_them_willie_boy_is_here.htm*), n.d.

Hell Up in Harlem (1973)
A: Leeds, Alan. Liner notes to *The Payback.* Polydor 517137, 1992. **B:** Wesley, Fred. *Hit Me, Fred: Recollections of a Sideman.* Durham, NC: Duke University Press, 2002, pp. 183–184.

The Seven-Ups (1973)
A: Lichtenfeld, Eric. Liner notes to *The Seven-Ups/The Verdict.* Intrada ISC 47, 2007.

The Exorcist (1973)
B: Bernstein, Elmer. "The Annoted Friedkin." *Elmer Bernstein's Film Music Notebook.* Los Angeles: The Film Music Society, 2004, pp. 52–58. **B:** Biskind, Peter. *Easy Riders, Raging Bulls.* NY: Touchstone, 2002, pp. 221–222. **B:** Smith, Steven C. *A Heart at Fire's Center.* Berkeley: University of California Press, 2002, p. 330. **P:** Park, George. "The Devil's Music." *FSM* vol. 4 no. 2, February 1999, pp. 24–30. **W:** Ordóñez, Miguel Á., and Pablo Nieto. "Interview with Lalo Schifrin." ScoreMagacine (*http://www.scoremagacine.com/Entrevistas_eng_det.php?Codigo=12*), 2004. **W:** "The Sound of Silence" from *The Exorcist*'s official website (http://theexorcist.warnerbros.com/cmp/silencebottom.html).

Chinatown (1974)
B: Bernstein, Elmer. "A Conversation with Jerry Goldsmith." *Elmer Bernstein's Film Music Notebook.* Los Angeles: The Film Music Society, 2004, p. 396. **B:** Lambro, Phillip. *Close Encounters of the Worst Kind.* Lulu.com, 2007, pp. 272–339.

Moses the Lawgiver (1974)
B: Burgess, Anthony. *This Man and His Music.* NY: McGraw-Hill, 1982, p. 39. **B:** Burgess, Anthony. *You've Had Your Time.* NY: Grove Press, 1990, p. 300. **B:** Phillips, Paul. *A Clockwork Counterpoint: The Music and Literature of Anthony Burgess.* Manchester (UK): Manchester University Press, 2011.

S*P*Y*S (1974)
W: Ramentol, Joaquim. "Interview with John Scott." ScoreMagacine (*http://www.scoremagacine.com/Entrevistas_eng_det.php?Codigo=28*), March 2006. **C:** Interview with Bruce Rowland, 15 January 2009. **C:** Interview with John Scott, 2 May 2008. **C:** Interview with Robert Townson, 28 September 2007.

Profondo Rosso (1975)
B: Luca M. Palmerini. *Spaghetti Nightmares: Il Cinema italiano della paura e del fantastico visto attraverso gli occhi dei suoi protagonisti.* Rome: M&P, 1996. (Translated by Alessandro Curci.) **C:** Interview with Giorgio Gaslini, 9 April 2008.

Robin and Marian (1976)
A: Burlingame, Jon. Liner notes to *Robin and Marian.* Silva Screen FILMCD 354, 2001. **A:** Burlingame, Jon. Liner notes to *Robin and Marian.* Prometheus Records PCR 522, 2008. **P:** Mangodt, Daniel. "Interview with John Barry." *Soundtrack!* vol. 15 no. 58, p. 23. **P:** Michaud, Stéphane. "The Man Who Loves Adventure: Michel Legrand." *FSM* vol. 12 no. 3, March 2007, p. 3.

Todo Modo (1976)
B: Priestly, Brian. *Mingus: A Critical Biography.* NY: Da Capo Press, 1994, p. 207–211. **B:** Santoro, Gene. *Myself When I Am Real: The Life and Music of Charles Mingus.* Oxford: Oxford University Press, 2001, pp. 349–361. **P:** Zenni, Stefano. *Behind the Plot: Charles Mingus,* Todo Modo *and the Italian Connection.* Lecture presented on 16 March 2006 at the Conference on Black Music Research (Center for Black Music Research, Columbia College, Chicago).

The Last Hard Men (1976)
P: Mangodt, Daniel. "Interview with Leonard Rosenman (Part 2)." *Soundtrack!* vol.15 no. 56, 1995, p. 5.

Fun with Dick and Jane (1977)
P: Phillips, James. "The King of TV Movie Music." *FSM* vol. 7 no. 6, August 2002, p. 27. **C:** Special thanks to David Schechter.

The White Buffalo (1977)
A: Southall, James. Liner notes to *The White Buffalo.* Prometheus Records, PCD 111, 1991. **B:** Schelle, Michael. *The Score.* Los Angeles: Silman-James Press, 2001, p. 19. **W:** Boggan, Justin. "Interview with David Shire." Rejected Film and TV Scores (*http://rejectedfilmscores.150m.com/davidshireinterview.html*), 3 July 2009.

Shoot the Sun Down (1978)
W: Panopticon. *Shoot the Sun Down* review and director interview. Walken Works (*http://www.walkenworks.com/sunleeds.html*), 2003.

Casey's Shadow (1978)
C: Original research at the Elmer Bernstein Archive, Univ. of Southern California. **C:** Interview with Peter Bernstein, 6 August 2007.

Dawn of the Dead / Zombi (1978)
B: Luca M. Palmerini. *Spaghetti nightmares: Il cinema italiano della paura e del fantastico visto attraverso gli occhi dei suoi protagonisti.* Rome: M&P, 1996 (Translated by Alessandro Curci.) **W:** Aloisio, Giovanni. *Goblin: La Musica, la paura, il fenomeno.* 2005. http://www.giovannialoisio.it/.

Patrick (1978)
B: Luca M. Palmerini. *Spaghetti nightmares: Il cinema italiano della paura e del fantastico visto attraverso gli occhi dei suoi protagonisti.* Rome: M&P, 1996. **W:** Aloisio, Giovanni. *Goblin: La Musica, la paura, il fenomeno.* 2005. http://www.giovannialoisio.it/.

Agatha (1979)
P: Carlsson, Mikael. Interview with Howard Blake. *Music from the Movies.* No. 12, 1996. pp. 34–39. **W:** Howard Blake's notes from his official website, *www.howardblake.com.*

The China Syndrome (1979)
A: Renick, Kyle. Liner notes to *The China Syndrome.* Intrada ISC 110, 2009. **C:** Discussion with Richard Fischoff, September 2008. **C:** Discussion with Lynn Small, 6 September 2007.

Apocalypse Now (1979)
V: Moog, Bob. "The Synthesizer Soundtrack," article from *Contemporary Keyboard* (January 1980), included in *Apocalypse Now: The Complete Dossier,* Paramount, 2006. **P:** Kraft, David. "A Conversation with David Shire." *CinemaScore* no. 13/14, 1985. **W:** Boggan, Justin. "Interview with David Shire." Rejected Film and TV Scores (*http://rejectedfilmscores.150m.com/davidshireinterview.html*), 3 July 2009.

Stalker (1979)
B: Johnson, Vida T., and Graham Petrie. *The Films of Andrei Tarkovsky: A Visual Fugue.* Bloomington: Indiana University Press, 1994, pp. 199–200. **W:** Varaldiev, Annaliese. "Interview with Eduard Artemyev." www.ElectroShock.ru (*http://www.electroshock.ru/eng/edward/interview/varaldiev/index.html*), 2004.

The Black Stallion (1979)
A: Takis, John. Liner notes to *The Black Stallion.* Intrada ISC 107, 2009. **B:** Schelle Michael. *The Score.* Los Angeles: Silman-James Press, 2001, p. 370–371. **C:** Discussions with Mark Adler, 2004.

Zombi Holocaust / Doctor Butcher M.D. (1980)
B: Harper, Jim. *Italian Horror.* Baltimore, MD: Luminary Press, 2005. **C:** Interview with Walter E. Sear, 3 August 2007.

The Shining (1980)
A: Carlos, Wendy. Liner notes to *Rediscovering Lost Scores, Vol. 1.* East Side Digital ESD 81752, 2005. **A:** Carlos, Wendy. Liner notes to *Rediscovering Lost Scores, Vol. 2.* East Side Digital ESD 81762, 2005.

Used Cars (1980)
C: Interview with Angela Morley, 5 August 2007. **C:** Interview with David Schechter, 5 March 2008. **C:** Interview with Patrick Williams, 12 November 2008.

The Hunter (1980)
A: Liner notes to *Le Mans/The Hunter.* Universal France 98489543, 2007. **C:** Interview with Charles Bernstein, 19 April 2008.

Captain Future—German Version (1980)
W: Christian Bruhn's official website, *www.christianbruhn.de.*

Flash Gordon (1980)
P: Carlsson, Mikael. Interview with Howard Blake. *Music from the Movies* no. 12, 1996. pp. 34–39. **W:** Howard Blake's notes from his official website, *www.howardblake.com.*

L'Ultimo squalo / Great White (1981)
A: Liner notes to *Act of Piracy/Great White*, Prometheus Records PCD 111, 1991.

Clash of the Titans (1981)
B: Webber, Roy P. *The Dinosaur Films of Ray Harryhausen: Features, Early 16mm Experiments and Unrealized Projects.* NY: McFarland & Company, 2004. **P:** French, Lawrence. "Ray Harryhausen, Film Music Fan." *FSM* vol. 11 no. 1, January 2006, p. 2.

Wolfen (1981)
P: Larson, Randall D. "Conversation with James Horner." *CinemaScore* nos. 11/12, 1983, p. 53. **W:** Foster, Jason. "A Tale of Two Scores, Part I." FSM (*http://www.filmscoremonthly.com/articles/1998/08_Sep---Tale_of_Two_Scores_Part_I.asp*), 8 September 1998. **W:** Foster, Jason. "Diamond in the Rough, Part II" FSM (*http://www.filmscoremonthly.com/articles/1998/17_Dec---Diamond_in_the_Rough_Part_II_Craig_Safan.asp*), 17 Dec. 1998. **C:** Interview with Craig Safan, 9 May 2008.

Le Professionnel (1981)
W: Thunus, Didier. "A Study of the Music of 'Chi Mai' Composed by Ennio Morricone." 18 August 2007. **C:** Interview with Loek Dikker, 7 April 2009.

Neighbors (1981)
A: Kirgo, Julie. Liner notes to *Neighbors.* Varèse Sarabande VCL 1107 1068, 2008. **B:** Woodward, Bob. *Wired: The Short Life and Fast Times of John Belushi.* NY: Pocket Books, 1985.

Lucifer Rising (1981)
A: Liner notes to *Kenneth Anger's Lucifer Rising.* Boleskine House Records, 1987.

Author! Author! (1982)
A: Kirgo, Julie. Liner notes to *Author! Author!* CD Club MO 0307 1061.2, 2007.

Jinxed! (1982)
C: Interview with Lalo Schifrin, 21 July 2008.

Five Days One Summer (1982)
B: Arnold, Alan. "On *Five Days One Summer.*" *Fred Zinnemann: Interviews.* Ed. George Miller. Jackson: University Press of Mississippi, 2004, pp. 71–79. **C:** Interview with Carl Davis, 21 September 2007. **C:** Interview with Neil R. Sinyard, 7 September 2007.

Fantasia—Re-recorded Version (1982)
B: Granata, Charles L. "Disney, Stokowski and the Genius of *Fantasia.*" *The Cartoon Music Book.* Ed. Daniel Goldmark. Chicago: A Capella Books, 2002, pp. 73–92.

Slapstick (of Another Kind) (1982)
C: Interview with Robert Townson, 28 September 2007.

Tender Mercies (1983)
A: Liner notes to *The Film Music of George Dreyfus, Vol. 2.* Move Records MD3238. **C:** Lecture by Bruce Beresford (Longford Lyell Lecture), 4 October 2006. **C:** Interview with George Dreyfus, 3 August 2007.

Something Wicked This Way Comes (1983)
A: Feigelson, Roger. Liner notes to *The Journey of Natty Gann.* Intrada ISC 95, 2009. **P:** Rebello, Stephen. "Something Wicked This Way Comes." *Cinefantastique* vol. 13 no. 5, June/July 1983, pp. 47–48. **C:** Interview with Colette Delerue, 11 March 2008. **C:** Interview with Neil R. Sinyard, 17 July 2007.

Yor, the Hunter from the Future (1983)
P: Kraft, Richard, and David Kraft. "An Interview with John Scott." *Soundtrack!* no. 18, June 1986, p. 5. **W:** Ramentol, Joaquim. "Interview with John Scott." ScoreMagacine (*http://www.scoremagacine.com/Entrevistas_eng_det.php?Codigo=28*), March 2006. **C:** Interview with John Scott, 2 May 2008.

Manimal (1983)
B: Phillips, Stu. *Stu Who?* Studio City, CA: Cissum Press, pp. 232, 237. **C:** Interview with Stu Phillips, 24 October 2008.

Mike's Murder (1984)
P: Lindway, Russ. "Interview with Joe Jackson." 17 May 2002. **P:** Gans, David. "Interview with Joe Jackson." *Musician*, February 1983. **P:** Promotional interview for *Mike's Murder*, 1984.

Greystoke: The Legend of Tarzan, Lord of the Apes (1984)
A: Bond, Jeff. Liner notes to *Greystoke: The Legend of Tarzan, Lord of the Apes*. La-La Land Records LLLCD 1144, 2010. **P:** Kraft, Richard, and David Kraft. "An Interview with John Scott." *Soundtrack!* no. 18, June 1986, p. 4. **C:** Interview with John Scott, 2 May 2008.

Misunderstood (1984)
C: Interview with Michael Hoppé, 6 April 2008. **C:** Interview with Jimmie Haskell. 25 October 2008.

V: The Final Battle (1984)
W: Koppl, Rudi. "Dennis McCarthy: Hot Rods to Hell: Blazing Roads from Television to Motion Picture Scoring." Reproduced at the composer's official website, www.dennismccarthy.com.

Streets of Fire (1984)
P: Schweiger, Daniel. "Partners in Crime." *FSM* vol. 1 no. 76, December 1996, p. 17. **P:** Simak, Stephen. "Horner on Scoring *Star Trek III*." *CinemaScore* nos. 13/14, 1984/1985, p. 17.

2010: The Year We Make Contact (1984)
P: Milano, Dominic. "Tony Banks and the Evolution of Genesis." *Keyboard* no. 10, November 1984. **P:** Kraft, David. "A Conversation with David Shire." *CinemaScore* nos. 13/14, 1985. **W:** Chellini, Jose Luis Díez. Interview with David Shire. BSO Spirit (*http://www.bsospirit.com/entrevistas/davidshire_e.php*), n.d.

Ordeal by Innocence (1984)
A: Liner notes to *Going Bananas/Déja Vu /Ordeal by Innocence*. Silva Screen/Edel Company SIL 5093-2, 1992. **A:** Kimmel, Bruce. Liner notes to *Ordeal by Innocence*. Kritzerland KR20018-5, 2011. **C:** Interview with Dave Brubeck. **C:** Spotting notes for *Ordeal by Innocence*, 1984. Letter from Richard S. Jeweler to John Nice, 6 September 1984.

The New Kids (1985)
C: Interview with Janet Greek, 14 September 2008. **C:** Interview with Harry Manfredini, 22 July 2008. **C:** Interview with Lalo Schifrin, 21 July 2008.

Doctor Who: The Mark of the Rani (1985)
W: Roberts, Steve, and Mark Ayres. "The Mark of the Rani." Purpleville (*purpleville.pwp.blueyonder.co.uk/rtwebsite*), 20 May 2006.

Heaven Help Us (1985)
P: Kraft, David. "*Heaven Help Us*: A James Horner Trilogy." *CinemaScore* nos. 13/14, 1984/1985.

Lifeforce (1985)
A: Larson, Randall D. Liner notes to *Lifeforce*. BSX Records BSXCD 8822, 2006. **P:** Kraft, David. "For Michael Kamen Film Music Must Engage His Heart." *Soundtrack!* vol. 7 no. 26, p. 26.

Crimewave (1985)
C: Interview with Carter Burwell, 1 December 2008. **C:** Interview with Joseph LoDuca, 30 October 2008.

The Journey of Natty Gann (1985)
A: Mori, Steven Y. Liner notes to *The Journey of Natty Gann*. Intrada ISC 103, 2009. A: Townson, Robert. "A Bernstein Revelation," liner notes to *Elmer Bernstein: Gangs of New York / The Journey of Natty Gann / The Scarlet Letter*. Varèse Sarabande, VCL 0608 1076-4.2, 2008. P: Mangodt, Daniel, and Luc Van de Ven. "Elmer Bernstein Interview Part Deux." *Soundtrack!* vol. 13 no. 49, March 1995, p. 8. **C:** Original research at the Elmer Bernstein Archive, Univ. of Southern California. **C:** Interview with Peter Bernstein, 6 August 2007.

Moonlighting: The Lady in the Iron Mask (1985)
W: Weinman, Jaime J. "Minor Moonlighting Mystery." *Something Old, Nothing New* (*http://zvbxrpl.blogspot.com/*), 15 May 2007.

Legend (1985)
A: MacLean, Paul Andrew. Liner Notes to *Legend*. Silva Screen FILMCD 045, 1992. **P:** Benair, Jonathan. "Interview on *Legend*." *Los Angeles Reader* 2 May 1986. **P:** Dursin, Andy. "*Legend* Resurrected", *FSM* vol. 7 no. 4, May/June

2002, pp. 13–15. **P:** Dursin, Andy. "Restoring *Legend*", *FSM* vol. 7 no. 4, May/June 2002, pp. 15–16. **P:** Larson, Randall D. "The Musics for *Legend*." *CinemaScore* no. 15, Summer 1987, p. 39. **P:** MacLean, Paul Andrew. "From a Legend to a Dream: A Comparative Critique of the Two *Legend* Scores." *Cinemascore* no. 15, Summer 1987, pp. 42–45. **W:** Bond, Jeff. "Wee the Mix: Jerry Goldsmith's *Legend* on Film." FSM 7 September 1998 (http://www.filmscoremonthly.com/daily/article.cfm?articleID=2411).

The Clan of the Cave Bear (1986)
P: Kraft, Richard, and David Kraft. "An Interview with John Scott." *Soundtrack!* no. 18, pp. 5–6. **C:** Interview with John Scott, 2 May 2008.

No Retreat, No Surrender (1986)
A: Harris, Frank. Liner notes to *No Retreat, No Surrender*, Frank Harris Music, 2008. **B:** Schelle, Michael. *The Score*. Los Angeles: Silman-James Press, 1999, p. 391. **C:** Interview with Frank Harris, 22 January 2009. **C:** Interview with Paul Gilreath, 24 November 2008. **C:** Conversation and email between Christopher Young and Jim Fox, September 2011.

Invaders from Mars (1986)
A: Sikoryak, Joe, and Douglass Fake. Liner notes to *Invaders from Mars*. Intrada ISE 1024, 2008. **A:** Young, Christopher. Liner notes to *Invaders from Mars/The Oasis*. Edel-Cinerama Records 0022032CIN, 1994. **B:** Schelle, Michael. *The Score*. Los Angeles: Silman-James Press, 2001, pp. 386–387. **C:** Conversation and email between Christopher Young and Jim Fox, September 2011.

The Golden Child (1986)
A: Burlingame, Jon. "The Chosen Ones": Liner notes to *The Golden Child*. La-La Land Records LLLCD 1180, 2011. **B:** Feldman, Edward S., and Tom Barton. *Tell Me How You Love the Picture: A Hollywood Life*. Beverly Hills: Creative Book Publishers, 2007, p. 156.

Class of Nuke 'Em High (1986)
W: West, Michael J. "Excerpt from Chapter 15." *Musical-Guru Blogspot*, 11 November 2007. **C:** Interview with Michael Perilstein, 28 November 2008.

Platoon (1986)
A: Liner notes to *Salvador/Platoon*. Prometheus PCD136, 2006. **C:** Interview with Colette Delerue, 11 March 2008.

Predator (1987)
C: Interview with Paul Kelly, 18 August 2008. **C:** Interview with Patrick Moraz, 27 January 2009.

A Prayer for the Dying (1987)
C: Interview with John Scott, 2 May 2008.

Hellraiser (1987)
W: Dickie, Tony. "Interview with John Balance." Compulsion (*http://www.compulsiononline.com/interview_coil.htm*), n. d.

The Belly of an Architect (1987)
C: Interview with Glenn Branca, 22 October 2008.

Witchfinder General / The Conqueror Worm—VHS (1987)
P: Larson, Randall D. "The Subtle Art of ReScoring: Kendall Schmidt and the World of Scoring Movie Trailers and Home Video Replacement Music." *Soundtrack!* no. 39, September 1991, pp. 41–47. **C:** Interview with Kenneth V. Jones, January 2008. **C:** Interview with Kendall Roclord Schmidt, November 2008.

The Serpent and the Rainbow (1988)
C: Interview with Charles Bernstein, 19 April 2008.

A Night in the Life of Jimmy Reardon (1988)
W: William Richert's official website, *www.williamrichert.com*. **C:** Original research at the Elmer Bernstein Archive, Univ. of Southern California. **C:** Interview with William Richert, 7 February 2008.

Stars and Bars (1988)
C: Original research at the Elmer Bernstein Archive, Univ. of Southern California. **C:** Interview with Robert Townson, 28 September 2007.

Cocktail (1988)
W: FilmzeneNet. "Between East and West." FilmzeneNet (*http://www.filmzene.net/read.php?u=interju_j_peter_robinson_english.html*), 2 April 2006.

Young Guns (1988)
C: Interview with Tony Hinnigan, 3 November 2007.

Alien Nation (1988)
A: Townson, Robert. Liner notes to *Alien Nation*. Varèse Sarabande VCL 0505 1035, 2005. **W:** Foster, Jason. "A Tale of Two Scores, Part II: Alien Nation" FSM (*http://www.filmscoremonthly.com/articles/1998/12_Nov---A_Tale_of_Two_Scores_Part_II_Alien_Nation.asp*), 12 November 1998.

The Accidental Tourist (1988)
A: Eldridge, Jeff. Liner notes to *The Accidental Tourist*. FSM vol. 11 no. 6, 2008. **C:** Interview with Bruce Broughton, 14 October 2008.

Apartment Zero (1988)
W: Goldwasser, Dan. "A Look at *Ronin* with Elia Cmiral." SoundtrackNet (*http://www.soundtrack.net/features/article/?id=9*),15 November 1998.

Alienator (1989)
W: Marty McKee. Reply from Chuck Cirino. Marty's Marquee (*http://pimannix.tripod.com/*), n.d.

Cyborg (1989)
A: Howlin' Wolf Records. Liner notes to *Cyborg: The Director's Cut*. Howlin' Wolf Records HWRCD-2005, 2011.

Say Anything... (1989)
B: Davis, Richard. *Complete Guide to Film Scoring*. Boston: Berklee Press, 1999, p. 288.

The Seinfeld Chronicles (1989)
W: Laskow, Michael. "TV Composer: Jonathan Wolff." Taxi (*http://www.taxi.com/music-business-faq/ftv/wolff-tv-1.html*), n.d. **C:** Interview with Eric Hester, 8 July 2008.

Koneko monogatari / The Adventures of Milo and Otis (1989)
C: Interview with David McHugh, 18 September 2008.

Trust Me (1989)
C: Interview with Frederic Talgorn, 22 April 2009. **C:** Interview with Dan Wool, 1 February 2008. **C:** Interview with Mason Daring, 7 April, 2008. **C:** Original research at the Elmer Bernstein Archive, Univ. of Southern California.

Tremors (1990)
W: Press clippings from Ernest Troost's official website, *www.ernesttroost.com*. **C:** Interview with Robert Folk, 7 October 2007.

White Fang (1991)
P: Cavanaugh, Darren, and Paul Andrew MacLean. "A Conversation with Basil Poledouris." *Soundtrack!* vol. 11 no. 54, December 1992. **W:** Black, Edwin. "New Hans Zimmer Interview." (*http://www.filmscoremonthly.com/features/zimmer.asp*), 1998.

New Jack City (1991)
C: Interview with Wally Badarou, 7 January 2009.

In the Heat of the Night: No Other Road (1991)
C: Interview with Larry Blank, 10 September 2008.

Regarding Henry (1991)
W: Black, Edwin. "New Hans Zimmer Interview." (*http://www.filmscoremonthly.com/features/zimmer.asp*), 1998. **C:** Interview with Colette Delerue, 11 March 2008.

The People Under the Stairs (1991)
A: Liner notes to *The People Under the Stairs*. Hitchcock-Media HMR9107, 2007. **W:** FilmzeneNet. "Interview with Graeme Revell." FilmzeneNet. (*http://www.filmzene.net/read.php?u=interju_graeme_revell_english.html*), 25 May 2005.

K2 (1991)
W: Black, Edwin. "New Hans Zimmer Interview." (*http://www.filmscoremonthly.com/features/zimmer.asp*), 1998. **C:** Interview with Jazz Jankel, 2007.

The Prince of Tides (1991)
B: Schelle, Michael. *The Score*. Los Angeles: Silman-James Press, 1999, p. 183.

Gladiator (1992)
W: Boggan, Justin. "Brad Fiedel Interview." Rejected Film and TV Scores (*http://rejectedfilmscores.150m.com/bradfiedel interview.html*), 4 October 2011.

Split Second (1992)
A: Carlos, Wendy. Liner notes to *Rediscovering Lost Scores, Vol. 2*. East Side Digital ESD 81762, 2005. **C:** Interview with Wendy Carlos, 23 May 2008.

CrissCross (1992)
C: Interview with Mark Howe, 31 March 2008.

Encino Man (1992)
W: FilmzeneNet. "Between East and West." FilmzeneNet (*http://www.filmzene.net/read.php?u=interju_j_peter_robinson_english.html*), 2 April 2006. C: Interview with Jonathan Sheffer, 7 April 2008.

Honeymoon in Vegas (1992)
W: Boggan, Justin. "Marc Shaiman: Bigger, Longer & Uncut." Rejected Film and TV Scores (*http://rejectedfilmscores.150m.com/marcshaimaninterview.html*), November 2004.

A River Runs Through It (1992):
C: Original research at the Elmer Bernstein Archive, Univ. of Southern California.

The Public Eye (1992)
W: Ordóñez, Miguel Á., and Pablo Nieto. "Interview with Mark Isham." Scoremagacine (*http://www.scoremagacine.com/Entrevistas_eng_det.php?Codigo=17*), 2005.

Jennifer 8 (1992)
B: Schelle, Michael. *The Score*. Los Angeles: Silman-James Press, 1999, pp. 406–408. P: Larson, Randall D. "Scoring Session: Christopher Young on the Man Who Knew Too Little." *Soundtrack!* vol. 16 no. 64, December 1997, p. 23. C: Conversation and email between Christopher Young and Jim Fox, September 2011.

Trespass (1992)
P: Schweiger, Daniel. "Partners in Crime." *FSM* vol. 1 no. 76, December 1996, p. 17–18.

McLintock!—Public Domain Version (1993)
P: Brown, Royal S. *Film Musings*. Lanham, MD: Scarecrow Press, 2007, p. 189. W: John Ottman's official website, *www.johnottman.com*.

Homeward Bound: The Incredible Journey (1993)
W: Boggan, Justin. "Interview with David Shire." Rejected Film and TV Scores (*http://rejectedfilmscores.150m.com/davidshireinterview.html*), 3 July 2009. W: Foster, Jason. "Diamond in the Rough, Part III." FSM (*http://www.filmscoremonthly.com/articles/1999/19_Jan---A_Conversation_with_David_Shire.asp*).19 January 1999. C: Interview with Bruce Broughton, 21 January 2008.

Point of No Return (1993)
C: Interview with John Badham, 24 January 2009.

Three of Hearts (1993)
C: Interview with Richard Gibbs, 4 November 2008.

La Belle et la bête / The Beauty and the Beast—Opera (1994)
W: Cott, Jonathan. "Interview with Philip Glass." *http://www.glasspages.org/belle.html*, 1995.

I Love Trouble (1994)
C: Original research at the Elmer Bernstein Archive, Univ. of Southern California. C: Interview with Robert Townson, 28 September 2007.

The River Wild (1994)
P: Mangodt, Daniel. "Interview with Maurice Jarre." *Soundtrack!* no. 60, December 1996, p. 22.

Sirens (1994)
C: Interview with Geoffrey Burgon, 23 October 2007.

Interview with the Vampire (1994)
C: Interview with Nicolas Cleobury, 21 January 2008.

Picture Bride (1995)
C: Interview with Mark Adler, 23 October 2008.

Johnny Mnemonic (1995)
P: Lebovici, Elisabeth. "J'ai nagé avec les requins et j'ai survécu: Robert Longo évoque son envie 'd'affronter le monde et les monstres.'" *Libération*, 22 November 1995. W: Epstein, Daniel Robert. Interview with William Gibson. Suicidegirls.com (*http://suicidegirls.com/interviews/602/William-Gibson/*), 23 February 2003. W: Mychael Danna, *www.originaltrilogy.com*.

The Indian in the Cupboard (1995)
W: Foster, Jason. "A Tale of Two Scores, Part I." FSM (*http://www.filmscoremonthly.com/articles/1998/08_Sep---Tale_of_Two_Scores_Part_I.asp*), 8 September 1998. W: Plume, Kenneth. Interview with Frank Oz. IGN (*http://movies.ign.com/articles/035/035842p1.html*), 10 February 2000.

Assassins (1995)
C: Interview with John van Tongeren, November 2008.

Waterworld (1995)
P: Carlson, Michael. Interview with Mark Isham. *Music from the Movies.* **C:** Interview with Richard Gibbs, 4 November 2008.

The Scarlet Letter (1995)
A: Townson, Robert. "A Bernstein Revelation." Varèse Sarabande, VCL 0608 1076-4.2, 2008. **B:** Schelle, Michael. *The Score.* Los Angeles: Silman-James Press, 2001, p. 35. **C:** Original research at the Elmer Bernstein Archive, Univ. of Southern California. **P:** Hoshowsky, Robert. "Exclusive Interview with John Barry." *FSM* vol 1 no. 76, December 1996, p. 13.

Silver Strand (1995)
C: Interview with Bruce Rowland, 15 January 2009.

Cutthroat Island (1995)
A: Tonks, Paul. Liner notes to *Cutthroat Island.* Prometheus XPCD 157, 2005. **C:** David Arnold interview during the third annual International Film Music Conference (Úbeda, Spain), July 2007.

White Squall (1996)
B: DesJardins, Christian. *Inside Film Music.* Los Angeles: Silman-James Press, 2006, p. 225. **B:** Rona, Jeff. *The Reel World.* San Francisco: Miller Freeman Books, 2000, pp. 13–20. **P:** Mangodt, Daniel. "Interview with Maurice Jarre." *Soundtrack!* no. 60, December 1996.

Mission: Impossible (1996)
B: Blumenfeld, Samuel, and Laurent Vachaud. *Brian De Palma.* Paris: Calmann-Lévy, 2001. **P:** Larson, Randall D. "Expecting the Impossible." *Soundtrack!* vol. 19 no. 74, Summer 2000, p. 40. **P:** Thaxton, Ford A., and Randall D. Larson. "Mission: Impossible: Composer Alan Silvestri Disavowed." *Soundtrack!* vol. 19 no. 74, Summer 2000, p. 39.

The Island of Dr. Moreau (1996)
C: Interview with Richard Stanley, 20 November 2008.

Last Man Standing (1996)
P: Schweiger, Daniel. "Partners in Crime." *FSM* vol. 1 no. 76, December 1996, p. 16.

The Winner (1996)
B: Schelle, Michael. *The Score.* Los Angeles: Silman-James Press, 2001, p. 242. **W:** Official website of Alex Cox, *www.alexcox.com.* **C:** Interview with Dan Wool, 1 February 2008.

2 Days in the Valley (1996)
W: Review on Jerry Goldsmith Online, (*http://www.jerrygoldsmithonline.com/two_days_in_the_valley_review.htm*), n.d.

Ransom (1996)
B: Schelle, Michael. *The Score.* Los Angeles: Silman-James Press, 2001, pp. 345–346.

Mariette in Ecstasy (1996)
C: Interview with Christopher Klatman, 7 July 2008. **C:** Interview with Ernest Thompson, 11 September 2008.

Rosewood (1997)
A: Wynton Marsalis. Liner notes to *Reeltime.* Sony Classical 51239, 1999. **P:** Levin, Jordan. "Movies on Location: Dredging in the Deep South. John Singleton Digs into the Story of Rosewood, a Town Burned by a Lynch Mob in 1923." *Los Angeles Times*, 30 June 1996.

Welcome to Woop Woop (1997)
W: Coverage of *Welcome to Woop Woop*: interviews, comments from cast & crew. Urban Cinefile (*http://www.urbancinefile.com.au/home/view.asp?a=1432&s=features*), n.d.

Breakdown (1997)
A: Bond, Jeff. Liner notes to *Breakdown.* La-La Land Records. **C:** Interview with Eric Colvin, 2008.

Air Force One (1997)
W: Black, Edwin. "New Hans Zimmer Interview." FSM (*http://www.filmscoremonthly.com/features/zimmer.asp*), 1998. **W:** Foster, Jason. "A Tale of Two Scores, Part I." FSM (*http://www.filmscoremonthly.com/articles/1998/08_Sep---Tale_of_Two_Scores_Part_I.asp*), 8 September 1998.

Drive (1997)
C: Interview with David C. Williams, 12 August 2008.

The Disappearance of García Lorca (1997)
P: Koppl, Rudy. Interview with Mark McKenzie. *Music from the Movies* no. 19, online re-publication at the composer's website, *www.markmckenzie.org* (at *http://www.markmckenzie.org/mm_interview_lorca.html*).

Kiss the Girls (1997)
B: Morgan, David. *Knowing the Score.* NY: Harper Collins, 2000, p. 182. W: Carter Burwell's official website, *www.thebodyinc.com.*

The House of Yes (1997)
B: Rona, Jeff. *The Reel World.* San Francisco: Miller Freeman Books, 2000 pp. 193–197. 207–215. W: Goldwasser, Dan. "Legally Kent." SoundtrackNet (available at *http://www.industrycentral.net/links_index1.html*), 27 July 2001.

The Gambler / A játékos (1997)
C: Interview with Gerard Schurmann, 7 December 2007.

The Wings of the Dove (1997)
W: Boggan, Justin. Interview with Gabriel Yared. Rejected Film and TV Scores (*http://rejectedfilmscores.150m.com/gabrielyaredinterview.html*), 22 July 2004.

Below Utopia (aka *Body Count*) (1997)
A: Liner notes to *Below Utopia: The Lost Score.* Virgin Records, 1998. W: Barshad, Amos. "RZA Debuts in *Derailed.*" The Michigan Daily (*http://www.michigandaily.com/content/rza-debuts-derailed*), 14 November 2005.

Babylon 5: The Gathering (Special Edition) (1998)
C: Message from J. Michael Straczynski, 4 November 1997.

Les Misérables (1998)
B: DesJardins, Christian. *Inside Film Music.* Los Angeles: Silman-James Press, 2006, pp. 183–184. W: Boggan, Justin. Interview with Gabriel Yared. Rejected Film and TV Scores (*http://rejectedfilmscores.150m.com/gabrielyaredinterview.html*), 22 July 2004.

The Horse Whisperer (1998)
C: Interview with Nic Raine, March 2008.

Halloween H20: 20 Years Later (1998)
P: Comeford, Jason. "Slicing and Dicing a Horror Score." *FSM* vol. 4 no. 5, June 1999, pp 26–30. W: Goldwasser, Dan. "John Ottman Gives Us the Scoop." SoundtrackNet (*http://www.soundtrack.net/features/article/?id=15*), 18 August 1998.

The Avengers (1998)
P: Lepretre, Didier. Interview with Michael Kamen, *Starfix*, September 1998.

Head On (1998)
C: Interview with Philip Brophy, 27 March 2008.

Shadowbuilder (1998)
W: Deppe, Roman. "*Shadowbuilder*: Temp Score to Final Score." FSM (*http://www.filmscoremonthly.com/daily/article.cfm?articleID=2424*), 9 October 1998. W: Deppe, Roman. "An Interview with Eckart Seeber." FSM (*http://www.filmscoremonthly.com/daily/article.cfm?articleID=2598*), 29 October 1998. C: Interview with Guy Zerafa, 6 October 2008.

The Eighteenth Angel (1998)
W: Broxton, Jonathan. "A Man Alone." *MovieMusicUK*, 2000. C: Interview with Simon Boswell, 9 July 2008. C: Interview with Starr Parodi, 19 November 2006.

What Dreams May Come (1998)
W: Goldwasser, Dan. "Dreams of Giants with Michael Kamen." SoundtrackNet (*http://www.soundtrack.net/features/article/?id=42*), 4 September 1999. W: I Am Legend Archive. Interview with Richard Matheson. I Am Legend Archive (*http://www.iamlegendarchive.com/ial.html*), n.d.

Practical Magic (1998)
B: Davis, Richard. *Complete Guide to Film Scoring.* Boston: Berklee Press, 1999, p. 87. W: Goldwasser, Dan. "The Practically Ravenous Michael Nyman." SoundtrackNet (*http://www.soundtrack.net/features/article/?id=53*), 16 March 2000.

Playing by Heart (1998)
W: Broxton, Jonathan. "Christopher Young in Conversation." *MovieMusicUK.* May 2000. A: Burlingame, Jon. Liner notes to *Playing by Heart.* Decca 466275, 1999. W: FilmzeneNet. "John Ottman Returns." FilmzeneNet (*http://www.filmzene.net/read.php?u=interju_john_ottman_english.html*), 10 June 2010.

Stepmom (1998)
W: Southall, James. "Review of *Stepmom.*" Movie Wave (*http://www.movie-wave.net/titles/stepmom.html*), 1998.

Cruel Intentions (1999)
W: Jarry, Jonathan. "Music for Super Fantastic Invaders." SoundtrackNet (*http://www.soundtrack.net/features/article/?id=237*), 27 June 2007. W: FilmzeneNet. "John Ottman Returns." FilmzeneNet (*http://www.filmzene.net/read.php?u=interju_john_ottman_english.html*), 10 June 2010. W: John Ottman's official website, *www.johnottman.com*.

A Midsummer Night's Dream (1999)
W: Broxton, Jonathan. "A Man Alone," *MovieMusicUK*, 2000. W: Flakus, Agnieszka. "Music: Speaking Your Own Language." Plus: Journal of Polish American Affairs (*http://www.pljournal.com/music/wojciech-kilar-interview.html*), 14 July 2007. C: Interview with Simon Boswell, 9 July 2008.

Mystery Men (1999):
P: Koppl, Rudy. "Scoring Session." *Soundtrack!* no. 71, Fall 1999, pp. 30–33. W: Gorjón, Sergio. Interview with Stephen Warbeck. BSO Spirit (*http://www.bsospirit.com/entrevistas/warbeck_e.php*), 2005. W: Robogeek. Interview with Stephen Warbeck. Ain't It Cool News (*http://images.aintitcool.com/node/3858*), 25 June 1999.

The 13th Warrior (1999)
A: Crichton, Michael. Liner notes to *The 13th Warrior*, Varèse Sarabande VSD 6038, 1999. W: Goldwasser, Dan. "Graeme's Sci-Fi Bonanza." SoundtrackNet (*http://www.soundtrack.net/features/article/?id=66*), 12 December 2000. W: Ordóñez, Miguel Á., and Demetris Christodoulides. Interview with Graeme Revell. ScoreMagacine (*http://www.scoremagacine.com/Entrevistas_det.php*), 2005.

Operation Condor 2: The Armour of the Gods (1999)
P: Renick, Kyle. "Punisher: Wandmacher Zone." FSM vol. 14 no. 1, January 2009.

La Lengua de las mariposas (1999)
W: Cornejo, Gorka. "Entrevista a Ángel Illarramendi (2a parte)." Score Magacine (*http://www.scoremagacine.com/Entrevistas_det.php*), 11 April 2007. W: Ordóñez, Miguel, and David Doncel. "Entrevista a Alejandro Amenábar." BSO Spirit (*http://www.bsospirit.com/entrevistas/alejandroamenabar_intro.php*), 2004.

Godzilla 2000 / Gojira ni-sen mireniamu (1999)
W: FilmzeneNet. "Between East and West." FilmzeneNet (*http://www.filmzene.net/read.php?u=interju_j_peter_robinson_english.html*), 2 April 2006.

Supernova (2000)
A: Liner notes to *Supernova*. Intrada ISE 1038, 2010. C: Interview with David C. Williams, 10 June 2008.

My Dog Skip (2000)
C: Interview with Richard Gibbs, 26 August 2009. C: Interview with Van Dyke Parks, 4 May 2008.

The Kid (aka ***Disney's The Kid***) (2000)
W: Boggan, Justin. "Marc Shaiman: Bigger, Longer & Uncut." Rejected Film and TV Scores (*http://rejectedfilmscores.150m.com/marcshaimaninterview.html*), November 2004.

Highlander: Endgame (2000)
W: Stephen Graziano's email to Justin Boggan. Rejected Film and TV Scores (*http://rejectedfilmscores.150m.com/info.html#HEG*), n.d.

Chinese Coffee (2000)
W: Broxton, Jonathan. "Howard Shore Questions His own eXistenZ." *MovieMusicUK*, 1999. W: Friedman, Roger. "Knowing the Score: The Wise Man of Movie Music Composition, Elmer Bernstein, Celebrates 50 Years in Hollywood." Reproduced on Elmer Bernstein official site, *www.elmerbernstein.com* (at *http://www.elmerbernstein.com/bio/interviews/redcarpet.html*), March 2003. C: Interview with Adam Glasser, 6 November 2008.

Into the Arms of Strangers: Stories of the Kindertransport (2000)
C: Interview with Mark Jonathan Harris, 16 August 2008. C: Interview with Lee Holdridge, 25 April 2009.

Harrison's Flowers (2000)
A: Liner notes to *Les Fleurs d'Harrison*. EMI Records 7243 531316 2, 2001.

All the Pretty Horses (2000)
W: Otto, Jeff. "Interview with Billy Bob Thornton." IGN (*http://movies.ign.com/articles/554/554690p1.html*), 7 October 2004.

Pollock (2000)
A: Schweiger, Daniel. Liner notes to *Martin/Pollock*. Perseverance Records PRD019, 2007. P: Buchsbaum, Tony. "Jeff Beal, Composer. Ed Harris, Director/Star: Pollock." *Soundtrack!* vol. 20 no. 77, Spring 2001. C: Interview with Donald Rubinstein, 13 August 2008.

Crossfire Trail (2001)
W: Boggan, Justin. "Interview with David Shire." Rejected Film Scores (*http://rejectedfilmscores.150m.com/davidshireinterview.html*), 3 July 2009. C: Interview with Eric Colvin, 2008.

Town & Country (2001)
W: Goldwasser, Dan. "Legally Kent." SoundtrackNet (available at *http://www.industrycentral.net/links_index1.html*), 24 July 2001.

What's the Worst That Could Happen? (2001)
W: Boggan, Justin. "Marc Shaiman: Bigger, Longer & Uncut." Rejected Film Scores (*http://rejectedfilmscores.150m.com/marcshaimaninterview.html*), November 2004. **C:** Interview with Larry Blank, 10 September 2008.

Lara Croft: Tomb Raider (aka ***Tomb Raider***) (2001)
W: FilmzeneNet. "Interview with Graeme Revell." FilmzeneNet (*http://www.filmzene.net/read.php?u=interju_graeme_revell_english.html*), 25 May 2005. **W:** Goldwasser, Dan. "Raiding the Tomb with Graeme Revell." SoundtrackNet (available at *http://www.industrycentral.net/content/music/revell1.shtml*), 28 July 2001.

Scary Movie 2 (2001)
W: FilmzeneNet. "Alternate Genres." FilmzeneNet (*http://www.filmzene.net/read.php?u=interju_george_s_clinton_english.html*), 16 July 2007.

Rat Race (2001)
C: Original research at the Elmer Bernstein Archive, Univ. of Southern California.

Behind Enemy Lines (2001)
W: CRMAV. "Composer Paul Haslinger Scores with Steinberg ." CRMAV (*http://www.crmav.com/composing/38/composer_paul_haslinger_scores_with_steinberg.shtml*), 2001. **C:** Interview with Richard Rich, 30 March 2008.

Texas Rangers (2001)
W: Coleman, Christopher. "Snakes on Refrain." Tracksounds (*http://www.tracksounds.com/specialfeatures/interviews/interview_trevor_rabin_2006.htm*), 2006. **W:** Mansell, John: "Interview with Marco Beltrami", Movie Music Italiano (*http://moviemusicitaliano.webs.com/hollywoodinfoandinterview.htm*), 2006. **C:** Interview with Marco Beltrami, 9 May 2008.

The Mothman Prophecies (2002)
B: DesJardins, Christian. *Inside Film Music.* Los Angeles: Silman-James Press, 2006, pp. 227–228.

The Bourne Identity (2002)
W: Notes from Carter Burwell's official website, *www.thebodyinc.com.* **C:** Interview with Carter Burwell, 1 December 2008. **C:** Interview with John Powell, 26 November 2006.

One Hour Photo (2002)
W: Reznor, Trent. "Access" feature, NIN.com (*http://access.nin.com/nearby/earth*), 7 May 2004.

Till Human Voices Wake Us (2002)
C: Interview with Amotz Plessner, 28 March 2008. **C:** Interview with Dale Cornelius, 12 March 2008.

The Tuxedo (2002)
W: Schweiger, Daniel. "On the Score with Hans Zimmer" (audio interview). Film Music Magazine (http://www.filmmusicmag.com/?p=7890), 16 May 2011.

Hellraiser: Hellseeker (2002)
C: Interview with Raz Mesinai, 3 March 2008.

Gangs of New York (2002)
P: Joy, Nick. "Ganging Up with Marty." *FSM* vol. 7 no. 8, October 2002, p. 27. **A:** Townson, Robert. "A Bernstein Revelation" (liner notes to *Elmer Bernstein: Gangs of New York / The Journey of Natty Gann / The Scarlet Letter*). Varèse Sarabande, VCL 0608 1076-4.2, 2008. **C:** Original research at the Elmer Bernstein Archive, Univ. of Southern California.

The Hours (2002)
B: DesJardins, Christian. *Inside Film Music.* Los Angeles: Silman-James Press, 2006, p. 116.

Confessions of a Dangerous Mind (2002)
W: Goldwasser, Dan. "Confessions of a Musical Mind." SoundtrackNet (*http://www.soundtrack.net/features/article/?id=158*), 5 August 2005.

Phone Booth (2002)
W: Boggan, Justin. Interview with Nathan Larson. Rejected Film and TV Scores (*http://rejectedfilmscores.150m.com/info.html#Larson*), 9 January 2008. **W:** Dan Goldwasser. "Composer on Fire." SoundtrackNet (*http://www.soundtrack.net/features/article/?id=122*), 7 May 2004.

Hulk (2003)
V: *Hulk* music featurette, Special Edition DVD, Universal Studios Home Entertainment, 2003. **P:** Bond, Jeff. "A Hulking Responsibility." *FSM* vol. 8 no. 5, June 2003, p. 24. **P:** Goldstein, Patrick. "Elfman Masters a Monster: Score One for *The Hulk.*" *Los Angeles Times*, 24 June 2003. **W:** B., Scott. "An Interview with Ang Lee,"

IGN (*http://movies.ign.com/articles/424/424621p1.html*), June 17, 2003. **W:** Benítez, Sergio, and Rubén Sánchez. "An Evening with Mychael Danna on the Phone." BSO Spirit (*http://www.bsospirit.com/entrevistas/danna1_e.php*), 2004.

Shade (2003)
W: Bruening, Erika. "Interview with Evan Evans." Composer's official website, *www.evanevans.org*, 19 Nov 2001. **C:** Conversation and email between Christopher Young and Jim Fox, September 2011.

Pirates of the Caribbean: The Curse of the Black Pearl (2003)
P: Bond, Jeff. "Shiver Me Timbres." *FSM* vol. 8 no. 6, pp. 24–26. **W:** Goldwasser, Dan. "The Honor of Composing." SoundtrackNet (*http://www.soundtrack.net/features/article/?id=112*),. 17 December 2003. **W:** Goldwasser, Dan. "Battling Monsters with Alan Silvestri." SoundtrackNet (*http://www.soundtrack.net/features/article/?id=137*), 21 January 2005.

Open Range (2003)
P: Bond Jeff. "Earning His Spurs." *FSM* vol. 8 no. 7, August 2003, p. 12. **C:** Interview with Eric Colvin, 2008.

Timeline (2003)
A: Townson, Robert. Liner notes to *Timeline*. Varèse Sarabande VSD-6600, 2004. **B:** DesJardins, Christian. *Inside Film Music*. Los Angeles: Silman-James Press, 2006, p. 267–268. **W:** DDBSpawn. Interview with Brian Tyler. BSO Spirit (*http://www.bsospirit.com/entrevistas/btyler_e.php*), n.d. **W:** Goldwasser, Dan. "Music for Hell." SoundtrackNet (*http://www.soundtrack.net/features/article/?id=141*), 22 March 2005.

Something's Gotta Give (2003)
W: Schweiger, Daniel. "On the Score with Hans Zimmer" (audio interview). Film Music Magazine (*http://www.filmmusicmag.com/?p=7890*), 16 May 2011.

The Passion of the Christ (2004)
P: Bond, Jeff. "Act of Faith: John Debney Brings His Own Passion to Mel Gibson's Controversial Film." *FSM* vol. 9 no. 2, February 2004, pp 12–15. **W:** Coleman, Christopher. "The Divine Inspiration of John Debney." TrackSounds (*http://www.tracksounds.com/specialfeatures/interviews/interview_john_debney.htm*), 2004.

Troy (2004)
P: Bond, Jeff. "The Fall of Troy" *FSM* vol. 9 no. 4, April/May 2004, pp 18–22. **P:** Coscina, David. "The Triumph of Troy." *FSM* vol. 9 no. 8, September 2004, pp. 28–31. **W:** Boggan, Justin. Interview with Gabriel Yared. Rejected Film and TV Scores (*http://rejectedfilmscores.150m.com/gabrielyaredinterview.html*), 22 July 2004. **W:** Schweiger, Daniel. "Interview with James Horner." *On the Score*. Audio interview. **W:** Yared, Gabriel. "The Score of Troy: A Mystery Unveiled." The Scream Online (*http://thescreamonline.com/film/film4-3/yared.html*), 2004.

I, Robot (2004)
V: Marco Beltrami audio commentary on All-Access Collector's Edition DVD, 2005. **P:** Bond, Jeff. "I, Marco." *FSM* vol. 9 no. 6, July 2004, pp. 11–12. **W:** Benítez, Sergio. "Interview with Trevor Jones." BSO Spirit (*http://www.bsospirit.com/entrevistas/tjones_e.php*), June 2004. **C:** Interview with Marco Beltrami, 9 May 2008.

Wimbledon (2004)
W: Official website of the London Metropolitan Orchestra, *www.lmo.co.uk*.

I ♥ Huckabees (2005)
P: Rhodes, S. Mark. "Brion of All Trades." *FSM* vol. 9 no. 8, September 2004, pp. 11–12, 42. **W:** Blunt, Emily. "Bluntly Speaking—Jon Brion: An Emily Blunt Interview." Blunt Review (*http://www.bluntreview.com/reviews/jonbrion.html*), 2005.

Being Julia (2004)
W: Carlsson, Mikael: "Mychael Danna: Being Julia" Music from the Movies (*http://www.musicfromthemovies.com/index5.php?option=com_content&view=article&id=' . (2819) . 'Mychael danna: being julia*), 2004.

Team America: World Police (2004)
W: Boggan, Justin. "Marc Shaiman: Bigger, Longer & Uncut." Rejected Film Scores (*http://rejectedfilmscores.150m.com/marcshaimaninterview.html*), November 2004.

Zoey 101: Episodes 2–5 (2005)
C: Interview with Eric Hester, 8 July 2008.

Hide and Seek (2005)
A: Liner notes for *Scenes of the Crime/A Child's Game*. BSX Records BSXCD 8837, 2008. **W:** Boggan, Justin. John Ottman interview excerpt. Rejected Film and TV Scores (*http://rejectedfilmscores.150m.com/info.html#NAYM*), n. d. **W:** John Ottman's official website, *www.johnottman.com*. **C:** Conversation and email between Christopher Young and Jim Fox, September 2011.

The Magic Roundabout/Doogal (2005).
A: Liner notes for *Doogal* soundtrack. Milan Records M2-36164, 2006.

Miss Congeniality 2: Armed and Fabulous (2005)
C: Interview with John van Tongeren, November 2008.

Major Dundee—Extended Version (2005)
P: Bond, Jeff. "Major Changes." *FSM* vol. 10 no. 2, May/June 2002, pp. 28–33, 52. **P**: Lasher, John Steven. "Major Dundee." *FSM* vol. 10 no. 5, November/December 2005. **W**: Dinman, Dick. Radio interview with Christopher Caliendo (*http://www.christophercaliendo.com/images/stories/FilmTV/01-Dick-Dinman-CC.mp3*). **W**: Christopher Caliendo's official website, *www.christophercaliendo.com.*

Constantine (2005)
W: Chellini, Jose Luis Díez. "Interview with Brian Tyler." BSO Spirit (*http://www.bsospirit.com/entrevistas/tylerconstantine_e.php*), Spring 2005. **W**: FilmzeneNet. "Brian Tyler: The Score of *Constantine.*" FilmzeneNet (*http://www.filmzene.net/read.php?u=interju_brian_tyler_english.html*), 26 March 2005. **W**: Goldwasser, Dan. "Music for Hell." SoundtrackNet (*http://www.soundtrack.net/features/article/?id=141*), 22 March 2005. **W**: Murray, Rebecca. "Composer Brian Tyler Talks About Working on *Constantine.*" About.com (*http://movies.about.com/od/constantine/a/constntbt021705.htm*), 17 February 2005.

La Marche de l'empereur / March of the Penguins (2005)
P: Vincentelli, Elisabeth. "Backstage with...Émilie Simon" *Time Out New York* no. 580, 9–15 November 2006. **W**: FilmzeneNet. "From Hollywood to Antarctica." FilmzeneNet (*http://www.filmzene.net/read.php?u=interju_alex_wurman_english.html*). 21 October 2005. **W**: Goldwasser, Dan. "Confessions of a Musical Mind." SoundtrackNet (*http://www.soundtrack.net/features/article/?id=158*), 5 August 2005.

An Unfinished Life (2005)
A: Townson, Robert. Liner notes to *An Unfinished Life.* Varèse Sarabande VCL 0706 1052, 2007. **W**: Rolewicz, Dominik. "Voyage of Suspense to Hollywood." *www.chrisyoung-filmmusic.info*, 2006. **C**: Interview with Robert Townson, 28 September 2007. **C**: Interview with Deborah Lurie, 24 June 2007.

Mrs. Harris (2005)
W: MarketWire. "Composer John Frizzell Scores *Mrs. Harris.*" MarketWire (*http://www.marketwire.com/press-release/composer-john-frizzell-scores-mrs-harris-560784.htm*), 16 September 2005.

Dreamer: Inspired by a True Story (2005)
W: Picard, Charles. Interview with Jan A. P. Kaczmarek. *Painted Saint Headquarters* (*http://www.paintedsaint.com/painted/jan_kaczmarek.html*), Fall 2005.

Aeon Flux (2005)
W: Coleman, Christopher. "The Flux Capacity of Graeme Revell." TrackSounds (*http://www.tracksounds.com/specialfeatures/interviews/interview_graeme_revell.htm*), 2005. **W**: Larson, Randall D. "The Music is Flux." Mania (*http://www.mania.com/music-flux_article_50243.html*), 8 December 2005.

King Kong (2005)
P: Burlingame, Jon. "Behind the Curtain: *King Kong*'s dueling scores." *Variety*, 30 November 2005. **W**: Carlsson, Mikael. "Behind the Scenes: Jeff Atmajian and King Kong." Music from the Movies (*http://www.musicfromthemovies.com/index5.php?option=com_content&view=article&id='.(2793).'mikael carlsson*), 2005. **W**: Fischer, Paul. "Interview: Peter Jackson." Dark Horizons (*http://www.darkhorizons.com/features/623/peter-jackson-for-king-kong*), 5 December 2005.

Transamerica (2005)
C: Interview with David Mansfield, 24 September 2008. **C**: Interview with Mason Daring, 14 September 2008.

Tsotsi (2005)
W: Carlini, Anne. "Storytelling at Its Finest." AnneCarlini.com (http://www.annecarlini.com/ex_interviews.php?id=492), 2005. W: Koran, David A. "Rendering Rendition." SoundtrackNet (http://www.soundtrack.net/features/article/?id=245), 5 November 2007. C: Interview with Guy Farley, 11 September 2008.

Nacho Libre (2006)
W: ScoreKeeper. "ScoreKeeper Unmasks Danny Elfman's NACHO LIBRE Score!!" Ain't It Cool News (*http://www.aintitcool.com/node/23558*), 10 June 2006.

You, Me and Dupree (2006)
W: Carlsson, Mikael. "Rolfe Kent to Score *You, Me and Dupree.*" Film Music Magazine (*http://www.filmmusicmag.com/?p=835*), 28 February 2006. **W**: Goldwasser, Dan. "Rolfe Kent Scores *You, Me and Dupree.*" Scoring Sessions (*http://www.scoringsessions.com/news/49/*), 12 June 2006. **W**: Rolfe Kent's blog, *www.rolfekent.com/blog.* 18 May 2006, 20 July 2006.

The Woods (2006)
A: Liner notes to *May and Other Selected Works of Jaye Barnes Luckett.* La-La Land Records LLLCD 1056, 2007. **W**: Hasan, Mark R. "Interview with Jaye Barnes Luckett." KQEK.com (*http://www.kqek.com/exclusives/Exclusives_Luckett_1.htm*), 2006.

Bonneville (2006)
C: Interview with Shie Rozow, 28 March 2008.

Open Season (2006)
W: Christodoulides, Demetris. "Interview with Ramin Djawadi" (audio interview). ScoreMagacine Composer Talk (interview available at *http://www.filmmusicsite.com/composers.cgi?go=interview&coid=205&firstname=Ramin&lastname=Djawadi&lang=en*), 30 September 2010. **W:** Doerschuk, Robert L. "Paul Westerberg: Grin and Bear It." *Harp* magazine (interview available at *http://wilco.yuku.com/topic/864/entire-harp-paul-interview*), November 2006.

The Queen (2006)
W: Boggan, Justin. "Interview with Nathan Larson." Rejected Film Scores *(http://rejectedfilmscores.150m.com/info.html#Larson)*, 9 January 2008. **W:** Goldwasser, Dan. "Painting Desplat's Musical Tapestry." SoundtrackNet (*http://www.soundtrack.net/features/article/?id=213*), 29 November 2006.

Payback: Straight Up (2006):
W: Kaufman, Debra. "The Self-Composed Music Editor." Editors Guild Magazine (*http://www.editorsguild.com/v2/magazine/archives/0506/features_article04.htm*), May 2006. **C:** Interview with Chris Boardman, 25 September 2007. **C:** Interview with Scott Stambler, 5 September 2007.

The Good German (2006)
W: Leo Abrahams' web diary, *www.leoabrahams.com/webdiary/*. 2006.

The Reaping (2007)
W: Goldwasser, Dan. "Notes for a Scandal." SoundtrackNet (*http://www.soundtrack.net/features/article/?id=216*), 12 November 2006. **W:** Goldwasser, Dan. "Frizzell replaces Glass on *The Reaping*." SoundtrackNet (*http://www.soundtrack.net/news/article/?id=883*), 12 December 2006. **W:** Hasan, Mark R. "Interview with John Frizzell." KQEK.com (*http://www.kqek.com/exclusives/Exclusives_Frizzell_1.htm*), 2007.

Before the Devil Knows You're Dead (2007)
W: Guillen, Michael. "*Before the Devil Knows You're Dead*: Interview with Producer Michael Cerenzie." TwitchFilm (*http://twitchfilm.com/interviews/2007/11/before-the-devil-knows-youre-deadinterview-with-producer-michael-cerenzie.php*), 19 November 2007. **W:** Carter Burwell's official website, *www.thebodyinc.com*. **C:** Phillips, James. Report on an interview with Richard Rodney Bennett, 2007. **C:** Interview with Carter Burwell, 1 December 2008.

Mr. Magorium's Wonder Emporium (2007)
P: Adams, Doug. "Risk, Passion" *FSM* vol. 12 no. 10, October 2007, p. 2. **W:** Lucas, Matthew. "*Mr. Magorium's Wonder Emporium*" From the Front Row (*http://www.fromthefrontrow.net/2007/08/mr-magoriums-wonder-emporium.html*), 30 August 2007.

Charlie Wilson's War (2007)
W: Southall, James: "Review of *Charlie Wilson's War*." Movie Wave (*http://www.movie-wave.net/titles/charlie_wilsons_war.html*), 2008.

Grace Is Gone (2007)
P: O'Neil, Tom. "Happy Oscars News for Harvey: Grace Is Gone, but Clint Is Here!" *Los Angeles Times*, 8 August 2007. **W:** Schieron, Sara. "Clint Eastwood Rescores John Cusack Indie *Grace Is Gone*." Rotten Tomatoes (*http://www.rottentomatoes.com/m/grace_is_gone/news/1661139/clint_eastwood_rescores_john_cusack_indie_grace_is_gone/#*), 9 August 2007. **W:** Weinberg, Scott. "Clint Eastwood Wants to Re-Score *Grace is Gone*"? Cinematical (*http://blog.moviefone.com/2007/08/08/clint-eastwood-wants-to-re-score-grace-is-gone*), 8 August 2007.

The Fugitive: Second Season—DVD Release (2008)
B: Burlingame, Jon. *TV's Biggest Hits: The Story of Television Themes from "Dragnet" to "Friends."* NY: Schirmer, 1996, p. 134. **P:** Bond, Jeff. "Trek Music Slips Through DVD Cracks." *FSM* vol. 5 no. 6, July 2000, pp. 4–5. **W:** Burlingame, Jon. "*The Fugitive* Music Debacle: Why It Happened." Film Music Society (*http://www.filmmusicsociety.org/news_events/features/2008/081508.html*), 15 August 2008.

The Mummy: Tomb of the Dragon Emperor (2008).
W: Scorenotes. Interview with John Debney. Scorenotes (*http://scorenotes.com/john_debney.html*), September 2008.

Gears of War 2 (2008)
W: Music 4 Games. "Interview with Steve Jablonsky." *Music 4 Games*. 17 October 2008. **W:** Riepl, Kevin. *Kevin Riepl Music Blog*. 25 February 2008, 12 November 2008. **W:** Greening, Chris. Interview with Kevin Riepl. Square Enix Music Online (*http://www.squareenixmusic.com/features/interviews/kevinriepl.shtml*), August 2010.

Index

T